Formal Syntax
and
Semantics of
Programming Languages

A Laboratory Based Approach

Kenneth Slonneger
University of Iowa

Barry L. Kurtz
Louisiana Tech University

Addison-Wesley Publishing Company

Reading, Massachusetts • Menlo Park, California • New York • Don Mills, Ontario

Wokingham, England • Amsterdam • Bonn • Sydney • Singapore

Tokyo • Madrid • San Juan • Milan • Paris

Senior Acquisitions Editor: *Tom Stone*
Assistant Editor: *Kathleen Billus*
Production Coordinator: *Marybeth Mooney*
Cover Designer: *Diana C. Coe*
Manufacturing Coordinator: *Evelyn Beaton*

The procedures and applications presented in this book have been included for their instructional value. They have been tested with care but are not guaranteed for any particular purpose. The publisher does not offer any warranties or representations, nor does it accept any liabilities with respect to the programs or applications.

Library of Congress Cataloging-in-Publication Data

Slonneger, Kenneth.
  Formal syntax and semantics of programming languages: a laboratory
  based approach / Kenneth Slonneger, Barry L. Kurtz.
      p.   cm.
  Includes bibliographical references and index.
  ISBN 0-201-65697-3
  1. Programming languages (Electronic computers)--Syntax.
  2. Programming languages (Electronic computers)--Semantics.
  I. Kurtz, Barry L.   II. Title.
  QA76.7.S59   1995
  005.13'1--dc20   94-4203
                                                                CIP

ISBN 0-201-65697-3
1 2 3 4 5 6 7 8 9 10-MA-979695

Dedications

To my father, Robert
> Barry L. Kurtz

To Marybeth and my family
> Ken Slonneger

Preface

This text developed out of our experiences teaching courses covering the formal semantics of programming languages. Independently we both developed laboratory exercises implementing small programming languages in Prolog following denotational definitions. Prolog proved to be an excellent tool for illustrating the formal semantics of programming languages. We found that these laboratory exercises were highly successful in motivating students since the hands-on experience helped demystify the study of formal semantics. At a professional meeting we became aware of each other's experiences with a laboratory approach to semantics, and this book evolved from that conference.

Although this text has been carefully written so that the laboratory activities can be omitted without loss of continuity, we hope that most readers will try the laboratory approach and experience the same success that we have observed in our classes.

Overall Goals

We have pursued a broad spectrum of definitional techniques, illustrated with numerous examples. Although the specification methods are formal, the presentation is "gentle", providing just enough in the way of mathematical underpinnings to produce an understanding of the metalanguages. We hope to supply enough coverage of mathematics and formal methods to justify the definitional techniques, but the text is accessible to students with a basic grounding in discrete mathematics as presented to undergraduate computer science students.

There has been a tendency in the area of formal semantics to create cryptic, overly concise semantic definitions that intimidate students new to the study of programming languages. The emphasis in this text is on clear notational conventions with the goals of readability and understandability foremost in our minds.

As with other textbooks in this field, we introduce the basic concepts using mini-languages that are rich enough to illustrate the fundamental concepts, yet sparse enough to avoid being overwhelming. We have named our mini-languages after birds.

Wren is a simple imperative language with two types, integer and Boolean, thus allowing for context-sensitive type and declaration checking. It has assignment, if, while, and input/output commands.

Pelican, a block-structured, imperative language, is an extension of Wren containing the declaration of constants, anonymous blocks, procedures, and recursive definitions.

The description of continuations in denotational semantics requires a modified version of Wren with goto statements, which we call *Gull*. This mini-language can be skipped without loss of continuity if continuations are not covered.

Organization of the Text

The primary target readership of our text is first-year graduate students, although by careful selection of materials it is also accessible to advanced undergraduate students. The text contains more material than can be covered in a one semester course. We have provided a wide variety of techniques so that instructors may choose materials to suit the particular needs of their students.

Dependencies between chapters are indicated in the graph below. We have purposely attempted to minimize mutual interdependencies and to make our presentation as broad as possible.

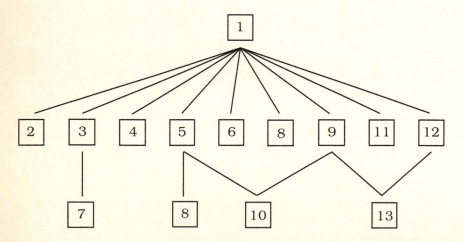

Only sections 2 and 3 of Chapter 8 depend on Chapter 5. The text contains a laboratory component that we describe in more detail in a moment. However, materials have been carefully organized so that no components of the non-laboratory sections of the text are dependent on any laboratory activities. All of the laboratory activities except those in Chapter 6 depend on Chapter 2.

Overview

The first four chapters deal primarily with the syntax of programming languages. Chapter 1 treats context-free syntax in the guise of BNF grammars and their variants. Since most methods of semantic specification use abstract syntax trees, the abstract syntax of languages is presented and contrasted with concrete syntax.

Language processing with Prolog is introduced in Chapter 2 by describing a scanner for Wren and a parser defined in terms of Prolog logic grammars. These utilities act as the front end for the prototype context checkers, interpreters, and translators developed later in the text. Extensions of BNF grammars that provide methods of verifying the context-sensitive aspects of programming languages—namely, attribute grammars and two-level grammars—are described in Chapters 3 and 4.

Chapters 5 through 8 are devoted to semantic formalisms that can be classified as operational semantics. Chapter 5 introduces the lambda calculus by describing its syntax and the evaluation of lambda expressions by reduction rules. Metacircular interpreters are consider in Chapter 6, which introduces the self-definition of programming languages.

Chapter 7 describes the translation of Wren into assembly language using an attribute grammar that constructs the target code as a program is parsed. Two well-known operational formalisms are treated in Chapter 8: the SECD machine—an abstract machine for evaluating the lambda calculus—and structural operational semantics—an operational methodology for describing the semantics of programming languages in terms of logical rules of inference. We use this technique to specify the semantics of Wren formally.

The last five chapters present three traditional methods of defining the semantics of programming languages formally and one recently proposed technique. Denotational semantics, one of the most complete and successful methods of specifying a programming language, is covered in Chapter 9. Specifications of several languages are provided, including a calculator language, Wren, Pelican, and Gull, a language whose semantics requires continuation semantics. Denotational semantics is also used to check the context constraints for Wren. Chapter 10 deals with the mathematical foundations of denotational semantics in domain theory by describing the data structures employed by denotational definitions. Chapter 10 also includes a justification for recursive definitions via fixed-point semantics, which is then applied in lambda calculus evaluation.

Axiomatic semantics, dealt with in Chapter 11, has become an important component of software development by means of proofs of correctness for algorithms. The approach here presents axiomatic specifications of Wren and Pelican, but the primary examples involve proofs of partial correctness and termination. The chapter concludes with a brief introduction to using assertions as program specifications and deriving program code based on these assertions. Chapter 12 investigates the algebraic specification of abstract data types and uses these formalisms to specify the context constraints and the semantics of Wren. Algebraic semantics also provides an explanation of abstract syntax.

Chapter 13 introduces a specification method, action semantics, that has been proposed recently in response to criticisms arising from the difficulty of using formal methods. Action semantics resembles denotational semantics but can be viewed in terms of operational behavior without sacrificing mathematical rigor. We use it to specify the semantics of the calculator language, Wren, and Pelican. The text concludes with two short appendices introducing the basics of programming in Prolog and Scheme, which is used in Chapter 6.

The Laboratory Component

A unique feature of this text is the laboratory component. Running throughout the text is a series of exercises and examples that involve implementing syntactic and semantic specifications on real systems. We have chosen Prolog as the primary vehicle for these implementations for several reasons:

1. Prolog provides high-level programming enabling the construction of derivation trees and abstract syntax trees as structures without using pointer programming as needed in most imperative languages.

2. Most Prolog systems provide a programming environment that is easy to use, especially in the context of rapid prototyping; large systems can be developed one predicate at a time and can be tested during their construction.

3. Logic programming creates a framework for drawing out the logical properties of abstract specifications that encourages students to approach problems in a disciplined and logical manner. Furthermore, the specifications described in logic become executable specifications with Prolog.

4. Prolog's logic grammars provide a simple-to-use parser that can serve as a front end to language processors. It also serves as a direct implementation of attribute grammars and provides an immediate application of BNF specifications of the context-free part of a language's grammar.

An appendix covering the basics of Prolog is provided for students unfamiliar with logic programming.

Our experience has shown that the laboratory practice greatly enhances the learning experience. The only way to master formal methods of language definition is to practice writing and reading language specifications. We involve students in the implementation of general tools that can be applied to a variety of examples and that provide increased motivation and feedback to the students. Submitting specifications to a prototyping system can uncover oversights and subtleties that are not apparent to a casual reader. As authors, we have frequently used these laboratory approaches to help "debug" our formal specifications!

Laboratory materials found in this textbook are available on the Internet via anonymous ftp from herky.cs.iowa.edu in the subdirectory pub/slonnegr.

Laboratory Activities

Chapter 2:   Scanning and parsing Wren

Chapter 3:   Context checking Wren using an attribute grammar

Chapter 4:   Context checking Hollerith literals using a two-level grammar

Chapter 5:   Evaluating the lambda calculus using its reduction rules

Chapter 6:   Self-definition of Scheme (Lisp)

Self-definition of Prolog

Chapter 7:   Translating (compiling) Wren programs following an attribute grammar

Chapter 8:   Interpreting the lambda calculus using the SECD machine

Interpreting Wren according to a definition using structural operational semantics

Chapter 9:   Interpreting Wren following a denotational specification

Chapter 10: Evaluating a lambda calculus that includes recursive definitions

Chapter 12: Interpreting Wren according to an algebraic specification of the language

Chapter 13: Translating Pelican programs into action notation following a specification in action semantics.

Acknowledgments

We would like to thank Addison-Wesley for their support in developing this text—in particular, Tom Stone, senior editor for Computer Science, Kathleen Billus, assistant editor, Marybeth Mooney, production coordinator, and the many other people who helped put this text together.

We would like to acknowledge the following reviewers for their valuable feedback that helped us improve the text: Doris Carver (Louisiana State University), Art Fleck (University of Iowa), Ray Ford (University of Montana), Phokion Kolaitis (Santa Cruz), William Purdy (Syracuse University), and Roy Rubinstein (Worcester Polytech). The comments and suggestions of a number of students contributed substantially to the text; those students include Matt Clay, David Frank, Sun Kim, Kent Lee, Terry Letsche, Sandeep Pal, Ruth Ruei, Matt Tucker, and Satish Viswanantham.

We used Microsoft Word and Aldus PageMaker for the Macintosh to develop this text. We owe a particular debt to the Internet, which allowed us to exchange and develop materials smoothly. Finally, we each would like to thank our respective family members whose encouragement and patience made this text possible.

Ken Slonneger
Barry L. Kurtz

Contents

Chapter 13
ACTION SEMANTICS   507

Chapter 1
SPECIFYING SYNTAX

L anguage provides a means of communication by sound and written symbols. Human beings learn language as a consequence of their life experiences, but in linguistics—the science of languages—the forms and meanings of languages are subjected to a more rigorous examination. This science can also be applied to the subject of this text, programming languages. In contrast to the natural languages, with which we communicate our thoughts and feelings, programming languages can be viewed as artificial languages defined by men and women initially for the purpose of communicating with computers but, as importantly, for communicating algorithms among people.

Many of the methods and much of the terminology of linguistics apply to programming languages. For example, language definitions consist of three components:

1. **Syntax** refers to the ways symbols may be combined to create well-formed sentences (or programs) in the language. Syntax defines the formal relations between the constituents of a language, thereby providing a structural description of the various expressions that make up legal strings in the language. Syntax deals solely with the form and structure of symbols in a language without any consideration given to their meaning.

2. **Semantics** reveals the meaning of syntactically valid strings in a language. For natural languages, this means correlating sentences and phrases with the objects, thoughts, and feelings of our experiences. For programming languages, semantics describes the behavior that a computer follows when executing a program in the language. We might disclose this behavior by describing the relationship between the input and output of a program or by a step-by-step explanation of how a program will execute on a real or an abstract machine.

3. **Pragmatics** alludes to those aspects of language that involve the users of the language, namely psychological and sociological phenomena such as utility, scope of application, and effects on the users. For programming languages, pragmatics includes issues such as ease of implementation, efficiency in application, and programming methodology.

1

Syntax must be specified prior to semantics since meaning can be given only to correctly formed expressions in a language. Similarly, semantics needs to be formulated before considering the issues of pragmatics, since interaction with human users can be considered only for expressions whose meaning is understood. In the current text, we are primarily concerned with syntax and semantics, leaving the subject of pragmatics to those who design and implement programming languages, chiefly compiler writers. Our paramount goal is to explain methods for furnishing a precise definition of the syntax and semantics of a programming language.

We begin by describing a metalanguage for syntax specification called BNF. We then use it to define the syntax of the main programming language employed in this text, a small imperative language called Wren. After a brief look at variants of BNF, the chapter concludes with a discussion of the abstract syntax of a programming language.

At the simplest level, languages are sets of sentences, each consisting of a finite sequence of symbols from some finite alphabet. Any really interesting language has an infinite number of sentences. This does not mean that it has an infinitely long sentence but that there is no maximum length for all the finite length sentences. The initial concern in describing languages is how to specify an infinite set with notation that is finite. We will see that a BNF grammar is a finite specification of a language that may be infinite.

1.1 GRAMMARS AND BNF

Formal methods have been more successful with describing the syntax of programming languages than with explaining their semantics. Defining the syntax of programming languages bears a close resemblance to formulating the grammar of a natural language, describing how symbols may be formed into the valid phrases of the language. The formal grammars that Noam Chomsky proposed for natural languages apply to programming languages as well.

Definition: A grammar $< \Sigma,N,P,S>$ consists of four parts:

1. A finite set Σ of **terminal symbols**, the **alphabet** of the language, that are assembled to make up the sentences in the language.

2. A finite set N of **nonterminal symbols** or **syntactic categories**, each of which represents some collection of subphrases of the sentences.

3. A finite set P of **productions** or **rules** that describe how each nonterminal is defined in terms of terminal symbols and nonterminals. The choice of

nonterminals determines the phrases of the language to which we ascribe meaning.

4. A distinguished nonterminal S, the **start symbol**, that specifies the principal category being defined—for example, sentence or program. ▮

In accordance with the traditional notation for programming language grammars, we represent nonterminals with the form "<category-name>" and productions as follows:

<declaration> ::= **var** <variable list> **:** <type> **;**

where "**var**", "**:**" , and "**;**" are terminal symbols in the language. The symbol "::=" is part of the language for describing grammars and can be read "is defined to be" or "may be composed of". When applied to programming languages, this notation is known as **Backus-Naur Form** or **BNF** for the researchers who first used it to describe Algol60. Note that BNF is a language for defining languages—that is, BNF is a **metalanguage**. By formalizing syntactic definitions, BNF greatly simplifies semantic specifications. Before considering BNF in more detail, we investigate various forms that grammars may take.

The **vocabulary** of a grammar includes its terminal and nonterminal symbols. An arbitrary production has the form α ::= β where α and β are strings of symbols from the vocabulary, and α has at least one nonterminal in it. Chomsky classified grammars according to the structure of their productions, suggesting four forms of particular usefulness, calling them type 0 through type 3.

Type 0: The most general grammars, the **unrestricted grammars**, require only that at least one nonterminal occur on the left side of a rule, "α ::= β"—for example,

a <thing> b ::= b <another thing>.

Type 1: When we add the restriction that the right side contains no fewer symbols than the left side, we get the **context-sensitive grammars**—for example, a rule of the form

<thing> b ::= b <thing>.

Equivalently, context-sensitive grammars can be built using only productions of the form "α <B> γ ::= $\alpha\beta\gamma$", where <B> is a nonterminal, α, β, and γ are strings over the vocabulary, and β is not an empty string. These rules are called context-sensitive because the replacement of a nonterminal by its definition depends on the surrounding symbols.

Type 2: The **context-free grammars** prescribe that the left side be a single nonterminal producing rules of the form "<A> ::= α", such as

<expression> ::= <expression> * <term>

where "*" is a terminal symbol. Type 2 grammars correspond to the BNF grammars and play a major role in defining programming languages, as will be described in this chapter.

Type 3: The most restrictive grammars, the **regular grammars**, allow only a terminal or a terminal followed by one nonterminal on the right side—that is, rules of the form "<A> ::= a" or "<A> ::= a <A>". A grammar describing binary numerals can be designed using the format of a regular grammar:

<binary numeral> ::= **0**

<binary numeral> ::= **1**

<binary numeral> ::= **0** <binary numeral>

<binary numeral> ::= **1** <binary numeral>.

The class of regular BNF grammars can be used to specify identifiers and numerals in most programming languages.

When a nonterminal has several alternative productions, the symbol "|" separates the right-hand sides of alternatives. The four type 3 productions given above are equivalent to the following consolidated production:

<binary numeral> ::= **0** | **1** | **0** <binary numeral> | **1** <binary numeral>.

Context-Free Grammars

As an example of a context-free grammar, consider the syntactic specification of a small fragment of English shown in Figure 1.1. The terminal symbols of the language are displayed in boldface. This grammar allows sentences such as "**the girl sang a song.**" and "**the cat surprised the boy with a song.**".

The grammar is context-free because only single nonterminals occur on the left sides of the rules. Note that the language defined by our grammar contains many nonsensical sentences, such as "**the telescope sang the cat by a boy.**". In other words, only syntax, and not semantics, is addressed by the grammar.

In addition to specifying the legal sentences of the language, a BNF definition establishes a structure for its phrases by virtue of the way a sentence can be derived. A derivation begins with the start symbol of the grammar, here the syntactic category <sentence>, replacing nonterminals by strings of symbols according to rules in the grammar.

    <sentence> ::= <noun phrase> <verb phrase> .

    <noun phrase> ::= <determiner> <noun>

                | <determiner> <noun> <prepositional phrase>

    <verb phrase> ::= <verb> | <verb> <noun phrase>

                | <verb> <noun phrase> <prepositional phrase>

    <prepositional phrase> ::= <preposition> <noun phrase>

    <noun> ::= **boy** | **girl** | **cat** | **telescope** | **song** | **feather**

    <determiner> ::= **a** | **the**

    <verb> ::= **saw** | **touched** | **surprised** | **sang**

    <preposition> ::= **by** | **with**

Figure 1.1: An English Grammar

An example of a derivation is given in Figure 1.2. It uniformly replaces the leftmost nonterminal in the string. Derivations can be constructed following other strategies, such as always replacing the rightmost nonterminal, but the outcome remains the same as long as the grammar is not ambiguous. We discuss ambiguity later. The symbol $\Rightarrow$ denotes the relation encompassing one step of a derivation.

The structure embodied in a derivation can be displayed by a **derivation tree** or **parse tree** in which each leaf node is labeled with a terminal symbol

---

  <sentence> $\Rightarrow$ <noun phrase> <verb phrase> .

            $\Rightarrow$ <determiner> <noun> <verb phrase> .

            $\Rightarrow$ **the** <noun> <verb phrase> .

            $\Rightarrow$ **the girl** <verb phrase> .

            $\Rightarrow$ **the girl** <verb> <noun phrase> <prepositional phrase> .

            $\Rightarrow$ **the girl touched** <noun phrase> <prepositional phrase> .

            $\Rightarrow$ **the girl touched** <determiner> <noun> <prepositional phrase> .

            $\Rightarrow$ **the girl touched the** <noun> <prepositional phrase> .

            $\Rightarrow$ **the girl touched the cat** <prepositional phrase> .

            $\Rightarrow$ **the girl touched the cat** <preposition> <noun phrase> .

            $\Rightarrow$ **the girl touched the cat with** <noun phrase> .

            $\Rightarrow$ **the girl touched the cat with** <determiner> <noun> .

            $\Rightarrow$ **the girl touched the cat with a** <noun> .

            $\Rightarrow$ **the girl touched the cat with a feather** .

Figure 1.2: A Derivation

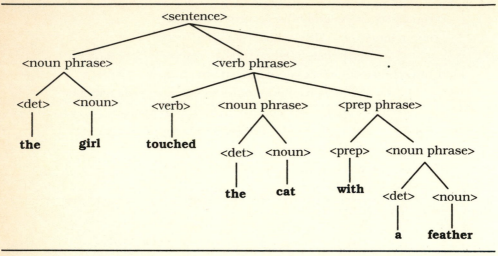

Figure 1.3: A Derivation Tree

and each interior node by a nonterminal whose children represent the right side of the production used for it in the derivation. A derivation tree for the sentence "**the girl touched the cat with a feather.**" is shown in Figure 1.3.

Definition: A grammar is **ambiguous** if some phrase in the language generated by the grammar has two distinct derivation trees.   ∎

Since the syntax of a phrase determines the structure needed to define its meaning, ambiguity in grammars presents a problem in language specification. The English language fragment defined in Figure 1.1 allows ambiguity as witnessed by a second derivation tree for the sentence "**the girl touched the cat with a feather.**" drawn in Figure 1.4. The first parsing of the sentence implies that a feather was used to touch the cat, while in the second it was the cat in possession of a feather that was touched.

We accept ambiguity in English since the context of a discourse frequently clarifies any confusions. In addition, thought and meaning can survive in spite of a certain amount of misunderstanding. But computers require a greater precision of expression in order to carry out tasks correctly. Therefore ambiguity needs to be minimized in programming language definitions, although, as we see later, some ambiguity may be acceptable.

At first glance it may not appear that our fragment of English defines an infinite language. The fact that some nonterminals are defined in terms of themselves—that is, using recursion—admits the construction of unbounded strings of terminals. In the case of our English fragment, the recursion is indirect, involving noun phrases and prepositional phrases. It allows the con-

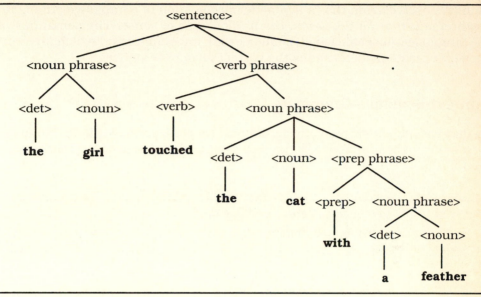

Figure 1.4: Another Derivation Tree

struction of sentences of the form "**the cat saw a boy with a girl with a boy with a girl with a boy with a girl.**" where there is no upper bound on the number of prepositional phrases.

To determine whether a nonterminal is defined recursively in a grammar, it suffices to build a directed graph that shows the dependencies among the nonterminals. If the graph contains a cycle, the nonterminals in the cycle are defined recursively. Figure 1.5 illustrates the **dependency graph** for the English grammar shown in Figure 1.1.

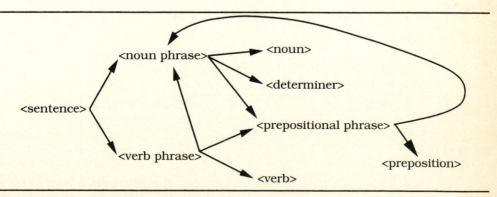

Figure 1.5: The Dependency Graph

Finally, observe again that a syntactic specification of a language entails no requirement that all the sentences it allows make sense. The semantics of the language will decide which sentences are meaningful and which are nonsense. Syntax only determines the correct form of sentences.

Context-Sensitive Grammars

To illustrate a context-sensitive grammar, we consider a synthetic language defined over the alphabet Σ = { **a**, **b**, **c** } using the productions portrayed in Figure 1.6.

<sentence> ::= **abc** | **a**<thing>**bc**

<thing>**b** ::= **b**<thing>

<thing>**c** ::= <other>**bcc**

a<other> ::= **aa** | **aa**<thing>

b<other> ::= <other>**b**

Figure 1.6: A Context-Sensitive Grammar

The language generated by this grammar consists of strings having equal numbers of **a**'s, **b**'s, and **c**'s in that order—namely, the set { **abc**, **aabbcc**, **aaabbbccc**, ... }. Notice that when replacing the nonterminal <thing>, the terminal symbol following the nonterminal determines which rule can be applied. This causes the grammar to be context-sensitive. In fact, a result in computation theory asserts that no context-free grammar produces this language. Figure 1.7 contains a derivation of a string in the language.

<sentence> => **a**<thing>**bc**

=> **ab**<thing>**c**

=> **ab**<other>**bcc**

=> **a**<other>**bbcc**

=> **aabbcc**

Figure 1.7: A Derivation

Exercises

1. Find two derivation trees for the sentence "**the girl saw a boy with a telescope.**" using the grammar in Figure 1.1 and show the derivations that correspond to the two trees.

2. Give two different derivations of the sentence "**the boy with a cat sang a song.**", but show that the derivations produce the same derivation tree.

3. Look up the following terms in a dictionary: *linguistics, semiotics, grammar, syntax, semantics,* and *pragmatics.*

4. Remove the syntactic category <prepositional phrase> and all related productions from the grammar in Figure 1.1. Show that the resulting grammar defines a finite language by counting all the sentences in it.

5. Using the grammar in Figure 1.6, derive the <sentence> **aaabbbccc** .

6. Consider the following two grammars, each of which generates strings of correctly balanced parentheses and brackets. Determine if either or both is ambiguous. The Greek letter ε represents an empty string.

    a) <string> ::= <string> <string> | **(** <string> **)** |**[** <string> **]** | ε

    b) <string> ::= **(** <string> **)** <string> | **[** <string> **]** <string> | ε

7. Describe the languages over the terminal set { **a**, **b** } defined by each of the following grammars:

    a) <string> ::= **a** <string> **b** | **ab**

    b) <string> ::= **a** <string> **a** | **b** <string> **b** | ε

    c) <string>::= **a** <B> | **b** <A>
       <A> ::= **a** | **a** <string> | **b** <A> <A>
       <B> ::= **b** | **b** <string> | **a** <B> <B>

8. Use the following grammar to construct a derivation tree for the sentence "**the girl that the cat that the boy touched saw sang a song.**":

    <sentence> ::= <noun phrase> <verb phrase> .
    <noun phrase> ::= <determiner> <noun>
                    | <determiner> <noun> <relative clause>
    <verb phrase> ::= <verb> | <verb> <noun phrase>
    <relative clause> ::= **that** <noun phrase> <verb phrase>
    <noun> ::= **boy** | **girl** | **cat** | **telescope** | **song** | **feather**
    <determiner> ::= **a** | **the**
    <verb> ::= **saw** | **touched** |**surprised** | **sang**

    Readers familiar with computation theory may show that the language generated by this grammar is context-free but not regular.

9. Identify which productions in the English grammar of Figure 1.1 can be reformulated as type 3 productions. It can be proved that productions of the form <A> ::= a_1 a_2 a_3 ...a_n <B> are also allowable in regular grammars. Given this fact, prove the English grammar is regular—that is, it can be defined by a type 3 grammar. Reduce the size of the language by limiting the terminal vocabulary to **boy**, **a**, **saw**, and **by** and omit the period. This exercise requires showing that the concatenation of two regular grammars is regular.

1.2 THE PROGRAMMING LANGUAGE WREN

In this text, the formal methods for programming language specification will be illustrated with an example language Wren and several extensions to it. Wren is a small imperative language whose only control structures are the **if** command for selection and the **while** command for iteration. The name of the language comes from its smallness and its dependence on the **while** command (**w** in Wren). Variables are explicitly typed as **integer** or **boolean**, and the semantics of Wren follows a strong typing discipline when using expressions.

A BNF definition of Wren may be found in Figure 1.8. Observe that terminal symbols, such as reserved words, special symbols (:=, +, ...), and the letters and digits that form numbers and identifiers, are shown in boldface for emphasis.

Reserved words are keywords provided in a language definition to make it easier to read and understand. Making keywords reserved prohibits their use as identifiers and facilitates the analysis of the language. Many programming languages treat some keywords as predefined identifiers—for example, "write" in Pascal. We take all keywords to be reserved words to simplify the presentation of semantics. Since declaration sequences may be empty, one of the production rules for Wren produces a string with no symbols, denoted by the Greek letter ε.

The syntax of a programming language is commonly divided into two parts, the **lexical syntax** that describes the smallest units with significance, called **tokens**, and the **phrase-structure syntax** that explains how tokens are arranged into programs. The lexical syntax recognizes identifiers, numerals, special symbols, and reserved words as if a syntactic category <token> had the definition:

<token> ::= <identifier> | <numeral> | <reserved word> | <relation>
        | <weak op> | <strong op> | := | (|) | , | ; | :

where

<program> ::= **program** <identifier> **is** <block>

<block> ::= <declaration seq> **begin** <command seq> **end**

<declaration seq> ::= ε | <declaration> <declaration seq>

<declaration> ::= **var** <variable list> : <type> ;

<type> ::= **integer** | **boolean**

<variable list> ::= <variable> | <variable> , <variable list>

<command seq> ::= <command> | <command> ; <command seq>

<command> ::= <variable> := <expr> | **skip**

   | **read** <variable> | **write** <integer expr>

   | **while** <boolean expr> **do** <command seq> **end while**

   | **if** <boolean expr> **then** <command seq> **end if**

   | **if** <boolean expr> **then** <command seq> **else** <command seq> **end if**

<expr> ::= <integer expr> | <boolean expr>

<integer expr> ::= <term> | <integer expr> <weak op> <term>

<term> ::= <element> | <term> <strong op> <element>

<element> ::= <numeral> | <variable> | (<integer expr>) | – <element>

<boolean expr> ::= <boolean term> | <boolean expr> **or** <boolean term>

<boolean term> ::= <boolean element>

                | <boolean term> **and** <boolean element>

<boolean element> ::= **true** | **false** | <variable> | <comparison>

                  | **not** (<boolean expr>) | (<boolean expr>)

<comparison> ::= <integer expr> <relation> <integer expr>

<variable> ::= <identifier>

<relation> ::= <= | < | = | > | >= | <>

<weak op> ::= + | –

<strong op> ::= * | /

<identifier> ::= <letter> | <identifier> <letter> | <identifier> <digit>

<letter> ::= **a** | **b** | **c** | **d** | **e** | **f** | **g** | **h** | **i** | **j** | **k** | **l** | **m**

        | **n** | **o** | **p** | **q** | **r** | **s** | **t** | **u** | **v** | **w** | **x** | **y** | **z**

<numeral> ::= <digit> | <digit> <numeral>

<digit> ::= **0** | **1** | **2** | **3** | **4** | **5** | **6** | **7** | **8** | **9**

Figure 1.8: BNF for Wren

<reserved word> ::= **program** | **is** | **begin** | **end** | **var** | **integer**

              | **boolean** | **read** | **write** | **skip** | **while** | **do** | **if**

              | **then** | **else** | **and** | **or** | **true** | **false** | **not**.

Such a division of syntax into lexical issues and the structure of programs in terms of tokens corresponds to the way programming languages are normally implemented. Programs as text are presented to a **lexical analyzer** or **scanner** that reads characters and produces a list of tokens taken from the **lexicon**, a collection of possible tokens of the language. Since semantics ascribes meaning to programs in terms of the structure of their phrases, the details of lexical syntax are irrelevant. The internal structure of tokens is immaterial, and only intelligible tokens take part in providing semantics to a program. In Figure 1.8, the productions defining <relation>, <weak op>, <strong op>, <identifier>, <letter>, <numeral>, and <digit> form the lexical syntax of Wren, although the first three rules may be used as abbreviations in the phrase-structure syntax of the language.

Ambiguity

The BNF definition for Wren is apparently free of ambiguity, but we still consider where ambiguity might enter into the syntactic definition of a programming language. Pascal allows the ambiguity of the "dangling else" by the definitions

<command> ::= **if** <boolean expr> **then** <command>
    | **if** <boolean expr> **then** <command> **else** <command>.

The string "**if** $expr_1$ **then if** $expr_2$ **then** cmd_1 **else** cmd_2" has two structural definitions, as shown in Figure 1.9. The Pascal definition mandates the second form as correct by adding the informal rule that an **else** clause goes with the nearest **if** command. In Wren this ambiguity is avoided by bracketing the **then** or **else** clause syntactically with **end if**. These examples illustrate that derivation trees can be constructed with any nonterminal at their root. Such trees can appear as subtrees in a derivation from the start symbol <program>.

Another source of ambiguity in the syntax of expressions is explored in an exercise. Note that these ambiguities arise in recursive productions that allow a particular nonterminal to be replaced at two different locations in the definition, as in the production

<command> ::= **if** <boolean expr> **then** <command> **else** <command>.

This observation does not provide a method for avoiding ambiguity; it only describes a situation to consider for possible problems. In fact, there exists no general method for determining whether an arbitrary BNF specification is ambiguous or not.

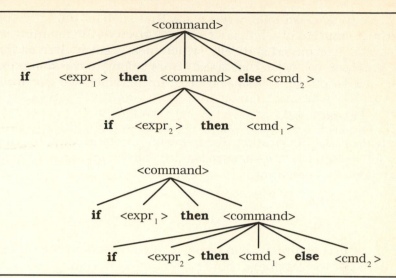

Figure 1.9: Two Structural Definitions

Context Constraints in Wren

Each program in Wren can be thought of as a string of tokens, although not every string of tokens is a legal Wren program. The BNF specification restricts the set of possible strings to those that can be obtained by a derivation from the nonterminal <program>. Even then, illegal programs remain. The BNF notation can define only those aspects of the syntax that are context-free, since each production can be applied regardless of the surrounding symbols. Therefore the program in Figure 1.10 passes the requirements prescribed by the BNF grammar for Wren.

---

program illegal **is**

    var a : **boolean**;

begin

    a := 5

end

Figure 1.10: An Illegal Wren Program

The error in the program "illegal" involves a violation of the context defined by a declaration. The variable "a" has been declared of Boolean type, but in the body of the program, an attempt is made to assign to it an integer value. The classification of such an error entails some controversy. Language implementers, such as compiler writers, say that such an infraction belongs to the **static semantics** of a language since it involves the meaning of symbols and can be determined statically, which means solely derived from the text of the program. We argue that static errors belong to the syntax, not the semantics, of a language. Consider a program in which we declare a constant:

> **const** c = 5;

In the context of this declaration, the following assignment commands are erroneous for essentially the same reason: It makes no sense to assign an expression value to a constant.

> 5 := 66;
>
> c := 66;

The error in the first command can be determined based on the context-free grammar (BNF) of the language, but the second is normally recognized as part of checking the context constraints. Our view is that both errors involve the incorrect formation of symbols in a command—that is, the syntax of the language. The basis of these syntactic restrictions is to avoid commands that are meaningless given the usual model of the language.

Though it may be difficult to draw the line accurately between syntax and semantics, we hold that issues normally dealt with from the static text should be called syntax, and those that involve a program's behavior during execution be called semantics. Therefore we consider syntax to have two components: the **context-free syntax** defined by a BNF specification and the **context-sensitive syntax** consisting of context conditions or constraints that legal programs must obey. While the context-free syntax can be defined easily with a formal metalanguage BNF, at this point we specify the context conditions for Wren informally in Figure 1.11.

---

1. The program name identifier may not be declared elsewhere in the program.

2. All identifiers that appear in a block must be declared in that block.

3. No identifier may be declared more than once in a block.

4. The identifier on the left side of an assignment command must be declared as a variable, and the expression on the right must be of the same type.

5. An identifier occurring as an (integer) element must be an integer variable.

6. An identifier occurring as a Boolean element must be a Boolean variable.

7. An identifier occurring in a read command must be an integer variable.

Figure 1.11: Context Conditions for Wren

In theory the context conditions can be prescribed using a context-sensitive grammar, but these grammars are unsuitable for several reasons. For one, they bear no resemblance to the techniques that are used to check context conditions in implementing a programming language. A second problem is that the expansion of a node in the derivation tree may depend on sibling nodes (the context). Therefore we lose the direct hierarchical relationships between nonterminals that furnish a basis for semantic descriptions. Finally, formal context-sensitive grammars are difficult to construct and understand. Later in the text, more pragmatic formal methods for defining the context-sensitive aspects of programming languages will be investigated using attribute grammars, two-level grammars, and the methods of denotational semantics and algebraic semantics.

An eighth rule may be added to the list of context conditions for Wren:

8. No reserved word may be used as an identifier.

Since a scanner recognizes reserved words and distinguishes them from identifiers, attaching tags of some sort to the identifiers, this problem can be handled by the requirements of the BNF grammar. If a reserved word occurs in a position where an identifier is expected, the context-free derivation fails. Therefore we omit rule 8 from the list of context conditions.

The relationships between the languages specified in defining Wren are shown in the diagram below:

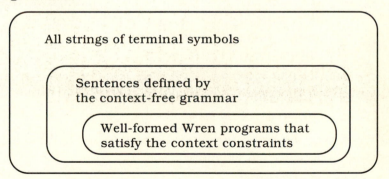

Semantic Errors in Wren

As any programmer knows, even after all syntax errors are removed from a program, it may still be defective. The fault may be that the program executes to completion but its behavior does not agree with the specification of the problem that the program is trying to solve. This notion of correctness will be dealt with in Chapter 11. A second possibility is that the program does not terminate normally because it has tried to carry out an operation that cannot be executed by the run-time system. We call these faults **seman-tic** or **dynamic errors**. The semantic errors that can be committed while executing a Wren program are listed in Figure 1.12.

---

1. An attempt is made to divide by zero.
2. A variable that has not been initialized is accessed.
3. A **read** command is executed when the input file is empty.
4. An iteration command (**while**) does not terminate.

Figure 1.12: Semantic Errors in Wren

We include nontermination as a semantic error in Wren even though some programs, such as real-time programs, are intended to run forever. In presenting the semantics of Wren, we will expect every valid Wren program to halt.

Exercises

1. Draw a dependency graph for the nonterminal <expr> in the BNF definition of Wren.

2. Consider the following specification of expressions:
    <expr> ::= <element> | <expr> <weak op> <expr>
    <element> ::= <numeral> | <variable>
    <weak op> ::= + | −

    Demonstrate its ambiguity by displaying two derivation trees for the expression "**a–b–c**". Explain how the Wren specification avoids this problem.

3. This Wren program has a number of errors. Classify them as context-free, context-sensitive, or semantic.

         program errors **was**
                 var a,b : **integer**;
                 var p,b ; **boolean**;
             begin
                 a := 34;
                 if b≠0 **then** p := **true else** p := (a+1);
                 write p; **write** q
             end

4. Modify the concrete syntax of Wren by adding an exponential operator ↑ whose precedence is higher than the other arithmetic operators (including unary minus) and whose associativity is right-to-left.

5. This BNF grammar defines expressions with three operations, *, -, and +, and the variables "a", "b", "c", and "d".

> <expr> ::= <thing> | <thing> * <expr>
>
> <object> ::= <element> | <elem> – <object>
>
> <thing> ::= <object> | <thing> + <object>
>
> <element> ::= **a** | **b** | **c** | **d** | (<object>)

a) Give the order of precedence among the three operations.

b) Give the order (left-to-right or right-to-left) of execution for each operation.

c) Explain how the parentheses defined for the nonterminal <element> may be used in these expressions. Describe their limitations.

6. Explain how the Wren productions for <identifier> and <numeral> can be written in the forms allowed for regular grammars (type 3)—namely, <A> ::= **a** or <A> ::= **a** <B>.

7. Explain the relation between left or right recursion in definition of expressions and terms, and the associativity of the binary operations (left-to-right or right-to-left).

8. Write a BNF specification of the syntax of the Roman numerals less than 100. Use this grammar to derive the string "XLVII".

9. Consider a language of expressions over lists of integers. List constants have the form: [3,-6,1], [86], [ ]. General list expressions may be formed using the binary infix operators

> +, –, *, and @ (for concatenation),

where * has the highest precedence, + and - have the same next lower precedence, and @ has the lowest precedence. @ is to be right associative and the other operations are to be left associative. Parentheses may be used to override these rules.

Example: [1,2,3] + [2,2,3] * [5,-1,0] @ [8,21] evaluates to [11,0,3,8,21].

Write a BNF specification for this language of list expressions. Assume that <integer> has already been defined. The conformity of lists for the arithmetic operations is not handled by the BNF grammar since it is a context-sensitive issue.

10. Show that the following grammar for expressions is ambiguous and pro-
    vide an alternative unambiguous grammar that defines the same set of
    expressions.

    <expr> ::= <term> | <factor>
    <term> ::= <factor> | <expr> + <term>
    <factor> ::= <ident> | (<expr>) | <expr> * <factor>
    <ident> ::= **a** | **b** | **c**

11. Consult [Naur63] to see how Algol solves the dangling else problem.

12. Explain how the syntactic ambiguity of the term "a(5)" in Ada is re-
    solved. (*Note*: Ada uses parentheses to enclose array subscripts.)

1.3 VARIANTS OF BNF

Several notational variations of BNF are in common usage for describing
context-free grammars. First we consider an alternate way of expressing regular grammars—namely, by **regular expressions**. Each regular expression E
denotes some language L(E) defined over an alphabet Σ. Figure 1.13 exhibits
the language of regular expressions with ε representing the empty string,
lowercase letters at the beginning of the alphabet portraying symbols in Σ,
and uppercase letters standing for regular expressions.

Regular Expression	Language Denoted
$\varnothing$	$\varnothing$
ε	$\{\varepsilon\}$
a	$\{a\}$
(E • F)	$\{uv \mid u \in L(E) \text{ and } v \in L(F)\} = L(E) \bullet L(F)$
(E | F)	$\{u \mid u \in L(E) \text{ or } u \in L(F)\} = L(E) \cup L(F)$
(E*)	$\{u_1 u_2 ... u_n \mid u_1, u_2, ..., u_n \in L(E) \text{ and } n \geq 0\}$

Figure 1.13: Regular Expressions

The normal precedence for these regular operations is, from highest to low-
est, "*" (Kleene closure or star), "•" (concatenation), and "|" (alternation), so
that some pairs of parentheses may be omitted. Observe that a language over
an alphabet Σ is a subset of Σ^*, the set of all finite length strings of symbols
from Σ.

The BNF definition of <digit> in Wren is already in the form of a regular expression. Numerals in Wren can be written as a regular expression using

<numeral> ::= <digit> • <digit>*.

The concatenation operator "•" is frequently omitted so that identifiers can be defined by

<identifier> ::= <letter> (<letter> | <digit>)*.

Several regular expressions have special abbreviations:

E^+ = E • E* represents the concatenation of one or more strings from L(E).

E^n represents the concatenation of exactly n≥0 strings from L(E).

$E^?$= ε | E represents zero or one string from L(E).

For example, in a language with signed numerals, their specification can be expressed as

<signed numeral> ::= (+ | –)$^?$ <digit>$^+$,

and the context-sensitive language defined in Figure 1.6 can be described as the set { $a^n b^n c^n$ | n≥1 }. Although this set is not regular, it can be described succinctly using this extension of the notation. The new operators "$^+$", "^{n}", and "$^?$" have the same precedence as "*".

The major reason for using the language of regular expressions is to avoid an unnecessary use of recursion in BNF specifications. Braces are also employed to represent zero or more copies of some syntactic category, for example:

<declaration seq> ::= { <declaration> },

<command seq> ::= <command> { ; <command> }, and

<integer expr> ::= <term> { <weak op> <term> }.

In general, braces are defined by { E } = E*. The braces used in this notation bear no relation to the braces that delimit a set. Since the sequencing of commands is an associative operation, these abbreviations for lists lose no information, but for integer expressions we no longer know the precedence for weak operators, left-to-right or right-to-left. Generally, we use only abbreviations in specifying syntax when the lost information is immaterial. The example of command sequences illustrates a place where ambiguity may be allowed in a grammar definition without impairing the accuracy of the definition, at least for program semantics. After all, a command sequence can be thought of simply as a list of commands. A derivation tree for a command sequence can be represented using a nested tree structure or the multibranch tree illustrated in Figure 1.14.

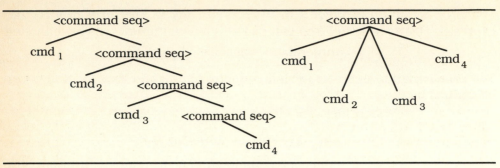

Figure 1.14: Derivation Trees for Command Sequences

Exercises

1. Use braces to replace recursion in specifying variable lists and terms in Wren.

2. Specify the syntax of the Roman numerals less that 100 using regular expressions.

3. Write a BNF grammar that specifies the language of regular expressions in Figure 1.13 over the alphabet $\Sigma = \{\mathbf{a},\mathbf{b},\mathbf{c}\}$. The grammar should enforce the precedence rules for the operators.

4. Investigate possible algebraic laws for the binary operators in regular expressions. Consider associative, commutative, and distributive laws for the operators "•" and "|". Prove properties that hold and give counterexamples for those that do not. Do these binary operations have identities?

5. Prove these special laws for "*":
   a) $E^* = \varepsilon \mid (E{\bullet}E^*)$
   b) $E^* = \varepsilon \mid (E^*{\bullet}E)$
   Hint: Show that the languages, sets of strings, denoted by the expressions are equal.

6. Use regular expressions to define the following token classes:
   a) Integer numerals (positive or negative) with no leading zeros.
   b) Fixed point decimal numerals that must have at least one digit before and after the decimal point.
   c) Identifiers that allow lowercase letters and underscores but with the properties that no underscore occurs at the beginning or the end of the identifier and that it contains no two consecutive underscores.

1.4 ABSTRACT SYNTAX

The BNF definition of a programming language is sometimes referred to as the **concrete syntax** of the language since it tells how to recognize the physical text of a program. Software utilities take a program as a file of characters, recognize that it satisfies the context-free syntax for the language, and produce a derivation tree exhibiting its structure. This software usually decomposes into two parts: a **scanner** or **lexical analyzer** that reads the text and creates a list of tokens and a **parser** or **syntactic analyzer** that forms a derivation tree from the token list based on the BNF definition. Figure 1.15 illustrates this process.

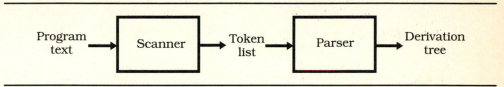

Figure 1.15: The Scanner and Parser

We can think of this process as two functions:

$$\text{scan} \ : \ \text{Character*} \rightarrow \text{Token*}$$

$$\text{parse} \ : \ \text{Token*} \rightarrow \text{Derivation Tree}$$

whose composition "parse ∘ scan" creates a derivation tree from a list of characters forming the physical program.

The success of this process "parse ∘ scan" depends on the accuracy and detail found in the syntactic specification, the BNF, of the programming language. In particular, ambiguity in a language specification may make it impossible to define this function.

Abstract Syntax Trees

Those qualities of a BNF definition that make parsing possible also create a resulting derivation tree containing far more information than necessary for a semantic specification. For example, the categories of terms and elements are required for accurate parsing, but when ascribing meaning to an expression, only its basic structure is needed. Consider the trees in Figures 1.16 and 1.17.

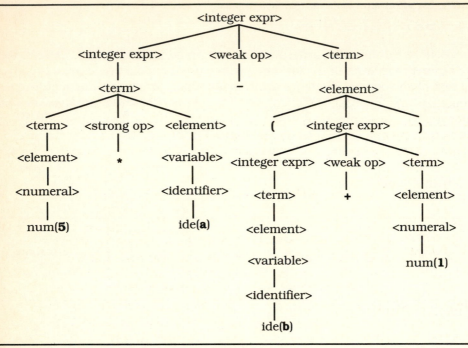

Figure 1.16: A Derivation Tree for **5*a– (b+1)**

The derivation tree retains all the information used in parsing including details that only the parser needs. On the other hand, an **abstract syntax tree** captures the syntactic structure of the expression completely in a much simpler form. After all, the crucial property of the expression "5*a – (b+1)" is that it is a difference of a product and a sum of certain numbers and variables. Any other information is redundant. Figure 1.17 shows two possible abstract syntax trees for the expression. In all three trees, we assume that the text has already been tokenized (scanned).

In transforming a derivation tree into an abstract syntax tree, we generally pull the terminal symbols representing operations and commands up to the root nodes of subtrees, leaving the operands as their children. The second tree in Figure 1.17 varies slightly from this principle in the interest of regularity in expressions. Using this approach, this expression can be thought of as a binary operation and two subexpressions. The choice of the left subtree for the binary operation is arbitrary; it seems to suggest a prefix notation for binary operations, but we are not talking about concrete syntax here, only an abstract representation of certain language constructs. We may choose any representation that we want as long as we can describe the constructs of the language adequately and maintain consistency.

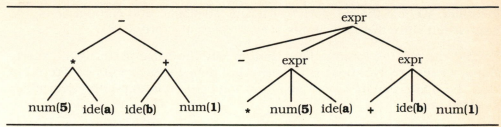

Figure 1.17: Abstract Syntax Trees for **5*a– (b+1)**

The literature of computer science contains considerable confusion between derivation trees and abstract syntax trees; the term parse tree has been used to refer to both kinds of trees. We explain the issue by viewing these trees as abstractions of phrases in a programming language. Derivation trees abstract derivations in the sense that one derivation tree can correspond to several different derivations—for example, leftmost or rightmost. Furthermore, abstract syntax trees abstract derivation trees, since several strings in the language may correspond to the same abstract syntax tree but yet have different derivation trees; for example, "(a+5)–x/2" and "a+5–(x/2)" have the same abstract syntax tree, although their derivation trees are different.

Abstract Syntax of a Programming Language

The point of abstract syntax is simply to communicate the structure of phrases in terms of their semantics in a programming language as trees. Semantics can be defined in terms of derivation trees and actually is with attribute grammars, but most semantic methods are far more understandable when based on a cleaner representation of the phrases in a language. As can be seen from Figure 1.17, designing patterns for abstract syntax allows freedom in format, but for a particular programming language specification, we want uniform templates for the various parts of a language. The blueprints for the abstract syntax trees of a programming language are specified by a collection of syntactic categories or domains and a set of rules telling how categories are decomposed into other categories or tokens.

To design the abstract syntax for a programming langauge, we need to determine which notions (nonterminals) are fundamental to the language and which basic forms the constructs of the language may take. As an example, consider the expressions in Wren—that is, those language phrases derivable from the nonterminal <expr>. By observing the concrete syntax for Wren (Figure 1.8), we see that expressions ultimately consist of operations (**+**, **–**, **and**, **not**, and so on) applied to numerals, identifiers, and Boolean constants (**true** and **false**). Therefore we reduce the nonterminals used to define expressions into three abstract syntactic categories: Expression, Numeral, and

Identifier. We fold the categories of terms, elements, and comparisons into Expression since they are simply special cases of expressions.

To find the abstract productions that specify the basic patterns of expressions, we first repeat those BNF rules that define expressions in Wren, but with the nonterminals <weak op>, <strong op>, <relation>, and <variable> factored out:

<expr> ::= <integer expr> | <boolean expr>

<integer expr> ::= <term>
                | <integer expr> **+** <term> | <integer expr> **–** <term>

<term> ::= <element> | <term> ***** <element> | <term> **/** <element>

<element> ::= <numeral> | <identifier> | **(** <integer expr> **)** | **–** <element>

<boolean expr> ::= <boolean term> | <boolean expr> **or** <boolean term>

<boolean term> ::= <boolean element>
                | <boolean term> **and** <boolean element>

<boolean element> ::= **true** | **false** | <identifier> | <comparison>
                | **not (** <boolean expr> **)** | **(** <boolean expr> **)**

<comparison> ::= <integer expr> **<=** <integer expr>
                | <integer expr> **<** <integer expr>
                | <integer expr> **=** <integer expr>
                | <integer expr> **>=** <integer expr>
                | <integer expr> **>** <integer expr>
                | <integer expr> **<>** <integer expr>

Observe that in a derivation

<expr> $\Rightarrow$ <integer expr> $\Rightarrow$ <term> $\Rightarrow$ <element> $\Rightarrow$ <numeral>,

the only essential information relative to Wren is that an expression can be a numeral. Outside of the parsing problem, the intervening nonterminals play no essential role in describing Wren. Therefore unit rules such as <integer expr> ::= <term>, can be ignored unless they involve basic components of expressions, such as numerals, identifiers, or essential nonterminals. So we select only those rules from the BNF that describe the structure of possible expressions. Omitting parenthesized expressions, the following list results:

<integer expr> **+** <term>

<integer expr> **–** <term>

<term> ***** <element>

<term> **/** <element>

<numeral>

<identifier>

– <element>

<boolean expr> **or** <boolean term>

<boolean term> **and** <boolean element>

true

false

not (<boolean expr> **)**

<integer expr> **<=** <integer expr>

<integer expr> **<** <integer expr>

<integer expr> **=** <integer expr>

<integer expr> **>=** <integer expr>

<integer expr> **>** <integer expr>

<integer expr> **<>** <integer expr>

After the redundant nonterminals are merged into Expression, these basic templates can be summarized by the following abstract production rules:

Expression ::= Numeral | Identifier | **true** | **false**
            | Expression Operator Expression | – Expression
            | **not(** Expression **)**

Operator ::= **+** | **–** | ***** | **/** | **or** | **and** | **<=** | **<** | **=** | **>** | **>=** | **<>**

An abstract syntax for Wren is given in Figure 1.18. This abstract syntax delineates the possible abstract syntax trees that may be produced by programs in the language. To avoid confusion with concrete syntax, we utilize a slightly different notation for abstract production rules, using identifiers starting with uppercase letters for syntactic categories.

Notice that a definition of abstract syntax tolerates more ambiguity since the concrete syntax has already determined the correct interpretation of the symbols in the program text. We investigate a formal description of abstract syntax in Chapter 12, using the terminology of algebraic semantics.

We suggested earlier that parsing a program results in the construction of a derivation tree for the program. As a consequence of adhering to the BNF syntax of a language, any parsing algorithm must at least implicitly create a derivation tree. But in fact we usually design a parser to generate an abstract syntax tree instead of a derivation tree. Therefore the syntax of "parse" is given by

                    parse : Token* → Abstract Syntax Tree.

Abstract Syntactic Categories

Program	Type	Operator
Block	Command	Numeral
Declaration	Expression	Identifier

Abstract Production Rules

Program ::= **program** Identifier **is** Block

Block ::= Declaration* **begin** Command$^+$ **end**

Declaration ::= **var** Identifier$^+$: Type ;

Type ::= **integer** | **boolean**

Command ::= Identifier **:=** Expression | **skip** | **read** Identifier

    | **write** Expression | **while** Expression **do** Command$^+$

    | **if** Expression **then** Command$^+$

    | **if** Expression **then** Command$^+$ **else** Command$^+$

Expression ::= Numeral | Identifier | **true** | **false**

    | Expression Operator Expression | – Expression

    | **not(** Expression**)**

Operator ::= **+** | **–** | ***** | **/** | **or** | **and** | **<=** | **<** | **=** | **>** | **>=** | **<>**

Figure 1.18: Abstract Syntax for Wren

Generally, this parse function will not be one to one. The token lists for the expressions "a+b-c" and "(a+b-c)" map to the same abstract syntax tree. The main point of abstract syntax is to omit the details of physical representation, leaving only the forms of the abstract trees that may be produced. For example, the abstract syntax has no need for parentheses since they are just used to disambiguate expressions. Once this assessment has been done by the parser, the resulting abstract trees have unambiguous meaning, since the branching of trees accurately conveys the hierarchical structure of a phrase. Whereas the concrete syntax defines the way programs in a language are actually written, the abstract syntax captures the pure structure of phrases in the language by specifying the logical relations (relative to the intended semantics) between parts of the language. We can think of an abstract syntax tree as embodying the derivation history of a phrase in the language without mentioning all of the terminal and nonterminal symbols.

When we implement a parser using Prolog in Chapter 2, the parsing operation applied to the token string for the expression "5*a – (b+1)" will create a Prolog structure:

```
expr(minus,expr(times,num(5),ide(a)),expr(plus,ide(b),num(1))),
```

which is a linear representation of one of the abstract syntax trees in Figure
1.17. See Appendix A for a definition of Prolog structures.

In the abstract production rules, lists of declarations, commands, and identifiers are described by means of the closure operators "*" and "+". An alternative approach used in many formal methods of specifying semantics involves direct recursion as in:

   command = command **;** command | identifier **:=** expression | **skip** | ....

The closure operator "+" on commands ignores the occurrence of semicolons
between commands, but in abstract syntax semicolons are only cosmetic.
Although the abstract production rules in Figure 1.18 use reserved words,
these act only as mnemonic devices to help us recognize the phrases being
formulated. In fact, not all the reserved words are used in the productions,
only enough to suggest the structure of the programming constructs. Note
that we have deleted **end if** and **end while** for the sake of conciseness.

An alternative way of describing the abstract production rules is displayed in
Figure 1.19 where the definitions are given as tagged record structures. Actually, the notation used to specify the abstract productions is not crucial.
The important property of abstract syntax is embodied in the relationships
between the categories; for example, a **while** command consists of an expression and a list of commands. As mathematical objects, the various categories are built from aggregations (Cartesian products), alternations (disjoint unions), and list structures. Any notations for these three constructors
can serve to define the abstract production rules. We explore these mathematical structures more carefully in Chapter 10.

As an example, consider abstract pattern of the command

while n>0 **do write** n; n:=n-1 **end while**.

Figure 1.20 shows an abstract syntax tree for this command based on the
abstract syntax defined in Figure 1.18. Since the body of a while command is
a command sequence, we need an extra level in the tree to represent the list
of commands. In contrast, following the abstract syntax specification in Figure 1.19 produces a structure representing a similar abstract syntax tree:

   while(*expr*(>,ide(n),num(0)),
         [*write*(ide(n)),*assign*(ide(n), *expr*(-,ide(n),num(1)))]).

The list of commands (a command sequence) in the body of the while command is represented as a list using brackets in the structure. This notation
agrees with that used by Prolog lists in the next chapter—namely, [a, b, c].
The abstract syntax tree of a complete Wren program as a Prolog structure
can be found at the beginning of Chapter 2. Notice the lists of variables,
declarations, and commands in the representation of that tree.

Abstract Production Rules

Program ::= *prog*(Identifier, Block)

Block ::= *block*(Declaration*, Command⁺)

Declaration ::= *dec*(Type, Identifier⁺)

Type ::= *integer* | *boolean*

Command ::= *assign*(Identifier, Expression) | *skip*

　　　| *read*(Identifier) | *write*(Expression)

　　　| *while*(Expression, Command⁺) | *if*(Expression, Command⁺)

　　　| *ifelse*(Expression, Command⁺, Command⁺)

Expression ::= Numeral | Identifier | *true* | *false* | *not*(Expression)

　　　| *expr*(Operator, Expression, Expression) | *minus*(Expression)

Operator ::= + | – | * | / | *or* | *and* | <= | < | = | > | >= | <>

Figure 1.19: Alternative Abstract Syntax for Wren

Although concrete syntax is essential to implementing programming languages, it is the abstract syntax that lies at the heart of semantic definitions. The concrete syntax is incidental to language specification, but it is important to users since it influences the way they think about a language. This aspect of pragmatics is not of direct concern to us in studying the semantics of programming languages.

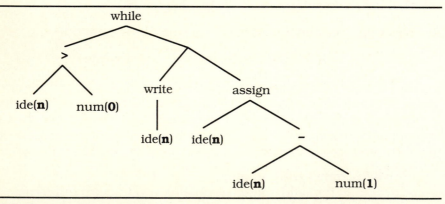

Figure 1.20: Abstract Syntax Tree

It can be argued that when designing a new programming language, we need to formulate the abstract syntax along with the semantics so that the meaning of a program emanates from a mapping

　　　meaning : Abstract Syntax Trees → Semantic Objects

where the semantic objects provide meaning for the various language constructs. Different approaches to semantics depend on the disparate kinds of objects used to define meaning. Later we will see that this discussion is skewed to the denotational approach to semantics, but viewing meaning as a function from syntactic phrases to some sort of semantic objects can be a useful way of organizing formal semantics.

Given the abstract syntax of a programming language, the concrete syntax can be defined by an operation

unparse : Abstract Syntax Trees → Concrete Syntax

where Concrete Syntax refers to derivation trees, to lists of tokens, or to lists of characters representing program texts. Since two different phrases following the concrete syntax may produce the same abstract syntax tree, *unparse* may not be a function at all. To ensure that *unparse* is a well-defined function, some canonical representation of concrete phrases must be specified— for example, taking expressions having the fewest parentheses. The correctness of a parsing algorithm can be demonstrated by showing that it is the inverse, in some sense, of the *unparse* function.

Exercises

1. Construct a derivation tree and an abstract syntax tree for the Wren command

    "if n>0 then a := 3 else skip end if".

    Also write the abstract tree as a Prolog structure.

2. Parse the following token list to produce an abstract syntax tree:
    [while, not, lparen, ide(done), rparen, do, ide(n), assign,
    ide(n), minus, num(1), semicolon, ide(done), assign,
    ide(n), greater, num(0), end, while]

3. Draw an abstract syntax tree for the following Wren program:
    program binary **is**
        var n,p : **integer**;
    begin
        read n; p := 2;
        while p<=n **do** p := 2*p **end while**;
        p := p/2;
        while p>0 **do**
            if n>= p **then write** 1; n := n–p **else write** 0 **end if**;
            p := p/2
        end while
    end

4. Using the concrete syntax of Wren, draw abstract syntax trees or record-like structures following the definition in Figure 1.19 for these language constructs:

   a) (a+7)*(n/2)

   b) **while** n>=0 **do** s:=s+(n*n); n:= n–1 **end while**

   c) **if** a **and** b **or** c **then read** m; **write** m **else** a:=**not**(b **and** c) **end if**

1.5 FURTHER READING

The concepts and terminology for describing the syntax of languages derives from Noam Chomsky's seminal work in the 1950s—for example, [Chomsky56] and [Chomsky59]. His classification of grammars and the related theory has been adopted for the study of programming languages. Most of this material falls into the area of the theory of computation. For additional material, see [Hopcroft79] and [Martin91]. These books and many others contain results on the expressiveness and limitations of the classes of grammars and on derivations, derivation trees, and syntactic ambiguity.

John Backus and Peter Naur defined BNF in conjunction with the group that developed Algol60. The report [Naur63] describing Algol syntax using BNF is still one of the clearest presentations of a programming language, although the semantics is given informally.

Most books on compiler writing contain extensive discussions of syntax specification, derivation trees, and parsing. These books sometimes confuse the notions of concrete and abstract syntax, but they usually contain extensive examples of lexical and syntactic analysis. We recommend [Aho86] and [Parsons92]. Compiler writers typically disagree with our distinction between syntax and semantics, putting context constraints with semantics under the name static semantics. Our view that static semantics is an oxymoron is supported by [Meek90].

Abstract syntax was first described by John McCarthy in the context of Lisp [McCarthy65a]. More material on abstract syntax and other issues pertaining to the syntax of programming languages can be found in various textbooks on formal syntax and semantics, including [Watt91] and [Meyer90]. The book by Roland Backhouse concentrates exclusively on the syntax of programming languages [Backhouse79].

Chapter 2
INTRODUCTION TO
LABORATORY ACTIVITIES

The laboratory activities introduced in this chapter and used elsewhere in the text are not required to understand definitional techniques and formal specifications, but we feel that laboratory practice will greatly enhance the learning experience. The laboratories provide a way not only to write language specifications but to test and debug them. Submitting specifications as a prototyping system will uncover oversights and subtleties that are not apparent to a casual reader. This laboratory approach also suggests that formal definitions of programming languages can be useful. The laboratory activities are carried out using Prolog. Readers not familiar with Prolog, should consult Appendix A or one of the references on Prolog (see the further readings at the end of this chapter) before proceeding.

In this chapter we develop a "front end" for a programming language processing system. Later we use this front end for a system that check the context-sensitive part of the Wren grammar and for prototype interpreters based on semantic specifications that provide implementations of programming languages.

The front end consists of two parts:
1. A scanner that reads a text file containing a Wren program and builds a Prolog list of tokens representing the meaningful atomic components of the program.
2. A parser that matches the tokens to the BNF definition of Wren, producing an abstract syntax tree corresponding to the Wren program.

Our intention here is not to construct production level software but to formulate an understandable, workable, and correct language system. The Prolog code will be kept simple and easy to read, since the main purpose here is to understand the definitional techniques studied in the text. Generally, only primitive error handling is provided, so that the scanner-parser system merely fails when a program has incorrect context-free syntax.

The system requests the name of a file containing a program, scans the program producing a token list, and parses it, creating an abstract syntax tree representing the structure of the program. The transcript below shows a typical execution of the scanner and parser. User input is depicted in boldface. The token list and abstract syntax tree have been formatted to make them easier to read.

```
| ?- go.
```

```
>>> Scanning and Parsing Wren <<<
```

Enter name of source file: **switch.wren**

```
    program switch is
       var sum,k : integer;
       var switch : boolean;
    begin
       switch := true; sum := 0;   k := 1;
       while k<10 do
          switch := not(switch);
          if switch then sum := sum+k end if;
          k := k+1
       end while;
       write sum
    end
```

```
Scan successful
```

```
[program,ide(switch),is,var,ide(sum),comma,ide(k),colon,integer,
 semicolon,var,ide(switch),colon,boolean,semicolon,begin,
 ide(switch),assign,true,semicolon,ide(sum),assign,num(0),
 semicolon,ide(k),assign,num(1),semicolon,while,ide(k),less,
 num(10),do,ide(switch),assign,not,lparen,ide(switch),rparen,
 semicolon,if,ide(switch),then,ide(sum),assign,ide(sum),plus,
 ide(k),end,if,semicolon,ide(k),assign,ide(k),plus,num(1),end,
 while,semicolon,write,ide(sum),end,eop]
```

```
Parse successful
```

```
prog([dec(integer,[sum,k]),dec(boolean,[switch])],
     [assign(switch,true),assign(sum,num(0)),assign(k,num(1)),
      while(exp(less,ide(k),num(10)),
          [assign(switch,bnot(ide(switch))),
           if(ide(switch),
               [assign(sum,exp(plus,ide(sum),ide(k)))],skip),
           assign(k,exp(plus,ide(k),num(1)))]),
      write(ide(sum))])
```

```
yes
```

Observe that the program "switch.wren", although satisfying the context-free syntax of Wren, is syntactically illegal. Review the context constraints in Figure 1.11 to identify the (minor) error. Several predefined predicates, primarily for input and output, are used to build the front end of the language processing system. See Appendix A for a brief description of these predicates.

2.1 SCANNING

The scanner reads the program text and produces a list of tokens according to the lexical syntax of the programming language. Recall that the lexical syntax can be defined using a regular grammar—for example,

> <numeral> ::= **0** | **1** | ... | **9** | **0** <numeral>
>
> | **1** <numeral> | ... | **9** <numeral>,

which we abbreviate as

> <numeral> ::= <digit> | <digit> <numeral>
>
> <digit> ::= **0** | **1** | **2** | **3** | **4** | **5** | **6** | **7** | **8** | **9**.

First we recognize a digit by specifying a span of ascii values.

> digit(C) :- 48 =< C, C =< 57.   % 0-9

The symbol "%" signals a comment that extends to the end of the line.

The form of these productions fits nicely with processing a stream of characters in Prolog. We name the predicate that collects a sequence of digits into a numeral getnum and write the productions for numeral as

> getnum ::= digit | digit getnum.

The first digit tells us that we have a numeral to process. We split the production into two parts, the first to start the processing of a numeral and the second to continue the processing until a nondigit occurs in the input stream.

> getnum ::= digit restnum
>
> restnum ::= ε | digit restnum   % ε represents an empty string

We describe these regular productions using the transition diagram shown in Figure 2.1.

Parameters are then added to the nonterminals, the first to hold a readahead character and the second to contain the numeral being constructed, either as a Prolog number or as a list of ascii values representing the digits.

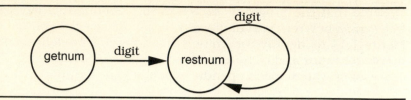

Figure 2.1: A Transition Diagram for getnum

The predicates are defined by

getnum(C,N) :- digit(C), get0(D), restnum(D,Lc), name(N,[C|Lc]).

restnum(C,[C|Lc]) :- digit(C), get0(D), restnum(D,Lc).

restnum(C,[ ]).   % end numeral if C is not a digit

and the numeral processor is initiated by the query

get0(C), getnum(C,N).

The first get0 acts as a priming read that gets (inputs) the first character, which is bound to C for getnum to process. Then getnum verifies that the first character is a digit, gets the next character, which is bound to D, and asks restnum to construct the tail Lc of the numeral. When restnum returns with the tail, the entire list [C|Lc] of digits passes to the predefined predicate name, which converts it into a Prolog number N. The predicate restnum reads characters forming them into a list until a nondigit is obtained, finishing the list with an empty tail.

Figure 2.2 shows a trace following the processing of the numeral given by the characters "905" followed by a return. This string generates the ascii values 57, 48, 53, and 10 on the input stream. Note that variables are numbered, since each recursive call requires a fresh set of variables to be instantiated. For example, the predicate get0 is called four times with the variables C, D, D1, and D2, respectively.

This example illustrates the basic principle behind the scanner—namely, to get the first item in a list and then call another predicate to construct the tail of the list. This second predicate is called repeatedly, with the items in the list being constructed as the first elements of the subsequent tails. When no more items are possible, the empty tail is returned. In order to comprehend the scanner better, we uniformly name the variables found in it:

Character (an ascii value): C, D, E

Token (a Prolog atom or simple structure): T, U

List of Characters: Lc

List of Tokens: Lt

Query	Bindings
get0(C)	C = 57
getnum(57,N)	
digit(57)	
get0(D)	D = 48
restnum(48,Lc)	Lc = [48|Lc1]
digit(48)	
get0(D1)	D1 = 53
restnum(53,Lc1)	Lc1 = [53|Lc2]
digit(53)	
get0(D2)	D2 = 10
restnum(10,Lc2)	Lc2 = [10|Lc3]
digit(10)	fails
restnum(10,Lc2)	Lc2 = [ ]
name(N,[57|Lc])	
where Lc = [48|Lc1] = [48,53|Lc2] = [48,53]	
name(N,[57,48,53]) gives N=905.	

Figure 2.2: Reading the Numeral 905

The predicates used in the scanner are described informally below, following the convention that input variables are marked by "+" and output variables by "–". Although most predicates in Prolog are invertible, meaning that variables can act as input or output parameters in different applications, the scanner needs to act in one direction only since it involves the side effect of reading a text file. The marking of parameters by "+" and "–" below will help the reader understand the execution of the scanner. Observe that some of the predicates have two variables for characters, one for the current lookahead character and one for the next lookahead character.

scan(Lt)

    – Construct a list of tokens Lt.

restprog(T,D,Lt)

    + T is the previous token.

    + D is the lookahead character.

    – Construct a list of tokens Lt from the rest of the program.

getch(C)

    – Get the next character C and echo the character.

gettoken(C,T,D)

+ C is the lookahead character.

− Construct the next token T and

−   find the next lookahead character D.

restnum(C,[C|Lc],E)

+ C is the lookahead character.

− Construct the tail of the number Lc and

−   find the next lookahead character E.

restid(C,[C|Lc],E)

+ C is the lookahead character.

− Construct the tail of the identifier or reserved word string Lc and

−   find the next lookahead character E.

To enable the scanner to recognize the different classes of characters, we define predicates, each representing a particular set of characters.

```
lower(C) :- 97=<C, C=<122.        % a-z
upper(C) :- 65=<C, C=<90.         % A-Z
digit(C) :- 48 =< C, C=< 57.      % 0-9
space(32).        tabch(9).           period(46).          slash(47).
endline(10).      endfile(26).        endfile(-1).
whitespace(C) :- space(C) ; tabch(C) ; endline(C).
idchar(C) :- lower(C) ; digit(C).
```

At the top level of the scanner, scan gets the first character, calls gettoken to find the first token, and then uses restprog to construct the rest of the token list. Each line of the program listing is indented four spaces by means of tab(4). Both scan and restprog invoke gettoken with a lookahead character C. When the end of the file is reached, gettoken returns a special atom eop symbolizing the end of the program. Note that getch performs special duties if the current character represents the end of a line or the end of the file.

```
scan([T|Lt]) :- tab(4), getch(C), gettoken(C,T,D), restprog(T,D,Lt).
getch(C) :- get0(C), (endline(C),nl,tab(4) ; endfile(C),nl ; put(C)).
restprog(eop,C,[ ]).            % end of file reached with previous character
restprog(T,C,[U|Lt]) :- gettoken(C,U,D), restprog(U,D,Lt).
```

To classify symbolic tokens, we need to identify those that are constructed from a single symbol and those that are constructed from two characters. Unfortunately, the first character in the two-character symbols may also stand alone. Therefore we classify symbols as single or double and provide a predicate to recognize the two-character symbols. Symbols specified by the predicate single consist of a single character. This predicate associates a token name with the ascii code of each character.

single(40,lparen).	single(41,rparen).	single(42,times).
single(43,plus).	single(44,comma).	single(45,minus).
single(47,divides).	single(59,semicolon).	single(61,equal).

Characters that may occur as a symbol by themselves or may be the first character in a string of length two are recognized by the predicate double. The second argument for double names the token given by the one-character symbol.

double(58,colon).	double(60,less).	double(62,grtr).

If, however, the symbol is two characters long, pair succeeds and provides the name of the token.

```
pair(58,61,assign).        % :=
pair(60,61,lteq).          % <=
pair(60,62,neq).           % <>
pair(62,61,gteq).          % >=
```

We also need to recognize the reserved words in Wren. The predicate reswd defines the set of reserved words.

reswd(program).	reswd(is).	reswd(begin).	reswd(end).
reswd(var).	reswd(integer).	reswd(boolean).	reswd(read).
reswd(write).	reswd(while).	reswd(do).	reswd(if).
reswd(then).	reswd(else).	reswd(skip).	reswd(or).
reswd(and).	reswd(true).	reswd(false).	reswd(not).

Figure 2.3 displays a transition diagram for analyzing the kinds of tokens in Wren. The Prolog code for scanning tokens is given below. Numerals are handled in the manner we discussed earlier. Although the productions for identifiers permit reserved words to be treated as identifiers, the scanner will first check each character string to see whether it is an identifier or a reserved word. Identifier tokens take the form ide(sum) while reserved words stand for themselves as Prolog atoms.

```
gettoken(C,num(N),E) :- digit(C), getch(D), restnum(D,Lc,E), name(N,[C|Lc]).
restnum(C,[C|Lc],E) :- digit(C), getch(D), restnum(D,Lc,E).
restnum(C,[ ],C).              % end of number if C is not a digit

gettoken(C,T,E) :- lower(C), getch(D), restid(D,Lc,E),
                   name(Id,[C|Lc]), (reswd(Id),T=Id ; T=ide(Id)).
restid(C,[C|Lc],E) :- idchar(C), getch(D), restid(D,Lc,E).
restid(C,[ ],C).               % end of identifier if C is not an id character
```

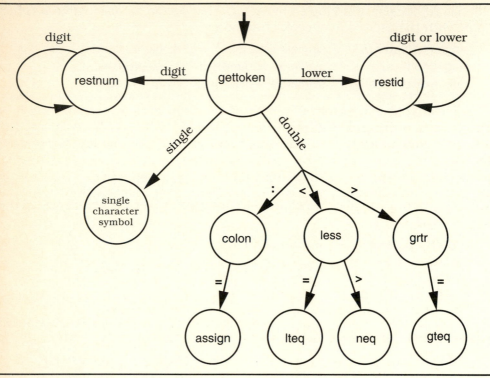

Figure 2.3: Classifying Tokens

gettoken(C,T,D) :- single(C,T), getch(D).

gettoken(C,T,E) :- double(C,U), getch(D), (pair(C,D,T),getch(E) ; T=U,E=D).

gettoken(C,eop,0) :- endfile(C).

gettoken(C,T,E) :- whitespace(C), getch(D), gettoken(D,T,E).

gettoken(C,T,E) :- write('Illegal character: '), put(C), nl, abort.

Single-character symbols are handled directly, while the two-character symbols require a decision guarded by pair. If pair succeeds, a new lookahead character is needed; otherwise, the token name is taken from the double predicate and the original lookahead character is used. When an end-of-file character occurs as the lookahead character, the token eop is returned. The predicate gettoken also allows for whitespace to be skipped, as seen in the next to the last clause. Finally, any illegal characters are trapped in the last clause, causing the scanner to abort with an error message.

To make the scanner easy to use, we define a predicate go that requests the name of the text file containing the Wren program to be scanned and invokes the scanner. Notice how it opens the text file for reading and closes it after the scanning is complete. The list of tokens is displayed by means of the predefined predicate write.

```
go :- nl, write('>>> Scanning Wren <<<'), nl, nl,
      write('Enter name of source file: '), nl, getfilename(fileName), nl,
      see(fileName), scan(Tokens), seen, write('Scan successful'), nl, nl,
      write(Tokens), nl.
```

The predicate for reading the file name is patterned on the code for scanning a numeral or an identifier. A priming read (get0) is followed by a predicate that accumulates a list of ascii values for the characters in the file name. We permit both uppercase and lowercase letters as well as digits, period, and slash in our file names. That enables the scanner to handle file names such as "gcd.wren" and "Programs/Factorial". Other symbols may be added at the user's discretion.

```
getfilename(W) :- get0(C), restfilename(C,Cs), name(W,Cs).
restfilename(C,[C|Cs]) :- filechar(C), get0(D), restfilename(D,Cs).
restfilename(C,[ ]).

filechar(C) :- lower(C) ; upper(C) ; digit(C) ; period(C) ; slash(C).
```

The transcript at the beginning of this chapter shows an execution of the scanner on a Wren program.

Exercises

1. Modify the scanner for Wren so that it accepts and recognizes the following classes of tokens:

   a) Character strings of the form "abcde".

   b) Character constants of the form 'a' or #\a.

   c) Fixed point numerals of the form 123.45.

2. Change the scanner for Wren so that "/=" is recognized instead of "<>".

3. Change the scanner for Wren so that "<=" and ">=" can also be entered as "=<" and "=>".

4. Add a repeat-until command to Wren and change the scanner appropriately.

5. Write a scanner for English using the alphabet of uppercase and lower-case letters and the following punctuation symbols: period, comma, ques-

tion mark, semicolon, colon, and exclamation. Each word and punctuation symbol in the text will be a token in the scanner.

6. Write a scanner that constructs a token list for a Roman numeral. Ignore any characters that are not part of the Roman numeral.

7. Write a scanner for the language of list expressions described in exercise 9 at the end of section 1.2.

2.2 LOGIC GRAMMARS

The parser forms the second part of the front end of our language processing system. It receives a token list from the scanner, and, following the BNF definition of the language, produces an abstract syntax tree. Prolog provides a mechanism, **definite clause grammars**, that makes the parser particularly easy to construct. Although the resulting system cannot compare in efficiency to present-day compilers for parsing, these grammars serve admirably for our prototype systems. Definite clause grammars are also called **logic grammars**, and we use these terms interchangeably.

Concrete Syntax

                \<sentence\> ::= \<noun phrase\> \<verb phrase\> **.**

                \<noun phrase\> ::= \<determiner\> \<noun\>

                \<verb phrase\> ::= \<verb\> | \<verb\> \<noun phrase\>

                \<determiner\> ::= **a** | **the**

                \<noun\> ::= **boy** | **girl** | **cat** | **telescope** | **song** | **feather**

                \<verb\> ::= **saw** | **touched** | **surprised** | **sang**

Abstract Syntax

                Sentence ::= NounPhrase Predicate

                NounPhrase ::= Determiner Noun

                Predicate ::= Verb | Verb NounPhrase

                Determiner ::= **a** | **the**

                Noun ::= **boy** | **girl** | **cat** | **telescope** | **song** | **feather**

                Verb ::= **saw** | **touched** | **surprised** | **sang**

Figure 2.4: An English Grammar

First, we motivate and explain the nature of parsing in Prolog with an example based on a subset of the English grammar found in Figure 1.1. To simplify the problem, we consider an English grammar without prepositional phrases. The BNF and abstract syntax are displayed in Figure 2.4. The abstract syntax closely resembles the concrete syntax with a slight change in names for syntactic categories and the deletion of the period.

Given a string from the language, say "**the girl sang a song.**", our goal is to construct an abstract syntax tree exhibiting the structure of this sentence— for example, the tree in Figure 2.5. This abstract syntax tree is quite similar to a derivation tree for the sentence.

Since we plan to carry out the parsing in Prolog, the resulting abstract syntax tree will be represented as a Prolog structure, with function symbols used to tag the syntactic categories:

sent(nounph(det(the), noun(girl)), pred(verb(sang), nounph(det(a), noun(song)))).

Observe how nicely Prolog describes a tree structure in a linear form. Recall that we view the front end for our English language grammar as a two-step process: the scanner takes a string of characters, "**the girl sang a song.**", and creates the token list [the, girl, sang, a, song, '.']; and the parser takes the token list and constructs an abstract syntax tree as a Prolog structure, such as the one above.

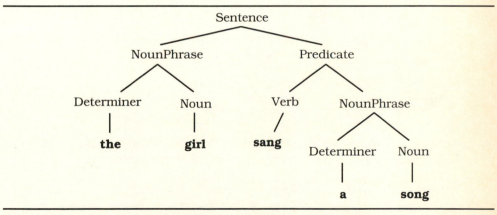

Figure 2.5: An Abstract Syntax Tree for "**the girl sang a song.**"

Motivating Logic Grammars

Although logic grammars in Prolog can be used without understanding how they work, we choose to explain their mechanism. The reader who wants to ignore this topic may skip to the subsection **Prolog Grammar Rules**.

Assume that the token list [the, girl, sang, a, song, '.'] has been generated by the scanner. The logic programming approach to analyzing a sentence according to a grammar can be seen in terms of a graph whose edges are labeled by the tokens that are terminals in the language.

Two terminals are contiguous in the original string if they share a common node in the graph.

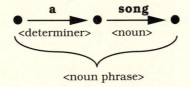

A sequence of contiguous labels constitutes a nonterminal if it corresponds to the right-hand side of a production rule for that nonterminal in the BNF grammar. For example, the three productions

<determiner> ::= **a**,

<noun> ::= **song**, and

<noun phrase> ::= <determiner> <noun>

tell us that "a song" can serve as a noun phrase. Since these two terminals lie next to each other in the graph, we know they constitute a noun phrase.

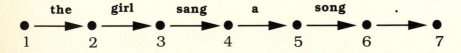

To enable these conditions to be expressed in logic, we give each node in the graph an arbitrary label—for example, using positive integers.

A predicate nounPhrase(K,L) is defined as asserting that the path from node K to node L can be interpreted as an instance of the nonterminal <noun phrase>. For example, nounPhrase(4,6) holds because edge <4,5> is labeled by a determiner **a** and edge <5,6> is labeled by a noun **song**.

The appropriate rule for <noun phrase> is

    nounPhrase(K,L) :- determiner(K,M), noun(M,L).

The common variable M makes the two edges contiguous. The complete BNF grammar written in logic is listed in Figure 2.6.

```
sentence(K,L) :- nounPhrase(K,M), predicate(M,N), period(N,L).
nounPhrase(K,L) :- determiner(K,M), noun(M,L).
predicate(K,L) :- verb(K,M), nounPhrase(M,L).
predicate(K,L) :- verb(K,L).
determiner(K,L) :- a(K,L).
determiner(K,L) :- the(K,L).
noun(K,L) :- boy(K,L).
noun(K,L) :- girl(K,L).
noun(K,L) :- cat(K,L).
noun(K,L) :- telescope(K,L).
noun(K,L) :- song(K,L).
noun(K,L) :- feather(K,L).
verb(K,L) :- saw(K,L).
verb(K,L) :- touched(K,L).
verb(K,L) :- surprised(K,L).
verb(K,L) :- sang(K,L).
```

Figure 2.6: Parsing in Prolog

The graph for the sentence **"the girl sang a song."** can be created by entering the following facts:

```
the(1,2).        girl(2,3).
sang(3,4).       a(4,5).
song(5,6).       period(6,7).
```

The syntactic correctness of the sentence, **"the girl sang a song."** can be determined by either of the following queries:

```
?- sentence(1,7).
yes

?- sentence(X,Y).
X = 1
Y = 7
yes
```

The sentence is recognized by the logic program when paths in the graph corresponding to the syntactic categories in the grammar are verified as building an instance of the nonterminal <sentence>.

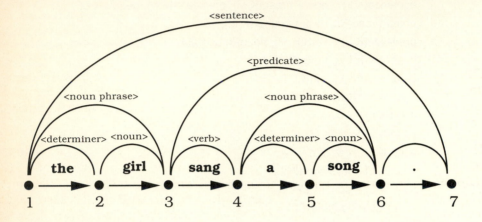

Note the similarity of the structure exhibited by the paths in the graph with the derivation tree for the sentence.

Improving the Parser

Two problems remain before this parser will be easy to use:

1. Entering the graph using predicates the(1,2), girl(2,3), ... is awkward since the scanner produces only a list of tokens—namely, [the,girl,sang a, song,'.'].

2. So far the logic program recognizes only a syntactically valid sentence and does not produce a representation of the abstract syntax tree for the sentence.

The first problem can be solved and the logic program simplified by using sublists of the token list to label the nodes of the graph. These lists are called **difference lists** since the difference between two adjacent node labels is the atom that labels the intervening edge.

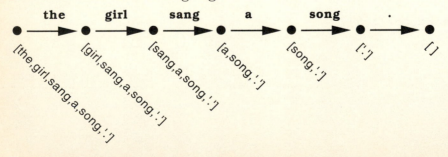

In general, a difference list is a Prolog structure consisting of two Prolog lists, with possibly uninstantiated components, having the property that the second list is or can be a suffix of the first one. Together they represent those items in the first list but not in the second list. For example,

difflist([a,b,c,d],[c,d]) represents the list [a,b], and

difflist([a,b,c|T],T) represents the list [a,b,c].

The concatenation of difference lists can be performed in constant time under certain conditions. Therefore many algorithms have very efficient versions using difference lists. For more on this technique of programming in Prolog, see the further readings at the end of the chapter.

The next version of the grammar exploits the same definitions for sentence, nounPhrase, and predicate, but it handles the tokens using a predicate 'C' (for "connect"), which is predefined in most Prolog implementations. The query 'C'(K,boy,L) succeeds if the edge joining the nodes K and L is labeled by the token boy. Figure 2.7 gives the Prolog code for the improved parser. The variables in the Prolog code stand for difference lists now instead of natural numbers.

```
sentence(K,L) :- nounPhrase(K,M), predicate(M,R), 'C'(R,'.',L).
nounPhrase(K,L) :- determiner(K,M), noun(M,L).
predicate(K,L) :- verb(K,M), nounPhrase(M,L).
predicate(K,L) :- verb(K,L).
determiner(K,L) :- 'C'(K,a,L).
determiner(K,L) :- 'C'(K,the,L).
noun(K,L) :- 'C'(K,boy,L).
noun(K,L) :- 'C'(K,girl,L).
noun(K,L) :- 'C'(K,cat,L).
noun(K,L) :- 'C'(K,telescope,L).
noun(K,L) :- 'C'(K,song,L).
noun(K,L) :- 'C'(K,feather,L).
verb(K,L) :- 'C'(K,saw,L).
verb(K,L) :- 'C'(K,touched,L).
verb(K,L) :- 'C'(K,surprised,L).
verb(K,L) :- 'C'(K,sang,L).
'C'([H|T],H,T).      % Edge from node [H|T] to node T is labeled with atom H
```

Figure 2.7: Improved Parsingin Prolog

An advantage of this approach is that the graph need not be explicitly created when this representation is employed. The syntactic correctness of the sentence "**the girl sang a song.**" can be recognized by the following query:

```
?- sentence([the,girl,sang,a,song,'.'],[ ]).
yes
```

The parsing succeeds because the node labeled with [the,girl,sang,a,song,'.'] can be joined to the node labeled with [ ] by a path representing the sentence predicate. Now the parsing query fits the scanner, since the arguments to sentence are the token list and the tail that remains when the tokens in the sentence are consumed.

By exploiting the invertibility of logic programming, it is possible to use the logic grammar to generate sentences in the language with the following query:

```
?- sentence(S, [ ]).
S = [a,boy,saw,a,boy,.] ;
S = [a,boy,saw,a,girl,.] ;
S = [a,boy,saw,a,cat,.] ;
S = [a,boy,saw,a,telescope,.] ;
S = [a,boy,saw,a,song,.] ;
S = [a,boy,saw,a,feather,.] ;
S = [a,boy,saw,the,boy,.] ;
S = [a,boy,saw,the,girl,.] ;
S = [a,boy,saw,the,cat,.]
yes
```

Using semicolons to resume the inference engine, we initiate the construction of all the sentences defined by the grammar. If the grammar contains a recursive rule, say with the conjunction **and**,

> NounPhrase ::= Determiner Noun
> | Determiner Noun **and** NounPhrase,

then the language allows infinitely many sentences, and the sentence generator will get stuck with ever-lengthening nounPhrase phrases, such as "**a boy saw a boy.**", "**a boy saw a boy and a boy.**", "**a boy saw a boy and a boy and a boy.**", and so on.

Prolog Grammar Rules

Most implementations of Prolog have a preprocessor that translates special grammar rules into regular Prolog clauses that allow the recognition of correct sentences as seen above. The BNF definition of the English subset takes the form of the logic grammar in Prolog shown in Figure 2.8. Logic grammars use a special predefined infix predicate "-->" to force this translation into normal Prolog code.

---

sentence --> nounPhrase, predicate, ['.'].
nounPhrase --> determiner, noun.
predicate --> verb, nounPhrase.
predicate --> verb.
determiner --> [a].
determiner --> [the].
noun --> [boy] ; [girl] ; [cat] ; [telescope] ; [song] ; [feather].
verb --> [saw] ; [touched] ; [surprised] ; [sang].

Figure 2.8: A Logic Grammar

The similarity between Figure 2.8 and the concrete syntax (BNF) in Figure 2.1 demonstrates the utility of logic grammars. Note that terminal symbols appear exactly as they do in the source text, but they are placed inside brackets. Since they are Prolog atoms, tokens starting with characters other than lowercase letters must be delimited by apostrophes. The Prolog interpreter automatically translates these special rules into normal Prolog clauses identical to those in Figure 2.7. Each predicate is automatically given two parameters in the translation. For example, the logic grammar clauses are translated as shown in the examples below:

nounPhrase --> determiner, noun.

becomes   nounPhrase(K,L) :- determiner(K,M),noun(M,L).

predicate --> verb.   becomes   predicate(K,L) :- verb(K,L).

noun --> [boy].   becomes   noun(K,L) :- 'C'(K,boy,L).

Since a Prolog system generates its own variable names, listing the translated code is unlikely to show the names K, L, and M, but the meaning will be the same.

Parameters in Grammars

The second problem, that of producing an abstract syntax tree as a sentence is parsed, can be handled by using parameters in the logic grammar rules. Predicates defined by using Prolog grammar rules may have arguments in addition to the implicit ones created by the preprocessor. These additional arguments are usually inserted by the translator in front of the implicit arguments. (Some Prolog implementations insert the additional arguments after the implicit ones.)

For example, the grammar rule

    sentence(sent(N,P)) --> nounPhrase(N), predicate(P), ['.'].

will be translated into the normal Prolog clause

    sentence(sent(N,P),K,L) :- nounPhrase(N,K,M), predicate(P,M,R), 'C'(R,'.',L).

Figure 2.9 presents the complete BNF grammar with parameters added to build a derivation tree.

---

sentence(sent(N,P)) --> nounPhrase(N), predicate(P), ['.'].
nounPhrase(nounph(D,N)) --> determiner(D), noun(N).
predicate(pred(V,N)) --> verb(V), nounPhrase(N).
predicate(pred(V)) --> verb(V).
determiner(det(a)) --> [a].
determiner(det(the)) --> [the].
noun(noun(boy)) --> [boy].
noun(noun(girl)) --> [girl].
noun(noun(cat)) --> [cat].
noun(noun(telescope)) --> [telescope].
noun(noun(song)) --> [song].
noun(noun(feather)) --> [feather].
verb(verb(saw)) --> [saw].
verb(verb(touched)) --> [telescope].
verb(verb(surprised)) --> [surprised].
verb(verb(sang)) --> [sang].

Figure 2.9: A Logic Grammar with Parameters

A query with a variable representing an abstract syntax tree produces that tree as its answer:

```
?- sentence(Tree, [the,girl,sang,a,song,'.'], []).
Tree = sent(nounph(det(the), noun(girl)),
            pred(verb(sang), nounph(det(a), noun(song))))
yes
```

A subphrase can be parsed as well.

```
?- predicate(Tree, [sang,a,song], []).
Tree = pred(verb(sang), nounph(det(a), noun(song)))
yes
```

Executing Goals in a Logic Grammar

Prolog terms placed within braces in a logic grammar are not translated by the preprocessor. They are executed as regular Prolog clauses unchanged. For example, the first clause in the English grammar can be written

    sentence(S) --> nounPhrase(N), predicate(P), ['.'], {S=sent(N,P)}.

The resulting Prolog clause after translation is

    sentence(S,K,L) :-
                nounPhrase(N,K,M), predicate(P,M,R), 'C'(R,'.',L), S=sent(N,P).

As a second example, we add a word-counting facility to the English grammar in Figure 2.9 (only those clauses that need to be changed are shown):

    sentence(WC,sent(N,P)) -->
                nounPhrase(W1,N), predicate(W2,P), ['.'], {WC is W1+W2}.

    nounPhrase(WC,nounph(D,N)) --> determiner(D), noun(N), {WC is 2}.

    predicate(WC,pred(V,N)) --> verb(V), nounPhrase(W,N), {WC is W+1}.

    predicate(1,pred(V)) --> verb(V).

If the word-counting feature is used, conditions may be placed on the sentences accepted by the grammar; for example, if only sentences with no more than ten words are to be accepted, the first clause can be written

    sentence(WC,sen(N,P)) -->
                nounPhrase(W1,N), predicate(W2,P), ['.'], {WC is W1+W2, WC <= 10}.

Any sentence with more than ten words will fail to parse in this augmented grammar because of the condition. Computing values and testing them illustrates the basic idea of attribute grammar, the subject of the next chapter.

The astute reader may have noticed that in the English grammar in this chapter, each sentence has exactly five words. The condition on word count makes more sense if applied to a grammar that includes prepositional phrases or allows **and**'s in the <noun phrase> strings.

Exercises

1. Write a definite clause grammar for an English grammar that includes prepositional phrases as in Chapter 1. To avoid ambiguity, add prepositional phrases only to noun phrases.

2.   Modify <noun phrase> to allow **and** according to the productions in Figure 2.4. Construct a logic grammar, and try to generate all the sentences. Make sure you recognize the shortest noun phrase first.

3.   This grammar is a BNF specification of the language of Roman numerals less than 500.

> <roman> ::= <hundreds> <tens> <units>
>
> <hundreds> ::= <empty> | **C** | **CC** | **CCC** | **CD**
>
> <tens> ::= <low tens> | **XL** | **L** <low tens> | **XC**
>
> <low tens> ::= <empty> | <low tens> **X**
>
> <units> ::= <low units> | **IV** | **V** <low units> | **IX**
>
> <low units> ::= <empty> | <low units> **I**

Write a logic grammar that parses strings in this language and also enforces a constraint that the number of X's in <low tens> and I's in <low units> can be no more than three.

4.   Write a logic grammar for the language of list expressions described in exercise 9 in section 1.2.

2.3 PARSING WREN

Prolog's definite clause grammars provide a mechanism for parsing Wren as well as our English language fragment. Again, we start with the BNF specification of Wren's concrete syntax and convert the productions into logic grammar clauses with as few changes as required. Parameters to the clauses construct an abstract syntax tree for the program being parsed.

We illustrate the process with a couple of the straightforward productions.

> <program> ::= **program** <identifier> **is** <block>

becomes

    program(AST) --> [program], [ide(I)], [is], block(AST).

and

> <block> ::= <declaration seq> **begin** <command seq> **end**

becomes

    block(prog(Decs,Cmds)) --> decs(Decs), [begin], cmds(Cmds), [end].

Observe that the reserved words and identifiers are recognized as Prolog atoms and ide structures inside brackets. The logic grammar needs to match the form of the tokens produced by the scanner. Also, note how the abstract syntax tree (AST) for a block is constructed from the two subtrees for declarations and commands.

The BNF specification for commands can be converted into logic grammar clauses with little modification.

> <command> ::= <variable> **:=** <expr>

becomes

> command(assign(V,E)) --> [ide(V)], [assign], expr(E).

and

> <command> ::= **while** <boolean expr> **do** <command seq> **end while**

becomes

> command(while(Test,Body)) -->
> > [while], boolexpr(Test), [do], cmds(Body), [end, while].

Parsing Wren involves collecting lists of items for several of its syntactic categories: command sequences, declaration sequences, and lists of variables. We describe the pattern for handling these lists by means of command sequences and leave the other two as exercises. Our approach follows the strategy for building a list in the scanner—that is, we obtain the first object in the list and then call a predicate to construct the (possibly empty) tail of the list. In each case, we use Prolog lists for the representation of the subtrees in the abstract syntax tree.

The productions

> <command seq> ::= <command> | <command> **;** <command seq>

become the two predicates

> cmds(Cmds) --> command(Cmd), restcmds(Cmd,Cmds).
> restcmds(Cmd,[Cmd|Cmds]) --> [semicolon], cmds(Cmds).
> restcmds(Cmd,[Cmd]) --> [ ].

A variable list can be formed in exactly the same way; but remember that declaration sequences may be empty, thereby producing an empty list [ ] as the abstract syntax subtree.

Handling Left Recursion

In defining the syntax of programming languages, BNF specifications frequently use left recursion to define lists and expressions; in fact, expressions with left associative operations are naturally formulated using left recursion. Unfortunately, parsing left recursion can lead the interpreter down an infinite branch of the search tree in the corresponding logic program.

As an example, consider a language of expressions with left associative addition and subtraction of numbers:

<expr> ::= <expr> <opr> <numeral>

<expr> ::= <numeral>

<opr> ::= + | –

<numeral> ::= ...   % as before

Using a Prolog definite clause grammar produces the following rules:

expr(plus(E1,E2)) --> expr(E1), ['+'], [num(E2)].

expr(minus(E1,E2)) --> expr(E1), ['–'], [num(E2)].

expr(E) --> [num(E)].

which translate into the following Prolog clauses:

expr(plus(E1,E2),K,L) :- expr(E1,K,M), 'C'(M,'+',N), 'C'(N,num(E2),L).

expr(minus(E1,E2),K,L) :- expr(E1,K,M), 'C'(M,'–',N), 'C'(N,num(E2),L).

expr(E,K,L) :- 'C'(K,num(E),L).

Suppose the string "5–2" runs through the scanner, and the logic grammar is invoked with the query

?- expr(E, [num(5), '–', num(2)], [ ]).

The Prolog interpreter repeatedly tries expr with an uninstantiated variable as the first argument, creating an endless search for a derivation, as shown in Figure 2.10.

The depth-first strategy for satisfying goals makes it impossible for Prolog to find the consequence defined by the logic program. The logic interpreter needs to satisfy the initial goal in the goal list first. The usual way to remove left recursion from a BNF grammar is to define a new syntactic category that handles all but the first token:

<expr> ::= <numeral> <rest of expr>

<rest of expr> ::= <opr> <numeral> <rest of expr>

<rest of expr> ::= ε

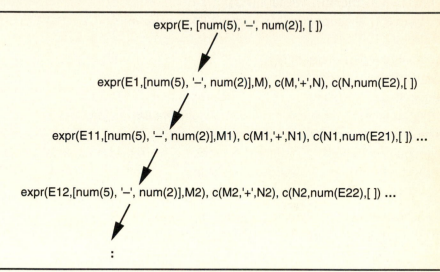

Figure 2.10: Parsing the expression "5–2"

The corresponding logic grammar has the property that each rule starts with a goal that can be verified without going down an infinite branch of the search tree. A careful definition of the parameters enables the grammar to construct a left associative parse tree even though the logic grammar is right recursive.

    expr(E) --> [num(E1)], restexpr(E1,E).

    restexpr(E1,E) --> ['+'], [num(E2)], restexpr(plus(E1,E2),E).

    restexpr(E1,E) --> ['–'], [num(E2)], restexpr(minus(E1,E2),E).

    restexpr(E,E) --> [ ].

The predicate restexpr(E1,E) means that the expression E1 has been constructed from the symbols encountered so far, and the resulting parse tree will be E once the rest of the symbols making up the expression have been processed. The last rule "restexpr(E,E) --> [ ]." states that when no tokens are left to build an expression, the result is the expression created so far—namely, the first argument.

For Wren, we use logic grammar clauses

    expr(E) --> intexpr(E).
    expr(E) --> boolexpr(E).

intexpr(E) --> term(T), restintexpr(T,E).
restintexpr(T,E) --> weakop(Op), term(T1), restintexpr(exp(Op,T,T1),E).
restintexpr(E,E) --> [ ].
term(T) --> element(P), restterm(P,T).
restterm(P,T) --> strongop(Op), element(P1), restterm(exp(Op,P,P1),T).
restterm(T,T) --> [ ].
element(num(N)) --> [num(N)].
element(Ide(I)) --> [ide(I)].
weakop(plus) --> [plus].   weakop(minus) --> [minus].
strongop(times) --> [times].   strongop(divides) --> [divides].
comparison(bexp(R,E1,E2)) --> intexpr(E1), rel(R), intexpr(E2).
rel(equal) --> [equal].   rel(neq) --> [neq].   rel(less) --> [less].
rel(grtr) --> [grtr].   rel(gteq) --> [gteq].   rel(lteq) --> [lteq].

following the pattern shown above for integer expressions. Many of the BNF
rules translate directly into logic grammar clauses. For example, the BNF
productions for handling parentheses and unary minus in integer expressions,

<element> ::= (<integer expr>)

<element> ::= – <element>

become the logic grammar clauses,

element(E) --> [lparen], expr(E), [rparen].
element(minus(E)) --> [minus], element(E).

Note that we can use the same function symbol minus for both unary minus
and subtraction since the number of parameters help define the structure.
Boolean expressions are handled in a similar manner.

Recall that we suggested two different formats for the abstract syntax of
expressions formed from binary operations:

exp(plus,E1,E2)

and

plus(E1,E2).

The choice between these two templates is largely subjective, depending on
the purpose for which the trees will be used. We elect to use the exp(plus,E1,E2)
format when we develop an interpreter for Wren in later chapters because it
eases the handling of arithmetic expressions. In this chapter we have used
both formats to emphasize that the difference is primarily cosmetic.

Left Factoring

Sometimes two productions have a common initial string of terminals and nonterminals to be processed. If the first production fails, the second one has to recognize that initial string all over again. Factoring the initial string as a separate rule leads to a more efficient parsing algorithm.

Suppose now that expressions have right associative operators at two precedence levels:

  expr(plus(E1,E2)) --> term(E1), ['+'], expr(E2).

  expr(minus(E1,E2)) --> term(E1), ['−'], expr(E2).

  expr(E) --> term(E).

  term(times(T1,T2)) --> [num(T1)], ['*'], term(T2).

  term(divides(T1,T2)) --> [num(T1)], ['/'], term(T2).

  term(T) --> [num(T)].

The problem here is that when processing a string such as "2*3*4*5*6 − 7", the term "2*3*4*5*6" must be recognized twice, once by the first clause that expects a plus sign next, and once by the second clause that matches the minus sign. This inefficiency is remedied by rewriting the grammar as follows:

  expr(E) --> term(E1), restexpr(E1,E).

  restexpr(E1,plus(E1,E2)) --> ['+'], expr(E2).

  restexpr(E1,minus(E1,E2)) --> ['−'], expr(E2).

  restexpr(E,E) --> [ ].

  term(T) --> [num(T1)], restterm(T1,T).

  restterm(T1,times(T1,T2)) --> ['*'], term(T2).

  restterm(T1,divides(T1,T2)) --> ['/'], term(T2).

  restterm(T,T) --> [ ].

Now the term "2*3*4*5*6" will be parsed only once.

Left factoring can also be used in processing the **if** commands in Wren.

  <command> ::= **if** <boolean expr> **then** <command seq> **end if**
    | **if** <boolean expr> **then** <command seq> **else** <command seq> **end if**

becomes

  command(Cmd) -->
        [if], boolexpr(Test), [then], cmds(Then), restif(Test,Then,Cmd).

```
restif(Test,Then,if(Test,Then,Else)) --> [else], cmds(Else), [end], [if].
restif(Test,Then,if(Test,Then)) --> [end], [if].
```

Observe that we construct either a ternary structure or a binary structure for the command, depending on whether we encounter **else** or not. Again, we use a predicate go to control the system:

```
go :-  nl,write('>>> Interpreting: Wren <<<'), nl, nl,
       write('Enter name of source file: '), nl, getfilename(fileName), nl,
       see(fileName), scan(Tokens), seen, write('Scan successful'), nl, !,
       write(Tokens), nl, nl,
       program(AST,Tokens,[eop]), write('Parse successful'), nl, !,
       write(AST), nl, nl.
```

Note that cut operations "!" have been inserted after the scanning and parsing phases of the language processing. This ensures that the Prolog interpreter never backtracks into the parser or scanner after each has completed successfully. Such backtracking can only generate spurious error messages. A cut acts as a one-way passage. It always succeeds once, but if the backtracking attempts the cut a second time, the entire query fails. Except for the go clause, we refrain from using cuts in our Prolog code because we want to avoid their nonlogical properties. See the references for details on the cut operation.

Exercises

1. Write the logic grammar clauses that parse declaration sequences and variable lists.

    <declaration seq> ::= ε | <declaration> <declaration seq>

    <declaration> ::= **var** <variable list> : <type> ;

    <type> ::= **integer** | **boolean**

    <variable list> ::= <variable> | <variable> , <variable list>

2. Write the logic grammar clauses that parse Boolean expressions. Use the tag bexp for these expressions.

    <boolean expr> ::= <boolean term>
                     | <boolean expr> **or** <boolean term>
    <boolean term> ::= <boolean element>
                     | <boolean term> **and** <boolean element>

<boolean element> ::= **true** | **false** | <variable> | <comparison>

|**not** (<boolean expr>) | (<boolean expr>)

3. Add these language constructs to Wren and modify the parser to handle them:

a) repeat-until commands

<command> ::= ... | **repeat** <command seq> **until** <boolean expr>

b) conditional expressions

<expression> ::= ... | **if** <boolean expr> **then** <expr> **else** <expr>

c) expressions with side effects

<expression> ::= ... | **begin** <command seq> **return** <expr> **end**

2.4 FURTHER READING

Many books provide a basic introduction to Prolog. Our favorites include the classic textbook by Clocksin and Mellish that is already in its third edition [Clocksin87]; Ivan Bratko's book [Bratko90], which emphasizes the use of Prolog in artificial intelligence; and the comprehensive text by Sterling and Shapiro [Sterling94]. These books also include descriptions of the operational semantics of Prolog with information on unification, the resolution proof strategy, and the depth-first search method used by Prolog. The last book has a good discussion of programming with difference lists in Prolog. The model for our scanner can be found in the Clocksin and Mellish text where the lexical analysis of an English sentence is presented.

Most Prolog texts cover the definite clause grammars that we used to build the parsers in this chapter. In addition to [Clocksin87] and [Sterling86], see [Kluzniak85], [Malpas87], [Covington88], and [Saint-Dizier90] for material on logic grammars.

The roots of Prolog lie in language processing. It has been said that Prolog was invented by Robert Kowalski in 1974 and implemented by Alain Colmerauer in 1973. To explain this apparent contradiction, we note that Prolog originated in Colmerauer's interest in using logic to express grammar rules and to formalize the parsing of natural language sentences. He developed the mechanism of syntactic analysis in logic before the power of Prolog as a general purpose programming language was made apparent by Kowalski. For more information on the early development of Prolog and logic grammars see [Colmerauer78] and [Kowalski79].

Some of the issues discussed in this chapter, such as left recursion and left factoring, are handled in compiler writing texts (see [Aho86] and [Parsons92]). Prolog was given credibility as a vehicle for language processing in 1980 by David Warren in a paper that describes a compiler written in Prolog [Warren80].

Chapter 3
ATTRIBUTE GRAMMARS

In Chapter 1 we discussed the hierarchy of formal grammars proposed by Noam Chomsky. We mentioned that context-sensitive conditions, such as ensuring the same value for n in a string $a^n b^n c^n$, cannot be tested using a context-free grammar. Although we showed a context-sensitive grammar for this particular problem, these grammars in general are impractical for specifying the context conditions for a programming language. In this chapter and the next we investigate two different techniques for augmenting a context-free grammar in order to verify context-sensitive conditions.

Attribute grammars can perform several useful functions in specifying the syntax and semantics of a programming language. An attribute grammar can be used to specify the context-sensitive aspects of the syntax of a language, such as checking that an item has been declared and that the use of the item is consistent with its declaration. As we will see in Chapter 7, attribute grammars can also be used in specifying an operational semantics of a programming language by defining a translation into lower-level code based on a specific machine architecture.

Attribute grammars were first developed by Donald Knuth in 1968 as a means of formalizing the semantics of a context-free language. Since their primary application has been in compiler writing, they are a tool mostly used by programming language implementers. In the first section, we use examples to introduce attribute grammars. We then provide a formal definition for an attribute grammar followed by additional examples. Next we develop an attribute grammar for Wren that is sensitive to the context conditions discussed in Chapter 1 (see Figure 1.11). Finally, as a laboratory activity, we develop a context-sensitive parser for Wren.

3.1 CONCEPTS AND EXAMPLES

An attribute grammar may be informally defined as a context-free grammar that has been extended to provide context sensitivity using a set of attributes, assignment of attribute values, evaluation rules, and conditions. A finite, possibly empty set of attributes is associated with each distinct symbol in the grammar. Each attribute has an associated domain of values, such as integers, character and string values, or more complex structures. Viewing the input sentence (or program) as a parse tree, attribute grammars can pass values from a node to its parent, using a synthesized attribute, or from the current node to a child, using an inherited attribute. In addition to passing attribute values up or down the parse tree, the attribute values may be assigned, modified, and checked at any node in the derivation tree. The following examples should clarify some of these points.

Examples of Attribute Grammars

We will attempt to write a grammar to recognize sentences of the form $a^n b^n c^n$. The sentences **aaabbbccc** and **abc** belong to this grammar but the sentences **aaabbbbbcc** and **aabbbcc** do not. Consider this first attempt to describe the language using a context-free grammar:

    <letter sequence> ::= <a sequence> <b sequence> <c sequence>

    <a sequence> ::= **a** | <a sequence> **a**

    <b sequence> ::= **b** | <b sequence> **b**

    <c sequence> ::= **c** | <c sequence> **c**

As seen in Figure 3.1, this grammar can generate the string **aaabbbccc**. It can also generate the string **aaabbbbbcc**, as seen in Figure 3.2.

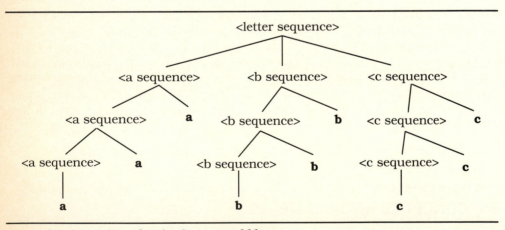

Figure 3.1: Parse Tree for the String **aaabbbccc**

As has already been noted in Chapter 1, it is impossible to write a context-free grammar to generate only those sentences of the form $a^n b^n c^n$. However, it is possible to write a context-sensitive grammar for sentences of this form. Attribute grammars provide another approach for defining context-sensitivity. If we augment our grammar with an attribute describing the length of a letter sequence, we can use these values to ensure that the sequences of **a**'s, **b**'s, and **c**'s all have the same length.

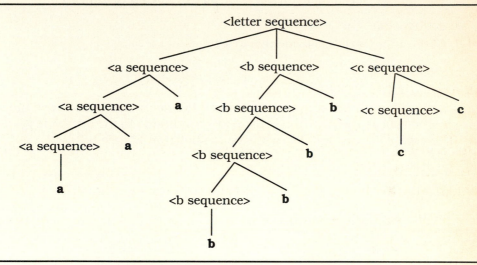

Figure 3.2: Parse Tree for the String **aaabbbbcc**

The first solution involves a synthesized attribute *Size* that is associated with the nonterminals <a sequence>, <b sequence>, and <c sequence>. We add the condition that, at the root of the tree, the *Size* attribute for each of the letter sequences has the same value. If a character sequence consists of a single character, *Size* is set to 1; if it consists of a character sequence followed by a single character, *Size* for the parent character sequence is the *Size* of the child character sequence plus one. We have added the necessary attribute assignments and conditions to the grammar shown below. Notice that we differentiate a parent sequence from a child sequence by adding subscripts to the nonterminal symbols.

<letter sequence> ::= <a sequence> <b sequence> <c sequence>
    condition:
        $Size$ (<a sequence>) = $Size$ (<b sequence>) = $Size$ (<c sequence>)

<a sequence> ::= **a**
        $Size$ (<a sequence>) $\leftarrow$ 1
    | <a sequence>$_2$ **a**
        $Size$ (<a sequence>) $\leftarrow$ $Size$ (<a sequence>$_2$) + 1

<b sequence> ::= **b**

        Size (<b sequence>) ← 1

    | <b sequence>$_2$ **b**

        Size (<b sequence>) ← *Size* (<b sequence>$_2$) + 1

<c sequence> ::= **c**

        Size (<c sequence>) ← 1

    | <c sequence>$_2$ **c**

        Size (<c sequence>) ←*Size* (<c sequence>$_2$) + 1

This attribute grammar successfully parses the sequence **aaabbbccc** since the sequence obeys the BNF and satisfies all conditions in the attribute grammar. The complete, decorated parse tree is shown in Figure 3.3.

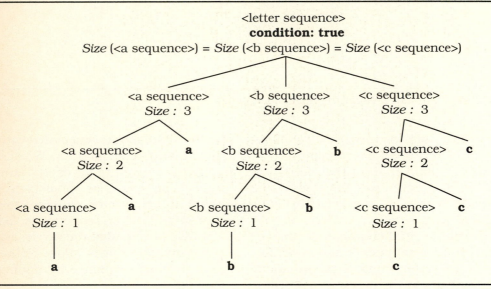

Figure 3.3: Parse Tree for **aaabbbccc** Using Synthesized Attributes

On the other hand, this attribute grammar cannot parse the sequence **aaabbbbcc**. Although this sequence satisfies the BNF part of the grammar, it does not satisfy the condition required of the attribute values, as shown in Figure 3.4.

When using only synthesized attributes, all of the relevant information is passed up to the root of the parse tree where the checking takes place. However, it is often more convenient to pass information up from one part of a tree, transfer it at some specified node, and then have it inherited down into other parts of the tree.

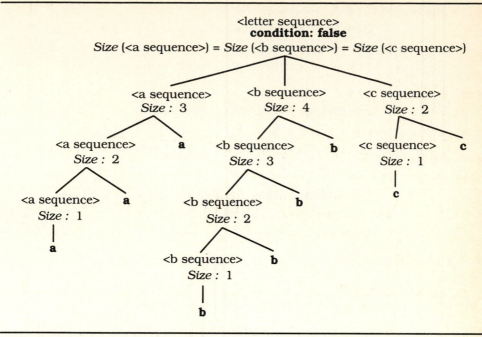

Figure 3.4: Parse Tree for **aaabbbbcc** Using Synthesized Attributes

Reconsider the problem of recognizing sequences of the form $a^n b^n c^n$. In this solution, we use the attribute *Size* as a synthesized attribute for the sequence of **a**'s and *InhSize* as inherited attributes for the sequences of **b**'s and **c**'s. As we have already seen, we can synthesize the size of the sequence of **a**'s to the root of the parse tree. In this solution we set the *InhSize* attribute for the **b** sequence and the **c** sequence to this value and inherit it down the tree, decrementing the value by one every time we see another character in the sequence. When we reach the node where the sequence has a child consisting of a single character, we check if the inherited *InhSize* attribute equals one. If so, the size of the sequence must be the same as the size of the sequences of **a**'s; otherwise, the two sizes do not match and the parse is unsuccessful. These ideas are expressed in the following attribute grammar:

<letter sequence> ::= <a sequence> <b sequence> <c sequence>

$$InhSize (<b sequence>) \leftarrow Size (<a sequence>)$$
$$InhSize (<c sequence>) \leftarrow Size (<a sequence>)$$

        <a sequence> ::= **a**

                Size (<a sequence>) ← 1

          | <a sequence>$_2$ **a**

                Size (<a sequence>) ← *Size* (<a sequence>$_2$) + 1

        <b sequence> ::= **b**

                condition: *InhSize* (<b sequence>) = 1

          | <b sequence>$_2$ **b**

                InhSize (<b sequence>$_2$) ← *InhSize* (<b sequence>) – 1

        <c sequence> ::= **c**

                condition: *InhSize* (<c sequence>) = 1

          | <c sequence>$_2$ **c**

                InhSize (<c sequence>$_2$) ← *InhSize* (<c sequence>) – 1

For the nonterminal <a sequence>, *Size* is a synthesized attribute, as we can see from the attribute assignment

$$Size \text{ (<a sequence>)} \leftarrow Size \text{ (<a sequence>}_2) + 1.$$

Here the value of the child is incremented by one and passed to the parent. For the nonterminals <b sequence> and <c sequence>, *InhSize* is an inherited attribute that is passed from parent to child. The assignment

$$InhSize \text{ (<b sequence>}_2) \leftarrow InhSize \text{ (<b sequence>)} - 1$$

shows that the value is decremented by one each time it is passed from the parent sequence to the child sequence. When the sequence is a single character, we check that the inherited size attribute value is one. Figure 3.5 shows a decorated attribute parse tree for the sequence **aaabbbccc**, which satisfies the attribute grammar since it satisfies the BNF and all attribute conditions are true. *Size* is synthesized up the left branch, passed over to the center and right branches at the root, inherited down the center branch, and inherited down the right branch as *InhSize*.

As before, we demonstrate that the attribute grammar cannot parse the sequence **aaabbbbcc**. Although this sequence satisfies the BNF part of the grammar, it does not satisfy all conditions associated with attribute values, as shown in Figure 3.6. In this case, the parse fails on two conditions. It only takes one false condition anywhere in the decorated parse tree to make the parse fail.

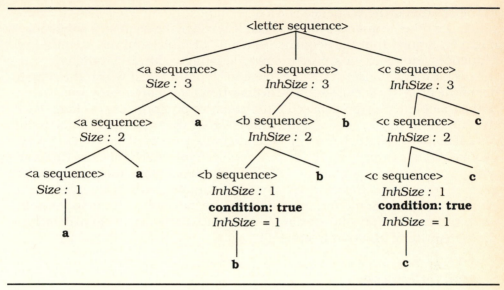

Figure 3.5: Parse Tree for **aaabbbccc** Using Inherited Attributes

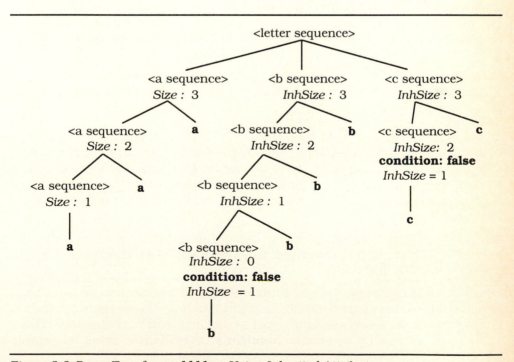

Figure 3.6: Parse Tree for **aaabbbbbcc** Using Inherited Attributes

In this grammar the sequence of **a**'s determines the "desired" length against which the other sequences are checked. Consider the sequence **aabbbccc**. It might be argued that the sequence of **a**'s is "at fault" and not the other two sequences. However, in a programming language with declarations, we use the declarations to determine the "desired" types against which the remainder of the program is checked. The declaration information is synthesized up to the root of the tree and passed into the entire program for checking. Using this approach makes it easier to localize errors that cause the parse to fail. Also, if both synthesized and inherited attributes are used, an attribute value may be threaded throughout a tree. We will see this mechanism in Chapter 7 when an attribute grammar is used to help determine label names in the generation of code. Before developing the complete attribute grammar for Wren, we provide some formal definitions associated with attribute grammars and examine one more example where attributes are used to determine the semantics of binary numerals.

Formal Definitions

Although the above examples were introduced in an informal way, attribute grammars furnish a formal mechanism for specifying a context-sensitive grammar, as indicated by the following definitions.

Definition: An **attribute grammar** is a context-free grammar augmented with attributes, semantic rules, and conditions.

Let $G = <N,\Sigma,P,S>$ be a context-free grammar (see Chapter 1).
Write a production $p \in P$ in the form:

$$p: X_0 ::= X_1 X_2 \ldots X_{n_p}$$

$$\text{where } n_p \geq 1, X_0 \in N \text{ and } X_k \in N \cup \Sigma \text{ for } 1 \leq k \leq n_p.$$

A derivation tree for a sentence in a context-free language, as defined in Chapter 1, has the property that each of its leaf nodes is labeled with a symbol from Σ and each interior node t corresponds to a production $p \in P$ such that t is labeled with X_0 and t has n_p children labeled with $X_1, X_2, \ldots, X_{n_p}$ in left-to-right order.

For each syntactic category $X \in N$ in the grammar, there are two finite disjoint sets $I(X)$ and $S(X)$ of **inherited** and **synthesized attributes**. For $X = S$, the start symbol, $I(X) = \emptyset$.

Let $A(X) = I(X) \cup S(X)$ be the set of attributes of X. Each attribute $Atb \in A(X)$ takes a value from some semantic domain (such as the integers, strings of characters, or structures of some type) associated with that attribute. These values are defined by **semantic functions** or **semantic rules** associated with the productions in P.

Consider again a production $p \in P$ of the form $X_0 ::= X_1 X_2 \ldots X_{n_p}$ Each synthesized attribute $Atb \in S(X_0)$ has its value defined in terms of the attributes in $A(X_1) \cup A(X_2) \cup \dots \cup A(X_{n_p}) \cup I(X_0)$. Each inherited attribute $Atb \in I(X_k)$ for $1 \le k \le n_p$ has its value defined in terms of the attributes in $A(X_0) \cup S(X_1) \cup S(X_2) \cup \dots \cup S(X_{n_p})$.

Each production may also have a set of conditions on the values of the attributes in $A(X_0) \cup A(X_1) \cup A(X_2) \cup \dots \cup A(X_{n_p})$ that further constrain an application of the production. The derivation (or parse) of a sentence in the attribute grammar is satisfied if and only if the context-free grammar is satisfied and all conditions are true. The semantics of a nonterminal can be considered to be a distinguished attribute evaluated at the root node of the derivation tree of that nonterminal. ∎

Semantics via Attribute Grammars

We illustrate the use of attribute grammars to specify meaning by developing the semantics of binary numerals. A binary numeral is a sequence of binary digits followed by a binary point (a period) and another sequence of binary digits—for example, 100.001 and 0.001101. For simplicity, we require at least one binary digit, which may be 0, for each sequence of binary digits. It is possible to relax this assumption—for example 101 or .11—but this flexibility adds to the complexity of the grammar without altering the semantics of binary numerals. Therefore we leave this modification as an exercise. We define the semantics of a binary numeral to be the real number value *Val* associated with the numeral, expressed in base-ten notation. For example, the semantics of the numeral 100.001 is 4.125.

The first version of an attribute grammar defining the meaning of binary numerals involves only synthesized attributes.

Nonterminals	Synthesized Attributes	Inherited Attributes
<binary numeral>	*Val*	—
<binary digits>	*Val, Len*	—
<bit>	*Val*	—

<binary numeral> ::= <binary digits>$_1$. <binary digits>$_2$
    Val (<binary numeral>) $\leftarrow Val$ (<binary digits>$_1$) +
        Val (<binary digits>$_2$) $/\ 2^{Len\ (<\text{binary digits}>_2)}$

<binary digits> ::=
    <binary digits>$_2$ <bit>
        Val (<binary digits>) $\leftarrow 2 \bullet Val$ (<binary digits>$_2$) + Val (<bit>)
        Len (<binary digits>) $\leftarrow Len$ (<binary digits>$_2$) + 1
    | <bit>
        Val (<binary digits>) $\leftarrow Val$ (<bit>)
        Len (<binary digits>) $\leftarrow 1$

\<bit\> ::=
    0
       Val (\<bit\>) ← 0
   | **1**
       Val (\<bit\>) ← 1

The derivation tree in Figure 3.7 illustrates the use of attributes that give the semantics for the binary numeral 1101.01 to be the real number 13.25.

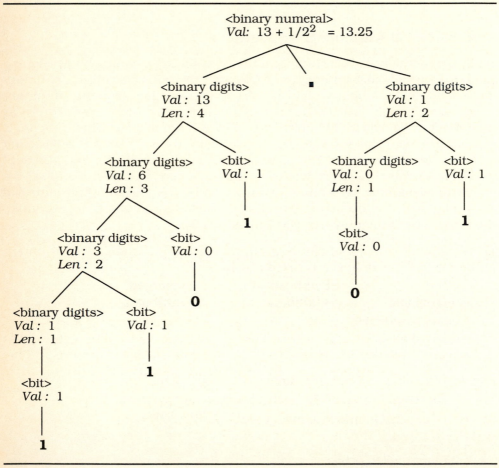

Figure 3.7: Binary Numeral Semantics Using Synthesized Attributes

The previous specification for the semantics of binary numerals was not based on positional information. As a result, the attribute values below the root do not represent the semantic meaning of the digits at the leaves. We now present an approach based on positional semantics, illustrated first in base 10,

$$123.45 = 1{\bullet}10^2 + 2{\bullet}10^1 + 3{\bullet}10^0 + 4{\bullet}10^{-1} + 5{\bullet}10^{-2}$$

and then in base 2,

$$110.101 = 1{\bullet}2^2 + 1{\bullet}2^1 + 0{\bullet}2^0 + 1{\bullet}2^{-1} + 0{\bullet}2^{-2} + 1{\bullet}2^{-3}$$
$$= 6.625 \text{ (base 10).}$$

We develop a positional semantics in which an inherited attribute called *Pos* is introduced. It is convenient to separate the sequence of binary digits to the left of the binary point, identified by the nonterminal <binary digits>, from the fractional binary digits to the right of the binary point, identified by the nonterminal <fraction digits>.

Nonterminals	Synthesized Attributes	Inherited Attributes
<binary numeral>	*Val*	—
<binary digits>	*Val*	*Pos*
<fraction digits>	*Val, Len*	—
<bit>	*Val*	*Pos*

We write our grammar in left recursive form, which means that the leftmost binary digit in a sequence of digits is "at the bottom" of the parse tree, as shown in Figure 3.7. For the binary digits to the left of the binary point, we initialize the *Pos* attribute to zero and increment it by one as we go down the tree structure. This technique provides the correct positional information for the binary digits in the integer part, but a different approach is needed for the fractional binary digits since the exponents from left to right are -1, -2, -3, ... Notice that this exponent information can be derived from the length of the binary sequence of digits from the binary point up to, and including, the digit itself. Therefore we add a length attribute for fractional digits that is transformed into a positional attribute for the individual bit. Notice that the *Val* attribute at any point in the tree contains the absolute value for the portion of the binary numeral in that subtree. Therefore the value of a parent node is the sum of the values for the children nodes. These ideas are implemented in the following attribute grammar:

<binary numeral> ::= <binary digits> . <fraction digits>

       Val (<binary numeral>) ← *Val* (<binary digits>)+*Val* (<fraction digits>)

       Pos (<binary digits>) ← 0

\<binary digits\> ::=

    \<binary digits\>$_2$ \<bit\>

        Val (\<binary digits\>) ← *Val* (\<binary digits\>$_2$) + *Val* (\<bit\>)

        Pos (\<binary digits\>$_2$) ← *Pos* (\<binary digits\>) + 1

        Pos (\<bit\>) ← *Pos* (\<binary digits\>)

   | \<bit\>

        Val (\<binary digits\>) ← *Val* (\<bit\>)

        Pos (\<bit\>) ← *Pos* (\<binary digits\>)

\<fraction digits\> ::=

    \<fraction digits\>$_2$ \<bit\>

        Val (\<fraction digits\>) ← *Val* (\<fraction digits\>$_2$) + *Val* (\<bit\>)

        Len (\<fraction digits\>) ← *Len* (\<fraction digits\>$_2$) + 1

        Pos (\<bit\>) ← - *Len* (\<fraction digits\>)

   | \<bit\>

        Val (\<fraction digits\>) ← *Val* (\<bit\>)

        Len (\<fraction digits\>) ← 1

        Pos (\<bit\>) ← - 1

\<bit\> ::=

     0

        Val (\<bit\>) ← 0

   | **1**

        Val (\<bit\>) ← $2^{Pos\,(\text{\<bit\>})}$

The parse tree in Figure 3.8 illustrates the use of positional attributes to generate the semantics of the binary numeral 110.101 to be the real number 6.625.

The two attribute grammars for binary numerals do not involve conditions. If we limit the size of binary numerals to match a particular machine architecture, conditionals can be introduced to ensure that the binary numerals are of proper size. Actually, this situation is fairly complex since real number representations in most computers are based on scientific notation, not the fractional notation that has been illustrated above. We examine this problem of checking the size of binary numerals in the exercises.

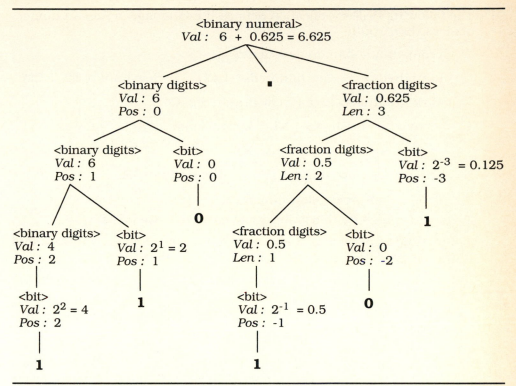

Figure 3.8: Binary Numeral Semantics Using Positional Attributes

Exercises

1. In old versions of Fortran that did not have the character data type, character strings were expressed in the following format:

    <string literal> ::= <numeral> H <string>

    where the <numeral> is a base-ten integer ($\geq$ 1), H is a keyword (named after Herman Hollerith), and <string> is a sequence of characters. The semantics of this string literal is correct if the numeric value of the base-ten numeral matches the length of the string. Write an attribute grammar using only synthesized attributes for the nonterminals in the definition of <string literal>.

2. Repeat exercise 1, using a synthesized attribute for <numeral> and an inherited attribute for <string>.

3. Repeat exercise 1, using an inherited attribute for <numeral> and a synthesized attribute for <string>.

4. The following BNF specification defines the language of Roman numerals less than 1000:

    <roman> ::= <hundreds> <tens> <units>

    <hundreds> ::= <low hundreds> | **CD** | **D** <low hundreds> | **CM**

    <low hundreds> ::= ε | <low hundreds> **C**

    <tens> ::= <low tens> | **XL** | **L** <low tens> | **XC**

    <low tens> ::= ε | <low tens> **X**

    <units> ::= <low units> | **IV** | **V** <low units> | **IX**

    <low units> ::= ε | <low units> **I**

    Define attributes for this grammar to carry out two tasks:

    a) Restrict the number of X's in <low tens>, the I's in <low units>, and the C's in <low hundreds> to no more than three.

    b) Provide an attribute for <roman> that gives the decimal value of the Roman numeral being defined.

    Define any other attributes needed for these tasks, but do not change the BNF grammar.

5. Expand the binary numeral attribute grammar (either version) to allow for binary numerals with no binary point (1101), binary fractions with no fraction part (101.), and binary fractions with no whole number part (.101).

6. Develop an attribute grammar for integers that allows a leading sign character (+ or -) and that ensures that the value of the integer does not exceed the capacity of the machine. Assume a two's complement representation; if the word-size is n bits, the values range from -2^{n-1} to $2^{n-1}-1$.

7. Develop an attribute grammar for binary numerals that represents signed integers using two's complement. Assume that a word-size attribute is inherited by the two's complement binary numeral. The meaning of the binary numeral should be present at the root of the tree.

8. Assume that we have a 32-bit machine where real numbers are represented in scientific notation with a 24-bit mantissa and an 8-bit exponent with 2 as the base. Both mantissa and exponent are two's complement binary numerals. Using the results from exercise 7, write an attribute grammar for <binary real number> where the meaning of the binary numeral is at the root of the tree in base-10 notation—for example, $0.5 \cdot 2^5$.

9. Assuming that we allow the left side of a binary fraction to be left recursive and the fractional part to be right recursive, simplify the positional attribute grammar for binary fractions.

10. Consider a language of expressions with only the variables a, b, and c and formed using the binary infix operators

   $+, -, *, /,$ and $\uparrow$ (for exponentiation)

   where $\uparrow$ has the highest precedence, $*$ and $/$ have the same next lower precedence, and $+$ and $-$ have the lowest precedence. $\uparrow$ is to be right associative and the other operations are to be left associative. Parentheses may be used to override these rules. Provide a BNF specification of this language of expressions. Add attributes to your BNF specification so that the following (unusual) conditions are satisfied by every valid expression accepted by the attribute grammar:

   a) The maximum depth of parenthesis nesting is three.

   b) No valid expression has more than eight applications of operators.

   c) If an expression has more divisions that multiplications, then subtractions are forbidden.

11. A binary tree consists of a root containing a value that is an integer, a (possibly empty) left subtree, and a (possibly empty) right subtree. Such a binary tree can be represented by a triple (Left subtree, Root, Right subtree). Let the symbol nil denote an empty tree. Examples of binary trees include:

   (nil,13,nil)
   > represents a tree with one node labeled with the value 13.

   ((nil,3,nil),8,nil)
   > represents a tree with 8 at the root, an empty right subtree, and a nonempty left subtree with root labeled by 3 and empty subtrees.

   The following BNF specification describes this representation of binary trees.

   <binary tree> ::= nil | (<binary tree> <value> <binary tree>)

   <value> ::= <digit> | <value> <digit>

   <digit> ::= 0 | 1 | 2 | 3 | 4 | 5 | 6 | 7 | 8 | 9

   Augment this grammar with attributes that carry out the following tasks:

   a) A binary tree is balanced if the heights of the subtrees at each interior node are within one of each other. Accept only balanced binary trees.

   b) A binary search tree is a binary tree with the property that all the values in the left subtree of any node N are less than the value at N, and all the value in the right subtree of N are greater than or equal to the value at node N. Accept only binary search trees.

3.2 AN ATTRIBUTE GRAMMAR FOR WREN

In this section we develop an attribute grammar for Wren that performs context checking that is the same as that done by a compiler. We concentrate on context-sensitive conditions for programs that obey the BNF of Wren, as summarized in Figure 1.11.

Wren, as we have defined it, is a flat language in the sense that there is only one block in a program. As a consequence, all declarations belong to a single declaration sequence at the main program level. In the exercises we extend Wren and investigate nested blocks, but for the moment we concentrate on developing an attribute grammar for our current version of Wren. It should be noted that there is one small exception to our single set of declarations: The program name itself is not part of the block structure. It is a language design decision whether an object can have the same name as the program name; at this point we have elected to require that the program name be unique and not be used elsewhere in the program.

The Symbol Table

We build our declaration information in an attribute called *Symbol-table*. This attribute is synthesized from the declaration sequence and inherited into the command sequence of a program. The attribute value is transferred at the block level, at which time the program name is added to the *Symbol-table* attribute. *Symbol-table* contains a set of pairs each associating a name with a type. All variables are of type *integer* or *boolean*, and we introduce a pseudo-type, called *program*, for the program name identifier, and a default value *undefined* to represent the absence of a type. Since all declarations in our current version of Wren are global, there is a single *Symbol-table* that is passed down to the command sequence. We will develop a number of utility operations to manipulate the *Symbol-table* attribute.

Since variable names and types cannot magically appear in the symbol table attribute at the internal nodes of our parse tree, all of this information must be synthesized into the tree using attributes such as *Name*, *Type*, and *Var-list*. Figure 3.9 contains a complete list of the attributes and associated value types. We have added the pseudo-type value of *program* to the attribute *Type* so that the program name is uniquely identified. A *Name* value is a string of one or more letters or digits. A *Var-list* value is a sequence of *Name* values. The *Symbol-table* attribute consists of a set of pairs containing a name and a type. The nonterminals and their associated attributes for the grammar are listed in Figure 3.10. Next we introduce our attribute grammar rules and associated conditions by first focusing on the declaration portion of a Wren program.

Attribute	Value Types
Type	{ *integer, boolean, program, undefined* }
Name	String of letters or digits
Var-list	Sequence of Name values
Symbol-table	Set of pairs of the form [Name, Type]

Figure 3.9: Attributes and Values

Nonterminals	Synthesized Attributes	Inherited Attributes
<block>	—	*Symbol-table*
<declaration sequence>	*Symbol-table*	—
<declaration>	*Symbol-table*	—
<variable list>	*Var-list*	—
<type>	*Type*	—
<command sequence>	—	*Symbol-table*
<command>	—	*Symbol-table*
<expr>	—	*Symbol-table, Type*
<integer expr>	—	*Symbol-table, Type*
<term>	—	*Symbol-table, Type*
<element>	—	*Symbol-table, Type*
<boolean expr>	—	*Symbol-table, Type*
<boolean term>	—	*Symbol-table, Type*
<boolean element>	—	*Symbol-table, Type*
<comparison>	—	*Symbol-table*
<variable>	*Name*	—
<identifier>	*Name*	—
<letter>	*Name*	—
<digit>	*Name*	—

Figure 3.10: Attributes Associated with Nonterminal Symbols

Consider the short program fragment:

```
program p is
    var x, y : integer;
    var a : boolean;
begin
    :
end
```

The *Symbol-table* attribute value passed to the command sequence will be

[['p', *program*], ['x', *integer*], ['y', *integer*], ['a', *boolean*]].

We have chosen to use list-like notation for both sets and sequences; however, we assume no significance for the ordering in the case of sets. The decorated parse tree for this program fragment appears in Figure 3.11.

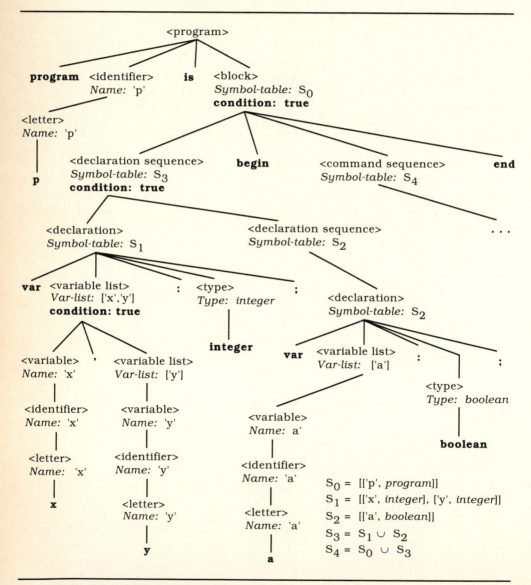

Figure 3.11: Decorated Parse Tree for Wren Program Fragment

The attribute *Symbol-table* is initialized with a pair of values: the *Name* value for the program identifier and the pseudo-type *program*. This *Symbol-table* attribute is inherited into <block>.

> <program> ::= **program** <identifier> **is** <block>
>> *Symbol-table*(<block>) ←
>>> add-item((*Name*(<identifier>), *program*), empty-table)

For the example in Figure 3.11, the *Symbol-table* attribute for <block> has the value [['p', *program*]]. A single declaration has the form

> **var** <var-list> **:** <type>;

The attribute grammar must construct a *Symbol-table* attribute value in which each variable in the list is entered separately in the table with the associated type. For example,

> **var** x, y **:** integer;

results in a symbol table value of [['x', *integer*], ['y', *integer*]]. In order to accomplish this, we need a synthesized attribute *Var-list* that collects a list of *Name* values, ['x', 'y'] in this case, and a utility function "build-symbol-table" to construct the required symbol table value.

> <declaration> ::= **var** <variable list> **:** <type>;
>> *Symbol-table*(<declaration>) ←
>>> build-symbol-table(*Var-list*(<variable list>), *Type*(<type>))

We first look at how the *Var-list* value is synthesized. Observe that the Lisp-like function "cons" builds the lists of variables.

> <variable list> ::=
>> <variable>
>>> *Var-list*(<variable list>) ←
>>>> cons(*Name*(<variable>), empty-list)
>> | <variable> **,** <variable list>₂
>>> *Var-list*(<variable list>) ←
>>>> cons(*Name*(<variable>), *Var-list*(<variable list>₂))
>> **condition:**
>> if *Name*(<variable>) is not a member of *Var-list*(<variable list>₂)
>>> then error("")
>>> else error("Duplicate variable in declaration list")

Every time we add a new *Name* value to the *Var-list* attribute, we must verify that it is not already present in the synthesized attribute value for variables that appear to the right. In the attribute grammars for strings of the form $a^n b^n c^n$, the conditions are either true or false. In this attribute grammar for Wren, we use a slightly different strategy that provides more precise information about any condition check that fails. We assume the existence of an error routine with a string parameter. Calling the error routine with an empty string means that the condition is true. Calling the error routine with a nonempty error message indicates that the condition is false and that the error message provides specific information about the nature of the error encountered.

For the nonterminal <type>, *Type* is a synthesized attribute with the values *integer* or *boolean*, depending on the declared type.

> <type> ::= **integer**
>
> > *Type*(<type>) ← *integer*
>
> | **boolean**
>
> > *Type*(<type>) ← *boolean*

We complete our discussion of <declaration> by looking at the utility functions involved. We have assumed some basic list manipulation functions, such as head, tail, and cons. These utility functions are described later, at the end of Figure 3.12, using pattern matching with Prolog-like list structures. The "build-symbol-table" utility function removes names from the variable listing one at a time and adds the pair [name, type] to the symbol table. The utility function "add-item" does the actual appending. This process continues until the entire symbol table is built.

> build-symbol-table(var-list, type) =
> > if empty(var-list)
> > > then empty-table
> > > else add-item(head(var-list), type,
> > > > > build-symbol-table(tail(var-list),type))
>
> add-item(name, type, table) = cons([name,type], table)

In situations where a declaration sequence is empty, the empty symbol table value is returned. When the declaration sequence is one declaration followed by another declaration sequence, the union of the two table values is passed up to the parent provided that the intersection of the two table values is empty; otherwise, an error condition occurs and the parse fails.

<declaration sequence> ::=

ε

    Symbol-table(<declaration sequence>) ← empty-table

| <declaration> <declaration sequence>$_2$

    Symbol-table(<declaration sequence>) ←

        table-union(*Symbol-table*(<declaration>),

                        Symbol-table(<declaration sequence>$_2$))

condition:

    if table-intersection(*Symbol-table*(<declaration>),

                   Symbol-table(<declaration sequence>$_2$)) = *empty*

    then error("")

    else error("Duplicate declaration of an identifier")

The utility function "table-union" glues the symbol tables together. Compare it with the Prolog function concat in Appendix A.

    table-union(table$_1$, table$_2$) =

        if empty(table$_1$)

           then table$_2$

           else if lookup-type(first-name(table$_1$),table$_2$) = *undefined*

               then add-item(head(table$_1$), table-union(tail(table$_1$), table$_2$))

               else table-union(tail(table$_1$), table$_2$))

The utility function "table-intersection" does not perform a set intersection, rather it returns only one of two values, *empty* or *nonempty*, as appropriate. This task is accomplished by removing items from table$_1$, one at a time, and looking up the type associated with the name in table$_2$. If the type is *undefined*, then the intersection process continues with the rest of table$_1$. However, if any other type is returned, the table intersection must be *nonempty* and this value is returned immediately without continuing the search.

    table-intersection(table$_1$, table$_2$) =

        if empty(table$_1$)

           then *empty*

           else if lookup-type(first-name(table$_1$),table$_2$) ≠ *undefined*

               then *nonempty*

               else table-intersection(tail(table$_1$), table$_2$)

The utility function "lookup-type" proceeds down a list using recursion, checking the first item as it goes to see if it matches the given name. If it does, the corresponding type is returned; if it does not, the search continues with the tail of the table. If the empty table is reached, the value *undefined* is returned.

> lookup-type(name, table) =
>> if empty(table)
>>> then *undefined*
>>> else if head(table) = [name, type]
>>>> then type
>>>> else lookup-type(name, tail(table))

Commands

The grammar rule for <block> is very similar to <declaration sequence> except that one of the symbol tables contains the program identifier. The union of these two tables is passed to <command sequence> in the rule for <block>, as shown in Figure 3.12. In the command section, *Symbol-table* is an inherited attribute that is passed down from <command sequence> to the various instances of <command>, except for **skip** which does not require any declaration or type checking.

> <command sequence> ::=
>> <command>
>> *Symbol-table*(<command>) ←
>>> *Symbol-table*(<command sequence>)
>> | <command> ; <command sequence>$_2$
>> *Symbol-table*(<command>) ←
>>> *Symbol-table*(<command sequence>)
>> *Symbol-table*(<command sequence>$_2$) ←
>>> *Symbol-table*(<command sequence>)

A **read** command requires an integer variable. Two context-sensitive errors are possible: The variable is not declared or the variable is not of type integer. In the condition check, the function lookup-type retrieves the variable type, which may be *undefined* if the variable is not found in *Symbol-table*; thus the type either satisfies the condition of being an integer or fails because it is not declared or not of the proper type.

> <command> ::= **read** <variable>
>> **condition:**
>> case lookup-type(*Name*(<variable>), *Symbol-table*(<command>)) is
>>> *integer*   : error("")
>>> *undefined* : error("Variable not declared")
>>> *boolean, program* : error("Integer variable expected for read")

A **write** command requires an integer expression. One way of specifying this is through a BNF production:

   <command> ::= **write** <integer expr>.

However, since <integer expr> is only one alternative for <expr>, we have elected to show a more relaxed BNF that expands to expression and to pass an inherited attribute *Type* to <expr> so that it can check that the expression is an integer expression. This attribute will be passed to each kind of expression so that the type consistency of variables is maintained. The symbol table is also inherited down to the <integer expr> nonterminal. The attribute grammar for <integer expr> ensures that any variables occurring in the expression are of type integer.

   <command> ::= **write** <expr>

   Symbol-table(<expr>) ← *Symbol-table*(<command>)

   Type(<expr>) ← *integer*

If the language has other types of expressions, such as character and string expressions, having output commands pass an inherited attribute *Type* provides a way of type checking the expressions.

In an assignment command, the *Symbol-table* and the type of the target variable are passed to the expression. We also look up the target variable in the *Symbol-table*. If the type of the target variable is *undefined* or *program*, an error occurs.

   <command> ::= <variable> **:=** <expr>

   Symbol-table(<expr>) ← *Symbol-table*(<command>)

   Type(<expr>) ←

                 lookup-type(*Name*(<var>),*Symbol-table*(<command>))

   condition:

   case lookup-type(*Name*(<variable>),*Symbol-table*(<command>)) is

     integer, boolean : error("")

     undefined   : error("Target variable not declared")

     program   : error("Target variable same as program name").

The control commands **while** and **if** pass the *Symbol-table* attribute to the <boolean expression> and <command sequence> levels and the expected type to <boolean expr>. Notice that in this case we have only allowed for <boolean expr> (and not <expr>) in the BNF since, even if other types are added such as character or string, the conditional still allows only a Boolean expression.

<command> ::=
    while <boolean expr> **do** <command sequence> **end while**
        Symbol-table(<boolean expr>) ← *Symbol-table*(<command>)
        Symbol-table(<cmd sequence>) ← *Symbol-table*(<command>)
        Type(<boolean expr>) ← *boolean*

<command> ::=
    if <boolean expr> **then** <command sequence> **end if**
        Symbol-table(<boolean expr>) ← *Symbol-table*(<command>)
        Symbol-table(<cmd sequence>) ←*Symbol-table*(<command>)
        Type(<boolean expr>) ← *boolean*
    | **if** <boolean expr> **then** <command sequence>$_1$
                        else <command sequence>$_2$ **end if**
        Symbol-table(<boolean expr>) ← *Symbol-table*(<command>)
        Symbol-table(<cmd sequence>$_1$) ← *Symbol-table*(<command>)
        Symbol-table(<cmd sequence>$_2$) ←*Symbol-table*(<command>)
        Type(<boolean expr>) ← *boolean*

Expressions

The *Symbol-table* and *Type* attributes of <expr> are passed to the two kinds
of expressions in Wren. To ensure that the proper alternative for expression
is chosen, a guard (condition) on each rule stops the derivation if the types
are not consistent. Other errors are handled at a lower level in the derivation.
If more sorts of data are available, the sets in the conditions can be expanded.

    <expr> ::=
        <integer expr>
           Symbol-table(<integer expr>) ← *Symbol-table*(<expr>)
           Type(<integer expr>) ← *Type*(<expr>)
           condition: *Type*(<expr>) ∉ { *boolean* }
        | <boolean expr>
           Symbol-table(<boolean expr>) ← *Symbol-table*(<expr>)
           Type(<boolean expr>) ← *Type*(<expr>)
           condition: *Type*(<expr>) ∉ { *integer* }

The nonterminals <integer expr> and <term> pass the *Symbol-table* and *Type*
attributes down to the children nodes, except for <weak op> and <strong
op>, which require no context checking.

<integer expr> ::=
    <term>
      Symbol-table(<term>) ← *Symbol-table*(<integer expr>)
      Type(<term>) ← *Type*(<integer expr>)

   | <integer expr>$_2$ <weak op> <term>
      Symbol-table(<integer expr>$_2$) ← *Symbol-table*(<integer expr>)
      Symbol-table(<term>) ← *Symbol-table*(<integer expr>)
      Type(<integer expr>$_2$) ← *Type*(<integer expr>)
      Type(<term>) ← *Type*(<integer expr>)

<term> ::=
    <element>
      Symbol-table(<element>) ← *Symbol-table*(<term>)
      Type(<element>) ← *Type*(<term>)
   | <term>$_2$ <strong op> <element>
      Symbol-table(<term>$_2$) ← *Symbol-table*(<term>)
      Symbol-table(<element>) ← *Symbol-table*(<term>)
      Type(<term>$_2$) ← *Type*(<term>)
      Type(<element>) ← *Type*(<term>)

The nonterminal <element> can expand to <numeral>, which requires no context checking, a parenthesized or negated expression, which receives *Symbol-table* and *Type*, or a variable, which is looked up in the symbol table. Normally, we expect this variable to be declared (not *undefined*) and to have type integer. On the other hand, if the inherited *Type* attribute is *undefined*, we have no expectations for the type of the variable, so no error is reported, thereby avoiding certain spurious errors.

<element> ::=
    <numeral>
   | <variable>
    condition:
    case lookup-type(*Name*(<variable>), *Symbol-table*(<element>)) is
      integer   : error("")
      undefined   : error("Variable not declared")
      boolean, program : if *Type*(<element>)=*undefined*
                       then error("")
                       else error("Integer variable expected")

| (<expr>)

    Symbol-table(<expr>) ← *Symbol-table*(<element>)

    Type(<expr>) ← *Type*(<element>)

| - <element>$_2$

    Symbol-table(<element>$_2$) ← *Symbol-table*(<element>)

    Type(<element>$_2$) ← *Type*(<element>)

The attribute grammar definitions for <boolean expr>, <boolean term>, and <boolean element> are similar to their integer counterparts and are shown in Figure 3.12. A comparison passes the *Symbol-table* and *Type* attributes down to both integer expressions.

<comparison> ::= <integer expr>$_1$ <relation> <integer expr>$_2$

    Symbol-table(<integer expr>$_1$) ← *Symbol-table*(<comparison>)

    Symbol-table(<integer expr>$_2$) ← *Symbol-table*(<comparison>)

    Type(<integer expr>$_1$) ← *integer*

    Type(<integer expr>$_2$) ← *integer*

Note that we have restricted comparisons to integer expressions only. Other alternatives are presented in the exercises.

This completes the context checking attribute grammar for Wren, except for the productions for <identifier>, <variable>, <letter>, and <digit>, which appear in the complete grammar in Figure 3.12.

<program> ::= **program** <identifier> **is** <block>

    Symbol-table(<block>) ←

        add-item((*Name*(<identifier>), *program*), empty-table)

<block> ::= <declaration sequence> **begin** <command sequence> **end**

    Symbol-table(<command sequence>) ←

        table-union(*Symbol-table*(<block>),

            Symbol-table(<declaration sequence>))

    condition:

    if table-intersection(*Symbol-table*(<block>),

        Symbol-table(<declaration sequence>)) = *empty*

    then error("")

    else error("Program name used as a variable")

<declaration> ::= **var** <variable list> : <type>;

    Symbol-table(<declaration>) ←

        build-symbol-table(*Var-list*(<variable list>), *Type*(<type>))

Figure 3.12: Context Checking Attribute Grammar for Wren (Part 1)

<declaration sequence> ::=

    ε

        Symbol-table(<declaration sequence>) ← empty-table

  | <declaration> <declaration sequence>$_2$

        Symbol-table(<declaration sequence>) ←

                table-union(*Symbol-table*(<declaration>),

                              Symbol-table(<declaration sequence>$_2$))

      condition:

      if table-intersection(*Symbol-table*(<declaration>),

                  Symbol-table(<declaration sequence>$_2$)) = *empty*

        then error("")

        else error("Duplicate declaration of identifier")

<variable list> ::=

     <variable>

     Var-list(<variable list>) ← cons(*Name*(<variable>), empty-list)

  | <variable> **,** <variable list>$_2$

     Var-list(<variable list>) ←

               cons(*Name*(<variable>), *Var-list*(<variable list>$_2$))

      condition:

      if *Name*(<variable>) is not a member of *Var-list*(<variable list>$_2$)

               then error("")

               else error("Duplicate variable in declaration list")

<type> ::=

    integer

        Type(<type>) ← *integer*

  | **boolean**

        Type(<type>) ← *boolean*

<command sequence> ::=

     <command>

     Symbol-table(<command>) ← *Symbol-table*(<command sequence>)

  | <command> **;** <command sequence>$_2$

     Symbol-table(<command>) ← *Symbol-table*(<command sequence>)

     Symbol-table(<cmd sequence>$_2$) ← *Symbol-table*(<command sequence>)

<command> ::=

   skip

  | **read** <variable>

      condition:

      case lookup-type(*Name*(<variable>), *Symbol-table*(<command>)) is

            integer : error("")

            undefined : error("Variable not declared")

            boolean, program : error("Integer variable expected for read")

Figure 3.12: Context Checking Attribute Grammar for Wren (Part 2)

| **write** <expr>
    Symbol-table(<expr>) ← *Symbol-table*(<command>)
    Type(<expr>) ← *integer*

| <variable> **:=** <expr>
        Symbol-table(<expr>) ← *Symbol-table*(<command>)
        condition:
        case lookup-type(*Name*(<variable>), *Symbol-table*(<command>)) is
                Type(<expr>) : error("")
                undefined : error("Target variable not declared")
                program : error("Target variable same as program name")

| **while** <boolean expr> **do** <command sequence> **end while**
        Symbol-table(<boolean expr>) ← *Symbol-table*(<command>)
        Symbol-table(<command sequence>) ← *Symbol-table*(<command>)
        Type(<boolean expr>) ← *boolean*

| **if** <boolean expr> **then** <command sequence>$_1$
                                else <command sequence>$_2$ **end if**
        Symbol-table(<boolean expr>) ← *Symbol-table*(<command>)
        Symbol-table(<command sequence>$_1$) ← *Symbol-table*(<command>)
        Symbol-table(<command sequence>$_2$) ← *Symbol-table*(<command>)
        Type(<boolean expr>) ← *boolean*

| **if** <boolean expr> **then** <command sequence> **end if**
        Symbol-table(<boolean expr>) ← *Symbol-table*(<command>)
        Symbol-table(<command sequence>) ← *Symbol-table*(<command>)
        Type(<boolean expr>) ← *boolean*

<expr> ::=
        <integer expr>
        Symbol-table(<integer expr>) ← *Symbol-table*(<expr>)
        Type(<integer expr>) ← *Type*(<expr>)
        condition: *Type*(<expr>) ∉ { *boolean* }

    | <boolean expr>
        Symbol-table(<boolean expr>) ← *Symbol-table*(<expr>)
        Type(<boolean expr>) ← *Type*(<expr>)
        condition: *Type*(<expr>) ∉ { *integer* }

<integer expr> ::=
        <term>
        Symbol-table(<term>) ← *Symbol-table*(<integer expr>)
        Type(<term>) ← *Type*(<integer expr>)
    | <integer expr>$_2$ <weak op> <term>
        Symbol-table(<integer expr>$_2$) ← *Symbol-table*(<integer expr>)
        Symbol-table(<term>) ← *Symbol-table*(<integer expr>)
        Type(<integer expr>$_2$) ← *Type*(<integer expr>)
        Type(<term>) ← *Type*(<integer expr>)

Figure 3.12: Context Checking Attribute Grammar for Wren (Part 3)

<term> ::=

    <element>

        Symbol-table(<element>) ← *Symbol-table*(<term>)

        Type(<element>) ← *Type*(<term>)

   | <term>$_2$ <strong op> <element>

        Symbol-table(<term>$_2$) ← *Symbol-table*(<term>)

        Symbol-table(<element>) ← *Symbol-table*(<term>)

        Type(<term>$_2$) ← *Type*(<term>)

        Type(<element>) ← *Type*(<term>)

<weak op> ::= **+** | **–**

<strong op> ::= ***** | **/**

<element> ::=

      <numeral>

    | <variable>

        condition:

        case lookup-type(*Name*(<variable>), *Symbol-table*(<element>)) is

            integer : error("")

            undefined : error("Variable not declared")

            boolean, program : if *Type*(<element>)=*undefined*

                        then error("")

                        else error("Integer variable expected")

    | **(** <expr> **)**

        Symbol-table(<expr>) ← *Symbol-table*(<element>)

        Type(<expr>) ← *Type*(<element>)

    | **-** <element>$_2$

        Symbol-table(<element>$_2$) ← *Symbol-table*(<element>)

        Type(<element>$_2$) ← *Type*(<element>)

<boolean expr> ::=

      <boolean term>

        Symbol-table(<boolean term>) ← *Symbol-table*(<boolean expr>)

        Type(<boolean term>) ← *Type*(<boolean expr>)

    | <boolean expr>$_2$ **or** <boolean term>

        Symbol-table(<boolean expr>$_2$) ←*Symbol-table*(<boolean expr>)

        Symbol-table(<boolean term>) ← *Symbol-table*(<boolean expr>)

        Type(<boolean expr>$_2$) ← *Type*(<boolean expr>)

        Type(<boolean term>) ← *Type*(<boolean expr>)

<boolean term> ::=

      <boolean element>

        Symbol-table(<boolean element>) ← *Symbol-table*(<boolean term>)

        Type(<boolean element>) ← *Type*(<boolean term>)

Figure 3.12: Context Checking Attribute Grammar for Wren (Part 4)

| <boolean term>$_2$ **and** <boolean element>

     Symbol-table(<boolean term>$_2$) ← *Symbol-table*(<boolean term>)

     Symbol-table(<boolean element>) ← *Symbol-table*(<boolean term>)

     Type(<boolean term>$_2$) ← *Type*(<boolean term>)

     Type(<boolean element>) ← *Type*(<boolean term>)

<boolean element> ::=

     true

     | **false**

     | <variable>

          condition:

          case lookup-type(*Name*(<variable>),*Symbol-table*(<boolean element>)) is

               boolean : error("")

               undefined : error("Variable not declared")

               integer, program : if *Type*(<element>) = *undefined*

                                then error("")

                                else error("Boolean variable expected")

     | <comparison>

          Symbol-table(<comparison>) ← *Symbol-table*(<boolean element>)

     | **not (** <boolean expr> **)**

          Symbol-table(<boolean expr>) ← *Symbol-table*(<boolean element>)

          Type(<boolean expr>) ← *Type*(<boolean element>)

     | **(** <boolean expr> **)**

          Symbol-table(<boolean expr>) ← *Symbol-table*(<boolean element>)

<comparison> ::= <integer expr>$_1$ <relation> <integer expr>$_2$

          Symbol-table(<integer expr>$_1$) ← *Symbol-table*(<comparison>)

          Symbol-table(<integer expr>$_2$) ← *Symbol-table*(<comparison>)

          Type(<integer expr>$_1$) ← *integer*

          Type(<integer expr>$_2$) ← *integer*

<relation> ::= **=** | **< >** | **<** | **< =** | **>** | **> =**

<variable> ::= <identifier>

          Name(<variable>) ← *Name*(<identifier>)

<identifier> ::=

     <letter>

          Name(<identifier>) ← *Name*(<letter>)

     | <identifier>$_2$ <letter>

          Name(<identifier>) ← str-concat(*Name*(<identifier>$_2$),*Name*(<letter>))

     | <identifier>$_2$ <digit>

          Name(<identifier>) ← str-concat(*Name*(<identifier>$_2$),*Name*(<digit>))

<letter> ::=

      a

          Name(<letter>) ← 'a'

      :   :   :

     | **z**

          Name(<letter>) ← 'z'

Figure 3.12: Context Checking Attribute Grammar for Wren (Part 5)

<numeral> ::= <digit> | <numeral> <digit>

<digit> ::=

    0

        Name(<digit>) ← '0'

    :   :   :

    | **9**

        Name(<digit>) ← '9'

Auxiliary Functions

build-symbol-table(var-list, type) =
    if empty(var-list)
        then empty-table
        else add-item(head(var-list),type,build-symbol-table(tail(var-list), type))

add-item(name, type, table) = cons([name,type], table)

table-union(table$_1$, table$_2$) =
    if empty(table$_1$)
        then table$_2$
        else if lookup-type(first-name(table$_1$),table$_2$) = *undefined*
            then add-item(head(table$_1$), table-union(tail(table$_1$), table$_2$))
            else table-union(tail(table$_1$), table$_2$))

table-intersection(table$_1$, table$_2$) =
    if empty(table$_1$)
        then *empty*
        else if lookup-type(first-name(table$_1$),table$_2$) ≠ *undefined*
            then *nonempty* else table-intersection(tail(table$_1$),table$_2$)

lookup-type(name, table) =
    if empty(table)
        then *undefined*
        else if head(table) = [name, type]
            then type else lookup-type(name,tail(table))

head([[name,type] | restTable]) = [name,type]

tail([[name,type] | restTable]) = restTable

first-name([[name,type] | restTable]) = name

cons([name,type], table) = [[name,type] | table]

empty-table = [ ]

empty(empty-table) = true

empty([name,type] | restTable]) = false

str-concat(char-sequence$_1$, char-sequence$_2$) returns the
        concatenation of char-sequence$_1$ followed by char-sequence$_2$

error(string) prints nonempty strings

Figure 3.12: Context Checking Attribute Grammar for Wren (Part 6)

Exercises

1   Draw the parse tree decorated with attributes for the following Wren program:

>   **program** p **is**
>   **var** b: **boolean;**
>   **var** m, n: **integer;**
>   **begin**
>   **read** m; **read** n;
>   b := m < n;
>   **if** b **then write** m
>   **else write** n
>   **end if**
>   **end**

2. Suppose the declarations in the above program are replaced by

    > **var** b, m, n: **integer;**

    Show the changes in the parse tree from exercise 1.

3. Modify the attribute grammar for Wren to allow for checking equality or inequality of Boolean expressions in comparisons, but none of the other relations.

4. Add the declaration types character and string to Wren. Allow the input of an integer and character (use **readch**), but not Boolean and string. Allow output of integer, character, and string (use **writech** and **writestr**), but not Boolean. Restrict a string literal to a sequence of lowercase alphabetic characters, digit characters, and the space character. Modify the attribute grammar to enforce the related context conditions. Overloading **read** and **write** makes this problem more difficult.

5. After completing exercise 4, add the following string expressions, character expressions, and additions to integer expressions.

    > String Expressions:
    >   concat(<str expr>,<str expr>) .
    >   substr(<str expr>,<int expr>,<int expr>)
    >   where the first integer expression is the start
    >   position and the second expression is the length
    >   toStr(<char expr>)
    >   "Example of a string literal"

Character Expressions:
    toChar(<str expr>,<int expr>)
        where the integer expression is the position of the
        character in the string
    char(<int expr>)
    'X'   character literal

Additions to Integer Expressions:
    ord(<char expr>)
    length(<str expr>)

After carefully specifying the BNF for these operations, add the appropriate context checking using attributes.

6. Suppose that we extend Wren to allow for the following alternative in declarations:

    <declaration> ::= **procedure** <identifier> **is** <block>

This alternative results in a new value for *Type*, which we name *procedure*. We also add a call command:

    <command> ::= **call** <identifier>

These changes allow nested blocks with local declarations. Modify the attribute grammar for Wren to accommodate these changes. Follow Pascal scope rules by requiring that an identifier must be declared before it is used. Furthermore, remove the first context condition concerning the program identifier and relax the second and third context condtions:

2. All identifiers that appear in a block must be declared in that block or in an enclosing block.

3. No identifier may be declared more than once at the top level of a block.

Hint: One attribute should synthesize declarations and a different attribute should inherit declarations since the declaration information has to be inherited into the declaration section itself because of the occurrence of a <block> in a procedure declaration.

7. Recall the language of expressions formed as lists of integers in exercise 9 in section 1.2. Augment the BNF grammar for the language with attributes that enforce the conformity of lists given to the arithmetic operations +, −, and *.

3.3 LABORATORY: CONTEXT CHECKING WREN

We have already seen how logic grammars in Prolog can be used to construct an abstract syntax tree for a Wren program. Using several utility predicates, we constructed a scanner that converts a text file containing a program into a sequence of tokens. We utilize this same "front-end" software for the current laboratory activity; however, we extend the parser using attributes to perform context-sensitive declaration and type checking.

Before proceeding directly into the development of the attribute grammar in Prolog, we need to make some important design decisions about the expected output from our context checker. The scanning and parsing front-end program from Chapter 2 assumes that the input program obeys the BNF for Wren. With attribute grammars, we have additional context-sensitive conditions at selected nodes that must be satisfied for the parse to succeed. The first question we need to address is what should be the output of the parser for a program that obeys the BNF but fails one of the context condition checks. We can elect to have the entire parse fail, with Prolog simply reporting "no", but this response seems less than satisfactory. Another alternative, the one we develop, is to allow the parse to succeed, provided the BNF is satisfied, and to insert error messages in cases where context-sensitive checking fails.

The second design decision we have to make is the form of the output of the parser in cases where the parse succeeds but may contain context checking errors. In Chapter 2 Wren programs were transformed into a compact form that contained only the relevant syntactic information—namely, abstract syntax trees. For example, the assignment statement in Wren

$$x := 3 + 2 * y$$

was tokenized by the scanner to:

[ide(x),assign,num(3),plus,num(2),times,ide(y)]

and then parsed to produce the abstract syntax tree:

assign(x,exp(plus,num(3),exp(times,num(2),ide(y)))).

This latter form will be useful when we develop an interpreter for Wren in later chapters. Since the current project deals with the detection of context condition violations, we elect to retain the stream of tokens output from the scanner with the possible error messages inserted to indicate any context condition violations. This approach is best illustrated by an example. The program below does not perform any useful function; it simply demonstrates a variety of commands and types.

```
?- go.
>>> Checking Context Constraints in Wren <<<
Enter name of source file: prog1.wren
     program prog1 is
        var x,y: integer;
        var b,c: boolean;
     begin
        read x;  read y;  write x+y;
        b := x < y;
        if x = y
           then c := x <= y
           else c := x > y end if;
        while c do x := x + 1 end while;
        b := b and (b or c)
     end
Scan successful
[program,ide(prog1),is,
    var,ide(x),comma,ide(y),colon,integer,semicolon,
    var,ide(b),comma,ide(c),colon,boolean,semicolon,
    begin,
       read,ide(x),semicolon,read,ide(y),semicolon,
       write,ide(x),plus,ide(y),semicolon,
       ide(b),assign,ide(x),less,ide(y),semicolon,
       if,ide(x),equal,ide(y),
          then,ide(c),assign,ide(x),lteq,ide(y),
          else,ide(c),assign,ide(x),grtr,ide(y),
       end,if,semicolon,
       while,ide(c),do,
          ide(x),assign,ide(x),plus,num(1),
       end,while,semicolon,
       ide(b),assign,ide(b),and,lparen,ide(b),or,ide(c),rparen,
  end,
eop]

Parse successful
[program,ide(prog1),is,
    var,ide(x),comma,ide(y),colon,integer,semicolon,
    var,ide(b),comma,ide(c),colon,boolean,semicolon,
    begin,
       read,ide(x),semicolon,read,ide(y),semicolon,
       write,ide(x),plus,ide(y),semicolon,
       ide(b),assign,ide(x),less,ide(y),semicolon,
       if,ide(x),equal,ide(y),
```

```
        then,ide(c),assign,ide(x),lteq,ide(y),
        else,ide(c),assign,ide(x),grtr,ide(y),
      end,if,semicolon,
      while,ide(c),do,
        ide(x),assign,ide(x),plus,num(1),
      end,while,semicolon,
      ide(b),assign,ide(b),and,lparen,ide(b),or,ide(c),rparen,
  end]
```

For readability, we have inserted line feeds and spacing for indentation in the listing shown above. The test program obeys the BNF and all context-sensitive conditions, so the output of the parser is the same as the output from the scanner, except for the removal of the final eop token. It may seem that we have done a lot of work to accomplish nothing, but introducing some context-sensitive errors will illustrate what the parser is doing for us.

```
?- go.
```
```
>>> Checking Context Constraints in Wren <<<
```
```
Enter name of source file: prog2.wren
    program prog2 is
      var x,y,b: integer;
      var b,c: boolean;
    begin
      read x;   read c;   write x+a;
      b := x < c;
      if x = y
          then c := x <= y
          else y := x > y
      end if;
      while c > b do x := x + 1 end while;
      b := b and (y or z)
    end
```
```
Scan successful
[program,ide(prog2),is,
  var,ide(x),comma,ide(y),comma,ide(b),colon,integer,semicolon,
  var,ide(b),comma,ide(c),colon,boolean,semicolon,
  begin,
    read,ide(x),semicolon,read,ide(c),semicolon,
    write,ide(x),plus,ide(a),semicolon,
    ide(b),assign,ide(x),less,ide(c),semicolon,
    if,ide(x),equal,ide(y),
        then,ide(c),assign,ide(x),lteq,ide(y),
        else,ide(y),assign,ide(x),grtr,ide(y),
      end,if,semicolon,
      while,ide(c),grtr,ide(b),do,
```

```
        ide(x),assign,ide(x),plus,num(1),
    end,while,semicolon,
      ide(b),assign,ide(b),and,lparen,ide(y),or,ide(z),rparen,
  end, eop]
Parse successful
[program,ide(prog2),is,
    var,ide(x),comma,ide(y),comma,ide(b),colon,integer,semicolon,
      ERROR: Duplicate declaration of an identifier,
      var,ide(b),comma,ide(c),colon,boolean,semicolon,
  begin,
    read,ide(x),semicolon,
    read,ide(c),
      ERROR: Integer variable expected for read,semicolon,
    write,ide(x),plus,ide(a),
      ERROR: Variable not declared,semicolon,
    ide(b),assign,ide(x),less,ide(c),
      ERROR: Integer variable expected,
      ERROR: Integer expression expected,
    semicolon,
    if,ide(x),equal,ide(y),
        then,ide(c),assign,ide(x),lteq,ide(y),
        else,ide(y),assign,ide(x),grtr,ide(y),
      ERROR: Integer expression expected,
    end,if,semicolon,
    while,ide(c),
      ERROR: Integer variable expected,grtr,ide(b),do,
        ide(x),assign,ide(x),plus,num(1),end,while,semicolon,
        ide(b),assign,ide(b),
      ERROR: Boolean variable expected,and,lparen,ide(y),
      ERROR: Boolean variable expected,or,ide(z),
      ERROR: Variable not declared,rparen,
      ERROR: Integer expression expected,
  end]
```

Again, we have formatted the output for readability. It should be noted that the error messages appear near the locations where the errors occur. As mentioned previously, for programs that obey the BNF, we allow the parse to succeed, although there may or may not be context-sensitive errors. The following strategy is implemented: An error variable is placed at all locations when a context-sensitive check is made. This variable is bound either to the atom noError or to an appropriate error message entered as an atom (a string inside apostrophes). During the final stage of processing, we flatten the parse tree into a linear list and strip away all noError values using a predicate called flattenplus, so only the real error messages remain.

Declarations

Now that we have formulated a goal for this laboratory exercise, we can proceed to develop the parser using stepwise refinement. Enough code is presented to introduce the idea of implementing the attribute grammar in Prolog. Those portions of code that are not detailed here are left as exercises.

```
program(TokenList) -->
        [program], [ide(I)], [is],
        { addItem(I,program,[ ],InitialSymbolTable) },
        block(Block, InitialSymbolTable),
        { flattenplus([program, ide(I), is, Block], TokenList) }.
```

After getting the program identifier name, we add it with the pseudo-type program to the InitialSymbolTable, which is passed to the predicate block. This predicate returns a structure (Block) that is used to build the list

```
[program, ide(I), is, Block],
```

which is flattened into a modified token list and given as the result of the context checker.

The utility functions in our attribute grammar use functional notation that can only be simulated in Prolog. We adopt the strategy that the return value is the last term in the parameter list, so addItem in Prolog becomes

```
addItem(Name, Type, Table, [[Name,Type] | Table]).
```

The code for block is the first place we do context checking to ensure that the program name is not declared elsewhere in the program.

```
block([ErrorMsg, Decs, begin, Cmds, end],InitialSymbolTable) -->
    decs(Decs,DecsSymbolTable),
    { tableIntersection(InitialSymbolTable, DecsSymbolTable,Result),
      tableUnion(InitialSymbolTable, DecsSymbolTable, SymbolTable),
     ( Result=nonEmpty,
         ErrorMsg='ERROR: Program name used as a variable'
       ; Result=empty, ErrorMsg=noError) },
    [begin], cmds(Cmds,SymbolTable), [end].
```

A block parses simply as

```
decs(Decs,DecsSymbolTable), [begin], cmds(Cmds,SymbolTable), [end],
```

but we have added some Prolog code to perform a table intersection, which returns one of two results: empty or nonEmpty. We bind the variable ErrorMsg to the atom noError if the intersection is empty or to an appropriate error message (another atom) if the program name appears in the declarations. We also form the union of the InitialSymbolTable and the DecsSymbolTable producing a value to be passed to the command sequence as SymbolTable.

The utility predicate tableIntersection follows directly from the definition of the utility function in the attribute grammar. Notice the use of lookupType that returns the value undefined if the identifier is not found in the table, or the associated type if the identifier is found. The predicate tableUnion also follows directly from the definition in the attribute grammar; its definition is left as an exercise.

tableIntersection([ ], Table2, empty).

tableIntersection(Table1, [ ], empty).

tableIntersection([[Name, Type1] | RestTable], Table2, nonEmpty) :-
      lookupType(Name, Table2,Type2), (Type2=integer; Type2=boolean).

tableIntersection([[Name, Type] | RestTable], Table2, Result) :-
      tableIntersection(RestTable, Table2, Result).

lookupType(Name, [ ], undefined).

lookupType(Name, [[Name,Type] | RestTable], Type).

lookupType(Name, [Name1 | RestTable], Type) :-
      lookupType(Name, RestTable, Type).

Observe that many of the variables in the heads of these clauses do not appear in the bodies of the clauses. Anonymous variables such as the following can be used in this situation:

tableIntersection([ ], _, empty).

tableIntersection(_, [ ], empty).

tableIntersection([[Name, _] | _], Table2, nonEmpty) :-
      lookupType(Name, Table2,Type2), (Type2=integer; Type2=boolean).

tableIntersection([[_ , _] | RestTable], Table2, Result) :-
      tableIntersection(RestTable, Table2, Result).

We prefer using variable names instead of anonymous variables because suggestive variable names make the clause definitions more intelligible. Substituting variable names in place of anonymous variables may result in warning messages from some Prolog systems, but the program still functions correctly.

Two types of multiple declarations may occur in Wren: duplicates within the same declaration, as in

    var x, y, z, x : **boolean**;

and duplicates between two different declarations, as in

    var x, y, z: **boolean**;
    var u, v, w, x: **integer**;

The context checker needs to recognize both errors. A variable list is a single variable followed by a list of variables, which may or may not be empty. In either case, we check if the current head of the variable list is a member of the list of remaining variables. If so, we have a duplicate variable error; otherwise, we pass forward the error message generated by the remainder of the list. Note that commas are inserted into the variable list that is returned since we want to construct the original token sequence.

```
varlist(Vars,ErrorMsg) --> [ide(Var)], restvars(ide(Var),Vars,ErrorMsg).

restvars(ide(Var),[ide(Var), comma |Vars],ErrorMsg) -->
                    [comma], varlist(Vars,ErrorMsg1),
                    { member(ide(Var),Vars),
                        ErrorMsg='ERROR: Duplicate variable in listing'
                      ; ErrorMsg = ErrorMsg1 }.

restvars(ide(Var),[ide(Var)],ErrorMsg) --> [ ], { ErrorMsg=noError }.
```

Once we have determined there are no duplicate variables within a single declaration, we check between declarations. The strategy is much the same: A sequence of declarations is a single declaration followed by any remaining declarations, which may or may not be empty. In each case, we check if the table intersection of the symbol table associated with the current declaration is disjoint from the symbol table of the remaining declarations. If it is not, an error message is generated. The code shown below is incomplete, as the table intersection test and the ERROR message are missing. Completing this code is left as an exercise.

```
decs(Decs,SymbolTable) --> dec(Dec,SymbolTable1),
                restdecs(Dec,SymbolTable1,Decs,SymbolTable).

decs([ ],[ ]) --> [ ].

restdecs(Dec,SymbolTable1,[Dec,ErrorMsg|Decs],SymbolTable) -->
                decs(Decs,SymbolTable2),
                { tableUnion(SymbolTable1,SymbolTable2,SymbolTable),
                  (ErrorMsg=noError) }.

restdecs(Dec,SymbolTable,[Dec],SymbolTable) --> [ ].
```

A single declaration results in a symbol table that is constructed by the utility predicate buildSymbolTable, which takes a list of variables and a single type and inserts a [Var, Type] pair into an initially empty symbol table for each variable name in the list. Observe that we remove commas from the variable list before passing it to buildSymbolTable. A predicate delete needs to be defined to perform this task.

```
dec([var, Vars, ErrorMsg, colon, Type, semicolon],SymbolTable) -->
            [var], varlist(Vars, ErrorMsg), [colon], type(Type), [semicolon],
            { delete(comma,Vars,NewVars),
                buildSymbolTable(NewVars, Type, SymbolTable) }.

type(integer) --> [integer].

type(boolean) --> [boolean].

buildSymbolTable([ ], Type, [ ]).

buildSymbolTable([ide(Var)|RestVars], Type, SymbolTable):-
                buildSymbolTable(RestVars,Type,SymbolTable1),
                addItem(Var, Type, SymbolTable1, SymbolTable).
```

Commands

We now turn our attention to the context checking within command sequences. A command sequence is a single command followed by the remaining commands, which may or may not be empty. We pass the symbol table attribute down the derivation tree to both the first command and to the remaining commands.

```
cmds(Cmds,SymbolTable) -->
        command(Cmd,SymbolTable), restcmds(Cmd,Cmds,SymbolTable).

restcmds(Cmd,[Cmd, semicolon|Cmds],SymbolTable) -->
                    [semicolon], cmds(Cmds,SymbolTable).

restcmds(Cmd,[Cmd],SymbolTable) --> [ ].
```

The **skip** command is very simple; it needs no type checking. The **read** command requires the associated variable to be of type integer. Two possible errors may occur in a **read** command: The variable has not been declared or the variable is of the wrong type.

```
command(skip,SymbolTable) --> [skip].

command([read, ide(I), ErrorMsg], SymbolTable) -->
    [read], [ide(I)],
    { lookupType(I,SymbolTable,Type),
        ( Type = integer, ErrorMsg=noError
        ; Type = undefined, ErrorMsg='ERROR: Variable not declared'
        ; (Type = boolean; Type = program),
                    ErrorMsg='ERROR: Integer variable expected') }.
```

The **write** command requests an integer expression by passing the value integer as an inherited attribute to the expression. This task is left as an exercise.

A correct assignment command has one of two forms: An integer variable is assigned the result of an integer expression or a Boolean variable is assigned the result of a Boolean expression. Two potential errors can occur: The target variable is not declared or the target variable and the expression are not the same type. The decision to have a successful parse whenever the BNF is satisfied complicates the code for the assignment command. No matter which errors occur, we must consume the symbols in the expression on the right-hand side. View the definition below as a case command controlled by the type of the target variable. Each case selection includes a call to parse the expression.

```
command([ide(V), assign, E, ErrorMsg], SymbolTable) -->
  [ide(V)], [assign],
  { lookupType(V,SymbolTable,VarType) },
  ({ VarType = integer },
      (expr(E,SymbolTable,integer), { ErrorMsg=noError }
        ; expr(E,SymbolTable,boolean),
                    { ErrorMsg='ERROR: Integer expression expected' }) ;
  { VarType = boolean },
      (expr(E,SymbolTable,boolean), { ErrorMsg=noError }
      ;  expr(E,SymbolTable,integer),
                    { ErrorMsg='ERROR: Boolean expression expected' }) ;
  { VarType = undefined, ErrorMsg='ERROR: Target of assign not declared' ;
    VarType = program,
                    ErrorMsg='ERROR: Program name used as a variable' },
          expr(E,SymbolTable,undefined)).
```

The **if** and **while** commands do no type checking directly; rather they pass the SymbolTable and Type attributes to their constituent parts. The **if-then-else** command is given; the **while** command is left as an exercise.

```
command([if,Test,then,Then,Else],SymbolTable) -->
                    [if], boolexpr(Test,SymbolTable,boolean), [then],
                cmds(Then,SymbolTable), restif(Else,SymbolTable).

restif([else,Else,end,if],SymbolTable) -->
                [else], cmds(Else,SymbolTable), [end], [if].

restif([end,if],SymbolTable) --> [end], [if].
```

Expressions

The inherited attribute passed from <expr> to <int expr> and <bool expr> may have the value undefined. We cannot let such a value cause failure in the parsing, so four clauses are needed in the logic grammar.

    expr(E,SymbolTable,integer) --> intexpr(E,SymbolTable,integer).
    expr(E,SymbolTable,boolean) --> boolexpr(E,SymbolTable,boolean).
    expr(E,SymbolTable,undefined) --> intexpr(E,SymbolTable,undefined).
    expr(E,SymbolTable,undefined) --> boolexpr(E,SymbolTable,undefined).

In the attribute grammar, we made expression and term left recursive since this matches the left associativity of the additive and multiplicative operations. Since we cannot use left recursion in logic grammars, we need to adopt a different strategy for producing the same parse tree. When we studied BNF, we learned that

    <int expr> ::= <int expr> <weak op> <term>

can also be expressed as

    <int expr> ::= <term> { <weak op> <term> }

where the braces mean zero or more occurrences. We use this technique to develop our logic grammar (see Chapter 2 for more on this issue).

    intexpr(E,SymbolTable,Type) -->
                term(T,SymbolTable,Type), restintexpr(T,E,SymbolTable,Type).
    restintexpr(T, E, SymbolTable,Type) -->
                                weakop(Op), term(T1, SymbolTable,Type),
                                restintexpr([T,Op,T1], E, SymbolTable,Type).
    restintexpr(E,E,SymbolTable,Type) --> [ ].
    weakop(plus) --> [plus].
    weakop(minus) --> [minus].

A term is an element, possibly followed by more elements separated by multiplication or division (strong operators). The code for term, restterm, and strongop is left as an exercise.

An element may be a constant number, in which case no type checking is required. If the element is a variable, it is looked up in the symbol table. Two errors are possible: The variable is not declared or it is the wrong type. No error occurs if it is an integer and we are expecting an integer or if the variable is defined, but we are not expecting any type in particular (the inherited attribute Type has the value undefined because the target variable in an assignment command was undeclared).

```
element(num(N),SymbolTable,Type) --> [num(N)].

element([ide(I),ErrorMsg],SymbolTable,Type) -->
    [ide(I)],
    { lookupType(I,SymbolTable,Type),
        (VarType = integer, Type = integer, ErrorMsg=noError
        ; VarType = undefined, ErrorMsg='ERROR: Variable not declared'
        ; Type = undefined, ErrorMsg=noError
        ; (VarType = boolean; VarType = program),
                ErrorMsg='ERROR: Integer variable expected') }.

element([lparen, E, rparen], SymbolTable,Type) -->
                [lparen], intexpr(E,SymbolTable,Type), [rparen].

element([minus|E],SymbolTable,Type) -->
                [minus], element(E, SymbolTable,Type).
```

We complete the discussion of the Prolog implementation of the attribute grammar for context checking by focusing on the code for Boolean expressions and for comparisons. Boolean expression, which handles the **or** operator, and Boolean term, which handles the **and** operator, are very similar to integer expression and term. A Boolean element may be a constant, **true** or **false**, a variable, whose declaration and type must be checked, a comparison, a parenthesized Boolean expression, or the unary Boolean operator **not**. Except for comparison, which is given below, this code is left as an exercise.

```
comparison([E1,R,E2],SymbolTable) -->
    intexpr(E1,SymbolTable,integer), rel(R), intexpr(E2,SymbolTable,integer).

rel(equal) --> [equal].  rel(neq) --> [neq].  rel(less) --> [less].

rel(grtr) --> [grtr].  rel(gteq) --> [gteq].  rel(lteq) --> [lteq].
```

This completes the discussion and partial implementation of our context checking attribute grammar. When the omitted code has been developed, the program will produce the output given at the start of the section.

Exercises

1. Complete the code for the following predicates that were omitted from the text:

    - the tableUnion utility function

    - the predicate restdecs by adding the tableIntersection test

    - the **write** command

- the **while** command

- term, restterm, and strongop

- boolexpr, boolterm, and boolelement

- a flatten utility predicate flattenplus that also removes noError

2. Modify the Prolog implementation of our Wren attribute grammar to allow checking equality or inequality of Boolean expressions in comparisons, but none of the other relations.

3. Following exercise 4 in Section 3.2, add the declaration types character and string to Wren. Implement the changes to the attribute grammar in Prolog.

4. Following exercise 5 in Section 3.2, add the commands for character and string manipulations. Use attributes to add any appropriate context checking.

5. Following exercise 6 in Section 3.2, add the declaration and calling of parameterless procedures.

3.4 FURTHER READING

The seminal paper in attribute grammars has been written by Donald Knuth [Knuth68]. Other papers have explored the mathematical semantics of attribute grammars [Mayoh81] or developed new concepts, such as ordered attribute grammars [Kastens80]. David Watt presents an extended attribute grammar for Pascal [Watt79].

The primary application of attribute grammars is in compiler construction [Bochman78]. Attribute grammars can be used both for type checking, as we have seen in this chapter, and code generation, as we will see in Chapter 7. Many automated tools have been written to aid in compiler construction. Kennedy and Warren discuss the generation of attribute grammar evaluators [Kennedy76]. Those familiar with Unix software may have used LEX, an automated lexical analyzer [Lesk75], and YACC, "Yet Another Compiler-Compiler" [Johnson78]. Automated tools can help generate production level compilers [Farrow84]. Readers wanting to explore the application of attribute grammars in compiler construction can consult any number of references, including [Aho86], [Fischer91], [Parsons92], and [Pittman92].

Recent research in attribute grammars includes work in attribute propagation by message passing [Demers85] and using attribute grammars to build language-based editors [Johnson85]. The Synthesizer-Generator [Reps89] is a modern software tool to build context-sensitive editors. This sophisticated, windows-based product is built on top of LEX and YACC (or equivalent tools). Editors are available for languages such as Pascal and C. We have used the Synthesizer-Generator as a teaching tool in a compiler class by asking students to build a context-sensitive editor for Wren. Uses of the Synthesizer-Generator include many diverse context-sensitive situations, such as calculations in a spreadsheet or balancing chemical equations.

Attribute grammars can also be used for type inferencing. It is possible to have a strongly typed language without requiring explicit declarations. ML is one such language. The first time an identifier appears in a program, its type is inferred from the usage. The type can be synthesized to the root of the parse tree. Other usage of the same identifier must be type consistent. Reps and Teitelbaum [Reps89] demonstrate type inferencing by using the Synthesizer-Generator to build a language editor that automatically inserts type declarations in a program based on the usage of identifiers.

Chapter 4
TWO-LEVEL GRAMMARS

We used attributes in Chapter 3 to augment a context-free grammar in order to verify context sensitivity. This chapter will focus on two-level grammars, another formal technique that starts with a context-free grammar, augmenting it with a higher-level grammar to test context-sensitive properties.

A BNF grammar involves a finite number of terminal symbols and production rules. We think of BNF as a "one-level grammar". The new approach of introducing "rules about rules" is called a "two-level grammar". Although we still have a finite number of terminal symbols, adding a second level to the grammar can be used to generate an infinite number of production rules. Consequently, a two-level grammar is inherently more powerful than a BNF grammar. Two-level grammars are sometimes called W-grammars, named after Aad van Wijngaarden, the researcher who developed this approach. The programming language Algol68 was defined using a two-level grammar to specify its complete syntax, including context-sensitive conditions.

This chapter begins with a brief introduction to two-level grammars; then in section 4.2, we develop a context-sensitive grammar for Wren. Two-level grammars can also be extended into the realm of operational semantics by building a programming language interpreter into the grammar, but this extension is beyond the scope of this text. Interested readers can consult the references described in the further reading section of this chapter. We end the chapter by showing how small two-level grammars can be implemented in Prolog. We also discuss the relationship of two-level grammars and logic programming.

4.1 CONCEPTS AND EXAMPLES

We begin by looking at the part of a two-level grammar that is equivalent to BNF. **Protonotions** correspond to nonterminals and terminals in a BNF grammar. We use a sequence of lowercase, boldface characters to represent protonotions. Terminals are distinguished by the final word **symbol**. Spaces can occur anywhere in a protonotion and do not change its meaning. Examples of protonotions are

    program is equivalent to the nonterminal <program>.

    program symbol is equivalent to the keyword **program**.

The correspondence between the protonotions ending in **symbol** and the actual terminal symbols is presented in a representation table.

A grammar rule for defining protonotions is called a **hyper-rule.** The following conventions are used in hyper-rules:

- A colon separates the left- and right-hand side of a rule.
- A comma indicates the juxtaposition of protonotions.
- A semicolon indicates alternatives on the right-hand side of a rule.
- A period terminates a hyper-rule.

For example, the following hyper-rule corresponds to the productions for <element> in Wren.

    element : numeral;
            variable;
            left paren symbol, integer expr, right paren symbol;
            negation symbol, element.

A complete (context-free) grammar for Wren using two-level grammar notation is shown in Figure 4.1, with the corresponding representation table given in Figure 4.2.

Next we look at the terms and notation associated with the "second level" of two-level grammars. A **metanotion** can stand for any number of protonotions. Metanotions are written in boldface, uppercase letters with no embedded spaces. The allowed protonotions are specified in the form of **metarules**, which use the following notational conventions:

---

program : program symbol, identifier, is symbol, block.

block : declaration seq, begin symbol, command seq, end symbol.

declaration seq : empty;
                 declaration, declaration seq.

empty : .

declaration : var symbol, variable list, colon symbol,
                             type, semicolon symbol.

type : integer symbol;
      boolean symbol.

variable list : variable;
              variable, comma symbol, variable list.

command seq : command;
               command, semicolon symbol, command seq.

Figure 4.1: Grammar for Wren Using Two-level Notation (Part 1)

```
command :   variable, assign symbol, expression;
            read symbol, variable;
            write symbol, integer expr;
            skip symbol;
            while symbol, boolean expr, do symbol,
                            command seq, end while symbol;
            if symbol, boolean expr, then symbol,
                            command seq, end if symbol;
            if symbol, boolean expr, then symbol, command seq,
                            else symbol, command seq, end if symbol.

expression :  integer expr;
              boolean expr.

integer expr :  term;
                integer expr, weak op, term.

term :  element;
        term, strong op, element.

element :  numeral;
           variable;
           left paren symbol, integer expr, right paren symbol;
           negation symbol, element.

boolean expr :  boolean term;
                boolean expr, or symbol, boolean term.

boolean term :  boolean element;
                boolean term, and symbol, boolean element.

boolean element : true symbol;
                  false symbol;
                  variable;
                  comparison;
                  left paren symbol, Boolean expr, right paren symbol;
                  not symbol, left paren symbol,
                                boolean expr, right paren symbol.

comparison :  integer expr, relation, integer expr.

variable :  identifier.
```

Figure 4.1: Grammar for Wren Using Two-level Notation (Part 2)

- A double colon (::) separates the left- and right-hand sides of a metarule.
- A space indicates the juxtaposition of items.
- A semicolon indicates alternatives on the right-hand side of a metarule.
- A period terminates a metarule.

---

relation : less or equal symbol;
         less symbol;
         equal symbol;
         greater symbol;
         greater or equal symbol;
         not equal symbol.

weak op : plus symbol;
         minus symbol.

strong op : multiply symbol;
          divide symbol.

identifier : letter;
          letter, identifier;
          letter, digit.

letter : a symbol;   b symbol;   c symbol;   d symbol;   e symbol;   f symbol;
       g symbol;   h symbol;   i symbol;   j symbol;   k symbol;   l symbol;
       m symbol;   n symbol;   o symbol;   p symbol;   q symbol;   r symbol;
       s symbol;   t symbol;   u symbol;   v symbol;   w symbol;   x symbol;
       y symbol;   z symbol.

numeral : digit;
         digit, numeral.

digit : zero symbol;   one symbol;   two symbol;   three symbol;
        four symbol;   five symbol;   six symbol;   seven symbol;
        eight symbol;   nine symbol.

Figure 4.1: Grammar for Wren Using Two-level Notation (Part 3)

The following metarule specifies that the metanotion **ALPHA** stands for 26 alternative protonotions.

ALPHA :: a; b; c; d; e; f; g; h; i; j; k; l; m;
                n; o; p; q; r; s; t; u; v; w; x; y; z.

A metarule can also contain metanotions on the right-hand side.

NOTION :: ALPHA; NOTION ALPHA.

In this case a **NOTION** is any sequence of bold, lowercase letters—in other words, a protonotion. Metanotions can also appear anywhere in a hyper-rule. For example, the following hyper-rule for Wren

program symbol	program	colon symbol	:
is symbol	is	semicolon symbol	;
begin symbol	begin	comma symbol	,
end symbol	end	assign symbol	:=
var symbol	var	plus symbol	+
integer symbol	integer	minus symbol	-
boolean symbol	boolean	multiply symbol	*
skip symbol	skip	divide symbol	/
read symbol	read	negation symbol	-
write symbol	write	left paren symbol	(
while symbol	while	right paren symbol	)
do symbol	do	less or equal symbol	<=
end while symbol	end while	less symbol	<
if symbol	if	equal symbol	=
then symbol	then	greater symbol	>
else symbol	else	greater or equal symbol	>=
end if symbol	end if	not equal symbol	<>
or symbol	or	a symbol	a
and symbol	and	: :	:
not symbol	not	z symbol	z
true symbol	true	zero symbol	0
false symbol	false	: :	:
		nine symbol	9

Figure 4.2: Representation Table for Wren

letter : a symbol; b symbol; c symbol; d symbol; e symbol; f symbol; g symbol; h symbol; i symbol; j symbol; k symbol; l symbol; m symbol; n symbol; o symbol; p symbol; q symbol; r symbol; s symbol; t symbol; u symbol; v symbol; w symbol; x symbol; y symbol; z symbol.

can now be written simply as

letter: ALPHA symbol.

By introducing a metanotion, we have one hyper-rule that stands for 26 possible rules: **letter : a symbol.**, **letter : b symbol.**, and so on.

Traditionally, two-level grammars are printed in boldface. The basic terms introduced so far can be summarized as follows:

- A **protonotion** is a sequence of lowercase, boldface characters that define a nonterminal; however, if the nonterminal is followed by the protonotion **symbol**, then protonotion corresponds to a terminal in the target language as given in a representation table.

- A **metanotion** is a sequence of uppercase characters, used to represent any number of protonotions.

- A **hyper-rule** is a production rule that define a protonotion or a class of protonotions; it may contain protonotions and metanotions on the left- and right-hand sides, and substitutions of protonotions for metanotions must be consistent.

- A **metarule** is a production rule that defines the single metanotion on its left-hand side using protonotions or metanotions on its right-hand side.

As indicated at the start of this chapter, it is possible to generate an infinite number of production rules. Suppose that we want to specify a nonempty list structure as a sequence of one or more items separated by commas. Wren uses a list structure to define lists of variables:

> **variable list : variable; variable, comma symbol, variable list.**

We can generalize this list concept by introducing the metanotion **NOTION** to provide a template for list construction:

> **NOTION list : NOTION; NOTION, comma symbol, NOTION list.**

If **NOTION** has the value **variable**, this hyper-rule specifies our metarule from Wren. If **NOTION** takes other values, say **integer** or **character**, then we are specifying a list of integers or a list of characters. We do require *consistent substitution* of protonotions for a metanotion within a hyper-rule, thus guaranteeing that our list contains elements of the same type. It will not be possible to produce a hyper-rule such as

> **integer list : character; integer, comma symbol, variable list.** (illegal!)

Since **NOTION** can match any protonotion (without embedded spaces), we have given a single hyper-rule that can match an infinite number of productions specifying nonempty lists containing items of the same kind.

We now introduce some notational conveniences. The metanotion **EMPTY** can stand for the empty protonotion:

> **EMPTY :: .**

Suppose that we want to use a tally notation to define the concept of number. For example, the tally **iiiiiiii** represents the number 8. We can specify a tally by the metarule

> **TALLY :: i ; TALLY i.**

We cannot represent the number zero by using **TALLY**, so we use the **EMPTY** protonotion

> **TALLETY :: EMPTY; TALLY.**

A conventional notation in two-level grammars is to have the suffix **-ETY** allow the **EMPTY** protonotion as one of the alternatives.

A second notational convenience allows us to relax (at least notationally) the consistent substitution principle. Consider the nonempty list example again. Initially assume lists can contain integers or characters, but not both.

> **LISTITEM list :**
>
> > **LISTITEM; LISTITEM, comma symbol, LISTITEM list.**
>
> **LISTITEM :: integer; character.**

Now suppose we want to mix integers and characters in a single list. A possible specification is

> **mixed list : LISTITEM; LISTITEM1, comma symbol, mixed list.**
> **LISTITEM1 :: LISTITEM.**

The hyper-rule **mixed list** has four different possibilities:

1. **mixed list : integer; integer, comma symbol, mixed list.**
2. **mixed list : integer; character, comma symbol, mixed list.**
3. **mixed list : character; character, comma symbol, mixed list.**
4. **mixed list : character; integer, comma symbol, mixed list.**

We adopt the convention that a metanotion ending in a digit stands for the same set of protonotions as the metanotion without the digit, so we do not have to specify metarules such as **LISTITEM1 :: LISTITEM.** given above. (It should be noted that **LISTITEM1** was not strictly required to produce the mixed list since **LISTITEM** and **LISTITEM1** appear only once in different alternatives; however, the intent of this example should be clear.)

Fortran String Literals

In older versions of Fortran having no character data type, character string literals were expressed in the following format:

> <string literal> ::= <numeral> H <string>

where the <numeral> is a base-ten integer (≥ 1), H is a keyword (named after Herman Hollerith), and <string> is a sequence of characters. The (context-sensitive) syntax of this string literal will be correct if the numeric value of the base-ten numeral matches the length of the string. A two-level grammar is developed for a Fortran string literal. The initial version assumes that the numeral is a single digit from 1 to 9. The hyper-rules for the digit symbols are as follows:

i digit : digit one symbol.

ii digit : digit two symbol.

iii digit : digit three symbol.

iiii digit : digit four symbol.

iiiii digit : digit five symbol.

iiiiii digit : digit six symbol.

iiiiiii digit : digit seven symbol.

iiiiiiii digit : digit eight symbol.

iiiiiiiii digit : digit nine symbol.

The string literal is a sequence of lowercase letters, which we call **LETTERSEQ**, as specified by the following metarules:

APLHA :: a; b; c; d; e; f; g; h; i; j; k; l; m;

$\qquad\qquad\qquad$ **n; o; p; q; r; s; t; u; v; w; x; y; z.**

LETTER :: letter ALPHA.

LETTERSEQ :: LETTER; LETTERSEQ LETTER.

The string literal, called **hollerith**, is specified by the following hyper-rule. Notice that the consistent substitution for **TALLY**, defined previously, provides the desired context sensitivity.

hollerith : TALLY digit, hollerith symbol, TALLY LETTERSEQ.

Finally, we need to show how a **TALLY LETTERSEQ** decomposes. The basic idea is that every time we remove an **i** from **TALLY** we also remove a **LETTER** from **LETTERSEQ**. We must eventually reach a single **i** followed by a single **LETTER**. The following two hyper-rules express these ideas.

TALLY i LETTER LETTERSEQ : i LETTER, TALLY LETTERSEQ.

i LETTER : LETTER symbol.

The representation table for this two-level grammar involves symbols for lowercase letters, digits, and the separator **H.**

Representation Table

letter a symbol	a	**digit one symbol**	1
: : :	:	: : :	:
letter z symbol	z	**digit nine symbol**	9
hollerith symbol	H		

Derivation Trees

Since two-level grammars are simply a variant of BNF, they support the idea of a derivation tree to exhibit the structure of a string of symbols.

Definition: A **derivation tree** of a string in a two-level grammar displays a derivation of a sentence in the grammar. The nodes in the tree are labeled with protonotions, and the protonotions for all leaf nodes end with **symbol**, indicating terminal symbols. Traversing the leaf nodes from left to right (a preorder traversal) and replacing the protonotion symbols with the corresponding tokens in the Representation Table produces the string being parsed. Empty leaves just disappear.   ∎

The derivation tree for "3Habc" is shown in Figure 4.3.

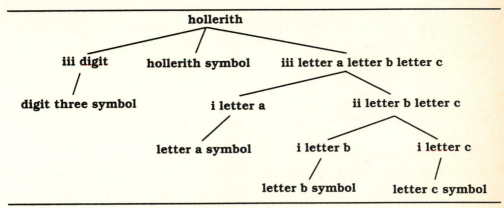

Figure 4.3: Derivation Tree for "3Habc"

When a string does not obey the context-sensitive conditions, no derivation is possible. Figure 4.4 shows an attempt to draw a derivation tree for "4Habc", but, as indicated, it is not possible to complete the tree.

If an arbitrary numeral is allowed to the left of the **hollerith symbol** in the previous example, a mechanism is needed to transform the base-ten numeral into a tally representation. For example, if the leaves of the subtree for a numeral are **digit two symbol** followed by **digit three symbol**, the **TALLY** will be **iiiiiiiiiiiiiiiiiiiiiii**, a sequence of 23 **i**'s. We need to allow for a zero digit at any position, other than the leading digit, and for the corresponding empty tally.

> **EMPTY digit** : **digit zero symbol.**
> **TALLETY** :: **TALLY; EMPTY.**

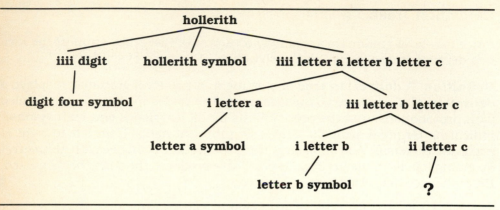

Figure 4.4: Attempted Derivation Tree for "4Habc"

We develop a hyper-rule for **TALLY constant** that captures the semantics of base-ten numerals. For a multiple digit numeral $d_1 d_2 \ldots d_{n-1} d_n$, we know that

value$(d_1 d_2 \ldots d_{n-1} d_n)$ is $10 \bullet$value$(d_1 d_2 \ldots d_{n-1})$ + value(d_n).

In a tally numeration system, multiplying by 10 is accomplished by concatenating ten copies of the tally together. So we rewrite our equation as

tally$(d_1 d_2 \ldots d_{n-1} d_n)$ is ten copies of tally$(d_1 d_2 \ldots d_{n-1})$
                           followed by one copy of tally(d_n).

A **where** clause gives us a mechanism for expressing this equality, as evidenced by the following hyper-rule that includes both the base case and the general case:

> **TALLETY constant :**
>
> > **TALLETY digit;**
> >
> > **TALLETY2 constant, TALLETY3 digit, where TALLETY is**
> >
> > > **TALLETY2 TALLETY2 TALLETY2 TALLETY2 TALLETY2**
> > >
> > > **TALLETY2 TALLETY2 TALLETY2 TALLETY2 TALLETY2**
> > >
> > > **TALLETY3.**
>
> **where TALLETY is TALLETY : EMPTY.**

The **where** clause is similar to condition checking in attribute grammars. If the condition holds, the **EMPTY** protonotion is the leaf on the tree; otherwise, the parse fails. This **where** clause is best illustrated by drawing the complete derivation tree, as shown for the numeral 23 in Figure 4.5. Notice that we rely on the fact that spaces in a protonotion do not change the protonotion.

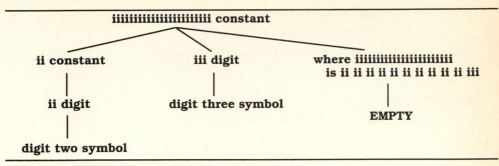

Figure 4.5: Derivation Tree for the Numeral 23

Exercises

1. Suppose that we have a programming language that allows mixed types for the arithmetic operations. Setting aside issues of precedence for the moment, we can describe expressions by the following two-level grammar:

   EXPRTYPE :: integer expression;
   real expression; complex expression.

   OPERATION :: addition; subtraction; multiplication; division.

   expression : EXPRTYPE, OPERATION, EXPRTYPE.

   How many different hyper-rules are possible for expression?

2. Suppose we have the following productions:

   TYPE :: integer; real; complex; character; string.

   assignment : TYPE1 name, assign symbol, TYPE2 expression,
   where TYPE1 is assignment compatible with TYPE2.

   Write the hyper-rules for this **where** condition assuming success if the types are the same, an integer expression can be assigned to a real or complex variable, a real expression can be assigned to a complex variable, and a character can be assigned to a string variable.

3. Develop a two-level grammar that parses only strings of the form $a^n b^n c^n$. Use the consistent substitution of a metanotion into a hyper-rule to guarantee that the values of n are the same. Test the grammar by drawing the derivation tree for "**aaabbbccc**". Also show why there is no valid derivation tree for "**aabbbcc**".

4. Some implementations of Pascal limit the size of identifiers to *eight or fewer* characters. The following hyper-rule expresses this constraint:

   identifier : letter, upto iiiiiii alphanum.

Develop a general hyper-rule to express the meaning of
> **upto TALLY NOTION**

Draw the derivation tree for the identifier "count".

4.2 A TWO-LEVEL GRAMMAR FOR WREN

The two-level grammar that we construct for Wren performs all necessary
context checking. The primary focus is on ensuring that identifiers are not
multiply declared, that variables used in the program have been declared,
and that their usage is consistent with their types (see Figure 1.11). All declaration information is present in a metanotion called DECLSEQ, which is
associated with the context-sensitive portions of commands. We use the following Wren program for illustration as we develop the two-level grammar:

> **program** p **is**
> > **var** x, y : **integer;**
> > **var** a : **boolean;**
> **begin**
> > **read** x; **read** y;
> > a := x < y;
> > **if** a **then write** x **else write** y **end if**
> **end**

The program is syntactically correct if we can build a complete derivation
tree for it. Recall that a tree is complete if every leaf is a terminal symbol or
empty and that a preorder traversal of the leaf nodes matches the target
program once the symbols have been replaced with the corresponding tokens from the representation table. We introduce metarules and hyper-rules
on an "as needed" basis while discussing the sample program. The complete
two-level grammar, with all rules identified by number, will appear later in
this chapter in Figures 4.12 and 4.13. The representation table for Wren has
already been presented in Figure 4.2.

We first introduce the metanotions that serve as some of the basic building
blocks in Wren.

(m1) **ALPHA :: a; b; c; d; e; f; g; h; i; j; k; l; m;**
> **n; o; p; q; r; s; t; u; v; w; x; y; z.**

(m2) **NUM :: zero; one; two; three; four; five; six; seven; eight; nine.**

(m3) **ALPHANUM :: ALPHA; NUM.**

(m4) **LETTER :: letter ALPHA.**

(m5) **DIGIT :: digit NUM.**

(m6) **LETTERDIGIT :: LETTER; DIGIT.**

A **NAME** starts with a letter followed by any sequence of letters or digits. One possible **NAME** is

  letter r digit two letter d digit two

A **NUMERAL** is a sequence of digits.

(m7) **NAME :: LETTER; NAME LETTERDIGIT.**

(m8) **NUMERAL :: DIGIT; NUMERAL DIGIT.**

Declarations

A declaration associates a name with a type. Suppose that a Wren program contains the following declarations:

>   **var** sum1 : **integer**;
>   **var** done : **boolean**;

These declarations will be represented in our two-level grammar derivation tree as

  letter s letter u letter m digit 1 type integer
  letter d letter o letter n letter e type boolean

The following metanotions define a declaration and a declaration sequence. Since a valid Wren program may have no declarations—for example, it may be a program that writes only constant values—we need to allow for an empty declaration sequence.

(m9) **DECL :: NAME type TYPE.**

(m10) **TYPE :: integer; boolean; program.**

(m11) **DECLSEQ :: DECL; DECLSEQ DECL.**

(m12) **DECLSEQETY :: DECLSEQ; EMPTY.**

(m13) **EMPTY :: .**

These metanotions are sufficient to begin construction of the declaration information for a Wren program. The most difficult aspect of gathering together the declaration information is the use of variable lists, such as

>   **var** w, x, y, z : **integer**;

which should produce the following **DECLSEQ**:

  letter w type integer letter x type integer
  letter y type integer letter z type integer

The difficulty is that **integer** appears only once as a terminal symbol and has to be "shared" with all the variables in the list. The following program fragments should produce this same **DECLSEQ**, despite the different syntactic form:

> **var** w : **integer;**
> **var** x : **integer;**
> **var** y : **integer;**
> **var** z : **integer;**

and

> **var** w, x : **integer;**
> **var** y, z : **integer;**

A DECLSEQ permits three alternatives: (1) a sequence followed by a single declaration, (2) a single declaration, or (3) an empty declaration.

(h3)   **DECLSEQ DECL declaration seq :**
> **DECLSEQ declaration seq, DECLSEQ declaration.**

(h4)   **DECLSEQ declaration seq : DECLSEQ declaration.**

(h5)   **EMPTY declaration seq : EMPTY.**

It should be noted that these three hyper-rules can be expressed as two rules (h4 is redundant), but we retain the three alternatives for the sake of clarity. If all variables are declared in a separate declaration, we will require a single hyper-rule for a declaration:

(h6)   **NAME type TYPE declaration : var symbol, NAME symbol,**
> **colon symbol, TYPE symbol, semicolon symbol.**

Figure 4.6 shows how h6, in combination with h3 and h4, can parse the definition of w, x, y, and z in separate declarations. For pedagogical emphasis, the corresponding metanotions are shown in italics to the left of the nodes in the tree, but these metanotions are not part of the tree itself. Observe that the specification of **NAME symbol** restricts identifier names to single characters. Since this makes the derivation tree more manageable with regard to depth, the example programs use only single letter identifiers. An exercise at the end of this section asks what modifications are needed in the grammar to allow for multiple character identifiers.

The same declaration sequence should be produced by the single declaration:

> **var** w, x, y, z : **integer;**

This is accomplished by adding three hyper-rules:

1. The first variable in the list, which must be preceded by **var symbol** and followed by **comma symbol**.

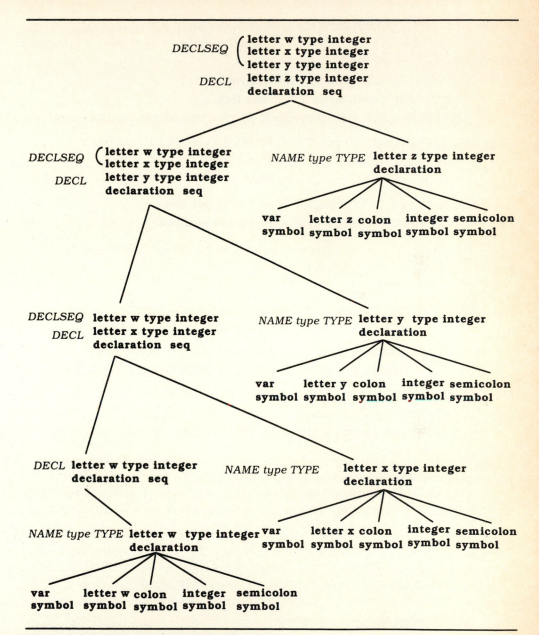

Figure 4.6: Parsing Individual Declarations

2. The last variable in the list, which must be followed by **colon symbol**, the type, and **semicolon symbol**

3. "In between" variables, each of which is followed by **comma symbol**

The general strategy is to have the type information passed from right to left. Here are the three hyper-rules that are used in conjunction with h4 to build the declaration information.

(h7)   **DECLSEQ NAME type TYPE declaration :**
      DECLSEQ NAME type TYPE var list,
      NAME symbol, colon symbol, TYPE symbol, semicolon symbol.

(h8)   **DECLSEQ NAME1 type TYPE NAME2 type TYPE var list :**
      DECLSEQ NAME1 type TYPE var list,
      NAME1 symbol, comma symbol.

(h9)   **NAME1 type TYPE NAME2 type TYPE var list :**
      var symbol, NAME1 symbol, comma symbol.

Figure 4.7 shows the derivation tree for the declaration of the variables w, x, y, and z in a single declaration statement.

We now return to our sample program. To develop the derivation tree from the program node, we need these hyper-rules for **program** and **block**.

(h1)   **program : program symbol, NAME symbol, is symbol,**
           block with NAME type program DECLSEQETY,
           where NAME type program DECLSEQETY unique.

(h2)   **block with NAME type program DECLSEQETY :**
      DECLSEQETY declaration seq, begin symbol,
      NAME type program DECLSEQETY command seq, end symbol.

Notice that the program identifier name is added to the declaration sequence with type **program**. This information is passed to the command sequence and is also checked for multiple declarations of the same identifier by a **where** rule. A top-level derivation tree for the example program is shown in Figure 4.8.

The **where** rule checks for the uniqueness of declarations. All leaf nodes for the **where** clauses will be **EMPTY** if the identifiers are unique. Since our hyper-rules for variable lists have produced separate declaration information for each identifier, this checking is relatively straightforward, albeit lengthy. The easiest case is a single declaration, which is obviously unique.

(h22) **where DECL unique : EMPTY.**

In the case of multiple declarations, we separate the last declaration in the list, and we use the following rule to ensure that the name is not contained in any declarations to the left

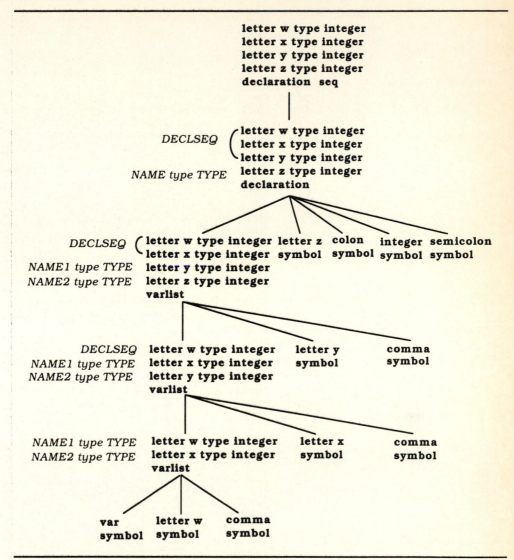

Figure 4.7: Parsing the Declaration: **var** w, x, y, z : **integer**;

(h23) **where DECLSEQ NAME type TYPE unique :**
      where DECLSEQ unique,
      where NAME not in DECLSEQ.

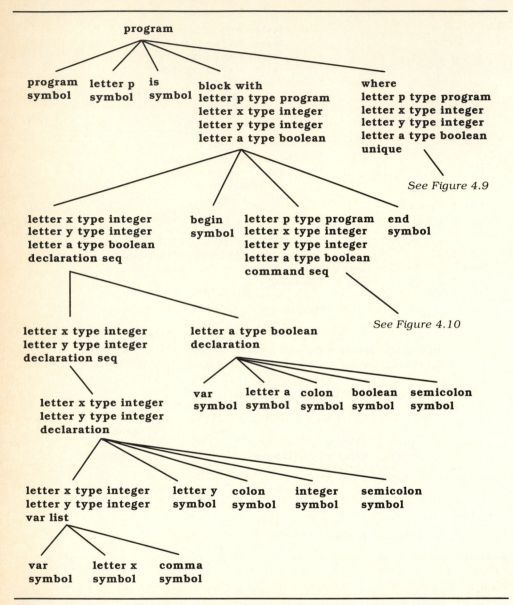

Figure 4.8: Top-Level Derivation Tree of Sample Program

To ensure that a name is not contained in a declaration sequence, we check one declaration at a time from right to left.

(h24) **where NAME not in DECLSEQ DECL :**
　　　　where NAME not in DECLSEQ,
　　　　where NAME not in DECL.

The type information in a declaration sequence is not needed to check for name uniqueness, so the hyper-rule simply checks that two names are not the same.

(h25) **where NAME1 not in NAME2 type TYPE :**
  where NAME1 is not NAME2.

Names are separated into a sequence of characters, which is possibly empty, followed by a final character. We need to use the metanotions for **NOTION** and **NOTETY** introduced in section 4.1.

(m14) **NOTION :: ALPHA; NOTION ALPHA.**

(m15) **NOTETY :: NOTION; EMPTY.**

The identifiers contain either alphabetic characters or digit characters. If characters are of different kind, they are not equal. If characters are of the same kind but they are not the same, then one character appears before the other character in the appropriate character set. This test is applied to all characters in the sequence until a mismatch is found.

(h26) **where NOTETY1 NOTION1 ALPHANUM1 is not**
    NOTETY2 NOTION2 ALPHANUM2 :
  where NOTETY1 is not NOTETY2;
  where NOTION1 different kind NOTION2;
  where ALPHANUM1 precedes ALPHANUM2
    in abcdefghijklmnopqrstuvwxyz;
  where ALPHANUM2 precedes ALPHANUM1
    in abcdefghijklmnopqrstuvwxyz;
  where ALPHANUM1 precedes ALPHANUM2
    in zero one two three four five six seven eight nine;
  where ALPHANUM2 precedes ALPHANUM1
    in zero one two three four five six seven eight nine.

A **letter** is always different than a **digit**.

(h27) **where letter different kind digit : EMPTY.**

(h28) **where digit different kind letter : EMPTY.**

Finally, two hyper-rules check whether a character or a digit precedes another.

(h29) **where ALPHA1 precedes ALPHA2**
    in NOTETY1 ALPHA1 NOTETY2 ALPHA2 NOTETY3 : EMPTY.

(h30) **where NUM1 precedes NUM2**
    in NOTETY1 NUM1 NOTETY2 NUM2 NOTETY3 : EMPTY.

Figure 4.9 shows the use of these **where** rules to check the uniqueness of the identifiers in our sample program.

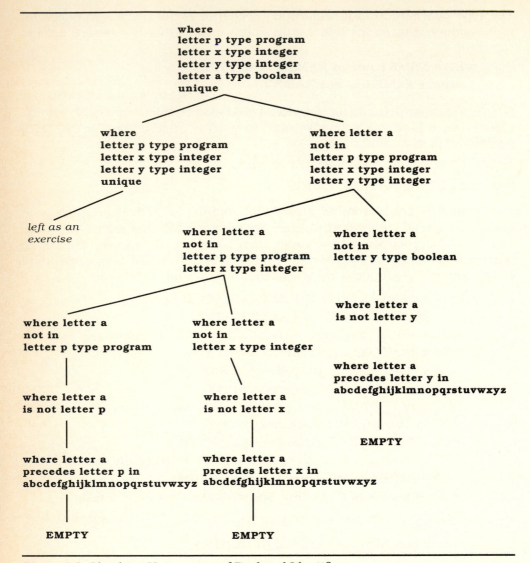

Figure 4.9: Checking Uniqueness of Declared Identifiers

Commands and Expressions

We complete the development of our two-level grammar for Wren by examining how declaration information is used to check for the proper use of variables that appear in commands. To reduce the number of hyper-rules, we introduce metanotions for the arithmetic operators and comparison operators.

(m16) **WEAKOP :: plus symbol; minus symbol.**

(m17) **STRONGOP :: multiply symbol; divide symbol.**

(m18) **RELATION ::**
> **less or equal symbol; less symbol; not equal symbol;**
> **greater symbol; greater or equal symbol; equal symbol.**

Declaration information is passed to each individual command. Note that an empty declaration sequence need not be allowed since every program must be named, even if no variables are declared.

(h10) **DECLSEQ command seq :**
> **DECLSEQ command;**
> **DECLSEQ command, semicolon symbol,**
> > **DECLSEQ command seq.**

Commands use the declaration information in different ways:

- The **skip** command uses no declaration information.
- The **write**, **while**, and **if** commands pass the declaration information to their constituent parts.
- The **read** command uses the declaration information to check that the associated variable is of type integer.

Here is the hyper-rule that separates these cases:

(h11) **DECLSEQ command :**
> **TYPE NAME in DECLSEQ, assign symbol,**
> > **TYPE expression in DECLSEQ;**
>
> **skip symbol;**
> **read symbol, integer NAME in DECLSEQ;**
> **write symbol, integer expression in DECLSEQ;**
>
> **while symbol, boolean expression in DECLSEQ, do symbol,**
> > **DECLSEQ command seq, end while symbol;**
>
> **if symbol, boolean expression in DECLSEQ, then symbol,**
> > **DECLSEQ command seq, end if symbol;**
>
> **if symbol, boolean expression in DECLSEQ, then symbol,**
> > **DECLSEQ command seq, else symbol,**
> > **DECLSEQ command seq, end if symbol.**

The **read** command illustrates hyper-rules of the form **TYPE NAME in DECLSEQ** that perform two important functions: They produce the appropriate **NAME** symbol and they check that the **NAME** appears in the **DECLSEQ** with the appropriate **TYPE**.

(h19)   **TYPE NAME in DECLSEQ :**
                  NAME symbol, where NAME type TYPE found in DECLSEQ.

The **DECLSEQ** is checked one declaration at a time from left to right. The **EMPTY** notion is produced if the appropriate declaration is found; otherwise, the parse fails.

(h20) **where NAME type TYPE found in**
                                NAME type TYPE DECLSEQETY : EMPTY.

(h21) **where NAME1 type TYPE1 found in NAME2 type TYPE2**
        DECLSEQETY : where NAME1 type TYPE1
                                    found in DECLSEQETY.

The remainder of the two-level grammar, dealing with expressions and comparisons, is straightforward. The portion of the grammar dealing with Boolean expressions has been left as an exercise.

(h12) **integer expression in DECLSEQ :**
        term in DECLSEQ;
        integer expression in DECLSEQ, WEAKOP, term in DECLSEQ.

(h13) **term in DECLSEQ :**
        element in DECLSEQ;
        term in DECLSEQ, STRONGOP, element in DECLSEQ.

(h14) **element in DECLSEQ :**
        NUMERAL symbol;
        integer NAME in DECLSEQ;
        left paren symbol, integer expression in DECLSEQ,
                                                        right paren symbol;
        negation symbol, element in DECLSEQ.

(h15) **boolean expression in DECLSEQ :** *left as an exercise.*

(h16) **boolean term in DECLSEQ :** *left as an exercise.*

(h17) **boolean element in DECLSEQ :** *left as an exercise.*

(h18) **comparison in DECLSEQ :**
        integer expression in DECLSEQ, RELATION,
                                        integer expression in DECLSEQ.

Figures 4.10 and 4.11 illustrate a partial derivation tree for the command sequence in the sample program. The unfinished branches in the tree are left as exercises.

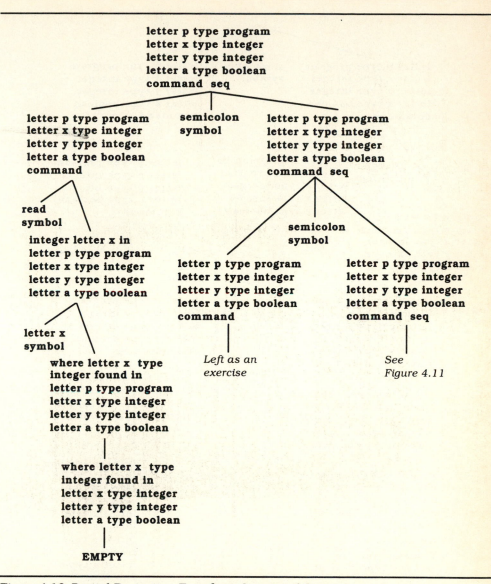

Figure 4.10: Partial Derivation Tree for a Command Sequence

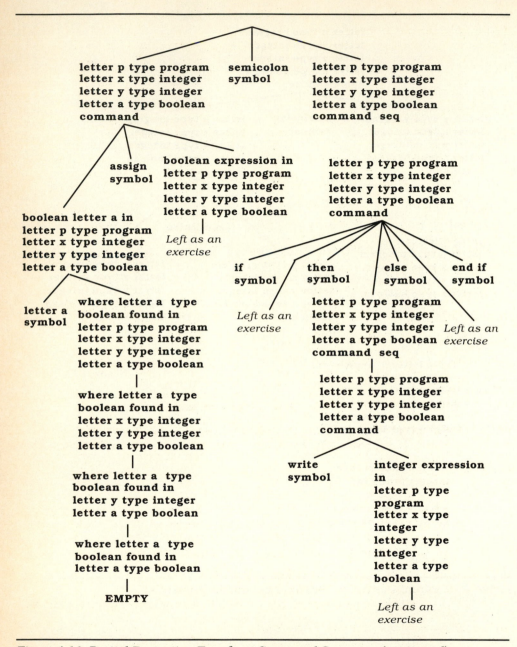

Figure 4.11: Partial Derivation Tree for a Command Sequence (continued)

(m1)	**ALPHA :: a; b; c; d; e; f; g; h; i; j; k; l; m; n; o; p; q; r; s; t; u; v; w; x; y; z.**
(m2)	**NUM :: zero; one; two; three; four; five; six; seven; eight; nine.**
(m3)	**ALPHANUM :: ALPHA; NUM.**
(m4)	**LETTER :: letter ALPHA.**
(m5)	**DIGIT :: digit NUM.**
(m6)	**LETTERDIGIT :: LETTER; DIGIT.**
(m7)	**NAME :: LETTER; NAME LETTERDIGIT.**
(m8)	**NUMERAL :: DIGIT; NUMERAL DIGIT.**
(m9)	**DECL :: NAME type TYPE.**
(m10)	**TYPE :: integer; boolean; program.**
(m11)	**DECLSEQ :: DECL; DECLSEQ DECL.**
(m12)	**DECLSEQETY :: DECLSEQ; EMPTY.**
(m13)	**EMPTY :: .**
(m14)	**NOTION :: ALPHA; NOTION ALPHA.**
(m15)	**NOTETY :: NOTION; EMPTY.**
(m16)	**WEAKOP :: plus symbol; minus symbol.**
(m17)	**STRONGOP :: multiply symbol; divide symbol.**
(m18)	**RELATION :: less or equal symbol; less symbol; not equal symbol; greater symbol; greater or equal symbol; equal symbol.**

Figure 4.12: Metarules for Wren

(h1)	**program : program symbol, NAME symbol, is symbol,
	              block with NAME type program DECLSEQETY,
	              where NAME type program DECLSEQETY unique.**

(h2)	**block with NAME type program DECLSEQETY :
	              DECLSEQETY declaration seq, begin symbol,
	              NAME type program DECLSEQETY command seq, end symbol.**

(h3)	**DECLSEQ DECL declaration seq : DECLSEQ declaration seq, DECLSEQ declaration.**
(h4)	**DECLSEQ declaration seq : DECLSEQ declaration.**
(h5)	**EMPTY declaration seq : EMPTY.**

Figure 4.13: Hyper-rules for Wren (Part 1)

(h6)   **NAME type TYPE declaration : var symbol, NAME symbol,**
          colon symbol, TYPE symbol, semicolon symbol.

(h7)   **DECLSEQ NAME type TYPE declaration :**
          DECLSEQ NAME type TYPE var list,
          NAME symbol, colon symbol, TYPE symbol, semicolon symbol.

(h8)   **DECLSEQ NAME1 type TYPE NAME2 type TYPE var list :**
          DECLSEQ NAME1 type TYPE var list,
          NAME1 symbol, comma symbol.

(h9)   **NAME1 type TYPE NAME2 type TYPE var list :**
          var symbol, NAME1 symbol, comma symbol.

(h10)   **DECLSEQ command seq :**
          DECLSEQ command;
          DECLSEQ command, semicolon symbol,
          DECLSEQ command seq.

(h11)   **DECLSEQ command :**
          TYPE NAME in DECLSEQ, assign symbol,
                    TYPE expression in DECLSEQ;
          skip symbol;
          read symbol, integer NAME in DECLSEQ;
          write symbol, integer expression in DECLSEQ;
          while symbol, boolean expression in DECLSEQ, do symbol,
                    DECLSEQ command seq, end while symbol;
          if symbol, boolean expression in DECLSEQ, then symbol,
                    DECLSEQ command seq, end if symbol;
          if symbol, boolean expression in DECLSEQ, then symbol,
                    DECLSEQ command seq, else symbol,
                    DECLSEQ command seq, end if symbol.

(h12)   **integer expression in DECLSEQ :**
          term in DECLSEQ;
          integer expression in DECLSEQ, WEAKOP, term in DECLSEQ.

(h13)   **term in DECLSEQ :**
          element in DECLSEQ;
          term in DECLSEQ, STRONGOP, element in DECLSEQ.

(h14)   **element in DECLSEQ :**
          NUMERAL symbol;
          integer NAME in DECLSEQ;
          left paren symbol, integer expression in DECLSEQ,
              right paren symbol;
          negation symbol, element in DECLSEQ.

(h15)   **boolean expression in DECLSEQ :** *left as exercise*

(h16)   **boolean term in DECLSEQ :** *left as exercise*

Figure 4.13: Hyper-rules for Wren (Part 2)

(h17) **boolean element in DECLSEQ :** *left as exercise*

(h18) **comparison in DECLSEQ :**
        integer expression in DECLSEQ, RELATION,
        integer expression in DECLSEQ.

(h19) **TYPE NAME in DECLSEQ :**
        NAME symbol, where NAME type TYPE found in DECLSEQ

(h20) **where NAME type TYPE found in NAME type TYPE DECLSEQETY :**
        EMPTY.

(h21) **where NAME1 type TYPE1 found in NAME2 type TYPE2**
        DECLSEQETY : where NAME1 type TYPE1 found in
                                    DECLSEQETY.

(h22) **where DECL unique : EMPTY.**

(h23) **where DECLSEQ NAME type TYPE unique :**
        where DECLSEQ unique,
        where NAME not in DECLSEQ.

(h24) **where NAME not in DECLSEQ DECL :**
        where NAME not in DECLSEQ,
        where NAME not in DECL.

(h25) **where NAME1 not in NAME2 type TYPE :**
        where NAME1 is not NAME2.

(h26) **where   NOTETY1 NOTION1 ALPHANUM1 is not**
        NOTETY2 NOTION2 ALPHANUM2 :
        where NOTETY1 is not NOTETY2;
        where NOTION1 different kind NOTION2;
        where ALPHANUM1 precedes ALPHANUM2
            in abcdefghijklmnopqrstuvwxyz;
        where ALPHANUM2 precedes ALPHANUM1
            in abcdefghijklmnopqrstuvwxyz;
        where ALPHANUM1 precedes ALPHANUM2
            in zero one two three four five six seven eight nine;
        where ALPHANUM2 precedes ALPHANUM1
            in zero one two three four five six seven eight nine.

(h27) **where letter different kind digit : EMPTY.**

(h28) **where digit different kind letter : EMPTY.**

(h29) **where ALPHA1 precedes ALPHA2**
        in NOTETY1 ALPHA1 NOTETY2 ALPHA2 NOTETY3 : EMPTY.

(h30) **where NUM1 precedes NUM2**
        in NOTETY1 NUM1 NOTETY2 NUM2 NOTETY3 : EMPTY.

Figure 4.13: Hyper-rules for Wren (Part 3)

Exercises

1. Show the derivation tree for the following declaration sequence:
     var w, x : **integer;**
     var y, z : **integer;**

2. Complete the remaining branches in Figure 4.9.

3. Complete the following hyper-rules:
     (h15) **boolean expression in DECLSEQ :**
     (h16) **boolean term in DECLSEQ :**
     (h17) **boolean element in DECLSEQ :**

4. Complete the remaining branches in Figures 4.10 and 4.11.

5. Draw the complete derivation tree for the following program:
   program p **is**
       var n, f : **integer;**
   begin
       read n; f := 1;
       while n > 0 **do** f := f * n; n := n − 1 **end while;**
       write f
   end

6. Suppose the declaration in exercise 5 is changed to
     var n : **integer;**
     var f : **boolean;**
   Show all locations in the command sequence where the parse fails, assuming the declaration sequence **letter n type integer letter f type boolean**.

7. Show all changes necessary to metarules and hyper-rules to allow for multiple character identifiers. Some rules already allow for multiple characters whereas others, such as those with **NAME symbol**, will have to be modified. Additional rules may be needed.

4.3 TWO-LEVEL GRAMMARS AND PROLOG

The consistent substitution of protonotions for a metanotion within a hyper-rule may seem similar to the binding of identifiers in a Prolog clause. In fact, a close relationship exists between two-level grammars and logic programming. Rather than present a complete implementation of the two-level grammar for Wren in this section, we present a brief example of implementing a two-level grammar in Prolog and then discuss some of the relationships between two-level grammars and logic programming.

Implementing Two-Level Grammars in Prolog

We implement the Hollerith string literal grammar from Section 4.1 to give the flavor a two-level grammar in Prolog. The top-level predicate, named hollerith, is called with three arguments:

> hollerith(<list of digit symbols>, hollerith, <list of lowercase letters>).

The program should print either "valid Hollerith string" or "invalid Hollerith string", as appropriate for the data. We assume the list of digits and list of letters are syntactically correct. A sample session appears below.

```
| ?- hollerith([digitSixSymbol], hollerith, [a,b,c,d,e,f]).
valid Hollerith string
yes

| ?- hollerith([digitSixSymbol], hollerith, [a,b,c,d,e]).
invalid Hollerith string
yes

| ?- hollerith([digitTwoSymbol,digitFiveSymbol], hollerith,
     [a,b,c,d,e,f,g,h,i,j,k,l,m,n,o,p,q,r,s,t,u,v,w,x,y]).
valid Hollerith string
yes

| ?- hollerith([digitTwoSymbol,digitFiveSymbol], hollerith,
     [a,b,c,d,e,f,g,h,i,j,k,l,m,n,o,p,q,r,s,t,u,v,w,x,y,z]).
invalid Hollerith string
yes
```

This interface is not very elegant, but it will serve adequately to illustrate the intended performance. An exercise suggests techniques for improving the interface. Observe that we have allowed for numerals of any size, so a **where** clause must be used in the grammar. The two-level grammar for Hollerith string literals is summarized in Figure 4.14.

---

hollerith : TALLY digit, hollerith symbol, TALLY LETTERSEQ.

TALLY i LETTER LETTERSEQ : i LETTER, TALLY LETTERSEQ.
i LETTER: LETTER symbol.

i digit : digit one symbol.
ii digit : digit two symbol.
iii digit : digit three symbol.
iiii digit : digit four symbol.
iiiii digit : digit five symbol.
iiiiii digit : digit six symbol.
iiiiiii digit : digit seven symbol.
iiiiiiii digit : digit eight symbol.
iiiiiiiii digit : digit nine symbol.

TALLETY constant :
    TALLETY digit;
    TALLETY2 constant, TALLETY3 digit, where TALLETY is
        TALLETY2 TALLETY2 TALLETY2 TALLETY2 TALLETY2
        TALLETY2 TALLETY2 TALLETY2 TALLETY2 TALLETY2
        TALLETY3.
where TALLETY is TALLETY : EMPTY.

EMPTY digit : digit zero symbol.
TALLETY :: TALLY; EMPTY.

APLHA :: a; b; c; d; e; f; g; h; i; j; k; l; m; n; o; p; q; r; s; t; u; v; w; x; y; z.
LETTER :: letter ALPHA.
LETTERSEQ :: LETTER; LETTERSEQ LETTER.

Figure 4.14: Two-level Grammar for Hollerith String Literals

The clauses for single digits are simple.

```
digit([digitZeroSymbol], [ ]).
digit([digitOneSymbol], [i]).
digit([digitTwoSymbol], [i,i]).
digit([digitThreeSymbol], [i,i,i]).
digit([digitFourSymbol], [i,i,i,i]).
digit([digitFiveSymbol], [i,i,i,i,i]).
digit([digitSixSymbol], [i,i,i,i,i,i]).
digit([digitSevenSymbol], [i,i,i,i,i,i,i]).
digit([digitEightSymbol], [i,i,i,i,i,i,i,i]).
digit([digitNineSymbol], [i,i,i,i,i,i,i,i,i]).
```

A constant is a single digit or a sequence of digits. We use the technique of concatenating ten copies of the tally for the leading digits to the tally for the units digit to produce a final tally. Supporting clauses are used to split the digits into the leading digits and units digit, to concatenate the ten copies of the leading digit's tally to the units digit's tally, and to perform the concatenation itself.

```
constant(DIGIT, TALLETY) :- digit(TALLETY, DIGIT).

constant(DIGITS, TALLETY) :-
                splitDigits(DIGITS, LeadingDIGITS, UnitDIGIT),
                constant(LeadingDIGITS, TALLETY2),
                digit(UnitDIGIT, TALLETY3),
                concatTenPlusDigit(TALLETY2, TALLETY3, TALLETY).

splitDigits([D], [ ], [D]).

splitDigits([Head|Tail],[Head|Result],Unit) :- splitDigits(Tail, Result, Unit).

concatTenPlusDigit(TALLETY2, TALLETY3, TALLETY) :-
                concat(TALLETY2, TALLETY2, TwoTimes),
                concat(TwoTimes, TwoTimes, FourTimes),
                concat(FourTimes, FourTimes, EightTimes),
                concat(EightTimes, TwoTimes, TenTimes),
                concat(TenTimes, TALLETY3, TALLETY).

concat([ ],L,L).

concat([Head|Tail],L,[Head|Result]) :- concat(Tail,L,Result).
```

The tally is generated from the number part, and it is used to check the length of the letter sequence. Each time a tally symbol is removed, a letter is removed. One base case is a single tally and a single letter, resulting in a valid hollerith string. If either the tally or the letter sequence becomes empty, the other base cases, the hollerith string is invalid. Each letter is checked to ensure that it is a lowercase character.

```
hollerith(Number,hollerith,Letters) :-  constant(Number, TALLETY),
                                letterSeq(TALLETY, Letters).
letterSeq([i],[Letter]) :-   alpha(Letter),
                        write('valid Hollerith string'), nl.

letterSeq([i|TALLETY],[Letter|Letters]) :-  alpha(Letter),
                                letterSeq(TALLETY, Letters).

letterSeq([ ],Letters) :- write('invalid Hollerith string'), nl.

letterSeq(Number,[ ]) :- write('invalid Hollerith string'), nl.
```

```
alpha(a).   alpha(b).   alpha(c).   alpha(d).   alpha(e).   alpha(f).
alpha(g).   alpha(h).   alpha(i).   alpha(j).   alpha(k).   alpha(l).
alpha(m).   alpha(n).   alpha(o).   alpha(p).   alpha(q).   alpha(r).
alpha(s).   alpha(t).   alpha(u).   alpha(v).   alpha(w).   alpha(x).
alpha(y).   alpha(z).
```

Two-level Grammars and Logic Programming

Hyper-rules in two-level grammars are similar to clauses in Prolog. In two-level grammars we have consistent substitution of the same value for a particular metanotion in a rule. In Prolog we have the consistent binding of the same value to a particular variable in a clause. Some of the syntax and pattern matching in two-level grammars are also similar to Prolog. Several researchers have investigated the relationships between two-level grammars (also known as W-grammars) and logic programming. We briefly summarize one of those approaches, originally presented by S. J. Turner in a paper entitled "W-Grammars for Logic Programming" [Turner84].

A programming language seldom completely represents a programming paradigm. For example, Common Lisp is not a purely functional language, and Prolog is not a purely logical language. Turner believes that two-level grammars as an implementation mechanism for logic programming have many advantages over Prolog, the most popular logic programming language. He implements a logic programming system based on a two-level (or W-) grammar in a system called WLOG. He claims this system overcomes some of the disadvantages of Prolog (see [Turner84], page 352).

- Understanding Prolog requires a detailed understanding of the backtracking mechanism built into the implementation of Prolog.

- The meaning of a Prolog program is highly dependent on the order of the clauses in the database, making the formal analysis of the semantics of Prolog very difficult.

- Many built-in predicates in Prolog have side effects that make parallel implementations difficult.

- Minor programming errors, such as misspelling, are difficult to find since the entire program fails with no indication of where the error occurred.

Consider the following example taken from Turner's paper:

MAN :: george; john; paul.

WOMAN :: jane; mary; sue.

PERSON :: MAN; WOMAN.
THING :: flowers; food; football; food; wine.
LEGAL :: PERSON likes THING; PERSON likes PERSON.

A fact is usually stated as a hyper-rule with an empty right side, such as:

mary likes football : .
john likes wine : .
paul likes mary : .
jane likes sue : .
paul likes food : .
george likes football : .

We can make a query, such as finding out what paul likes:

paul likes THING?

which succeeds with THING matching mary and food. We can have compound queries, such as:

PERSON1 likes PERSON, PERSON likes THING?

which succeeds with paul likes mary and mary likes football. Hyper-rules with right-hand sides are used to express rules of logic. Consider the logical rule: Two people who like the same object like each other, which is expressed as:

PERSON1 likes PERSON2 : PERSON1 likes OBJECT,
PERSON2 likes OBJECT.

From the database given above, we can conclude that mary likes john.

Turner's paper gives a formal definition of WLOG and discusses an implementation based on non-deterministic finite automata. This implementation uses a breadth-first search, which means that the order of the database is not critical and that certain types of parallelism can be realized. The system also handles *not* in a more understandable manner than Prolog. With the database given above, if we pose the query

paul likes WOMAN?

then only mary is found in the database. In WLOG, if we make the query

not [paul likes WOMAN]?

then the values of sue and jane satisfy the query. This should be compared with Prolog where this query fails. In WLOG, not[not[X]]? is satisfied by the same values as X?, but this is not true in Prolog, which is based on negation as failure. This completes our brief look at the relationship between two-level grammars and pure logic programming.

Exercises

1. Build a "front end" for the Hollerith string checker to prompt the user for string input and then print the appropriate evaluation message. Use the built-in Prolog clause name for converting a string to a sequence of ascii codes.

2. Implement a two-level grammar that parses strings of the form $a^n b^n c^n$. The program should either print that the string obeys the grammar or that it does not. Assume that the strings are syntactically correct, in the sense that they are a sequence of **a**'s followed by a sequence of **b**'s, followed by a sequence of **c**'s.

3. Implement a two-level grammar to recognize valid Pascal identifiers assuming that an identifier starts with a letter followed by a sequence of alphanumeric characters and that the length of the identifier is eight or fewer characters (see exercise 4 in section 4.1).

4.4 FURTHER READING

Two-level grammars are also called W-grammars after their developer, Aad van Wijngaarden, who described them in an early paper [van Wijngaarden66]. The formal definition of Algol68 using two-level grammars appears in [van Wijngaarden76]. [Kupka80] has applied two-level grammars to model information processing.

Several references include two-level grammars as part of an overview of formal techniques. Most notable are [Pagan81], [Marcotty76], and [Cleaveland77]. Pagan develops an interpreter for a language with parameterized procedures using a two-level grammar.

Some of the theoretical issues relating to two-level grammars are discussed in [Deussen75] and [Slintzoff67]. The relationship between two-level grammars and programming language design is explored in [van Wijngaarden82], [Maluszynski84], and [Turner84].

The most active group of researchers in the United States working on two-level grammars is at the University of Alabama, Birmingham. Barrett Bryant and Balanjaninath Edupuganty are coauthors of several papers dealing with applications of two-level grammars to a wide variety of problem domains [Bryant86a], [Bryant86b], [Bryant88], [Edupuganty85], [Edupuganty88], [Edupuganty89], and [Sundararaghavan87].

Chapter 5
THE LAMBDA CALCULUS

F
unctions play a prominent role in describing the semantics of a programming language, since the meaning of a computer program can be considered as a function from input values to output values. In addition, functions play an essential role in mathematics, which means that much of the theory of functions, including the issue of computability, unfolded as part of mathematical logic before the advent of computers. In particular, Alonzo Church developed the lambda calculus in the 1930s as a theory of functions that provides rules for manipulating functions in a purely syntactic manner.

Although the lambda calculus arose as a branch of mathematical logic to provide a foundation for mathematics, it has led to considerable ramifications in the theory of programming languages. Beyond the influence of the lambda calculus in the area of computation theory, it has contributed important results to the formal semantics of programming languages:

- Although the lambda calculus has the power to represent all computable functions, its uncomplicated syntax and semantics provide an excellent vehicle for studying the meaning of programming language concepts.

- All functional programming languages can be viewed as syntactic variations of the lambda calculus, so that both their semantics and implementation can be analyzed in the context of the lambda calculus.

- Denotational semantics, one of the foremost methods of formal specification of languages, grew out of research in the lambda calculus and expresses its definitions using the higher-order functions of the lambda calculus.

In this chapter we take a brief but careful look at the lambda calculus, first defining it as a language and then viewing it as a computational formalism in light of its reduction rules. We end the chapter by implementing a lambda calculus evaluator in Prolog. In Chapter 10 we continue the study of functions with the goal of explaining recursive definitions.

5.1 CONCEPTS AND EXAMPLES

Our description of the lambda calculus begins with some motivation for the notation. A function is a mapping from the elements of a domain set to the elements of a codomain set given by a rule—for example,

cube : Integer → Integer   where cube(n) = n^3.

Certain questions arise from such a function definition:

- What is the value of the identifier "cube"?
- How can we represent the object bound to "cube"?
- Can this function be defined without giving it a name?

Church's lambda notation allows the definition of an anonymous function, that is, a function without a name:

λn . n^3 defines the function that maps each n in the domain to n^3.

We say that the expression represented by λn . n^3 is the value bound to the identifier "cube". The number and order of the parameters to the function are specified between the λ symbol and an expression. For instance, the expression n^2+m is ambiguous as the definition of a function rule:

(3,4) ↦ 3^2+4 = 13   or   (3,4) ↦ 4^2+3 = 19.

Lambda notation resolves the ambiguity by specifying the order of the parameters:

λn . λm . n^2+m   or   λm . λn . n^2+m.

Most functional programming languages allow anonymous functions as values; for example, the function λn . n^3 is represented as

(lambda (n) (* n n n))   in Scheme and

fn n => n * n * n   in Standard ML.

Syntax of the Lambda Calculus

The lambda calculus derives its usefulness from having a sparse syntax and a simple semantics, and yet it retains sufficient power to represent all computable functions. Lambda expressions come in four varieties:

1. Variables, which are usually taken to be any lowercase letters.

2. Predefined constants, which act as values and operations are allowed in an impure or **applied lambda calculus**.

3. Function applications (combinations).

4. Lambda abstractions (function definitions).

The simplicity of lambda calculus syntax is apparent from a BNF specification for it:

<expression> ::= <variable>   ; lowercase identifiers

        | <constant>   ; predefined objects

        | (<expression> <expression>)   ; combinations

        | (λ <variable> . <expression>)   ; abstractions.

In the spirit of software engineering, we allow identifiers of more than one letter to stand as variables and constants. The pure lambda calculus has no predefined constants, but it still allows the definition of all of the common constants and functions of arithmetic and list manipulation. We will say more about the expressibility of the pure lambda calculus later in this chapter. For now, predefined constants will be allowed in our examples, including numerals (for example, 34), add (for addition), mul (for multiplication), succ (the successor function), and sqr (the squaring function).

In an abstraction, the variable named is referred to as the **bound variable** and the associated lambda expression is the **body** of the abstraction. With a function application $(E_1 \ E_2)$, it is expected that E_1 evaluates to a predefined function (a constant) or an abstraction, say $(\lambda x \ . \ E_3)$, in which case the result of the application will be the evaluation of E_3 after every "free" occurrence of x in E_3 has been replaced by E_2. In a combination $(E_1 \ E_2)$, the function or ope**rator** E_1 is called the **rator** and its argument or ope**rand** E_2 is called the **rand**. Formal definitions of free occurrences of variables and the replacement operation will be provided shortly.

Lambda expressions will be illustrated with several examples in which we use prefix notation as in Lisp for predefined binary operations and so avoid the issue of precedence among operations.

- The lambda expression λx . x denotes the identity function in the sense that ((λx . x) E) = E for any lambda expression E. Functions that allow arguments of many types, such as this identity function, are known as **polymorphic** operations. The lambda expression (λx . x) acts as an identity function on the set of integers, on a set of functions of some type, or on any other kind of object.

- The expression λn . (add n 1) denotes the successor function on the integers so that ((λn . (add n 1)) 5) = 6. Note that "add" and 1 need to be predefined constants to define this function, and 5 must be predefined to apply the function as we have done.

- The abstraction $(\lambda f . (\lambda x . (f (f x))))$ describes a function with two arguments, a function and a value, that applies the function to the value twice. If sqr is the (predefined) integer function that squares its argument, then

$$(((\lambda f . (\lambda x . (f (f x)))) \text{ sqr}) 3) \quad = ((\lambda x . (\text{sqr (sqr x)})) 3)$$
$$= (\text{sqr (sqr 3)}) = (\text{sqr 9}) = 81.$$

Here f is replaced by sqr and then x by 3. These examples show that the number of parentheses in lambda expressions can become quite large. The following notational conventions allow abbreviations that reduce the number of parentheses:

1. Uppercase letters and identifiers beginning with capital letters will be used as metavariables ranging over lambda expressions.

2. Function application associates to the left.

$$E_1 E_2 E_3 \text{ means } ((E_1 E_2) E_3)$$

3. The scope of "λ<variable>" in an abstraction extends as far to the right as possible.

$$\lambda x . E_1 E_2 E_3 \text{ means } (\lambda x . (E_1 E_2 E_3)) \text{ and not } ((\lambda x . E_1 E_2) E_3).$$

So application has a higher precedence than abstraction, and parentheses are needed for $(\lambda x . E_1 E_2) E_3$, where E_3 is intended to be an argument to the function $\lambda x . E_1 E_2$ and not part of the body of the function as above.

4. An abstraction allows a list of variables that abbreviates a series of lambda abstractions.

$$\lambda x\ y\ z . E \text{ means } (\lambda x . (\lambda y . (\lambda z . E)))$$

5. Functions defined as lambda expression abstractions are anonymous, so the lambda expression itself denotes the function. As a notational convention, lambda expressions may be named using the syntax

define <name> = <expression>

For example, given *define* Twice = $\lambda f . \lambda x . f (f x)$, it follows that

$$(\text{Twice } (\lambda n . (\text{add n 1})) 5) = 7.$$

We follow a convention of starting defined names with uppercase letters to distinguish them from variables. Imagine that "Twice" is replaced by its definition as with a macro expansion before the lambda expression is reduced. Later we show a step-by-step reduction of this lambda expression to 7.

Example: Because of the sparse syntax of the lambda calculus, correctly parenthesizing (parsing) a lambda expression can be challenging. We illustrate the problem by grouping the terms in the following lambda expression:

$$(\lambda n . \lambda f . \lambda x . f (n f x)) (\lambda g . \lambda y . g y).$$

We first identify the lambda abstractions, using the rule that the scope of lambda variable extends as far as possible. Observe that the lambda abstractions in the first term are ended by an existing set of parentheses.

$(\lambda x . f (n f x))$ $(\lambda y . g y)$

$(\lambda f . (\lambda x . f (n f x)))$ $(\lambda g . (\lambda y . g y))$

$(\lambda n . (\lambda f . (\lambda x . f (n f x))))$

Then grouping the combinations by associating them to the left yields the completely parenthesized expression:

$$((\lambda n . (\lambda f . (\lambda x . (f ((n f) x))))) (\lambda g . (\lambda y . (g y)))).$$ ∎

Curried Functions

Lambda calculus as described above seems to permit functions of a single variable only. The abstraction mechanism allows for only one parameter at a time. However, many useful functions, such as binary arithmetic operations, require more than one parameter; for example, sum(a,b) = a+b matches the syntactic specification sum : NxN $\rightarrow$ N, where N denotes the natural numbers.

Lambda calculus admits two solutions to this problem:

1. Allow ordered pairs as lambda expressions, say using the notation <x,y>, and define the addition function on pairs:

    sum <a,b> = a + b

    Pairs can be provided by using a predefined "cons" operation as in Lisp, or the pairing operation can be defined in terms of primitive lambda expressions in the pure lambda calculus, as will be seen later in the chapter.

2. Use the **curried** version of the function with the property that arguments are supplied one at a time:

    add : N $\rightarrow$ N $\rightarrow$ N   ($\rightarrow$ associates to the right)

    where add a b = a + b   (function application associates to the left).

Now (add a) : N $\rightarrow$ N is a function with the property that ((add a) b) = a + b. In this way, the successor function can be defined as (add 1).

Note that the notational conventions of associating → to the right and function application to the left agree. The terms "curried" and "currying" honor Haskell Curry who used the mechanism in his study of functions. Moses Schönfinkel actually developed the idea of currying before Curry, which means that it might more accurately be called "Schönfinkeling".

The operations of currying and uncurrying a function can be expressed in the lambda calculus as

define Curry = λf . λx . λy . f <x,y>

define Uncurry = λf . λp . f (head p) (tail p)

provided the pairing operation <x,y> = (cons x y) and the functions (head p) and (tail p) are available, either as predefined functions or as functions defined in the pure lambda calculus, as we will see later.

Therefore the two versions of the addition operation are related as follows:

Curry sum = add   and   Uncurry add = sum.

One advantage of currying is that it permits the "partial application" of a function. Consider an example using Twice that takes advantage of the currying of functions:

define Twice = λf . λx . f (f x).

Note that Twice is another example of a polymorphic function in the sense that it may be applied to any function and element as long as that element is in the domain of the function and its image under the function is also in that domain. The mechanism that allows functions to be defined to work on a number of types of data is also known as **parametric polymorphism**.

If D is any domain, the syntax (or signature) for Twice can be described as

Twice : (D → D) → D → D.

Given the square function, sqr : N → N where N stands for the natural numbers, it follows that

(Twice sqr) : N → N

is itself a function. This new function can be named

define FourthPower = Twice sqr.

Observe that FourthPower is defined without any reference to its argument. Defining new functions in this way embodies the spirit of functional programming. Much of the power of a functional programming language lies in its ability to define and apply higher-order functions—that is, functions that take functions as arguments and/or return a function as their result. Twice is higher-order since it maps one function to another.

Semantics of Lambda Expressions

A lambda expression has as its meaning the lambda expression that results after all its function applications (combinations) are carried out. Evaluating a lambda expression is called **reduction**. The basic reduction rule involves substituting expressions for free variables in a manner similar to the way that the parameters in a function definition are passed as arguments in a function call. We start by defining the concepts of free occurrences of variables and the substitution of expressions for variables.

Definition: An *occurrence* of a variable v in a lambda expression is called **bound** if it is within the scope of a "λv"; otherwise it is called **free**.   ∎

A variable may occur both bound and free in the same lambda expression; for example, in λx . y λy . y x the first occurrence of y is free and the other two are bound. Note the care we take in distinguishing between a variable and occurrences of that variable in a lambda expression.

The notation **E[v→E₁]** refers to the lambda expression obtained by replacing each free occurrence of the variable v in E by the lambda expression E_1. Such a substitution is called **valid** or **safe** if no free variable in E_1 becomes bound as a result of the substitution $E[v→E_1]$. An invalid substitution involves a **variable capture** or **name clash**.

For example, the naive substitution (λx . (mul y x))[y→x] to get (λx . (mul x x)) is unsafe since the result represents a squaring operation whereas the original lambda expression does not. We cannot allow the change in semantics engendered by this naive substitution, since we want to preserve the semantics of lambda expressions as we manipulate them.

The definition of substitution requires some care to avoid variable capture. We first need to identify the variables in E that are free by defining an operation that lists the variables that occur free in an expression. For example, $FV(λx . y λy . y x z) = \{y,z\}$.

Definition: The **set of free variables** (variables that occur free) in an expression E, denoted by **FV(E)**, is defined as follows:

   a) $FV(c) = ∅$ for any constant c

   b) $FV(x) = \{x\}$ for any variable x

   c) $FV(E_1\ E_2) = FV(E_1) ∪ FV(E_2)$

   d) $FV(λx . E) = FV(E) - \{x\}$ ∎

A lambda expression E with no free variables ($FV(E) = ∅$) is called **closed**.

Definition: The **substitution** of an expression for a (free) variable in a lambda expression is denoted by **E[v→E$_1$]** and is defined as follows:

a) $v[v→E_1]$ = E_1 for any variable v

b) $x[v→E_1]$ = x   for any variable x≠v

c) $c[v→E_1]$ = c   for any constant c

d) $(E_{rator}\ E_{rand})[v→E_1]$ = $((E_{rator}[v→E_1])\ (E_{rand}[v→E_1]))$

e) $(\lambda v\ .\ E)[v→E_1]$ = $(\lambda v\ .\ E)$

f) $(\lambda x\ .\ E)[v→E_1]$ = $\lambda x\ .\ (E[v→E_1])$ when x≠v and x∉ $FV(E_1)$

g) $(\lambda x\ .\ E)[v→E_1]$ = $\lambda z\ .\ (E[x→z][v→E_1])$ when x≠v and x∈ $FV(E_1)$,

where z≠v and z∉ $FV(E\ E_1)$ ∎

In part g) the first substitution E[x→z] replaces the bound variable x that will capture the free x's in E$_1$ by an entirely new bound variable z. Then the intended substitution can be performed safely.

Example: $(\lambda y\ .\ (\lambda f\ .\ f\ x)\ y)[x→f\ y]$

$(\lambda y\ .\ (\lambda f\ .\ f\ x)\ y)[x→f\ y]$

= $\lambda z\ .\ ((\lambda f\ .\ f\ x)\ z)[x→f\ y]$	by g) since y∈ $FV(f\ y)$
= $\lambda z\ .\ ((\lambda f\ .\ f\ x)[x→f\ y]\ z[x→f\ y])$	by d)
= $\lambda z\ .\ ((\lambda f\ .\ f\ x)[x→f\ y]\ z)$	by b)
= $\lambda z\ .\ (\lambda g\ .\ (g\ x)[x→f\ y])\ z$	by g) since f∈ $FV(f\ y)$
= $\lambda z\ .\ (\lambda g\ .\ g\ (f\ y))\ z$	by d), b), and a) ∎

Observe that if v∉ $FV(E)$, then E[v→E$_1$] is essentially the same lambda expression as E; there may be a change of bound variables, but the structure of the expression remains unchanged.

The substitution operation provides the mechanism for implementing function application. In the next section we define the rules for simplifying lambda expressions based on this idea of substitution.

Exercises

1.   Correctly parenthesize each of these lambda expressions:

a) $\lambda x\ .\ x\ \lambda y\ .\ y\ x$

b) $(\lambda x . x) (\lambda y . y) \lambda x . x (\lambda y . y) z$

c) $(\lambda f . \lambda y . \lambda z . f z y z) p x$

d) $\lambda x . x \lambda y . y \lambda z . z \lambda w . w z y x$

2. Find the set of free variables for each of the following lambda expressions:

a) $\lambda x . x y \lambda z . x z$

b) $(\lambda x . x y) \lambda z . w \lambda w . w z y x$

c) $x \lambda z . x \lambda w . w z y$

d) $\lambda x . x y \lambda x . y x$

3. Carry out the following substitutions:

a) $(f (\lambda x . x y) \lambda z . x y z)[x \rightarrow g]$ b) $(\lambda x . \lambda y . f x y)[y \rightarrow x]$

c) $((\lambda x . f x) \lambda f . f x)[f \rightarrow g x]$ d) $(\lambda f . \lambda y . f x y)[x \rightarrow f y]$

4. Using the function Twice and the successor function succ, define a function that

a) adds four to its argument.

b) adds sixteen to its argument.

5. Give a definition of the set of bound variables in a lambda expression E, denoted by $BV(E)$.

6. Show by an example that substitutions can be carried out that alter the intended semantics if part g) of the substitution rule is replaced by:

g') $(\lambda x . E)[v \rightarrow E_1] = \lambda z . (E[x \rightarrow z][v \rightarrow E_1])$ when $x \neq v$ and $x \in FV(E_1)$,

where $z \notin FV(E \; E_1)$

5.2 LAMBDA REDUCTION

Simplifying or evaluating a lambda expression involves reducing the expression until no more reduction rules apply. The main rule for simplifying a lambda expression, called β-reduction, encompasses the operation of function application. Since substituting for free variables in an expression may cause variable capture, we first need a mechanism for changing the name of a bound variable in an expression—namely, α-reduction.

Definition: α-reduction

If v and w are variables and E is a lambda expression,

$$\lambda v \,.\, E \;\Rightarrow_\alpha\; \lambda w \,.\, E[v{\rightarrow}w]$$

provided that w does not occur at all in E, which makes the substitution E[v→w] safe. The equivalence of expressions under α-reduction is what makes part g) of the definition of substitution correct.

The α-reduction rule simply allows the changing of bound variables as long as there is no capture of a free variable occurrence. The two sides of the rule can be thought of as variants of each other, both members of an equivalence class of "congruent" lambda expressions.   ∎

The example substitution at the end of the previous section contains two α-reductions:

$$\lambda y \,.\, (\lambda f \,.\, f\, x)\, y \;\Rightarrow_\alpha\; \lambda z \,.\, (\lambda f \,.\, f\, x)\, z$$

$$\lambda z \,.\, (\lambda f \,.\, f\, x)\, z \;\Rightarrow_\alpha\; \lambda z \,.\, (\lambda g \,.\, g\, x)\, z$$

Now that we have a justification of the substitution mechanism, the main simplification rule can be formally defined.

Definition: β-reduction

If v is a variable and E and E_1 are lambda expressions,

$$(\lambda v \,.\, E)\, E_1 \;\Rightarrow_\beta\; E[v{\rightarrow}E_1]$$

provided that the substitution $E[v{\rightarrow}E_1]$ is carried out according to the rules for a safe substitution.

This β-reduction rule describes the function application rule in which the actual parameter or argument E_1 is "passed to" the function (λv . E) by substituting the argument for the formal parameter v in the function. The left side (λv . E) E_1 of a β-reduction is called a β-**redex**—a term derived from the terms "reduction expression" and meaning an expression that can be β-reduced. β-reduction serves as the main rule of evaluation in the lambda calculus. α-reduction is simply used to make the substitutions for variables valid.   ∎

The evaluation of a lambda expression consists of a series of β-reductions, possibly interspersed with α-reductions to change bound variables to avoid confusion. Take **E ⇒ F** to mean E $\Rightarrow_\beta$ F or E $\Rightarrow_\alpha$ F and let ⇒* be the reflexive and transitive closure of ⇒. That means for any expression E, E ⇒* E and for any three expressions, (E_1 ⇒* E_2 and E_2 ⇒* E_3) implies E_1 ⇒* E_3. The goal of evaluation in the lambda calculus is to reduce a lambda expression via ⇒ until it contains no more β-redexes.

To define an "equality" relation on lambda expressions, we also allow a β-reduction rule to work backward.

Definition: Reversing β-reduction produces the β-**abstraction** rule,

$$E[v{\rightarrow}E_1] \Rightarrow_\beta (\lambda v \,.\, E)\, E_1,$$

and the two rules taken together give β-**conversion**, denoted by $\Leftrightarrow_\beta$. Therefore $E \Leftrightarrow_\beta F$ if $E \Rightarrow_\beta F$ or $F \Rightarrow_\beta E$. Take $E \Leftrightarrow F$ to mean $E \Leftrightarrow_\beta F$, $E \Rightarrow_\alpha F$ or $F \Rightarrow_\alpha E$ and let $\Leftrightarrow^*$ be the reflexive and transitive closure of $\Leftrightarrow$. Two lambda expressions E and F are **equivalent** or **equal** if $E \Leftrightarrow^* F$. ∎

We also allow reductions (both α and β) to subexpressions in a lambda expression. In particular, the following three rules expand the notion of reduction to components of combinations and abstractions:

1. $E_1 \Rightarrow E_2$ implies $E_1\, E \Rightarrow E_2\, E$.
2. $E_1 \Rightarrow E_2$ implies $E\, E_1 \Rightarrow E\, E_2$.
3. $E_1 \Rightarrow E_2$ implies $\lambda x \,.\, E_1 \Rightarrow \lambda x \,.\, E_2$.

A third rule, η-reduction, justifies an extensional view of functions; that is, two functions are equal if they produce the same values when given the same arguments. The rule is not strictly necessary for reducing lambda expressions and may cause problems in the presence of constants, but we include it for completeness.

Definition: η-**reduction**

If v is a variable, E is a lambda expression (denoting a function), and v has no free occurrence in E,

$$\lambda v \,.\, (E\, v) \Rightarrow_\eta E.$$ ∎

Note that in the pure lambda calculus every expression is a function, but the rule fails when E represents some constants; for example, if 5 is a predefined constant numeral, $\lambda x \,.\, (5\, x)$ and 5 are not equivalent or even related.

However, if E stands for a predefined function, the rule remains valid as suggested by these examples:

$$\lambda x \,.\, (\text{sqr } x) \Rightarrow_\eta \text{sqr}$$

$$\lambda x \,.\, (\text{add } 5\, x) \Rightarrow_\eta (\text{add } 5).$$

Remember, (add 5 x) abbreviates ((add 5) x).

The requirement that x should have no free occurrences in E is necessary to avoid a reduction such as

$$\lambda x \,.\, (\text{add } x\, x) \Rightarrow (\text{add } x),$$

which is clearly invalid.

Take $E \Leftrightarrow_\eta F$ to mean $E \Rightarrow_\eta F$ or $F \Rightarrow_\eta E$.

The η-reduction rule can be used to justify the extensionality of functions; namely, if f(x) = g(x) for all x, then f = g. In the framework of the lambda calculus, we can prove an extensionality property.

Extensionality Theorem: If F_1 x ⇒* E and F_2 x ⇒* E where x∉ $FV(F_1 F_2)$, then F_1 ⇔* F_2 where ⇔* includes η-reductions.

Proof: F_1 ⇔$_η$ λx . (F_1 x) ⇔* λx . E ⇔* λx . (F_2 x) ⇔$_η$ F_2. ∎

Finally, in an applied lambda calculus containing predefined values and operations, we need a justification for evaluating combinations of constant objects. Such a rule is known as δ-reduction.

Definition: δ-reduction

If the lambda calculus has predefined constants (that is, if it is not pure), rules associated with those predefined values and functions are called δ rules; for example, (add 3 5) ⇒$_δ$ 8 and (not true) ⇒$_δ$ false. ∎

Example: Consider the following reduction of Twice (λn . (add n 1)) 5 where the leftmost β-redex is simplified in each step. For each β-reduction, the redex has its bound variable and argument highlighted in boldface.

Twice (λn . (add n 1)) 5 ⇒ (λ**f** . λx . (f (f x))) (λ**n . (add n 1))** 5

⇒$_β$ (λ**x** . ((λn . (add n 1)) ((λn . (add n 1)) x))) **5**

⇒$_β$ (λ**n** . (add n 1)) ((λn . (add n 1)) 5)

⇒$_β$ (add ((λ**n** . (add n 1)) **5**) 1)

⇒$_β$ (add (add 5 1) 1) ⇒$_δ$ 7. ∎

The key to performing a reduction of a lambda calculus expression lies in recognizing a β-redex, (λv . E) E_1. Observe that such a lambda expression is a combination whose left subexpression is a lambda abstraction. In terms of the abstract syntax, we are looking for a structure with the form illustrated by the following tree:

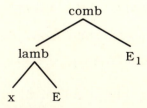

Reduction Strategies

The main goal of manipulating a lambda expression is to reduce it to a "simplest form" and consider that as the value of the lambda expression.

Definition: A lambda expression is in **normal form** if it contains no β-redexes (and no δ-rules in an applied lambda calculus), so that it cannot be further reduced using the β-rule or the δ-rule. An expression in normal form has no more function applications to evaluate. ∎

The concepts of normal form and reduction strategy can be investigated by asking four questions:

1. Can every lambda expression be reduced to a normal form?

2. Is there more than one way to reduce a particular lambda expression?

3. If there is more than one reduction strategy, does each one lead to the same normal form expression?

4. Is there a reduction strategy that will guarantee that a normal form expression will be produced?

The first question has a negative answer, as shown by the lambda expression (λx . x x) (λx . x x). This β-redex reduces to itself, meaning that the only reduction path continues forever:

$$(λ\mathbf{x} . x x) (λ\mathbf{x} . \mathbf{x} \mathbf{x}) \Rightarrow_β$$

$$(λ\mathbf{x} . x x) (λ\mathbf{x} . \mathbf{x} \mathbf{x}) \Rightarrow_β (λ\mathbf{x} . x x) (λ\mathbf{x} . \mathbf{x} \mathbf{x}) \Rightarrow_β \ ...$$

The second question has an affirmative answer, as evidenced by the different reduction paths in the following examples.

Example: (λx . λy . (add y ((λz . (mul x z)) 3))) 7 5

Path 1: (λ**x** . λy . (add y ((λz . (mul x z)) 3))) **7** 5

$\Rightarrow_β$ (λ**y** . (add y ((λz . (mul 7 z)) 3))) **5**

$\Rightarrow_β$ (add 5 ((λ**z** . (mul 7 z)) **3**))

$\Rightarrow_β$ (add 5 (**mul 7 3**)) $\Rightarrow_δ$ (**add 5 21**) $\Rightarrow_δ$ 26

Path 2: (λx . λy . (add y ((λ**z** . (mul x z)) 3))) 7 5

$\Rightarrow_β$ (λ**x** . λy . (add y (mul x 3))) **7** 5

$\Rightarrow_β$ (λ**y** . (add y (mul 7 3))) **5**

$\Rightarrow_δ$ (λ**y** . (add y 21)) **5** $\Rightarrow_β$ (**add 5 21**) $\Rightarrow_δ$ 26

In this example both paths lead to the same result, which is clearly in normal form. Note that in both paths λx must be reduced before λy because at this point in the reduction, λy is not part of a β-redex.   ∎

Example: (λy . 5) ((λx . x x) (λx . x x))

Path 1:   (λ**y** . 5) (**(λx . x x) (λx . x x))** ⇒_β 5

Path 2:   (λy . 5) ((λ**x** . x x) (λ**x . x x**))

$$⇒_β \quad (λy . 5) ((λ\mathbf{x} . x x) (λ\mathbf{x . x x}))$$

$$⇒_β \quad (λy . 5) ((λ\mathbf{x} . x x) (λ\mathbf{x . x x})) ...$$

With this example the first path, which reduces the leftmost redex first, leads to a normal form expression, but the second path, which evaluates the rightmost application each time, results in a nonterminating calculation.   ∎

These two reduction strategies have names.

Definition: A **normal order** reduction always reduces the leftmost outermost β-redex (or δ-redex) first. An **applicative order** reduction always reduces the leftmost innermost β-redex (or δ-redex) first.   ∎

The operative words in this definition are "outermost" and "innermost". Only when more than one outermost or innermost redex occur in a lambda expresion do we choose the leftmost of these redexes.

Definition: For any lambda expression of the form E = ((λx . B) A), we say that β-redex E is **outside** any β-redex that occurs in B or A and that these are **inside** E. A β-redex in a lambda expression is **outermost** if there is no β-redex outside of it, and it is **innermost** if there is no β-redex inside of it.   ∎

Sometimes constructing an abstract syntax tree for the lambda expression can help show the pertinent β-redexes. For example, in Figure 5.1 the tree has the outermost and innermost β-redexes marked for the lambda expression (((λx . λy . (add x y)) ((λz . (succ z)) 5)) ((λw . (sqr w)) 7)). The two kinds of structured subexpressions are tagged by *comb* for combinations and *lamb* for lambda abstractions. From the tree, we can identify the leftmost outermost β-redex as ((λx . λy . (add x y)) ((λz . (succ z)) 5)) and the leftmost innermost as ((λz . (succ z)) 5). Remember that a β-redex (λv . E) E$_1$ is a combination consisting of an abstraction joined with another expression to be passed to the function. Some abstractions cannot be considered as innermost or outermost because they are not part of β-redexes.

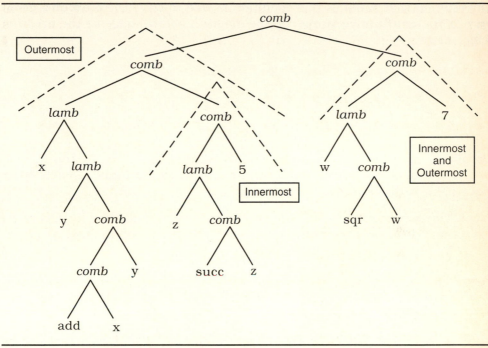

Figure 5.1: β-redexes in $(((\lambda x.\lambda y.(add\ x\ y))\ ((\lambda z.(succ\ z))\ 5))\ ((\lambda w.(sqr\ w))\ 7))$

When reducing lambda expressions in an applied lambda calculus, use a reduction strategy to decide when both β-reductions and δ-reductions are carried out. For predefined binary operations, we complete the δ-reduction only when both arguments have been evaluated. Strictly following an applicative order reduction strategy requires that $((\lambda n\ .\ (add\ 5\ n))\ 8)$ be reduced to the lambda expression $((\lambda n\ .\ add5\ n)\ 8)$ where $add5 : N \to N$ is the function that adds 5 to its argument. To avoid making up unary functions from partially evaluated curried binary functions, we postpone the evaluation of add until both of its arguments are evaluated. So the reduction proceeds as follows:

$$((\lambda \mathbf{n}\ .\ (add\ 5\ n))\ \mathbf{8}) \Rightarrow_\beta (\mathbf{add\ 5\ 8}) \Rightarrow_\delta 13.$$

The two remaining questions can be answered by applying the results proved by Alonzo Church and J. Barkley Rosser in 1936.

Church-Rosser Theorem I: For any lambda expressions E, F, and G, if $E \Rightarrow^*$ F and $E \Rightarrow^* G$, there is a lambda expression Z such that $F \Rightarrow^* Z$ and $G \Rightarrow^* Z$.

Proof: The somewhat technical proof of this theorem can be found in [Barendregt84] or [MacLennan90]. ∎

Any relation that satisfies this condition is said to have the **diamond property** or the **confluence property**.The diagram below suggests the origin of these terms.

$$E$$

$$* \swarrow \qquad \searrow *$$

$$F \qquad\qquad G$$

$$\searrow * \qquad * \swarrow$$

$$Z$$

Corollary: For any lambda expressions E, M, and N, if E $\Rightarrow$* M and E $\Rightarrow$* N where M and N are in normal form, M and N are variants of each other (equivalent with respect to α-reduction).

Proof: The only reduction possible for an expression in normal form is an α-reduction. Therefore the lambda expression Z in the theorem must be a variant of M and N by α-reduction only.   ∎

This corollary states that if a lambda expression has a normal form, that normal form is unique up to a change of bound variables, thereby answering the third question.

Church-Rosser Theorem II: For any lambda expressions E and N, if E $\Rightarrow$* N where N is in normal form, there is a normal order reduction from E to N.

Proof: Again see [Barendregt84].   ∎

The second Church-Rosser theorem answers the fourth question by stating that normal order reduction will produce a normal form lambda expression if one exists.

A normal order reduction can have either of the following outcomes:
1. It reaches a unique (up to α-conversion) normal form lambda expression.
2. It never terminates.

Unfortunately, there is no algorithmic way to determine for an arbitrary lambda expression which of these two outcomes will occur.

Turing machines are abstract machines designed in the 1930s by Alan Turing to model computable functions. It has been shown that the lambda calculus is equivalent to Turing machines in the sense that every lambda expression has an equivalent function defined by some Turing machine and vice versa. This equivalence gives credibility to Church's thesis.

Church's Thesis: The effectively computable functions on the positive integers are precisely those functions definable in the pure lambda calculus (and computable by Turing machines).   ∎

The term "thesis" means a conjecture. In the case of Church's thesis, the conjecture cannot be proved since the informal notion of "effectively computable function" is not defined precisely. But since all methods developed for computing functions have been proved to be no more powerful than the lambda calculus, it captures the idea of computable functions as well as we can hope.

Alan Turing proved a fundamental result, called the undecidability of the **halting problem**, which states that there is no algorithmic way to determine whether or not an arbitrary Turing machine will ever stop running. Therefore there are lambda expressions for which it cannot be determined whether a normal order reduction will ever terminate.

Correlation with Parameter Passing

The two fundamental reduction strategies, normal and applicative order, are related to techniques for passing parameters to a procedure or function in a programming language. Recall that an abstraction $\lambda x . B$ is an anonymous function whose formal parameter is x and whose body is the lambda expression B.

1. **Call by name** is the same as normal order reduction except that no redex in a lambda expression that lies within an abstraction (within a function body) is reduced. With call by name, an actual parameter is passed as an unevaluated expression that is evaluated in the body of the function being executed each time the corresponding formal parameter is referenced. Normal order is ensured by choosing the leftmost redex, which will always be an outermost one with an unevaluated operand.

2. **Call by value** is the same as applicative order reduction except that no redex in a lambda expression that lies within an abstraction is reduced. This restriction corresponds to the principle that the body of a function is not evaluated until the function is called (in a β-reduction). Applicative order means the argument to a function is evaluated before the function is applied.

Example: The call by value reduction of

$(\lambda x . (\lambda f . f (succ \; x)) (\lambda z . (\lambda g . (\lambda y . (add (mul (g \; y) \; x)) \; z))) ((\lambda z . (add \; z \; 3)) \; 5)$

proceeds as follows:

(λx . (λf . f (succ x)) (λz . (λg . (λy . (add (mul (g y) x))) z))) ((λ**z** . (add z 3)) **5**)

   ⇒_β (λx . (λf . f (succ x)) (λz . (λg . (λy . (add (mul (g y) x))) z))) (**add 5 3**)

   ⇒_δ (λ**x** . (λf . f (succ x)) (λz . (λg . (λy . (add (mul (g y) x))) z))) **8**

   ⇒_β (λ**f** . f (succ 8)) (λ**z** . (λg . (λy . (add (mul (g y) 8))) z))

   ⇒_β (λz . (λg . (λy . (add (mul (g y) 8))) z)) (**succ 8**)

   ⇒_δ (λ**z** . (λg . (λy . (add (mul (g y) 8))) z)) **9**

   ⇒_β (λg . (λy . (add (mul (g y) 8))) 9)   ■

In this example, the reduction of the argument, ((λz . (add z 3)) 5), can be thought of as an optimization, since we pass in a value and not an unevaluated expression that would be evaluated twice in the body of the function. Observe that the final result stops short of normal form with call by value semantics.

Constants in the Pure Lambda Calculus

If Church's thesis is to be credible, there must be a way to define the nonnegative integers in the pure lambda calculus. Furthermore, to allow the definition of uncurried binary functions, we need to be able to define a list constructor and list selectors. Since so many functions employ conditional definitions, we also need to define Boolean constants and operations. Although all of these constants can be defined as functions in the pure lambda calculus, we consider only a few examples here.

The function "Pair" encapsulates two values in a given order; it is essentially the dotted pair notion (cons) in Lisp.

     define Pair = λa . λb . λf . f a b

Two selector functions "Head" and "Tail" confirm that Pair implements the cons operation.

     define Head = λg . g (λa . λb . a)

     define Tail = λg . g (λa . λb . b)

Now the correctness of the definitions is verified by reductions:

  Head (Pair p q) ⇒   (λ**g** . g (λa . λb . a)) **((λa . λb . λf . f a b) p q)**

                  ⇒_β ((λ**a** . λb . λf . f a b) **p** q) (λa . λb . a)

                  ⇒_β ((λ**b** . λf . f p b) **q**) (λa . λb . a)

                  ⇒_β (λ**f** . f p q) (λ**a** . λ**b** . **a**)

                  ⇒_β (λ**a** . λb . a) **p** q ⇒_β (λ**b** . p) **q** ⇒_β p

As with "cons" in Lisp, "Pair" is sufficient to construct lists of arbitrary length; for example, assuming we have positive integers and a special constant,

define Nil = λx . λa . λb . a,

a list can be constructed as follows:

define [1, 2, 3, 4] = Pair 1 (Pair 2 (Pair 3 (Pair 4 Nil))).

Combinations of the selector functions can choose items from the list:

Head (Tail (Tail [1, 2, 3, 4])) ⇒ 3.

Several ways have been proposed for representing the natural numbers in the pure lambda calculus. In each case, cardinal values are encoded as patterns in function definitions. Our approach will be to code a natural number by the number of times a function parameter is applied:

define 0 = λf . λx . x

define 1 = λf . λx . f x

define 2 = λf . λx . f (f x)

define 3 = λf . λx . f (f (f x)) and so on.

Based on this definition of numerals, the standard arithmetic operations can be defined as functions in the lambda calculus. We give two examples here.

Successor function, Succ : N → N

define Succ = λn . λf . λx . f (n f x)

Addition operation, Add : N → N → N

define Add = λm . λn . λf . λx . m f (n f x).

As an example of a reduction using this arithmetic of pure lambda expressions, consider the successor of 2. The bound variables are altered in 2 to make the reduction easier to follow, but the changes are really unnecessary.

Succ 2   ⇒   (λ**n** . λf . λx . f (n f x)) (λ**g** . λ**y** . **g** (**g y**))

⇒$_\beta$ λf . λx . f ((λ**g** . λy . g (g y)) **f** x)

⇒$_\beta$ λf . λx . f ((λ**y** . f (f y)) **x**)

⇒$_\beta$ λf . λx . f (f (f x)) = 3

Functional Programming Languages

All functional programming languages can be viewed as syntactic variations of the lambda calculus. Certainly the fundamental operations in all functional languages are the creation of functions—namely, lambda abstraction—and the application of functions, the two basic operations in the lambda calculus. The naming of functions or other objects is pure syntactic sugar since the values named can be substituted directly for their identifiers, at least for nonrecursive definitions. Recursive definitions can be made nonrecursive using a fixed point finder, an issue that we cover in Chapter 10.

Most current functional programming languages follow static scoping to resolve references to identifiers not declared in a local scope. Static or lexical scoping means that nonlocal variables refer to bindings created in the textually enclosing blocks. In contrast, with dynamic scoping nonlocal references are resolved by following the calling chain. We examine these two possibilities more carefully in Chapters 6 and 8.

Nested scopes are naturally created by the activations of nested function calls where the formal parameters designate the local identifiers. A **let** expression is an alternate means of writing a lambda expression that is a function application.

> **let** x=5 **in** (add x 3) means (λx . (add x 3)) 5.

In some functional languages, a **where** expression acts as an alternative to the let expression.

> (add x 3) **where** x=5 also means (λx . (add x 3)) 5.

A recursive let or where, sometimes called "letrec" or "whererec", requires the fixed point operator, but we postpone a discussion of that until Chapter 10. At any rate, the syntactic forms of a functional programming language can be translated into the lambda calculus and studied in that context. For more on this translation process, see the further readings at the end of this chapter.

Exercises

1. Identify the innermost and outermost β-redexes in the following lambda expression and draw its abstract syntax tree:

    (λx y z . (add x (mul y z))) ((λx . (succ x)) 5) 12 ((λw . (w 4)) sqr)

2. Use both normal order reduction and applicative order reduction to reduce the following lambda expressions. Reach a normal form representation if possible.

   a) (λg . g 5) (λx . (add x 3))

   b) (λx . (λy z . z y) x) p (λx . x)

   c) (λx . x x x) (λx . x x x)

   d) (λx . λy . (add x ((λx . (sub x 3)) y))) 5 6

   e) (λc . c (λa . λb . b)) ((λa . λb . λf . f a b) p q)

   f) Twice (λn . (mul 2 (add n 1))) 5

   g) Twice (Twice (λn . (mul 2 (add n 1)))) 5

   h) Twice Twice sqr 2

   i) (λx . ((λz . (add x x)) ((λx . λz . (z 13 x)) 0 div))) ((λx . (x 5)) sqr)

3. Use call by value semantics to reduce the following lambda expressions:

   a) (λf . f add (f mul (f add 5)) (λg . λx . g x x))

   b) (λx . λf . f (f x)) ((λy . (add y 2)) ((λz . (sqr z)) ((λy . (succ y)) 1))) sqr

4. Show that Tail (Pair p q) ⇒β q.

5. Using constants defined in the *pure* lambda calculus, verify the following reductions:

   a) Succ 0 ⇒ 1

   b) Add 2 3 ⇒ 5

6. Using the definitions of Pair, Head, Tail, Curry, and Uncurry, where

   > *define* Curry = λf . λx . λy . f (Pair x y)

   > *define* Uncurry = λf . λp . f (Head p) (Tail p)

   carry out the following reductions:

   a) Curry (Uncurry h) ⇒β h

   b) Uncurry (Curry h) ⇒β h

7. Translate these "let" expressions into lambda expressions and reduce them. Also write the expressions using "where" instead of "let".

   a) **let** x = 5 **in let** y = (add x 3) **in** (mul x y)

   b) **let** a = 7 **in let** g = λx . (mul a x) **in let** a = 2 **in** (g 10)

5.3 LABORATORY: A LAMBDA CALCULUS EVALUATOR

In this section we implement a lambda calculus evaluator in Prolog for an applied lambda calculus with a few constants. Extensions are suggested in the exercises. The implementation was inspired by a lambda calculus evaluator written in Lisp and described in [Gordon88].

The evaluator expects to read a file containing one lambda expression to be reduced according to a normal order reduction strategy. A sample execution follows:

```
>>> Evaluating an Applied Lambda Calculus <<<
Enter name of source file: twice
    ((L f x (f (f x))) (L n (mul 2 (add n 1))) 5)
Successful Scan
Successful Parse
Result =   26
yes
```

Since Greek letters are missing from the ascii character set, we use "L" to stand for λ in lambda expressions. The concrete syntax recognized by our implementation, displayed in Figure 5.2, allows only two abbreviations for eliminating parentheses:

(L x y E) means (L x (L y E)), which stands for $\lambda x \, . \, \lambda y \, . \, E$ and

$(E_1 \, E_2 \, E_3)$ means $((E_1 \, E_2) \, E_3)$.

In particular, outermost parentheses are never omitted.

<expression> ::= <identifier> | <constant>

| **(L** <identifier>$^+$ <expression> **)**

| **(** <expression>$^+$ <expression> **)**

<constant> ::= <numeral> | **true** | **false** | **succ** | **sqr**

| **add** | **sub** | **mul**

Figure 5.2: Concrete Syntax for an Applied Lambda Calculus

Scanner and Parser

The scanner for the implementation needs to recognize identifiers starting with lowercase letters, numerals (only nonnegative to simplify the example), parentheses, and the reserved words "L", "true", and "false", together with the identifiers for the predefined operations. The scanner for Wren can be adapted to recognize these tokens for the lambda calculus. Remember that an atom starting with an uppercase letter, such as L, must be written within apostrophes in Prolog.

The parser takes the list of tokens Tokens from the scanner and constructs an abstract syntax tree for the lambda expression as a Prolog structure. The examples below illustrate the tags used by the abstract syntax.

Lambda Expression: λx . (sqr x)

Concrete Syntax: (L x (sqr x))

Abstract Syntax Tree: *lamb(x,comb(con(sqr),var(x)))*

Lambda Expression: (λx . λy . (add x y)) 5 8

Concrete Syntax: ((L x y (add x y)) 5 8)

Abstract Syntax Tree: *comb(comb(lamb(x,lamb(y,comb(comb(con(add),*
var(x)),var(y)))),con(5)),con(8))

The abstract syntax tree for the second example is displayed in Figure 5.3.

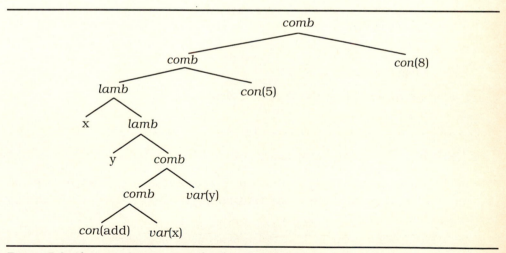

Figure 5.3: Abstract Syntax Tree for (λx . λy . (add x y)) 5 8

Figure 5.4 gives the abstract syntax used by the lambda calculus evaluator following a tagged structure format. Identifiers and constants are left unspecified since they are handled by the scanner.

Expression ::= *var*(Identifier) | *con*(Constant)

| *lamb*(Identifier,Expression)

| *comb*(Expression,Expression)

Figure 5.4: Abstract Syntax for an Applied Lambda Calculus

We invoke the parser by means of program(expr(E),Tokens,[eop]). Following the concrete syntax, we obtain the logic grammar shown in Figure 5.5 that recognizes variables, constants, lambda abstractions, and combinations.

```
program(expr(E)) --> expr(E).

expr(lamb(X,E)) --> [lparen],['L'],[var(X)],expr(E1),restlamb(E1,E).
      restlamb(E,E) --> [rparen].
      restlamb(var(Y),lamb(Y,E)) --> expr(E1),restlamb(E1,E).

expr(E) --> [lparen],expr(E1),expr(E2),restcomb(E1,E2,E).
      restcomb(E1,E2,comb(E1,E2)) --> [rparen].
      restcomb(E1,E2,E) --> expr(E3), restcomb(comb(E1,E2),E3,E).

expr(var(X)) --> [var(X)].          expr(con(N)) --> [num(N)].
expr(con(true)) --> [true].         expr(con(false)) --> [false].
expr(con(succ)) --> [succ].         expr(con(sqr)) --> [sqr].
expr(con(add)) --> [add].           expr(con(sub)) --> [sub].
expr(con(mul)) --> [mul].
```

Figure 5.5: Logic Grammar for the Lambda Calculus

The Lambda Calculus Evaluator

The evaluator proceeds by reducing the given lambda expression until no further reduction is possible. That reduction can be carried out in Prolog using

    evaluate(E,NewE) :- reduce(E,TempE), evaluate(TempE,NewE).

    evaluate(E,E).

When reduce fails, the second clause terminates the evaluation, returning the current lambda expression.

Before we can describe the reduction predicate reduce, which encompasses the β-reduction rule, the δ-reduction rule, and the overall normal order reduction strategy, we need to define the substitution operation used by β-reduction. As a first step, we formulate a predicate for determining the free variables in a lambda expression:

    freevars(var(X),[X]).

    freevars(con(C),[ ]).

    freevars(comb(Rator,Rand),FV) :-   freevars(Rator,RatorFV),
                                        freevars(Rand,RandFV),
                                        union(RatorFV,RandFV,FV).

    freevars(lamb(X,E),FV) :- freevars(E,F), delete(X,F,FV).

The utility predicates union(S1,S2,S3), forming S3 as the union of lists S1 and S2, and delete(X,S1,S2), which removes the item X from the list S1 producing S2, are left for the reader to supply. Compare the Prolog definition of freevars with the specification of *FV*(E) in section 5.1.

The substitution predicate follows the definition in section 5.1 case by case, except that parts f) and g) combine into one clause with a guard, member(X,F1), where F1 holds the free variables in E1, to distinguish the cases. If the guard fails, we are in part f) and just carry out the substitution in E. If, however, X is a free variable in E1, we construct a new variable Z using the predicate variant and perform the two substitutions shown in the definition of part g).

    subst(var(V),V,E1,E1).   % a)

    subst(var(X),V,E1,var(X)).   % b)

    subst(con(C),V,E1,con(C)).   % c)

    subst(comb(Rator,Rand),V,E1,comb(NewRator,NewRand)) :-   % d)
                            subst(Rator,V,E1,NewRator),
                            subst(Rand,V,E1,NewRand).

    subst(lamb(V,E),V,E1,lamb(V,E)).   % e)

    subst(lamb(X,E),V,E1,lamb(Z,NewE)) :- freevars(E1,F1),
            (member(X,F1), freevars(E,F),   % g)
                    union(F,[V],F2), union(F1,F2,FV),
                    variant(X,FV,Z),
                    subst(E,X,var(Z),TempE),
                    subst(TempE,V,E1,NewE)
            ;   subst(E,V,E1,NewE), Z=X) .   % f)

The predicate variant(X,L,NewX) builds a variable that is different from all the variables in the list L by adding apostrophes to the end of the variable bound to X.

variant(X,L,NewX) :- member(X,L),prime(X,PrimeX),variant(PrimeX,L,NewX).

variant(X,L,X).

prime(X,PrimeX) :- name(X,L), concat(L,[39],NewL), name(PrimeX,NewL).

The ascii value 39 indicates an apostrophe. The reader needs to furnish the utility predicates member and concat to finish the specification of the substitution operation. See Appendix A for definitions of these predicates.

The reduce predicate performs a one-step reduction of a lambda expression, using pattern matching to provide a normal order reduction strategy. Since no clauses match a variable or a constant, no reduction exists for them—they are already in normal form. The first clause handles a β-reduction because the pattern is the outermost β-redex. The second clause executes a predefined function (δ-reduction) by calling a predicate compute to carry out the arithmetic and Boolean operations. The third and fourth clauses reduce the rator and rand expressions in that order, thus ensuring the evaluation of outermost β-redexes from left to right. Finally, the last clause simplifies a lambda expression by reducing its body.

reduce(comb(lamb(X,Body),Arg),R) :- subst(Body,X,Arg,R).   % 1

reduce(comb(con(C),con(Arg)),R) :- compute(C,Arg,R).   % 2

reduce(comb(Rator,Rand),comb(NewRator,Rand)) :-
                                            reduce(Rator,NewRator).   % 3

reduce(comb(Rator,Rand),comb(Rator,NewRand)) :-
                                            reduce(Rand,NewRand).   % 4

reduce(lamb(X,Body),lamb(X,NewBody)) :- reduce(Body,NewBody).   % 5

The compute predicate evaluates the arithmetic operations using Prolog's native numerical operations. We give it the responsibility for attaching the con tag to the result because some predefined operations may not need a tag. An exercise asks the reader to implement an "if" operation, which produces an untagged answer since it only evaluates one of its branches.

compute(succ,N,con(R)) :- R is N+1.

compute(sqr,N,con(R)) :- R is N*N.

compute(add,N,con(add(N))).   compute(add(M),N,con(R)) :- R is M+N.

compute(sub,N,con(sub(N))).   compute(sub(M),N,con(R)) :- R is M-N.

compute(mul,N,con(mul(N))).   compute(mul(M),N,con(R)) :- R is M*N.

Notice how the curried binary operations are handled by constructing a Prolog term containing the left operand, tagged by the operation name to represent the partially evaluated operation. To compute (add 2 3), which has as its abstract syntax tree

> comb(comb(con(add),con(2)),con(3)),

the evaluation proceeds as follows using add(2) to represent the partially applied operation:

$$\text{comb(comb(con(add),con(2)),con(3))} \Rightarrow \text{comb(con(add(2)),con(3))}$$
$$\Rightarrow \text{con(5)}.$$

The final result can be printed by a pretty-printer predicate pp. To visualize the progress of the reduction, insert pp(TempE) in the evaluate predicate.

pp(var(X)) :- write(X).

pp(con(C)) :- write(C).

pp(lamb(X,E)) :- write('(L '),write(X),tab(1),pp(E),write(')').

pp(comb(Rator,Rand)) :- write('('),pp(Rator),tab(1),pp(Rand),write(')').

If the parser produces a structure of the form expr(Exp), the lambda calculus evaluator can be invoked using the query

evaluate(Exp,Result), nl, write('Result = '), pp(Result), nl.

Although the lambda calculus evaluator in Prolog suffers from a lack of efficiency, it provides an effective tool for describing the reduction of lambda expressions. The reader will find that the task of matching parentheses correctly in an expression inflicts the most discomfort to a user of the evaluator.

Exercises

1. Complete the Prolog code for the lambda calculus evaluator by writing the missing utility predicates and test the evaluator on some of the lambda expressions in section 5.2.

2. Define a Prolog predicate boundvars(E,List) that produces a list containing the bound variables in E.

3. Add the operations "div", "pred" (for predecessor), "and", "or", "not", "zerop" (testing whether an expression equals zero), and "(if E_1,E_2,E_3)" to the evaluator. Test the evaluator on the lambda expression:

   ((L x (if (zerop x) 5 (div 100 x))) 0).

4. Add lists of arbitrary lambda expressions "[E_1, E_2, ..., E_n]", the operations "cons", "head", "tail", and "nullp" (testing whether a list is empty), and the constant "nil" to the evaluator.

5. Change the evaluator to applicative order reduction and test it by comparing it to the normal order reducer.

6. Add a mechanism to the evaluator for giving definitions prior to the lambda expression to be evaluated. An example program is

> define Twice = (L f x (f (f x)))
>
> define Thrice = (L f x (f (f (f x))))
>
> define Double = (L x (add x x))
>
> (Thrice Twice Double 3).

Provide a predicate elaborate that enters the definitions into an environment structure, say

env(Double,lamb(x,comb(comb(con(add),var(x)),var(x))),

   env(Thrice,lamb(f,lamb(x,comb(var(f),comb(var(f),comb(var(f),var(x))))))),

      env(Twice,lamb(f,lamb(x,comb(var(f),comb(var(f),var(x))))),nil)))

where nil represents an empty environment, and a predicate expand that replaces the defined names by their bindings in the environment. Design the mechanism so that definitions may refer to names that have already been defined in the list of declarations. This modification will require changes to the scanner and parser as well as the evaluator.

5.4 FURTHER READING

Many books on functional programming contain material on the lambda calculus, including [Michaelson89], [Revesz88], [Field88], and [Reade89]. For a short but very clear presentation of the lambda calculus, we recommend [Gordon88], which contains a lambda calculus evaluator written in Lisp. The text by Bruce MacLennan [MacLennan90] contains readable proofs for some of the theoretical results that we skipped in this chapter. For an advanced and exhaustive look at the lambda calculus, see [Barendregt84].

Several books describe a methodology for translating programs in a functional language into the lambda calculus, among them [Peyton Jones87] and [Diller88].

Chapter 6
SELF-DEFINITION OF PROGRAMMING LANGUAGES

The execution of a program written in a high-level language provides an informal, operational specification of the program. Two primary approaches are used to implement high-level languages: as an interpreter for the language or as a compiler for the language. Since interpreters and compilers are able to process any syntactically legal program, they themselves can provide an operational definition for a programming level language. Program translation will be discussed in Chapter 7. In this chapter we focus on program interpreters—in particular, a Lisp interpreter written in Lisp and a Prolog interpreter written in Prolog. In each case, the interpreter itself is written in the programming language it is interpreting. We call such an approach an operational self-definition of a programming language and refer to the implementation as a **metacircular interpreter**.

6.1 SELF-DEFINITION OF LISP

Lisp, initially developed by John McCarthy in 1958, is the second oldest programming language (after Fortran) in common use today. In the early 1960s McCarthy realized that the semantics of Lisp can be defined in terms of a few Lisp primitives and that an interpreter for Lisp can be written as a very small, concise Lisp program. Such an interpreter, referred to as a metacircular interpreter, can handle function definitions, parameter passing, and recursion as well as simple S-expressions of Lisp. The small size of the interpreter is striking, considering the thousands of lines of code needed to write a compiler for an imperative language.

We have elected to construct the interpreter in Scheme, a popular dialect of Lisp. Although we implement a subset of Scheme in Scheme, the interpreter is similar to the original self-definition given by McCarthy. The basic operations to decompose a list, **car** and **cdr**, and the list constructor **cons** are described in Figure 6.1. Combined with a predicate **null?** to test for an empty list, a conditional expression **cond**, and a method to define functions using

define, it is possible to write useful Scheme functions. See Appendix B for a more detailed description of Scheme. Our first example concatenates two lists. A function for concatenating lists is usually predefined in Lisp systems and goes by the name "append".

```
(define (concat lst1 lst2)
    (cond   ((null? lst1) lst2)
                    (#t (cons (car lst1) (concat (cdr lst1) lst2)))))
```

List Operations

(car <list>)	return the first item in <list>
(cdr <list>)	return <list> with the first item removed
(cons <item> <list>)	add <item> as first element of <list>

Arithmetic Operations

(+ <e_1> <e_2>)	return sum of the values of <e_1> and <e_2>
(- <e_1> <e_2>)	return difference of the values of <e_1> and <e_2>
(* <e_1><e_2>)	return product of the values of <e_1> and <e_2>
(/ <e_1> <e_2>)	return quotient of the values of <e_1> and <e_2>

Predicates

(null? <list>)	test if <list> is empty
(equal? <s_1> <s_2>)	test the equality of S-expressions <s_1> and <s_2>
(atom? <s>)	test if <s> is an atom

Conditional

(cond (<p_1> <e_1>)	sequentially evaluate predicates <p_1>, <p_2>, ... till
(<p_2> <e_2>)	one of them, say <p_i>, returns a not false (not #f)
: :	result; then the corresponding expression e_i is
(<p_n> <e_n>))	evaluated and its value returned from the cond

Function Definition and Anonymous Functions

(define (<name>	allow user to define function <name> with formal
<formals>)	parameters <formals> and function body <body>
<body>)	
(lambda (<formals>)	create an anonymous function
<body>)	
(let (<var-bindings>)	an alternative to function application;
<body>)	<var-bindings> is a list of (variable S-expression)
	pairs and the body is a list of S-expressions; let
	returns the value of last S-expression in <body>

Other

(quote <item>)	return <item> without evaluating it
(display <expr>)	print the value of <expr> and return that value
(newline)	print a carriage return and return ( )

Figure 6.1: Built-in Functions of Scheme

The symbols #t and #f represent the constant values true and false. Anonymous functions can be defined as **lambda** expressions. The **let** expression is a variant of function application. If we add an equality predicate **equal?** and an atom-testing predicate **atom?**, we can write other useful list processing functions with this small set of built-in functions. In the replace function below, all occurrences of the item s are replaced with the item r at the top level in the list lst.

```
(define (replace s r lst)
   (cond  ((null? lst) lst)
          ((equal? (car lst) s) (cons r (replace s r (cdr lst))))
          (#t (cons (car lst) (replace s r (cdr lst))))))
```

In order to test the metacircular interpreter, it is necessary to have a function **quote** that returns its argument unevaluated and a function **display** that prints the value of an S-expression. The basic built-in functions of Scheme are shown in Figure 6.1.

We have elected to expand the basic interpreter by adding four arithmetic operations, **+**, **-**, *****, and **/**, so that we can execute some recursive arithmetic functions that are familiar from imperative programming.

```
(define (fibonacci n)
   (cond  ((equal? n 0) 1)
          ((equal? n 1) 1)
          (#t (+ (fibonacci (- n 1)) (fibonacci (- n 2))))))

(define (factorial n)
   (cond  ((equal? n 0) 1)
          (#t (* n (factorial (- n 1))))))
```

Metacircular Interpreter

When designing a metacircular interpreter, it is easy to confuse those expressions belonging to the language being interpreted and those belonging to the language that is doing the interpreting, since both are Scheme. To reduce confusion, we use two different fonts: san-serif font for the interpreter code and normal serif font for the interpreted language. We need three major functions to construct the interpreter:

- The top-level function **micro-rep** **r**eads an S-expression (an atom or a list), **e**valuates it, and **p**rints the result, thus the name **rep**. The function micro-rep begins with an empty environment in which all identifiers are unbound.

- The function **micro-eval** accepts an S-expression and an environment and returns the value of the S-expression in the context of the environment.

- The function **micro-apply** accepts a function name or lambda abstraction, a list of the results from evaluating the actual parameters, and an environment, and returns the result of applying the given function to the parameters in the given environment.

The functions micro-eval and micro-apply are mutually recursive and continue simplifying the task at hand until they reach a base case that can be solved directly. An environment is an association list, a list of (name value) pairs. Function definitions and variable bindings share the same association list.

The recursive function micro-rep repeatedly reads an S-expression after printing a prompt, evaluates the expression, prints the result, and calls itself with the new environment reflecting any definitions that have been elaborated. The function micro-rep handles two situations:

- If the S-expression is the atom quit, micro-rep prints "Goodbye" and exits the interpreter.

- If the S-expression is a function definition, micro-rep uses the utility function updateEnv to add the function name to the environment with an associated value, which is a lambda expression encapsulating the parameter list and the body of the function. Then micro-rep displays the name of the function.

All other S-expressions are passed on to micro-eval for evaluation. Note that atoms are recognized first so that we only apply car to a list.

```
(define (micro-rep env)
    (let ((prompt (display ">> ")) (s (read)))
        (if   (equal? s 'quit)
            (begin (newline) (display "Goodbye") (newline))
            (cond
                ((atom? s) (begin   (newline)
                                    (display (micro-eval s env))
                                    (newline)
                                    (micro-rep env)))
                ((equal? (car s) 'define)
                        (let ((newenv (updateEnv env
                                (caadr s)
                                (list 'lambda (cdadr s) (caddr s)))))
                            (begin   (newline)
                                    (display (caadr s))
                                    (newline)
                                    (micro-rep newenv))))
```

```
(#t  (begin  (newline)
             (display (micro-eval s env))
             (newline)
             (micro-rep env)))))))
```

The utility function updateEnv adds a new binding onto the front of the given environment.

```
(define (updateEnv env ide binding) (cons (list ide binding) env))
```

The function micro-eval deals with several forms of S-expressions as described below:

• An atom is either a constant (#t, #f, or a numeral) or a variable whose value is returned.

• A quoted expression is returned unevaluated.

• The function "display" evaluates its argument, displays that value, and returns the value of the expression printed.

• The function "newline" prints a carriage return.

• A conditional expression "cond" is handled separately since, unlike most other functions, its arguments are only evaluated on an "as needed" basis.

• A "let" expression augments the environment with the new variable bindings and evaluates the body of the let in this environment.

All other S-expressions are function calls to be processed by micro-apply, which receives three arguments:

• A function object, either an identifier bound to a function or a lambda expression.

• The actual parameters after their evaluation, accomplished by mapping micro-eval over the actual parameter list.

• The current environment.

We first present the main function micro-eval. The environment is an association list where the first item in each entry is an identifier. The utility function applyEnv uses the built-in function assoc to search for a given identifier in an association list and return the first list entry that matches the identifier.

```
(define (applyEnv ide env) (cadr (assoc s env)))
```

Map, which is used to evaluate a list of actual parameters, is a built-in function that applies a functional argument to every item in a list and returns the list of results.

```
(define (micro-eval s env)
    (cond ((atom? s)
                (cond  ((equal? s #t) #t)
                       ((equal? s #f) #f)
                       ((number? s) s)
                       (else (applyEnv s env))))
           ((equal? (car s) 'quote) (cadr s))
           ((equal? (car s) 'lambda) s)
           ((equal? (car s) 'display)
                (let ((expr-value (micro-eval (cadr s) env)))
                      (display expr-value) expr-value))
           ((equal? (car s) 'newline) (begin (newline) '( )))
           ((equal? (car s) 'cond) (micro-evalcond (cdr s) env))
           ((equal? (car s) 'let)
                (micro-evallet (cddr s) (micro-let-bind (cadr s) env)))
           (else (micro-apply  (car s)
                                (map (lambda (x) (micro-eval x env )) (cdr s))
                                env))))
```

Observe that the value of a lambda expression in this implementation is the lambda expression itself. So lambda expressions are handled in the same way as boolean constants and numerals, and the internal representation of a function is identical to its syntactic representation.

The arguments for the cond function are a sequence of lists, each with two parts: a predicate to be tested and an expression to be evaluated if the result of the test is non-#f (not false). These lists are evaluated sequentially until the first non-#f predicate is encountered. If all predicates return #f, cond returns #f. The function micro-evalcond is used to perform the necessary evaluations on an "as needed" basis.

```
(define (micro-evalcond clauses env)
    (cond    ((null? clauses) #f)
             ((micro-eval (caar clauses) env) (micro-eval (cadar clauses) env))
             (else (micro-evalcond (cdr clauses) env))))
```

We show two simple uses of the let expression before discussing its implementation. The following let expression returns 5:

```
(let ((a 2) (b 3)) (+ a b))
```

In the case of nested let's, the nearest local binding is used.

```
(let ((a 5))   (display a)
           (let ((a 6)) (display a))
           (display (display a)))
```

prints (all on one line)

5 *from the first display*
6 *from the second display inside the inner let*
5 *from the final nested display*
5 *from the final outer display*
5 *from the outer let.*

Notice that the value returned from the inner let is not displayed since it is not the final S-expression in the outer let. The function micro-evallet receives a list of one or more S-expressions from the body of the let and the environment constructed using micro-let-bind applied to the list of bindings. These S-expressions are evaluated until the final one is reached, and that one is returned after being evaluated.

```
(define (micro-evallet exprlist env)
    (if   (null? (cdr exprlist))
          (micro-eval (car exprlist) env)
          (begin  (micro-eval (car exprlist) env)
                  (micro-evallet (cdr exprlist) env))))
```

The environment for the execution of a let is the current environment of the let augmented by the bindings created by the list of (identifier value) pairs.

```
(define (micro-let-bind pairlist env)
    (if   (null? pairlist)
          env
          (cons (list (caar pairlist) (micro-eval (cadar pairlist) env))
                      (micro-let-bind (cdr pairlist) env))))
```

We now turn our attention to micro-apply. If the object passed to micro-apply is one of the predefined functions car, cdr, cons, atom?, null?, equal?, +, -, *, or /, the appropriate function is executed. If the object is a user-defined function, micro-apply is called recursively with the value (a lambda expression) associated with the function identifier, retrieved from the environment using micro-eval, as the first parameter. If fn, the first formal parameter of micro-apply, is not an atom, it must already be a lambda expression (an explicit check can be added if desired). Calling micro-apply with a lambda expression causes micro-eval to be called with the body of the function as the S-expression and the environment augmented by the binding of the formal parameters to the actual parameter values. This binding is accomplished by micro-bind, which accepts a list of formal parameters, a list of values, and the current environment and adds the (identifier value) pairs, one at a time, to the environment. Notice that the bindings are added to the front of the environ-

ment, which acts like a stack, so that the most recent value is always retrieved by applyEnv.

```
(define (micro-apply fn args env)
    (if   (atom? fn)
        (cond   ((equal? fn 'car) (caar args))
                ((equal? fn 'cdr) (cdar args))
                ((equal? fn 'cons) (cons (car args) (cadr args)))
                ((equal? fn 'atom?) (atom? (car args)))
                ((equal? fn 'null?) (null? (car args)))
                ((equal? fn 'equal?) (equal? (car args) (cadr args)))
                ((equal? fn '+) (+ (car args) (cadr args)))
                ((equal? fn '-) (- (car args) (cadr args)))
                ((equal? fn '*) (* (car args) (cadr args)))
                ((equal? fn '/) (/ (car args) (cadr args)))
                (else (micro-apply (micro-eval fn env) args env)))
        (micro-eval (caddr fn) (micro-bind (cadr fn) args env))))

(define (micro-bind key-list value-list env)
    (if   (or (null? key-list) (null? value-list))
        env
        (cons (list (car key-list) (car value-list))
                        (micro-bind (cdr key-list) (cdr value-list) env))))
```

This completes the code for our interpreter, which is initiated by entering

(micro-rep '( )).

Running the Interpreter

To illustrate its operation, we trace the interpretation of a simple user-defined function "first" that is a renaming of the built-in function car.

>> (define (first lst) (car lst))

first

Now consider the execution of the function call:

>> (first (quote (a b c)))

a

This S-expression is not dealt with by micro-eval, but is passed to micro-apply
with three arguments:

first	a function identifier
((a b c))	evaluation of the actual parameters
((first (lambda (lst) (car lst))))	the current environment

The evaluation of the actual parameters results from mapping micro-eval onto the actual parameter list. In this case, the only actual parameter is an expression that calls the function quote, which is handled by micro-eval directly.

Since micro-apply does not recognize the object first, it appeals to micro-eval to evaluate first. So micro-eval looks up a value for first in the environment and returns a lambda expression to micro-apply, which then calls itself recursively with the following arguments:

((lambda (lst) (car lst)))	a function object
((a b c))	evaluation of the actual parameter
((first (lambda (lst) (car lst))))	the current environment

Since the object is not an atom, this results in a call to micro-eval, with the function body as the first parameter and the environment, augmented by the binding of formal parameters to actual values.

(car lst)	S-expression to be evaluated
((lst (a b c))	
(first (lambda (lst) (car lst))))	the current environment

But micro-eval does not deal with car directly; it now calls micro-apply with the first parameter as car, the evaluation of the actual parameters, and the environment.

car	a function identifier
((a b c))	evaluation of the actual parameters
((lst (a b c))	
(first (lambda (lst) (car lst))))	the current environment

The actual parameter value is supplied when micro-eval evaluates the actual parameter lst. The function car is something that micro-apply knows how to deal with directly; it returns the caar of the arguments, namely the atom a. This result is returned through all the function calls back to micro-rep, which displays the result.

This interpreter can handle simple recursion, as illustrated by the Fibonacci and factorial functions given earlier, and it can also handle nested recursion, as illustrated by Ackermann's function shown below. We illustrate by calling Ackermann's with values 3,2 and 3,3, but with no higher values due to the explosion of recursion calls.

```
>> (define (ackermann x y)
        (cond   ((equal? x 0) (+ y 1))
                ((equal? y 0) (ackermann (- x 1) 1))
                (#t (ackermann (- x 1)  (ackermann x (- y 1))))))
ackermann

>> (ackermann 3 2)
29

>> (ackermann 3 3)
61
```

The interpreter can also deal with anonymous lambda functions, as illustrated by

```
>> ((lambda (lst) (car (cdr lst))) (quote (1 2 3)))
2
```

A let expression can also bind identifiers to lambda expressions, as illustrated by:

```
>> (let ((addition (lambda (x y) (+ x y))) (a 2) (b 3)) (addition a b))
5
```

Let expressions that are nested use the innermost binding, including lambda functions.

```
>> (let ((addb 4) (b 2))
        (let ((addb (lambda (x) (+ b x))) (b 3)) (display (addb b))))
```

6   *from the display itself*
6   *from the inner let passing its result back through the outer let.*

These values are printed on the same line.

Because of the way our interpreter works, let can be recursive (a letrec in Scheme), as illustrated by the following example:

```
>> (let ((fact (quote (lambda (n)
                  (cond   ((equal? n 0) 1)
                          (#t (* n (fact (- n 1)))))))))
        (fact 5))
120
```

We complete our discussion of the Scheme interpreter by examining two strategies for evaluating nonlocal variables. Most programming languages, including Scheme and Common Lisp, use static scoping—that is, nonlocal variables are evaluated in their lexical environment. However, our interpreter and early versions of Lisp use dynamic scoping for which nonlocal variables are evaluated in the environment of the caller. This scoping strategy results in the **funarg** (**fun**ction **arg**ument) problem, which is best illustrated by an example. We first define a function twice that has a function argument and a value. The function twice returns the application of the function argument to the value, and a second application of the function to the result.

```
>> (define (twice func val) (func (func val)))
twice
```

Suppose we define a function double that multiplies its argument times two.

```
>> (define (double n) (* n 2))
double
```

Now we call twice passing double as the function and three as the value:

```
>> (twice double 3)
12
```

The value returned is 12, as expected, since doubling 3 once gives 6, and doubling it again gives 12. We now generalize the double function by writing a function, called times, that multiplies its argument by a preset value, called val.

```
>> (define (times x)  (* x val))
```

If val is set to 2, we expect the times function to perform just like the double function. Consider the following let expression:

```
>> (let ((val 2)) (twice times 3))
27
```

Surprisingly, the value of 27 is returned rather than the value 12. To understand what is happening, we must carefully examine the environment at each step of execution. At the time of the function call the environment has three bindings:

```
((times (lambda (x) (* x val)))
 (twice (lambda (func val) (func (func val))))
 (val 2))
```

The execution of twice adds its parameter bindings to the environment before executing the body of the function.

```
((val 3)
 (func times)
 (times (lambda (x) (* x val)))
 (twice (lambda (func val) (func (func val))))
 (val 2))
```

Now we see the source of difficulty; when we start executing the function body for times and it fetches a value for val, it fetches 3 instead of 2. So, times became a tripling function, and tripling 3 twice gives 27. Once the execution of the function is completed, all parameter bindings disappear from the environment.

Although dynamic scoping is easy to implement, unexpected results, as illustrated above, have led designers of modern programming languages to abandon this approach. The exercises suggest some modifications to the interpreter so that it implements static scoping.

Exercises

1. Given the following function definition
    ```
    >> (define (even n)
              (cond  ((equal? n (* (/ n 2) 2)) #t)
                     (#t #f))),
    ```

    trace the evaluation of the function call:

    ```
    >> (even 3)
    ```

2. Add predicates to the interpreter for the five arithmetic relational operations: <, <=, =, >, and >=.

3. Add the functions "add1" and "sub1" to the interpreter.

4. Add the functions (actually special forms since they do not always evaluate all of their parameters) "if", "and", and "or" to the interpreter.

5. Modify the interpreter to save the environment of function definition at the time of a define. Make sure that this new interpreter solves the funarg problem and gives the expected results, as shown by the following sequence of S-expressions:

>> (define (twice func val) (func (func val)))

>> (define (times x) (* x val))

>> (let ((val 2)) (twice times 3))   ; returns 12

>> (let ((val 4)) (twice times 3))   ; returns 48

6. Implement the predicate zero? and change cond so that an else clause is allowed. Test the resulting implementation by applying these functions:

>> (define (even n)
            (cond ((zero? n) #t)
                   (else (odd (- n 1))))))

>> (define (odd n)
            (cond ((zero? n) #f)
                   (else (even (- n 1))))))

7. The implementation of Scheme in this section allows the definition only of functions using a particular format. Augment the implementation so that the following definitions are also allowed:

>> (define n 55)

>> (define map (lambda (fn lst)
                (cond ((null? lst) (quote ()))
                       (#t (cons (fn (car lst)) (map fn (cdr lst)))))))

6.2 SELF-DEFINITION OF PROLOG

We first build a very simple meta-interpreter in Prolog that handles only the conjunction of goals and the chaining goals. A goal succeeds for one of three reasons:

1. The goal is true.

2. The goal is a conjunction and both conjuncts are true.

3. The goal is the head of a clause whose body is true.

All other goals fail. A predefined Prolog predicate clause searches the user database for a clause whose head matches the first argument; the body of the clause is returned as the second argument.

prove(true).

prove((Goal1, Goal2)) :- prove(Goal1), prove(Goal2).

prove(Goal) :- clause(Goal, Body), prove(Body).

prove(Goal) :- fail.

We define a membership function, called memb so it will not conflict with any built-in membership operation.

memb(X,[X|Rest]).
memb(X,[Y|Rest]) :- memb(X,Rest).

Here is the result of the testing:

```
:- prove((memb(X,[a,b,c]),memb(X,[b,c,d]))).
X = b ;     % semicolon requests the next answer, if any
X = c ;
no
:- prove((memb(X,[a,b,c]),memb(X,[d,e,f]))).
no
:- prove(((memb(X,[a,b,c]),memb(X,[b,c,d])),memb(X,[c,d,e]))).
X = c ;
no
```

These results are correct, but they provide little insight into how they are obtained. We can overcome this problem by returning a "proof tree" for each clause that succeeds. The proof for true is simply true, the proof of a conjunction of goals is a conjunction of the individual proofs, and a proof of a clause whose head is true because the body is true will be represented as "Goal<==Proof". We introduce a new infix binary operator <== for this purpose. The proof tree for failure is simply fail.

:- op(500,xfy,<==).

prove(true, true).

prove((Goal1, Goal2),(Proof1, Proof2)) :-   prove(Goal1,Proof1),
                                            prove(Goal2,Proof2).

prove(Goal, Goal<==Proof) :- clause(Goal, Body), prove(Body, Proof).

prove(Goal,fail) :- fail.

Here are the results of our test cases:

```
:- prove((memb(X,[a,b,c]),memb(X,[b,c,d])),Proof).
X = b
Proof = memb(b,[a,b,c])<==memb(b,[b,c])<==true,
memb(b,[b,c,d])<==true

:- prove((memb(X,[a,b,c]),memb(X,[d,e,f])), Proof).
no

:- prove(((memb(X,[a,b,c]),memb(X,[b,c,d])),
                          memb(X,[c,d,e])), Proof).
X = c
Proof =
(memb(c,[a,b,c])<==memb(c,[b,c])<==memb(c,[c])<==true,
         memb(c,[b,c,d])<==memb(c,[c,d])<==true),
         memb(c,[c,d,e])<==true
```

Displaying Failure

We still have no display for the second test where the proof fails. Another alternative is to add a trace facility to show each step in a proof, whether it succeeds or fails. This capability can be added to the second version of the meta-interpreter, but for simplicity we return to the first version of the program and add a tracing facility. Every time we chain a rule from a goal to a body, we will indent the trace two spaces. Therefore we add an argument that provides the level of indentation. This argument is initialized to zero and is incremented by two every time we prove a clause from its body.

Before the application of a user-defined rule, we print "Call: " and the goal. If we exit from the body of the goal successfully, we print "Exit: " and the goal. If a subsequent goal fails, we have to backtrack and retry a goal that previously succeeded. We add a predicate retry that is true the first time it is called but prints "Retry: ", the goal, and fails on subsequent calls. When a goal fails, "Fail: " and the goal are printed. Here is the meta-interpreter implementing these changes.

```
    prove(Goal) :- prove(Goal, 0).

    prove(true, _).

    prove((Goal1, Goal2), Level) :- prove(Goal1, Level), prove(Goal2, Level).

    prove(Goal, Level) :-  tab(Level), write('Call: '), write(Goal), nl,
                           clause(Goal, Body),
                           NewLevel is Level + 2,
                           prove(Body, NewLevel),
                           tab(Level), write('Exit: '), write(Goal), nl,
                           retry(Goal, Level).
```

```
prove(Goal, Level) :- tab(Level), write('Fail: '), write(Goal), nl, fail.
retry(Goal, Level) :-  true ;
                       tab(Level), write('Retry: '), write(Goal), nl,
                       fail.
```

In the first test we call prove with the query

prove((memb(X,[a,b,c]),memb(X,[b,c,d])))).

X first binds to a, but this fails for the second list. The predicate memb is retried for the first list and X binds to b. This succeeds for the second list, so the binding of X to b succeeds for both clauses.

```
Call: memb(_483,[a,b,c])
Exit: memb(a,[a,b,c])
Call: memb(a,[b,c,d])
  Call: memb(a,[c,d])
    Call: memb(a,[d])
      Call: memb(a,[])
      Fail: memb(a,[])
    Fail: memb(a,[d])
  Fail: memb(a,[c,d])
Fail: memb(a,[b,c,d])
Retry: memb(a,[a,b,c])
  Call: memb(_483,[b,c])
  Exit: memb(b,[b,c])
Exit: memb(b,[a,b,c])
Call: memb(b,[b,c,d])
Exit: memb(b,[b,c,d])
```

Consider the second query, which has no solution.

prove((memb(X,[a,b,c]),memb(X,[d,e,f])))).

X binds to a, then b, then c, all of which fail to be found in the second list. When the program backtracks to find any other bindings for X in the first list, it fails and the entire proof thus fails.

```
Call: memb(_483,[a,b,c])
Exit: memb(a,[a,b,c])
Call: memb(a,[d,e,f])
  Call: memb(a,[e,f])
    Call: memb(a,[f])
      Call: memb(a,[])
      Fail: memb(a,[])
    Fail: memb(a,[f])
  Fail: memb(a,[e,f])
```

```
Fail: memb(a,[d,e,f])
Retry: memb(a,[a,b,c])
  Call: memb(_483,[b,c])
  Exit: memb(b,[b,c])
Exit: memb(b,[a,b,c])
Call: memb(b,[d,e,f])
  Call: memb(b,[e,f])
    Call: memb(b,[f])
       Call: memb(b,[])
       Fail: memb(b,[])
    Fail: memb(b,[f])
  Fail: memb(b,[e,f])
Fail: memb(b,[d,e,f])
Retry: memb(b,[a,b,c])
  Retry: memb(b,[b,c])
    Call: memb(_483,[c])
    Exit: memb(c,[c])
  Exit: memb(c,[b,c])
Exit: memb(c,[a,b,c])
Call: memb(c,[d,e,f])
  Call: memb(c,[e,f])
    Call: memb(c,[f])
       Call: memb(c,[])
       Fail: memb(c,[])
    Fail: memb(c,[f])
  Fail: memb(c,[e,f])
Fail: memb(c,[d,e,f])
Retry: memb(c,[a,b,c])
  Retry: memb(c,[b,c])
    Retry: memb(c,[c])
       Call: memb(_483,[])
       Fail: memb(_483,[])
    Fail: memb(_483,[c])
  Fail: memb(_483,[b,c])
Fail: memb(_483,[a,b,c])
```

The final query succeeds.

> **prove(((memb(X,[a,b,c]),memb(X,[b,c,d])),memb(X,[c,d,e]))).**

X first binds to a, but this fails for the second list. Backtracking to the first list, X binds to b, which succeeds for the second list but fails for the third list. There are no other occurrences of b in the second list, so the program backtracks to the first list and binds X to c. This succeeds for the second and third lists.

```
Call: memb(_486,[a,b,c])
Exit: memb(a,[a,b,c])
Call: memb(a,[b,c,d])
  Call: memb(a,[c,d])
    Call: memb(a,[d])
      Call: memb(a,[])
      Fail: memb(a,[])
    Fail: memb(a,[d])
  Fail: memb(a,[c,d])
Fail: memb(a,[b,c,d])
Retry: memb(a,[a,b,c])
  Call: memb(_486,[b,c])
  Exit: memb(b,[b,c])
Exit: memb(b,[a,b,c])
Call: memb(b,[b,c,d])
Exit: memb(b,[b,c,d])
Call: memb(b,[c,d,e])
  Call: memb(b,[d,e])
    Call: memb(b,[e])
      Call: memb(b,[])
      Fail: memb(b,[])
    Fail: memb(b,[e])
  Fail: memb(b,[d,e])
Fail: memb(b,[c,d,e])
Retry: memb(b,[b,c,d])
  Call: memb(b,[c,d])
    Call: memb(b,[d])
      Call: memb(b,[])
      Fail: memb(b,[])
    Fail: memb(b,[d])
  Fail: memb(b,[c,d])
Fail: memb(b,[b,c,d])
Retry: memb(b,[a,b,c])
  Retry: memb(b,[b,c])
    Call: memb(_486,[c])
    Exit: memb(c,[c])
  Exit: memb(c,[b,c])
Exit: memb(c,[a,b,c])
Call: memb(c,[b,c,d])
  Call: memb(c,[c,d])
  Exit: memb(c,[c,d])
Exit: memb(c,[b,c,d])
```

```
Call: memb(c,[c,d,e])
Exit: memb(c,[c,d,e])
```

Other improvements can be made to the interpreter, but these are left as exercises. The interpreter works only with user-defined clauses. This limitation is fairly easy to overcome by adding *call* for built-in clauses. There is no provision for disjunction. Perhaps the most difficult problem to handle is the addition of the cut clause to control the underlying search mechanism. Peter Ross discusses some alternatives that can handle the cut correctly. (See the further readings at the end of this chapter).

Our Prolog interpreter written in Prolog does not explicitly implement the built-in backtracking of Prolog or show the unification process. The trace facility allows us to follow the backtracking but does not illustrate its implementation. It is also possible to develop a simple Prolog interpreter written in Lisp where both the backtracking and unification are explicit. The interested reader may consult the references at the end of the chapter.

Exercises

1. Add a rule for prove that handles built-in predicates correctly by using call. Be careful to ensure that user-defined clauses are not called twice.

2. Add the capability to handle the disjunction of clauses correctly.

3. Research the implementation of the cut clause (see the references). Implement cut in the meta-interpreter.

4. Investigate the implementation of a unification function in Lisp or Scheme. Write and test your function.

5. Use your unification function from exercise 4 to build a logic interpreter in Lisp or Scheme.

6.3 **FURTHER READING**

The self-definition of a programming language is a special case of a more general technique: using a high-level programming language as a metalanguage for defining the semantics of a high-level programming language. The use of programming languages as metalanguages is discussed in [Pagan76] and [Anderson76]. [Pagan81] gives a definition of the minilanguage Pam using Algol68 as a metalanguage.

Lisp was developed during the late 1950s; the seminal publication was [McCarthy60]. Our self-definition of Scheme using Scheme, a variant of Lisp, is similar to the original presentation of a Lisp interpreter written in Lisp given in [McCarthy65b]. Other versions appear in many textbooks on programming languages. The use of Scheme as a metalanguage to define a logic interpreter is described in [Abelson85]. Other good references for the Scheme programing language include [Springer89] and [Dybvig87].

We present Prolog as a metalanguage throughout this text. A variety of issues dealing with the implementation of Prolog are discussed in [Campbell84]. [Nillson84] presents a very concise interpreter for Prolog written in Lisp. Our treatment of a Prolog interpreter written in Prolog closely follows the more detailed presentation by [Ross89].

Chapter 7
TRANSLATIONAL SEMANTICS

The previous chapter provided a definition of the semantics of a programming language in terms of the programming language itself. The primary example was based on a Lisp interpreter programmed in Lisp. Although this is an interesting academic exercise, it has little practical importance. However, programming language compilers are an integral part of the study of computer science. Compilers perform a translation of a high-level language into a low-level language. Executing this target program on a computer captures the semantics of the program in a high-level language.

In Chapter 3 we investigated the use of attribute grammars for context checking. These same techniques can be used to translate Wren into a machine-oriented language. Translational semantics is based on two notions:

1. The semantics of a programming language can be preserved when the language is translated into another form, called the target language.

2. The target language can be defined by a small number of primitive constructs that are closely related to an actual or a hypothetical machine architecture.

We first introduce the target language and then build an attribute grammar that is capable of translating a Wren program into this language. Finally, we implement this attribute grammar in the laboratory.

7.1 CONCEPTS AND EXAMPLES

In order to focus on issues relating to the translation process, we assume that the Wren program being translated obeys the context-sensitive conditions for the language as well as the context-free grammar. We parse the declaration section to ensure that the BNF is correct, but no attributes are associated with the declaration section. Context checking can be combined with code generation in a single attribute grammar, but we leave this task unfinished at this time.

The machine code is based on a primitive architecture with a single accumulator (Acc) and a memory addressable with symbolic labels and capable of holding integer values. In this translation, Boolean values are simulated by integers. We use names to indicate symbolic locations. The hypothetical machine has a load/store architecture:

- The LOAD instruction copies a value from a named location, whose value is not changed, to the accumulator, whose old value is overwritten, or transfers an integer constant into the accumulator.

- The STO instruction copies the value of the accumulator, whose value is not changed, to a named location, whose previous value is overwritten.

The target language has two input/output commands:

- GET transfers an integer value from the input device to the named location.

- PUT transfers the value stored at the named location to the output device.

There are four arithmetic operations—ADD, SUB, MULT and DIV—and three logical operations—AND, OR, and NOT. For the binary operations, the first operand is the current accumulator value and the second operand is specified in the instruction itself. The second operand can be either the contents of a named location or an integer constant. For Boolean values, the integer 1 is used to represent true and the integer 0 to represent false. The result of an operation is placed in the accumulator. The NOT operation has no argument; it simply inverts the 0 or 1 in the accumulator.

The target language contains one unconditional jump J and one conditional jump JF where the conditional jump is executed if the value in the accumulator is false (equal to zero). The argument of a jump instruction is a label instruction. For example, J L3 means to jump unconditionally to label L3, which appears in an instruction of the form L3 LABEL. The label instruction has no operand.

There are six test instructions; they test the value of the accumulator relative to zero. For example, TSTEQ tests whether the accumulator is equal to zero. The test instructions are destructive in the sense that the value in the accumulator is replaced by a 1 if the test is true and a 0 if the test is false. We will find this approach to be convenient when processing Boolean expressions. The five other test instructions are: TSTLT (less than zero), TSTLE (less than or equal zero), TSTNE (not equal zero), TSTGE (greater than or equal zero), and TSTGT (greater than zero). The NO-OP instruction performs no operation. Finally, the target language includes a HALT instruction. The complete instruction set is shown in Figure 7.1.

LOAD	<name> or <const>	Load accumulator from named
		location or load constant value
STO	<name>	Store accumulator to named location
GET	<name>	Input value to named location
PUT	<name>	Output value from named location
ADD	<name> or <const>	Acc ← Acc + <operand>
SUB	<name> or <const>	Acc ← Acc – <operand>
MULT	<name> or <const>	Acc ← Acc • <operand>
DIV	<name> or <const>	Acc ← Acc / <operand>
AND	<name> or 0 or 1	Acc ← Acc and <operand>
OR	<name> or 0 or 1	Acc ← Acc or <operand>
NOT		Acc ← not Acc
J	<label>	Jump unconditionally
JF	<label>	Jump on false (Acc = 0)
LABEL		Label instruction
TSTLT		Test if Acc **L**ess **T**han zero
TSTLE		Test if Acc **L**ess than or **E**qual zero
TSTNE		Test if Acc **N**ot **E**qual zero
TSTEQ		Test if Acc **EQ**ual zero
TSTGE		Test if Acc **G**reater than or **E**qual zero
TSTGT		Test if Acc **G**reater **T**han zero
NO-OP		No operation
HALT		Halt execution

Figure 7.1: Machine-oriented Target Language

A Program Translation

Consider a greatest common divisor (gcd) program:

```
program gcd is
    var m,n : integer;
begin
    read m; read n;
    while m < > n do
            if m < n  then n := n – m
                    else m := m – n
            end if
    end while;
    write m
end
```

This program translates into the following object code:

```
    GET    M
    GET    N
L1  LABEL
    LOAD   M
```

```
        SUB    N
        TSTNE
        JF     L2
        LOAD   M
        SUB    N
        TSTLT
        JF     L3
        LOAD   N
        SUB    M
        STO    N
        J      L4
L3   LABEL
        LOAD   M
        SUB    N
        STO    M
L4   LABEL
        J      L1
L2   LABEL
        LOAD   M
        STO    T1
        PUT    T1
        HALT
```

In Chapter 3 we saw that the semantics of a binary numeral can be expressed as the final value of a synthesized attribute at the root of the parse tree. We use the same approach here: The synthesized attribute *Code* integrates the pieces of object code in the target language from lower levels in the tree, and the final value at the root of the tree expresses the semantics of the Wren program in the form of its translation into object code in the target language.

We begin by discussing the constraints imposed by labels and temporary locations in the target language. Labels throughout the object program must be unique. With nested control structures, the labels do not appear in order, as we see from the sample program above. The labels L1 and L2 are associated with the **while** loop, the outer control structure, and the labels L3 and L4 are associated with the nested **if** structure. We use both an inherited attribute *InhLabel* and a synthesized attribute *SynLabel* working together to thread the current label value throughout the derivation tree.

The intermediate language uses temporary named locations, labeled T1, T2, T3, and so forth, to evaluate Boolean and arithmetic expressions. For our purposes, it is immaterial if these named locations are thought of as registers or as an area of main memory. One location must not be used for two different purposes at the same time within a subexpression, but it can be reused once the final value for a subexpression has been processed. Since temporary locations need not be unique throughout the program, there is no need to maintain a synthesized attribute returning the last location used. However, we do need an inherited attribute, called *Temp*, that transfers the starting temporary location value to subexpressions.

Exercises

1. Generate object code that is semantically equivalent to the following Wren program that multiplies two numbers.

   program multiply **is**
     var m, n, product : **integer**;
   begin
     read m; **read** n;
     product := 0;
     while n > 0 **do**
        if 2 * (n / 2) < > n **then**   (* if n is odd *)
              product := product + m
        end if;
        m := 2 * m;
        n := n / 2
     end while;
     write product
   end

2. Generate object code that evaluates the following expression:
   2 * (x – 1) * (y / 4) – (12 * z + y)

7.2 ATTRIBUTE GRAMMAR CODE GENERATION

Figure 7.2 gives all of the attributes and the associated value types necessary to develop this attribute grammar. The nonterminals <variable>, <identifier>, <letter>, <numeral>, and <digit> all have an associated *Name* attribute that synthesizes an internal representation of identifier names and of base-ten numerals, as was done in the attribute grammar for Wren in Chapter 3. Since the source language uses lowercase letters as variable names, and the target language uses uppercase, we make a conversion between the two in the production for <letter>.

Attribute	Value
Name	Sequences of letters and/or digits
Temp	Natural numbers (integers ≥ 0)
SynLabel	Natural numbers
InhLabel	Natural numbers
OpCode	ADD, SUB, MULT, DIV
TestCode	TSTLT, TSTLE, TSTNE, TSTEQ, TSTGE, TSTGT
Code	Sequence of instructions of the following forms:
	(Load/Store, Name) as in (LOAD, X)
	(Input/Output, Name) as in (GET, X)
	(OpCode, Name) as in (ADD, 5)
	(BooleanOp, Name) as in (AND, T2)
	(Jump, Name) as in (J, L2)
	(Name, LABEL) as in (L3, LABEL)
	TestCode as in TSTNE
	NOT, NO-OP, or HALT

Figure 7.2: Attributes and Values

<variable> ::= <identifier>

      Name(<variable>) ← *Name*(<identifier>)

<identifier> ::=

      <letter>

      Name(<identifier>) ← *Name*(<letter>)

  | <identifier>$_2$ <letter>

      Name(<identifier>) ← concat(*Name*(<identifier>$_2$),*Name*(<letter>))

  | <identifier>$_2$ <digit>

      Name(<identifier>) ← concat(*Name*(<identifier>$_2$),*Name*(<digit>))

<letter> ::=

      a

      Name(<letter>) ← 'A'

        :   :   :

  | **z**

      Name(<letter>) ← 'Z'

<numeral> ::= <digit>

      Name(<numeral>) ← *Name*(<digit>)

  | <numeral>$_2$ <digit>

      Name(<numeral>) ← concat(*Name*(<numeral>$_2$),*Name*(<digit>))

<digit> ::=

   0

     Name(<digit>) ← '0'

       :   :   :

  | **9**

     Name(<digit>) ← '9'

Expressions

We now turn our attention to the code generation for binary arithmetic expressions. Consider the general form

<left operand>   <operator>   <right operand>

where the left and right operands may be simple, as in the case of a variable name or numeral, or compound, as in the case of another operation or a parenthesized expression. The general case can be handled by the following code sequence, assuming that n is the value of the inherited attribute *Temp*:

```
code for <left operand>
STO        T<n+1>              (for example, if n = 0, this is T1)
code for <right operand>
STO        T<n+2>              (for example, if n = 0, this is T2)
LOAD       T<n+1>
OpCode     T<n+2>
```

In this situation, OpCode is determined by the <operator>. The inherited value for *Temp* is passed to the left operand while that value, incremented by one, is passed to the right operand, since the location T<n+1> is not available for use when generating code for the right operand. In general, the value of *Temp* represents the highest value used so far in the current subexpression.

As an example of translating expressions, consider the compound expression

    x / (y − 5) * (z + 2 * y).

The expression expands to <term> that then expands to <term> <strong op> <element>. So, assuming *Temp* initially equals zero, the code expansion becomes

```
code for x/(y − 5)
STO    T1
code for (z + 2 * y)
STO    T2
LOAD   T1
MULT   T2
```

We show object code in bold when it first appears. *Temp* is passed unchanged to the code for the left operand and is incremented by 1 and passed to the right operand. When we expand the code for x/(y – 5) we have

```
code for x
STO    T1
code for (y – 5)
STO    T2
LOAD   T1
DIV    T2
STO    T1
code for (z + 2 * y)
STO    T2
LOAD   T1
MULT   T2
```

The code for x is LOAD X, so we proceed with the expansion of (y – 5) with *Temp* equal to 1, obtaining

```
LOAD   X
STO    T1
code for y
STO    T2
code for 5
STO    T3
LOAD   T2
SUB    T3
STO    T2
LOAD   T1
DIV    T2
STO    T1
code for (z + 2 * y)
STO    T2
LOAD   T1
MULT   T2
```

The code for y and for 5 is LOAD Y and LOAD 5, respectively. We now need to expand the code for (z + 2 * y) with *Temp* equal to 1.

```
LOAD   X
STO    T1
LOAD   Y
STO    T2
LOAD   5
```

```
STO    T3
LOAD   T2
SUB    T3
STO    T2
LOAD   T1
DIV    T2
STO    T1
```
code for z
```
STO    T2
```
code for 2 * y
```
STO    T3
LOAD   T2
ADD    T3
STO    T2
LOAD   T1
MULT   T2
```

The code for z is LOAD Z. When we expand the code for 2 * y, we use a *Temp* value of 2, the inherited value incremented by 1. We complete the code by using LOAD 2 and LOAD Y as the code for 2 and code for y, respectively. The complete code expansion is shown below.

```
LOAD   X
STO    T1
LOAD   Y
STO    T2
LOAD   5
STO    T3
LOAD   T2
SUB    T3
STO    T2
LOAD   T1
DIV    T2
STO    T1
LOAD   Z
STO    T2
LOAD   2
STO    T3
LOAD   Y
STO    T4
LOAD   T3
MULT   T4
```

```
STO    T3
LOAD   T2
ADD    T3
STO    T2
LOAD   T1
MULT   T2
```

If the result of this expression, which is currently in the accumulator, is to be saved, one more store instruction will be needed. The code generated in this way is correct but very lengthy. A human hand-generating code for the same expression can do much better. Working "from the inside out" and taking advantage of known arithmetic properties, such as the commutativity of addition, a human might produce the following code sequence:

```
LOAD   Y
SUB    5
STO    T1          -- T1 contains y – 5
LOAD   X
DIV    T1
STO    T1          -- T1 contains x/(y – 5)
LOAD   2
MULT   Y
ADD    Z
MULT   T1          -- accumulator contains x / (y – 5) * (z + 2 * y)
```

Only ten instructions and one temporary location are needed, as compared with 26 instructions and four temporary locations for the code developed previously. We do not attempt to match hand-compiled code generated by a human for efficiency; however, there is one small optimization we can make that improves the code generation. Consider the special case

<left operand>   <operator>   <variable or numeral>

If we follow the previous scheme, the generated code is

```
code for <left operand>
STO        T<n+1>
code for <variable or numeral>
STO        T<n+2>
LOAD       T<n+1>
OpCode   T<n+2>
```

When the second operand is a variable or numeral, this code can be optimized to

```
code for <left operand>
OpCode     <variable or numeral>
```

This saves four instructions and two temporary locations. This code pattern occurs twice in the expression we were evaluating. The code for y−5

```
LOAD  Y        becomes    LOAD  Y
STO   T2                  SUB   5
LOAD  5
STO   T3
LOAD  T2
SUB   T3
```

The code for 2*y

```
LOAD  2        becomes    LOAD  2
STO   T3                  MULT  Y
LOAD  Y
STO   T4
LOAD  T3
MULT  T4
```

When this one optimization technique is used, the code for the expression is reduced to 18 instructions and three temporary locations, as shown below.

```
LOAD  X
STO   T1
LOAD  Y
SUB   5
STO   T2
LOAD  T1
DIV   T2
STO   T1
LOAD  Z
STO   T2
LOAD  2
MULT  Y
STO   T3
LOAD  T2
ADD   T3
STO   T2
LOAD  T1
MULT  T2
```

Code optimization, a major topic in compiler theory, is very complex and occurs at many levels. A detailed discussion is beyond the scope of this text, and we will do no further optimization beyond this one technique.

We now turn our attention to the attribute grammar itself. Four of the attributes listed in Figure 7.2 are utilized in generating the code for arithmetic expressions: *Name*, *OpCode*, *Code*, and *Temp*.

First consider the attribute grammar for integer expression.

```
<integer expr> ::=
      <term>
         Code(<integer expr>) ← Code(<term>)
         Temp(<term>) ← Temp(<integer expr>)
   | <integer expr>₂ <weak op> <term>
         Code(<integer expr>) ←
                  concat(Code(<integer expr>₂),
                           optimize(Code(<term>),Temp(<integer expr>),
                                                OpCode(<weak op>)))
         Temp(<integer expr>₂) ← Temp(<integer expr>)
         Temp(<term>) ← Temp(<integer expr>)+1

<weak op> ::=
      +
         OpCode(<weak op>) ← ADD
   | −
         OpCode(<weak op>) ← SUB
```

Temp is inherited, as expected, *OpCode* synthesizes the appropriate object code operation, and *Code* is synthesized, as previously described. However, we need to say something about the utility procedure "optimize".

```
optimize(code, temp, opcode) =
      if length(code) = 1 then                    -- a variable or numeral
                     [(opcode, secondField(first(code)))]
                else
                     concat([(STO, temporary(temp+1))],
                            code,
                            [(STO, temporary(temp+2))],
                            [(LOAD, temporary(temp+1))],
                            [(opcode, temporary(temp+2))])
```

If the code for the second operand is a single item, indicating either a variable or a numeral, we generate a single instruction, the appropriate operation with that operand. Otherwise, we generate the more lengthy set of instructions and use two temporary locations. The utility procedure "temporary" accepts an integer argument and produces the corresponding temporary symbol as a string. This requires another utility function "string" to convert an integer into the corresponding base-ten numeral.

temporary(integer) = concat('T',string(integer))

string(n) = if n = 0 then '0'

$\qquad$: $\qquad$:

$\qquad$ else if n = 9 then '9'

$\qquad$ else concat(string(n/10), string(n mod 10))

The code for <term> and <element> is very similar and will be given later in Figure 7.8. The sharp-eyed reader may notice that we have ignored negation as one of the alternatives for <element>. Developing this portion of the attribute grammar is left as an exercise. The complete, decorated parse tree for x / (y – 5) * (z + 2 * y) is shown in Figure 7.3 where we have used an infix operator @ to represent concatenation.

The code for <boolean expr> is similar to integer expression, except that the single operator is **or**. Since the Boolean operations are commutative, there is no need for a second temporary location. A Boolean term is similar to an integer term. In <boolean element> the constants **false** and **true** result in loading 0 and 1, respectively. Variables and parenthesized Boolean expressions are handled as expected. A <comparison> is another alternative for a Boolean element; we will discuss comparisons in a moment. The **not** operation results in the NOT instruction being appended after the code for the Boolean expression being negated. The complete code for Boolean expressions is given in Figure 7.8.

A comparison has the general form

$\qquad$ <integer expr>$_1$ <relation> <integer expr>$_2$

Since the target language has test instructions based on comparisons with zero, we rewrite the comparison as

$\qquad$ <integer expr>$_1$ – <integer expr>$_2$ <relation> 0

The generated code will be the code defined for the left side expression minus the right side expression followed by the test instruction. This code will be optimized if the right side expression is a constant or a variable. Here is an example with code optimization: x < y translates into

```
LOAD  X
SUB   Y
TSTLT
```

If the right side expression is complex, the code will not be optimized, as seen by x >= 2 * y, which translates to

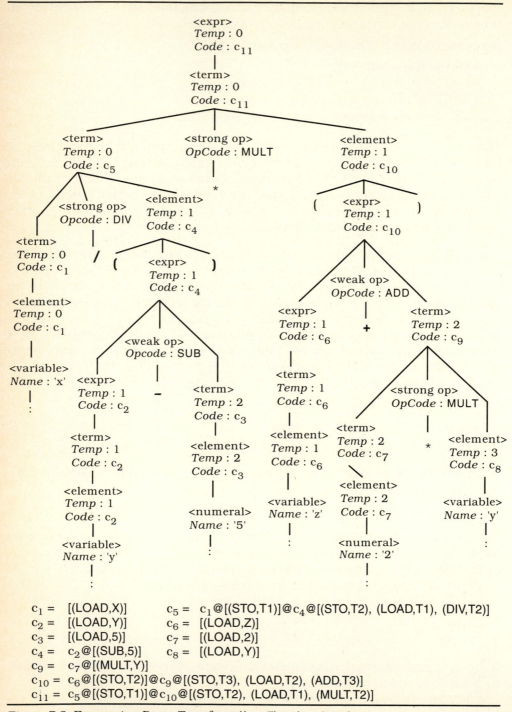

$c_1 = $ [(LOAD,X)] $c_5 = $ c_1@[(STO,T1)]@c_4@[(STO,T2), (LOAD,T1), (DIV,T2)]
$c_2 = $ [(LOAD,Y)] $c_6 = $ [(LOAD,Z)]
$c_3 = $ [(LOAD,5)] $c_7 = $ [(LOAD,2)]
$c_4 = $ c_2@[(SUB,5)] $c_8 = $ [(LOAD,Y)]
$c_9 = $ c_7@[(MULT,Y)]
$c_{10} = $ c_6@[(STO,T2)]@c_9@[(STO,T3), (LOAD,T2), (ADD,T3)]
$c_{11} = $ c_5@[(STO,T1)]@c_{10}@[(STO,T2), (LOAD,T1), (MULT,T2)]

Figure 7.3: Expression Parse Tree for x/(y − 5) * (z + 2 * y)

```
LOAD   X
STO    T1
LOAD   2
MULT   Y
STO    T2
LOAD   T1
SUB    T2
TSTGE
```

There is a direct correspondence between the comparison operators in Wren and the test instructions in the target language:

<	becomes	TSTLT
<=	becomes	TSTLE
=	becomes	TSTEQ
>	becomes	TSTGT
>=	becomes	TSTGE
<>	becomes	TSTNE.

The following attribute grammar rules follow directly from this discussion.

<comparison> ::= <integer expr>$_1$ <relation> <integer expr>$_2$

    Code(<comparison>) ← concat(*Code*(<integer expr>$_1$),

        optimize(*Code*(<integer expr>$_1$),*Temp*(<comparison>),SUB),

        TestCode(<relation>))

    Temp(<integer expr>$_1$) ← *Temp*(<comparison>)

    Temp(<integer expr>$_2$) ← *Temp*(<comparison>)+1

<relation> ::=

  >

    TestCode(<relation>) ← TSTGT

  | >=

    TestCode(<relation>) ← TSTGE

  | <>

    TestCode(<relation>) ← TSTNE

  | =

    TestCode(<relation>) ← TSTEQ

  | <=

    TestCode(<relation>) ← TSTLE

  | <

    TestCode(<relation>) ← TSTLT

Commands

The next major task is the generation of code for the commands in Wren. As mentioned earlier, all labeled locations must be unique throughout the object code. We use two attributes, *InhLabel* and *SynLabel*, to thread the current label value throughout the tree. The <program> node concatenates HALT to the code generated by <block>. The program identifier provides source code documentation but does not contribute to the code generation.

<program> ::= **program** <identifier> **is** <block>

   Code(<program>) ← concat(*Code*(<block>), [HALT])

The code for <block> is synthesized directly from the code for <command sequence>. The inherited attributes *Temp* and *InhLabel* are initialized to zero at this time. Parsing a declaration sequence does not involve any attributes for code generation.

<block> ::= <declaration sequence> **begin** <command sequence> **end**

   Code(<block>) ← *Code*(<command sequence>)

   Temp(<command sequence>) ← 0

   InhLabel(<command sequence>) ← 0

The BNF for <declaration sequence> will be given in Figure 7.8, but no attributes are calculated for this nonterminal. The nonterminal <command sequence> allows two alternatives, a single command or a command followed by a command sequence. The first case, which describes a single command, passes the inherited attributes *Temp* and *InhLabel* to the child and synthesizes the attributes *Code* and *SynLabel* from the child. When the command sequence is a command followed by a second command sequence, the *Code* attributes from each of the children are concatenated and passed up to the parent. The inherited attribute *Temp* passes down to both children. The inherited attribute *InhLabel* is passed down to the first child <command>, synthesized out as *SynLabel*, passed over and inherited into <command sequence>$_2$. Finally *SynLabel* for <command sequence>$_2$ is passed back to <command sequence>. The attribute grammar for a command sequence appears below.

<command sequence> ::=

   <command>

   Code(<command sequence>) ← *Code*(<command>)

   Temp(<command>) ← *Temp*(<command sequence>)

   InhLabel(<command>) ← *InhLabel*(<command sequence>)

   SynLabel(<command sequence>) ← *SynLabel*(<command>)

   | <command> ; <command sequence>$_2$

   Code(<command sequence>) ←

       concat(*Code*(<command>),*Code*(<command sequence>$_2$))

   Temp(<command>) ← *Temp*(<command sequence>)

   Temp(<command sequence>$_2$) ← *Temp*(<command sequence>)

   InhLabel(<command>) ← *InhLabel*(<command sequence>)

$$InhLabel(\text{<command sequence>}_2) \leftarrow SynLabel(\text{<command>})$$
$$SynLabel(\text{<command sequence>}) \leftarrow SynLabel(\text{<command sequence>}_2)$$

This threading of label values in and out of commands is important and is illustrated in Figure 7.4.

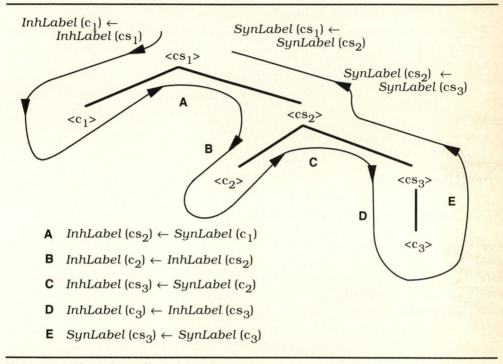

A $InhLabel(cs_2) \leftarrow SynLabel(c_1)$

B $InhLabel(c_2) \leftarrow InhLabel(cs_2)$

C $InhLabel(cs_3) \leftarrow SynLabel(c_2)$

D $InhLabel(c_3) \leftarrow InhLabel(cs_3)$

E $SynLabel(cs_3) \leftarrow SynLabel(c_3)$

Figure 7.4: Threading of Label Attributes

Some commands, such as assignment, do not affect label values while others, such as **while** or **if**, require one or two label values. The threaded label value is incremented appropriately as it passes through the tree and, in this way, it ensures that all labeled locations are unique throughout the target code.

A command takes one of seven alternatives: input, output, **skip**, assignment, a single alternative **if**, a double alternative **if**, or **while**. Four of the commands—input, output, **skip**, and assignment—do not generate code with labels, so the inherited label value *InhLabel* is "turned around" unmodified and synthesized back as *SynLabel*. The **if** and **while** commands receive the inherited attribute *InhLabel* and synthesize back a different value for *SynLabel*.

The input, output, and **skip** commands are very simple. Input of a variable generates the code of GET followed by the variable name. Output generates code for the expression, stores the reult in a temporary location, and then does a PUT of that temporary location. Finally, **skip** generates a NO-OP (no operation) instruction.

<command> ::= **read** <variable>

     Code(<command>) ← [(GET, *Name*(<variable>))]

     SynLabel(<command>) ← *InhLabel*(<command>)

<command> ::= **write** <expr>

     Code(<command>) ← concat(*Code*(<expr>),

                          [(STO, temporary(temp+1))])

                          [(PUT, temporary(temp+1))])

     Temp(<expr>) ← *Temp*(<command>)

     SynLabel(<command>) ← *InhLabel*(<command>)

<command> ::= **skip**

     Code(<command>) ← [NO-OP]

     SynLabel(<command>) ← *InhLabel*(<command>)

We have already discussed in detail the code generation for both integer and Boolean expressions. The result of an expression is left in the accumulator, so the assignment command concatenates code to store that result in the target variable name for the assignment. Since an expression may need to use temporary locations, the inherited attribute *Temp* is passed down to <expr>.

<command> ::= <variable> **:=** <expr>

     Code(<command>) ←

                  concat(*Code*(<expr>),[(STO, *Name*(<variable>))])

     Temp(<expr>) ← *Temp*(<command>)

     SynLabel(<command>) ← *InhLabel*(<command>)

The **while** command has the form

    while <boolean expr> **do** <command sequence> **end while**

where the code generated by the Boolean expression is followed by a conditional jump on false. A flow diagram of the **while** command and the corresponding code appears in Figure 7.5. We assume that the incoming value of the *InhLabel* attribute is n. The attribute grammar definition for the **while** command follows directly.

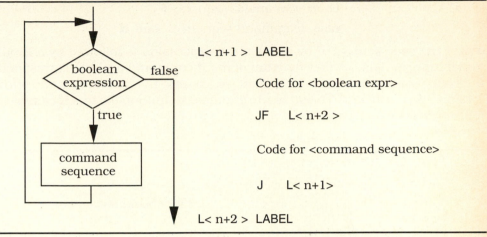

Figure 7.5: Flow Diagram and Code Generation for a **while** Command

<command> ::=

> **while** <boolean expr> **do** <command sequence> **end while**
>> *Code*(<command>) ← concat(
>>> [(label(*InhLabel*(<command>)+1),LABEL)],
>>> *Code*(<boolean expr>),
>>> [(JF,label(*InhLabel*(<command>)+2))],
>>> *Code*(<command sequence>),
>>> [(J,label(*InhLabel*(<command>)+1))],
>>> [(label(*InhLabel*(<command>)+2),LABEL)])
>>
>> *Temp*(<boolean expr>) ← *Temp*(<command>)
>> *Temp*(<command sequence>) ← *Temp*(<command>)
>> *InhLabel*(<command sequence>) ← *InhLabel*(<command>)+2
>> *SynLabel*(<command>) ← *SynLabel*(<command sequence>)

Since the **while** command itself needs two labels, *InhLabel* is incremented by two before being passed down to *InhLabel* for the command sequence, which may or may not generate new labels of its own. The *SynLabel* coming out of the command sequence is passed out of the **while** command. The inherited attribute *Temp* is passed down to both the Boolean expression and the command sequence. The utility function "label" converts an integer value into an appropriate label name.

> label(integer) = concat('L', string(integer))

The **if** command has two forms; we concentrate on the one with two alternatives

>   **if** \<boolean expr\> **then** \<command sequence\>
>
>   **else** \<command sequence\> **end if**

where the code generated by the Boolean expression is followed by a conditional jump on false. A flow diagram of the **if** command and the corresponding code appears in Figure 7.6. Again we assume the incoming value of the *InhLabel* attribute is n. The attribute grammar definition for this **if** command follows directly.

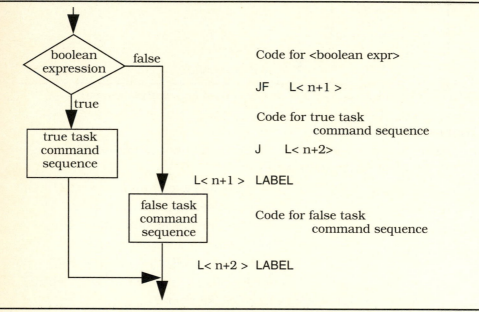

Figure 7.6: Flow Diagram and Code Generation for an **if** Command

\<command\> ::= **if** \<boolean expr\> **then** \<command sequence\>$_1$
> **else** \<command sequence\>$_2$ **end if**

$Code$(\<command\>) $\leftarrow$ concat($Code$(\<boolean expr\>),

> [JF,label($InhLabel$(\<command\>)+1))],
>
> $Code$(\<command sequence\>$_1$),
>
> [(J,label($InhLabel$(\<command\>)+2))],
>
> [(label($InhLabel$(\<command\>)+1),LABEL)],
>
> $Code$(\<command sequence\>$_2$),
>
> [(label($InhLabel$(\<command\>)+2),LABEL)])

$Temp$(\<boolean expr\>) $\leftarrow$ $Temp$(\<command\>)

$Temp$(\<command sequence\>$_1$) $\leftarrow$ $Temp$(\<command\>)

$Temp$(\<command sequence\>$_2$) $\leftarrow$ $Temp$(\<command\>)

$$InhLabel(\text{<command sequence>}_1) \leftarrow InhLabel(\text{<command>})+2$$
$$InhLabel(\text{<command sequence>}_2) \leftarrow SynLabel(\text{<command sequence>}_1)$$
$$SynLabel(\text{<command>}) \leftarrow SynLabel(\text{<command sequence>}_2)$$

Since the **if** command with two alternatives needs two labels, *InhLabel* is incremented by two before being passed down to the first command sequence. The *SynLabel* coming out of the first command sequence is threaded over as the input to *InhLabel* for the second command sequence. The *SynLabel* from the second command sequence is passed out of the **if** command. The inherited attribute *Temp* is passed down to the Boolean expression and to both command sequences.

The single alternative **if** command is simpler since it needs to generate only one label instruction. This attribute grammar clause will be presented in Figure 7.8. The attribute grammar for code generation for Wren is now complete. A summary of the synthesized and inherited attributes associated with each nonterminal is presented in Figure 7.7. The entire attribute grammar is given without interruption in Figure 7.8.

Nonterminal	Inherited Attributes	Synthesized Attributes
<program>	—	*Code*
<block>	—	*Code*
<declaration sequence>	—	—
<declaration>	—	—
<variable list>	—	—
<type>	—	—
<command sequence>	*Temp, InhLabel*	*Code, SynLabel*
<command>	*Temp, InhLabel*	*Code, SynLabel*
<expr>	*Temp*	*Code*
<integer expr>	*Temp*	*Code*
<term>	*Temp*	*Code*
<element>	*Temp*	*Code*
<weak op>	—	*OpCode*
<strong op>	—	*OpCode*
<boolean expr>	*Temp*	*Code*
<boolean term>	*Temp*	*Code*
<boolean element>	*Temp*	*Code*
<comparison>	*Temp*	*Code*
<relation>	—	*TestCode*
<variable>	—	*Name*
<identifier>	—	*Name*
<numeral>	—	*Name*
<letter>	—	*Name*
<digit>	—	*Name*

Figure 7.7: Attributes Associated with Nonterminal Symbols

<program> ::= **program** <identifier> **is** <block>
    Code(<program>) ← concat(Code(<block>), [HALT])

<block> ::= <declaration sequence> **begin** <command sequence> **end**
    Code(<block>) ← Code(<command sequence>)
    Temp(<command sequence>) ← 0
    InhLabel(<command sequence>) ← 0

<declaration sequence> ::= ε | <declaration> <declaration sequence>₂

<declaration> ::= **var** <variable list> **:** <type>**;**

<variable list> ::= <variable> | <variable> **,** <variable list>₂

<type> ::= **integer** | **boolean**

<command sequence> ::= <command>
    Code(<command sequence>) ← Code(<command>)
    Temp(<command>) ← Temp(<command sequence>)
    InhLabel(<command>) ← InhLabel(<command sequence>)
    SynLabel(<command sequence>) ← SynLabel(<command>)
    | <command> **;** <command sequence>₂
    Code(<command sequence>) ←
                    concat(Code(<command>),Code(<command sequence>₂))
    Temp(<command>) ← Temp(<command sequence>
    Temp(<command sequence>₂) ← Temp(<command sequence>)
    InhLabel(<command>) ← InhLabel(<command sequence>)
    InhLabel(<command sequence>₂) ← SynLabel(<command>)
    SynLabel(<command sequence>) ← SynLabel(<command sequence>₂)

<command> ::= <variable> **:=** <expr>
    Code(<command>) ← concat(Code(<expr>),[(STO, Name(<variable>))]])
    Temp(<expr>) ← Temp(<command>)
    SynLabel(<command>) ← InhLabel(<command>)

<command> ::= **read** <variable>
    Code(<command>) ← [(GET, Name(<variable>))]]
    SynLabel(<command>) ← InhLabel(<command>)

<command> ::= **write** <expr>
    Code(<command>) ←
                    concat(Code(<expr>),[(STO, temporary(temp+1))],
                            [(PUT, temporary(temp+1))]])
    Temp(<expr>) ← Temp(<command>)
    SynLabel(<command>) ← InhLabel(<command>)

Figure 7.8: Complete Attribute Grammar for Wren (Part 1)

<command> ::= **skip**
  Code(<command>) ← [NO-OP]
  SynLabel(<command>) ← *InhLabel*(<command>)

<command> ::= **while** <boolean expr> **do** <command sequence> **end while**
  Code(<command>) ← concat([[(label(*InhLabel*(<command>)+1),LABEL)],
                          Code(<boolean expr>),
                          [JF,label(*InhLabel*(<command>)+2))]],
                          Code(<command sequence>),
                          [(J,label(*InhLabel*(<command>)+1))]],
                          [(label(*InhLabel*(<command>)+2),LABEL)]]),
  Temp(<boolean expr>) ← *Temp*(<command>)
  Temp(<command sequence>) ← *Temp*(<command>)
  InhLabel(<command sequence>) ← *InhLabel*(<command>)+2
  SynLabel(<command>) ← *SynLabel*(<command sequence>)

<command> ::= **if** <boolean expr> **then** <command sequence> **end if**
  Code(<command>) ← concat(*Code*(<boolean expr>),
                          [JF,label(*InhLabel*(<command>)+1))]],
                          Code(<command sequence>),
                          [(label(*InhLabel*(<command>)+1),LABEL)]])
  Temp(<boolean expr>) ← *Temp*(<command>)
  Temp(<command sequence>) ← *Temp*(<command>)
  InhLabel(<command sequence>) ← *InhLabel*(<command>)+1
  SynLabel(<command>) ← *SynLabel*(<command sequence>)

<command> ::= **if** <boolean expr> **then** <command sequence>$_1$
                          else <command sequence>$_2$ **end if**
  Code(<command>) ← concat(*Code*(<boolean expr>),
                          [JF,label(*InhLabel*(<command>)+1))]],
                          Code(<command sequence>$_1$),
                          [(J,label(*InhLabel*(<command>)+2))]],
                          [(label(*InhLabel*(<command>)+1),LABEL)],
                          Code(<command sequence>$_2$),
                          [(label(*InhLabel*(<command>)+2),LABEL)]])
  Temp(<boolean expr>) ← *Temp*(<command>)
  Temp(<command sequence>$_1$) ← *Temp*(<command>)
  Temp(<command sequence>$_2$) ← *Temp*(<command>)
  InhLabel(<command sequence>$_1$) ← *InhLabel*(<command>)+2
  InhLabel(<command sequence>$_2$) ← *SynLabel*(<command sequence>$_1$)
  SynLabel(<command>) ← *SynLabel*(<command sequence>$_2$)

Figure 7.8: Complete Attribute Grammar for Wren (Part 2)

<expr> ::=
    <integer expr>
      Code(<expr>) ← *Code*(<integer expr>)
      Temp(<integer expr>) ← *Temp*(<expr>)
  | <boolean expr>
      Code(<expr>) ← *Code*(<boolean expr>)
      Temp(<integer expr>) ← *Temp*(<expr>)

<integer expr> ::=
    <term>
      Code(<integer expr>) ← *Code*(<term>)
      Temp(<term>) ← *Temp*(<integer expr>)
  | <integer expr>$_2$ <weak op> <term>
      Code(<integer expr>) ← concat(*Code*(<integer expr>$_2$),
            optimize(*Code*(<term>),*Temp*(<integer expr>),*OpCode*(<weak op>)))
      Temp(<integer expr>$_2$) ← *Temp*(<integer expr>)
      Temp(<term>) ← *Temp*(<integer expr>)+1

<weak op> ::=
    +
      OpCode(<weak op>) ← ADD
  | −
      OpCode(<weak op>) ← SUB

<term> ::=
    <element>
      Code(<term>) ← *Code*(<element>)
      Temp(<element>) ← *Temp*(<term>)
  | <term>$_2$ <strong op> <element>
      Code(<term>) ← concat(*Code*(<term>$_2$),
            optimize(*Code*(<element>),*Temp*(<term>),*OpCode*(<strong op>)))
      Temp(<term>$_2$) ← *Temp*(<term>)
      Temp(<element>) ← *Temp*(<term>)+1

<strong op> ::=
    *
      OpCode(<strong op>) ← MULT
  | /
      OpCode(<strong op>) ← DIV

<element> ::=
    <numeral>
      Code(<element>) ← [(LOAD, *Name*(<numeral>))]
  | <variable>
      Code(<element>) ← [(LOAD, *Name*(<variable>))]
  | (<integer expr>)
      Code(<element>) ← *Code*(<integer expr>)
      Temp(<integer expr>) ← *Temp*(<element>)

Figure 7.8: Complete Attribute Grammar for Wren (Part 3)

<boolean expr> ::=
    <boolean term>
      Code(<boolean expr>) ← *Code*(<boolean term>)
      Temp(<boolean term>) ← *Temp*(<boolean expr>)
  | <boolean expr>$_2$ **or** <boolean term>
      Code(<boolean expr>) ← concat(*Code*(<boolean expr>$_2$),
                               [(STO, temporary(temp+1))],
                               Code(<boolean term>,
                               [(OR, temporary(temp+1))]])
      Temp(<boolean expr>$_2$) ← *Temp*(<boolean expr>)
      Temp(<boolean term>) ← *Temp*(<boolean expr>)+1
<boolean term> ::=
    <boolean element>
      Code(<boolean term>) ← *Code*(<boolean element>)
      Temp(<boolean element>) ← *Temp*(<boolean term>)
  | <boolean term>$_2$ **and** <boolean element>
      Code(<boolean term>) ← concat(*Code*(<boolean term>$_2$),
                               [(STO, temporary(temp+1))],
                               Code(<boolean element>,
                               [(AND, temporary(temp+1))]])
      Temp(<boolean term>$_2$) ← *Temp*(<boolean term>)
      Temp(<boolean element>) ← *Temp*(<boolean term>)+2

<boolean element> ::=
    false
      Code(<boolean element>) ← [(LOAD, 0)]
  | **true**
      Code(<boolean element>) ← [(LOAD, 1)]
  | <variable>
      Code(<boolean element>) ← [(LOAD, *Name*(<variable>))]
  | <comparison>
      Code(<boolean element>) ← *Code*(<comparison>)
      Temp(<comparison>) ← *Temp*(<boolean element>)
  | (<boolean expr>)
      Code(<boolean element>) ← *Code*(<boolean expr>)
      Temp(<boolean expr>) ← *Temp*(<boolean element>)
  | **not** (<boolean expr>)
      Code(<boolean element>) ← concat(*Code*(<boolean expr>), [NOT]),
      Temp(<boolean expr>) ← *Temp*(<boolean element>)

<comparison> ::= <integer expr>$_1$ <relation> <integer expr>$_2$
      Code(<comparison>) ← concat(*Code*(<integer expr>$_1$),
           optimize(*Code*(<integer expr>$_1$),*Temp*(<comparison>),SUB),
           TestCode(<relation>))
      Temp(<integer expr>$_1$) ← *Temp*(<comparison>)
      Temp(<integer expr>$_2$) ← *Temp*(<comparison>)+1

Figure 7.8: Complete Attribute Grammar for Wren (Part 4)

<relation> ::=
>
  TestCode(<relation>) ← TSTGT
| >=
  TestCode(<relation>) ← TSTGE
| <>
  TestCode(<relation>) ← TSTNE
| =
  TestCode(<relation>) ← TSTEQ
| <=
  TestCode(<relation>) ← TSTLE
| <
  TestCode(<relation>) ← TSTLT

<variable> ::= <identifier>
  Name(<variable>) ← *Name*(<identifier>)

<identifier> ::=
  <letter>
  Name(<identifier>) ← *Name*(<letter>)
| <identifier>$_2$ <letter>
  Name(<identifier>) ← concat(*Name*(<identifier>$_2$),*Name*(<letter>))
| <identifier>$_2$ <digit>
  Name(<identifier>) ← concat(*Name*(<identifier>$_2$),*Name*(<digit>))

<letter> ::=
  a
  Name(<letter>) ← 'A'
        :   :
| **z**
  Name(<letter>) ← 'Z'

<numeral> ::=
  <digit>
  Name(<numeral>) ← *Name*(<digit>)
| <numeral>$_2$ <digit>
  Name(<numeral>) ← concat(*Name*(<numeral>$_2$),*Name*(<digit>))

<digit> ::=
  0
  Name(<digit>) ← '0'
        :   :
| **9**
  Name(<digit>) ← '9'

Figure 7.8: Complete Attribute Grammar for Wren (Part 5)

Auxiliary Functions

```
optimize(code, temp, opcode) =
    if length(code) = 1 then                -- a variable or numeral
                    [(opcode, secondField(first(code)))]
            else
                concat([[(STO, temporary(temp+1))],
                        code,
                        [(STO, temporary(temp+2))],
                        [(LOAD, temporary(temp+1))],
                        [(opcode, temporary(temp+2))]])

temporary(integer) =  concat('T',string(integer))

label(integer) = concat('L', string(integer))

string(n) =   if n = 0 then '0'
            :  :        :
            else if n = 9 then '9'
            else concat(string(n/10), string(n mod 10))
```

Figure 7.8: Complete Attribute Grammar for Wren (Part 6)

Exercises

1. The negation of an element was not specified in the attribute grammar of Figure 7.8. Add this alternative to the production for <element> without adding any new instructions to the object code.

2. Draw the complete, decorated tree for the arithmetic expression

    $$2 * x * y + z / 3$$

3. Draw the complete, decorated tree for the command sequence in the following program:

    ```
    program mod is
      var m, n : integer;
    begin
      read m;  read n;
      while m > n do
            m := m - n
      end while;
      write m
    end
    ```

4. Without drawing the complete tree, show the code generated by attribute grammar for the following Wren program:

    program multiply **is**
       var m, n, product : **integer**;
    begin
       read m; **read** n;
       product := 0;
       while n > 0 **do**
             if 2 * (n / 2) < > n **then** (* if n is odd *)
                   product := product + m
             end if;
             m := 2 * m; n := n / 2
       end while;
       write product
    end

    Compare the answer for this problem with the answer for exercise 1 in section 7.1. Is there any difference in efficiency between hand-generated and machine-generated code?

5. Change the semantic rules for the **write** command so that the code is optimized when the expression being printed is a variable or a numeral.

6. The Boolean expressions in the grammar given are fully evaluated. Some programming languages short-circuit Boolean expression evaluation once the final result is known. Is it possible to modify the grammar in a *simple way* so that short-circuit evaluation is performed?

7. We did not include an optimization for Boolean expressions. Will such an optimization be possible? If it is, add it to the attribute grammar; if it is not, explain why.

8. Add the command

        repeat <command sequence> **until** <boolean expr>

    to Wren and modify the attribute grammar so that the generated code causes the loop to be exited when the Boolean expression is true.

9. Add the conditional expression

        if <boolean expr> **then** <expr> **else** <expr>

    to Wren and modify the attribute grammar accordingly.

10. Add expressions with side effects

        begin <command sequence> **return** <expr> **end**

    to Wren and modify the attribute grammar so that the value returned is evaluated with the state produced by executing the command sequence.

11. Reverse Polish notation is used on some calculators to evaluate arith-
    metic expressions. For a binary operation, the first operand is pushed
    on a stack, the second operand is pushed on the stack, and, when the
    operation is performed, both operands are popped off the stack and the
    result of the operation is pushed back onto the stack. Introduce appro-
    priate machine instructions for a stack architecture for arithmetic expres-
    sion evaluation and modify the attribute grammar for Wren accordingly.

12. The following BNF grammar defines an expression language with binary
    operations +, –, *, and /, unary -, and the variables a, b, and c.

    <expr> ::= <term> | <expr> + <term> | <expr> – <term>

    <term> ::= <elem> | <term> * <elem> | <term> / <elem>

    <elem> ::= a | b | c | (<expr>) | - <expr>

    Convert this definition into an attribute grammar whose main attribute
    Val is an abstract syntax tree for the expression represented in the form
    of a tagged structure similar to a Prolog structure. For example,

    Val("(a–b)*-(b+c)/a") = times(minus(a,b),divides(negative(plus(b,c)),a)).

7.3 LABORATORY: IMPLEMENTING CODE GENERATION

As in Chapter 3, we will be developing an attribute grammar written in Prolog,
but unlike that previous laboratory project, our goal now is the generation of
intermediate code, as described in section 7.1. Although we parse the declaration section of the program, we do not use this information in the generation of code.

As before, we assume "front end" code to read the text from a file and convert
it into a sequence of tokens. We also add a pretty-printing capability on the
"back end" so that the resulting program looks like assembly code. An example illustrates the code generator.

```
>>> Translating Wren <<<
Enter name of source file: gcd.wren
    program gcd is
    var m,n: integer;
    begin
      read m; read n;
      while m <> n do
        if m < n then n := n - m
                 else m := m - n
        end if
```

```
        end while;
        write m
    end
Scan successful
[program,ide(gcd),is,var,ide(m),comma,ide(n),colon,integer,
 semicolon,begin,read,ide(m),semicolon,read,ide(n),semicolon,
 while,ide(m),neq,ide(n),do,if,ide(m),less,ide(n),then,ide(n),
 assign,ide(n),minus,ide(m),else,ide(m),assign,ide(m),minus,
 ide(n),end,if,end,while,semicolon,write,ide(m),end,eop]
Parse successful
[[[GET,m],[GET,n],[L1,LABEL],[LOAD,m],[SUB,n],[TSTNE],[JF,L2],[LOAD,m],[SUB,n],
 [TSTGT],[JF,L3],[LOAD,n],[SUB,m],[STO,n],[J,L4],[L3,LABEL],
 [LOAD,m],[SUB,N],[STO,m],[L4,LABEL],[J,L1],[L2,LABEL],
 [LOAD,m],[STO,T1],[PUT,T1],[HALT]]]
        GET     M
        GET     N
L1      LABEL
        LOAD    M
        SUB     N
        TSTNE
        JF      L2
        LOAD    M
        SUB     N
        TSTGT
        JF      L3
        LOAD    N
        SUB     M
        STO     N
        J       L4
L3      LABEL
        LOAD    M
        SUB     N
        STO     M
L4      LABEL
        J       L1
L2      LABEL
        LOAD    M
        STO     T1
        PUT     T1
        HALT
yes
```

The transcript above shows the token list produced by the scanner and the
list of assembly language instructions constructed by the attribute grammar

woven throughout the parser. A pretty-print routine capitalizes symbols in the code and formats the output. The program above is the gcd program in Wren that was discussed in section 7.1.

This example illustrates the code generated by the Prolog translator once it is fully implemented. As in previous laboratory sections, we provide only a partial implementation and leave the unimplemented components as exercises.

The generated code for the synthesized attribute *Code* is maintained as a Prolog list of assembly language instructions, each of which is a Prolog list itself.

The program clause adds the instruction ['HALT'] to the generated code; at the same time it ignores the program identifier since that value does not affect the code generated. Because uppercase has particular significance in Prolog, generated opcodes must be enclosed in apostrophes. At the block level, the synthesized *Code* attribute is passed to the program level and the inherited attributes for *Temp* and *InhLabel* are initialized to zero.

```
program(Code) -->   [program, ide(Ident), is], block(Code1),
                       { concat(Code1, [['HALT']], Code) }.

block(Code) --> decs, [begin], commandSeq(Code,0,0,SynLabel), [end].
```

Commands

Implementing decs following the example in Chapter 2 is left as an exercise. We break a command sequence into the first command followed by the rest of the commands, if any. The *Temp* attribute is passed to both children, the *InhLabel* attribute from the command sequence is inherited by the first command, the *SynLabel* attribute from the first command becomes the *InhLabel* attribute of the rest of the commands, and the *SynLabel* of the rest of the commands is passed to the parent command sequence. The two code sequences are concatenated in a list structure. The rest of the commands are handled in a similar manner except that when no more commands remain, the resulting code list is empty.

```
commandSeq(Code,Temp,InhLab,SynLab) -->
                          command(Code1,Temp,InhLab,SynLab1),
                          restcmds(Code2,Temp,SynLab1,SynLab),
                          { concat(Code1, Code2, Code) }.
restcmds(Code,Temp,InhLab,SynLab) -->
                          [semicolon],
                          command(Code1,Temp,InhLab,SynLab1),
                          restcmds(Code2,Temp,SynLab1,SynLab),
                          { concat(Code1, Code2, Code) }.
restcmds([ ],Temp,InhLab,InhLab) --> [ ].
```

The input and **skip** commands do not use the *Temp* attribute and simply turn the label attribute around and feed it back out by placing the same variable Label in both argument places. The assignment and output commands use the *Temp* attribute and turn around the label attribute. Some of these commands appear below, others are left as exercises.

```
command([['GET', Var]], Temp, Label, Label) --> [read,ide(Var)].

command(Code, Temp, Label, Label) -->
                    [ide(Var), assign], expr(Code1,Temp),
                    { concat(Code1, [['STO',Var]], Code) }.
```

The input of a variable is translated into the GET of the same variable. The output of an expression is the code generated for the expression, followed by the store of its result in a temporary location and a PUT of this location. The **skip** command generates a NO-OP. The assignment command concatenates a STO of the target variable after the code generated by expression. The reader is encouraged to complete the **write** and **skip** commands.

The single alternative **if** command consists of the code for the Boolean expression that includes a test operation, a conditional jump, the code for the body, and a label instruction that is the target of the conditional jump. Notice the use of the built-in Prolog predicate is to evaluate an arithmetic expression and bind the result. We have also used a utility predicate label to combine L with the label number. Note that we need to define a concat predicate that concatenates three lists (see Appendix A).

```
command(Code,Temp,InhLab,SynLab) -->
                [if], { InhLab1 is InhLab+1, label(InhLab1,Lab) },
                booleanExpr(Code1,Temp),
                [then], commandSeq(Code2,Temp,InhLab1,SynLab), [end,if],
                { concat(Code1, [['JF',Lab]|Code2], [[Lab,'LABEL']], Code) }.

label(Number,Label) :-
        name('L',L1), name(Number,L2), concat(L1,L2,L), name(Label,L).
```

The two-alternative **if** command has the most complex code sequence:
- The code from the Boolean expression
- A conditional jump to the false task
- The code from the true task
- An unconditional jump to the label instruction following the entire command
- A label instruction for entry into the false task
- The code for the false task itself
- The final label instruction for the jump out of the true task.

The same *Temp* attribute is passed to all three children. Since the two-alternative **if** command requires two unique labels, the *InhLabel* for the true command sequence has been incremented by two. The *SynLabel* out of the true command sequence is threaded into the false command sequence. The *SynLabel* of the false command sequence is passed to the parent. Here we need a concat predicate that concatenates four lists.

```
command(Code,Temp,InhLab,SynLab) -->
                    [if], { InhLab1 is InhLab+1, InhLab2 is InhLab+2,
                            label(InhLab1,Lab1), label(InhLab2,Lab2) },
                    booleanExpr(Code1,Temp),
                    [then], commandSeq(Code2,Temp,InhLab2,SynLab2),
                    [else], commandSeq(Code3,Temp,SynLab2,SynLab), [end,if],
                    { concat(Code1, [['JF',Lab1]|Code2],
                        [['J',Lab2], [Lab1,'LABEL']|Code3], [[Lab2,'LABEL']], Code) }.
```

The **while** command begins with a label instruction that is the target for the unconditional jump at the bottom of the loop, which is followed by the code for the Boolean expression, a conditional jump out of the **while**, the code for the loop body, an unconditional jump to the top of the loop, and a final label instruction for exiting the **while** loop. The *Temp* attribute is inherited down to the Boolean expression and loop body. Since two labels are used, the InhLabel to the loop body is incremented by two and the *SynLabel* from the loop body is passed back up to the parent. Completion of the code for a **while** command is left as an exercise.

Expressions

The code generated by arithmetic expressions does not involve labels, so the label attributes are not used at all. As we saw earlier in Chapter 2, we have to transform our left recursive attribute grammar into a right recursive format when implemented as a logic grammar. If an expression goes directly to a single term, then *Temp* is passed in and Code is passed out. If an expression is a term followed by one or more subsequent terms, then the inherited *Temp* value is passed down to the left-hand term and this value incremented by one is passed to the right-hand term. There may be still more terms to the right, but since the additive operations are left associative, we have completed the operation on the left two terms and the temporary locations can be used again. Therefore the original *Temp* value is passed down to the clause for the remaining terms.

The generated code for an integer expression is the code from the first term followed by the optimized code from any remaining terms. If the code from the right-hand term is simply the load of a variable or a numeral, the code is optimized by having the opcode associated with the binary operation applied directly to the simple operand. If this is not the case, the result from the left operand is stored in a temporary, the code is generated for the right operand that is stored in a second temporary, the first temporary is loaded, and the operation is applied to the second temporary. The predicate optimize allows two forms due to the two possible list structures. Notice the use of the utility predicate temporary to build temporary location names. The resulting code from an expression with multiple terms is the code from the first term, the code from the second term, and the code from the remaining terms, if any.

```
integerExpr(Code,Temp) -->   term(Code1,Temp), restExpr(Code2,Temp),
                             { concat(Code1, Code2, Code) }.

restExpr(Code,Temp) -->   weakop(Op), { Temp1 is Temp+1 },
                          term(Code1,Temp1),
                          { optimize(Code1,OptCode1,Temp,Op) },
                          restExpr(Code2,Temp),
                          { concat(OptCode1, Code2, Code) }.

restExpr([ ],Temp) --> [ ].

weakop('ADD') --> [plus].

weakop('SUB') --> [minus].

optimize([['LOAD',Operand]],[[Opcode,Operand]],Temp,Opcode).
optimize(Code,OptCode,Temp,Op) :-
        Temp1 is Temp+1, Temp2 is Temp+2,
        temporary(Temp1,T1), temporary(Temp2,T2),
        concat([['STO',T1]|Code], [['STO',T2], ['LOAD',T1], [Op,T2]], OptCode).

temporary(Number,Temp) :-
        name('T',T1), name(Number,T2), concat(T1,T2,T), name(Temp,T).
```

Terms are similar to expressions and are left as an exercise. For now, we give a clause for terms that enables the current specification of the attribute grammar to work correctly on a restrict subset of Wren with only the "weak" arithmetic operators. This clause will have to be replaced to produce correct translations of terms in Wren.

```
term(Code,Temp) --> element(Code,Temp).
```

An element can expand to a number, an identifier, or a parenthesized expression, in which case the *Temp* attribute is passed in. The negation of an element is left as an exercise.

```
element(['LOAD',Number], Temp) --> [num(Number)].

element(['LOAD',Name], Temp) --> [ide(Name)].

element(Code,Temp) --> [lparen], expression(Code,Temp), [rparen].
```

The code for expressions, Boolean expressions, Boolean terms, and Boolean elements is left as an exercise.

The final task is to generate the code for comparisons. We generate code for the left-side expression, recognize the relation, generate code for the right-side expression, and then call optimize for the right side using the subtract operation. The code for the comparison is the concatenation of the code for the left-side expresion, the optimized code for the right-side expression, and the test instruction. In the code below, the variable Tst holds the value of the test operation returned by testcode. The reader is encouraged to write the clauses for testcode.

```
comparison(Code,Temp) -->
            { Temp1 is Temp+1 },
            integerExpr(Code1,Temp),
            testcode(Tst), integerExpr(Code2,Temp1),
            { optimize(Code2,OptCode2,Temp,'SUB') },
            { concat(Code1,OptCode2,[Tst]], Code) }.
```

This completes our partial code generator for Wren. The exercises below describe the steps needed to complete this Wren translator. Other exercises deal with extensions to Wren that can be translated into intermediate code.

Exercises

1. Complete the implementation given in this section by adding the following featues:

    • The output and **skip** commands

    • The **while** command

    • Clauses for term, remterm, and strongop

    • Clauses for expression, boolExpr, boolTerm, and boolElement

    • Clauses for testcode

2. Write a pretty-print routine for the intermediate code. Add a routine to capitalize all identifiers. All commands, except for labels, are indented by one tab and there is a tab between an opcode and its argument. A tab character is generated by put(9) and a return is accomplished by nl. Recursion in the pretty-print predicte can stop once the halt instruction is encountered and printed.

3. The negation of an element (unary minus) was not specified in the production that defines elements. Add this alternative using the *existing* intermediate code instructions.

4. Modify the output command to print a list of expression values. Add a new intermediate code command for a line feed that is generated after the list of expressions is printed.

5. Add the repeat .. until command, as described in exercise 7, section 7.2.

6. Add a conditional expression, as described in exercise 8, section 7.2.

7. Add expressions with side effects, as described in exercise 9, section 7.2.

8. Follow exercise 10 in section 7.2 to change the code generation for a stack architecture machine and to implement these changes in the Prolog code generator.

7.4 FURTHER READING

The use of attribute grammars for code generation is of primary interest to the compiler writer. Lewis, Rosenkrantz, and Stearns presented an early paper on attributed translations [Lewis74]. Several references in compiler construction have already been noted in Section 3.4 [Aho86], [Fischer91], [Parsons92], and [Pittman92].

Frank Pagan presents a code-generating attribute grammar for the language Pam [Pagan81]. Pam is somewhat simpler than Wren since all variables are of type integer. Because there is no need to generate Boolean values, as our TST instructions do, his target language has six conditional jumps that use the same instruction both to test and jump.

We have assigned programs for students to use the Synthesizer-Generator [Reps89] to implement code generation for Wren. Our code generator in Prolog operates in batch mode whereas the Synthesizer-Generator code-generating editor operates in incremental mode. Two windows appear on the screen, one for the source code and one for the object code. As the code is entered in the source window, the corresponding object code appears immediately. Changes in the source code, including deletions, result in "instantaneous" changes in the object code, even when this involves changes in label numbers and temporary location numbers.

Chapter 8
TRADITIONAL OPERATIONAL SEMANTICS

In contrast to a semantics that describes only what a program does, the purpose of operational semantics is to describe how a computation is performed. An introduction to computers and programming languages is usually presented in terms of operational concepts. For example, an assignment statement "V := E" might be described by the steps that it performs: Evaluate the expression E and then change the value bound to the variable V to be this result. In another example, pointer assignments might be made clearer by drawing boxes and arrows of the configurations before and after the assignments.

Informal operational semantics illustrates the basic components of the operational approach to meaning. A state or configuration of the machine is described by means of some representation of symbols, such as labeled boxes, values in the boxes, and arrows between them. One configuration assumes the role of the initial state, and a function, determined by the program whose meaning is being explained, maps one configuration into another. When the program (or programmer) is exhausted or the transition function is undefined for some reason, the process halts producing a "final" configuration that we take to be the result of the program.

In this chapter we first discuss how earlier chapters have already presented the operational semantics of languages. We then briefly describe a well-known but seldom-used method of specifying a programming language by means of formal operational semantics—namely, the Vienna Definition Language.

The main part of this chapter looks at the SECD abstract machine defined by Peter Landin, an early method of describing expression evaluation in the context of the lambda calculus. The chapter concludes with an introduction to a formal specification method known as structural operational semantics. This method describes semantics by means of a logical system of deductive rules that model the operational behavior of language constructs in an abstract manner.

The laboratory exercises for this chapter include implementing the SECD machine for evaluating expressions in the lambda calculus following the pattern used in Chapter 5 and implementing a prototype interpreter of Wren based on its structural operational semantics using the scanner and parser developed in Chapter 2.

8.1 CONCEPTS AND EXAMPLES

We have already considered several versions of operational semantics in this text. For the lambda calculus in Chapter 5, the β-reduction and δ-reduction rules provide a definition of a computation step for reducing a lambda expression to its normal form, if possible. A configuration consists of the current lambda expression still to be reduced, and the transition function simply carries out reductions according to a predetermined strategy. The occurrence of a lambda expression in normal form signals the termination of the computation. As with most operational semantics, the computation may continue forever.

One view of operational semantics is to take the meaning of a programming language as the collection of results obtained by executing programs on a particular interpreter or as the assembly language program produced by a compiler for the language. This approach to meaning is called **concrete operational semantics**. The translational semantics of a compiler, such as the one discussed in Chapter 7 using an attribute grammar, can be understood as a definition of a programming language. The diagram below shows the structure of a translational system for a programming language.

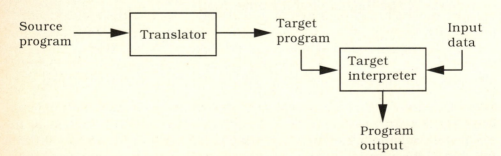

The translational approach entails two major disadvantages as a formal specification tool:

1. The source language is defined only as well as the target language of the translator. The correctness and completeness of the specification relies on a complete understanding of the target language.

2. A translator can carefully describe the relation between a source program and its translation in the target language, but it may at the same time provide little insight into the essential nature of the source language.

More commonly, concrete operational semantics refers to an interpreter approach in which a source language program is simulated directly. An interpretive definition of a programming language is generally less complex than following a translational method. The diagram below shows the basic structure of an interpretation system.

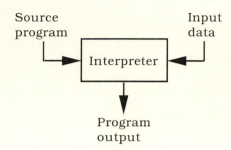

Defining the meaning of a programming language in terms of a real interpreter also has shortcomings as a specification mechanism:

1. For complex languages, correct interpreters (as well as compilers) are difficult to write. Moreover, these definitions are too machine dependent to serve as formal specifications for a programming language.

2. Interpreters are written to provide practical program development tools, and they do not provide the mathematical precision needed in a formal definition.

The metacircular interpreters in Chapter 6 describe the operation of a Lisp machine and a simplified Prolog machine using the languages themselves to express the descriptions. These descriptions represent the configurations directly as structures in the language being defined. John McCarthy's definition of Lisp in Lisp [McCarthy65b] was an early landmark in providing the semantics of a programming language. Although such meta-interpreters can give insight into a programming language to someone who is already familiar with the language, they are not suitable as formal definitions because of the circularity.

Formal semantics demands a better approach, using a precisely defined hypothetical abstract machine described in a formal mathematical or logical language with no limitations on memory, word size, precision of arithmetic, and other such implementation-dependent aspects of a language, and rigorously defined rules that reveal the way the state of the machine is altered when a program is executed.

VDL

The most ambitious attempt at defining an abstract machine for operational semantics was the Vienna Definition Language (VDL) developed at the Vienna IBM laboratory in 1969. All the nonprimitive objects in VDL are modeled as trees. This includes the program being interpreted (an abstract syntax tree), memory, input and output lists, environments, and even the control mechanism that performs the interpretation. Figure 8.1 shows a typical VDL configuration that is represented as a collection of subtrees. A set of instruction definitions, in effect a "microprogram", interprets an abstract representation of a program on the abstract machine defined by this tree structure.

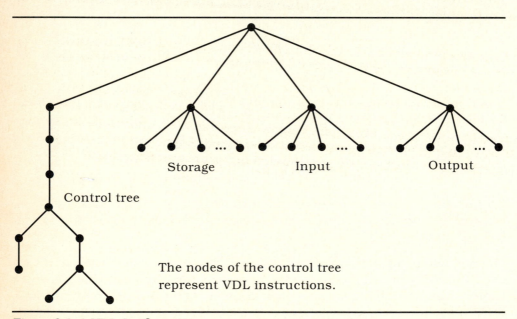

Figure 8.1: A VDL Configuration

Starting with an initial configuration or state that has all the components of storage properly initialized (probably to "undefined"), input defined as a tree representing the list of input values, output set as an empty tree, and the control tree defined as a single instruction to execute the entire program, the transition function given by the instructions of the VDL interpreter performs the steps of a computation. One step consists of selecting a leaf node of the control tree and evaluating it according to the microprogram, producing a new state with a modified control tree. As the leaf nodes of the control tree are evaluated, a sequence of configurations results:

$$\text{configuration}_0 \rightarrow \text{configuration}_1 \rightarrow \text{configuration}_2 \rightarrow \text{configuration}_3 \rightarrow \dots$$

An interpretation of a program terminates normally when the control tree becomes empty, signaling that the program has completed. The VDL interpreter also recognizes certain error conditions that may occur during an execution, and the computation may execute forever.

The major accomplishment of the VDL effort was a specification of PL/I. Unfortunately, the complexity of definitions in VDL hampers its usefulness. The tree structures do not relate to any actual implementation, and the details of the representation can overwhelm the users of a VDL specification to the point of raising questions about its correctness. Any hope of practical application of formal semantics depends on providing a certain amount of clarity and conciseness in language definitions.

Our venture into traditional operational semantics considers two examples that are more accessible. The first technique illustrates the use of an abstract machine, called the SECD machine, to interpret the lambda calculus. Developed in the mid 1960s, it provides an elegant example of traditional operation semantics that has become the basis for some implementations of functional programming languages. The second method of language specification, called structural operational semantics, finds its roots in logic deduction systems. It is a more abstract approach to operational specifications, recently supporting applications in type theory.

Exercises

1. List several ways that programming languages are described to beginners using informal operational semantics.

2. How well does the translational semantics of Chapter 7 provide a formal definition of the programming language Wren? Can it be used to prove the equivalence of language constructs?

3. Enumerate some of the advantages and disadvantages of using an actual interpreter or compiler as the definition of Pascal.

8.2 SECD: AN ABSTRACT MACHINE

In 1964 Peter Landin proposed an abstract machine, called the **SECD machine**, for the mechanical evaluation of lambda expressions. This machine has become a classic example of operational semantics, involving computational techniques that have been adopted in practical implementations of functional programming languages. With the SECD machine, evaluation of a function application entails maintaining an environment that records the bindings of formal parameters to arguments in a way similar to the method of implementing function application in some real implementations. The SECD machine surpasses the efficiency of a lambda calculus evaluator based on β-reductions, but it lends itself primarily to an applicative order evaluation strategy. In fact, the SECD machine as described by Landin follows pass by value semantics in the sense that combinations in the body of a lambda expression are not reduced unless the lambda abstraction is applied to an argument; so the evaluator stops short of normal form in some instances.

The states in the abstract machine consist of four components, all exhibiting stack behavior. The names of these four stacks, S, E, C, and D, provide the title of the machine.

S for **Stack**: A structure for storing partial results awaiting subsequent use.

E for **Environment**: A collection of bindings of values (actual parameters) to variables (formal parameters).

C for **Control**: A stack of lambda expressions yet to be evaluated plus a special symbol "@" meaning that an application can be performed; the top expression on the stack is the next one to be evaluated.

D for **Dump**: A stack of complete states corresponding to evaluations in progress but suspended while other expressions (inner redexes) are evaluated.

In describing the SECD interpreter we represent a state, also called a configuration, as a structured object with four components:

cfg(S, E, C, D).

Borrowing notation from Prolog and mixing it with a few functional operations, we depict the S and C stacks as lists of the form [a,b,c,d] with the top at the left and define *head* and *tail* so that

head([a,b,c,d]) = a, and

tail([a,b,c,d]) = [b,c,d].

To push an item X onto the stack S, we simply write [X|S] for the new stack. The empty list [ ] acts as an empty stack.

Environments, which provide bindings for variables, are portrayed as lists of pairs, say $[x \mapsto 3, y \mapsto 8]$, with the intention that bindings have precedence from left to right. An empty environment is denoted by the atom "nil". In describing the SECD machine, we let E(x) denote the value bound to x in E, and let $[y \mapsto val]E$ be the environment E_1 that extends E with the property

$$E_1(x) = E(x) \text{ if } x \neq y, \text{ and}$$

$$E_1(y) = val.$$

So if $E = [y \mapsto 5][x \mapsto 3, y \mapsto 8] = [y \mapsto 5, x \mapsto 3]$, E(y) = 5. If an identifier x has not been bound in E, the application E(x) returns the variable x itself.

The D stack is represented as a structure. Since a dump is a stack of configurations (states), we display it using notation with the pattern

$$cfg(S_1,E_1,C_1,cfg(S_2,E_2,C_2,cfg(S_3,E_3,C_3,nil)))$$

for a dump that stacks three states. An empty dump is also given by "nil".

When a lambda abstraction ($\lambda V . B$) appears on the top of the control stack, it is moved to the partial result stack while its argument is evaluated. The object that is placed on the stack is a package containing the bound variable V and body B of the abstraction, together with the current environment Env, so that the meaning of the free variables can be resolved when the abstraction is applied. This bundle of three items is known as a **closure** since the term represented is a closed expression in the sense that it carries along the meanings of its free variables. We represent such a closure by the structure "closure(V,B,Env)", which we abbreviate as "cl(V,B,Env)" when space is short.

To evaluate a lambda expression expr, the SECD machine starts with the initial configuration cfg([ ],nil,[expr],nil) that has empty stacks for S, E, and D. The one item on the control stack is the expression to be evaluated. The SECD machine is defined by a transition function,

$$transform : \text{State} \rightarrow \text{State},$$

that maps the current configuration to the next configuration until a final state results, if it ever does. A final state is recognized by its having an empty control stack and an empty dump, indicating that no further computation is possible. Figure 8.2 gives a definition of the *transform* function as a conditional expression returning a new configuration when given the current configuration.

---

transform cfg(S, E, C, D) =

    (1)   if *head*(C) is a constant

            then cfg([*head*(C) | S], E, *tail*(C), D)

    (2)   else if *head*(C) is a variable

            then cfg([E(*head*(C)) | S], E, *tail*(C), D)

    (3)   else if *head*(C) is an application (Rator Rand)

            then cfg(S, E, [Rator,Rand,@ | *tail*(C)], D)

    (4)   else if *head*(C) is a lambda abstraction $\lambda V . B$

            then cfg([closure(V,B,E) | S], E, *tail*(C), D)

    (5)   else if *head*(C) = @ and *head*(*tail*(S)) is a predefined function f

            then cfg([f(*head*(S)) | *tail*(*tail*(S))], E, *tail*(C), D)

    (6)   else if *head*(C) = @ and *head*(*tail*(S)) = closure(V,B,E_1)

            then cfg([ ], [V$\mapsto$*head*(S)]E_1, [B], cfg(*tail*(*tail*(S)),E,*tail*(C),D))

    (7)   else if C = [ ]

            then cfg([*head*(S) | S_1], E_1, C_1, D_1) where D = cfg(S_1,E_1,C_1,D_1)

Figure 8.2: Transition Function for the SECD Machine

In order to explain the SECD machine, we will discuss each case in the definition of the transition function. The cases are determined primarily by the
top element of the control stack C.

1. If the next expression to be evaluated is a constant, move it as is from the
control stack to the partial result stack S.

2. If the next expression is a variable, push its binding in the current environment onto S. If no binding exists, push the variable itself.

3. If the next expression is an application (Rator Rand), decompose it and
reenter the parts onto the control stack C with the Rator at the top, the
Rand next, and the special application symbol @ following the Rand.
(In his original machine, Landin placed the Rand above the Rator to be
evaluated first, but that results in rightmost-innermost evaluation instead of leftmost-innermost—redexes in the Rator before the Rand—that
we described for applicative order evaluation in Chapter 5.)

4. If the next expression is a lambda abstraction, form a closure incorporating the current environment and add that closure to the partial result
stack. The use of a closure ensures that when the lambda abstraction is
applied, its free variables are resolved in the environment of its definition, thereby providing static scoping.

5. If the next expression is @ and the function in the second place on the S stack is a predefined function, apply that function to the evaluated argument at the top of the S stack and replace the two of them with the result.

6. If the next expression is @ and the function in the second place of the S stack is a closure, after popping @ and the top two elements of S, push the current configuration onto the dump. Then initiate a new computation to evaluate the body of the closure in the closure's environment augmented with the binding of the bound variable in the closure, the formal parameter, to the argument at the top of the partial result stack.

7. If the control stack is empty, that means the current evaluation is completed and its result is on the top of the partial result stack. Pop the configuration on the top of the dump, making it the new current state with the result of the previous computation appended to the top of its partial result stack.

If the control stack and the dump are both empty, the transition function is undefined, and the SECD machine halts in a final state. The value at the top of the partial result stack is the outcome of the original evaluation.

Example

Shown below are the state transitions as the lambda expression

$$((\lambda x . (\text{mul } x ((\lambda y . \text{sqr } y) 5))) 3)$$

is evaluated by the SECD machine. The numbers at the far right identify which alternative of the definition by cases is employed at each step. Closures are represented as cl(V,B,E), and g stands for $(\lambda y.\text{sqr } y)$ to save space in describing the computation.

S	E	C	D	
[ ]	nil	[((λx.(mul x ((λy.sqr y) 5))) 3)]	nil	
[ ]	nil	[(λx.(mul x (g 5))), 3, @]	nil	(3)
[cl(x,(mul x (g 5)),nil)]	nil	[3, @]	nil	(4)
[3, cl(x,(mul x (g 5)),nil)]	nil	[@]	nil	(1)
[ ]	[x↦3]	[(mul x (g 5))]	d_1	(6)
	where d_1 = cfg([ ],nil,[ ],nil)			
[ ]	[x↦3]	[(mul x), (g 5), @]	d_1	(3)

| [ ] | [x↦3] | [mul, x, @, (g 5), @] | d_1 | (3) |

| [mul] | [x↦3] | [x, @, (g 5), @] | d_1 | (1) |

| [3, mul] | [x↦3] | [@, ((λy.sqr y) 5), @] | d_1 | (2) |

| [mul3] | [x↦3] | [((λy.sqr y) 5), @] | d_1 | (5) |

where mul3 is the unary function that multiplies its argument by 3

| [mul3] | [x↦3] | [(λy.sqr y), 5, @, @] | d_1 | (3) |

| [cl(y,(sqr y),E_1), mul3] | [x↦3] | [5, @, @] | d_1 | (4) |

where E_1 = [x↦3]

| [5, cl(y,(sqr y),E_1), mul3] | [x↦3] | [@, @] | d_1 | (1) |

| [ ] | [y↦5, x↦3] | [(sqr y)] | d_2 | (6) |

where d_2 = cfg([mul3],[x↦3],[@],d_1)

| [ ] | [y↦5, x↦3] | [sqr, y, @] | d_2 | (3) |

| [sqr] | [y↦5, x↦3] | [y, @] | d_2 | (1) |

| [5, sqr] | [y↦5, x↦3] | [@] | d_2 | (2) |

| [25] | [y↦5, x↦3] | [ ] | d_2 | (5) |

| [25, mul3] | [x↦3] | [@] | d_1 | (7) |

| [75] | [x↦3] | [ ] | d_1 | (5) |

| [75] | nil | [ ] | nil | (7) |

The transition function has no definition when both the control stack and the dump are empty. The result of the evaluation is the value 75 at the top of the S stack.

Parameter Passing

As mentioned earlier, the SECD machine evaluates redexes following a leftmost-innermost strategy but fails to continue reducing in the body of a lambda expression. The next example illustrates this pass by value approach to the lambda calculus by evaluating the lambda expression ((λf . λx . f x)(λy . y)).

S	E	C	D	
[ ]	nil	$[((\lambda f.\lambda x.f\ x)(\lambda y.y))]$	nil	
[ ]	nil	$[(\lambda f.\lambda x.f\ x),\ (\lambda y.y),\ @]$	nil	(3)
$[cl(f,(\lambda x.f\ x),nil)]$	nil	$[(\lambda y.y),\ @]$	nil	(4)
$[cl(y,y,nil),\ cl(f,(\lambda x.f\ x),nil)]$	nil	$[@]$	nil	(4)
[ ]	$[f{\mapsto}cl(y,y,nil)]$	$[(\lambda x.f\ x)]$	d_1	(6)
where $d_1 = cfg([\ ],nil,[\ ],nil)$				
$[cl(x,(f\ x),[f{\mapsto}cl(y,y,nil)])]$	$[f{\mapsto}cl(y,y,nil)]$	[ ]	d_1	(4)
$[cl(x,(f\ x),[f{\mapsto}cl(y,y,nil)])]$	nil	[ ]	nil	(7)

This final state produces the closure $cl(x,(f\ x),[f{\mapsto}cl(y,y,nil)])$ as the result of the computation. Unfolding the environment that binds f to $cl(y,y,nil)$ in the closure and extracting the lambda abstraction $(\lambda x\ .\ f\ x)$ from the closure, we get $(\lambda x\ .\ ((\lambda y\ .\ y)\ x))$ as the final result following a pass by value reduction. In true applicative order evaluation, the reduction continues by simplifying the body of the abstraction giving the lambda expression $(\lambda x\ .\ x)$, which is in normal form, but pass by value reduction does not reduce the bodies of abstractions that are not applied to arguments.

Static Scoping

The easiest way to see that lambda calculus reduction adheres to static scoping is to review **let**-expressions, which we discussed briefly at the end of section 5.2. For example, consider the following expression:

> **let** x=5
> > **in let** f = $\lambda y\ .$ (add x y)
> > > **in let** x = 3
> > > > **in** f x

Here the variable x is bound to two different values at different points in the expression. When the function f is applied to 3, to which value is 3 added? By translating the **let**-expression into a lambda expression

$$(\lambda x\ .\ (\lambda f\ .\ ((\lambda x\ .\ f\ x)\ 3))\ (\lambda y\ .\ (add\ x\ y)))\ 5$$

and reducing, following either a normal order or an applicative order strategy, we get the value 8 as the normal form. To match this behavior in the SECD machine, the function f must carry along the binding of x to 5 that is in effect when f is bound to (λy . (add x y)). That is precisely the role of closures in the interpretation.

In contrast, a slight change to the definition of the transition function turns the SECD machine into an adherent to dynamic scoping. Simply change case 6 to read:

> else if *head*(C) = @ and *head*(*tail*(S)) = closure(V,B,E$_1$)
>
>> then cfg([ ], [V$\mapsto$*head*(S)]E, [B], cfg(*tail*(*tail*(S)),E,*tail*(C),D))

Now the body of the lambda abstraction is evaluated in the environment in effect at the application of f to x—namely, binding x to 3, so that the computation produces the value 6. With dynamic scoping, closures can be dispensed with altogether, and case 4 need only move the lambda abstraction from the top of the control stack to the top of the partial result stack S.

Exercises

1. Trace the execution of the SECD machine on the following lambda expressions in the applied lambda calculus that we have defined:

   a) (succ 4)

   b) (λx . (add x 2)) 5

   c) (λf . λx . (f (f x))) sqr 2

   d) (λx ((λy . λz . z y) x)) p (λx . x)

2. In the pure lambda calculus, both the successor function and the numeral 0 are defined as lambda expressions (see section 5.2). The expression (succ 0) takes the form

   $$(\lambda n . \lambda f . \lambda x . f (n f x)) (\lambda f . \lambda x . x)$$

   in the pure lambda calculus. Use the SECD machine and β-reduction to evaluate this expression. Explain the discrepancy.

3. Trace the execution of the SECD machine on the lambda expression that corresponds to the **let**-expresssion discussed in the text:

   $$(\lambda x . (\lambda f . ((\lambda x . f x) 3)) (\lambda y . (add x y))) 5$$

4. Trace a few steps of the SECD machine when evaluating the lambda expression (λx . x x) (λx . x x).

5. Modify the SECD machine so that it follows a normal order reduction strategy. Use a new data structure, a suspension, to model unevaluated expressions. See [Field88] or [Glaser84] for help on this exercise.

8.3 LABORATORY: IMPLEMENTING THE SECD MACHINE

If we use the scanner and parser from the lambda calculus evaluator in Chapter 5, the implementation of the SECD machine is a simple task. We already use Prolog structures for some of the components of a configuration. All we need to add is a Prolog data structure for environments. We design the SECD interpreter to be used in the same way as the evaluator, prompting for the name of a file that contains one lambda expression. The transcript below shows the SECD machine as it evaluates the lambda expression from the example in section 8.2.

```
>>> SECD: Interpreting an Applied Lambda Calculus <<<
Enter name of source file: text
    ((L x (mul x ((L y (sqr y)) 5))) 3)
Successful Scan
Successful Parse
Result = 75
yes
```

We represent the stack S and control C using Prolog lists, as in the definition of the transition function in the previous section, but now we implement *head* and *tail* by pattern matching.

Environments are implemented as structures of the form env(x, 3, env(y, 8, nil)) for the environment $[x \mapsto 3, y \mapsto 8]$. An empty environment is given by nil. A predicate extendEnv(Env,X,Val,NewEnv) appends a new binding to an existing environment, producing a new environment. A single Prolog clause defines this predicate:

    extendEnv(Env,Ide,Val,env(Ide,Val,Env)).

For example, if Env is bound to the structure env(x, 3, env(y, 8, nil)) and we execute extendEnv(Env,z,13,NewEnv), NewEnv will be bound to the structure env(z, 13, env(x, 3, env(y, 8, nil))).

The predicate applyEnv(Env,Ide,Val) performs the application of an environment to a variable to find its binding. Three clauses define this predicate, the first clause tries to match the binding at the top of the environment:

    applyEnv(env(Ide,Val,Env),Ide,Val).

If the first clause fails, the second continues the search in the "tail" of the environment:

    applyEnv(env(Ide1,Val1,Env),Ide,Val) :- applyEnv(Env,Ide,Val).

Finally, the third clause applies to an empty environment signaling a failed search for the variable. In this case the value returned is the variable itself marked with a tag:

    applyEnv(nil,Ide,var(Ide)).

In agreement with the conventions of Chapter 5, variables and constants have tags (var and con) provided by the parser to make the pattern matching easier to understand. Dumps are implemented as Prolog structures following the pattern used in the previous section:

    cfg(S1,E1,C1,cfg(S2,E2,C2,cfg(S3,E3,C3,nil))).

The transition function for the SECD machine is embodied in a Prolog predicate transform(Config, NewConfig) that carries out one step of the interpreter each time it is invoked. Seven clauses implement the seven cases in Figure 8.2.

    transform(cfg(S,E,[con(C)|T],D), cfg([con(C)|S],E,T,D)).   % 1

    transform(cfg(S,E,[var(X)|T],D), cfg([Val|S],E,T,D)) :- applyEnv(E,X,Val).   % 2

    transform(cfg(S,E,[comb(Rator,Rand)|T],D), cfg(S,E,[Rator,Rand,@|T],D)).   % 3

    transform(cfg(S,E,[lamb(X,B)|T],D), cfg([closure(X,B,E)|S],E,T,D)).   % 4

    transform(cfg([con(Rand),con(Rator)|T],E,[@|T1],D), cfg([Val|T],E,T1,D)) :- % 5
                                                    compute(Rator,Rand,Val).

    transform(cfg([Rand,closure(V,B,E1)|T],E,[@|T1],D),   % 6
                                cfg([ ],E2,[B],cfg(T,E,T1,D))) :-
                                                    extendEnv(E1,V,Rand,E2).

    transform(cfg([H|S],E,[ ],cfg(S1,E1,C1,D1)), cfg([H|S1],E1,C1,D1)).   % 7

Recall the abstract syntax and the associated tags for the lambda calculus. Each lambda expression is a variable (var), a constant (con), a lambda abstraction (lamb), or a combination (comb). The compute predicate used in step 5 is identical to the one in the evaluator in Chapter 5. Notice how well pattern matching performs tests such as the one in step 6

        if $head(C)$ = @ and $head(tail(S))$ = closure(V,B,E_1),
becomes

    transform(cfg([Rand,closure(V,B,E1)|T],E,[@|T1],D), ...).

The SECD interpreter is driven by a predicate interpret(Config,Result) that watches for a final state to terminate the machine:

    interpret(cfg([Result|S],Env,[ ],nil), Result).

Otherwise it performs one transition step and calls itself with the new configuration:

```
interpret(Config,Result) :- transform(Config,NewConfig),
                            interpret(NewConfig,Result).
```

If the parser produces a structure of the form expr(Exp), the SECD machine can be invoked using the query:

```
interpret(cfg([ ],nil,[Exp],nil), Result), nl, write('Result = '), pp(Result), nl.
```

where cfg([ ],nil,[Exp],nil), Result) serves as the initial configuration and the predicate pp prints the result (see Chapter 5).

Exercises

1. Following the directions above, implement the SECD machine in Prolog and test it on some of the lambda expressions in the exercises for section 8.2.

2. Change the Prolog implementation of the SECD machine so that it follows the semantics of dynamic scoping instead of static scoping. Illustrate the difference between static and dynamic scoping by evaluating the lambda expression that corresponds to the following let expression:

   let a = 7 **in let** g = λx . (mul a x) **in let** a = 2 **in** (g 10)

3. Add a conditional expression (if E_1 E_2 E_3) to the interpreter. Since the SECD machine follows an applicative order evaluation strategy, "if" cannot be handled by compute, which expects its arguments to be evaluated already. A new case can be added to the definition of transform that manipulates the top few items on the control stack. Test the machine on the following lambda expressions:

   ((L x (if (zerop x) 5 (div 100 x))) 0)

   ((L x (if (zerop x) 2 ((L x (x x)) (L x (x x))))) 0)

4. Extend the lambda calculus to include a "label" expression of the form

   <expression> ::= ... | (label <variable> <expression>)

   whose semantics requires that the expression be bound to the variable in the environment before the expression is evaluated. This mechanism allows recursive functions to be defined (the original approach in Lisp). This definition of the factorial function exemplifies the use of a label expression:

   ((label f (L n (if (zerop n) 1 (mul n (f (pred n)))))) 8)

5. Compare the efficiency of the lambda calculus evaluator in Chapter 5
    with the SECD machine in this chapter. Use combinations of "Twice"
    and "Thrice" as test expressions, where

    $\qquad$ Twice = λf . λx . f (f x) and

    $\qquad$ Thrice = λf . λx . f (f (f x)).

    For example, try Twice (λz . (add z 1))

    $\qquad\qquad\qquad$ Thrice (λz . (add z 1))

    $\qquad\qquad\qquad$ Twice Thrice (λz . (add z 1))

    $\qquad\qquad\qquad$ Thrice Twice (λz . (add z 1))

    $\qquad\qquad\qquad$ Twice Twice Thrice (λz . (add z 1))

    $\qquad\qquad\qquad$ Twice Thrice Twice (λz . (add z 1)) and so on.

8.4 STRUCTURAL OPERATIONAL SEMANTICS: INTRODUCTION

Proving properties of programs and the constructs of programming languages
provides one of the main justifications of formal descriptions of languages.
Operational semantics specifies programming languages in terms of program
execution on abstract machines. **Structural operational semantics**, developed by Gordon Plotkin in 1981, represents computation by means of deductive systems that turn the abstract machine into a system of logical inferences. Since the semantic descriptions are based on deductive logic, proofs
of program properties are derived directly from the definitions of language
constructs.

With structural operational semantics, definitions are given by **inference
rules** consisting of a conclusion that follows from a set of premises, possibly
under control of some condition. The general form of an inference rule has
the premises listed above a horizontal line, the conclusion below, and the
condition, if present, to the right.

$$\frac{\text{premise}_1 \quad \text{premise}_2 \quad ... \quad \text{premise}_n}{\text{conclusion}} \quad \text{condition}$$

If the number of premises is zero, n=0 in the example, the line is omitted, and
we refer to the rule as an **axiom**. This method of presenting rules evolved
from a form of logic called **natural deduction**. As an example in natural
deduction, three inference rules express the logical properties of the conjunction (and) connective:

$$\frac{p \wedge q}{p} \qquad \frac{p \wedge q}{q} \qquad \frac{p \quad q}{p \wedge q}$$

The principle that allows the introduction of a universal quantifier exhibits a rule with a condition:

$$\frac{P(a)}{\forall x P(x)} \quad \text{a does not occur in P(x) or in any assumption on which P(a) depends.}$$

For more on natural deduction, see the further readings at the end of this chapter.

Rather than investigate this method of expressing logical deductions, we concentrate on the use of inference rules of this form in structural operational semantics. But before we consider the semantics of Wren, we see how an inference system can be used to describe the syntax of Wren.

Specifying Syntax

For the present, we ignore the declarations in a Wren program, assuming that any program whose semantics is to be explained has been verified as syntactically correct (including the context-sensitive syntax), and that all integer identifiers in the program are included in a set Id and Boolean identifiers in a set Bid. Furthermore, we concern ourselves only with abstract syntax, since any program submitted for semantic analysis comes in the form of an abstract syntax tree.

The abstract syntax of these Wren programs is formed from the syntactic sets defined in Figure 8.3. The elements of the sets are identified by the designated metavariables, possibly with subscripts, attached to each syntactic category.

When describing the abstract syntax of a programming language, we strive to fit the description to the structure of the semantic formalism that uses it. The precise notational form of abstract syntax is not intrinsic to a language, as is the concrete syntax. We simply need to give the patterns of the structures that capture the essential components of constructs in the language. For instance, the fundamental property of an assignment is that it consists of an identifier and an expression of the same type.

n ∈ Num = Set of numerals

b ∈ { **true**, **false** } = Set of Boolean values

id ∈ Id = Set of integer identifiers

bid ∈ Bid = Set of Boolean identifiers

iop ∈ Iop = { +, −, *, / }

rop ∈ Rop = { <, ≤, =, ≥, >, <> }

bop ∈ Bop = { **and**, **or** }

ie ∈ Iexp = Set of integer expressions

be ∈ Bexp = Set of Boolean expressions

c ∈ Cmd = Set of commands

Figure 8.3: Syntactic Categories

Figure 8.4 gives a version of the abstract syntax of Wren specially adapted to a structural operational semantic description. In particular, the patterns that abstract syntax trees may take are specified by inference rules and axioms, some with conditions. The statements that make up the premises and conclusions have the form of type assertions; for example,

n : iexp with the condition n ∈ Num

asserts that objects taken from Num may serve as integer expressions. In this context, "n : iexp" states that n is of type iexp, the sort of objects corresponding to the set Iexp defined in Figure 8.3. The types iexp, bexp, and cmd correspond to the sets Iexp, Bexp, and Cmd, respectively.

The biggest difference between this specification of abstract syntax and that in Chapter 1 is the way we handle lists of commands. The inference rule that permits a command to be a sequence of two commands enables the type "cmd" to include arbitrary finite sequences of commands. Since we ignore declarations in this presentation, a Wren program may be thought of simply as a command. Moreover, a combination of symbols c is a command if we can construct a derivation of the assertion "c : cmd". In fact, the derivation parallels an abstract syntax tree for the group of symbols. Later we give semantics to Wren programs by describing the meaning of a command relative to this specification of abstract syntax.

Assuming that the identifier x is a member of Id because of a declaration that has already been elaborated, a deduction showing the abstract structure of the command "x := 5 ; **while not**(x=0) **do** x := x-1 ; **write** x" is displayed in Figure 8.5. Conditions have been omitted to save space, but each condition should be obvious to the reader. Compare this deduction in the inference system with a derivation according to an abstract syntax given by a BNF-type specification.

$n : iexp \qquad n \in Num$

$b : bexp \qquad b \in \{\textbf{true}, \textbf{false}\}$

$id : iexp \qquad id \in Id$

$bid : iexp \qquad bid \in Bid$

$$\frac{ie_1 : iexp \qquad ie_2 : iexp}{ie_1 \; iop \; ie_2 : iexp} \; iop \in Iop$$

$$\frac{ie_1 : iexp \qquad ie_2 : iexp}{ie_1 \; rop \; ie_2 : bexp} \; rop \in Rop$$

$$\frac{be_1 : bexp \qquad be_2 : bexp}{be_1 \; bop \; be_2 : bexp} \; bop \in Bop$$

$$\frac{be : bexp}{\textbf{not}(\, be) : bexp}$$

$\textbf{skip} : cmd$

$$\frac{ie : iexp}{- \, ie : iexp}$$

$$\frac{ie : iexp}{id := ie : cmd} \; id \in Id$$

$$\frac{be : bexp}{bid := be : cmd} \; bid \in Bid$$

$$\frac{be : bexp \qquad c : cmd}{\textbf{if} \; be \; \textbf{then} \; c : cmd}$$

$$\frac{be : bexp \qquad c_1 : cmd \qquad c_2 : cmd}{\textbf{if} \; be \; \textbf{then} \; c_1 \; \textbf{else} \; c_2 : cmd}$$

$$\frac{c_1 : cmd \qquad c_2 : cmd}{c_1 \; ; \; c_2 : cmd}$$

$$\frac{be : bexp \qquad c : cmd}{\textbf{while} \; be \; \textbf{do} \; c : cmd}$$

$\textbf{read} \; id : cmd \qquad id \in Id$

$$\frac{ie : iexp}{\textbf{write} \; ie : cmd}$$

Figure 8.4: Abstract Syntax for Wren

As with most definitions of abstract syntax, this approach allows ambiguity. For the derivation in Figure 8.5, the command sequence can be associated to the left instead of to the right. The choice of grouping command sequences is known as an **inessential ambiguity** since it has no effect on the semantics of the language. Essential ambiguities, such as those in expressions (associativity of minus) and **if** commands (dangling else), are handled by the concrete syntax that is used to construct abstract syntax trees from the program text. Since we represent these tree structures with a linear notation, we insert (meta-)parentheses in abstract syntax expressions whose structure is not obvious.

$$\frac{\dfrac{\dfrac{\dfrac{\dfrac{x : iexp \quad 0 : iexp}{x=0 : bexp}}{\mathbf{not}(x=0) : bexp} \quad \dfrac{\dfrac{x : iexp \quad 1 : iexp}{x-1 : iexp}}{x := x-1 : cmd}}{\mathbf{while\ not}(x=0)\ \mathbf{do}\ x := x-1 : cmd} \quad \dfrac{x : iexp}{\mathbf{write}\ x : cmd}}{\dfrac{5 : iexp}{x := 5 : cmd} \quad \mathbf{while\ not}(x=0)\ \mathbf{do}\ x := x-1\ ;\ \mathbf{write}\ x : cmd}}{x := 5\ ;\ \mathbf{while\ not}(x=0)\ \mathbf{do}\ x := x-1\ ;\ \mathbf{write}\ x : cmd}$$

Figure 8.5: Derivation in the Abstract Syntax

Inference Systems and Structural Induction

The abstract syntax for Wren presented in Figure 8.4 can be defined just as well using a BNF specification or even other notational conventions (see [Astesiano91]). The common thread between these presentations of syntax is the inductive nature of the definitions. A set of objects, say Iexp, is specified by describing certain atomic elements—$n \in$ Iexp for each $n \in$ Num and $id \in$ Iexp for each $id \in$ Id—and then describing how more complex objects are constructed from already existing objects,

$\{ie_1, ie_2 \in$ Iexp and $iop \in$ Iop$\}$ implies $\{(ie_1 \ iop \ ie_2) \in$ Iexp$\}$.

The fundamental structure remains the same whether the set is defined by inference rules or by BNF rules:

    iexp ::= n | id | ie_1 iop ie_2 and

    iop ::= + | – | * | /   where $n \in$ Num, $id \in$ Id, and $ie_1, ie_2 \in$ Iexp.

Structured objects described using inductive definitions support a proof method, a version of mathematical induction, known as **structural induction**. This induction technique depends on the property that each object in some collection is either an atomic element with no structure or is created from other objects using well-defined constructor operations.

Principle of Structural Induction: To prove that a property holds for all phrases in some syntactic category, we need to confirm two conditions:

1. **Basis**: The property must be established for each atomic (nondecomposable) syntactic element.

2. **Induction step**: The property must be proved for any composite element given that it holds for each of its immediate subphrases (the induction hypothesis).   ∎

For objects defined by a system of inference rules, the axioms create atomic items that are handled by the basis of the induction, and the rules with premises correspond to the induction step. The induction hypothesis assumes that the property being proved holds for all the objects occurring in premises, and we must show that the property holds for the object in the conclusion of the rule.

The syntactic categories defined for the abstract syntax of Wren are so general that few interesting properties can be proven about them. For a simple example, consider the set of all expressions, Exp = Iexp ∪ Bexp. The elementary components of expressions can be divided into two classes:

1. The operands, Rand = Num ∪ {**true**,**false**} ∪ Id ∪ Bid.

2. The operators, Rator = Iop ∪ Rop ∪ Bop ∪ {**not**}.

We can prove a lemma about the number of operands and operators in any Wren expression using structural induction.

Lemma: For any expression e ∈ (Iexp ∪ Bexp) containing no unary operations (without **not** and unary minus), the number of operands in e is greater than the number of operators in e. Write #rand(e) > #rator(e) to express this relation.

Proof: These expressions are defined by the first seven rules in Figure 8.4.

Basis: Atomic expressions are formed by the four axioms corresponding to numerals, Boolean constants, integer identifiers, and Boolean identifiers. In each case the expression defined has one operand and zero operators, satisfying the property of the lemma.

Induction Step: We consider three cases corresponding to the three inference rules that create structured expressions using a binary operator.

Case 1: $e = ie_1$ iop ie_2 for some iop ∈ Iop where ie_1, ie_2 : iexp. By the induction hypothesis, #rator(ie_1) < #rand(ie_1) and #rator(ie_2) < #rand(ie_2). It follows that #rator(ie_2)+1 ≤ #rand(ie_2). But #rator(ie_1 iop ie_2) = #rator(ie_1) + #rator(ie_2) + 1 and #rand(ie_1 iop ie_2) = #rand(ie_1) + #rand(ie_2). Therefore, #rator(ie_1 iop ie_2) = #rator(ie_1) + #rator(ie_2) + 1 < #rand(ie_1) + #rand(ie_2) = #rand(ie_1 iop ie_2).

Case 2: $e = ie_1$ rop ie_2 for some rop ∈ Rop where ie_1, ie_2 : iexp. This case is similar to case 1.

Case 3: $e = be_1$ bop be_2 for some bop ∈ Bop where be_1, be_2 : bexp. This case is also similar to case 1.

Therefore, by the principle of structural induction, the property #rator(e) < #rand(e) holds for all expressions $e \in$ (Iexp $\cup$ Bexp) containing no unary operations. ∎

Exercises

1. Construct derivations of these Wren constructs using the abstract syntax inference system in Figure 8.4. Refer to the concrete syntax to resolve ambiguities. Assume that all identifiers have been properly declared.

   a) a*b + c*d

   b) -n-k-5 = n/2*k

   c) n>0 **and not**(switch)

   d) **if** a>=b **then while** a>=c **do write** a ; a := a-1 **else skip**

2. Define (part of) the concrete syntax of Wren using inference rules and axioms in a manner similar to the definition of the abstract syntax of Wren in Figure 8.4.

3. Use the definition of concrete syntax from exercise 2 and structural induction to prove the following properties:

   a) Every expression in Wren has the same number of left and right parentheses.

   b) Each command in Wren has at least as many occurrences of the reserved word **then** as of the reserved word **else**.

4. The following two inference rules define a language comprising lists of integers using "::" as an infix operator denoting the operation of prefixing an element to a list (cons in Lisp):

$$[\,] : \text{intList} \qquad \frac{\text{tail} : \text{intList}}{m :: \text{tail} : \text{intList}} \ m \in \text{Num}$$

These are similar to the lists in ML where "::" is a right associative operator and lists can be abbreviated as follows: [1,2,3,4] = 1 :: 2 :: 3 :: 4 :: [ ].

Functions on these lists of integers can be defined inductively by describing their behavior on the two kinds of lists established by the definitions.

length([ ]) = 0

length(m::tail) = 1+length(tail) where $m \in$ Num and tail:intList concat([ ],L) = L where L:intList

concat(m::tail,L) = m :: concat(tail,L) where m∈ Num and tail,L:intList

reverse([ ]) = [ ]

reverse(m::tail) = concat(reverse(tail), m::[ ])
$$\text{where } m∈ \text{Num and tail:intList}$$

Use structural induction to prove the following properties concerning the functions just defined on integer lists where the variables L, L_1, L_2, and L_3 range over intList. Some properties depend on earlier ones.

a) concat(L,[ ]) = L

b) length(concat(L_1,L_2)) = length(L_1)+length(L_2)

c) concat(L_1,concat(L_2,L_3)) = concat(concat(L_1,L_2),L_3)

d) length(reverse(L)) = length(L)

e) reverse(concat(L_1,L_2)) = concat(reverse(L_2),reverse(L_1))

f) reverse(reverse(L)) = L

8.5 STRUCTURAL OPERATIONAL SEMANTICS: EXPRESSIONS

We now develop a description of the semantics of Wren using an inference system according to structural operational semantics. The task can be separated into two parts, the first specifying the semantics of expressions in Wren and the second specifying the semantics of commands.

Semantics of Expressions in Wren

Structural operational semantics provides a deductive system, based on the abstract syntax of a programming language, that allows a syntactic transformation of language elements to normal form values that serve as their meaning. Such a definition includes a notion of configurations representing the progress of computations and an inference system that defines transitions between the configurations. We concentrate first on the meaning (evaluation) of expressions in Wren.

Since expressions in Wren permit identifiers, their meaning depends on the values of identifiers recorded in a structure, called the **store**, that models the memory of a computer. Any expression (even any program) contains only a finite set of identifiers, which means that the store structure can be viewed as a finite set of pairs binding values to identifiers, sometimes referred to as a **finite function**. For any store sto, let *dom*(sto) denote the (finite) set of identifiers with bindings in sto.

Thinking of a store as a set of pairs, we informally use a notation of the form {x↦3, y↦5, p↦true} to represent a store with three bindings. For this store, *dom*(sto) = {x,y,p}. Let Store with sto as its metavariable stand for the category of stores. The actual implementation of stores is immaterial to the specification of a programming language, so we rely on three abstract operations to describe the manipulation of stores:

1. *emptySto* represents a store with no bindings; that is, all identifiers are undefined.

2. *updateSto*(sto,id,n) and *updateSto*(sto,bid,b) represent the store that agrees with sto but contains one new binding, either id↦n or bid↦b.

3. *applySto*(sto,id) and *applySto*(sto,bid) return the value associated with id or bid; if no binding exists, the operation fails blocking the deduction.

Observe that *applySto*(sto,id) is defined if and only if id∈ *dom*(sto), and the corresponding property holds for Boolean identifiers. Expressions in Wren have no way to modify bindings in a store, so the operation *updateSto* is not used in defining their semantics in Wren.

In a manner similar to the store actions, the binary operations allowed in Wren expressions are abstracted into an all-purpose function *compute*(op,arg_1,arg_2) that performs the actual computations. For example, *compute*(+,3,5) returns the numeral 8, *compute*(<,3,5) returns **true**, and *compute*(**and**,**true**,**false**) returns **false**. Since *compute*(/,n,0) is not defined, the evaluation of any expression in which this computation appears must fail. We say that such an evaluation is **stuck**, since no rule can be successfully applied to an expression of the form "n/0". A stuck computation cannot proceed. This concept is different from a nonterminating computation, which proceeds forever.

For evaluating expressions, a configuration consists of a pair containing an expression to examine and a store that provides a context for the computation. A particular evaluation starts with a configuration, and under control of an inference system, allows a reduction of the configuration to a final or terminating configuration that acts as a normal form value for the expression. In Wren, final configurations for expressions have a first value that is a numeral or a Boolean constant: <n,sto> or <b,sto>.

The inference system for Wren expressions, shown in Figure 8.6, provides rules for each syntactic form that is not in normal form. The symbol → serves to represent a transition from one configuration to another. Note that some rules—namely, axioms (7), (12), and (13)—have conditions.

(1)
$$\frac{<ie_1,sto> \rightarrow <ie_1',sto>}{<ie_1 \; iop \; ie_2,sto> \rightarrow <ie_1' \; iop \; ie_2,sto>}$$

(2)
$$\frac{<ie_1,sto> \rightarrow <ie_1',sto>}{<ie_1 \; rop \; ie_2,sto> \rightarrow <ie_1' \; rop \; ie_2,sto>}$$

(3)
$$\frac{<be_1,sto> \rightarrow <be_1',sto>}{<be_1 \; bop \; be_2,sto> \rightarrow <be_1' \; bop \; be_2,sto>}$$

(4)
$$\frac{<ie_2,sto> \rightarrow <ie_2',sto>}{<n \; iop \; ie_2,sto> \rightarrow <n \; iop \; ie_2',sto>}$$

(5)
$$\frac{<ie_2,sto> \rightarrow <ie_2',sto>}{<n \; rop \; ie_2,sto> \rightarrow <n \; rop \; ie_2',sto>}$$

(6)
$$\frac{<be_2,sto> \rightarrow <be_2',sto>}{<b \; bop \; be_2,sto> \rightarrow <b \; bop \; be_2',sto>}$$

(7) $<n_1 \; iop \; n_2, sto> \rightarrow <compute(iop,n_1,n_2), sto>$ $(iop \neq \; /)$ or $(n_2 \neq 0)$

(8) $<n_1 \; rop \; n_2, sto> \rightarrow <compute(rop,n_1,n_2), sto>$

(9) $<b_1 \; bop \; b_2, sto> \rightarrow <compute(bop,b_1,b_2), sto>$

(10)
$$\frac{<be,sto> \rightarrow <be',sto>}{<\mathbf{not}(be),sto> \rightarrow <\mathbf{not}(be'),sto>}$$

(11) $<\mathbf{not}(\mathbf{true}),sto> \rightarrow <\mathbf{false},sto>$ $<\mathbf{not}(\mathbf{false}),sto> \rightarrow <\mathbf{true},sto>$

(12) $<id,sto> \rightarrow <applySto(sto,id),sto>$ $id \in dom(sto)$

(13) $<bid,sto> \rightarrow <applySto(sto,bid),sto>$ $bid \in dom(sto)$

Figure 8.6: Inference System for Expressions

The inference rules enforce a definite strategy for evaluating expressions. Rules (1) through (3) require that the left argument in a binary expression be simplified first. Only when the left argument has been reduced to a constant (n or b) can rules (4) through (6) proceed by evaluating the right argument. Finally, when both arguments are constants, rules (7) through (9) permit the binary operation to be calculated using *compute*. The only other rules handle the unary operation **not** and the atomic expressions that are identifiers. Atomic expressions that are numerals or Boolean constants have already been reduced to normal form. Unary minus has been left as an exercise at the end of this section.

We can view a computation describing the meaning of an expression as a sequence of configurations where each transition is justified using rules (1) through (13):

$$<e_1,sto> \rightarrow <e_2,sto> \rightarrow <e_3,sto> \rightarrow \ldots \rightarrow <e_{n-1},sto> \rightarrow <e_n,sto>.$$

Then by adding a rule (14), which makes the $\rightarrow$ relation transitive, we can deduce $<e_1,sto> \rightarrow <e_n,sto>$ by applying the new rule n-1 times.

$$(14) \quad \frac{<e_1,sto> \rightarrow <e_2,sto> \qquad <e_2,sto> \rightarrow <e_3,sto>}{<e_1,sto> \rightarrow <e_3,sto>} \quad \begin{array}{c} e_1,e_2,e_3 \in \text{Iexp} \\ \text{or} \\ e_1,e_2,e_3 \in \text{Bexp} \end{array}$$

In addition to having $\rightarrow$ be transitive, it makes sense to assume that $\rightarrow$ is also reflexive, so that $<e,sto> \rightarrow <e,sto>$ for any expression e and store sto. Then when we write $<e_1,sto> \rightarrow <e_2,sto>$, we mean that one configuration $<e_1,sto>$ can be reduced to another configuration $<e_2,sto>$, possibly the same one, by zero or more applications of inference rules from Figure 8.6.

The rules in these inference systems are really **rule schemes**, representing classes of actual rules in which specific identifiers, numerals, Boolean constants, and specific operators replace the metavariables in the inference rules. For example, "$<5 \geq 12,emptySto> \rightarrow <\textbf{false},emptySto>$" is an instance of rule (8) since $compute(\geq,5,12) = \textbf{false}$.

Example

Consider an evaluation of the expression "x+y+6" with sto = {x$\mapsto$17, y$\mapsto$25} given as the store. The sequence of computations depends on the structure of the abstract syntax tree that "x+y+6" represents. We distinguish between the two possibilities by inserting parentheses as structuring devices. We carry out the computation for "x+(y+6)" and leave the alternative grouping as an exercise. Observe that in Wren an abstract syntax tree with this form must have come from a text string that originally had parentheses.

We first display the computation sequence for "x+(y+6)" as a linear derivation:

a)	<y,sto>	→ <25,sto> since *applySto*(sto,y)=25	(12)
b)	<y+6,sto>	→ <25+6,sto>	(1) and a
c)	<25+6,sto>	→ <31,sto> since *compute*(+,25,6)=31	(7)
d)	<y+6,sto>	→ <31,sto>	(14), b, and c
e)	<x,sto>	→ <17,sto> since *applySto*(sto,x)=17	(12)
f)	<x+(y+6),sto>	→ <17+(y+6),sto>	(1) and e
g)	<17+(y+6),sto>	→ <17+31,sto>	(4) and d
h)	<x+(y+6),sto>	→ <17+31,sto>	(14), f, and g
i)	<17+31,sto>	→ <48,sto> since *compute*(+,17,31)=48	(7)
j)	<x+(y+6),sto>	→ <48,sto>	(14), h, and i

The last configuration is terminal since <48,sto> is in normal form. Note the use of rule (14) that makes → a transitive relation. Using a proof by mathematical induction, we can establish a derived rule that allows any finite sequence of transitions as premises for the rule:

$$\frac{<e_1,sto> \rightarrow <e_2,sto> \quad <e_2,sto> \rightarrow <e_3,sto> \quad \ldots \quad <e_{n-1},sto> \rightarrow <e_n,sto>}{<e_1,sto> \rightarrow <e_n,sto>}$$

provided that $n \geq 2$ and every e_i comes from Iexp or every e_i comes from Bexp.

Figure 8.7 depicts the derivation tree corresponding to the inferences that evaluate "x+(y+6)". To save space, the store argument is shortened to "s". The last step of the deduction uses the generalization of rule (14) seen immediately above.

$$\frac{\dfrac{\dfrac{<y,s> \rightarrow <25,s>}{<y+6,s> \rightarrow <25+6,s>} \quad <25+6,s> \rightarrow <31,s>}{<x,s> \rightarrow <17,s> \qquad <y+6,s> \rightarrow <31,s>}}{<x+(y+6),s> \rightarrow <17+(y+6),s> \quad <17+(y+6),s> \rightarrow <17+31,s> \quad <17+31,s> \rightarrow <48,s>}{<x+(y+6),s> \rightarrow <48,s>}$$

Figure 8.7: A Derivation Tree

Notice from the previous example that the step-by-step computation semantics prescribes a left-to-right evaluation strategy for expressions. For an expression such as "(2*x)+(3*y)", with parentheses to show the structure of the abstract syntax tree, the subexpression "2*x" is evaluated before the subexpression "3*y". Some language designers complain that such ordering amounts to over specification of the semantics of expressions. However, slight changes in the inference rules can make expression evaluation nondeterministic in terms of this order. The problem is left to the reader as an exercise.

Outcomes

We say the computation has terminated or halted if no rule applies to the final configuration $<e_n,sto>$. This happens if the configuration is in normal form or if no rule can be applied because of unsatisfied conditions. Since we solely consider syntactically correct expressions, the only conditions whose failure may cause the computation to become stuck result from the dynamic errors of Wren. These conditions are as follows:

1. $(iop\ne/)$ or $(n\ne0)$ for rule (7)
2. $id\in dom(sto)$ for rule (12)
3. $bid\in dom(sto)$ for rule (13)

Taking the conditions into account, we can establish a completeness result for the inference system that defines the semantics of Wren expressions.

Definition: For any expression e, let *var*(e) be the set of variable identifiers that occur in e.   ∎

Completeness Theorem:

1. For any $ie\in(Iexp - Num)$ and $sto\in Store$ with $var(ie)\subseteq dom(sto)$ and no occurrence of the division operator in ie, there is a numeral $n\in Num$ such that $<ie,sto> \rightarrow <n,sto>$.
2. For any $be\in(Bexp - \{\textbf{true},\textbf{false}\})$ and $sto\in Store$ with $var(be)\subseteq dom(sto)$ and no occurrence of the division operator in be, there is a Boolean constant $b\in\{\textbf{true},\textbf{false}\}$ such that $<be,sto> \rightarrow <b,sto>$.

Proof: The proof is by structural induction following the abstract syntax of expressions in Wren.

1. Let $ie\in(Iexp - Num)$ and $sto\in Store$ with $var(ie)\subseteq dom(sto)$, and suppose ie has no occurrence of the division operator. According to the definition of abstract syntax presented in Figure 8.4, ie must be of the form $id\in Id$ or $(ie_1 iop ie_2)$ where $iop\in Iop-\{/\}$ and $ie_1,ie_2 : iexp$ also have no occurrence of /.

    Case 1: $ie = id\in Id$. Then $id\in dom(sto)$ and $<id,sto> \rightarrow <n,sto>$ where $n = applySto(sto,id)$ using rule (12).

Case 2: $ie = ie_1$ iop ie_2 where $iop \in Iop-\{/\}$ and ie_1, ie_2 : iexp, and for $i=1,2$, $var(ie_i) \subseteq dom(sto)$ and ie_i contains no occurrence of $/$.

Subcase a: $ie_1 = n_1 \in Num$ and $ie_2 = n_2 \in Num$. Then $<ie,sto> = <n_1$ iop $n_2,sto> \to <n,sto>$ where $n = compute(iop,n_1,n_2)$ by rule (7), whose condition is satisfied since $iop \neq /$.

Subcase b: $ie_1 = n_1 \in Num$ and $ie_2 \in (Iexp - Num)$. By the induction hypothesis, $<ie_2,sto> \to <n_2,sto>$ for some $n_2 \in Num$. We then use rule (4) to get $<ie,sto> = <n_1$ iop $ie_2,sto> \to <n_1$ iop $n_2,sto>$, to which we can apply subcase a.

Subcase c: $ie_1 \in (Iexp - Num)$ and $ie_2 \in Iexp$. By the induction hypothesis, $<ie_1,sto> \to <n_1,sto>$ for some $n_1 \in Num$. We then use rule (1) to get $<ie,sto> = <ie_1$ iop $ie_2,sto> \to <n_1$ iop $ie_2,sto>$, to which we can apply subcase a or subcase b.

Therefore, the conditions for structural induction on integer expressions are satisfied and the theorem holds for all $ie \in (Iexp-Num)$.

2. An exercise. ∎

A companion theorem, called the consistency theorem, asserts that every computation has a unique result.

Consistency Theorem:

1. For any $ie \in (Iexp - Num)$ and $sto \in Store$, if $<ie,sto> \to <n_1,sto>$ and $<ie,sto> \to <n_2,sto>$ with $n_1,n_2 \in Num$, it follows that $n_1 = n_2$.

2. For any $be \in (Bexp - \{\textbf{true},\textbf{false}\})$ and $sto \in Store$, if $<be,sto> \to <b_1,sto>$ and $<be,sto> \to <b_2,sto>$ with $b_1,b_2 \in \{\textbf{true},\textbf{false}\}$, it follows that $b_1 = b_2$.

Proof: Use structural induction again.

1. Let $ie \in (Iexp - Num)$ and $sto \in Store$ with $<ie,sto> \to <n_1,sto>$ and $<ie,sto> \to <n_2,sto>$ for $n_1,n_2 \in Num$.

   Case 1: $ie = id \in Id$. Then both computations must use rule (12), and $n_1 = applySto(sto,id) = n_2$.

   Case 2: $ie = ie_1$ iop ie_2. The last step in the computations $<ie_1$ iop $ie_2,sto> \to <n_1,sto>$ and $<ie_1$ iop $ie_2,sto> \to <n_2,sto>$ must be obtained by applying rule (7) to expressions of the form k_1 iop k_2 and m_1 iop m_2 where $k_1,k_2,m_1,m_2 \in Num$,
   $$<ie_1,sto> \to <k_1,sto>, <ie_2,sto> \to <k_2,sto>,$$
   $$<ie_1,sto> \to <m_1,sto>, <ie_2,sto> \to <m_2,sto>,$$
   $$compute(iop,k_1,k_2) = n_1, \text{ and } compute(iop,m_1,m_2) = n_2.$$
   Then by the induction hypothesis, $k_1 = m_1$ and $k_2 = m_2$.
   Therefore $n_1 = compute(iop,k_1,k_2) = compute(iop,m_1,m_2) = n_2$.

Now the result follows by structural induction.

2.   An exercise.   ∎

Exercises

1. Evaluate the Wren expression "(x+y)+6" using the store, sto = {x↦17, y↦25}. Draw a derivation tree that shows the applications of the inference rules.

2. Evaluate the following Wren expressions using the structural operational specification in Figure 8.6 and the store sto = {a↦6, b↦9, p↦true, q↦false}.
    a) (a<>0) **and not**(p **and** q)
    b) a − (b − (a −1))
    c) (a > 10) **or** (c=0)
    d) b / (a-6)

3. Prove the derived rule for the semantics of Wren expressions:

$$\frac{<e_1,sto> \rightarrow <e_2,sto> \quad <e_2,sto> \rightarrow <e_3,sto> \quad \ldots \quad <e_{n-1},sto> \rightarrow <e_n,sto>}{<e_1,sto> \rightarrow <e_n,sto>}$$

with the condition that $n \geq 2$ and every e_i comes from Iexp or every e_i comes from Bexp.

4. Provide additional inference rules in Figure 8.6 so that the system gives meaning to Wren expressions using the unary minus operation. *Hint:* Use *compute* for the arithmetic.

5. Modify the inference system for Wren expressions so that binary expressions can have either the left or the right argument evaluated first.

6. Complete the proof of the completeness theorem for Boolean expressions in Wren.

7. Complete the proof of the consistency theorem for Boolean expressions in Wren.

8. Define rules that specify the meaning of Boolean expressions of the form "b_1 **and** b_2" and "b_1 **or** b_2" directly in the manner of rule (11) for **not**. Then rewrite the specification of Wren expressions so that **and then** and **or else** are interpreted as conditional (short-circuit) operators. A conditional **and**—for example, "b_1 **and then** b_2"—is equivalent to "**if** b_1 **then** b_2 **else false**".

9. Extend Wren to include conditional integer expressions with the abstract syntax

$$be : bexp \qquad ie_1 : iexp \qquad ie_2 : iexp$$

$$\textbf{if } be \textbf{ then } ie_1 \textbf{ else } ie_2 : iexp$$

and add inference rule(s) to give them meaning.

8.6 STRUCTURAL OPERATIONAL SEMANTICS: COMMANDS

The structural operational semantics of a command in Wren describes the steps of a computation as the command modifies the state of a machine. We now consider language features—assignment and input—that can change the values bound to identifiers in the store. In addition, the **read** and **write** commands affect the input and output lists associated with the execution of a program. A triple of values represents the state of our abstract machine: the current input list, the current output list, and the current store. Input and output sequences are finite lists of numerals. We use structures of the form st(in,out,sto) to describe the state of a machine at a particular instant, where "in" and "out" are finite lists of numerals, represented using the notation [3,5,8].

A configuration on which the transition system operates contains a command to be executed and a state. Given a command c_0 and an initial state $st(in_0,out_0,sto_0)$, a computation proceeds following a set of inference rules.

$$<c_0,st(in_0,out_0,sto_0)> \rightarrow <c_1,st(in_1,out_1,sto_1)> \rightarrow <c_2,st(in_2,out_2,sto_2)> \rightarrow \;....$$

The inference rules for the structural operational semantics of commands in Wren are listed in Figure 8.8. Observe that most commands need not delve into the internal structure of states; in fact, only assignment, **read**, and **write** explicitly modify components of the state. The input and output lists are manipulated by auxiliary functions, *head*, *tail*, and *affix*. The **write** command uses *affix* to append a numeral onto the right end of the output list. For example, $affix([2,3,5],8) = [2,3,5,8]$.

Again, the inference rules promote a well-defined strategy for the execution of commands. When the action of a command depends on the value of some expression that serves as a component in the command, we use a rule whose premise describes one step in the reduction of the expression and whose conclusion assimilates that change into the command. See rules (1), (3), and (11) for illustrations of this strategy. When the expression has been reduced to its normal form (a numeral or a Boolean constant), the command carries out its action. See rules (2), (4), (5), and (12) for examples.

(1a) $$\frac{<ie,sto> \rightarrow <ie',sto>}{<id := ie,st(in,out,sto)> \rightarrow <id := ie',st(in,out,sto)>}$$

(1b) $$\frac{<bie,sto> \rightarrow <bie',sto>}{<bid:=bie,st(in,out,sto)> \rightarrow <bid:=bie',st(in,out,sto)>}$$

(2a) $<id := n,st(in,out,sto)> \rightarrow <$**skip**$,st(in,out,updateSto(sto,id,n))>$

(2b) $<bid := b,st(in,out,sto)> \rightarrow <$**skip**$,st(in,out,updateSto(sto,bid,b))>$

(3) $$\frac{<be,sto> \rightarrow <be',sto>}{<\text{if } be \text{ then } c_1 \text{ else } c_2,st(in,out,sto)> \rightarrow <\text{if } be' \text{ then } c_1 \text{ else } c_2,st(in,out,sto)>}$$

(4) $<$**if true then** c_1 **else** c_2,state$> \rightarrow <c_1$,state$>$

(5) $<$**if false then** c_1 **else** c_2,state$> \rightarrow <c_2$,state$>$

(6) $<$**if** be **then** c,state$> \rightarrow <$**if** be **then** c **else skip**,state$>$

(7) $<$**while** be **do** c,state$> \rightarrow <$**if** be **then** (c ; **while** be **do** c) **else skip**,state$>$

(8) $$\frac{<c_1,state> \rightarrow <c_1',state'>}{<c_1 ; c_2,state> \rightarrow <c_1' ; c_2,state'>}$$

(9) $<$**skip** ; c,state$> \rightarrow <$c,state$>$

(10) $<$**read** id,st(in,out,sto)$> \rightarrow$ $\qquad\qquad\qquad$ in $\neq$ [ ]
$\qquad\qquad\qquad\qquad <$**skip**$,st(tail(in),out,updateSto(sto,id,head(in)))>$

(11) $$\frac{<ie,sto> \rightarrow <ie',sto>}{<\textbf{write } ie,st(in,out,sto)> \rightarrow <\textbf{write } ie',st(in,out,sto)>}$$

(12) $<$**write** n,st(in,out,sto)$> \rightarrow <$**skip**$,st(in,affix(out,n),sto)$

Figure 8.8: Semantics for Commands

Note that assignment and the **read** and **write** commands are elementary actions, so they reduce to an "empty command" represented by **skip**. Two commands, **if-then** and **while**, are handled by translation into forms that are treated elsewhere (see rules (6) and (7)). Finally, command sequencing (semicolon) needs two rules—one to bring about the reduction of the first command to **skip**, and the second to discard the first command when it has been simplified to **skip**. Observe that now we have the possibility that a computation may continue forever because of the **while** command in Wren. Rule (7) defines "**while** be **do** c" in terms of itself.

For completeness, we again included an inference rule that makes the transition relation $\rightarrow$ transitive:

$$(13) \quad \frac{<c_1,state_1> \rightarrow <c_2,state_2> \qquad <c_2,state_2> \rightarrow <c_3,state_3>}{<c_1,state_1> \rightarrow <c_3,state_3>}$$

and furthermore assume that $\rightarrow$ is a reflexive relation.

Given a Wren program whose declarations have been elaborated, verifying that it satisfies the context conditions of its syntax, and whose body is the command c, and given a list $[n_1, n_2, n_3, ..., n_k]$ of numerals as input, the transition rules defined by the inference system in Figure 8.8 are applied to the initial configuration, $<c, st([n_1,n_2,n_3,...,n_k],[\ ],emptySto)>$, to produce the meaning of the Wren program.

A configuration with the pattern $<$**skip**,state$>$ serves as a normal form for computations. No rule applies to configurations in this form, and their state embodies the result of the computation—namely, the output list and the final store—when all of the commands have been executed. We have three possible outcomes of a computation that starts with a command and an initial state:

1. After a finite number of transitions, we reach a configuration $<$**skip**,state$>$ in normal form.

2. After a finite number of transitions, we reach a configuration that is not in normal form but for which no further transition is defined. This can happen when an expression evaluation becomes stuck because of an undefined identifier or division by zero, or upon the failure of the condition on rule (10), which specifies that the input list is nonempty when a **read** command is to be executed next.

3. A computation sequence continues without end when describing the semantics of a **while** command that never terminates. As a simple example, consider the transitions:

   $<$**while true do skip**,state$>$

   $\quad \rightarrow <$**if true then** (**skip** ; **while true do skip**) **else skip**,state$>$ (7)

$\rightarrow$ <**skip** ; **while true do skip**,state>   (4)

$\rightarrow$ <**while true do skip**,state>   (9)

$\rightarrow$ <**if true then** (**skip** ; **while true do skip**) **else skip**,state>   (7)

$\rightarrow$ <**skip** ; **while true do skip**,state>   (4)

$\rightarrow$ <**while true do skip**,state>   (9)

$\rightarrow$ ....

We use the notation <**c,state**> $\rightarrow \infty$ to denote the property that a computation sequence starting with the configuration <c,state> fails to terminate. It should be obvious from the example above that for any state st, <**while true do skip**,st> $\rightarrow \infty$.

Using rules (8) and (9) we can derive a new inference rule (9') that will make deductions a bit more concise.

$$(9') \quad \frac{<c_1,\text{state}> \rightarrow <\textbf{skip},\text{state'}>}{<c_1 ; c_2,\text{state}> \rightarrow <c_2,\text{state'}>}$$

Verifying this new rule provides an example of a derivation following the inference system.

$$\frac{\dfrac{<c_1,\text{state}> \rightarrow <\textbf{skip},\text{state'}>}{<c_1 ; c_2,\text{state}> \rightarrow <\textbf{skip} ; c_2,\text{state'}>} \; (8) \qquad <\textbf{skip} ; c_2,\text{state'}> \rightarrow <c_2,\text{state'}> \; (9)}{<c_1 ; c_2,\text{state}> \rightarrow <c_2,\text{state'}>} \qquad (13)$$

A Sample Computation

Since the steps in a computation following structural operational semantics are very small, derivation sequences for even simple programs can get quite lengthy. We illustrate the semantics with an example that may well be a test of endurance. The Wren program under consideration consists of the command sequence

mx := 0; **read** z; **while** z$\geq$0 **do** ((**if** z>mx **then** mx:=z);read z); **write** mx

where we assume that all identifiers have been appropriately declared. Meta-parentheses clarify the grouping of this representation of the abstract syntax. The program is given the input list: [5,8,3,-1].

To shorten the description of the derivation, a number of abbreviations will be employed:

c_1 = (mx:=0)

c_2 = **read** z

c_3 = **while** $z \geq 0$ **do** ((**if** z>mx **then** mx:=z);read z)

c_4 = **write** mx

c_w = (**if** z>mx **then** mx:=z);read z

{ } = *emptySto*

We start the transition system with the initial state, st([5,8,3,-1],[ ],{ }).

Throughout the derivation, assume that "**if** z>mx **then** mx:=z" is an abbreviation of "**if** z>mx **then** mx:=z **else skip**" to avoid the extra steps using rule (6). For each step in the derivation, the number of the rule being applied will appear at the far right. The details of expression evaluation are suppressed, so we just use "(expr)" to signify a derivation for an expression even though it may consist of several steps. The rule (13) that makes → transitive is generally ignored, but its result is implied. Here then is the computation according to structural operational semantics.

<mx:=0,st([5,8,3,-1],[ ],{ })> → <**skip**,st([5,8,3,-1],[ ],{mx↦0})>   (2)

<mx:=0;c_2;c_3;c_4,st([5,8,3,-1],[ ],{ })> →

    <**read** z;c_3;c_4,st([5,8,3,-1],[ ],{mx↦0})>   (9')

<**read** z,st([5,8,3,-1],[ ],{mx↦0})> → <**skip**,st([8,3,-1],[ ],{mx↦0,z↦5})>   (10)

<**read** z;c_3;c_4,st([5,8,3,-1],[ ],{mx↦0})> →

    <(**while** $z \geq 0$ **do** c_w);c_4,st([8,3,-1],[ ],{mx↦0,z↦5})>   (9')

<**while** $z \geq 0$ **do** c_w,st([8,3,-1],[ ],{mx↦0,z↦5})> →

    <**if** $z \geq 0$ **then**(c_w;c_3) **else skip**,st([8,3,-1],[ ],{mx↦0,z↦5})>   (7)

<$z \geq 0$,{mx↦0,z↦5}> → <**true**,{mx↦0,z↦5}>   (expr)

<**if** $z \geq 0$ **then**(c_w;c_3) **else skip**,st([8,3,-1],[ ],{mx↦0,z↦5})> →   (3)

    <**if true then**(c_w; c_3) **else skip**,st([8,3,-1],[ ],{mx↦0,z↦5})>

<**if true then**(c_w;c_3) **else skip**,st([8,3,-1],[ ],{mx↦0,z↦5})> →   (4)

                         <c_w;c_3,st([8,3,-1],[ ],{mx↦0,z↦5})> =

    <(**if** z>mx **then** mx:=z);read z;**while** $z \geq 0$ **do** c_w,st([8,3,-1],[ ],{mx↦0,z↦5}>

<z>mx,{mx↦0,z↦5}> → <**true**,{mx↦0,z↦5}>   (expr)

<**if** z>mx **then** mx:=z,st([8,3,-1],[ ],{mx↦0,z↦5}> →   (3)

    <**if true then** mx:=z,st([8,3,-1],[ ],{mx↦0,z↦5}>

<**if true then** mx:=z,st([8,3,-1],[ ],{mx↦0,z↦5}> →   (4)

    <mx:=z,st([8,3,-1],[ ],{mx↦0,z↦5}>

<z,{mx↦0,z↦5}> → <5,{mx↦0,z↦5}>   (expr)

$\langle mx:=z, st([8,3,-1],[\ ],\{mx \mapsto 0, z \mapsto 5\})\rangle \rightarrow$ (1)
    $\langle mx:=5, st([8,3,-1],[\ ],\{mx \mapsto 0, z \mapsto 5\})\rangle$

$\langle mx:=5, st([8,3,-1],[\ ],\{mx \mapsto 0, z \mapsto 5\})\rangle \rightarrow$ (2)
    $\langle \mathbf{skip}, st([8,3,-1],[\ ],\{mx \mapsto 5, z \mapsto 5\})\rangle$

$\langle \mathbf{if}\ z>mx\ \mathbf{then}\ mx:=z, st([8,3,-1],[\ ],\{mx \mapsto 0, z \mapsto 5\})\rangle \rightarrow$ (13)
    $\langle \mathbf{skip}, st([8,3,-1],[\ ],\{mx \mapsto 5, z \mapsto 5\})\rangle$

$\langle (\mathbf{if}\ z>mx\ \mathbf{then}\ mx:=z);\mathbf{read}\ z;\mathbf{while}\ z{\geq}0\ \mathbf{do}\ c_w, st([8,3,-1],[\ ],\{mx \mapsto 0, z \mapsto 5\})\rangle \rightarrow$
    $\langle \mathbf{read}\ z;\mathbf{while}\ z{\geq}0\ \mathbf{do}\ c_w, st([8,3,-1],[\ ],\{mx \mapsto 5, z \mapsto 5\})\rangle$ (9')

$\langle \mathbf{read}\ z, st([8,3,-1],[\ ],\{mx \mapsto 5, z \mapsto 5\})\rangle \rightarrow \langle \mathbf{skip}, st([3,-1],[\ ],\{mx \mapsto 5, z \mapsto 8\})\rangle$ (10)

$\langle \mathbf{read}\ z;\mathbf{while}\ z{\geq}0\ \mathbf{do}\ c_w, st([8,3,-1],[\ ],\{mx \mapsto 5, z \mapsto 5\})\rangle \rightarrow$ (9')
    $\langle \mathbf{while}\ z{\geq}0\ \mathbf{do}\ c_w, st([3,-1],[\ ],\{mx \mapsto 5, \mapsto 8\})\rangle$

$\langle \mathbf{while}\ z{\geq}0\ \mathbf{do}\ c_w, st([3,-1],[\ ],\{mx \mapsto 5, z \mapsto 8\})\rangle \rightarrow$ (7)
    $\langle \mathbf{if}\ z{\geq}0\ \mathbf{then}(c_w;c_3)\ \mathbf{else\ skip}, st([3,-1],[\ ],\{mx \mapsto 5, \mapsto 8\})\rangle$

$\langle z{\geq}0, \{mx \mapsto 5, z \mapsto 8\}\rangle \rightarrow \langle \mathbf{true}, \{m \mapsto 5, \mapsto 8\}\rangle$ (expr)

$\langle \mathbf{if}\ z{\geq}0\ \mathbf{then}(c_w;c_3)\ \mathbf{else\ skip}, st([3,-1],[\ ],\{mx \mapsto 5, \mapsto 8\})\rangle \rightarrow$ (3)
    $\langle \mathbf{if\ true\ then}(c_w;c_3)\ \mathbf{else\ skip}, st([3,-1],[\ ],\{mx \mapsto 5, z \mapsto 8\})\rangle$

$\langle \mathbf{if\ true\ then}(c_w;c_3)\ \mathbf{else\ skip}, st([3,-1],[\ ],\{mx \mapsto 5, z \mapsto 8\})\rangle \rightarrow$ (4)
                $\langle c_w;c_3, st([3,-1],[\ ],\{mx \mapsto 5, \mapsto 8\})\rangle =$
    $\langle (\mathbf{if}\ z>mx\ \mathbf{then}\ mx:=z);\mathbf{read}\ z;\mathbf{while}\ z{\geq}0\ \mathbf{do}\ c_w, st([3,-1],[\ ],\{mx \mapsto 5, \mapsto 8\}\rangle$

$\langle z>mx, \{mx \mapsto 5, z \mapsto 8\}\rangle \rightarrow \langle \mathbf{true}, \{m \mapsto 5, z \mapsto 8\}\rangle$ (expr)

$\langle \mathbf{if}\ z>mx\ \mathbf{then}\ mx:=z, st([3,-1],[\ ],\{mx \mapsto 5, z \mapsto 8\})\rangle \rightarrow$
    $\langle \mathbf{if\ true\ then}\ mx:=z, st([3,-1],[\ ],\{mx \mapsto 5, z \mapsto 8\})\rangle$ (3)

$\langle \mathbf{if\ true\ then}\ mx:=z, st([3,-1],[\ ],\{mx \mapsto 5, z \mapsto 8\})\rangle \rightarrow$
    $\langle mx:=z, st([3,-1],[\ ],\{mx \mapsto 5, z \mapsto 8\})\rangle$ (4)

$\langle z, \{mx \mapsto 5, z \mapsto 8\}\rangle \rightarrow \langle 8, \{mx \mapsto 5, z \mapsto 8\}\rangle$ (expr)

$\langle mx:=z, st([3,-1],[\ ],\{mx \mapsto 5, z \mapsto 8\})\rangle \rightarrow$
    $\langle mx:=8, st([3,-1],[\ ],\{mx \mapsto 5, z \mapsto 8\})\rangle$ (1)

$\langle mx:=8, st([3,-1],[\ ],\{mx \mapsto 5, \mapsto 8\}\rangle \rightarrow$ (2)
    $\langle \mathbf{skip}, st([3,-1],[\ ],\{mx \mapsto 8, z \mapsto 8\}\rangle$

$\langle \mathbf{if}\ z>mx\ \mathbf{then}\ mx:=z, st([3,-1],[\ ],\{mx \mapsto 5, z \mapsto 8\})\rangle \rightarrow$ (13)
    $\langle \mathbf{skip}, st([3,-1],[\ ],\{mx \mapsto 8, z \mapsto 8\})\rangle$

$<$(**if** $z>mx$ **then** $mx:=z$);**read** z;**while** $z\geq0$ **do** c_w,st([3,-1],[ ],\{mx$\mapsto$5,z$\mapsto$8\})$> \rightarrow$

$<$**read** z;**while** $z\geq0$ **do** c_w,st([3,-1],[ ],\{mx$\mapsto$8,$\mapsto$8\})$>$ (9')

$<$**read** z,st([3,-1],[ ],\{mx$\mapsto$8,z$\mapsto$8\})$> \rightarrow <$**skip**,st([-1],[ ],\{mx$\mapsto$8,z$\mapsto$3\})$>$ (10)

$<$**read** z;**while** $z\geq0$ **do** c_w,st([3,-1],[ ],\{mx$\mapsto$8,z$\mapsto$8\})$> \rightarrow$ (9')

$<$**while** $z\geq0$ **do** c_w,st([-1],[ ],\{mx$\mapsto$8,z$\mapsto$3\})$>$

$<$**while** $z\geq0$ **do** c_w,st([-1],[ ],\{mx$\mapsto$8,z$\mapsto$3\})$> \rightarrow$ (7)

$<$**if** $z\geq0$ **then**$(c_w;c_3)$ **else skip**,st([-1],[ ],\{mx$\mapsto$8,z$\mapsto$3\})$>$

$<z\geq0$,\{mx$\mapsto$8,z$\mapsto$3\}$> \rightarrow <$**true**,\{mx$\mapsto$8,z$\mapsto$3\}$>$ (expr)

$<$**if** $z\geq0$ **then**$(c_w;c_3)$ **else skip**,st([-1],[ ],\{mx$\mapsto$8,z$\mapsto$3\})$> \rightarrow$ (3)

$<$**if true then**$(c_w;c_3)$ **else skip**,st([-1],[ ],\{mx$\mapsto$8,z$\mapsto$3\})$>$

$<$**if true then**$(c_w;c_3)$ **else skip**,st([-1],[ ],\{mx$\mapsto$8,z$\mapsto$3\})$> \rightarrow$ (4)

$<c_w;c_3$,st([-1],[ ],\{mx$\mapsto$8,z$\mapsto$3\})$> =$

$<$(**if** $z>mx$ **then** $mx:=z$);**read** z;**while** $z\geq0$ **do** c_w,st([-1],[ ],\{m$\mapsto$8,z$\mapsto$3\}$>$

$<z>mx$,\{mx$\mapsto$8,z$\mapsto$3\}$> \rightarrow <$**false**,\{mx$\mapsto$8,z$\mapsto$3\})$>$ (expr)

$<$**if** $z>mx$ **then** $mx:=z$,st([-1],[ ],\{mx$\mapsto$8,z$\mapsto$3\})$> \rightarrow$ (3)

$<$**if false then** $mx:=z$,st([-1],[ ],\{mx$\mapsto$8,z$\mapsto$3\})$>$

$<$**if false then** $mx:=z$,st([-1],[ ],\{mx$\mapsto$8,z$\mapsto$3\})$> \rightarrow$ (5)

$<$**skip**,st([-1],[ ],\{mx$\mapsto$8,z$\mapsto$3\})$>$

$<$(**if** $z>mx$ **then** $mx:=z$);**read** z;**while** $z\geq0$ **do** c_w,st([-1],[ ],\{mx$\mapsto$8,z$\mapsto$3\})$>$ (9')

$<$**read** z;**while** $z\geq0$ **do** c_w,st([-1],[ ],\{mx$\mapsto$8,z$\mapsto$3\})$>$

$<$**read** z,st([-1],[ ],\{mx$\mapsto$8,z$\mapsto$3\})$> \rightarrow <$**skip**,st([ ],[ ],\{mx$\mapsto$8,z$\mapsto$-1\})$>$ (10)

$<$**read** z;**while** $z\geq0$ **do** c_w,st([-1],[ ],\{mx$\mapsto$8,z$\mapsto$3\})$> \rightarrow$ (9')

$<$**while** $z\geq0$ **do** c_w,st([ ],[ ],\{mx$\mapsto$8,z$\mapsto$-1\})$>$

$<$**while** $z\geq0$ **do** c_w,st([ ],[ ],\{m$\mapsto$8,z$\mapsto$-1\})$> \rightarrow$ (7)

$<$**if** $z\geq0$ **then**$(c_w;c_3)$ **else skip**,st([ ],[ ],\{mx$\mapsto$8,z$\mapsto$-1\})$>$

$<z\geq0$,\{mx$\mapsto$8,z$\mapsto$-1\}$> \rightarrow <$**false**,\{mx$\mapsto$8,z$\mapsto$-1\}$>$ (expr)

$<$**if** $z\geq0$ **then**$(c_w;c_3)$ **else skip**,st([ ],[ ],\{mx$\mapsto$8,z$\mapsto$-1\})$> \rightarrow$ (3)

$<$**if false then**$(c_w;c_3)$ **else skip**,st([ ],[ ],\{mx$\mapsto$8,z$\mapsto$-1\})$>$

$<$**if false then**$(c_w;c_3)$ **else skip**,st([ ],[ ],\{mx$\mapsto$8,z$\mapsto$-1\})$> \rightarrow$ (5)

$<$**skip**,st([ ],[ ],\{mx$\mapsto$8,z$\mapsto$-1\})$>$

<**while** $z \geq 0$ **do** c_w,st([ ],[ ],{mx$\mapsto$8,z$\mapsto$-1})> $\rightarrow$ (13)

    <**skip**,st([ ],[ ],{mx$\mapsto$8,z$\mapsto$-1})>

<**while** $z \geq 0$ **do** c_w ;**write** mx,st([8,3,-1],[ ],{mx$\mapsto$0,z$\mapsto$5})> $\rightarrow$ (9')

    <**write** mx,st([ ],[ ],{mx$\mapsto$8,z$\mapsto$-1})>

<mx,{mx$\mapsto$8,z$\mapsto$-1})> $\rightarrow$ <8,{mx$\mapsto$8,z$\mapsto$-1}>   (expr)

<**write** mx,st([ ],[ ],{mx$\mapsto$8,z$\mapsto$-1})> $\rightarrow$ (11)

    <**write** 8,st([ ],[ ],{mx$\mapsto$8,z$\mapsto$-1})>

<**write** 8,st([ ],[ ],{mx$\mapsto$8,z$\mapsto$-1})> $\rightarrow$ (12)

    <**skip** ,st([ ],[8],{mx$\mapsto$8,z$\mapsto$-1})>

<c_1;c_2;c_3;c_4,st([5,8,3,-1],[ ],{ })> $\rightarrow$ (13)

    <**skip** ,st([ ],[8],{mx$\mapsto$8,z$\mapsto$-1})>

This linear deduction of the final state represents a derivation tree with axioms at its leaf nodes and the configuration <**skip**, st([ ],[8],{mx$\mapsto$8,z$\mapsto$-1})> at its root. Clearly, there is no reasonable way we can show the tree for this derivation.

Semantic Equivalence

One justification for formal definitions of programming languages is to provide a method for determining when two commands have the same effect. In the framework of structural operational semantics, we can define semantic equivalence in terms of the computation sequences produced by the two commands.

Definition: Commands c_1 and c_2 are **semantically equivalent,** written $c_1 \equiv c_2$, if both of the following two properties hold:

1. For any two states s and s_f,

        <c_1,s> $\rightarrow$ <**skip**,s_f> if and only if <c_2,s> $\rightarrow$ <**skip**,s_f>, and

2. For any state s,

        <c_1,s> $\rightarrow$ ∞ if and only if <c_2,s> $\rightarrow$ ∞.   ∎

It follows that for semantically equivalent commands, if one gets stuck in a nonfinal configuration, the other must also.

Example: For any c_1,c_2 : cmd and be : bexp,

    if be **then** c_1 **else** c_2 $\equiv$ **if not**(be) **then** c_2 **else** c_1.

Proof: Let be : bexp and let c_1 and c_2 be any two commands. Suppose that s = st(in,out,sto) is an arbitrary state.

Case 1: <be,sto> → <**true**,sto> by some computation sequence. Then <**not**(be),sto> → <**not**(**true**),sto> → <**false**,sto> by rules (10) and (11) for expressions in Figure 8.6. Now use rules (3), (4), and (5) for commands to get:

<**if** be **then** c_1 **else** c_2,s> → <**if true then** c_1 **else** c_2,s> → <c_1,s> and

<**if not**(be) **then** c_2 **else** c_1,s> → <**if false then** c_2 **else** c_1,s> → <c_1,s>.

From here on the two computations from <c_1,s> must be identical.

Case 2: <be,sto> → <**false**,sto> by some computation. Proceed as in case 1.

Case 3: <be,sto> → <be',sto> where be' is not a Boolean constant and the computation is stuck. Then both

<**if** be **then** c_1 **else** c_2,s> → <**if** be' **then** c_1 **else** c_2,s> and

<**if not**(be) **then** c_2 **else** c_1,s> → <**if not**(be') **then** c_2 **else** c_1,s>

are stuck computations.   ∎

Our definition of semantic equivalence entails a slight anomaly in that any two nonterminating computations are viewed as equivalent. In particular, this means that a program that prints the number 5 endlessly is considered equivalent to another program that runs forever without any output. For terminating computations, however, the definition of semantic equivalence agrees with our intuition for programs having the same behavior.

Natural Semantics

Structural operational semantics takes as its mission the description of the individual steps of a computation. It strives to capture the smallest possible changes in configurations. For this reason, structural operational semantics is sometimes called **small-step semantics**. An alternative semantics takes the opposite view—namely, to describe the computation in large steps providing a direct relation between initial and final states. This version of operational semantics is defined by inference systems to create a so-called **big-step semantics**. The most developed version of big-step semantics, called **natural semantics**, was proposed by a group in France led by Gilles Kahn.

To suggest the flavor of natural semantics, we show in Figure 8.9 several of the inference rules that are used to define the meaning of Wren. In natural semantics, configurations have several possible forms for each kind of language construct:

Expressions: <e,sto>, n, or b, and

Commands: <c,state> or state.

A transition defines a final result in one step, namely

<e,sto> ➡ n or <e,sto> ➡ b, and

<c,state> ➡ state',

We chose to investigate small-step semantics because big-step semantics closely resembles denotational semantics and, in fact, can be viewed as a notational variant of it. See Chapter 9 for a description of denotational semantics. For more on natural semantics as well as structural operational semantics, see the further readings at the end of this chapter.

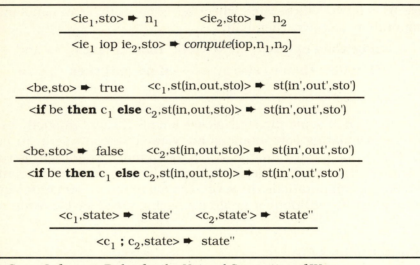

$$\frac{<ie_1,sto> ➡ n_1 \qquad <ie_2,sto> ➡ n_2}{<ie_1 \; iop \; ie_2,sto> ➡ compute(iop,n_1,n_2)}$$

$$\frac{<be,sto> ➡ true \qquad <c_1,st(in,out,sto)> ➡ st(in',out',sto')}{<if \; be \; then \; c_1 \; else \; c_2,st(in,out,sto)> ➡ st(in',out',sto')}$$

$$\frac{<be,sto> ➡ false \qquad <c_2,st(in,out,sto)> ➡ st(in',out',sto')}{<if \; be \; then \; c_1 \; else \; c_2,st(in,out,sto)> ➡ st(in',out',sto')}$$

$$\frac{<c_1,state> ➡ state' \qquad <c_2,state'> ➡ state''}{<c_1 \; ; \; c_2,state> ➡ state''}$$

Figure 8.9: Some Inference Rules for the Natural Semantics of Wren

Exercises

1. Derive the computation sequence for the following Wren programs. Use [8,13,-1] as the input list.

    a) **read** a; **read** b; c:=a; a:=b; b:=c; **write** a; **write** b

    b) n:=3; f:=1; **while** n>1 **do** (f:=f*n; n:=n-1); **write** f

    c) s:=0; **read** a; **while** a≥0 **do** (s:=s+a; **read** a); **write** s

    d) **read** x; **if** x>5 **then** y := x+2 **else** y := 0

    e) p:=**true**; **read** m; **while** p **do** (**read** a; m:=m*a; p:=**not**(p)); **write** m

2. The following rule provides an alternate definition of the **while** command in Wren:

    (7')
    $$\frac{\text{<if } be \text{ then } (c \text{ ; while } be \text{ do } c) \text{ else skip},\text{state>} \rightarrow \text{<skip},\text{state'>}}{\text{<while } be \text{ do } c,\text{state>} \rightarrow \text{<skip},\text{state'>}}$$

    Show that the inference system with rule (7) replaced by this new rule is equivalent to the original system.

3. Add these language constructs to Wren and provide meaning for them by defining inference rules for their semantics.

    a)
    $$\frac{be : bexp \qquad c : cmd}{\textbf{repeat } c \textbf{ until } be : cmd}$$

    b)
    $$\frac{c : cmd \qquad ie : iexp}{\textbf{begin } c \textbf{ return } ie \textbf{ end} : iexp}$$

    c)   **swap** (id_1, id_2) : cmd $id_1, id_2 \in$ Id

    d) Parallel assignment:
    $$\frac{ie_1, ie_2 : iexp}{id_1, id_2 := ie_1, ie_2 : cmd} \qquad id_1, id_2 \in \text{Id}$$

4. Verify the following semantic equivalences.

    a) For any c:cmd, c ; **skip** $\equiv$ c.

    b) For any c:cmd, **skip** ; c $\equiv$ c.

    c) For any be:bexp and c:cmd, **if** be **then** c **else** c $\equiv$ c, assuming the reduction of be does not become stuck.

    d) For any be:bexp and c_1, c_2, c_3:cmd,
    (**if** be **then** c_1 **else** c_2) ; c_3 $\equiv$ **if** be **then** $(c_1 ; c_3)$ **else** $(c_2 ; c_3)$.

5. Prove that these pairs of commands are not semantically equivalent:

    a) c_3 ; (**if** be **then** c_1 **else** c_2) and **if** be **then** $(c_3 ; c_1)$ **else** $(c_3 ; c_2)$

    b) $id_1, id_2 := ie_1, ie_2$ and $id_1 := ie_1$; $id_2 := ie_2$

6. Extend Wren to include a definite iteration command of the form
    $$\frac{ie_1 : iexp \qquad ie_2 : iexp \qquad c : cmd}{\textbf{for } id := ie_1 \textbf{ to } ie_2 \textbf{ do } c \textbf{ end} : cmd} \qquad id \in \text{Id}$$

whose informal semantics agrees with the **for** command in Pascal. Add inference rules to the structural operational semantics of Wren to give a formal semantics for this new command.

8.7 LABORATORY: IMPLEMENTING STRUCTURAL OPERATIONAL SEMANTICS

In Chapter 2 we developed a scanner and parser that take a text file containing a Wren program and produce an abstract syntax tree. Now we continue, creating a prototype implementation of Wren based on its structural operational semantics.

The transcript below shows a sample execution with the operational interpreter. The program reads a positive decimal integer and converts it into binary by subtracting powers of two. The example illustrates how the input list can be handled in Prolog.

```
>>> Interpreting Wren via Operational Semantics <<<
Enter name of source file: tobinary.wren
    program tobinary is
          var n,p : integer;
    begin
        read n; p := 2;
        while p<=n do p := 2*p end while;
        p := p/2;
        while p>0 do
            if n>= p then write 1; n := n-p
                     else write 0 end if;
            p := p/2
        end while
    end
Scan successful
Parse successful
Enter input list followed by a period: [321].
Output = [1,0,1,0,0,0,0,0,1]
Final Store:
    n      int(0)
    p      int(0)
yes
```

Commands

As with the implementation of the SECD machine in section 8.3, we define a predicate transform(Config,NewConfig) that carries out one computation step for the transition function. A configuration is represented just as it was in section 8.6—namely, st(In,Out,Sto)—except that we need uppercase for Prolog variables. Then rules (3), (4), and (5) defining transitions for **if-then-else** commands become three Prolog clauses whose order requires rule (3) to be last, which means that its more general pattern applies only if the Boolean expression is not in normal form.

transform(cfg(if(bool(true),C1,C2),State), cfg(C1,State)).   % 4

transform(cfg(if(bool(false),C1,C2),State), cfg(C2,State)).   % 5

transform(cfg(if(Be,C1,C2),st(In,Out,Sto)),   % 3
    cfg(if(Be1,C1,C2),st(In,Out,Sto))) :- transform(cfg(Be,Sto),cfg(Be1,Sto)).

The predicate transform that reduces expressions is defined later. Rules (6) and (7) in Figure 8.8 translate **while** and **if** commands according to their meaning. Two Prolog clauses perform the required translations.

transform(cfg(if(Be,C),State), cfg(if(Be,C,skip),State)).   % 6

transform(cfg(while(Be,C),State), cfg(if(Be,[C,while(Be,C)],skip),State)).   % 7

Remember from Chapter 2 that the parser produces a Prolog list of commands as the abstract syntax tree for a sequence of commands. Therefore the command "$c_1 ; c_2 ; c_3 ; c_4$" comes from the parser as $[c_1, c_2, c_3, c_4]$. So rule (9) becomes

transform(cfg([skip|Cs],State), cfg(Cs,State)).   % 9

and rule (8), which must follow rule (9), becomes

transform(cfg([C|Cs],State), cfg([C1|Cs],State1)) :-   % 8
    transform(cfg(C,State),cfg(C1,State1)).

Since a list of commands may become empty, we need an additional clause that has no analogue in Figure 8.8:

transform(cfg([ ],State), cfg(skip,State)).

Before considering the assignment command, we discuss how to model the finite function that comprises the store. We portray the store as a Prolog structure of the form

sto(a, int(3), sto(b, int(8), sto(c, bocl(false), nil)))

for the store {a↦3, b↦8, c↦false}. The empty store is given by the Prolog atom nil. The auxiliary functions for manipulating the store become predicates defined as follows:

updateSto(sto(Ide,V,Sto),Ide,Val,sto(Ide,Val,Sto)).

updateSto(sto(I,V,Sto),Ide,Val,sto(I,V,NewSto)) :-
                               updateSto(Sto,Ide,Val,NewSto).

updateSto(nil,Ide,Val,sto(Ide,Val,nil)).

applySto(sto(Ide,Val,Sto),Ide,Val).

applySto(sto(I,V,Sto),Ide,Val) :- applySto(Sto,Ide,Val).

applySto(nil,Ide,undefined) :- write('Undefined variable'), nl, abort.

Note that when an identifier cannot be found in the store, applySto prints an error message and aborts the execution of the operational interpreter.

If the right side of an assignment is already in normal form, the new binding can be entered into the store immediately. Two clauses correspond to the two parts of rule (2).

transform(cfg(assign(Ide,int(N)),st(In,Out,Sto)),   % 2a
    cfg(skip,st(In,Out,Sto1))) :- updateSto(Sto,Ide,int(N),Sto1).

transform(cfg(assign(Ide,bool(B)),st(In,Out,Sto)),   % 2b
    cfg(skip,st(In,Out,Sto1))) :- updateSto(Sto,Ide,bool(B),Sto1).

We leave the tags produced by the scanner and parser on constants as we place the values in memory.

If the right side of an assignment is not yet in normal form, we call on the transition function for expressions to reduce the right side using the predicate transform(cfg(E,Sto),cfg(E1,Sto)) that provides the operational semantics for expressions. We can combine the two parts of rule (1) in the Prolog implementation, since Prolog is not strongly typed.

transform(cfg(assign(Ide,E),st(In,Out,Sto)),   % 1
    cfg(assign(Ide,E1),st(In,Out,Sto))) :- transform(cfg(E,Sto),cfg(E1,Sto)).

Again, because of pattern matching, the more specialized clause head must precede the more general—that is, rule (2) comes before rule (1).

The **read** command is handled by two clauses, one to catch the dynamic error when the input list is empty and one to carry out the operation. Note that the head and tail functions are replaced by pattern matching.

transform(cfg(read(Ide),st([ ],Out,Sto)),cfg(skip,st([ ],Out,Sto))) :-   % 10
    write('Attempted read of empty file'), nl, abort.

transform(cfg(read(Ide),st([N|T],Out,Sto)), cfg(skip,st(T,Out,Sto1))) :-   % 10
    updateSto(Sto,Ide,int(N),Sto1).

The **write** command uses a Prolog predicate concat that concatenates two lists to affix a value to the right end of the output list.

```
transform(cfg(write(int(N)),st(In,Out,Sto)), cfg(skip,st(In,Out1,Sto))) :-     % 12
    concat(Out,[N],Out1).

transform(cfg(write(E),st(In,Out,Sto)), cfg(write(E1),st(In,Out,Sto))) :-     % 11
    transform(cfg(E,Sto),cfg(E1,Sto)).
```

We need a driver predicate interpret to call the transition predicate transform repeatedly until a normal form configuration with the **skip** command turns up or until the program aborts, if ever.

```
interpret(cfg(skip,FinalState),FinalState).

interpret(Config,FinalState) :-  transform(Config,NewConfig),
                                 interpret(NewConfig,FinalState).
```

Expressions

The three groups of rules for binary expressions must be handled from the most specific to the most general. Rules (7), (8), and (9), having both arguments in normal form, must come first.

```
transform(cfg(exp(Opr,int(N1),int(N2)),Sto), cfg(Val,Sto)) :-     % 7
    compute(Opr,int(N1),int(N2),Val).

transform(cfg(bexp(Opr,int(N1),int(N2)),Sto), cfg(Val,Sto)) :-     % 8
    compute(Opr,int(N1),int(N2),Val).

transform(cfg(bexp(Opr,bool(B1),bool(B2)),Sto), cfg(Val,Sto)) :-     % 9
    compute(Opr,bool(B1),bool(B2),Val).
```

For all three rules, the actual computation is isolated in the predicate compute(Opr,A1,A2,Result).

Expressions whose first argument is in normal form are treated in rules (4), (5), and (6). We use E2p for E2'.

```
transform(cfg(exp(Opr,int(N),E2),Sto), cfg(exp(Opr,int(N),E2p),Sto)) :-     % 4
    transform(cfg(E2,Sto),cfg(E2p,Sto)).

transform(cfg(bexp(Opr,int(N),E2),Sto), cfg(bexp(Opr,int(N),E2p),Sto)) :-     % 5
    transform(cfg(E2,Sto),cfg(E2p,Sto)).

transform(cfg(bexp(Opr,bool(B),E2),Sto),
                         cfg(bexp(Opr,bool(B),E2p),Sto)) :-     % 6
                         transform(cfg(E2,Sto),cfg(E2p,Sto)).
```

Those rules in which the left argument is not yet in normal form—namely (1), (2), and (3)—must come last.

```
transform(cfg(exp(Opr,E1,E2),Sto),cfg(exp(Opr,E1p,E2),Sto)) :-          % 1
    transform(cfg(E1,Sto),cfg(E1p,Sto)).

transform(cfg(bexp(Opr,E1,E2),Sto),cfg(bexp(Opr,E1p,E2),Sto)) :-        % 2+3
    transform(cfg(E1,Sto),cfg(E1p,Sto)).
```

Rules (2) and (3) can be folded together by letting Opr stand for both comparisons and Boolean operators. The compute predicate relies on native arithmetic in Prolog and simple pattern matching to carry out the computations. A few examples of clauses for this predicate are listed below.

```
compute(plus,int(M),int(N),int(R)) :- R is M+N.

compute(divides,int(M),int(0),int(0)) :- write('Division by zero'), nl, abort.
compute(divides,int(M),int(N),int(R)) :- R is M//N.

compute(equal,int(M),int(N),bool(true)) :- M =:= N.
compute(equal,int(M),int(N),bool(false)).

compute(neq,int(M),int(N),bool(false)) :- M =:= N.
compute(neq,int(M),int(N),bool(true)).

compute(less,int(M),int(N),bool(true)) :- M < N.
compute(less,int(M),int(N),bool(false)).

compute(and,bool(true),bool(true),bool(true)).
compute(and,bool(P),bool(Q),bool(false)).
```

Observe how a division by zero error causes the interpreter to abort. We use abort to signal a stuck configuration. Also note that the clauses for each operator depend on their order for correctness.

To complete the transition function for the operational semantics of expressions, we still need to handle the two unary operations, logical **not** and unary minus, which are left as exercises, and to deal with identifiers by probing the store (rules 12 and 13 for expressions). One clause defines the transition function for both integer and Boolean identifiers.

```
transform(cfg(ide(Ide),Sto), cfg(Val,Sto)) :- applySto(Sto,Ide,Val).      % 12+13
```

Finally, we need to define the driver predicate evaluate that propels and monitors the computation steps for expressions.

```
evaluate(cfg(int(N),Sto), int(N)).

evaluate(cfg(bool(B),Sto), bool(B)).

evaluate(Config, FinalValue) :-  transform(Config, NewConfig),
                                 evaluate(NewConfig, FinalValue).
```

Top-Level Driver

At the top level we call interpret with an initial configuration containing the command Cmd that makes up the body of the Wren program together with an initial state st(In,[ ],nil)) where In holds the input list obtained from the user. We depend on a predicate go to request the input and print the output.

```
go :-   nl,write('>>> Interpreting Wren via Operational Semantics <<<'), nl, nl,
        write('Enter name of source file: '), nl, readfilename(File), nl,
        see(File), scan(Tokens), seen, write('Scan successful'), nl, !,
        program(prog(Dec,Cmd),Tokens,[eop]), write('Parse successful'), nl, !,
        write('Enter input list followed by a period: '), nl, read(In), nl,
        interpret(cfg(Cmd,st(In,[ ],nil)),st(FinalIn,Out,Sto)), nl,
        write('Output = '), write(Out), nl, nl,
        write('Final Store:'), nl, printSto(Sto), nl.
```

Exercises

1. Supply Prolog definitions for the transition rules for the remaining expression types: **not** and unary minus.

2. Complete the definition of the compute predicate.

3. Extend the prototype interpreter to include the following language constructs.
   a) repeat-until commands
        Command ::= ... | **repeat** Command **until** Expression
   b) conditional expressions
        Expression ::= ... | **if** Expression **then** Expression **else** Expression
   c) expressions with side effects
        Expression ::= ... | **begin** Command **return** Expression **end**

4. Give a definition of the Prolog predicate printSto(Sto) that prints the bindings in the store Sto, one to a line.

8.8 FURTHER READING

Structural operational semantics originated in a seminal technical report by Gordon Plotkin [Plotkin81]. This initial presentation of an operational semantics based on inference rules defines a number of imperative programming constructs using small-step semantics. Early work with big-step semantics, called natural semantics by the group at INRIA, can be found in

[Kahn87]. The logic text [Reeves90] contains an introduction to natural deduction, the logic methodology that provides a basis for structural operational semantics. Also see [Prawitz65] for a more advanced description of natural deduction.

The introduction to formal semantics by Nielson and Nielson [Nielson92] treats both structural operational semantics and natural deduction. They suggest translating such operational definitions of programming languages into prototype implementations using Miranda.

Matthew Hennessy [Hennessy90] has aimed his text at an undergraduate audience, providing many examples of operational specifications using both small-step and big-step semantics, using the terms computation semantics and evaluation semantics. Hennessy considers imperative, functional, and concurrent programming languages in his examples. He also includes an extensive discussion of structural induction with numerous examples.

Egidio Astesiano [Astesiano91] gives a clear and logical presentation of operational semantics based on inference systems. He discusses the use of inference rules to specify abstract syntax and compares small-step and big-step operational semantics. Astesiano also describes the relation between natural semantics and denotational semantics.

Peter Landin's description of the SECD machine appears in [Landin64] and [Landin66]. Many recent texts on functional programming also contain material on SECD machines and their variants, including [Glaser84], [Henson87], [Field88], and [Reade89].

Peter Wegner's survey paper [Wegner72] covers the basics of the Vienna Definition Language. [Pagan81] describes VDL succinctly, using two small programming languages to illustrate this specification method.

Chapter 9
DENOTATIONAL SEMANTICS

W ith formal semantics we give programs meaning by mapping them into some abstract but precise domain of objects. Using denotational semantics, we provide meaning in terms of mathematical objects, such as integers, truth values, tuples of values, and functions. For this reason, denotational semantics was originally called mathematical semantics.

Christopher Strachey and his Programming Research Group at Oxford developed denotational semantics in the mid 1960s; Dana Scott supplied the mathematical foundations in 1969. Although originally intended as a mechanism for the analysis of programming languages, denotational semantics has become a powerful tool for language design and implementation.

In this chapter we take a careful look at denotational semantics. We illustrate the methodology by specifying the language of a simple calculator and three programming languages: (1) Wren, (2) a language with procedures called Pelican, and (3) a language with goto's called Gull. The presentation differs from some of the literature on denotational semantics in that we enhance the readability of the specifications by avoiding the Greek alphabet and single character identifiers found in the traditional presentations.

9.1 CONCEPTS AND EXAMPLES

Denotational semantics is based on the recognition that programs and the objects they manipulate are symbolic realizations of abstract mathematical objects, for example,

strings of digits realize numbers, and

function subprograms realize (approximate) mathematical functions.

The exact meaning of "approximate" as used here will be made clear in Chapter 10. The idea of denotational semantics is to associate an appropriate mathematical object, such as a number, a tuple, or a function, with each phrase of the language. The phrase is said to **denote** the mathematical object, and the object is called the **denotation** of the phrase.

Syntactically, a phrase in a programming language is defined in terms of its constituent parts by its BNF specification. The decomposition of language phrases into their subphrases is reflected in the abstract syntax of the programming language as well. A fundamental principle of denotational semantics is that the definition be **compositional**. That means the denotation of a language construct is defined in terms of the denotations of its subphrases. Later we discuss reasons for having compositional definitions.

Traditionally, denotational definitions use special brackets, the emphatic brackets $[\![\ ]\!]$, to separate the syntactic world from the semantic world. If p is a syntactic phrase in a programming language, then a denotational specification of the language will define a mapping *meaning*, so that *meaning* $[\![p]\!]$ is the denotation of p—namely, an abstract mathematical entity that models the semantics of p.

For example, the expressions "**2∗4**", "**(5+3)**", "**008**", and "**8**" are syntactic phrases that all denote the same abstract object, namely the integer 8. Therefore with a denotational definition of expressions we should be able to show that

$$meaning\ [\![2*4]\!] = meaning\ [\![(5+3)]\!] = meaning\ [\![008]\!] = meaning\ [\![8]\!] = 8.$$

Functions play a prominent role in denotational semantics, modeling the bindings in stores and environments as well as control abstractions in programming languages. For example, the "program"

$$fact(n) = if\ n=0\ then\ 1\ else\ n*fact(n-1)$$

denotes the factorial function, a mathematical object that can be viewed as the set of ordered pairs,

$$\{ <0,1>, <1,1>, <2,2>, <3,6>, <4,24>, <5,120>, <6,720>, \dots \},$$

and a denotational semantics should confirm this relationship.

A denotational specification of a programming language consists of five components, two specifying the syntactic world, one describing the semantic domains, and two defining the functions that map the syntactic objects to the semantic objects.

The Syntactic World

Syntactic categories or **syntactic domains** name collections of syntactic objects that may occur in phrases in the definition of the syntax of the language—for example,

Numeral, Command, and Expression.

Commonly, each syntactic domain has a special metavariable associated with it to stand for elements in the domain—for example,

> C : Command
>
> E : Expression
>
> N : Numeral
>
> I : Identifier.

With this traditional notation, the colon means "element of". Subscripts will be used to provide additional instances of the metavariables.

Abstract production rules describe the ways that objects from the syntactic categories may be combined in accordance with the BNF definition of the language. They provide the possible patterns that the abstract syntax trees of language phrases may take. These abstract production rules can be defined using the syntactic categories or using the metavariables for elements of the categories as an abbreviation mechanism.

> Command ::= **while** Expression **do** Command$^+$ **end while**
>
> E ::= N | I | E O E | − E

These rules are the abstract productions that were discussed in Chapter 1. They do not fully specify the details of syntax with respect to parsing items in the language but simply portray the possible forms of syntactic constructs that have been verified as correct by some other means.

The Semantic World

Semantic domains are "sets" of mathematical objects of a particular form. The sets serving as domains have a lattice-like structure that will be described in Chapter 10. For now we view these semantic domains as normal mathematical sets and structures—for example,

> Boolean = { true, false } is the set of truth values,
>
> Integer = { ... , -2, -1, 0, 1, 2, 3, 4, ... } is the set of integers, and
>
> Store = (Variable → Integer)   consists of sets of bindings (functions mapping variable names to values).

We use the notation A → B to denote the set of functions with domain A and codomain B.

The Connection between Syntax and Semantics

Semantic functions map objects of the syntactic world into objects in the semantic world. Constructs of the subject language—namely elements of the syntactic domains—are mapped into the semantic domains. These functions are specified by giving their syntax (domain and codomain), called their **signatures**—for example,

$meaning$: Program $\to$ Store

$evaluate$: Expression $\to$ (Store $\to$ Value)

and by using **semantic equations** to specify how the functions act on each pattern in the syntactic definition of the language phrases. For example,

$evaluate$ $[\![E_1 + E_2]\!]$ sto = $plus(evaluate$ $[\![E_1]\!]$ sto, $evaluate$ $[\![E_2]\!]$ sto)

states that the value of an expression "$E_1 + E_2$" is the mathematical sum of the values of its component subexpressions. Note that the value of an expression will depend on the current bindings in the store, here represented by the variable "sto". The function $evaluate$ maps syntactic expressions to semantic values—namely, integers—using mathematical operations such as $plus$. We refer to these operations as **auxiliary functions** in the denotational definition.

Figure 9.1 contains a complete denotational specification of a simple language of nonnegative integer numerals. This definition requires two auxiliary functions defined in the semantic world, where Number x Number denotes the Cartesian product.

$plus$: Number x Number $\to$ Number

$times$: Number x Number $\to$ Number.

Syntactic Domains

    N : Numeral   -- nonnegative numerals

    D : Digit   -- decimal digits

Abstract Production Rules

    Numeral ::= Digit | Numeral Digit

    Digit ::= **0** | **1** | **2** | **3** | **4** | **5** | **6** | **7** | **8** | **9**

Semantic Domain

    Number = { 0, 1, 2, 3, 4, ... }   -- natural numbers

Semantic Functions

    $value$: Numeral $\to$ Number

    $digit$: Digit $\to$ Number

Semantic Equations

    $value$ $[\![N\ D]\!]$ = $plus$ $(times(10,\ value$ $[\![N]\!]),\ digit$ $[\![D]\!])$

    $value$ $[\![D]\!]$ = $digit$ $[\![D]\!]$

    $digit$ $[\![\mathbf{0}]\!]$ = 0 $digit$ $[\![\mathbf{3}]\!]$ = 3 $digit$ $[\![\mathbf{6}]\!]$ = 6 $digit$ $[\![\mathbf{8}]\!]$ = 8

    $digit$ $[\![\mathbf{1}]\!]$ = 1 $digit$ $[\![\mathbf{4}]\!]$ = 4 $digit$ $[\![\mathbf{7}]\!]$ = 7 $digit$ $[\![\mathbf{9}]\!]$ = 9

    $digit$ $[\![\mathbf{2}]\!]$ = 2 $digit$ $[\![\mathbf{5}]\!]$ = 5

Figure 9.1: A Language of Numerals

We need two syntactic domains for the language of numerals. Phrases in this language are mapped into the mathematical domain of natural numbers. Generally we have one semantic function for each syntactic domain and one semantic equation for each production in the abstract syntax. To distinguish numerals (syntax) from numbers (semantics), different typefaces are employed. Note the compositionality of the definition in that the value of a phrase "N D" is defined in terms of the value of N and the value of D.

As an example of evaluating a numeral according to this denotational definition, we find the value of the numeral **65**:

$$value [\![\mathbf{65}]\!] = plus(times(10, value [\![\mathbf{6}]\!]), digit [\![\mathbf{5}]\!])$$
$$= plus(times(10, digit [\![\mathbf{6}]\!]), 5)$$
$$= plus(times(10, 6), 5)$$
$$= plus(60, 5) = 65$$

Solely using the specification of the semantics of numerals, we can easily prove that $value [\![\mathbf{008}]\!] = value [\![\mathbf{8}]\!]$:

$$value [\![\mathbf{008}]\!] = plus(times(10, value [\![\mathbf{00}]\!]), digit [\![\mathbf{8}]\!])$$
$$= plus(times(10, plus(times(10, value [\![\mathbf{0}]\!]), digit [\![\mathbf{0}]\!])), 8)$$
$$= plus(times(10, plus(times(10, digit [\![\mathbf{0}]\!]), 0)), 8)$$
$$= plus(times(10, plus(times(10, 0), 0)), 8)$$
$$= 8 = digit [\![\mathbf{8}]\!] = value [\![\mathbf{8}]\!]$$

Although the syntactic expression "**008**" inside the emphatic brackets is written in linear form, it actually represents the abstract syntax tree shown in Figure 9.2 that reflects its derivation

<numeral> ⇒ <numeral> <digit> ⇒ <numeral> <digit> <digit> ⇒
<digit> <digit> <digit> ⇒ **0** <digit> <digit> ⇒ **0 0** <digit> ⇒ **0 0 8**.

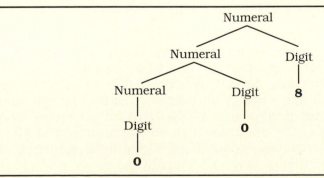

Figure 9.2: An Abstract Syntax Tree

The elements of the syntactic world inside of the emphatic brackets are always abstract syntax trees. We write them in a linear form only for convenience. The abstract production rules will be used to describe the abstract syntax trees and the concrete syntax to disambiguate them.

Compositionality

The principle of compositionality has a long history in mathematics and the specification of languages (see the further readings at the end of this chapter). In his book [Tennent91] on the semantics of programming languages, Tennent suggests three reasons for using compositional definitions:

1. In a denotational definition, each phrase of a language is given a meaning that describes its contribution to the meaning of a complete program that contains it. Furthermore, the meaning of each phrase is formulated as a function of the denotations of its immediate subphrases. As a result, whenever two phrases have the same denotation, one can be replaced by the other without changing the meaning of the program. Therefore a denotational semantics supports the substituition of semantically equivalent phrases.

2. Since a denotational definition parallels the syntactic structure of its BNF specification, properties of constructs in the language can be verified by **structural induction**, the version of mathematical induction introduced in Chapter 8 that follows the syntactic structure of phrases in the language.

3. Compositionality lends a certain elegance to denotational definitions, since the semantic equations are structured by the syntax of the language. Moreover, this structure allows the individual language constructs to be analyzed and evaluated in relative isolation from other features in the language.

As a consequence of compositionality, the semantic function *value* is a homomorphism, which means that the function respects operations. As an illustration, consider a function $H : A \rightarrow B$ where A has a binary operation $f : A \times A \rightarrow A$ and B has a binary operation $g : B \times B \rightarrow B$. The function H is a **homomorphism** if $H(f(x,y)) = g(H(x),H(y))$ for all $x,y \in A$. For the example in Figure 9.1, the operation f is concatenation and $g(m,n) = plus(times(10, m), n)$. Therefore $value(f(x,y)) = g(value(x),value(y))$, which thus demonstrates that *value* is a homomorphism.

Exercises

1. Using the language of numerals in Figure 9.1, draw abstract syntax trees for the numerals "**5**" and "**6789**".

2. Use the denotational semantics for numerals to derive the value of "**3087**".

3. Define a denotational semantics for the language of numerals in which the meaning of a string of digits is the number of digits in the string.

4. Define a denotational semantics for the language of octal (base 8) numerals. Use the definition to find the value of "**752**".

5. This is a BNF specification (and abstract syntax) of the language of Roman numerals less than five hundred.

   Roman ::= Hundreds Tens Units

   Hundreds ::= ε | **C** | **CC** | **CCC** | **CD**

   Tens ::= LowTens | **XL** | **L** LowTens | **XC**

   LowTens ::= ε | LowTens **X**

   Units ::= LowUnits | **IV** | **V** LowUnits | **IX**

   LowUnits ::= ε | LowUnits **I**

   The language of Roman numerals is subject to context constraints that the number of X's in LowTens and I's in LowUnits can be no more than three. Remember ε represents the empty string.

   Provide semantic functions and semantic equations for a denotational definition of Roman numerals that furnishes the numeric value of each string in the language. Assume that the context constraints have been verified by other means.

9.2 A CALCULATOR LANGUAGE

In this section we develop the denotational semantics for the language of the simple three-function calculator shown in Figure 9.3. A "program" on this calculator consists of a sequence of keystrokes generally alternating between operands and operators. The concrete syntax in Figure 9.4 gives those combinations that we call legal on the calculator. For instance,

$$6 + 33 \times 2 =$$

produces the value **78** on the display of the calculator. Observe that unlike more complex calculators, keystrokes are entered and processed from left to right, so that the addition is performed before the multiplication.

Figure 9.3: A Three-Function Calculator

In fact calculators usually accept any sequence of key presses, but we have limited our syntax to those collections that a user is most likely to employ. We outlaw combinations such as

$$5 + + 6 = \qquad \text{and} \qquad 88 \text{ x }^+/\text{- } 11 + \textbf{M}^\textbf{R}\ \textbf{M}^\textbf{R}$$

that provide no new meaningful calculations although many real calculators allow them. The **Clear** key occurs in several productions because a user is likely to press it at almost any time. The plus-minus key $^+/\text{-}$ changes the sign of the displayed value.

<program> ::= <expression sequence>

<expression sequence> ::= <expression> | <expression> <expression sequence>

<expression> ::= <term> | <expression> <operator> <term> | **Clear**
        | <expression> <answer> | <expression> <answer> $^+/\text{-}$

<term> ::= <numeral> | **M**$^\textbf{R}$ | **Clear** | <term> $^+/\text{-}$

<operator> ::= + | − | x

<answer> ::= **M**$^\textbf{+}$ | =

<numeral> ::= <digit> | <numeral> <digit>

<digit> ::= **0** | **1** | **2** | **3** | **4** | **5** | **6** | **7** | **8** | **9**

Figure 9.4: Concrete Syntax for the Calculator Language

To simplify the definition of the denotational semantics for the calculator, the abstract syntax in Figure 9.5 considerably reduces the complexity of the notation while still representing all the key sequences allowed by the concrete syntax. Since $^+$/- acts in much the same way as the answer keys, it has been included with them in the abstract syntax.

Abstract Syntactic Domains

P : Program	O : Operator	N : Numeral
S : ExprSequence	A : Answer	D : Digit
E : Expression		

Abstract Production Rules

Program ::= ExprSequence

ExprSequence ::= Expression | Expression ExprSequence

Expression ::= Numeral | **M^R** | **Clear** | Expression Answer

            | Expression Operator Expression

Operator ::= + | − | **x**

Answer ::= **M^+** | = | $^+$/-

Numeral ::= see Figure 9.1

Figure 9.5: Abstract Syntax for the Calculator Language

Following the concrete syntax for the calculator language, given the sequence of keystrokes

$$10\ M^+ + 6\ ^+/\!\!- = x\ M^R =$$

a parser will construct the abstract syntax tree shown in Figure 9.6. Notice that most operations associate to the left because of the way keystrokes are processed from left to right.

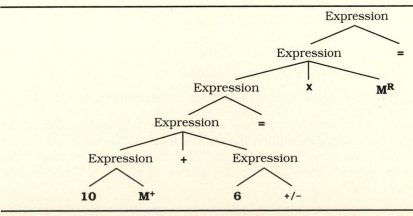

Figure 9.6: An Abstract Syntax Tree for **$10\ M^+ + 6\ ^+/\!\!- = x\ M^R =$**

The syntax of the calculator language encompasses six syntactic domains if we ignore the structure of numerals. In providing semantics for the calculator we define a semantic function for each of these domains. But before these functions can be specified, we need to describe the semantic domains into which they map, and to do so requires that we understand the operation of the calculator.

Calculator Semantics

The description presented here for the meaning of calculator expressions is slightly more complicated than it needs to be so that some extensions of the meaning can be implemented easily. See the exercises at the end of this section for an alternative model of the calculator. To define the semantics of the calculator, we use a state that maintains four registers or values to capture its internal working:

1. An internal accumulator maintains a running total value reflecting the operations that have been carried out so far.

2. An operator flag indicates the pending operation that will be executed when another operand is made available.

3. The current display portrays the latest numeral that has been entered, the memory value that has been recalled using M^R, or the total computed so far whenever the = or M^+ key has been pressed.

4. The memory of the calculator contains a value, initially zero; it is controlled by the M^+ and M^R keys.

Calculator arithmetic will be modeled by several auxiliary functions that carry out the three basic binary operations and an "identity" operation for the case when no operator is pending:

$$plus : \text{Integer x Integer} \rightarrow \text{Integer}$$

$$minus : \text{Integer x Integer} \rightarrow \text{Integer}$$

$$times : \text{Integer x Integer} \rightarrow \text{Integer}$$

$$nop : \text{Integer x Integer} \rightarrow \text{Integer} \quad \text{where } nop(a,d) = d.$$

We use the same names for the values of the operator flag and for the auxiliary operations, assuming an implicit function that identifies the flag values with the auxiliary functions. To understand how the state varies under the control of the keystrokes, consider the calculation in Figure 9.7 and how it effects these four values.

Keystroke	Accumulator	Operator Flag	Display	Memory
	0	*nop*	0	0
12	0	*nop*	12	0
+	12	*plus*	12	0
5	12	*plus*	5	0
⁺/-	12	*plus*	-5	0
=	12	*nop*	7	0
x	7	*times*	7	0
2	7	*times*	2	0
M⁺	7	*nop*	14	14
123	7	*nop*	123	14
M⁺	7	*nop*	123	137
Mᴿ	7	*nop*	137	137
⁺/-	7	*nop*	-137	137
-	-137	*minus*	-137	137
25	-137	*minus*	25	137
=	-137	*nop*	-162	137
+	-162	*plus*	-162	137
Mᴿ	-162	*plus*	137	137
=	-162	*nop*	-25	137

Figure 9.7: Sample Calculation of **12 + 5 ⁺/- = x 2 M⁺ 123 M⁺ Mᴿ ⁺/- - 25 = + Mᴿ =**

Although the meaning of a calculator program will be the final integer value shown on the display, we are also interested in the behavior of the calculator in response to individual keystrokes and partial results. This meaning depends on the following semantic domains:

Integer = { ... , -2, -1, 0, 1, 2, 3, 4, ... }

Operation = { *plus, minus, times, nop* }

State = Integer x Operation x Integer x Integer.

The Operation domain can be compared to an enumerated type in Pascal. These four values act as flags inside the calculator by saving the last operator keystroke. Integer represents the abstract collection of mathematical integers, and State takes values that are quadruples embodying the internal accumulator, the pending operation, the display, and the memory. In particular, observe which entries change the various values in the State tuple:

State tuple value	Tokens that may alter the value
Accumulator	**Clear**, **+**, **–**, and **x**
Operator Flag	**Clear**, **+**, **–**, **x**, **=**, and **M⁺**
Display	**Clear**, numeral, **=**, **M⁺**, **Mᴿ**, and **⁺/-**
Memory	**Clear** and **M⁺**

The trace in Figure 9.7 shows the changing state in response to various keystrokes.

Semantic Functions

The denotational semantics for this calculator has a semantic function for each of the syntactic domains.

meaning : Program $\rightarrow$ Integer

perform : ExprSequence $\rightarrow$ (State $\rightarrow$ State)

evaluate : Expression $\rightarrow$ (State $\rightarrow$ State)

compute : Operator $\rightarrow$ (State $\rightarrow$ State)

calculate : Answer $\rightarrow$ (State $\rightarrow$ State)

value   : Numeral $\rightarrow$ Integer   -- uses only nonnegative integers

Semantic equations specifying the functions are defined in Figure 9.8, with one equation for each production rule in the abstract syntax. Inspection of the semantics for individual keystrokes will provide an understanding of the calculator operation. The semantic function *meaning* calls *perform* on a sequence of one or more expressions that makes up a program, giving *perform* an initial state (0,*nop*,0,0) as its argument. An expression sequence is evaluated one expression at a time by composing executions of the *evaluate* function. Finally, *meaning* returns the display value given as a result of evaluating the last expression in the sequence.

The semantic function *evaluate* produces a function in State $\rightarrow$ State as its result when applied to an expression. The functions *compute* and *calculate* give meaning to operators and "totaling" keys. For example, **+** computes the pending operation with the accumulator and the display, updating the accumulator but leaving the display unchanged. Furthermore, *plus* becomes the new pending operation. On the other hand, **=** places the computed value into the display with *nop* signaling that there is no longer a pending operation.

Observe that **Mᴿ** and **⁺/-** act only on the display. Compound keystrokes are handled as compositions, eliminating the need to give the argument tuple. The semantic equation, given here as a composition,

$$evaluate [\![E\ A]\!] = calculate [\![A]\!] \circ evaluate [\![E]\!]$$

is equivalent to writing

$$evaluate [\![E\ A]\!] (a,op,d,m) = calculate [\![A]\!] (evaluate [\![E]\!] (a,op,d,m)).$$

meaning [[P]] = d where *perform* [[P]](0,*nop*,0,0) = (a,op,d,m)

perform [[E S]] = *perform* [[S]] ∘ *evaluate* [[E]]

perform [[E]] = *evaluate* [[E]]

evaluate [[N]] (a,op,d,m) = (a,op,v,m) where v = *value* [[N]]

evaluate [[M^R]] (a,op,d,m) = (a,op,m,m)

evaluate [[**Clear**]] (a,op,d,m) = (0,*nop*,0,0)

evaluate [[E_1 O E_2]] = *evaluate* [[E_2]] ∘ *compute* [[O]] ∘ *evaluate* [[E_1]]

evaluate [[E A]] = *calculate* [[A]] ∘ *evaluate* [[E]]

compute [[**+**]] (a,op,d,m) = (op(a,d),*plus*,d,m)

compute [[**–**]] (a,op,d,m) = (op(a,d),*minus*,d,m)

compute [[**x**]] (a,op,d,m) = (op(a,d),*times*,d,m)

calculate [[**=**]] (a,op,d,m) = (a,*nop*,op(a,d),m)

calculate [[M^+]] (a,op,d,m) = (a,*nop*,v,*plus*(m,v)) where v = op(a,d)

calculate [[$^+$/-]] (a,op,d,m) = (a,op,*minus*(0,d),m)

value [[N]] = see Figure 9.1

Figure 9.8: Semantic Equations for the Calculator Language

Denotational definitions commonly use this technique of factoring out arguments to semantic equations whenever possible. It was for this reason that the syntax of *evaluate* and the other semantic functions are given in a curried form (see Chapter 5 for a discussion of curried functions)

   evaluate : Expression → (State → State)

instead of as an uncurried function acting on a tuple

   evaluate : (Expression x State) → State.

A Sample Calculation

As an example of an evaluation according to the definition, consider the series of keystrokes "**2 + 3 =**". The meaning of the sequence is given by

   meaning [[**2 + 3 =**]] = d where *perform* [[**2 + 3 =**]](0,*nop*,0,0) = (a,op,d,m).

The evaluation proceeds as follows:

perform [[**2 + 3 =**]](0,*nop*,0,0)

   = *evaluate* [[**2 + 3 =**]](0,*nop*,0,0)

   = (*calculate* [[**=**]] ∘ *evaluate* [[**2 + 3**]]) (0,*nop*,0,0)

   = (*calculate* [[**=**]] ∘ *evaluate* [[**3**]] ∘ *compute* [[**+**]] ∘ *evaluate* [[**2**]]) (0,*nop*,0,0)

= *calculate* [[=]] (*evaluate* [[**3**]] (*compute* [[**+**]] (*evaluate* [[**2**]] (0,*nop*,0,0))))

= *calculate* [[=]] (*evaluate* [[**3**]] (*compute* [[**+**]] (0,*nop*,2,0))), since *value* [[**2**]] = 2

= *calculate* [[=]] (*evaluate* [[**3**]] (2,*plus*,2,0)), since *nop*(0,2) = 2

= *calculate* [[=]] (2,*plus*,3,0), since *value* [[**3**]] = 3

= (2,*nop*,5,0), since *plus*(2,3) = 5.

Therefore *meaning* [[**2 + 3 =**]] = 5.

A similar evaluation corresponding to the computation in Figure 9.7 will provide a useful example of elaborating the semantics of the calculator—namely, to demonstrate that

$$\text{\textit{meaning}} \; [\![\mathbf{12 + 5 \;^{+}/- = x \; 2 \; M^{+} \; 123 \; M^{+} \; M^{R} \;^{+}/- - 25 = + \; M^{R} =}]\!] = \text{-25.}$$

Remember that the ambiguity in the abstract syntax is resolved by viewing the keystrokes from left to right.

Real calculators have two conditions that produce errors when evaluating integer arithmetic: arithmetic overflow and division by zero. Our calculator has no division so that we can avoid handling the problem of division by zero as a means of reducing the complexity of the example. Furthermore, we assume unlimited integers so that overflow is not a problem.

Exercises

1. Draw the abstract syntax tree that results from parsing the series of keystrokes

      12 + 5 $^{+}$/- M^{+} M^{+} - 55 =.

   Remember, keystrokes are entered and evaluated from left to right.

2. Evaluate the semantics of these combinations of keystrokes using the denotational definition in this section:

   a) **8 $^{+}$/- + 5 x 3 =**

   b) **7 x 2 M^{+} M^{+} M^{+} – 15 + M^{R} =**

   c) **10 - 5 $^{+}$/- M^{+} 6 x M^{R} M^{+} =**

3. Prove that for any expression E, *evaluate* [[E **Clear**]] = *evaluate* [[**Clear**]].

4. Some calculators treat = differently from the calculator in this section, repeating the most recent operation, so that "**2 + 5 = =**" leaves 12 on the display and "**2 + 5 = = =**" leaves 17. Describe the changes that must be made in the denotational semantics to model this alternative interpretation.

5. Prove that for any expression E, *meaning* $[\![E = \mathbf{M^+}]\!]$ = *meaning* $[\![E\ \mathbf{M^+} =]\!]$.

6. Add to the calculator a key **sqr** that computes the square of the value in the display. Alter the semantics to model the action of this key. Its syntax should be similar to that of the $\mathbf{^+/\text{-}}$ key.

7. Alter the calculator semantics so that **Clear** leaves the memory unchanged. Modify the semantic equations to reflect this change.

8. Explain how the *evaluate* function for the semantics of the calculator language can be thought of as a homomorphism.

9. Rewrite the denotational definition of the calculator semantics taking the state to be State = Integer x Integer, representing the display and memory only. Delete the semantic functions *compute* and *calculate*, and use the following abstract syntax:

    Abstract Syntactic Domains

    > P : Program   E : Expression   D: Digit
    > S : ExprSequence   N : Numeral

    Abstract Production Rules

    > Program ::= ExprSequence
    > ExprSequence ::= Expression | Expression ExprSequence
    > Expression ::= Numeral | $\mathbf{M^R}$ | **Clear** | Expression $\mathbf{M^+}$
    > | Expression = | Expression $\mathbf{^+/\text{-}}$
    > | Expression + Expression | Expression - Expression
    > | Expression x Expression

9.3 THE DENOTATIONAL SEMANTICS OF WREN

The programming language Wren exemplifies a class of languages referred to as **imperative**. Several properties characterize imperative programming languages:

1. Programs consist of commands, thereby explaining the term "imperative".

2. Programs operate on a global data structure, called a store, in which results are generally computed by incrementally updating values until a final result is produced.

3. The dominant command is the assignment instruction, which modifies a location in the store.

4. Program control entails sequencing, selection, and iteration, represented by the semicolon, the **if** command, and the **while** command in Wren.

The abstract syntax for Wren appears in Figure 9.9. Compare this version with the one in Figure 1.17. Note that lists of commands are handled somewhat differently. Instead of using the postfix operator "+", a command is allowed to be a pair of commands that by repetition produces a sequence of commands. However, the definition still provides abstract syntax trees for the same collection of programs. As a second change, input and output have been omitted from Wren for the time being. This simplifies our initial discussion of denotational semantics. The issues involved with defining input and output will be considered later.

Abstract Syntactic Domains

P : Program	C : Command	N : Numeral
D : Declaration	E : Expression	I : Identifier
T : Type	O : Operator	

Abstract Production Rules

Program ::= **program** Identifier **is** Declaration* **begin** Command **end**

Declaration ::= **var** Identifier$^+$: Type ;

Type ::= **integer** | **boolean**

Command ::= Command ; Command | Identifier := Expression
    | **skip** | **if** Expression **then** Command **else** Command
    | **if** Expression **then** Command | **while** Expression **do** Command

Expression ::= Numeral | Identifier | **true** | **false** | - Expression
    | Expression Operator Expression | **not(** Expression**)**

Operator ::= **+** | **–** | ***** | **/** | **or** | **and** | **<=** | **<** | **=** | **>** | **>=** | **<>**

Figure 9.9: Abstract Syntax for Wren

Semantic Domains

To provide a denotational semantics for Wren, we need to specify semantic domains into which the syntactic constructs map. Wren uses two primitive domains that can be described by listing (or suggesting) their values:

    Integer = { ..., -2, -1, 0, 1, 2, 3, 4, ... }

    Boolean = { true, false }.

Primitive domains are combined into more complex structures by certain mathematical constructions. The calculator language uses two of these structures, the Cartesian product and the function domain. The State in the semantics of the calculator is a Cartesian product of four primitive domains, so that each element of the State is a quadruple. Although we do not name the function domains, we use them in the semantic functions—for example, *evaluate* maps an Expression into a set of functions State $\rightarrow$ State. The notation for a function domain A $\rightarrow$ B agrees with normal mathematical notation. We view this expression as representing the set of functions from A into B; that the function f is a member of this set can be described by f : A $\rightarrow$ B using a colon as the symbol for membership.

Wren without input and output needs no Cartesian product for its semantics, but function domains are essential. The Store (memory) is modeled as a function from Identifiers to values,

$$\text{Store} = \text{Identifier} \rightarrow (\text{SV} + undefined),$$

where SV represents the collection of values that may be placed in the store, the so-called **storable values**, and *undefined* is a special value indicating that an identifier has not yet been assigned a value. The constant function mapping each identifier to *undefined* serves as the initial store provided to a Wren program. Wren allows integers and Boolean values to be storable. To specify the domain of storable values, we take the union of the primitive domains Integer and Boolean. The notion of set union will not keep the sets separate if they contain common elements. For this reason, we use the notion of **disjoint union** or **disjoint sum** that requires tags on the elements from each set so that their origin can be determined. We exploit the notation

$$\text{SV} = int(\text{Integer}) + bool(\text{Boolean})$$

for the disjoint union of Integer and Boolean, where the tag *int* indicates the integer values and the tag *bool* specifies the Boolean values. Typical elements of SV are *int*(5), *int*(-99), and *bool*(true). Such elements can be viewed as Prolog structures where the function symbols provide the tags or as items in a Standard ML datatype. The important feature of disjoint unions is that we can always determine the origin of an element of SV by inspecting its tag. In the disjoint sum for Store, *undefined* is a tagged value with no data field. Chapter 10 provides a more formal definition of the structure of disjoint unions.

We assume several properties about the store that make it an abstraction of the physical memory of a computer—namely, that it has an unbounded number of locations and that each location will be large enough to contain any storable value. Formal semantics usually does not concern itself with implementation restrictions imposed when executing programs on an actual computer.

Language Constructs in Wren

Structurally, Wren includes three main varieties of language constructs: declarations, commands, and expressions. In programming languages, declarations define bindings of names (identifiers) to objects such as memory locations, literals (constants), procedures, and functions. These bindings are recorded in a structure, called an **environment**, that is active over some part of a program known as the **scope** of the bindings. Since a Wren program has only one scope, the entire program, environments can be ignored in its semantics. Thus the environment of a Wren program is constant, in effect determined at the start of the program, and need not be modeled at all in the dynamic semantics of Wren. The declarations in Wren act solely as part of the context-sensitive syntax that we assume has already been verified by some other means, say an attribute grammar. Later we show that denotational semantics can be used to verify context conditions. For now, we assume that any Wren program to be analyzed by our denotational semantics has no inconsistency in its use of types. At this stage, we also ignore the program identifier, taking it as documentation only.

Expressions in a programming language produce values. An important defining trait of a language is the sorts of values that expressions can produce, called the **expressible values** or the **first-class values** of the language. The expressible values in Wren are the same as the storable values:

$$EV = int(\text{Integer}) + bool(\text{Boolean}).$$

The value of an expression will depend on the values associated with its identifiers in the store. Therefore the semantic function *evaluate* for expressions has as its signature

evaluate : Expression $\rightarrow$ (Store $\rightarrow$ EV).

The syntax of *evaluate* can also be given by

evaluate : Expression x Store $\rightarrow$ EV,

but we prefer the first (curried) version since it allows partial evaluation of the semantic function. The object *evaluate* $[\![I]\!]$ makes sense as a function from the store to an expressible value when we use the curried version. This approach to defining functions sometimes allows us to factor out rightmost arguments (see command sequencing in the denotational definition given later in this section).

Commands may modify the store, so we define the meaning of a command to be a function from the current store to a new store. We mentioned earlier that the store is global and implied that only one store exists. When we speak of the "current store" and the "new store", we mean snapshots of the same store. The signature of the semantic function *execute* for commands is given by

execute : Command $\rightarrow$ (Store $\rightarrow$ Store).

The meaning of a command is thus a function from Store to Store.

As for primitive syntactic domains, Numerals will be handled by the semantic function *value* as with the calculator language, and the Boolean values **true** and **false** will be defined directly by *evaluate*. Note that the syntactic domain Identifier is used in defining the semantic domain Store. To make sense of this mixing of syntactic and semantic worlds, we assume that the denotational semantics of Wren has an implicit semantic function that maps each Identifier in the syntactic world to a value in the semantic world that is the identifier itself, as the attribute *Name* did in the attribute grammars for Wren. We can pretend that we have an invisible semantic function defined by *id* $[\![I]\!]$ = I.

Since input and output commands have been omitted from Wren for the time being, we consider the final values of the variables of the program to be the semantics of the program. So the signature of *meaning* is

> *meaning* : Program → Store.

The semantic domains for Wren and the signatures of the semantic functions are summarized in Figure 9.10. Remember that the syntactic domain Store allows its maps to take the special value *undefined* to represent identifiers that have not yet been assigned a value and that in the disjoint sum, *undefined* stands for a tag with an empty "value". By the way, in constructing semantic domains we assume that disjoint sum "+" has a higher precedence than the forming of a function domain, so some parentheses may be omitted—for example, those around SV + *undefined* in the definiton of Store.

Semantic Domains

> Integer = { ... , -2, -1, 0, 1, 2, 3, 4, ... }
>
> Boolean = { true, false }
>
> EV = *int*(Integer) + *bool*(Boolean)   -- expressible values
>
> SV = *int*(Integer) + *bool*(Boolean)   -- storable values
>
> Store = Identifier → SV + *undefined*

Semantic Functions

> *meaning* : Program → Store
>
> *execute* : Command → (Store → Store)
>
> *evaluate* : Expression → (Store → EV)
>
> *value*   : Numeral → EV

Figure 9.10: Semantic Domains and Functions for Wren

Auxiliary Functions

To complete our denotational definition of Wren, we need several auxiliary functions representing the normal operations on the primitive semantic domains and others to make the semantic equations easier to read. Since Wren is an algorithmic language, its operations must map to mathematical operations in the semantic world. Here we use the semantic operations *plus, minus, times, divides, less, lesseq, greater, greatereq, equal, neq* defined on the integers with their normal mathematical meanings. The relational operators have syntax following the pattern

$$less : \text{Integer x Integer} \rightarrow \text{Boolean}.$$

Operations that update and access the store can be threaded into the definitions of the semantic functions, but we get a cleaner specification by factoring these operations out of the semantic equations, thereby treating the store as an abstract data type. In defining these auxiliary functions and Wren's semantic functions, we make use of semantic metavariables in a way similar to the syntactic domains. We use "sto" for elements of Store and "val" for values in either EV or SV. Three auxiliary functions manipulate the store:

$emptySto$: Store

$emptySto$ I = *undefined*   or $emptySto = \lambda$ I . *undefined*

$updateSto$: Store x Identifier x SV $\rightarrow$ Store

$updateSto(\text{sto},I,\text{val})$ I_1 = (if I = I_1 then val else sto(I_1))

$applySto$: Store x Identifier $\rightarrow$ SV + *undefined*

$applySto(\text{sto},I)$ = sto(I)

The definition of *updateSto* means that *updateSto*(sto,I,val) is the function Identifier $\rightarrow$ SV + *undefined* that is identical to sto except that I is bound to val. Denotational definitions frequently use lambda notation to describe functions, as seen above in the definition of *emptySto*. See Chapter 5 for an explanation of the lambda calculus.

Semantic Equations

The semantic equations for the denotational semantics of Wren are listed in Figure 9.11. Notice how we simply ignore the declarations in the first equation by defining the meaning of a program to be the store that results from executing the commands of the program starting with the store in which all identifiers are undefined. Command sequencing follows the pattern shown in the calculator language. Observe that *execute* [[**skip**]] is the identity function on Store. Some semantic equations for expressions are omitted in Figure 9.11—they follow the pattern given for the operations addition and less than.

---

meaning [[**program** I **is** D **begin** C **end**]] = *execute* [[C]] *emptySto*

execute [[C$_1$; C$_2$]] = *execute* [[C$_2$]] ∘ *execute* [[C$_1$]]

execute [[**skip**]] sto = sto

execute [[I := E]] sto = *updateSto*(sto, I, (*evaluate* [[E]] sto))

execute [[**if** E **then** C]] sto = if p then *execute* [[C]] sto else sto
　　　　　　　where *bool*(p) = *evaluate* [[E]] sto

execute [[**if** E **then** C$_1$ **else** C$_2$]] sto =
　　if p then *execute* [[C$_1$]] sto else *execute* [[C$_2$]] sto
　　　　　　where *bool*(p) = *evaluate* [[E]] sto

execute [[**while** E **do** C]] = loop
　　　　　　where loop sto = if p then loop(*execute* [[C]] sto) else sto
　　　　　　　　　　　　　　where *bool*(p) = *evaluate* [[E]] sto

evaluate [[I]] sto = if val=*undefined* then *error* else val
　　　　　　where val = *applySto*(sto, I)

evaluate [[N]] sto = *int*(*value* [[N]])

evaluate [[**true**]] sto = *bool*(true)　　　　　　*evaluate* [[**false**]] sto = *bool*(false)

evaluate [[E$_1$ + E$_2$]] sto = *int*(*plus*(m,n))
　　　　　　where *int*(m) = *evaluate* [[E$_1$]] sto and *int*(n) = *evaluate* [[E$_2$]] sto

．
．

evaluate [[E$_1$ / E$_2$]] sto = if n=0 then *error* else *int*(*divides*(m,n))
　　　　　　where *int*(m) = *evaluate* [[E$_1$]] sto and *int*(n) = *evaluate* [[E$_2$]] sto

evaluate [[E$_1$ < E$_2$]] sto = if *less*(m,n) then *bool*(true) else *bool*(false)
　　　　　　where *int*(m) = *evaluate* [[E$_1$]] sto and *int*(n) = *evaluate* [[E$_2$]] sto

．
．

evaluate [[E$_1$ **and** E$_2$]] sto = if p then *bool*(q) else *bool*(false)
　　　　　　where *bool*(p) = *evaluate* [[E$_1$]] sto and *bool*(q) = *evaluate* [[E$_2$]] sto

evaluate [[E$_1$ **or** E$_2$]] sto = if p then *bool*(true) else *bool*(q)
　　　　　　where *bool*(p) = *evaluate* [[E$_1$]] sto and *bool*(q) = *evaluate* [[E$_2$]] sto

evaluate [[- E]] sto = *int*(*minus*(0,m)) where *int*(m) = *evaluate* [[E]] sto

evaluate [[**not**(E)]] sto = if p then *bool*(false) else *bool*(true)
　　　　　　where *bool*(p) = *evaluate* [[E]] sto

Figure 9.11: Semantic Equations for Wren

An assignment evaluates the expression on the right and updates the store accordingly. To illustrate the change in the store caused by the *updateSto* operation, we use the notation "{x ↦ *int*(3), y ↦ *int*(5), z ↦ *int*(8)}" to represent a store with those three bindings where every other identifier maps to *undefined*. Observe that for any Wren program, no matter how long or complex, the current store function will always be finite in the sense that all but a finite set of identifiers will map to *undefined*. We also use the notation "{x↦*int*(25) y↦*int*(-1)}sto" to stand for the store that is identical to sto except that x has the value 25 and y the value -1. Therefore we can write

$$updateSto(updateSto(emptySto, a, int(0)), b, int(1))$$
$$= updateSto(\{a↦int(0)\}emptySto, b, int(1))$$
$$= \{a↦int(0), b↦int(1)\}emptySto$$
$$= \{a↦int(0), b↦int(1)\}.$$

Incidentally, this store is the meaning of *execute* [[a := 0; b := 1]] *emptySto*. To tie these two notations together, we view {a↦*int*(0), b↦*int*(1)}as an abbreviation for {a↦int(0), b↦*int*(1)}*emptySto*.

One other point needs to be made about our functional notation. It has been implicitly assumed that function application associates to the left as with the lambda calculus, so that

$$execute \text{ [[a := 0; b := 1]] } emptySto = (execute \text{ [[a := 0; b := 1]]}) \text{ } emptySto.$$

Furthermore, the arrow forming a function domain associates to the right, so that

$$execute : \text{Command} → \text{Store} → \text{Store}$$

means

$$execute : \text{Command} → (\text{Store} → \text{Store}).$$

Surprisingly, these two conventions, associating application to the left and → to the right, agree, as shown by the following signatures:

$$execute : \text{Command} → \text{Store} → \text{Store}$$

$$execute \text{ [[a := 0; b := 1]] } : \text{Store} → \text{Store}$$

$$execute \text{ [[a := 0; b := 1]] } emptySto : \text{Store}.$$

Also remember that composition "∘" is an associative operation so that no convention is required to disambiguate f∘g∘h.

When we inspect primitive values, as in the selection (**if**) commands, we must account for the tags provided by the disjoint sum. Maintaining correct tags is also an important part of defining the *evaluate* semantic function.

The **while** command presents special difficulties in a denotational definition. A naive approach to its meaning follows its operational description—namely, to evaluate the test and, if its value is true, to execute the body of the **while** and repeat the entire command, whereas if it is false, to do nothing (more). The corresponding semantic equation can be written:

$$execute \text{ [[while E do C]] sto} =$$
$$\text{if p then } execute \text{ [[while E do C]]}(execute \text{ [[C]] sto) else sto}$$
$$\text{where } bool(p) = evaluate \text{ [[E]] sto}.$$

Although this equation captures the operational explanation, it fails to adhere to a fundamental tenet of denotational semantics—namely, that each semantic equation be compositional. The meaning of the **while** command is defined in terms of itself, not just its constituent parts. Using a technique common to functional programming we transform this equation into a definition that is compositional:

$$execute \ [\![\textbf{while} \ \text{E} \ \textbf{do} \ \text{C}]\!] = \text{loop}$$
$$\text{where loop sto} = \text{if p then loop}(execute \ [\![\text{C}]\!] \ \text{sto}) \ \text{else sto}$$
$$\text{where} \ bool(\text{p}) = evaluate \ [\![\text{E}]\!] \ \text{sto}.$$

In this definition we have factored out a function embodying the effect of the meaning of a **while** command; "loop: Store → Store" is a function that models *execute* [[**while** E **do** C]] compositionally as a recursive function defined on stores. This approach will be justified in Chapter 10, where we also ensure that recursive definitions of functions are really describing mathematical objects.

The meaning of expressions is straightforward, consisting of evaluating the operands and then passing the values to auxiliary functions in the semantic world. The Boolean operations **and**, **or**, and **not** are defined directly as conditional expressions in the metalanguage.

Error Handling

We take a simple approach to dynamic errors in Wren, automatically adding a special element *error* to each of the semantic domains and assuming that all semantic functions produce *error* when given *error* as an argument; that is, errors propagate. In an actual programming language, a program aborts when a dynamic (or runtime) error occurs, but the kind of denotational semantics described in this section—namely, **direct denotational semantics**— makes this sort of termination very difficult to define.

Nontermination of a **while** command is also not modeled directly by our semantics, but it will be considered when we study semantic domains more carefully in Chapter 10. We tolerate an operational point of view in the sense that a nonterminating **while** command gives no value at all under the *execute* semantic function, making *execute* a partial function. For example, we consider *execute* [[**while true do skip**]] to be an undefined function on any store.

The semantic equations in Figure 9.11 are heavily dependent on pattern matching, such as "*int*(m) = *evaluate* [[E]] sto", for their definition. The question may arise as to whether this pattern matching can fail—for example, what if "*evaluate* [[E]] sto" in a numeric expression produces the value *bool*(true)? Since we assume that programs that are analyzed by the denotational semantics have already been verified as syntactically valid according to both the context-free and context-sensitive syntax of Wren, a numeric expression cannot produce a Boolean value. If, on the other hand, such an expression produces *error*, say by accessing an undefined variable, then the *error* value is propagated through the equations.

Semantic Equivalence

Denotational semantics provides a method for formulating the equivalence of two language phrases.

Definition: Two language constructs are **semantically equivalent** if they share the same denotation according to their denotational definition.   ∎

For example, for any command C, since

execute ⟦C; **skip**⟧ sto = *execute* ⟦**skip**⟧ (*execute* ⟦C⟧ sto) = *execute* ⟦C⟧ sto,

we conclude that "C; **skip**" is semantically equivalent to C.

Furthermore, we can show that the following denotations are mathematically the same function:

execute ⟦a := **0**; b := **1**⟧ sto = {a ↦ *int*(0), b ↦ *int*(1)}sto

execute ⟦b := **1**; a := b–b⟧ sto = *execute* ⟦a := b–b⟧ {b ↦ *int*(1)}sto
$$= \{b \mapsto int(1), a \mapsto int(0)\}sto,$$

since 0 = *minus*(1,1). Therefore "a := **0**; b := **1**" is semantically equivalent to "b := **1**; a := b–b".

As a consequence of this definition of semantic equivalence, we cannot distinguish nonterminating computations since they have no denotation. Hence, the commands "**while true do** m:=m+1" and "**while true do skip**" are semantically equivalent. (Since we consider only abstract syntax trees when analyzing syntax, we omit "**end while**" from these commands.)

Input and Output

Remember, Wren allows only integer values for input and output. The **read** and **write** commands permit Wren to communicate with entities outside of programs—namely, files of integers. We model these files as semantic domains that are sets of finite lists where any particular file is an element of one of these sets:

Input = Integer*
Output = Integer*.

At each point during the execution of a program, the values in these lists influence the current computation and the final result of the program. We define the meaning of a program as a function between two files taken from Input and Output:

$$meaning : \text{Program} \rightarrow (\text{Input} \rightarrow \text{Output}).$$

Since input and output are performed by commands, the semantic function for them must encompass the values of the input and output files. We describe the state of a machine executing a Wren program with input and output as a semantic domain containing the store and two lists of integers:

$$\text{State} = \text{Store x Input x Output}.$$

The signature of the *execute* semantic function for commands becomes

$$execute : \text{Command} \rightarrow \text{State} \rightarrow \text{State}.$$

Again, we rely on auxiliary functions to handle the manipulation of the input and output files to simplify the semantic equations. We represent an arbitrary list of integers by the notation $[n_1,n_2, ..., n_k]$ where $k \geq 0$. A list with $k=0$ is empty and is represented as [ ]. We need four auxiliary functions that are similar to those found in a list-processing language such as Scheme (see Chapter 6).

head : Integer* $\rightarrow$ Integer

    head $[n_1,n_2, ..., n_k] = n_1$ provided $k \geq 1$.

tail : Integer* $\rightarrow$ Integer*

    tail $[n_1,n_2, ..., n_k] = [n_2, ..., n_k]$ provided $k \geq 1$.

null : Integer* $\rightarrow$ Boolean

    null $[n_1,n_2, ..., n_k] = (k=0)$

affix : Integer* x Integer $\rightarrow$ Integer*

    affix $([n_1,n_2, ..., n_k],m) = [n_1,n_2, ..., n_k,m]$.

Although all the semantic equations for *meaning* and *execute* must be altered to reflect the new signature, the changes for most commands are merely cosmetic and are left to the reader as an exercise. We list only those semantic equations that are totally new, using "inp" and "outp" as metavariables ranging over Input and Output:

meaning [[**program** I **is** D **begin** C **end**]] inp = outp

       where (sto, inp_1, outp) = *execute* [[C]] (*emptySto*, inp, [ ])

execute [[**read** I]] (sto,inp,outp) =

    if *null*(inp) then *error*

          else (*updateSto*(sto,I,*int*(*head*(inp))), *tail*(inp), outp)

execute [[**write** E]] (sto,inp,outp) = (sto, inp, *affix*(outp,val))
$$\text{where } int(\text{val}) = evaluate \text{ [[E]] sto.}$$

In the next section where Wren is implemented in the laboratory, we develop a prototype implementation of Wren based on its denotational semantics. We consider two methods for implementing input and output, one based on these denotational definitions, and one that ignores the denotational approach, handling input and output interactively.

Elaborating a Denotational Definition

The denotational semantics for Wren supplies a meaning to each Wren program. Here we apply the semantic functions defined for Wren to give meaning to the following Wren program that contains both input and output. This example illustrates that a complete denotational description of even a small program entails a considerable amount of patience and attention to detail.

```
program sample is
        var sum,num : integer;
    begin
        sum := 0;
        read num;
        while num>=0 do
            if num>9 and num<100
                    then sum := sum+num
            end if;
            read num
        end while;
        write sum
    end
```

The meaning of the program is defined by

meaning [[**program** I **is** D **begin** C **end**]] inp = outp
$$\text{where (sto, inp1, outp)} = execute \text{ [[C]] } (emptySto, \text{ inp, [ ]).}$$

The semantic equations for *execute* must be altered to reflect the use of states. For example, the meaning of an assignment command is defined as

execute [[I := E]] (sto,inp,outp) =
$$(updateSto(\text{sto,I,}(evaluate \text{ [[E]] sto})),\text{inp,outp}).$$

Let the input list be [5,22,-1]. To simplify the work, the elaboration employs several abbreviations.

d = **var** sum,num : **integer**

c_1 = sum := 0

c_2 = **read** num

c_3 = **while** num>=0 **do** $c_{3.1}$; $c_{3.2}$

   $c_{3.1}$ = **if** num>9 **and** num<100 **then** sum := sum+num

   $c_{3.2}$ = **read** num

 c_4 = **write** sum

Using these abbreviations for the abstract syntax trees that make up the program, the meaning of sample unfolds as follows:

meaning [[**program** sample **is** d **begin** c_1 ; c_2 ; c_3 ; c_4 **end**]] [5,22,-1] = outp
  where (sto, inp$_1$, outp) = *execute* [[c_1 ; c_2 ; c_3 ; c_4]] (*emptySto*, [5,22,-1], [ ]).

In Wren the semantics of a program reduces to the meaning of its sequence of commands.

execute [[c_1 ; c_2 ; c_3 ; c_4]] (*emptySto*, [5,22,-1], [ ])
  = (*execute* [[c_4]] ∘ *execute* [[c_3]] ∘ *execute* [[c_2]] ∘ *execute* [[c_1]])
                                    (*emptySto*, [5,22,-1], [ ])
  = *execute* [[c_4]] (*execute* [[c_3]] (*execute* [[c_2]] (*execute* [[c_1]]
                                    (*emptySto*, [5,22,-1], [ ])))).

The commands are executed from the inside out, starting with c_1.

execute [[sum := 0]] (*emptySto*, [5,22,-1], [ ])
        = (*updateSto*(*emptySto*, sum, (*evaluate* [[0]] *emptySto*)), [5,22,-1], [ ])
        = (*updateSto*(*emptySto*, sum, *int*(0)), [5,22,-1], [ ])
        = ({sum |→*int*(0)}, [5,22,-1], [ ]).

execute [[**read** num]] ({sum |→*int*(0)}, [5,22,-1], [ ])
        = (*updateSto*({sum |→*int*(0)},num, *int*(5)), [22,-1], [ ])
        = ({sum |→*int*(0),num |→*int*(5)}, [22,-1], [ ]).

Let $sto_{0.5}$ = {sum |→*int*(0),num |→*int*(5)}.

execute [[**while** num>=0 **do** $c_{3.1}$; $c_{3.2}$]] ($sto_{0.5}$, [22,-1], [ ])
                     = loop ($sto_{0.5}$, [22,-1], [ ])
      where loop (sto,in,out) =
          if p then loop(*execute* [[$c_{3.1}$; $c_{3.2}$]] (sto,in,out)) else (sto,in,out)
                     where *bool*(p) = *evaluate* [[num>=0]] sto.

We work on the Boolean expression first.

evaluate [[num]] $sto_{0.5}$ = *applySto*($sto_{0.5}$, num) = *int*(5).

evaluate [[0]] $sto_{0.5}$ = *int*(0).

evaluate [[num>=0]] $sto_{0.5}$
      = if *greatereq*(m,n) then *bool*(true) else *bool*(false)
          where *int*(m) = *evaluate* [[num]] $sto_{0.5}$
            and *int*(n) = *evaluate* -0]] $sto_{0.5}$
      = if *greatereq*(5,0) then *bool*(true) else *bool*(false)
      = *bool*(true).

Now we can execute loop for the first time.

loop (sto$_{0.5}$, [22,-1], [ ])
    = if p then loop(*execute* $[\![c_{3.1} ; c_{3.2}]\!]$ (sto$_{0.5}$, [22,-1], [ ]))
                else (sto$_{0.5}$, [22,-1], [ ])
                    where *bool*(p) = *evaluate* $[\![num>=0]\!]$ sto$_{0.5}$
    = if true then loop(*execute* $[\![c_{3.1} ; c_{3.2}]\!]$ (sto$_{0.5}$, [22,-1], [ ]))
                else (sto$_{0.5}$, [22,-1], [ ])
    = loop(*execute* $[\![c_{3.1} ; c_{3.2}]\!]$ (sto$_{0.5}$, [22,-1], [ ])).

To complete the execution of loop, we need to execute the body of the **while** command.

execute $[\![c_{3.1} ; c_{3.2}]\!]$ (sto$_{0.5}$, [22,-1], [ ])
    = *execute* $[\![$**read** num$]\!]$
        (*execute* $[\![$**if** num>9 **and** num<100 **then** sum := sum+num$]\!]$
                                    (sto$_{0.5}$, [22,-1], [ ])).

We need the value of the Boolean expression in the **if** command next.

evaluate $[\![num>9]\!]$ sto$_{0.5}$
    = if *greater*(m,n) then *bool*(true) else *bool*(false)
        where *int*(m) = *evaluate* $[\![num]\!]$ sto$_{0.5}$
            and *int*(n) = *evaluate* $[\![9]\!]$ sto$_{0.5}$
    = if *greater*(5,9) then *bool*(true) else *bool*(false)
    = *bool*(false)

evaluate $[\![num<100]\!]$ sto$_{0.5}$
    = if *less*(m,n) then *bool*(true) else *bool*(false)
        where *int*(m) = *evaluate* $[\![num]\!]$ sto$_{0.5}$
            and *int*(n) = *evaluate* $[\![100]\!]$ sto$_{0.5}$
    = if *less*(5,100) then *bool*(true) else *bool*(false)
    = *bool*(true)

evaluate $[\![num>9$ **and** num<100$]\!]$ sto$_{0.5}$
    = if p then *bool*(q) else *bool*(false)
        where *bool*(p) = *evaluate* $[\![num>9]\!]$ sto$_{0.5}$
            and *bool*(q) = *evaluate* $[\![num<100]\!]$ sto$_{0.5}$
    = if false then *bool*(true) else *bool*(false)
    = *bool*(false).

Continuing with the **if** command, we get the following.

execute $[\![$**if** num>9 **and** num<100 **then** sum := sum+num$]\!]$ (sto$_{0.5}$, [22,-1], [ ])
    = if p then *execute* $[\![$sum := sum+num$]\!]$ (sto$_{0.5}$, [22,-1], [ ])
            else (sto$_{0.5}$, [22,-1], [ ])
                    where *bool*(p) = *evaluate* $[\![num>9$ **and** num<100$]\!]$ sto$_{0.5}$
    = if false then *execute* $[\![$sum := sum+num$]\!]$ (sto$_{0.5}$, [22,-1], [ ])
            else (sto$_{0.5}$, [22,-1], [ ])
    = (sto$_{0.5}$, [22,-1], [ ]).

After finishing with the **if** command, we proceed with the second command in the body of the **while**.

$execute$ [[**read** num]] $(sto_{0.5}, [22,-1], [\;]))$
$= (updateSto(sto_{0.5},num,int(22)), [-1], [\;])$
$= (\{sum \mapsto int(0),num \mapsto int(22)\}, [-1], [\;]).$

Let $sto_{0.22} = \{sum \mapsto int(0),num \mapsto int(22)\}.$

Summarizing the execution of the body of the **while** command, we have the result

$execute$ [[$c_{3.1}$; $c_{3.2}$]] $(sto_{0.5}, [22,-1], [\;]) = (sto_{0.22}, [-1], [\;]).$

This completes the first pass through loop.

$loop\,(sto_{0.5}, [22,-1], [\;])$
$= loop\,(execute\,[[c_{3.1}\,;\,c_{3.2}]]\,(sto_{0.5}, [22,-1], [\;]))$
$= loop\,(sto_{0.22}, [-1], [\;]).$

Again, we work on the Boolean expression from the **while** command first.

$evaluate$ [[num]] $sto_{0.22} = applySto(sto_{0.22}, num) = int(22).$

$evaluate$ [[0]] $sto_{0.22} = int(0).$

$evaluate$ [[num>=0]] $sto_{0.22}$
$= $ if $greatereq(m,n)$ then $bool(true)$ else $bool(false)$
    where $int(m) = evaluate$ [[num]] $sto_{0.22}$
    and $int(n) = evaluate$ [[0]] $sto_{0.22}$
$= $ if $greatereq(22,0)$ then $bool(true)$ else $bool(false)$
$= bool(true).$

Now we can execute loop for the second time.

$loop\,(sto_{0.22}, [-1], [\;])$
$= $ if p then $loop(execute\,[[c_{3.1}\,;\,c_{3.2}]]\,(sto_{0.22}, [-1], [\;]))$
        else $(sto_{0.22}, [-1], [\;])$
                where $bool(p) = evaluate$ [[num>=0]] $sto_{0.22}$
$= $ if true then $loop(execute\,[[c_{3.1}\,;\,c_{3.2}]]\,(sto_{0.22}, [-1], [\;]))$
        else $(sto_{0.22}, [-1], [\;])$
$= loop(execute\,[[c_{3.1}\,;\,c_{3.2}]]\,(sto_{0.22}, [-1], [\;])).$

Again we execute the body of the **while** command.

$execute$ [[$c_{3.1}$; $c_{3.2}$]] $(sto_{0.22}, [-1], [\;])$
$= execute$ [[**read** num]]
        $(execute$ [[**if** num>9 **and** num<100
                    then sum := sum+num]] $(sto_{0.22}, [-1], [\;])).$

The Boolean expression in the **if** command must be evaluated again.

evaluate $[\![$num>9$]\!]$ $sto_{0,22}$
   = if *greater*(m,n) then *bool*(true) else *bool*(false)
      where *int*(m) = *evaluate* $[\![$num$]\!]$ $sto_{0,22}$
         and *int*(n) = *evaluate* $[\![$9$]\!]$ $sto_{0,22}$
   = if *greater*(22,9) then *bool*(true) else *bool*(false)
   = *bool*(true)

evaluate $[\![$num<100$]\!]$ $sto_{0,22}$
   = if *less*(m,n) then *bool*(true) else *bool*(false)
      where *int*(m) = *evaluate* $[\![$num$]\!]$ $sto_{0,22}$
         and *int*(n) = *evaluate* $[\![$99$]\!]$ $sto_{0,22}$
   = if *less*(22,99) then *bool*(true) else *bool*(false)
   = *bool*(true)

evaluate $[\![$num>9 **and** num<100$]\!]$ $sto_{0,22}$
   = if p then *bool*(q) else *bool*(false)
      where *bool*(p) = *evaluate* $[\![$num>9$]\!]$ $sto_{0,22}$
         and *bool*(q) = *evaluate* $[\![$num<100$]\!]$ $sto_{0,22}$
   = if true then *bool*(true) else *bool*(false)
   = *bool*(true).

This time we execute the **then** clause in the **if** command.

execute $[\![$**if** num>9 **and** num<100 **then** sum := sum+num$]\!]$ $(sto_{0,22}, [-1], [\ ])$
   = if p then *execute* $[\![$sum := sum+num$]\!]$ $(sto_{0,22}, [-1], [\ ])$
      else $(sto_{0,22}, [-1], [\ ])$
            where *bool*(p) = *evaluate* $[\![$num>9 **and** num<100$]\!]$ $sto_{0,22}$
   = if true then *execute* $[\![$sum := sum+num$]\!]$ $(sto_{0,22}, [-1], [\ ])$
      else $(sto_{0,22}, [-1], [\ ])$
   = *execute* $[\![$sum := sum+num$]\!]$ $(sto_{0,22}, [-1], [\ ])$.

Therefore we need the value of the right side of the assignment command.

evaluate $[\![$sum+num$]\!]$ $sto_{0,22}$
         = *int*(plus(m,n))
                  where *int*(m) = *evaluate* $[\![$sum$]\!]$ $sto_{0,22}$
                     and *int*(n) = *evaluate* $[\![$num$]\!]$ $sto_{0,22}$
         = *int*(plus(0,22)) = *int*(22).

Completing the assignment provides the state produced by the **if** command.

execute $[\![$sum := sum+num$]\!]$ $(sto_{0,22}, [-1], [\ ])$
   = $(updateSto(sto_{0,22}, sum, (evaluate [\![sum+num]\!] sto_{0,22})), [-1], [\ ])$
   = $(updateSto(sto_{0,22}, sum, int(22)), [-1], [\ ])$
   = $(\{sum \mapsto int(22), num \mapsto int(22)\}, [-1], [\ ])$.

Let $sto_{22,22} = \{sum \mapsto int(22), num \mapsto int(22)\}$.

Continuing with the body of the **while** command for its second pass yields a state with a new store after executing the **read** command.

$execute$ [[**read** num]] $(sto_{22.22}, [-1], [\ ]))$
$\qquad\qquad = (updateSto(sto_{22.22}, num, int(-1)), [\ ], [\ ])$
$\qquad\qquad = (\{sum \mapsto int(22), num \mapsto int(-1)\}, [\ ], [\ ]).$

Let $sto_{22,-1} = \{sum \mapsto int(22), num \mapsto int(-1)\}.$

Summarizing the second execution of the body of the **while** command, we have the result

$execute$ [[$c_{3.1}$; $c_{3.2}$]] $(sto_{0.22}, [-1], [\ ]) = (sto_{22,-1}, [\ ], [\ ]).$

This completes the second pass through loop.

$loop (sto_{0.22}, [-1], [\ ])$
$\qquad = loop (execute$ [[$c_{3.1}$; $c_{3.2}$]] $(sto_{0.22}, [-1], [\ ]))$
$\qquad = loop(sto_{22,-1}, [\ ], [\ ]).$

Again we work on the Boolean expression from the **while** command first.

$evaluate$ [[num]] $sto_{22,-1} = applySto(sto_{22,-1}, num) = int(-1).$

$evaluate$ [[0]] $sto_{22,-1} = int(0).$

$evaluate$ [[num>=0]] $sto_{22,-1}$
$\qquad = if\ greatereq(m,n)\ then\ bool(true)\ else\ bool(false)$
$\qquad\qquad where\ int(m) = evaluate$ [[num]] $sto_{22,-1}$
$\qquad\qquad\qquad and\ int(n) = evaluate$ [[0]] $sto_{22,-1}$
$\qquad = if\ greatereq(-1,0)\ then\ bool(true)\ else\ bool(false)$
$\qquad = bool(false).$

When we execute loop for the third time, we exit the **while** command.

$loop (sto_{22,-1}, [\ ], [\ ])$
$\qquad = if\ p\ then\ loop(execute$ [[$c_{3.1}$; $c_{3.2}$]] $(sto_{22,-1}, [\ ], [\ ]))$
$\qquad\qquad\qquad else\ (sto_{22,-1}, [\ ], [\ ])$
$\qquad\qquad\qquad\qquad where\ bool(p) = evaluate$ [[num>=0]] $sto_{22,-1}$
$\qquad = if\ false\ then\ loop(execute$ [[$c_{3.1}$; $c_{3.2}$]] $(sto_{22,-1}, [\ ], [\ ]))$
$\qquad\qquad\qquad else\ (sto_{22,-1}, [\ ], [\ ])$
$\qquad = (sto_{22,-1}, [\ ], [\ ]).$

Recapping the execution of the **while** command, we conclude:

$execute$ [[**while** num>=0 **do** $c_{3.1}$; $c_{3.2}$]] $(sto_{0.5}, [22,-1], [\ ])$
$\qquad = loop (sto_{0.5}, [22,-1], [\ ])$
$\qquad = (sto_{22,-1}, [\ ], [\ ]).$

Now we continue with the fourth command in the program.

$evaluate$ [[sum]] $sto_{22,-1} = applySto(sto_{22,-1}, sum) = int(22).$

execute [[**write** sum]] $(sto_{22,-1}, [\,], [\,])$
     $= (sto_{22,-1}, [\,], affix([\,],val))$ where $int(val) = evaluate$ [[sum]] $sto_{22,-1}$
     $= (sto_{22,-1}, [\,], [22]))$.

Finally, we summarize the execution of the four commands to obtain the meaning of the program.

   execute [[c_1 ; c_2 ; c_3 ; c_4]] $(emptySto, [5,22,-1], [\,]) = (sto_{22,-1}, [\,], [22]))$.
and so

   meaning [[**program** sample **is** d **begin** c_1 ; c_2 ; c_3 ; c_4 **end**]] $[5,22,-1] = [22]$.

Exercises

1. Add these language constructs to Wren and provide their denotational semantics.

    a) repeat-until command
         Command ::= ... | **repeat** Command **until** Expression

    b) conditional expression
         Expression ::= ... | **if** Expression **then** Expression **else** Expression
        Use your definition to prove the semantic equivalence of
         m := **if** E_1 **then** E_2 **else** E_3 and   **if** E_1 **then** m:=E_2 **else** m:=E_3.

    c) expression with side effects
         Expression ::= ... | **begin** Command **return** Expression **end**.

    d) case command
         Command ::= **case** IntegerExpr **of** (**when** Numeral$^+$ **=>** Command)$^+$

2. Express the denotational meaning of this code fragment as a function Store $\rightarrow$ Store using the notation described in this section for representing stores:

         switch := **true**; sum := 0; k := 1;
         while k<4 **do**
             switch := **not**(switch);
             if switch **then** sum := sum+k **end if**;
             k := k+1
         end while

3. Modify the remaining semantic equations for *execute* to reflect the inclusion of input and output in Wren.

4. Carefully prove: *execute* [[m:=5; n:=m+3]] = *execute* [[n:=8; m:=n-3]].

5. Prove the semantic equivalence of these language phrases:

   a) **while** E **do** C and **if** E **then** (C; **while** E **do** C) **else skip**

   b) **if** E **then** C_1 **else** C_2 and **if not**(E) **then** C_2 **else** C_1

   c) x := 5; y := 2*x and y := 10; x := y/2

   d) $E_1 + E_2$ and $E_2 + E_1$

   e) **if** E **then** (**if** E **then** C_1 **else** C_2) **else** C_3 and **if** E **then** C_1 **else** C_2

   f) (**while** E **do** C_1); **if** E **then** C_2 **else** C_3 and (**while** E **do** C_1); C_2.

6. Elaborate the denotational meaning of the following Wren program us-
   ing the function, meaning: Program $\rightarrow$ Input $\rightarrow$ Output, taking [5,22,-1]
   as the input list:

   ```
   program bool is
      var a,b : boolean;
   begin
      a := true;     b := true;
      while a or b do
            write 5;
            if not(a) then b := not(b) end if;
            if b then a := not(a) end if
      end while
   end
   ```

7. Discuss the ambiguity in binary operations that occurs when expressions can have side effects—for example, the expressions in exercise 1c
   or in a language with function subprograms. Give an example of this
   ambiguity. Where is this issue dealt with in a denotational definition?

8. A vending machine takes nickels, dimes, and quarters and has buttons
   to select gum (30¢), a candy bar (50¢), or a brownie (65¢), or to return
   the coins entered. After entering a sequence of coins and pressing a
   button, the user receives the selected item (or nothing) and the change
   from the purchase. When the value of the coins is insufficient for the
   button pressed, the outcome is the same as from return.

   The following two examples show how the vending machine might be
   used:
   > "dime, dime, dime, quarter, candy bar button"
   >> produces a candy bar and 5 cents in change.
   > "quarter, nickel, return" or "quarter, nickel, candy"
   >> produce nothing and 30 cents in change.

The language of the vending machine has the following abstract syntax:

> Program ::= CoinSeq Button
> CoinSeq ::= ε | Coin CoinSeq
> Coin ::= Nickel | Dime | Quarter
> Button ::= Gum | Candy | Brownie | Return

Using the semantic domains

> Result = { gum, candy, brownie, naught } and
> Number = { 0, 1, 2, 3, 4, ... },

provide a denotational semantics for the language of the vending machine.

9. Consider the language of propositional logic, which contains symbols from the following syntactic domains:

var : Var = { p, q, r, p_1, q_1, r_1, p_2, q_2, ... }	Propositional variables
con : Con = { **t**, **f** }	Propositional constants
uop : Uop = { ~ }	Unary operation
bop : Bop = { ∧, ∨, ⊃, ↔ }	Binary operations

a) Give a BNF grammar for the concrete syntax of the language (well-formed formulas) of propositional logic.

b) Describe an abstract syntax of this language in terms of the syntactic variables for the syntactic domains.

c) Provide a denotational defintion that gives meaning to the formulas in the language of propositional logic, specifying the semantic domain(s), the syntax of the semantic function(s), and the semantic equations that define the semantics of the language. One parameter to the semantic functions will be a function assigning Boolean values to the propositional variables.

9.4 LABORATORY: IMPLEMENTING DENOTATIONAL SEMANTICS

In Chapter 2 we developed a scanner and parser that take a text file containing a Wren program and produce an abstract syntax tree. Now we continue, creating a prototype implementation of Wren based on its denotational semantics. The semantic equations are translated into Prolog clauses that carry out the denotational definition when executed.

We illustrate the result of this exercise with a Wren program that tests whether positive integers are prime. It expects a list of integers terminated by a negative number or zero as input and returns those integers that are prime and zero for those that are not. A sample execution of a version of the interpreter using interactive (nondenotational) input and output is shown below:

```
>>> Interpreting Wren via Denotational Semantics <<<
Enter name of source file: prime.wren
     program prime is
        var num,div : integer;
        var done : boolean;
     begin
        read num;
        while num>0 do
           div := 2; done := false;
           while div<= num/2 and not(done) do
              done := num = div*(num/div);
              div := div+1
            end while;
           if done then write 0
                    else write num
           end if;
           read num
        end while
     end
Scan successful
Parse successful
Input: 23
Output = 23
Input: 91
Output = 0
Input: 149
Output = 149
Input: 0
Final store:
        num    int(0)
        div    int(75)
        done   bool(false)
yes
```

If the denotational approach to input and output is followed using a state containing an input list, an output list, and the store (see section 9.3), the results look like this:

```
Enter input list followed by a period:
[23,79,91,129,149,177,0].
```

```
Output = [23,79,0,0,149,0]
yes
```

We consider the version with interactive input and output in this section, leaving the denotational version as an exercise. To implement a denotational definition in Prolog, we translate semantic functions into relations given by Prolog predicates. Since functions *are* relations, this approach works nicely. For example, the *execute* function

> *execute* : Command → Store → Store

becomes the predicate execute(Cmd, Sto, NewSto). In the abstract syntax tree produced by the parser, command sequencing is handled by using a Prolog list of commands. In the semantic equations, execute processes the first command producing a temporary store that is given to another application of execute on the rest of the commands. Executing an empty list results in the identity relation on stores.

> execute([Cmd|Cmds],Sto,NewSto) :- execute(Cmd,Sto,TempSto),
>   execute(Cmds,TempSto,NewSto).
> execute([ ],Sto,Sto).

Both the **if** and **while** commands require auxiliary predicates in their Prolog versions. We illustrate the **while** command since it is a bit more complex:

> execute(while(Test,Body),Sto,NewSto) :- loop(Test,Body,Sto,NewSto).
>
> loop(Test,Body,Sto,NewSto) :- evaluate(Test,Sto,Val),
>   iterate(Val,Test,Body,Sto,NewSto).
>
> iterate(bool(true),Test,Body,Sto,NewSto) :- execute(Body,Sto,TempSto),
>   loop(Test,Body,TempSto,NewSto).
> iterate(bool(false),Test,Body,Sto,Sto).

Before considering the assignment command, we need to discuss how to model the finite function that comprises the store. We portray the store as a Prolog structure of the form

> sto(a, int(3), sto(b, int(8), sto(c, bool(false), nil)))

for the store {a |→*int*(3), b |→*int*(8), c |→*bool*(false)}. The empty store is given by the Prolog atom nil. The auxiliary functions for manipulating the store become predicates defined as follows:

> updateSto(sto(Ide,V,Sto),Ide,Val,sto(Ide,Val,Sto)).
>
> updateSto(sto(I,V,Sto),Ide,Val,sto(I,V,NewSto)) :-
>   updateSto(Sto,Ide,Val,NewSto).
>
> updateSto(nil,Ide,Val,sto(Ide,Val,nil)).

The predicate updateSto(Sto,Ide,Val,NewSto) searches the current store for a match with Ide. If the identifier is found, its binding is changed to Val in the new store. If Ide is not found, the binding Ide |→Val is inserted at the end of the store. A value binding for an identifier is found using the predicate applySto.

> applySto(sto(Ide,Val,Sto),Ide,Val).
>
> applySto(sto(I,V,Sto),Ide,Val) :- applySto(Sto,Ide,Val).
>
> applySto(nil,Ide,undefined) :- write('Undefined variable'), nl, abort.

Note that when an identifier cannot be found in the store, applySto prints an error message and aborts the execution of the denotational interpreter to indicate the runtime error.

The assignment command evaluates the expression on the right and updates the identifier in the store:

> execute(assign(Ide,Exp),Sto,NewSto) :- evaluate(Exp,Sto,Val),
>
> $\qquad\qquad\qquad\qquad\qquad$ updateSto(Sto,Ide,Val,NewSto).

The *evaluate* function, *evaluate* : Expression → Store → EV, takes an expression and the current store and produces an expressible value. For literals, we use the value given by the scanner and attach the appropriate tag:

> evaluate(num(N),Sto,int(N)).
>
> evaluate(true,Sto,bool(true)).
>
> evaluate(false,Sto,bool(false)).

For identifiers, evaluate simply fetches a value from the store:

> evaluate(ide(Ide),Sto,Val) :- applySto(Sto,Ide,Val).

Numeric binary operations are handled by evaluating the two operands using evaluate and calling a predicate compute that carries out the operations using the native arithmetic in Prolog. We illustrate a few of the operations:

> evaluate(exp(Opr,E1,E2),Sto,Val) :- evaluate(E1,Sto,V1), evaluate(E2,Sto,V2),
>
> $\qquad\qquad\qquad\qquad\qquad$ compute(Opr,V1,V2,Val).
>
> compute(times,int(M),int(N),int(R)) :- R is M*N.
>
> compute(divides,int(M),int(0),int(0)) :- write('Division by zero'), nl, abort.
>
> compute(divides,int(M),int(N),int(R)) :- R is M//N.

Observe how a division-by-zero error causes the interpreter to abort. This action does not follow the denotational definition but avoids the problem of propagating errors in the prototype interpreter.

Comparisons and Boolean operations can be dealt with in a similar manner, except that some operations are implemented using pattern matching:

evaluate(bexp(Opr,E1,E2),Sto,Val) :-   evaluate(E1,Sto,V1), evaluate(E2,Sto,V2),
                                        compute(Opr,V1,V2,Val).

compute(equal,int(M),int(N),bool(true)) :- M =:= N.
compute(equal,int(M),int(N),bool(false)).

compute(neq,int(M),int(N),bool(false)) :- M =:= N.
compute(neq,int(M),int(N),bool(true)).

compute(lteq,int(M),int(N),bool(true)) :- M =< N.
compute(lteq,int(M),int(N),bool(false)).

compute(and,bool(true),bool(true),bool(true)).
compute(and,bool(P),bool(Q),bool(false)).

For an entire program, meaning calls execute with an empty store and returns the final store, which is printed by the predicate controlling the system.

meaning(prog(Dec,Cmd),Sto) :- execute(Cmd,nil,Sto).

We now consider the two approaches to input and output. For the interactive version, we disregard the denotational definitions for **read** and **write** and simply rely on Prolog to fetch an input value from the keyboard and print an integer on the screen. Executing the **read** command this way requires an auxiliary predicate readnum that can be based on the part of the scanner for processing integers.

execute(read(Ide),Sto,NewSto) :- write('Input: '), nl, readnum(N),
                                        updateSto(Sto,Ide,int(N),NewSto).

execute(write(Exp),Sto,Sto) :- evaluate(Exp,Sto,Val), Val=int(M),
                                        write('Output = '), write(M), nl.

The denotational approach complicates the semantic equations for execute, as was discussed in section 9.3. Then the **read** and **write** commands act directly on the input and output lists in the state, modeled by a Prolog structure, state(Sto,Intp,Outp).

execute(read(Ide),state(Sto,[H|T],Outp),state(NewSto,T,Outp)) :-
                                        updateSto(Sto,Ide,int(H),NewSto).

execute(read(Ide),state(Sto,[ ],Outp),state(NewSto,[ ],Outp)) :-
                                        write('Attempt to read empty input'), nl, abort.

execute(write(Exp),state(Sto,Inp,Outp),state(Sto,Inp,Outp1)) :-
                                        evaluate(Exp,Sto,Val), int(M)=Val, concat(Outp,[M],Outp1).

Note that in both versions of **write**, we use a variable as the third parameter of evaluate, and then use unification, denoted by =, to pull the integer out of the structure. This convention ensures that if evaluate involves a store lookup that fails, the failure comes in the body of the third clause applySto and not because undefined in the head of that clause failed to pattern match with int(M).

The top-level meaning predicate calls execute with the original input list and produces the output list as its result. We depend on a predicate go to request the input and print the output.

```
meaning(prog(Dec,Cmd),Inp,Outp)) :-
                    execute(Cmd,state(nil,Inp,[ ]),state(Sto,Inp1,Outp)).

go :-  nl, write('>>> Interpreting Wren <<<'), nl, nl,
       write('Enter name of source file: '), nl, getfilename(FileName), nl,
       see(FileName), scan(Tokens), seen, write('Scan successful'), nl, !,
       program(Parse,Tokens,[eop]), write('Parse successful'), nl, !,
       write('Enter input list followed by a period: '), nl, read(Inp), nl,
       meaning(Parse,Inp,Outp),nl,write('Output = '), write(Outp), nl.
```

All of the clauses defining execute must correctly maintain the state; for example, the assignment command has no effect on the input or output list but needs access to the store argument inside the state:

```
execute(assign(Ide,Exp),state(Sto,Inp,Outp),state(Sto1,Inp,Outp)) :-
                    evaluate(Exp,Sto,Val),  updateSto(Sto,Ide,Val,Sto1).
```

Exercises

1. Supply Prolog definitions for the remaining commands: **skip** and **if**.

2. Supply Prolog definitions for subtraction, multiplication **or**, unary minus, **not**, and the remaining relations. Be careful in handling the tags on the values.

3. Write a Prolog predicate readnum that accepts a string of digits from the terminal and forms an integer. Modify the predicate to accept an optional minus sign immediately preceding the digits.

4. Complete the Prolog definition of the prototype interpreter for both interactive input and output and for the denotational version.

5. Extend the prototype interpreter to include the following language constructs:

   a) repeat-until commands
      Command ::= ... | **repeat** Command **until** Expression

   b) conditional expressions
      Expression ::= ... | **if** Expression **then** Expression **else** Expression

c) expressions with side effects

Expression ::= ... | **begin** Command **return** Expression **end**

6. Write a scanner, parser, and denotational interpreter for the calculator language described in section 9.2.

9.5 DENOTATIONAL SEMANTICS WITH ENVIRONMENTS

In this section we extend Wren to a programming language in which declarations contribute to the semantics as well as the context-sensitive syntax of the language. The addition of procedures significantly enlarges the language, and we thus take the P from procedure to give it a new name, Pelican. Figure 9.12 contains a definition of its abstract syntax. Notice the features that make Pelican different from Wren:

Abstract Syntactic Domains

P : Program	C : Command	N : Numeral
B : Block	E : Expression	I : Identifier
D : Declaration	O : Operator	L : Identifier$^+$
T : Type		

Abstract Production Rules

Program ::= **program** Identifier **is** Block

Block ::= Declaration **begin** Command **end**

Declaration ::= ε | Declaration Declaration
     | **const** Identifier = Expression
     | **var** Identifier : Type | **var** Identifier, Identifier$^+$: Type
     | **procedure** Identifier **is** Block
     | **procedure** Identifier (Identifier : Type) **is** Block

Type ::= **integer** | **boolean**

Command ::= Command ; Command | Identifier := Expression
     | **skip** | **if** Expression **then** Command **else** Command
     | **if** Expression **then** Command | **while** Expression **do** Command
     | **declare** Block | Identifier | Identifier(Expression)
     | **read** Identifier | **write** Expression

Expression ::= Numeral | Identifier | **true** | **false** | - Expression
     | Expression Operator Expression | **not**(Expression)

Operator ::= + | − | * | / | **or** | **and** | <= | < | = | > | >= | <>

Figure 9.12: Abstract Syntax for Pelican

1. A program may consist of several scopes corresponding to the syntactic domain Block that occurs in the main program, in anonymous blocks headed by **declare**, and in procedures.

2. Each block may contain constant declarations indicated by **const** as well as variable declarations.

3. Pelican permits the declaration of procedures with zero or one value parameter and their use as commands. We limit procedures to no more than one parameter for the sake of simplicity. Multiple parameters will be left as an exercise.

We have slightly modified the specification of lists of declarations to make the semantic equations easier to define. In particular, the nonempty lists of identifiers in variable declarations are specified with two clauses: the first handles a basis case of one identifier, and the second manages lists of two or more identifiers. In addition, we specify Pelican without the **read** and **write** commands, whose definitions are left as an exercise at the end of this section.

Environments

In a block structured language with more than one scope, such as Pelican, the same identifier can refer to different objects in different parts of the program. The region where an identifier has a unique meaning is called the **scope** of the identifier, and this meaning is recorded in a structure called an **environment**. Therefore in Pelican the bindings between a variable identifier and a value split into two parts: (1) a binding between the identifier and a location, modeling a memory address, and (2) a binding of the location to its value in the store. The record of bindings between identifiers and locations as well as bindings of other sorts of objects, such as literals and procedures, to identifiers is maintained in the environment. Those values that are bindable to identifiers are known as **denotable values**, and in Pelican they are given by the semantic domain

$$DV = int(\text{Integer}) + bool(\text{Boolean}) + var(\text{Location}) + \text{Procedure},$$

where Procedure represents the domain of procedure objects in Pelican. We defer the discussion of Pelican procedures until later. The first two terms in the disjoint sum for DV provide the literal values that can be bound to identifiers by a **const** declaration.

As with stores, we use auxiliary functions to manipulate environments, thereby treating them as an abstract data type:

$emptyEnv$: Environment

$\quad emptyEnv$ I = $unbound$

extendEnv : Environment x Identifier x DV $\rightarrow$ Environment

$\quad$ *extendEnv*(env,I,dval) I_1 = (if I = I_1 then dval else env(I_1))

applyEnv : Environment x Identifier $\rightarrow$ DV + *unbound*

$\quad$ *applyEnv*(env,I) = env(I).

Stores

A store in Pelican becomes a function from locations, here modeled by the natural numbers, to the storable values, augmented by two special values: (1) *unused* for those locations that have not been bound to an identifier by a declaration, and (2) *undefined* for locations that have been associated with a variable identifier but do not have a value yet. Locations serve as an abstraction of memory addresses and should not be confused with them. In fact, any ordinal set can be used to model locations; we take the natural numbers for convenience.

The auxiliary functions for stores now include operations for allocating and deallocating memory locations at block entry and exit:

emptySto : Store

$\quad$ *emptySto* loc = *unused*

updateSto : Store x Location x (SV + *undefined* + *unused*) $\rightarrow$ Store

$\quad$ *updateSto*(sto,loc,val) loc_1 = (if loc = loc_1 then val else sto(loc_1))

applySto : Store x Location $\rightarrow$ SV + *undefined* + *unused*

$\quad$ *applySto*(sto,loc) = sto(loc)

allocate : Store $\rightarrow$ Store x Location

$\quad$ *allocate* sto = (*updateSto*(sto,loc,*undefined*),loc)

$\qquad\qquad\qquad$ where loc = *minimum* { k | sto(k) = *unused* }

deallocate : Store x Location $\rightarrow$ Store

$\quad$ *deallocate*(sto,loc) = *updateSto*(sto,loc,*unused*).

The semantic domains for Pelican are summarized in Figure 9.13. We save the explanation of the Procedure domain until later in this section.

Figures 9.14 and 9.15 show how a Pelican program with multiple scopes influences environments and the store. We use a notation for environments that is similar to the one employed to display the store. The expression "[a$\mapsto$*int*(5),b$\mapsto$*var*(0)]" indicates that the identifier a is bound to the constant 5 and b is bound to the location 0, while all other identifiers are *unbound*. Furthermore, "[x$\mapsto$*var*(3),y$\mapsto$*var*(4)]env" denotes the environment that is identical to env except that x and y have new bindings.

Semantic Domains

Integer = { ... , -2, -1, 0, 1, 2, 3, 4, ... }

Boolean = { true, false }

EV = *int*(Integer) + *bool*(Boolean)   -- expressible values

SV = *int*(Integer) + *bool*(Boolean)   -- storable values

DV = EV + *var*(Location) + Procedure   -- denotable values

Location = Natural Number = { 0, 1 2, 3, 4, ... }

Store = Location → SV + *unused* + *undefined*

Environment = Identifier → DV + *unbound*

Procedure = *proc0*(Store → Store) + *proc1*(Location → Store → Store)

Semantic Functions

meaning	: Program → Store
perform	: Block → Environment → Store → Store
elaborate	: Declaration → Environment → Store → Environment x Store
execute	: Command → Environment → Store → Store
evaluate	: Expression → Environment → Store → EV
value	: Numeral → EV

Figure 9.13: Semantic Domains and Functions for Pelican

In the representation of the stores in Figure 9.15, locations that are unused are simply omitted, whereas locations that are allocated but without a meaningful value are indicated within the brackets as bound to *undefined*. So the empty store with all locations bound to *unused* can be depicted by { }. Note that seven different locations are allocated for the seven variables declared in the program.

Semantic Functions

The main alteration in the semantic functions for Pelican is to add Environment as an argument and to include functions providing meaning to Blocks and Declarations. The semantic function *elaborate* constructs a new environment on top of the given environment reflecting the declarations that are processed in the current block. Observe that *elaborate* produces a new store as well as a new environment, since the declaration of variable identifiers requires the allocation of locations, which thereby changes the state of the store. On the other hand, constant and procedure declarations have no effect on the store. The function *perform* has the same signature as *execute*, but it elaborates the declarations in the block before its commands are executed. The signatures of the semantic functions may be found in Figure 9.13.

program scope **is**   **Environment**
    const c = 9; $[\,c\mapsto int(9)\,]$
    var : **integer**; $[\,a\mapsto var(0),\,c\mapsto int(9)\,]$
    var b : **boolean**; $[\,b\mapsto var(1),\,a\mapsto var(0),\,c\mapsto int(9)\,]$
  begin
    a := 10; env_1
    b := a>0; env_1
    declare
      const a = 0; $[\,a\mapsto int(0)\,]\,env_1$
      var x,y : **integer**; $[\,y\mapsto var(3),\,x\mapsto var(2),\,a\mapsto int(0)\,]\,env_1$
    begin
      x := a; env_2
      y := c–2; env_2
      declare
        var x : **boolean**; $[\,x\mapsto var(4)\,]\,env_2$
        var c,d : **integer**; $[\,d\mapsto var(6),\,c\mapsto var(5),\,x\mapsto var(4)\,]\,env_2$
      begin
        x := **not**(b); env_3
        c := y+5; env_3
        d := 17 env_3
      end;
      x := –c env_2
    end;
    a := a+5 env_1
  end

where env_1 = $[\,b\mapsto var(1),\,a\mapsto var(0),\,c\mapsto int(9)\,]$
      env_2 = $[\,y\mapsto var(3),\,x\mapsto var(2),\,a\mapsto int(0)\,]\,env_1$
          = $[\,y\mapsto var(3),\,x\mapsto var(2),\,a\mapsto int(0),\,b\mapsto var(1),\,c\mapsto int(9)\,]$
      env_3 = $[\,d\mapsto var(6),\,c\mapsto var(5),\,x\mapsto var(4)\,]\,env_2$
          = $[\,d\mapsto var(6),\,c\mapsto var(5),\,x\mapsto var(4),\,y\mapsto var(3),\,a\mapsto int(0),\,b\mapsto var(1)\,]$

Figure 9.14: Environments for the Program "scope"

	Store
program scope **is**	
const c = 9;	{ }
var a : **integer**;	{ 0|→*ud* }
var b : **boolean**;	{ 0|→*ud*, 1|→*ud* }
begin	
a := 10;	{ 0|→*int*(10), 1|→*ud* }
b := a>0;	{ 0|→*int*(10), 1|→*bool*(true) }
declare	
const a = 0;	{ 0|→*int*(10), 1|→*bool*(true) }
var x,y : **integer**;	{ 0|→*int*(10), 1|→*bool*(true), 2|→*ud*, 3|→*ud* }
begin	
x := a;	{ 0|→*int*(10), 1|→*bool*(true), 2|→*int*(0), 3|→*ud* }
y := c–2;	{ 0|→*int*(10), 1|→*bool*(true), 2|→*int*(0), 3|→*int*(7) }
declare	
var x : **boolean**;	{ 0|→*int*(10), 1|→*bool*(true), 2|→*int*(0), 3|→*int*(7), 4|→*ud* }
var c,d : **integer**;	{ 0|→*int*(10), 1|→*bool*(true), 2|→*int*(0), 3|→*int*(7), 4|→*ud*, 5|→*ud*, 6|→*ud* }
begin	
x := **not**(b);	{ 0|→*int*(10), 1|→*bool*(true), 2|→*int*(0), 3|→*int*(7), 4|→*bool*(false), 5|→*ud*, 6|→*ud* }
c := y+5;	{ 0|→*int*(10), 1|→*bool*(true), 2|→*int*(0), 3|→*int*(7), 4|→*bool*(false), 5|→*int*(12), 6|→*ud* }
d := 17	{ 0|→*int*(10), 1|→*bool*(true), 2|→*int*(0), 3|→*int*(7), 4|→*bool*(false), 5|→*int*(12), 6|→*int*(17) }
end;	
x := –c	{ 0|→*int*(10), 1|→*bool*(true), 2|→*int*(-9), 3|→*int*(7), 4|→*bool*(false), 5|→*int*(12), 6|→*int*(17)) }
end;	
a := a+5	{ 0|→*int*(15), 1|→*bool*(true), 2|→*int*(-9), 3|→*int*(7), 4|→*bool*(false), 5|→*int*(12), 6|→*int*(17) }
end	
where *ud* = *undefined*	

Figure 9.15: The Store for the Program "scope"

Semantic Equations

Many of the semantic equations are straightforward extensions of those for
Wren, especially for those language constructs that are defined in the
denotational semantics of Wren. Figure 9.16 shows the semantic equations
except that we have omitted many of the *evaluate* equations since they all
follow the pattern established by the addition operation. We focus on those
functions that are entirely new—namely, *perform* and *elaborate*. The function *perform* is invoked by *meaning* for the whole program and by *execute* for
an anonymous block (**declare**). It also is encapsulated in the procedure objects declared in a program, but these will be considered in detail later.

---

meaning [[**program** I **is** B]] = *perform* [[B]] *emptyEnv emptySto*

perform [[D **begin** C **end**]] env sto = *execute* [[C]] env_1 sto_1
　　　　　where (env_1, sto_1) = *elaborate* [[D]] env sto

elaborate [[ε]] env sto = (env, sto)
elaborate [[D_1 D_2]] env sto = *elaborate* [[D_2]] env_1 sto_1
　　　　　where (env_1, sto_1) = *elaborate* [[D_1]] env sto
elaborate [[**const** I = E]] env sto = (*extendEnv*(env,I,*evaluate* [[E]] env sto), sto)
elaborate [[**var** I : T]] env sto = (*extendEnv*(env,I,*var*(loc)), sto_1)
　　　　　where (sto_1, loc) = *allocate* sto
elaborate [[**var** I, L : T]] env sto = *elaborate* [[**var** L : T]] env_1 sto_1
　　　　　where (env_1, sto_1) = *elaborate* [[**var** I : T]] env sto
elaborate [[**procedure** I **is** B]] env sto = (env_1, sto)
　　　　　where env_1 = *extendEnv*(env,I,*proc0*(proc))
　　　　　and proc = *perform* [[B]] env_1
elaborate [[**procedure** I_1(I_2 : T) **is** B]] env sto = (env_1, sto)
　　　　　where env_1 = (*extendEnv*(env,I_1,*proc1*(proc))
　　　　　and proc loc = *perform* [[B]] *extendEnv*(env,I_2,*var*(loc))

Figure 9.16: Semantic Equations for Pelican (Part 1)

Compare the equation for elaborating a sequence of declarations with that
for executing a pair of commands. Since *elaborate* produces a pair of values,
Environment and Store, the composition operator cannot be used. Of course,
an empty declaration leaves the environment and store unchanged.

execute $[\![C_1 \; ; \; C_2]\!]$ env sto = *execute* $[\![C_2]\!]$ env (*execute* $[\![C_1]\!]$ env sto)

execute $[\![\textbf{skip}]\!]$ env sto = sto

execute $[\![I := E]\!]$ env sto = *updateSto*(sto, loc, (*evaluate* $[\![E]\!]$ env sto))
    where *var*(loc) = *applyEnv*(env,I)

execute $[\![\textbf{if } E \textbf{ then } C]\!]$ env sto = if p then *execute* $[\![C]\!]$ env sto else sto
    where *bool*(p) = *evaluate* $[\![E]\!]$ env sto

execute $[\![\textbf{if } E \textbf{ then } C_1 \textbf{ else } C_2]\!]$ env sto =
    if p then *execute* $[\![C_1]\!]$ env sto else *execute* $[\![C_2]\!]$ env sto
        where *bool*(p) = *evaluate* $[\![E]\!]$ env sto

execute $[\![\textbf{while } E \textbf{ do } C]\!]$ = loop
    where loop env sto = if p then loop env (*execute* $[\![C]\!]$ env sto) else sto
                    where *bool*(p) = *evaluate* $[\![E]\!]$ env sto

execute $[\![\textbf{declare } B]\!]$ env sto = *perform* $[\![B]\!]$ env sto

execute $[\![I]\!]$ env sto = proc sto
    where *proc0*(proc) = *applyEnv*(env,I)

execute $[\![I(E)]\!]$ env sto = proc loc *updateSto*(sto$_1$,loc,*evaluate* $[\![E]\!]$ env sto)
    where *proc1*(proc) = *applyEnv*(env,I) and (sto$_1$,loc) = *allocate* sto

evaluate $[\![I]\!]$ env sto =
    if dval = *int*(n) or dval = *bool*(p) then dval
                else if dval = *var*(loc)
                            then if *applySto*(sto,loc) = *undefined*
                                then *error*
                                else *applySto*(sto,loc)
            where dval = *applyEnv*(env,I)

evaluate $[\![N]\!]$ env sto = *int*(*value* $[\![N]\!]$)

evaluate $[\![\textbf{true}]\!]$ env sto = *bool*(true)

evaluate $[\![\textbf{false}]\!]$ env sto = *bool*(false)

evaluate $[\![E_1 + E_2]\!]$ env sto = *int*(plus(m,n))
    where *int*(m) = *evaluate* $[\![E_1]\!]$ env sto and *int*(n) = *evaluate* $[\![E_2]\!]$ env sto
    :

evaluate $[\![E_1 \; / \; E_2]\!]$ env sto = if n=0 then *error* else *int*(divides(m,n))
    where *int*(m) = *evaluate* $[\![E_1]\!]$ env sto and *int*(n) = *evaluate* $[\![E_2]\!]$ env sto
    :

Figure 9.16: Semantic Equations for Pelican (Part 2)

The declaration of a list of variable identifiers is reduced to declarations of individual variable identifiers by elaborating the single identifier (the head of the list) to produce a new environment and store and then by elaborating the list of identifiers (the tail of the list) using that environment and store. In the equation for "**var** I : T", *allocate* produces a new state of the store because a location with the value *undefined* has been reserved for the variable. Recall that L is the metavariable for nonempty lists of identifiers. The equation for "**const** I = E" simply binds the current value of E to the identifier I in the environment, leaving the store unchanged. Note that these constant identifiers are bound to dynamic expressions whose values may not be known until run-time.

Observe that when a sequence of commands is executed, both commands receive the same environment; only the store is modified by the commands. The semantic equations may also be written using compositon:

$$execute \; [\![C_1 \; ; \; C_2]\!] \; \text{env} = (execute \; [\![C_2]\!] \; \text{env}) \circ (execute \; [\![C_1]\!] \; \text{env})$$

An assignment command depends on the environment for the location of the target variable and on the store for the value of the expression on the right side. Executing an assignment results in a modification of the store using *updateSto*.

Because we assume Pelican programs have already been checked for syntax errors (both context-free and context-sensitive), only syntactically correct programs are submitted for semantic analysis. Therefore identifiers used in assignment commands, in expression, and in procedure calls are bound to values of the appropriate type. The following semantic decisions need to be handled in the semantic equations (in the absence of the **read** command):

1. Whether an identifier in an expression represents a constant or a variable.

2. Whether the location bound to a variable identifier has a value when it is accessed (whether it is defined).

3. Whether the second operand to a divides operation is zero.

Procedures

A procedure declaration assembles a new binding in the environment. We consider procedures without parameters first.

$elaborate \; [\![\mathbf{procedure} \; I \; \mathbf{is} \; B]\!] \; \text{env} \; \text{sto} = (\text{env}_1, \text{sto})$
    where $\text{env}_1 = (extendEnv(\text{env},I,proc0(\text{proc})))$
    and $\text{proc} = perform \; [\![B]\!] \; \text{env}_1$.

The procedure object proc, constructed to complete the binding, encapsulates a call of *perform* on the body of the procedure in the environment now being defined, thus ensuring two important properties:

1. Since a procedure object carries along an extension of the environment in effect at its definition, we get **static scoping**. That means nonlocal variables in the procedure will refer to variables in the scope of the declaration, not in the scope of the call of the procedure (dynamic scoping). A procedure object constructed this way is an example of a closure (see Chapter 5).

2. Since the environment env_1 inserted into the procedure object contains the binding of the procedure identifier with this object, recursive references to the procedure are permitted. If recursion is forbidden, the procedure object can be defined by

$$proc = \textit{perform } [\![B]\!] \text{ env}.$$

When such a procedure object is invoked by "*execute* $[\![I]\!]$ env sto", the object is found by accessing the current environment and is executed by passing the current store to it, after first removing the tag *proc0*.

$\qquad$ *execute* $[\![I]\!]$ env sto = proc sto
$\qquad\qquad$ where *proc0*(proc) = *applyEnv*(env,I).

For procedures that take a parameter, the object defined in the declaration is a function of a location corresponding to the formal parameter that will be provided at procedure invocation time when the value of the actual parameter passed to the procedure is stored in the location.

$\qquad$ *elaborate* $[\![$**procedure** $I_1(I_2 : T)$ **is** $B]\!]$ env sto = $(env_1,$ sto$)$
$\qquad\qquad$ where env_1 = *extendEnv*(env,I_1,*proc1*(proc))
$\qquad\qquad$ and proc loc = *perform* $[\![B]\!]$ *extendEnv*(env_1,I_2,*var*(loc)).

The environment encapsulated with the procedure object includes a binding of the unspecified location "loc" to the formal parameter I_2. Note that the actual location must be allocated at the point of call, thus providing "call by value" semantics for the parameter.

$\qquad$ *execute* $[\![I(E)]\!]$ env sto = proc loc *updateSto*(sto_1,loc,*evaluate* $[\![E]\!]$ env sto)
$\qquad\qquad$ where *proc1*(proc) = *applyEnv*(env,I) and $(sto_1,$loc$)$ = *allocate* sto.

The procedure object then executes with a store having the allocated location loc bound to the value of the actual parameter "*evaluate* $[\![E]\!]$ env sto". Again the environment env_1, provided to the procedure object proc, contains the binding of the procedure name, so that recursion can take place.

Figure 9.17 shows a Pelican program with the declaration of a recursive procedure along with the environments at points of the program. Because Pelican adheres to static scoping, we can identify the bound identifiers at each position in the program. Since the procedure has no local variables other than the formal parameter, the procedure object proc disregards the elaboration of its (empty) declarations. The four calls, sum(3), sum(2), sum(1), and

---

program summation **is**	**Environment**
var s : **integer**;	$[s \mapsto var(0)]$
procedure sum(n:integer) **is**	$[s \mapsto var(0), sum \mapsto proc1(proc)]$
begin	
if n>0	$env_{2,loc}$
then s := s+n;	$env_{2,loc}$
sum(n–1) **end if**	$env_{2,loc}$
end;	
begin	
s := 0;	env_1
sum(3)	env_1
end	

where

proc = λ loc . *execute* [[**if** n>0 **then** s := s+n; sum(n–1)]]

extendEnv(env$_1$,n,var(loc))

$env_1 = [s \mapsto var(0), sum \mapsto proc1(proc)]$

$env_{2,1} = [s \mapsto var(0), sum \mapsto proc1(proc), n \mapsto var(1)]$

$env_{2,2} = [s \mapsto var(0), sum \mapsto proc1(proc), n \mapsto var(2)]$

$env_{2,3} = [s \mapsto var(0), sum \mapsto proc1(proc), n \mapsto var(3)]$

$env_{2,4} = [s \mapsto var(0), sum \mapsto proc1(proc), n \mapsto var(4)]$

Figure 9.17: A Procedure Declaration in Pelican

---

sum(0), result in four environments $env_{2,1}$, $env_{2,2}$, $env_{2,3}$, and $env_{2,4}$, respectively, as new locations are allocated.

In Figure 9.18 we describe the status of the store as the declarations and commands of the program summation are processed according to the denotational semantics of Pelican, showing the store only when it changes. Each time sum is invoked, a new location is allocated and bound to n as the value of loc in the procedure object proc. Therefore $env_{2,loc}$ stands for four different environments for the body of the procedure depending on the current value of loc—namely, 1, 2, 3, or 4. These four locations in the store correspond to the four activation records that an implementation of Pelican creates when executing this program.

8. Suppose that Pelican is extended to include functions of one parameter, passed by value. The abstract syntax now has productions of the form:

> Declaration ::= ... | **function** Identifier (Identifier) **is** Declaration
> **begin** Command **return** Expression **end**

and

> Expressions ::= ... | Identifier (Expression)

Make all the necessary changes in the denotational definition of Pelican to incorporate this new language construct.

9. Some programming languages allow functions with no parameters but require an empty parameter list at the time of the call, as in f(). Why do these languages have this requirement?

10. Remove the assignment command, the **read** command, and the **while** command from Pelican, calling the new language BabyPelican. Use structural induction (see Chapter 8) to prove that every command in BabyPelican is semantically equivalent to **skip**.

11. Construct a prototype denotational interpreter for Pelican in Prolog.

9.6 CHECKING CONTEXT-SENSITIVE SYNTAX

In Chapter 3 we developed an attribute grammar to check the context constraints imposed by the declarations and type regime of a programming language. Here we solve the same problem in the framework of denotational semantics, mapping a program into the semantic domain Boolean in such a way that the resulting truth value records whether the program satisfies the requirements of the context-sensitive syntax. We assume that programs analyzed in this way already agree with the context-free syntax of the language.

A slightly modified Pelican serves as an example for illustrating this process of verifying context conditions. We leave procedure declarations and calls to be handled in an exercise and include the **read** and **write** commands now. The context conditions for Pelican are listed in Figure 9.19, including those for procedures that will be treated in an exercise.

The context checker has radically simplified denotational semantics since run-time behavior need not be modeled. In particular, we drop the store and register only the types of objects in environments, not their values. Figure 9.20 lists the semantic domains and the signatures of the semantic functions. The semantic function *elaborate* enters the type information given by declarations into the environment in much the same way the attribute grammar constructed a symbol table in Chapter 3. *Typify* produces the type of an expression given the types of the identifiers recorded in the (type) environment.

1. The program name identifier has no restrictions.

2. All identifiers that appear in a block must be declared in that block or in an enclosing block.

3. No identifier may be declared more than once at the top level of a block.

4. The identifier on the left side of an assignment command must be declared as a variable, and the expression on the right side must be of the same type.

5. An identifier occurring as an (integer) element must be an integer variable or an integer constant.

6. An identifier occurring as a Boolean element must be a Boolean variable or a Boolean constant.

7. An identifier occurring in a read command must be an integer variable.

8. An identifier used in a procedure call must be defined in a procedure declaration with the same (zero or one) number of parameters.

9. The identifier defined as the formal parameter in a procedure declaration is considered to belong to the top level declarations of the block that forms the body of the procedure.

10. The expression in a procedure call must match the type of the formal parameter in the procedure's declaration.

Figure 9.19: Context Conditions for Pelican

Since environments map identifiers to types, we need a semantic domain Sort to assemble the possible types. Note that we distinguish between constants (*integer* and *boolean*) and variables (*intvar* and *boolvar*). It is important to remember that every domain is automatically augmented with an *error* value, and every semantic function and auxiliary function propagates *error*.

Semantic Domains

Boolean = { true, false }

Sort = { *integer, boolean, intvar, boolvar, program, unbound* }

Environment = Identifier → Sort

Semantic Functions

validate	:	Program → Boolean
examine	:	Block → Environment → Boolean
elaborate	:	Declaration → Environment → Environment
check	:	Command → Environment → Boolean
typify	:	Expression → Environment → Sort

Figure 9.20: Semantic Domains and Functions for Context Checking

The auxiliary functions for Pelican need to altered so that we can distinguish between two ways of modifying the environment:

1. By adding a binding to an environment while processing a sequence of declarations (*extendEnv*).

2. By establishing a new environment that may hide previous bindings to some of the identifiers when entering a new block (*overlay*).

The auxiliary functions for maintaining environments are listed below (see section 9.5 for the missing definitions):

emptyEnv : Environment

extendEnv : Environment x Identifier x Sort → Environment

overlay : Environment x Environment → Environment

    overlay(env_1,env_2) I = (if I∈ *domain*(env_1) then env_1(I) else env_2(I))

applyEnv : Environment x Identifier → Sort

type : Type → Sort

    type(**integer**) = *intvar*

    type(**boolean**) = *boolvar*.

The semantic equations in Figure 9.21 show that each time a block is initialized, we build a type environment starting with the empty environment, and that new environment overlays the previous environment. The first equation indicates that the program identifier is viewed as lying in a block of its own, and so it does not conflict with any other occurrences of identifiers. This alteration in the context conditions for program identifiers as compared to Wren makes this denotational specification considerably simpler.

As declarations are processed, the environment for the current block is constructed incrementally, adding a binding of identifiers to a type for each individual declaration while checking for multiple declarations of an identifier. If an attempt is made to declare an identifier that is not *unbound*, the *error* value results. We assume that all semantic functions propagate an *error* value.

Checking commands involves finding Boolean or integer expressions where required and recursively checking sequences of commands that might occur. The semantic function *check* applied to a **declare** command just calls the *examine* function for the block.

Simple expressions have their types determined directly. When we *typify* a compound expression, we must verify that its operands have the proper types and then specify the appropriate result type. If any part of the verification fails, *error* becomes the type value to be propagated.

validate ⟦**program** I **is** B⟧ =
    examine ⟦B⟧ *extendEnv*(*emptyEnv*,I,*program*)

examine ⟦D **begin** C **end**⟧ env =
    check ⟦C⟧ *overlay*((*elaborate* ⟦D⟧ *emptyEnv*, env))

elaborate ⟦ε⟧ env = env
elaborate ⟦D₁ D₂⟧ env = *elaborate* ⟦D₂⟧ (*elaborate* ⟦D₁⟧ env)
elaborate ⟦**const** I = E⟧ env = if *applyEnv*(env,I) = *unbound*
                        then *extendEnv*(env,I,*typify* ⟦E⟧ env) else *error*
elaborate ⟦**var** I : T⟧ env = if *applyEnv*(env,I) = *unbound*
                        then *extendEnv*(env,I,*type* (T)) else *error*
elaborate ⟦**var** I, L : T⟧ env = *elaborate* ⟦**var** L : T⟧ (*elaborate* ⟦**var** I : T⟧ env)

check ⟦C₁ ; C₂⟧ env = (*check* ⟦C₁⟧ env) and (*check* ⟦C₂⟧ env)
check ⟦**skip**⟧ env = true
check ⟦I := E⟧ env =
            (*applyEnv* (env,I) = *intvar* and *typify* ⟦E⟧ env = *integer*)
        or (*applyEnv* (env,I) = *boolvar* and *typify* ⟦E⟧ env = *boolean*)
check ⟦**if** E **then** C⟧ env = (*typify* ⟦E⟧ env = *boolean*) and (*check* ⟦C⟧ env)
check ⟦**if** E **then** C₁ **else** C₂⟧ env =
    (*typify* ⟦E⟧ env = *boolean*) and (*check* ⟦C₁⟧ env) and (*check* ⟦C₂⟧ env)
check ⟦**while** E **do** C⟧ env = (*typify* ⟦E⟧ env = *boolean*) and (*check* ⟦C⟧ env)
check ⟦**declare** B⟧ env = *examine* ⟦B⟧ env
check ⟦**read** I⟧ env = (*applyEnv*(I, env) = *intvar*)
check ⟦**write** E⟧ env = (*typify* ⟦E⟧ env = *integer*)

Figure 9.21: Checking Context Constraints in Pelican (Part 1)

A program satisfies the context-sensitive syntax of Pelican if *validate* produces true when applied to it. A final value of false or *error* means that the
program does not fulfill the context constraints of the programming language.

typify ⟦I⟧ env = case *applyEnv*(env,I) of

                   intvar, integer   : *integer*

                   boolvar, boolean : *boolean*

                   program   : *program*

                   unbound   : *error*

typify ⟦N⟧ env = *integer*

typify ⟦**true**⟧ env = *boolean*

typify ⟦**false**⟧ env = *boolean*

typify ⟦E_1 + E_2⟧ env =

        if (*typify* ⟦E_1⟧ env = *integer*) and (*typify* ⟦E_2⟧ env = *integer*)

            then *integer* else *error*

    ⋮

typify ⟦E_1 **and** E_2⟧ env =

        if (*typify* ⟦E_1⟧ env = *boolean*) and (*typify* ⟦E_2⟧ env = *boolean*)

            then *boolean* else *error*

    ⋮

typify ⟦E_1 < E_2⟧ env =

        if (*typify* ⟦E_1⟧ env = *integer*) and (*typify* ⟦E_2⟧ env = *integer*)

            then *boolean* else *error*

    ⋮

Figure 9.21: Checking Context Constraints in Pelican (Part 2)

Exercises

1. Apply the *validate* semantic function to these Pelican programs and elaborate the definitions that check the context constraints for Pelican.

a) **program** a **is**
    const c = 99;
    var n : **integer**;
   begin
    read n;
    n := c-n;
    write c+1;
    write n
   end

b) **program** b **is**
    const c = 99;
    var b : **boolean**;
   begin
    b := **false**;
    if b **and true**
      then b := c **end if**;
    b := c>0
   end

c) **program** c **is**
   var x,y,z : **integer**;
  begin
    read x;
    y := z;
    declare
     var x,z : **integer**;
    begin
     while x>0 **do**
      x := x-1 **end while**;
    declare
     var x,y : **boolean**;
     const y = **false**;
    begin
     skip
    end
   end
  end

d) **program** d **is**
   var b : **boolean**;
   const c = **true**;
  begin
    b := **not**(c) **or false**;
    read b;
    write 1109
  end

e) **program** e **is**
   var m,n : **integer**;
  begin
    read m;
    n := m/5;
    write n+k
  end

2. Extend the denotational semantics for context checking Pelican to include procedure declarations and calls.

3. Extend the result in exercise 2 to incorporate procedures with an arbitrary number of parameters.

4. Reformulate the denotational semantics for context checking Pelican using false in place of *error* and changing the signature of *elaborate* to

    elaborate : Declaration → Environment → Environment x Boolean

    Let *typify* applied to an expression with a type error or an unbound identifier take the value *unbound*.

5. Following the denotational approach in this section, implement a context checker for Pelican in Prolog.

9.7 CONTINUATION SEMANTICS

All the denotational definitions studied so far in this chapter embody what is known as **direct denotational semantics**. With this approach, each semantic equation for a language construct describes a transformation of argument domain values, such as environment and store, directly into results in some semantic domain, such as a new environment, an updated store, or an expressible value. Furthermore, the results from one construct pass directly to the language construct that immediately follows it physically in the code. The semantic equation for command sequencing shows this property best:

$$execute \; [\![C_1 \; ; \; C_2]\!] \; sto = execute \; [\![C_2]\!] \; (execute \; [\![C_1]\!]sto).$$

Observe that this semantic equation has the second command C_2 working directly on the store produced by the first command. We return to Wren for these examples since the points to be made here do not depend on environments as found in Pelican. As an example, consider the following Wren program fragment processed by the semantic function $execute$: Command $\rightarrow$ Store $\rightarrow$ Store.

```
s := 0; n := 5;
while n>1 do
        s := s+n; n := n–2
end while;
mean := s/2
```

Figure 9.22 outlines the modifications through which the store progresses as $execute$ is applied to this sequence of commands. At the same time we suppress the applications of $evaluate$ that must be carried out in the analysis— for example, $evaluate \; [\![5]\!]$ and $evaluate \; [\![n>1]\!]$. Our purpose is to illustrate the flow of data through commands in direct denotational semantics.

Although many language constructs have perspicuous descriptions in direct denotational semantics, two problems reduce the applicability of this approach:

1. When an error occurs in determining the meaning of a language construct, the error must propagate through all of the remaining denotational transformations in the definition of the construct in a program. If semantic equations detail all the aspects of this propagation, they become cluttered with error testing. We avoided such confusion in our semantic equations by informally describing the nature of error propagation at the cost of lost precision in the definitions. Furthermore, most programming language implementations do not propagate errors in this manner; they abort (terminate) execution on finding a dynamic error. Of course, denotational definitions do not have to adhere to real implementations, but aborting execution is an easier way to handle errors, if we only have a way of describing it.

2. Most programing languages allow radical transfers of control during the execution of a program—in particular, by means of the **goto** command. Such constructs cannot be modeled easily with direct denotational semantics.

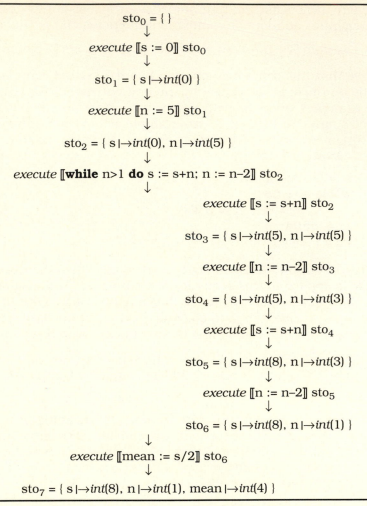

$$sto_0 = \{\ \}$$
$$\downarrow$$
$$execute\ [\![s := 0]\!]\ sto_0$$
$$\downarrow$$
$$sto_1 = \{\ s\!\mapsto\!int(0)\ \}$$
$$\downarrow$$
$$execute\ [\![n := 5]\!]\ sto_1$$
$$\downarrow$$
$$sto_2 = \{\ s\!\mapsto\!int(0),\ n\!\mapsto\!int(5)\ \}$$
$$\downarrow$$
$$execute\ [\![\textbf{while}\ n{>}1\ \textbf{do}\ s := s{+}n;\ n := n{-}2]\!]\ sto_2$$
$$\downarrow$$

$$execute\ [\![s := s{+}n]\!]\ sto_2$$
$$\downarrow$$
$$sto_3 = \{\ s\!\mapsto\!int(5),\ n\!\mapsto\!int(5)\ \}$$
$$\downarrow$$
$$execute\ [\![n := n{-}2]\!]\ sto_3$$
$$\downarrow$$
$$sto_4 = \{\ s\!\mapsto\!int(5),\ n\!\mapsto\!int(3)\ \}$$
$$\downarrow$$
$$execute\ [\![s := s{+}n]\!]\ sto_4$$
$$\downarrow$$
$$sto_5 = \{\ s\!\mapsto\!int(8),\ n\!\mapsto\!int(3)\ \}$$
$$\downarrow$$
$$execute\ [\![n := n{-}2]\!]\ sto_5$$
$$\downarrow$$
$$sto_6 = \{\ s\!\mapsto\!int(8),\ n\!\mapsto\!int(1)\ \}$$

$$\downarrow$$
$$execute\ [\![mean := s/2]\!]\ sto_6$$
$$\downarrow$$
$$sto_7 = \{\ s\!\mapsto\!int(8),\ n\!\mapsto\!int(1),\ mean\!\mapsto\!int(4)\ \}$$

Figure 9.22: Passing the Store through a Denotational Analysis

Consider again the meaning of command sequencing, "*execute* $[\![C_1 ; C_2]\!]$".
Direct denotational semantics assumes that C_2 will be executed immediately
following C_1 and that it depends on receiving a store from "*execute* $[\![C_1]\!]$ sto".
But what happens if C_1 does not pass control on to C_2, producing a new store
for C_2 to act on? The reasons that C_1 may not be immediately followed by C_2
include the occurrence of a dynamic error in C_1, or because C_1 may belong to
a class of commands, called **sequencers**, including **goto**, **stop**, **return**, **exit**
(Ada or Modula-2), **break** (C), **continue** (C), **raise** (a language with excep-
tions), and **resume** (a language with coroutines). Sequencers have the property that computation generally does not proceed with the next command in
the physical text of the program.

Returning to a concrete example, regard a sequence (block) of four labeled commands:

$$\textbf{begin } L_1 : C_1; \ L_2 : C_2; \ L_3 : C_3; \ L_4 : C_4 \textbf{ end}.$$

With direct semantics, the sequence has as its meaning

$$\textit{execute } [\![C_4]\!] \circ \textit{execute } [\![C_3]\!] \circ \textit{execute } [\![C_2]\!] \circ \textit{execute } [\![C_1]\!],$$

if we ignore the denotations of the labels for now. As a store transformation, the sequence can be viewed as follows:

$$\text{sto}_0 \to \textit{execute } [\![C_1]\!] \to \textit{execute } [\![C_2]\!] \to \textit{execute } [\![C_3]\!] \to \textit{execute } [\![C_4]\!] \to \text{sto}_{\text{final}}.$$

But what if C_3 is the command "**goto** L_1"? Then the store transformation must develop as follows:

$$\text{sto}_0 \to \textit{execute } [\![C_1]\!] \to \textit{execute } [\![C_2]\!] \to \textit{execute } [\![C_3]\!] \to \textit{execute } [\![C_1]\!] \to \ \dots.$$

To handle these two possibilities, "*execute* $[\![C_3]\!]$" must be able to make the choice of sending its result, a store, on to "*execute* $[\![C_4]\!]$" or to somewhere else, such as "*execute* $[\![C_1]\!]$". Before describing how this choice can be made, we need to establish the meaning of a label. We take the label L_k, for k=1, 2, 3, or 4, to denote the computation starting with the command C_k and running to the termination of the program. This meaning is encapsulated as a function from the current store to a final store for the entire program. Such functions are known as **continuations**, and a denotational definition involving them is called **continuation semantics** or **standard semantics**.

Continuations

A continuation describes the change of state (store in this case) that occurs as a result of executing the program from a particular point until the program terminates; that is, a continuation models the **remainder of the program** from a point in the code. The semantic domain of continuations,

$$\text{Continuation} = \text{Store} \to \text{Store}$$

is included with the denotable values since they can be bound to identifiers (labels). Each label in a program is bound to a continuation in the environment of the block containing that label.

For the previous block with four commands and *no sequencers*, we have an environment env with the following bindings:

Identifier	Denotable Value
L_1	$\text{cont}_1 = \textit{execute } [\![C_1; \ C_2; \ C_3; \ C_4]\!] \text{ env}$
L_2	$\text{cont}_2 = \textit{execute } [\![C_2; \ C_3; \ C_4]\!] \text{ env}$
L_3	$\text{cont}_3 = \textit{execute } [\![C_3; \ C_4]\!] \text{ env}$
L_4	$\text{cont}_4 = \textit{execute } [\![C_4]\!] \text{ env}$

Note that each continuation depends on an environment that contains the bindings of all the labels being elaborated so that jumps anywhere in the block can be made when we allow sequencers. Therefore the signature of *execute* includes an environment domain:

$$execute : \text{Command} \rightarrow \text{Environment} \rightarrow \text{Store} \rightarrow \text{Store}$$

This is not, however, the final signature for *execute* since we have one more issue to deal with.

Suppose that C_2 is not a sequencer. Then "*execute* $[\![C_2]\!]$" passes its resulting store to the rest of the computation starting at C_3—namely, the "normal" continuation $cont_3$. On the other hand, if C_3 is "**goto** L_1", it passes its resulting store to the continuation bound to L_1—namely, $cont_1$. To allow these two possibilities, we make the normal continuation an argument to "*execute* $[\![C_k]\!]$" to be executed with normal program flow (as with C_2) or to be discarded when a sequencer occurs (as with C_3). Therefore the final signature of *execute* has the form

$$execute : \text{Command} \rightarrow \text{Environment} \rightarrow \text{Continuation} \rightarrow \text{Store} \rightarrow \text{Store},$$

and the corresponding semantic equation for command sequencing becomes

$$execute\ [\![C_1 ; C_2]\!]\ env\ cont\ sto = execute\ [\![C_1]\!]\ env\ \{execute\ [\![C_2]\!]\ env\ cont\}\ sto$$

where "*execute* $[\![C_2]\!]$ env cont" is the normal continuation for C_1. The continuation given to the execution of C_1 encapsulates the execution of C_2 followed by the execution of the original continuation. Traditionally, braces are used to delimit this constructed continuation. Observe the functionality of this normal continuation:

$$execute\ [\![C_2]\!]\ env\ cont : \text{Store} \rightarrow \text{Store}.$$

The semantic equation for the **goto** command shows that the continuation bound to the label comes from the environment and is executed with the store passed as a parameter,

$$execute\ [\![\textbf{goto } L]\!]\ env\ cont\ sto = applyEnv(env,L)\ sto$$

with the effect that the normal continuation is simply discarded. In the previous example, where C_2 is **skip** and C_3 is "**goto** L_1",

$$execute\ [\![C_2]\!]\ env\ cont_3 = cont_3$$

and $execute\ [\![C_3]\!]\ env\ cont_4 = applyEnv(env,L_1).$

Observe that the store argument has been factored out of both of these semantic equations.

The Programming Language Gull

We illustrate continuation semantics with Gull (G for **goto**), a programming language that is similar to Wren but contains two sequencers, **goto** and **stop**. Figure 9.23 provides the abstract syntax for Gull.

Syntactic Domains

P : Program	L : Label	O : Operator
S : Series	I : Identifier	N : Numeral
C : Command	E : Expression	

Abstract Production Rules

Program ::= **program** Identifier **is begin** Series **end**

Series ::= Command

Command ::= Command **;** Command | Identifier **:=** Expression
      | **if** Expression **then** Series **else** Series
      | **while** Expression **do** Series | **skip** | **stop**
      | **goto** Label | **begin** Series **end** | Label **:** Command

Expression ::= Identifier | Numeral | - Expression
      | Expression Operator Expression

Operator ::= **+** | **−** | * | **/** | **=** | **<=** | **<** | **>** | **>=** | **<>**

Label ::= Identifier

Figure 9.23: Abstract Syntax of Gull

Gull permits only integer variables and has simply the **if-then-else** selection command for economy. The syntactic domain "Series" acts as the syntactic domain that corresponds to blocks, thus making the bodies of **if** and **while** commands into local scoping regions. A local environment for labels can also be created by an anonymous block using "**begin** Series **end**". Although a series is only a command in the abstract syntax, it serves as a separate syntactic category to allow for the elaboration of labels in the command. The syntax of Gull must have context constraints that forbid multiple labels with the same identifier in a series and a jump to an undefined label.

We need to elaborate labels at the top level and also inside compound commands, ensuring correct denotations for language constructs, such as those found in the program shown below. This poorly written program is designed to illustrate the environments created by labels in Gull. Figure 9.24 displays the nesting of the five environments that bind the labels in the program.

program labels **is**

    begin

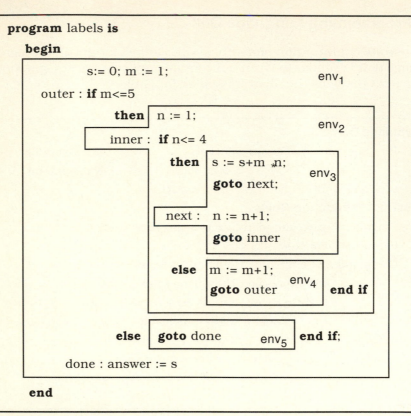

    end

Figure 9.24: A Gull Program

Figure 9.25 provides the semantic domains and the signatures of the semantic functions for the continuation semantics of Gull. As already mentioned, continuations are functions from store to store, and environments map labels to continuations, the only denotable values in Gull. Therefore we do not bother to put tags on them. The semantic functions indicate that only commands depend on continuations, sometimes called **command continuations**. A deeper investigation of continuation semantics would study **expression continuations** and **declaration continuations**. An expression continuation encapsulates the rest of the computation following the expression being evaluated. These are the continuations in Scheme, which allows the manipulation of such continuations as first-class objects in the same way as any other functions. Declaration continuations are necessary to model an escape from the elaboration of a declaration, say because of an error. These other kinds of continuations are beyond the scope of this text. They are covered in other books (see the further readings at the end of the chapter).

Semantic Domains

EV = *int*(Integer) + *bool*(Boolean)

SV = *int*(Integer)

DV = Continuation

Store = Identifier $\rightarrow$ SV + *undefined*

Continuation = Store $\rightarrow$ Store

Environment = Label $\rightarrow$ Continuation + *unbound*

Semantic Functions

meaning : Program $\rightarrow$ Store

perform : Series $\rightarrow$ Environment $\rightarrow$ Continuation $\rightarrow$ Store $\rightarrow$ Store

execute : Command $\rightarrow$ Environment $\rightarrow$ Continuation $\rightarrow$ Store $\rightarrow$ Store

evaluate : Expression $\rightarrow$ Store $\rightarrow$ EV

Figure 9.25: Semantic Domains and Semantic Functions of Gull

Auxiliary Functions

The semantic equations defining the semantic functions require a number of auxiliary functions that have been presented previously. When we specify the meaning of a program, an initial environment, *emptyEnv*, an initial store, *emptySto*, and an initial continuation, *identityCont*, must be supplied. The initial continuation is a function that takes the store resulting at the end of the execution of the entire program and produces the final "answer". We take the final store as the answer of a program, since Gull has no output. The initial continuation can thus be the identity function.

emptySto : Store

updateSto : Store x Identifier x SV $\rightarrow$ Store

applySto : Store x Identifier $\rightarrow$ SV

emptyEnv : Environment

extendEnv : Environment x Label[+] x Continuation[+] $\rightarrow$ Environment

applyEnv : Environment x Label $\rightarrow$ Continuation

identityCont : Continuation

$\quad$ *identityCont* = λ sto . sto.

Since the denotational semantics of Gull elaborates all the labels in a series in one semantic equation, *extendEnv* takes lists of labels and continuations as arguments. An exercise asks the reader to define this auxiliary function.

Semantic Equations

The semantic equations for Gull are detailed in Figure 9.26. We examine the specification of *execute* first, assuming that the environment argument already contains bindings for all visible labels. Command sequencing has already been described. Executing the **skip** command makes no change in the store, so the current store is passed to the current continuation to continue the execution of the program. The **stop** command abandons the current continuation and returns the current store, which thereby becomes the final store terminating the denotational analysis. The **if** and **while** commands are analogues of those for direct semantics, passing the current continuation to appropriate series. The only exception occurs when the **while** test is false and the effect is like a **skip** command. The assignment command calls the current continuation with a store reflecting the new value that has been stored.

Since our denotational specification of Gull ignores expression continuations, the semantic equations for *evaluate* remain the same as those for Wren.

The function *perform*, specifying the meaning of a series, assumes a list of n commands, all possessing labels. It proceeds by binding each label to the appropriate continuation that encapsulates the rest of the code from the point of the label in the program together with an environment that includes all the bindings being established in the series. Observe that each defined continuation executes one command with the continuation that follows the command. The last continuation $cont_n$ executes the last command with the continuation that was originally passed to the series, representing the rest of the program following the series. Once the labels have been elaborated, the first continuation $cont_1$, which embodies the entire list of commands, is invoked.

The Error Continuation

Gull does not handle errors any better than Wren, even though we suggested earlier that continuation semantics allows us to abort execution when a dynamic error occurs. To treat errors properly, we need expression continuations, so that when division by zero or accessing an undefined variable happens, an error continuation can be called at that point. Our specification of Gull has to inspect the result of evaluating an expression at the command level and call an error (command) continuation there. The semantic equation for the assignment command then takes the form

execute $[\![I := E]\!]$ env cont sto =
    if *evaluate* $[\![E]\!]$ sto=*error*
        then *errCont* sto else cont *updateSto*(sto,I,*evaluate* $[\![E]\!]$ sto).

meaning ⟦program I is begin S end⟧ =
            perform ⟦S⟧ emptyEnv identityCont emptySto

perform ⟦L_1: C_1; L_2: C_2; ... ; L_n: C_n ⟧ env cont = $cont_1$
        where $cont_1$ = *execute* ⟦C_1⟧ env_1 $cont_2$
                    $cont_2$ = *execute* ⟦C_2⟧ env_1 $cont_3$
                                :
                    $cont_n$ = *execute* ⟦C_n⟧ env_1 cont
        and env_1 = extendEnv(env,[L_1, L_2, ... , L_n],[$cont_1$, $cont_2$, ... , $cont_n$])

execute ⟦I := E⟧ env cont sto = cont *updateSto*(sto,I,*evaluate* ⟦E⟧ sto)
execute ⟦**skip**⟧ env cont sto = cont sto
execute ⟦**stop**⟧ env cont sto = sto
execute ⟦**if** E **then** S_1 **else** S_2 ⟧ env cont sto =
                if p then *perform* ⟦S_1⟧ env cont sto else *perform* ⟦S_2⟧ env cont sto
                                where *bool*(p) = *evaluate* ⟦E⟧ sto
execute ⟦**while** E **do** S⟧ env cont sto = loop
        where loop env cont sto = if p then *perform* ⟦S⟧ env {loop env cont} sto
                                else cont sto
                            where *bool*(p) = *evaluate* ⟦E⟧ sto
execute ⟦C_1 ; C_2⟧ env cont sto = *execute* ⟦C_1⟧ env {*execute* ⟦C_2⟧ env cont} sto
execute ⟦**begin** S **end**⟧ env cont sto = *perform* ⟦S⟧ env cont sto
execute ⟦**goto** L⟧ env cont sto = *applyEnv*(env,L) sto
execute ⟦L : C⟧ = *execute* ⟦C⟧

evaluate ⟦I⟧ sto = *applySto*(sto,I)
evaluate ⟦N⟧ sto = *value* ⟦N⟧
evaluate ⟦-E⟧ = *int*(*minus*(0,m)) where *int*(m) = *evaluate* ⟦E_1⟧ sto
evaluate ⟦E_1 + E_2⟧ sto = *int*(*plus*(m,n))
                where *int*(m) = *evaluate* ⟦E_1⟧ sto and *int*(n) = *evaluate* ⟦E_2⟧ sto
        :

Figure 9.26: Semantic Equations for Gull

For the **if** command, the value of "*evaluate* ⟦E⟧ sto" must be examined before
executing one of the branches.

$execute$ ⟦**if** E **then** S_1 **else** S_2⟧ env cont sto =
   if $evaluate$ ⟦E⟧ sto=$error$
       then $errCont$ sto
         else if p then $perform$ ⟦S_1⟧ env cont sto
             else $perform$ ⟦S_2⟧ env cont sto
                where $bool(p)$ = $evaluate$ ⟦E⟧ sto.

The error continuation $errCont$ performs in the same way as the identity continuation, except that it should signal an error condition some way, say by displaying an error message. For our purposes, we simply take $errCont$ = $identityCont$.

Exercises

1. Give a definition of $extendEnv$ for lists of identifiers and continuations.

2. Describe the continuations used in analyzing the following program denotationally, and give the bindings in its environment:

   program fact **is**
   begin
           f := 1; n := 6;
      start : **if** n>=1 **then goto** rest **else stop end if**;
       rest : f := f*n; n := n–1; **goto** start
   end

3. Add an **exit** command to Gull and provide a denotational definition for its semantics. Executing an **exit** causes control to transfer to the point following the closest enclosing **begin**-**end** construct. Explain why it is not sufficient to exit from the enclosing series.

4. Define the denotational semantics of a programming language that combines the features of Gull and Pelican.

5. Construct a denotational interpreter for Gull in Prolog. See the further readings for a suggestion on handling continuations as Prolog structures.

9.8 FURTHER READING

Denotational semantics grew out of the tradition of mathematical logic, and early versions were characterized by single-letter identifiers, the Greek alphabet, and a heavy use of concise and sometimes cryptic mathematical notation. Under the influence of the principles of good software design, more recent expositions of denotational semantics possess enhanced readability as a result of the use of meaningful identifiers and the concepts of data abstraction.

One of the best descriptions of denotational semantics can be found in David Schmidt's book [Schmidt88], which covers most of the material that we describe in this chapter as well as additional material and examples treating compound data structures, applicative languages, expression continuations, and concurrency.

The traditional reference for denotational semantics has been the book by Joseph Stoy [Stoy77]. Many of the later books were based on his work. The books by Michael Gordon [Gordon79], Frank Pagan [Pagan81], and Lloyd Allison [Allison86] contain short but thorough explanations of denotational semantics with many good examples, although the dense notation in them requires careful reading. The books by Allison and Gordon have clear presentations of continuation semantics. Moreover, Allison discusses at some length the possibility of implementing a denotational definition using an imperative programming language to construct interpreters. His examples were one of the inspirations for our denotational interpreter of Wren written in Prolog.

Several textbooks published in the past few years provide additional examples of denotational specifications and a look at the various notational conventions employed in denotational semantics. These books, [Meyer90], [Watt91], and [Nielson92], are written at about the same level as our presentation. The Nielson book discusses implementing denotational definitions using the functional language Miranda. David Watt's very readable text uses notational conventions that are close to ours. Watt also suggests using denotational semantics to verify the context constraints on programming languages. His text contains a complete denotational specification of an imperative programming language called Triangle. He suggests using Standard ML as a vehicle for constructing a denotational interpreter for Triangle based on the specification. Watt coined the term **semantic prototyping** for the process of implementing formal specifications of programming languages. Susan Stepney gives a denotational semantics for a small imperative programming language and a hypothetical machine language (using continuation semantics). After describing a compiler from one the other, she verifies it relative to the formal specifications and implements the system in Prolog [Stepney93].

More formal treatments of denotational semantics can be found in [Mosses90], [Tennent91], and [Winskel93]. The book by Tennent contains an interesting discussion of compositionality. He suggests [Janssen86] for a historical review of the notion of compositional definitions. Tennent has also written an undergraduate textbook on the concepts of programming languages that is based on denotational principles [Tennent81].

Most of the descriptions of implementing denotational semantics have avoided the problems inherent in continuation semantics. For a short presentation of denotational interpreters that handle continuations, see [Slonneger93], where implementations in Standard ML and Prolog are explained and compared.

Chapter 10
DOMAIN THEORY AND
FIXED-POINT SEMANTICS

Although we did not stress the point in Chapter 9, the notation of denotational semantics is built upon that of the lambda calculus. The purpose of denotational semantics is to provide mathematical descriptions of programming languages independent of their operational behavior. The extended lambda calculus serves as a mathematical formalism, a metalanguage, for denotational definitions. As with all mathematical formalisms, we need to know that the lambda calculus has a model to ensure that the definitions are not meaningless.

Furthermore, denotational definitions, as well as programming languages in general, rely heavily on recursion, a mechanism whose description we deferred in the discussion of the lambda calculus in Chapter 5. Normally a user of a programming language does not care about the logical foundations of declarations, but we maintain that serious questions can be raised concerning the validity of recursion. In this chapter we justify recursive definitions to guarantee that they actually define meaningful objects.

10.1 CONCEPTS AND EXAMPLES

Programmers use recursion to define functions and procedures as subprograms that call themselves and also to define recursive data structures. Most imperative programming languages require the use of pointers to declare recursive data types such as (linked) lists and trees. In contrast, many functional programming languages allow the direct declaration of recursive types. Rather than investigating recursive types in an actual programming language, we study recursive data declarations in a wider context. In this introductory section we consider the problems inherent in recursively defined functions and data and the related issue of nontermination.

Recursive Definitions of Functions

When we define a symbol in a denotational definition or in a program, we expect that the symbol can be replaced by its meaning wherever it occurs. In particular, we expect that the symbol is defined in terms of other (preferably simpler) concepts so that any expression involving the symbol can be expressed by substituting its definition. With this concept in mind, consider two simple recursive definitions:

$f(n) = $ if $n=0$ then 1 else $f(n-1)$

$g(n) = $ if $n=0$ then 1 else $g(n+1)$.

The purpose of these definitions is to give meaning to the symbols "f" and "g". Both definitions can be expressed in the applied lambda calculus as

define $f = \lambda n$. (if (zerop n) 1 (f (sub n 1)))

define $g = \lambda n$. (if (zerop n) 1 (g (succ n))).

Either way, these definitions fail the condition that the defined symbol can be replaced by its meaning, since that meaning also contains the symbol. The definitions are circular. The best we can say is that recursive "definitions" are equations in the newly defined symbol. The meaning of the symbol will be a solution to the equation, if a solution exists. If the equation has more than one solution, we need some reason for choosing one of those solutions as the meaning of the new symbol.

An analogous situation can be seen with a mathematical equation that resembles the recursive definitions:

$x = x^2 - 4x + 6$.

This "definition" of x has two solutions, $x=2$ and $x=3$. Other similar definitions of x, such as $x = x+5$, have no solutions at all, while $x = x^2/x$ has infinitely many solutions. We need to describe conditions on a recursive definition of a function, really a recursion equation, to guarantee that at least one solution exists and a reason for choosing one particular solution as the meaning of the function.

For the examples considered earlier, we will describe in this chapter a methodology that enables us to show that the equation in f has only one solution $(\lambda n . 1)$, but the equation in g has many solutions, including

$(\lambda n . 1)$ and $(\lambda n . $ if $n=0$ then 1 else *undefined*).

One purpose of this chapter is to develop a "fixed-point" semantics that gives a consistent meaning to recursive definitions of functions.

Recursive Definitions of Sets (Types)

Recursively defined sets occur in both programming languages and specifications of languages. Consider the following examples:

1. The BNF specification of Wren uses direct recursion in specifying the syntactic category of identifiers,

    <identifier> ::= <letter> | <identifier> <letter> | <identifier> <digit>,

    and indirect recursion in many places, such as,

    <command> ::= **if** <boolean expr> **then** <command seq> **end if**

    <command seq> ::= <command> | <command> ; <command seq>.

2. The domain of lists of natural numbers N may be provided in a functional programming language according to the definition:

    List = {*nil*} $\cup$ (N x List) where *nil* represents the empty list.

    Scheme lists have essentially this form using "cons" as the constructor operation forming ordered pairs in N x List. Standard ML allows data type declarations following this pattern.

3. A model for the (pure) lambda calculus requires a domain of values that are manipulated by the rules of the system. These values incorporate variables as primitive objects and functions that may act on any values in the domain, including any of the functions. If V denotes the set of variables and D→D represents the set of functions from set D to D, the domain of values for the lambda calculus can be "defined" by D = V $\cup$ (D→D).

The third example presents major problems if we analyze the cardinality of the sets involved. We give the critical results without going into the details of measuring the cardinality of sets. It suffices to mention that the sizes of sets are compared by putting their elements into a one-to-one correspondence. We denote the cardinality of a set A by |A| with the following properties:

1. |A| ≤ |B| if there is a one-to-one function A→B.

2. |A| = |B| if there is a one-to-one and onto function A→B (which can be shown to be equivalent to |A| ≤ |B| and |B| ≤ |A|).

3. |A| < |B| if |A| ≤ |B| but not |A| ≥ |B|.

Two results about cardinalities of sets establish the problem with the recursive "definition" of D:

1. In the first use of "diagonalization" as a proof method, Georg Cantor proved that for any set A, |A| < |$\mathcal{P}$(A)| where $\mathcal{P}$(A) is the power set of A—that is, the set of all subsets of A.

2. If $|A| > 1$, then $|\mathcal{P}(A)| \leq |A{\to}A|$.

Since $D{\to}D$ is a subset of D by the definition, $|D{\to}D| \leq |D|$. Therefore,
$$|D{\to}D| \leq |D| < |\mathcal{P}(D)| \leq |D{\to}D|,$$
which is clearly a contradiction.

One way to provide a solution to the recursion equation $D = V \cup (D{\to}D)$ is to restrict the membership in the set of functions $D{\to}D$ by putting a "structure" on the sets under consideration and by requiring that functions are well-behaved relative to the structure. Although the solution to this recursion equation is beyond the scope of this book (see the further readings at the end of this chapter), we study this structure carefully for the intuition that it provides about recursively defined functions and sets.

Modeling Nontermination

Any programming language that provides (indefinite) iteration or recursively defined functions unfortunately also allows a programmer to write nonterminating programs. Specifying the semantics of such a language requires a mechanism for representing nontermination. At this point we preview domain theory by considering how it handles nontermination. Domain theory is based on a relation of definedness. We say $x \sqsubseteq y$ if x is less defined than or equal to y. This means that the information content of x is contained in the information content of y. Each domain (structured set) contains a least element $\perp$, called bottom, representing the absence of information. Bottom can be viewed as the result of a computation that fails to terminate normally. By adding a bottom element to every domain, values that produce no outcome under a function can be represented by taking $\perp$ as the result. This simple idea enables us to avoid partial functions in describing the semantics of a programming language, since values for which a function is undefined map to the bottom element in the codomain.

Dana Scott developed domain theory to provide a model for the lambda calculus and thereby provide a consistent foundation for denotational semantics. Without such a foundation, we have no reason to believe that denotational definitions really have mathematical meaning. At the same time, domain theory gives us a valid interpretation for recursively defined functions and types.

In this chapter we first describe the structure supplied to sets by domain theory, and then we investigate the semantics of recursively defined functions via fixed-point theory. Finally, we use fixed points to give meaning to recursively defined functions in the lambda calculus, implementing them by extending the lambda calculus evaluator described in Chapter 5.

Exercises

1. Write a recursive definition of the factorial function in the lambda calculus using *define*.

2. Give a recursive definition of binary trees whose leaf nodes contain natural number values.

3. Suppose A is a finite set with $|A| = n$. Show that $|\mathcal{P}(A)| = 2^n$ and $|A \rightarrow A| = n^n$.

4. Let A be an arbitrary set. Show that it is impossible for $f : A \rightarrow \mathcal{P}(A)$ to be a one-to-one and onto function. *Hint*: Consider the set $X = \{a \in A \mid a \notin f(a)\}$.

5. Prove that $|\mathcal{P}(A)| \leq |A \rightarrow A|$ for any set A with $|A| \geq 2$. *Hint*: Consider the characteristic functions of the sets in $\mathcal{P}(A)$.

10.2 DOMAIN THEORY

The structured sets that serve as semantic domains in denotational semantics are similar to the structured sets called lattices, but these domains have several distinctive properties. Domains possess a special element $\perp$, called **bottom**, that denotes an undefined element or simply the absence of information. A computation that fails to complete normally produces $\perp$ as its result. Later in this section we describe how the bottom element of a domain can be used to represent the nontermination of programs, since a program that never halts is certainly an undefined object. But first we need to define the structural properties of the sets that serve as domains.

Definition: A **partial order** on a set S is a relation $\subseteq$ with the following properties:

1. $\subseteq$ is **reflexive**: $x \subseteq x$ for all $x \in S$.
2. $\subseteq$ is **transitive**: $(x \subseteq y$ and $y \subseteq z)$ implies $x \subseteq z$ for all $x,y,z \in S$.
3. $\subseteq$ is **antisymmetric**: $(x \subseteq y$ and $y \subseteq x)$ implies $x = y$ for all $x,y \in S$. ∎

Definition: Let A be a subset of S.

1. A **lower bound** of A is an element $b \in S$ such that $b \subseteq x$ for all $x \in A$.
2. An **upper bound** of A is an element $u \in S$ such that $x \subseteq u$ for all $x \in A$.
3. A **least upper bound** of A, written *lub* A, is an upper bound of A with the property that for any upper bound m of A, $lub\ A \subseteq m$. ∎

Example 1: The subset relation $\subseteq$ on the power set $\mathcal{P}(\{1,2,3\})$ is a partial order as shown by the **Hasse diagram** in Figure 10.1. The main idea of a Hasse diagram is to represent links between distinct items where no other values intervene. The reflexive and transitive closure of this "minimal" relation forms the ordering being defined. We know that the subset relation is reflexive, transitive, and antisymmetric. Any subset of $\mathcal{P}(\{1,2,3\})$ has lower, upper, and least upper bounds. For example, if A = { {1}, {1,3}, {3} }, both {1,2,3} and {1,3} are upper bounds of A, ∅ is a lower bound of A, and *lub* A = {1,3}. ∎

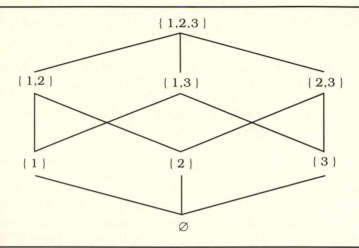

Figure 10.1: Partial order on $\mathcal{P}(\{1,2,3\})$

In addition to possessing a partial ordering, the structured sets of domain theory require a "smallest" element and the existence of limits for sequences that admit a certain conformity.

Definition: An **ascending chain** in a partially ordered set S is a sequence of elements {x_1, x_2, x_3, x_4, ...} with the property $x_1 \subseteq x_2 \subseteq x_3 \subseteq x_4 \subseteq$ .... ∎

Remember that the symbol $\subseteq$ stands for an arbitrary partial order, not necessarily the subset relation. Each item in an ascending chain must contain information that is consistent with its predecessor in the chain; it may be equal to its predecessor or it may provide additional information.

Definition: A **complete partial order** (**cpo**) on a set S is a partial order $\subseteq$ with the following properties:

1. There is an element $\bot \in S$ for which $\bot \subseteq x$ for all $x \in S$.
2. Every ascending chain in S has a least upper bound in S. ∎

Sets with complete partial orders serve as the semantic domains in denotational semantics. On these domains, $\subseteq$ is thought of as the relation **approximates** or **is less defined than or equal to**. View $x \subseteq y$ as asserting that y has at least as much information content as x does, and that the information in y is consistent with that in x. In other words, y is a consistent (possibly trivial) extension of x in terms of information.

The least upper bound of an ascending chain summarizes the information that has been accumulated in a consistent manner as the chain progresses. Since an ascending chain may have an infinite number of distinct values, the least upper bound acts as a limit value for the infinite sequence. On the other hand, a chain may have duplicate elements, since $\subseteq$ includes equality, and a chain may take a constant value from some point onward. Then the least upper bound is that constant value.

Example 1 (revisited): $\mathcal{P}(\{1,2,3\})$ with $\subseteq$ is a complete partial order. If S is a set of subsets of $\{1,2,3\}$, lub S = $\cup\{X \mid X \in S\}$, and $\emptyset$ serves as bottom. Note that every ascending chain in $\mathcal{P}(\{1,2,3\})$ is a finite subset of $\mathcal{P}(\{1,2,3\})$—for example, the chain with $x_1=\{2\}$, $x_2=\{2,3\}$, $x_3=\{1,2,3\}$, and $x_i=\{1,2,3\}$ for all $i\geq4$. ∎

Example 2: Define m $\subseteq$ n on the set S = $\{1,2,3,5,6,15\}$ as the divides relation, m|n (n is a multiple of m). The set S with the divides ordering is a complete partial order with 1 as the bottom element, and since each ascending chain is finite, its last element serves as the least upper bound. Figure 10.2 gives a Hasse diagram for this ordered set. Observe that the elements of the set lie on three levels. Therefore no ascending chain can have more than three distinct values. ∎

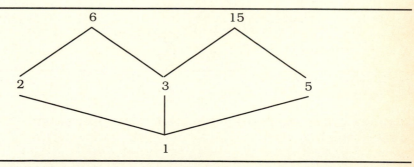

Figure 10.2: Partial order "divides" on $\{1,2,3,5,6,15\}$

These complete partially ordered sets have a lattice-like structure but need not be lattices. Lattices possess the property that any two elements have a least upper bound and a greatest lower bound. A complete lattice also satisfies the condition that *any* subset has a least upper bound and a greatest lower bound. Observe that $\{1,2,3,5,6,15\}$ with "divides" is not a lattice since $\{6,15\}$ has no least upper bound.

Any finite set with a partial order and a bottom element $\perp$ is a cpo since each ascending chain is a finite set and its last component will be the least upper bound. A partially ordered set with an infinite number of distinct elements that lie on an infinite number of "levels" may not be a cpo.

Elementary Domains

Common mathematical sets such as the natural numbers and the Boolean values are converted into complete partial orders by adding a bottom element $\perp$ and defining the **discrete partial order** $\subseteq$ as follows:

for $x,y \in S$, $x \subseteq y$ iff $x = y$ or $x = \perp$.

In denotational semantics, elementary domains correspond to "answers" or results produced by programs. A typical program produces a stream of these atomic values as its result.

Example 3: The domain of Boolean values T has the structure shown in Figure 10.3. With a discrete partial order, bottom is called an **improper** value, and the original elements of the set are called **proper**. Each proper value, true or false, contains more information than $\perp$, but they are incomparable with each other. The value true has no more information content than false; it is just different information. ∎

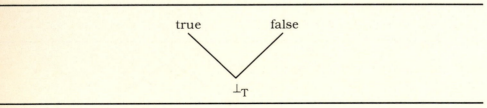

Figure 10.3: Boolean Domain

Example 4: The domain of natural numbers N has the structure portrayed in Figure 10.4. ∎

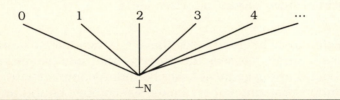

Figure 10.4: Domain of natural numbers

Do not confuse the "approximates" ordering $\subseteq$ with the numeric ordering $\leq$ on the natural numbers. Under $\subseteq$, no pair of natural numbers is comparable, since neither contains more or even the same information as the other. These primitive complete partially ordered sets are also called **elementary** or **flat domains**. More complex domains are formed by three domain constructors.

Product Domains

Definition: If A with ordering $\subseteq_A$ and B with ordering $\subseteq_B$ are complete partial orders, the **product domain** of A and B is A×B with the ordering $\subseteq_{A×B}$ where

$$A×B = \{<a,b> \mid a \in A \text{ and } b \in B\} \text{ and}$$

$$<a,b> \subseteq_{A×B} <c,d> \text{ iff } a \subseteq_A c \text{ and } b \subseteq_B d. \qquad \blacksquare$$

It is a simple matter to show that $\subseteq_{A×B}$ is a partial order on A×B, which we invite the reader to try as an exercise. Assuming that a product domain is a partial order, we need a bottom element and least upper bound for ascending chains to guarantee it is a cpo.

Theorem: $\subseteq_{A×B}$ is a complete partial order on A×B.

Proof: $\perp_{A×B} = <\perp_A, \perp_B>$ acts as bottom for A×B, since $\perp_A \subseteq_A a$ and $\perp_B \subseteq_B b$ for each $a \in A$ and $b \in B$. If $<a_1,b_1> \subseteq <a_2,b_2> \subseteq <a_3,b_3> \subseteq$ ... is an ascending chain in A×B, then $a_1 \subseteq_A a_2 \subseteq_A a_3 \subseteq_A$ ... is a chain in A with a least upper bound $lub\{a_i \mid i \geq 1\} \in A$, and $b_1 \subseteq_B b_2 \subseteq_B b_3 \subseteq_B$ ... is a chain in B with a least upper bound $lub\{b_i \mid i \geq 1\} \in B$. Therefore $lub\{<a_i,b_i> \mid i \geq 1\} = <lub\{a_i \mid i \geq 1\}, lub\{b_i \mid i \geq 1\}> \in A×B$ is the least upper bound for the original chain. $\qquad \blacksquare$

A product domain can be constructed with any finite set of domains in the same manner. If $D_1, D_2, ..., D_n$ are domains (sets with complete partial orders), then $D_1×D_2×...×D_n$ with the induced partial order is a domain. If the original domains are identical, then the product domain is written D^n.

Example 5: Consider a classification of university students according to two domains.

1. Level = $\{\perp_L,$ undergraduate, graduate, nondegree$\}$

2. Gender = $\{\perp_G,$ female, male$\}$

The product domain Level x Gender allows 12 different values as depicted in the diagram in Figure 10.5, which shows the partial ordering between the elements using only the first letters to symbolize the values. Notice that six values are "partial", containing incomplete information for the classification. We can interpret these partial values by imagining two processes, one to determine the level of a student and the other to ascertain the gender. The six incomplete values fit into one of three patterns.

<$\perp_L,\perp_G$>   Both processes fail to terminate normally.

<$\perp_L$,male>   The Gender process terminates with a result but the Level process fails.

<graduate,$\perp_G$> The Level process completes but the Gender one does not terminate normally.   ∎

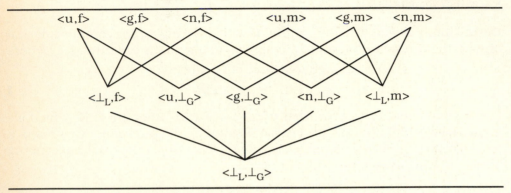

Figure 10.5: Level x Gender

To choose components from an element of a product domain, selector functions are defined on the structured domain.

Definition: Assume that for any product domain AxB, there are **projection** functions

   first : AxB→A, defined by *first* <a,b> = a for any <a,b>∈AxB, and

   second : AxB→B, defined by *second* <a,b> = b for any <a,b>∈AxB.   ∎

Selector functions of this sort may be applied to arbitrary product domains, D_1xD_2x...xD_n. As a shorthand notation we sometimes use *1st, 2nd, 3rd,* ..., *nth,* for the names of the selector functions.

Example 6: We used a product domain IntegerxOperationxIntegerxInteger to represent the states of the calculator in Chapter 9. In the semantic equations of Figure 9.8, pattern matching simulates the projection functions— for example, the equation

   meaning ⟦P⟧ = d where (a,op,d,m) = *perform* ⟦P⟧ (0,*nop*,0,0)

abbreviates the equation

   meaning ⟦P⟧ = *third*(*perform* ⟦P⟧ (0,*nop*,0,0)).

Similarly,

   evaluate ⟦$\mathbf{M^R}$⟧ (a,op,d,m) = (a,op,m,m)

is a more readable translation of

$$evaluate\ [\![\mathbf{M^R}]\!]\ st = (first(st), second(st), fourth(st), fourth(st)).\qquad\blacksquare$$

Generally, using pattern matching to select components from a structure leads to more understandable definitions, as witnessed by its use in Prolog and many functional programming languages, such as Standard ML.

Sum Domains (Disjoint Unions)

Definition: If A with ordering $\subseteq_A$ and B with ordering $\subseteq_B$ are complete partial orders, the **sum domain** of A and B is A+B with the ordering $\subseteq_{A+B}$ defined by

$$A+B = \{<a,1> \mid a\in A\} \cup \{<b,2> \mid b\in B\} \cup \{\perp_{A+B}\},$$

$$<a,1> \subseteq_{A+B} <c,1> \text{ if } a \subseteq_A c,$$

$$<b,2> \subseteq_{A+B} <d,2> \text{ if } b \subseteq_B d,$$

$$\perp_{A+B} \subseteq_{A+B} <a,1> \text{ for each } a\in A,$$

$$\perp_{A+B} \subseteq_{A+B} <b,2> \text{ for each } b\in B, \text{ and}$$

$$\perp_{A+B} \subseteq_{A+B} \perp_{A+B}.\qquad\blacksquare$$

The choice of "1" and "2" as tags in a disjoint union is purely arbitrary. Any two distinguishable values can serve the purpose. In Chapter 9 we used the symbols int and $bool$ as tags for the sum domain of storable values when specifying the semantics of Wren,

$$SV = int(\text{Integer}) + bool(\text{Boolean}),$$

which can be thought of as an abbreviation of $\{<i,int> \mid i\in \text{Integer}\} \cup \{<b,bool> \mid b\in \text{Boolean}\} \cup \{\perp\}$.

Again it is not difficult to show that $\subseteq_{A+B}$ is a partial order on A+B, and the proof is left as an exercise.

Theorem: $\subseteq_{A+B}$ is a complete partial order on A+B.

Proof: $\perp_{A+B} \subseteq x$ for any $x\in A+B$ by definition. An ascending chain $x_1 \subseteq x_2 \subseteq x_3 \subseteq \ldots$ in A+B may repeat $\perp_{A+B}$ forever or eventually climb into either $A\times\{1\}$ or $B\times\{2\}$. In the first case, the least upper bound will be $\perp_{A+B}$, and in the other two cases the least upper bound will exist in A or B. $\qquad\blacksquare$

Example 7: The sum domain T+N (Boolean values and natural numbers) may be viewed as the structure portrayed in Figure 10.6, where the tags have been omitted to simplify the diagram. $\qquad\blacksquare$

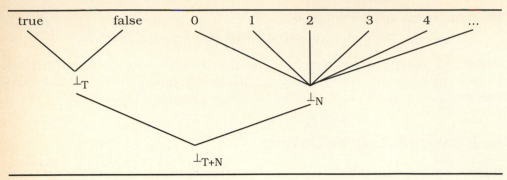

Figure 10.6: The sum domain T+N

A sum domain can be constructed with any finite set of domains in the same manner as with two domains. If D_1, D_2, ..., D_n are domains (sets with complete partial orders), then $D_1 + D_2 + ... + D_n = \{<d,i> \mid d \in D_i, 1 \le i \le n\}$ with the induced partial order is a domain.

Functions on sum domains include a constructor, a selector, and a testing function.

Definition: Let S = A+B, where A and B are two domains.

1. Injection (creation):

    inS : A→S is defined for $a \in A$ as inS a = $<a,1> \in S$

    inS : B→S is defined for $b \in B$ as inS b = $<b,2> \in S$

2. Projection (selection):

    $outA$: S→A is defined for $s \in S$ as $outA$ s = $a \in A$ if s=$<a,1>$, and
                                  $outA$ s = $\perp_A \in A$ if s=$<b,2>$ or s=$\perp_S$.

    $outB$: S→B is defined for $s \in S$ as $outB$ s = $b \in B$ if s=$<b,2>$, and
                                  $outB$ s = $\perp_B \in B$ if s=$<a,1>$ or s=$\perp_S$.

3. Inspection (testing): Recall that T = {true, false, $\perp_T$}.

    isA : S→T is defined for $s \in S$ as
           (isA s) if and only if there exists $a \in A$ with s=$<a,1>$.

    isB : S→T is defined for $s \in S$ as
           (isB s) if and only if there exists $b \in B$ with s=$<b,2>$.

    In both cases, $\perp_S$ is mapped to $\perp_T$.   ∎

Example 8: In the semantic domain of storable values for Wren shown in Figure 9.10, the identifiers *int* and *bool* act as the tags to specify the separate sets of integers and Boolean values. The notation

SV = *int*(Integer) + *bool*(Boolean)
  = {*int*(n) | n∈ Integer} ∪ {*bool*(b) | b∈ Boolean} ∪ {⊥$_{SV}$}

represents the sum domain

SV = (Integer x {*int*}) ∪ (Boolean x {*bool*}) ∪ {⊥$_{SV}$}.

Then an injection function is defined by

inSV : Integer → SV where *inSV* n = *int*(n).   ∎

Actually, the tags themselves can be thought of as constituting the injection function (or as constructors) with the syntax *int* : Integer → SV and *bool* : Boolean → SV, so that we can dispense with the special injection function *inSV*.

A projection function takes the form

outInteger : SV → Integer where *outInteger int*(n) = n
                                    outInteger bool(b) = ⊥.

Inspection is handled by pattern matching, as in the semantic equation

execute ⟦**if** E **then** C⟧ sto = if p then *execute* ⟦C⟧ sto else sto
    where *bool*(p) = *evaluate* ⟦E⟧ sto,

which stands for

execute ⟦**if** E **then** C⟧ sto =
    if *isBoolean*(val)
        then if *outBoolean*(val) then *execute* ⟦C⟧ sto else sto
        else ⊥
    where val = *evaluate* ⟦E⟧ sto.

Example 9: In the sum domain Level + Gender shown in Figure 10.7, tags *lv* for level and *gd* for gender are attached to the elements from the two component domains. If a computation attempts to identify either the level or the gender of a particular student (but not both), it may utterly fail giving ⊥, it may be able to identify the level or the gender of the student, or as a middle ground it may know that the computation is working on the level value but may not be able to complete its work, thus producing the result ⊥$_L$.   ∎

An infinite sum domain may be defined in a similar way. If D_1, D_2, D_3, ... are domains, then $D_1 + D_2 + D_3 + ...$ contains elements of the form <d,i> where d∈ D_i for i≥1.

This infinite sum domain construction allows the definition of the domain of all finite sequences (lists) formed using elements from a domain D and denoted by D*.

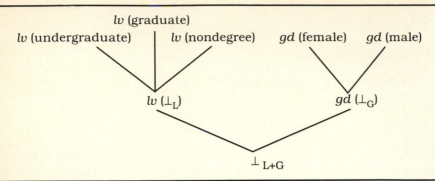

Figure 10.7: Level + Gender

D* = {*nil*}+D+D^2+D^3+D^4+... where *nil* represents the empty sequence.

An element of D* is either the empty list *nil*, a finite ordered tuple from D^k for some k≥1, or ⊥.

Special selector and constructor functions are defined on D*.

Definition: Let L∈ D* and e∈ D. Then L=<d,k> for d∈ D^k for some k≥0 where D^0 = {*nil*}.

1. *head* : D*→D where
   head(L) = *first*(*outD*^{k}(L)) if k>0 and *head*(<*nil*,0>) = ⊥.

2. *tail* : D*→D* where
   tail(L) = *inD**(<2*nd*(*outD*^{k}(L)),3*rd*(*outD*^{k}(L)),...,*kth*(*outD*^{k}(L))>) if k>0 and
   tail(<*nil*,0>) = ⊥.

3. *null* : D*→T where
   null(<*nil*,0>) = true and *null*(L) = false if L = <d,k> with k>0.
   Therefore *null*(L) = *isD*^{0}(L).

4. *prefix* : DxD*→D* where
   prefix(e,L) = *inD**(<e,1*st*(*outD*^{k}(L)),2*nd*(*outD*^{k}(L)),...,*kth*(*outD*^{k}(L))>) and
   prefix(e,<*nil*,0>)) = <<e>,1>

5. *affix* : D*xD→D* where
   affix(L,e) = *inD**(<1*st*(*outD*^{k}(L)),2*nd*(*outD*^{k}(L)),...,*kth*(*outD*^{k}(L)),e>) and
   affix(<*nil*,0>,e) = <<e>,1>. ∎

Each of these five functions on lists maps bottom to bottom. The binary functions *prefix* and *affix* produce ⊥ if either argument is bottom.

Function Domains

Definition: A function from a set A to a set B is **total** if $f(x) \in B$ is defined for every $x \in A$. If A with ordering $\subseteq_A$ and B with ordering $\subseteq_B$ are complete partial orders, define **Fun(A,B)** to be the set of all total functions from A to B. (This set of functions will be restricted later.) Define $\subseteq$ on Fun(A,B) as follows:

For $f,g \in$ Fun(A,B), $f \subseteq g$ if $f(x) \subseteq_B g(x)$ for all $x \in A$. ∎

Lemma: $\subseteq$ is a partial order on Fun(A,B).

Proof:
1. Reflexive: Since $\subseteq_B$ is reflexive, $f(x) \subseteq_B f(x)$ for all $x \in A$, so $f \subseteq f$ for any $f \in$ Fun(A,B).
2. Transitive: Suppose $f \subseteq g$ and $g \subseteq h$. Then $f(x) \subseteq_B g(x)$ and $g(x) \subseteq_B h(x)$ for all $x \in A$. Since $\subseteq_B$ is transitive, $f(x) \subseteq_B h(x)$ for all $x \in A$, and so $f \subseteq h$.
3. Antisymmetric: Suppose $f \subseteq g$ and $g \subseteq f$. Then $f(x) \subseteq_B g(x)$ and $g(x) \subseteq_B f(x)$ for all $x \in A$. Since $\subseteq_B$ is antisymmetric, $f(x) = g(x)$ for all $x \in A$, and so $f = g$. ∎

Theorem: $\subseteq$ is a complete partial order on Fun(A,B).

Proof: Define bottom for Fun(A,B) as the function $\perp(x) = \perp_B$ for all $x \in A$. Since $\perp(x) = \perp_B \subseteq_B f(x)$ for all $x \in A$ and $f \in$ Fun(A,B), $\perp \subseteq f$ for any $f \in$ Fun(A,B). Let $f_1 \subseteq f_2 \subseteq f_3 \subseteq \ldots$ be an ascending chain in Fun(A,B). Then for any $x \in A$, $f_1(x) \subseteq_B f_2(x) \subseteq_B f_3(x) \subseteq_B \ldots$ is a chain in B, which has a least upper bound, $y_x \in B$. Note that y_x is $lub\{f_i(x) \mid i \geq 1\}$. Define the function $F(x) = y_x$ for each $x \in A$. F serves as a least upper bound for the original chain. Set $lub\{f_i \mid i \geq 1\} = F$. ∎

The set Fun(A,B) of all total functions from A to B contains many functions with abnormal behavior that precludes calculating or even approximating them on a computer. For example, consider a function H : $(N \rightarrow N) \rightarrow (N \rightarrow N)$ defined by

for $g \in N \rightarrow N$, H g = λn . if $g(n) = \perp$ then 0 else 1.

Certainly $H \in$ Fun($N \rightarrow N, N \rightarrow N$), but if we make this function acceptable in the domain theory that provides a foundation for denotational definitions, we have accepted a function that solves the halting problem—that is, whether an arbitrary function halts normally on given data. To exclude this and other abnormal functions, we place two restrictions on functions to ensure that they have agreeable behavior.

Definition: A function f in Fun(A,B) is **monotonic** if $x \subseteq_A y$ implies $f(x) \subseteq_B f(y)$ for all $x,y \in A$. ∎

Since we interpret $\subseteq$ to mean "approximates", whenever y has at least as much information as x, it follows that f(y) has at least as much information as f(x). We get more information out of a function by putting more information into it.

An ascending chain in a parially order set can be viewed as a subset of the partially ordered set on which the ordering is total (any two elements are comparable).

Definition: A function $f \in Fun(A,B)$ is **continuous** if it preserves least upper bounds—that is, if $x_1 \subseteq_A x_2 \subseteq_A x_3 \subseteq_A \ldots$ is an ascending chain in A, then $f(lub\{x_i \mid i \geq 1\}) = lub\{f(x_i) \mid i \geq 1\}$.   ∎

Note that if f is also monotonic, then $f(x_1) \subseteq_B f(x_2) \subseteq_B f(x_3) \subseteq_B \ldots$ is an ascending chain. Intuitively, continuity means that there are no surprises when taking the least upper bounds (limits) of approximations. The diagram in Figure 10.8 shows the relation between the two chains.

$$x_1 \quad \subseteq_A \quad x_2 \quad \subseteq_A \quad x_3 \quad \subseteq_A \quad \ldots \quad \Rightarrow \qquad\qquad lub\{x_i \mid i \geq 1\}$$
$$\downarrow \qquad\qquad \downarrow \qquad\qquad \downarrow \qquad\qquad\qquad\qquad\qquad\qquad \downarrow$$
$$f(x_1) \quad \subseteq_B \quad f(x_2) \quad \subseteq_B \quad f(x_3) \quad \subseteq_B \quad \ldots \quad \Rightarrow \quad lub\{f(x_i) \mid i \geq 1\} = f(lub\{x_i \mid i \geq 1\})$$

Figure 10.8: Continuity

A continuous function f has predictable behavior in the sense that if we know its value on the terms of an ascending chain $x_1 \subseteq x_2 \subseteq x_3 \subseteq \ldots$, we also know its value on the least upper bound of the chain since $f(lub\{x_i \mid i \geq 1\})$ is the least upper bound of the chain $f(x_1) \subseteq f(x_2) \subseteq f(x_3) \subseteq \ldots$. It is possible to predict the value of f on $lub\{x_i \mid i \geq 1\}$ by its behavior on each x_i.

Lemma: If $f \in Fun(A,B)$ is continuous, it is also monotonic.

Proof: Suppose f is continuous and $x \subseteq_A y$. Then $x \subseteq_A y \subseteq_A y \subseteq_A y \subseteq_A \ldots$ is an ascending chain in A, and so by the continuity of f,

$$f(x) \subseteq_B lub_B\{f(x), f(y)\} = f(lub_A\{x,y\}) = f(y).$$ ∎

Definition: Define **A→B** to be the set of functions in Fun(A,B) that are (monotonic and) continuous. This set is ordered by the relation $\subseteq$ from Fun(A,B).   ∎

Lemma: The relation $\subseteq$ restricted to A→B is a partial order.

Proof: The properties reflexive, transitive, and antisymmetric are inherited by a subset.   ∎

The example function H : (N→N) → (N→N) defined by

for $g \in N \rightarrow N$, H g = λn . if g(n)=⊥ then 0 else 1

is neither monotonic nor continuous. It suffices to show that it is not monotonic by a counterexample.

Let $g_1 = \lambda n . \perp$ and $g_2 = \lambda n . 0$. Then $g_1 \subseteq g_2$. But $H(g_1) = \lambda n . 0$, $H(g_2) = \lambda n . 1$, and the functions $\lambda n . 0$ and $\lambda n . 1$ are not related by $\subseteq$ at all.

Two lemmas will be useful in proving the continuity of functions.

Lub Lemma: If $x_1 \subseteq x_2 \subseteq x_3 \subseteq \ldots$ is an ascending chain in a cpo A, and $x_i \subseteq$ d$\in$A for each i$\geq$1, it follows that $lub\{x_i \mid i \geq 1\} \subseteq d$.

Proof: By the definition of least upper bound, if d is a bound for the chain, the least upper bound $lub\{x_i \mid i \geq 1\}$ must be no larger than d.   ∎

Limit Lemma: If $x_1 \subseteq x_2 \subseteq x_3 \subseteq \ldots$ and $y_1 \subseteq y_2 \subseteq y_3 \subseteq \ldots$ are ascending chains in a cpo A, and $x_i \subseteq y_i$ for each i$\geq$1, then $lub\{x_i \mid i \geq 1\} \subseteq lub\{y_i \mid i \geq 1\}$.

Proof: For each i$\geq$1, $x_i \subseteq y_i \subseteq lub\{y_i \mid i \geq 1\}$. Therefore $lub\{x_i \mid i \geq 1\} \subseteq lub\{y_i \mid i \geq 1\}$ by the Lub lemma (take d = $lub\{y_i \mid i \geq 1\}$).   ∎

Theorem: The relation $\subseteq$ on A$\rightarrow$B, the set of functions in Fun(A,B) that are monotonic and continuous, is a complete partial order.

Proof: Since $\subseteq$ is a partial order on A$\rightarrow$B, two properties need to be verified.

1. The bottom element in Fun(A,B) is also in A$\rightarrow$B, which can be proved by showing that the function $\perp(x) = \perp_B$ is monotonic and continuous.

2. For any ascending chain in A$\rightarrow$B, its least upper bound, which is an element of Fun(A,B), is also in A$\rightarrow$B, which means that it is monotonic and continuous.

Part 1: If $x \subseteq_A y$ for some x,y$\in$A, then $\perp(x) = \perp_B = \perp(y)$, which means $\perp(x) \subseteq_B \perp(y)$, and so $\perp$ is a monotonic function. If $x_1 \subseteq_A x_2 \subseteq_A x_3 \subseteq_A \ldots$ is an ascending chain in A, then its image under the function $\perp$ will be the ascending chain $\perp_B \subseteq_B \perp_B \subseteq_B \perp_B \subseteq_B \ldots$, whose least upper bound is $\perp_B$. Therefore $\perp(lub\{x_i \mid i \geq 1\})$ = $\perp_B = lub\{\perp(x_i) \mid i \geq 1\}$, and $\perp$ is a continuous function.

Part 2: Let $f_1 \subseteq f_2 \subseteq f_3 \subseteq \ldots$ be an ascending chain in A$\rightarrow$B, and let F = $lub\{f_i \mid i \geq 1\}$ be its least upper bound (in Fun(A,B)). Remember the definition of F, F(x) = $lub\{f_i(x) \mid i \geq 1\}$ for each x$\in$A. We need to show that F is monotonic and continuous so that we know F is a member of A$\rightarrow$B.

Monotonic: If $x \subseteq_A y$, then $f_i(x) \subseteq_B f_i(y) \subseteq_B lub\{f_i(y) \mid i \geq 1\}$ for any i since each f_i is monotonic. Therefore F(y) = $lub\{f_i(y) \mid i \geq 1\}$ is an upper bound for each $f_i(x)$, and so the least upper bound of all the $f_i(x)$ satisfies F(x) = $lub\{f_i(x) \mid i \geq 1\} \subseteq F(y)$, and F is monotonic. This result can also be proved using the Limit lemma. Since $f_i(x) \subseteq_B f_i(y)$ for each i$\geq$1, F(x) = $lub\{f_i(x) \mid i \geq 1\} \subseteq lub\{f_i(y) \mid i \geq 1\}$ = F(y).

Continuous: Let $x_1 \subseteq_A x_2 \subseteq_A x_3 \subseteq_A \ldots$ be an ascending chain in A. We need to show that $F(lub\{x_j \mid j \geq 1\}) = lub\{F(x_j) \mid j \geq 1\}$ where $F(x) = lub\{f_i(x) \mid i \geq 1\}$ for each $x \in A$. Note that "i" is used to index the ascending chain of functions from $A \to B$ while "j" is used to index the ascending chains of elements in A and B. So F is continuous if $F(lub\{x_j \mid j \geq 1\}) = lub\{F(x_j) \mid j \geq 1\}$.

Recall these definitions and properties.

1. Each f_i is continuous: $f_i(lub\{x_j \mid j \geq 1\}) = lub\{f_i(x_j) \mid j \geq 1\}$ for each chain $\{x_j \mid j \geq 1\}$ in A.

2. Definition of F: $F(x) = lub\{f_i(x) \mid i \geq 1\}$ for each $x \in A$.

Thus
$$
\begin{aligned}
F(lub\{x_j \mid j \geq 1\}) &= lub\{f_i(lub\{x_j \mid j \geq 1\}) \mid i \geq 1\} && \text{by 2} \\
&= lub\{lub\{f_i(x_j) \mid j \geq 1\} \mid i \geq 1\} && \text{by 1} \\
&= lub\{lub\{f_i(x_j) \mid i \geq 1\} \mid j \geq 1\} && \ddagger \text{ needs to be shown} \\
&= lub\{F(x_j) \mid j \geq 1\} && \text{by 2.}
\end{aligned}
$$

The condition $\ddagger$ to be proved is illustrated in Figure 10.9.

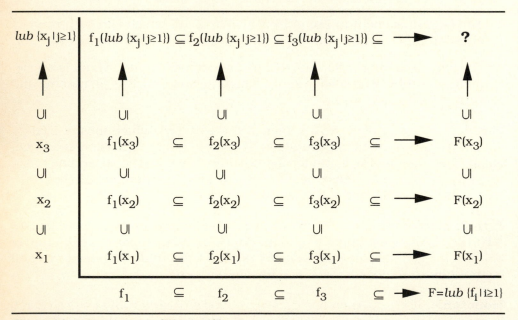

Figure 10.9: Continuity of $F = lub\{f_i \mid i \geq 1\}$

The rows in the diagram correspond to the definition of F as the least upper bound of the ascending chain of functions $lub\{f_i \mid i \geq 1\}$. The columns correspond to the continuity of each f_i—namely, that $lub\{f_i(x_j) \mid j \geq 1\} = f_i(lub\{x_j \mid j \geq 1\})$ for each i and each ascending chain $\{x_j \mid j \geq 1\}$ in A.

First Half: $lub\{lub\{f_i(x_j) \mid j \geq 1\} \mid i \geq 1\} \subseteq lub\{lub\{f_i(x_j) \mid i \geq 1\} \mid j \geq 1\}$

For all k and j, $f_k(x_j) \subseteq lub\{f_i(x_j) \mid i \geq 1\}$ by the definition of F (the rows of Figure 10.9). We have ascending chains $f_k(x_1) \subseteq f_k(x_2) \subseteq f_k(x_3) \subseteq \ldots$ for each k and $lub\{f_i(x_1) \mid i \geq 1\} \subseteq lub\{f_i(x_2) \mid i \geq 1\} \subseteq lub\{f_i(x_3) \mid i \geq 1\} \subseteq \ldots$. So for each k, $lub\{f_k(x_j) \mid j \geq 1\} \subseteq lub\{lub\{f_i(x_j) \mid i \geq 1\} \mid j \geq 1\}$ by the Limit lemma. This corresponds to the top row. Hence $lub\{lub\{f_k(x_j) \mid j \geq 1\} \mid k \geq 1\} \subseteq lub\{lub\{f_i(x_j) \mid i \geq 1\} \mid j \geq 1\}$ by the Lub lemma. Now change k to i.

Second Half: $lub\{lub\{f_i(x_j) \mid i \geq 1\} \mid j \geq 1\} \subseteq lub\{lub\{f_i(x_j) \mid j \geq 1\} \mid i \geq 1\}$

For all i and k, $f_i(x_k) \subseteq f_i(lub\{x_j \mid j \geq 1\}) = lub\{f_i(x_j) \mid j \geq 1\}$ by using the fact that each f_i is monotonic and continuous (the columns of Figure 10.9). So for each k, $lub\{f_i(x_k) \mid i \geq 1\} \subseteq lub\{lub\{f_i(x_j) \mid j \geq 1\} \mid i \geq 1\}$ by the Limit lemma. This corresponds to the rightmost column. Hence $lub\{lub\{f_i(x_k) \mid i \geq 1\} \mid k \geq 1\} \subseteq lub\{lub\{f_i(x_j) \mid j \geq 1\} \mid i \geq 1\}$ by the Lub lemma. Now change k to j.

Therefore F is continuous. ∎

Corollary: Let $f_1 \subseteq f_2 \subseteq f_3 \subseteq \ldots$ be an ascending chain of continuous functions in A→B. Then $F = lub\{f_i \mid i \geq 1\}$ is a continuous function.

Proof: This corollary was proved in Part 2 of the proof of the previous theorem. ∎

In agreement with the notation for denotational semantics in Chapter 9, as a domain constructor, we treat → as a right associative operation. The domain A→B→C means A→(B→C), which is the set of continuous functions from A into the set of continuous functions from B to C. If f∈ A→B→C, then for a∈ A, f(a)∈ B→C. Generally, we write ":" to represent membership in a domain. So we write g : A→B for g∈ A→B.

Example 10: Consider the functions from a small domain of students,

Student = {⊥, Autry, Bates}

to the domain of levels,

Level = {⊥, undergraduate, graduate, nondegree}.

We can think of the functions in Fun(Student,Level) as descriptions of our success in classifying two students, Autry and Bates. The set of all total functions, Fun(Student,Level), contains 64 (4^3) elements, but only 19 of these functions are monotonic and continuous. The structure of Student → Level is portrayed by the lattice-like structure in Figure 10.10, where the values in the domains are denoted by only their first letters. ∎

Since the domain Student of a function in Student→Level is finite, it is enough to show that the function is monotonic as we show in the next theorem.

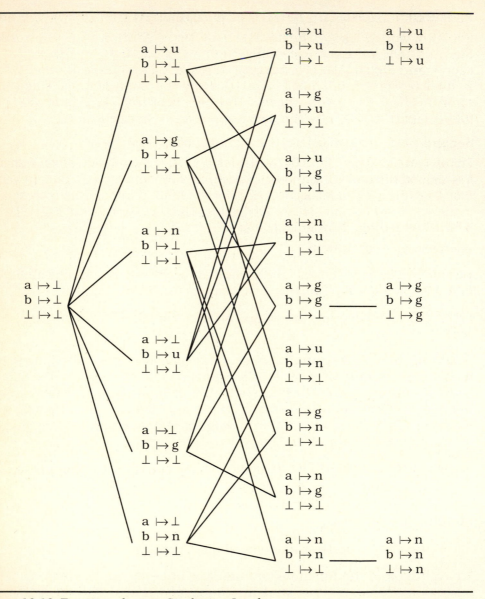

Figure 10.10: Function domain Student → Level

Theorem: If A and B are cpo's, A is a finite set, and f∈ Fun(A,B) is monotonic, then f is also continuous.

Proof: Let $x_1 \subseteq_A x_2 \subseteq_A x_3 \subseteq_A$ ... be an ascending chain in A. Since A is finite, for some k, $x_k = x_{k+1} = x_{k+2} =$ .... So the chain is a finite set $\{x_1, x_2, x_3, ..., x_k\}$ whose least upper bound is x_k. Since f is monotonic, $f(x_1) \subseteq_B f(x_2) \subseteq_B f(x_3) \subseteq_B$

$\ldots \subseteq_B f(x_k) = f(x_{k+1}) = f(x_{k+2}) = \ldots$ is an ascending chain in B, which is also a finite set—namely, $\{f(x_1), f(x_2), f(x_3), \ldots, f(x_k)\}$ with $f(x_k)$ as its least upper bound. Therefore, $f(lub\{x_i \mid i \geq 1\}) = f(x_k) = lub\{f(x_i) \mid i \geq 1\}$, and f is continuous. ∎

Lemma: The function f : Student → Level defined by

$$f(\bot) = graduate, \quad f(Autry) = nondegree, \quad f(Bates) = graduate$$

is neither monotonic nor continuous.

Proof: Clearly, $\bot \subseteq$ Autry. But $f(\bot) = graduate$ and $f(Autry) = nondegree$ are incomparable. Therefore, f is not monotonic. By the contrapositive of an earlier theorem, if f is not monotonic, it is also not continuous. ∎

Continuity of Functions on Domains

The notation used for the special functions defined on domains implied that they were continuous—for example, *first* : A×B→A. To justify this notation, a theorem is needed.

Theorem: The following functions on domains and their analogs are continuous:

1. *first* : A×B→A

2. *inS* : A→S where S = A+B

3. *outA* : A+B→A

4. *isA* : A+B→T

Proof:

1. Let $<a_1,b_1> \subseteq <a_2,b_2> \subseteq <a_3,b_3> \subseteq \ldots$ be an ascending chain in A×B. Then $lub\{first <a_i,b_i> \mid i \geq 1\} = lub\{a_i \mid i \geq 1\}$
$$= first <lub\{a_i \mid i \geq 1\}, lub\{b_i \mid i \geq 1\}> = first(lub_{A \times B}\{<a_i,b_i> \mid i \geq 1\}).$$

2. An exercise.

3. An exercise.

4. An ascending chain $x_1 \subseteq x_2 \subseteq x_3 \subseteq \ldots$ in A+B may repeat $\bot_{A+B}$ forever or eventually climb into either A×{1} or B×{2}. In the first case, the least upper bound will be $\bot_{A+B}$, and in the other two cases the *lub* will be some $a \in A$ or some $b \in B$.

   Case 1: $\{x_i \mid i \geq 1\} = \{\bot_{A+B}\}$. Then $isA(lub_{A+B}\{x_i \mid i \geq 1\}) = isA(\bot_{A+B}) = \bot_T$, and $lub_T\{isA(x_i) \mid i \geq 1\} = lub_T\{isA(\bot_{A+B})\} = lub_T\{\bot_T\} = \bot_T$.

   Case 2: $\{x_i \mid i \geq 1\} = \{\bot_{A+B}, \ldots, \bot_{A+B}, <a_1,1>, <a_2,1>, \ldots\}$ where $a_1 \subseteq_A a_2 \subseteq_A a_3 \subseteq_A \ldots$ is a chain in A. Suppose $a = lub\{a_i \mid i \geq 1\}$. Then $isA(lub_{A+B}\{x_i \mid i \geq 1\}) = isA(<a,1>) = true$, and $lub_T\{isA(x_i) \mid i \geq 1\} = lub_T\{\bot, \ldots, \bot, true, true, \ldots\} = true$.

Case 3: $\{x_i \mid i \geq 1\} = \{\perp_{A+B}, \ldots, \perp_{A+B}, <b_1,2>, <b_2,2>, \ldots\}$ where $b_1 \sqsubseteq_B b_2 \sqsubseteq_B b_3 \sqsubseteq_B \ldots$ is a chain in B. Suppose $b = lub\{b_i \mid i \geq 1\}$. Then $isA(lub_{A+B}\{x_i \mid i \geq 1\}) = isA(<b,2>) = $ false, and $lub_T\{isA(x_i) \mid i \geq 1\} = lub_T\{\perp, \ldots, \perp, \text{false}, \text{false}, \ldots\} = $ false. ∎

The functions defined on lists, such as *head* and *tail*, are mostly built from the selector functions for products and sums. The list functions can be shown to be continuous by proving that composition preserves the continuity of functions.

Theorem: The composition of continuous functions is continuous.

Proof: Suppose $f : A \to B$ and $g : B \to C$ are continuous functions. Let $a_1 \sqsubseteq a_2 \sqsubseteq a_3 \sqsubseteq \ldots$ be an ascending chain in A. Then $f(a_1) \sqsubseteq f(a_2) \sqsubseteq f(a_3) \sqsubseteq \ldots$ is an ascending chain in B with $f(lub\{a_i \mid i \geq 1\}) = lub\{f(a_i) \mid i \geq 1\}$ by the continuity of f. Since g is continuous, $g(f(a_1)) \sqsubseteq g(f(a_2)) \sqsubseteq g(f(a_3)) \sqsubseteq \ldots$ is an ascending chain in C with $g(lub\{f(a_i) \mid i \geq 1\}) = lub\{g(f(a_i)) \mid i \geq 1\}$. Therefore $g(f(lub\{a_i \mid i \geq 1\})) = g(lub\{f(a_i) \mid i \geq 1\}) = lub\{g(f(a_i)) \mid i \geq 1\}$ and $g \circ f$ is continuous. ∎

To handle *tail*, *prefix*, and *affix* we need a generalization of this theorem to allow for tuples of continuous functions, a result that appears as an exercise.

Theorem: The following functions on lists are continuous:

1. *head* : $D^* \to D$
2. *tail* : $D^* \to D^*$
3. *null* : $D^* \to T$
4. *prefix* : $D \times D^* \to D^*$
5. *affix* : $D^* \times D \to D^*$

Proof: For 1, 2, 4, 5 use the continuity of the compositions of continuous functions and the previous theorems. A case analysis is needed to deal with ascending sequences that contain mostly *nil* values.

3. An ascending chain $x_1 \sqsubseteq x_2 \sqsubseteq x_3 \sqsubseteq \ldots$ in D^* may repeat $\perp_{D^*}$ forever or eventually climb into D^k, where $k \geq 0$ and $D^0 = \{nil\}$.

Case 1: $\{x_i \mid i \geq 1\} = \{\perp_{D^*}\}$. $null(lub_{D^*}\{x_i \mid i \geq 1\}) = null(\perp_{D^*}) = \perp_T$, and $lub_T\{null(x_i) \mid i \geq 1\} = lub_T\{\perp_T\} = \perp_T$.

Case 2: $\{x_i \mid i \geq 1\} = \{\perp_{D^*}, \perp_{D^*}, \ldots, \perp_{D^*}, <nil,0>, <nil,0>, \ldots\}$. $null(lub_{D^*}\{x_i \mid i \geq 1\}) = null(<nil,0>) = $ true, and $lub_T\{null(x_i) \mid i \geq 1\} = lub_T\{\perp_T, \perp_T, \ldots, \perp_T, \text{true}, \text{true}, \ldots\} = $ true.

Case 3: $\{x_i \mid i \geq 1\} = \{\perp_{D^*}, \ldots, \perp_{D^*}, <d_1,k>, <d_2,k>, \ldots\}$ where $d_i \in D^k$ for some $k > 0$ and $d_1 \sqsubseteq_{D^k} d_2 \sqsubseteq_{D^k} d_3 \sqsubseteq_{D^k} \ldots$ is a chain in D^k. $null(lub_{D^*}\{x_i \mid i \geq 1\}) = null(<lub_{D^k}\{d_i \mid i \geq 1\}, k>) = $ false since $(lub_{D^k}\{d_i \mid i \geq 1\}) \in D^k$, and $lub_D\{null(x_i) \mid i \geq 1\} = lub_D\{null<d_1,k>, null<d_2,k>, \ldots\} = lub_D\{\text{false}, \text{false}, \ldots\} = $ false. ∎

Exercises

1. Determine which of the following ordered sets are complete partial orders:

   a) Divides ordering on {1,3,6,9,12,18}.

   b) Divides ordering on {2,3,6,12,18}.

   c) Divides ordering on {2,4,6,8,10,12}.

   d) Divides ordering on the set of positive integers.

   e) Divides ordering on the set P of prime numbers.

   f) Divides ordering on the set P $\cup$ {1}.

   g) $\subseteq$ (subset) on the nonempty subsets of {a,b,c,d}.

   h) $\subseteq$ (subset) on the collection of all finite subsets of the natural numbers.

   i) $\subseteq$ (subset) on the collection of all subsets of the natural numbers whose complement is finite.

2. Which of the partially ordered sets in exercise 1 are also lattices?

3. Let S = {1,2,3,4,5,6,9,15,25,30} be ordered by the divides relation.

   a) Find all lower bounds for {6,30}.

   b) Find all lower bounds for {4,6,15}.

   c) Find all upper bounds for {1,2,3}.

   d) Does {4,9,25} have an upper bound?

4. Show that $\subseteq_{AxB}$ is a partial order on AxB.

5. Show that $\subseteq_{A+B}$ is a partial order on A+B.

6. Prove that the least upper bound of an ascending chain $x_1 \subseteq x_2 \subseteq x_3 \subseteq \ldots$ in a domain D is unique.

7. Let Hair = {$\perp$,black,blond,brown} and Eyes = {$\perp$,blue,brown,gray} be two elementary domains (flat complete partially ordered sets).

   a) Sketch a Hasse diagram showing all the elements of Hair x Eyes and the relationships between its elements under $\subseteq$.

   b) Sketch a Hasse diagram showing all the elements of Hair+Eyes and the relationships between its elements under $\subseteq$.

8. Suppose that $A = \{\perp, a\}$ and $B = \{\perp, b, c, d\}$ are elementary domains.

    a) Sketch a Hasse diagram showing all seven elements of $A \rightarrow B$ and the relationships between its elements under $\subseteq$.

    b) Give an example of one function in $Fun(A, B)$ that is not monotonic.

    c) Sketch a Hasse diagram showing all the elements of $A \times B$ and the relationships between its elements under $\subseteq$.

9. Suppose $A = \{\perp, a, b\}$ and $B = \{\perp, c\}$ are elementary domains.

    a) Sketch a Hasse diagram showing all the elements of $(A \rightarrow B) + (A \times B)$ and their ordering under the induced partial order. Represent functions as sets of ordered pairs. Since $A \rightarrow B$ and $A \times B$ are disjoint, omit the tags on the elements, but provide subscripts for the bottom elements.

    b) Give one example of a function in $Fun(A \rightarrow B, A \times B)$ that is continuous and one that is not monotonic.

10. Prove the following property:

    A function f in $Fun(A, B)$ is continuous if and only if both of the following conditions hold.

    a) f is monotonic.

    b) For any ascending chain $x_1 \subseteq x_2 \subseteq x_3 \subseteq \ldots$ in A, $f(lub_A\{x_i \mid i \geq 1\}) \subseteq lub_B\{f(x_i) \mid i \geq 1\}$.

11. Let $A = \{\perp, a_1, a_2, \ldots, a_m\}$ and $B = \{\perp, b_1, b_2, \ldots, b_n\}$ be flat domains. Show that

    a) $Fun(A, B)$ has $(n+1)^{m+1}$ elements.

    b) $A \rightarrow B$ has $n + (n+1)^m$ elements.

12. Prove that *inS* and *outA* are continuous functions.

13. Prove that *head* and *tail* are continuous functions.

14. Tell whether these functions $F : (N \rightarrow N) \rightarrow (N \rightarrow N)$ are monotonic and/or continuous.

    a) $F \, g \, n = $ if *total(g)* then $g(n)$ else $\perp$, where *total(g)* is true if and only if $g(n)$ is defined (not $\perp$) for all $n \in N$.

    b) $F \, g \, n = $ if $g = (\lambda n \, . 0)$ then 1 else 0.

    c) $F \, g \, n = $ if $n \notin dom(g)$ then 0 else $\perp$, where $dom(g) = \{n \in N \mid g(n) \neq \perp\}$ denotes the domain of g.

15. Let $N = \{\bot, 0, 1, 2, 3, \ldots\}$ be the elementary domain of natural numbers. A function $f : N \rightarrow N$ is called **strict** if $f(\bot) = \bot$. Consider the function $add1 : N \rightarrow N$ defined by $add1(n) = n+1$ for all $n \in N$ with $n \neq \bot$. Prove that if $add1$ is monotonic, it must also be strict.

16. Consider the function $F : (N \rightarrow N) \rightarrow (N \rightarrow N)$ defined by

    for $g \in N \rightarrow N$, $F g = \lambda n$. if $g(n) = \bot$ then 0 else 1

    Describe $F g_1$, $F g_2$, and $F g_3$ where the $g_k : N \rightarrow N$ are defined by

    $g_1(n) = n$

    $g_2(n) = $ if $n > 0$ then $n/0$ else $\bot$

    $g_3(n) = $ if *even*(n) then $n+1$ else $\bot$

17. Prove that if $f \in Fun(A,B)$, where A and B are domains (cpo's), is a constant function (there is a $b \in B$ such that $f(a) = b$ for all $a \in A$), then f is continuous.

18. An ascending chain $x_1 \subseteq x_2 \subseteq x_3 \subseteq \ldots$ in a cpo A is called **stationary** if there is an $n \geq 1$ such that for all $i \geq n$, $x_i = x_n$. Carefully prove the following properties:

    a) If every ascending chain in A is stationary and $f \in Fun(A,B)$ is monotonic, then f must be continuous.

    b) If an ascending chain $x_1 \subseteq x_2 \subseteq x_3 \subseteq \ldots$ is not stationary, then for all $i \geq 1$, $x_i \neq lub\{x_j \mid j \geq 1\}$. *Hint:* Prove the contrapositive.

19. Prove the following lemma: If $a_1 \subseteq a_2 \subseteq a_3 \subseteq \ldots$ and $b_1 \subseteq b_2 \subseteq b_3 \subseteq \ldots$ are ascending chains with the property that for each $m \geq 1$ there exists an $n \geq 1$ such that $a_m \subseteq b_n$, it follows that $lub\{a_i \mid i \geq 1\} \subseteq lub\{b_i \mid i \geq 1\}$.

10.3 FIXED-POINT SEMANTICS

Functions, and in particular recursively defined functions, are central to computer science. Functions are used not only in programming but also in describing the semantics of programming languages as witnessed by the recursive definitions in denotational specifications. Recursion definitions entail a circularity that can make them suspect. Many of the paradoxes of logic and mathematics revolve about circular definitions—for example, the set of all sets. Considering the suspicious nature of circular definitions, how can we be certain that function definitions have a consistent model? The use of domains (complete partially ordered sets) and the associated fixed-point theory to be developed below put recursive function definitions and denotational semantics on a firm, consistent foundation.

Our goal is to develop a coherent theory of functions that makes sense out of recursive definitions. In describing fixed-point semantics we restate some of the definitions from section 10.2 as we motivate the concepts. The discussion breaks into two parts: (1) interpreting partial functions so that they are total, and (2) giving meaning to a recursively defined function as an approximation of a sequence of "finite" functions.

First Step

We transform partial functions into analogous total functions.

Example 11: Let f be a function on a few natural numbers with domain D = {0,1,2} and codomain C = {0,1,2} and with its rule given as

$f(n) = 2/n$ or as a set of ordered pairs: $f = \{<1,2>,<2,1>\}$.

Note that f(0) is undefined; therefore f is a partial function. Now extend f to make it a total function.

$f = \{<0,?>,<1,2>,<2,1>\}$.

Add an undefined element to the codomain, $C^+ = \{\perp_{C^+},0,1,2\}$, and for symmetry, do likewise with the domain, $D^+ = \{\perp_{D^+},0,1,2\}$.

Then define the **natural extension** of f by having $\perp_{D^+}$ map to $\perp_{C^+}$ under f.

$f^+ = \{<\perp,\perp>,<0,\perp>,<1,2>,<2,1>\}$.

From this point on, we drop the subscripts on $\perp$ unless they are needed to clarify an example. Finally, define a relationship that orders functions and domains according to how "defined" they are, putting a lattice-like structure on the elementary domains: For $x,y \in D^+$, $x \subseteq y$ if $x=\perp$ or $x=y$. It follows that $f \subseteq f^+$. ∎

This relation is read "f approximates f^+" or "f is less defined than or equal to f^+". D^+ and C^+ are examples of the flat domains of the previous section.

Consider the function $g = \{<\perp,\perp>,<0,0>,<1,2>,<2,1>\}$, which is an extension of f^+ that is slightly more defined. The relationship between the two functions is denoted by $f^+ \subseteq g$. Observe that the two functions agree where they are both defined (do not map to $\perp$).

Theorem: Let f^+ be a natural extension of a function between two sets D and C so that f^+ is a total function from D^+ to C^+. Then f^+ is monotonic and continuous.

Proof: Let $x_1 \subseteq x_2 \subseteq x_3 \subseteq \ldots$ be an ascending chain in the domain $D^+ = D \cup \{\bot_{D^+}\}$. There are two possibilities for the behavior of the chain.

Case 1: $x_i = \bot_{D^+}$ for all $i \geq 1$. Then $lub\{x_i \mid i \geq 1\} = \bot_{D^+}$, and $f^+(lub\{x_i \mid i \geq 1\}) = f^+(\bot_{D^+})$ $= \bot_{C^+} = lub\{\bot_{C^+}\} = lub\{f^+(x_i) \mid i \geq 1\}$.

Case 2: $x_i = \bot_{D^+}$ for $1 \leq i \leq k$ and $\bot_{D^+} \neq x_{k+1} = x_{k+2} = x_{k+3} = \ldots$, since once the terms move above bottom, the sequence is constant in a flat domain. Then $lub\{x_i \mid i \geq 1\} = x_{k+1}$, and $f^+(lub\{x_i \mid i \geq 1\}) = f^+(x_{k+1}) = lub\{\bot_{C^+}, f^+(x_{k+1})\} = lub\{f^+(x_i) \mid i \geq 1\}$. If f^+ is continuous, it is also monotonic. ∎

Since many functions used in programming, such as "addition", "less than", and "or", are binary operations, their natural extensions need to be clarified.

Definition: The **natural extension** of a function whose domain is a Cartesian product—namely, $f : D_1^+ \times D_2^+ \times \ldots \times D_n^+ \to C^+$—has the property that $f^+(x_1, x_2, \ldots, x_n) = \bot_C$ whenever at least one $x_i = \bot$. Any function that satisfies this property is known as a **strict** function. ∎

Theorem: If $f^+: D_1^+ \times D_2^+ \times \ldots \times D_n^+ \to C^+$ is a natural extension where D_i^+, $1 \leq i \leq n$, and C^+ are elementary domains, then f^+ is monotonic and continuous.

Proof: Consider the case where $n=2$. We show f^+ is continuous.

Let $<x_1, y_1> \subseteq <x_2, y_2> \subseteq <x_3, y_3> \subseteq \ldots$ be an ascending chain in $D_1^+ \times D_2^+$. Since D_1^+ and D_2^+ are elementary domains, the chains $\{x_i \mid i \geq 1\}$ and $\{y_i \mid i \geq 1\}$ must follow one of the two cases in the previous proof—namely, all $\bot$ or eventually constant proper values in D_1^+ and D_2^+, respectively.

Case 1: $lub\{x_i \mid i \geq 1\} = \bot_{D_1^+}$ or $lub\{y_i \mid i \geq 1\} = \bot_{D_2^+}$ (or both). Then $f^+(lub\{<x_i, y_i> \mid i \geq 1\})$ $= f^+(<lub\{x_i \mid i \geq 1\}, lub\{y_i \mid i \geq 1\}>) = \bot_C$ because f^+ is a natural extension and one of its arguments is $\bot$; furthermore, $lub\{f^+(<x_i, y_i>) \mid i \geq 1\} = lub\{\bot_{C^+}\} = \bot_{C^+}$, since at least one of the chains must be all $\bot$.

Case 2: $lub\{x_i \mid i \geq 1\} = x \in D_1$ and $lub\{y_i \mid i \geq 1\} = y \in D_2$ (neither is $\bot$). Since D_1^+ and D_2^+ are both elementary domains, there is an integer k such that $x_i = x$ and $y_i = y$ for all $i \geq k$. So $f^+(lub\{<x_i, y_i> \mid i \geq 1\}) = f^+(<lub\{x_i \mid i \geq 1\}, lub\{y_i \mid i \geq 1\}>) = f^+(<x, y>) \in C^+$ and $lub\{f^+(<x_i, y_i>) \mid i \geq 1\} = lub\{\bot_{C^+}, f^+(<x, y>)\} = f^+(<x, y>)$. ∎

Example 12: Consider the natural extension of the conditional expression operation (if a b c) = if a then b else c.

The natural extension unduly restricts the meaning of the conditional expression—for example, we prefer that the following expression returns 0 when m=1 and n=0 instead of causing a fatal error: if n>0 then m/n else 0.

But if we interpret the undefined operation 1/0 as $\bot$, when m=1 and n=0,

$$(if^+ \ n>0 \ m/n \ 0) = (if^+ \ false \ \bot \ 0) = \bot \ \text{for a natural extension.} \quad ∎$$

As we continue with the development of fixed-point semantics, we drop the superscript plus sign ($^+$) on sets and functions since all sets will be assumed to be domains (cpo's) and all functions will be naturally extended unless otherwise specified.

Second Step

We now define the meaning of a recursive definition of a function defined on complete partially ordered sets (domains) as the limit of a sequence of approximations.

Example 13: Consider a recursively defined function $f : N \rightarrow N$ where $N = \{\perp,0,1,2,3,...\}$ and

$$f(n) = \text{if } n=0 \text{ then } 5 \text{ else if } n=1 \text{ then } f(n+2) \text{ else } f(n-2). \qquad (\dagger)$$

Two questions can be asked about a recursive definition of a function.

1. What function, if any, does this equation in f denote?

2. If the equation specifies more than one function, which one should be selected?

Define a **functional** F, a function on functions, by

$F : (N \rightarrow N) \rightarrow (N \rightarrow N)$ where
$(F(f)) (n) = \text{if } n=0 \text{ then } 5 \text{ else if } n=1 \text{ then } f(n+2) \text{ else } f(n-2). \qquad (\ddagger)$

Assuming function application associates to the left, we usually omit the parentheses with multiple applications, writing F f n for (F(f)) (n). A function, $f : N \rightarrow N$, satisfies the original definition ($\dagger$) if and only if it is a **fixed point** of the definition of F ($\ddagger$)—namely, F f n $= f(n)$ for all $n \in N$ or just F f = f.   ∎

Just in case this equivalence has not been understood, we go through it once more carefully. Suppose $f : D \rightarrow C$ is a function defined recursively by $f(x) = \alpha(x,f)$ for each $x \in D$ where $\alpha(x,f)$ is some expression in x and f. Furthermore, let $F : (D \rightarrow C) \rightarrow (D \rightarrow C)$ be the functional defined by F f x $= \alpha(x,f)$. Then $F(f) = f$ if and only if F f x = f x for all $x \in D$ if and only if $\alpha(x,f) = f$ x for all $x \in D$, which is the same as $f(x) = \alpha(x,f)$ for all $x \in D$. Observe that the symbol "f" plays different roles in ($\dagger$) and ($\ddagger$). In the recursive definition ($\dagger$), "f" is the name of the function being defined, whereas in the functional definition ($\ddagger$), "f" is a formal parameter to the (nonrecursive) functional F being defined.

The notation of the lambda calculus is frequently used to define these functionals.

F f = λn . if n=0 then 5 else if n=1 then f(n+2) else f(n-2)
    or
F = λf . λn . if n=0 then 5 else if n=1 then f(n+2) else f(n-2).

Fixed points occur frequently in mathematics. For instance, solving simple equations can be framed as fixed-point problems. Consider functions defined on the set of natural numbers N and consider fixed points of the functions—namely, $n \in N$ such that g(n) = n.

Function	Fixed points
$g(n) = n^2\text{-}6n$	0 and 7
$g(n) = n$	all $n \in N$
$g(n) = n+5$	none
$g(n) = 2$	2

For the first function, $g(0) = 0^2\text{-}6 \bullet 0 = 0$ and $g(7) = 7^2\text{-}6 \bullet 7 = 7$.

Certainly the function specified by a recursive definition must be a fixed point of the functional F. But that is not enough. The function $g = \lambda n \ . \ 5$ is a fixed point of F in example 13 as shown by the following calculation:

F g = λn . if n=0 then 5 else if n=1 then g(n+2) else g(n-2)
    = λn . if n=0 then 5 else if n=1 then 5 else 5
    = λn . 5 = g.

The only problem is that this fixed point does not agree with the operational view of the function definition. It appears that f(1) = f(3) = f(5) = ... does not produce a value, whereas g(1) = 5. We need to find a fixed point for F that captures the entire operational behavior of the recursive definition.

When the functional corresponding to a recursive definition (equation) has more than one fixed point, we need to choose one of them as *the* function specified by the definition. It turns out that the fixed points of a suitable functional are partially ordered by $\subseteq$ in such a way that one of those functions is less defined than all of the other fixed points. Considering all the fixed points of a functional F, the least defined one makes sense as the function specified because of the following reasons:

1. Any fixed point of F embodies the information that can be deduced from F.

2. The least fixed point includes no more information than what *must* be deduced.

Define the meaning of a recursive definition of a function to be the least fixed point with respect to $\subseteq$ of the corresponding functional F. We show next that a unique least fixed point exists for a continuous functional. The following theorem proves the existence and provides a method for constructing the least fixed point.

Notation: We define f^k for each k≥0 inductively using the rules:
        $f^0(x) = x$ is the identity function and
        $f^{n+1}(x) = f(f^n(x))$ for n≥0.

Fixed-Point Theorem: If D with $\subseteq$ is a complete partial order and g : D→D is any monotonic and continuous function on D, then g has a least fixed point in D with respect to $\subseteq$.

Proof:

Part 1: g has a fixed point. Since D is a cpo, $g^0(\bot) = \bot \subseteq g(\bot)$. Also, since g is monotonic, $g(\bot) \subseteq g(g(\bot)) = g^2(\bot)$. In general, since g is monotonic, $g^i(\bot) \subseteq g^{i+1}(\bot)$ implies $g^{i+1}(\bot) = g(g^i(\bot)) \subseteq g(g^{i+1}(\bot)) = g^{i+2}(\bot)$. So by induction, $\bot \subseteq g(\bot) \subseteq g^2(\bot) \subseteq g^3(\bot) \subseteq g^4(\bot) \subseteq \dots$ is an ascending chain in D, which must have a least upper bound $u = lub\{g^i(\bot) \mid i \geq 0\} \in D$.

Then $g(u) = g(lub\{g^i(\bot) \mid i \geq 0\})$

$\qquad\qquad = lub\{g(g^i(\bot)) \mid i \geq 0\}$ because g is continuous

$\qquad\qquad = lub\{g^{i+1}(\bot) \mid i \geq 0\}$

$\qquad\qquad = lub\{g^i(\bot) \mid i > 0\} = u$.

That is, u is a fixed point for g. Note that $g^0(\bot) = \bot$ has no effect on the least upper bound of $\{g^i(\bot) \mid i \geq 0\}$.

Part 2: u is the least fixed point. Let $v \in D$ be another fixed point for g. Then $\bot \subseteq v$ and $g(\bot) \subseteq g(v) = v$, the basis step for induction. Suppose $g^i(\bot) \subseteq v$. Then since g is monotonic, $g^{i+1}(\bot) = g(g^i(\bot)) \subseteq g(v) = v$, the induction step. Therefore, by mathematical induction, $g^i(\bot) \subseteq v$ for all $i \geq 0$. So v is an upper bound for $\{g^i(\bot) \mid i \geq 0\}$. Hence $u \subseteq v$ by the Lub lemma, since u is the least upper bound for $\{g^i(\bot) \mid i \geq 0\}$. ∎

Corollary: Every continuous functional F : (A→B)→(A→B), where A and B are domains, has a least fixed point F_{fp} : A→B, which can be taken as the meaning of the (recursive) definition corresponding to F.

Proof: This is an immediate application of the fixed-point theorem. ∎

Example 13 (revisited): Consider the functional F : (N→N)→(N→N) that we defined earlier corresponding to the recursive definition (†),

$\qquad$ F f n = if n=0 then 5 else if n=1 then f(n+2) else f(n-2). $\qquad$ (‡)

Construct the ascending sequence

$$\bot \subseteq F(\bot) \subseteq F^2(\bot) \subseteq F^3(\bot) \subseteq F^4(\bot) \subseteq \dots$$

and its least upper bound following the proof of the fixed-point theorem.

Use the following abbreviations:

$\qquad f_0(n) = F^0 \bot n = \bot(n)$

$\qquad f_1(n) = F \bot n = F f_0 n$

$\qquad f_2(n) = F (F \bot) n = F f_1 n$

$\qquad f_{k+1}(n) = F^{k+1} \bot n = F f_k n$, in general.

Now calculate a few terms in the ascending chain

$$f_0 \subseteq f_1 \subseteq f_2 \subseteq f_3 \subseteq \ldots.$$

$f_0(n) = F^0 \perp n = \perp(n) = \perp$ for $n \in N$, the everywhere undefined function.

$f_1(n) = F \perp n = F f_0 \, n$
$\quad =$ if n=0 then 5 else if n=1 then $f_0(n+2)$ else $f_0(n-2)$
$\quad =$ if n=0 then 5 else if n=1 then $\perp(n+2)$ else $\perp(n-2)$
$\quad =$ if n=0 then 5 else $\perp$

$f_2(n) = F^2 \perp n = F f_1 \, n$
$\quad =$ if n=0 then 5 else if n=1 then $f_1(n+2)$ else $f_1(n-2)$
$\quad =$ if n=0 then 5
$\qquad\qquad$ else if n=1 then $f_1(3)$
$\qquad\qquad\qquad$ else (if n-2=0 then 5 else $\perp$)
$\quad =$ if n=0 then 5
$\qquad\qquad$ else if n=1 then $\perp$
$\qquad\qquad\qquad$ else if n=2 then 5 else $\perp$

$f_3(n) = F^3 \perp n = F f_2 \, n$
$\quad =$ if n=0 then 5 else if n=1 then $f_2(n+2)$ else $f_2(n-2)$
$\quad =$ if n=0 then 5
$\qquad\qquad$ else if n=1 then $f_2(3)$
$\qquad\qquad\qquad$ else (if n-2=0 then 5
$\qquad\qquad\qquad\qquad\qquad$ else if n-2=1 then $\perp$
$\qquad\qquad\qquad\qquad\qquad\qquad$ else if n-2=2 then 5 else $\perp$)
$\quad =$ if n=0 then 5
$\qquad\qquad$ else if n=1 then $\perp$
$\qquad\qquad\qquad$ else if n=2 then 5
$\qquad\qquad\qquad\qquad$ else if n=3 then $\perp$
$\qquad\qquad\qquad\qquad\qquad$ else if n=4 then 5 else $\perp$

$f_4(n) = F^4 \perp n = F f_3 \, n$
$\quad =$ if n=0 then 5 else if n=1 then $f_3(n+2)$ else $f_3(n-2)$
$\quad =$ if n=0 then 5
$\qquad\qquad$ else if n=1 then $f_3(3)$
$\qquad\qquad\qquad$ else (if n-2=0 then 5
$\qquad\qquad\qquad\qquad\qquad$ else if n-2=1 then $\perp$
$\qquad\qquad\qquad\qquad\qquad\qquad$ else if n-2=2 then 5
$\qquad\qquad\qquad\qquad\qquad\qquad\qquad$ else if n-2=3 then $\perp$
$\qquad\qquad\qquad\qquad\qquad\qquad\qquad\qquad$ else if n-2=4 then 5 else $\perp$)

$$= \text{if } n=0 \text{ then } 5$$
$$\text{else if } n=1 \text{ then } \bot$$
$$\text{else if } n=2 \text{ then } 5$$
$$\text{else if } n=3 \text{ then } \bot$$
$$\text{else if } n=4 \text{ then } 5$$
$$\text{else if } n=5 \text{ then } \bot$$
$$\text{else if } n=6 \text{ then } 5 \text{ else } \bot$$

A pattern seems to be developing.

Lemma: For all $i \geq 0$, $f_i(n) = $ if $n < 2i$ and *even*(n) then 5 else $\bot$
$$= \text{if } n < 2i \text{ then (if } even(n) \text{ then } 5 \text{ else } \bot) \text{ else } \bot.$$

Proof: The proof proceeds by induction on i.

1. By the previous computations, for $i = 0$ (also $i = 1, 2, 3$, and 4)
   $$f_i(n) = \text{if } n < 2i \text{ then (if } even(n) \text{ then } 5 \text{ else } \bot) \text{ else } \bot$$

2. As the induction hypothesis, assume that $f_i(n) = $ if $n < 2i$ then (if *even*(n) then 5 else $\bot$) else $\bot$, for some arbitrary $i \geq 0$.
   Then
   $$f_{i+1}(n) = F\, f_i\, n$$
   $$= \text{if } n=0 \text{ then } 5 \text{ else if } n=1 \text{ then } f_i(n+2) \text{ else } f_i(n-2)$$
   $$= \text{if } n=0 \text{ then } 5$$
   $$\text{else if } n=1 \text{ then } f_i(3)$$
   $$\text{else (if } n-2 < 2i \text{ then (if } even(n-2) \text{ then } 5 \text{ else } \bot) \text{ else } \bot)$$
   $$= \text{if } n=0 \text{ then } 5$$
   $$\text{else if } n=1 \text{ then } \bot$$
   $$\text{else (if } n < 2i+2 \text{ then (if } even(n) \text{ then } 5 \text{ else } \bot) \text{ else } \bot)$$
   $$= \text{if } n < 2(i+1) \text{ then (if } even(n) \text{ then } 5 \text{ else } \bot) \text{ else } \bot.$$

Therefore our pattern for the f_i is correct.   ∎

The least upper bound of the ascending chain $f_0 \subseteq f_1 \subseteq f_2 \subseteq f_3 \subseteq \ldots$, where $f_i(n)$ = if $n < 2i$ then (if *even*(n) then 5 else $\bot$) else $\bot$, must be defined (not $\bot$) for any n where some f_i is defined, and must take the value 5 there. Hence the least upper bound is

$$F_{fp}(n) = (lub\{f_i \mid i \geq 0\})\, n$$
$$= (lub\{F^i \bot \mid i \geq 0\})\, n$$
$$= \text{if } even(n) \text{ then } 5 \text{ else } \bot, \text{ for all } n \in N,$$

and this function can be taken as the meaning of the original recursive definition. Figure 10.11 shows the chain of approximating functions as sets of ordered pairs, omitting the undefined ($\bot$) values. Following this set theoretic viewpoint, the least upper bound of the ascending chain can be taken as the union of all these functions, $lub\{f_i \mid i \geq 0\} = \cup\{f_i \mid i \geq 0\}$, to get a function that is undefined for all odd values.

$f_0 = \varnothing$

$f_1 = \{\ <0,5>\ \}$

$f_2 = \{\ <0,5>,<2,5>\ \}$

$f_3 = \{\ <0,5>,<2,5>,<4,5>\ \}$

$f_4 = \{\ <0,5>,<2,5>,<4,5>,<6,5>\ \}$

$f_5 = \{\ <0,5>,<2,5>,<4,5>,<6,5>,<8,5>\ \}$

$f_6 = \{\ <0,5>,<2,5>,<4,5>,<6,5>,<8,5>,<10,5>\ \}$

$\vdots$ $\vdots$

$f_k = \{\ <0,5>,<2,5>,<4,5>,<6,5>,<8,5>,<10,5>,....,<2\bullet k-2,5>\ \}$

$\vdots$ $\vdots$

Figure 10.11: Approximations to F_{fp}

Remember that the definition of the function $lub\{f_i \mid i \geq 0\}$ is given as the least upper bound of the f_i's on individual values of n,

$$(lub\{f_i \mid i \geq 0\})\ n = lub\{f_i(n) \mid i \geq 0\}.$$

The procedure for computing a least fixed point for a functional can be described as an operator on functions $F : D{\rightarrow}D$.

$$fix : (D{\rightarrow}D){\rightarrow}D \text{ where}$$
$$fix = \lambda F\ .\ lub\{F^i(\bot) \mid i \geq 0\}.$$

The least fixed point of the functional

$$F = \lambda f\ .\ \lambda n\ .\ \text{if n=0 then 5 else if n=1 then f(n+2) else f(n-2)}$$

can then be expressed as $F_{fp} = fix\ F$ where $D = N{\rightarrow}N$.

For $F : (N{\rightarrow}N){\rightarrow}(N{\rightarrow}N)$, fix has type $fix : ((N{\rightarrow}N){\rightarrow}(N{\rightarrow}N)){\rightarrow}(N{\rightarrow}N)$.

The fixed-point operator fix provides a fixed point for any continuous functional—namely, the least defined function with this fixed-point property.

Fixed-Point Identity: $F(fix\ F) = fix\ F$.

Summary: Recapping the fixed-point semantics of functions, we start with a recursive definition, say fac : $N{\rightarrow}N$, where

fac n = if n=0 then 1 else n•fac(n-1) or

fac = λn . if n=0 then 1 else n•fac(n-1)

Operationally, the meaning of fac on a value $n \in N$ results from unfolding the definition enough times, necessarily a finite number of times, until the basis case is reached. For example, we calculate fac(4) by the following process:

fac(4) = if 4=0 then 1 else 4•fac(3) = 4•fac(3)
       = 4•(if 3=0 then 1 else 3•fac(2)) = 4•3•fac(2)

$$= 4 \bullet 3 \bullet (\text{if } 2=0 \text{ then } 1 \text{ else } 2 \bullet \text{fac}(1)) = 4 \bullet 3 \bullet 2 \bullet \text{fac}(1)$$
$$= 4 \bullet 3 \bullet 2 \bullet (\text{if } 1=0 \text{ then } 1 \text{ else } 1 \bullet \text{fac}(0)) = 4 \bullet 3 \bullet 2 \bullet 1 \bullet \text{fac}(0)$$
$$= 4 \bullet 3 \bullet 2 \bullet 1 \bullet 1 = 24$$

The problem with providing a mathematical interpretation of this unfolding process is that we cannot predict ahead of time how many unfoldings of the definition are required. The idea of fixed-point semantics is to consider a corresponding (nonrecursive) functional

Fac : $(N{\rightarrow}N){\rightarrow}(N{\rightarrow}N)$ where

Fac = $\lambda f . \lambda n .$ if n=0 then 1 else n$\bullet$f(n-1)

and construct terms in the ascending chain

$$\bot \subseteq \text{Fac}(\bot) \subseteq \text{Fac}^2(\bot) \subseteq \text{Fac}^3(\bot) \subseteq \text{Fac}^4(\bot) \subseteq \dots.$$

Using the abbreviations $\text{fac}_i = \text{Fac}^i(\bot)$ for $i{\geq}0$, the chain can also be viewed as
$$\text{fac}_0 \subseteq \text{fac}_1 \subseteq \text{fac}_2 \subseteq \text{fac}_3 \subseteq \text{fac}_4 \subseteq \dots.$$

A careful investigation of these "partial" functions $\text{fac}_i : N{\rightarrow}N$ reveals that

$$\text{fac}_0 \, n = \bot$$

$$\begin{aligned}\text{fac}_i \, n &= \text{Fac}^i(\bot) \, n \\ &= \text{Fac}(\text{fac}_{i-1}) \, n \\ &= \text{if } n{<}i \text{ then } n! \text{ else } \bot \text{ for } i{\geq}1.\end{aligned}$$

The proof that this pattern is correct for the functions in the ascending chain is left as an exercise. It follows that any application of fac to a natural number can be handled by one of these nonrecursive approximating functions fac_i. For instance, fac 4 = fac_5 4, fac 100 = fac_{101} 100, and in general fac m = fac_{m+1} m.

The purpose of each approximating function $\text{fac}_i = \text{Fac}^i(\bot)$ is to embody any calculation of the factorial function that entails fewer than i unfoldings of the recursive definition. Fixed-point semantics gives the least upper bound of these approximating functions as the *meaning* of the original recursive definition of fac. The ascending chain, whose limit is the least upper bound, $lub\{\text{fac}_i \,|\, i{\geq}0\} = lub\{\text{Fac}^i \bot \,|\, i{\geq}0\}$, is made up of finite functions, each consistent with its predecessor in the chain, and having the property that any computation of fac can be obtained by one of the functions far enough out in the chain.

Continuous Functionals

To apply the theorem about the existence of a least fixed point to the functionals F as described in the previous examples, it must be established that these functionals are continuous.

Writing the conditional expression function if-then-else as a function if : T×N×N→N or alternatively taking a curried version if : T→N→N→N, these functionals take the form

$$F\ f\ n = if(n=0,\ 5,\ if(n=1,\ f(n+2),\ f(n-2)))) \qquad \text{uncurried if}$$

$$Fac\ f\ n = (if\ n=0\ 1\ n\bullet f(n-1)) \qquad \text{curried if}$$

Since it has already been proved that the natural extension of an arbitrary function on elementary domains is continuous, parts of these definitions are known to be continuous—namely, the functions defined by the expressions "n=0", "n+2", and "n−1". Several lemmas will fill in the remaining properties needed to verify the continuity of these and other functionals.

Lemma: A constant function f : D→C, where f(x) = k for some fixed k∈ C and for all x∈ D, is continuous given either of the two extensions

1. The natural extension where $f(\bot_D) = \bot_C$.
2. The "unnatural" extension where $f(\bot_D) = k$.

Proof: Part 1 follows by a proof similar to the one for the earlier theorem about the continuity of natural extensions, and part 2 is left as an exercise at the end of this section. ∎

Lemma: An identity function f : D→D, where f(x) = x for all x in a domain D, is continuous.

Proof: If $x_1 \subseteq x_2 \subseteq x_3 \subseteq \ldots$ is an ascending chain in D, it follows that $f(lub\{x_i \mid i \geq 1\})$ = $lub\{x_i \mid i \geq 1\}$ = $lub\{f(x_i) \mid i \geq 1\}$. ∎

In defining the meaning of the conditional expression function,

if(a,b,c) = if a then b else c.

where if : T×D×D→D for some domain D and T = $\{\bot, true, false\}$,

the natural extension is considered too restrictive. The preferred approach is to define this function by

(if true then b else c) = b for any b,c∈ D
(if false then b else c) = c for any b,c∈ D
(if ⊥ then b else c) = $\bot_D$ for any b,c∈ D

Note that this is not a natural extension. It allows an undefined or "erroneous" expression in one branch of a conditional as long as that branch is avoided when the expression is undefined. For example, h(*nil*) is defined for the function

h(L) = if L≠*nil* then *head*(L) else *nil.*

Lemma: The uncurried "if" function as defined above is continuous.

Proof: Let $\langle t_1, b_1, c_1 \rangle \subseteq \langle t_2, b_2, c_2 \rangle \subseteq \langle t_3, b_3, c_3 \rangle \subseteq \ldots$ be an ascending chain in TxDxD. Three cases need to be considered:

   Case 1: $t_i = \perp_T$ for all $i \geq 1$.

   Case 2: $t_i =$ true for all $i \geq k$, for some fixed k.

   Case 3: $t_i =$ false for all $i \geq k$, for some fixed k.

The details of this proof are left as an exercise. ∎

Lemma: A generalized composition of continuous functions is continuous—namely, if $f : C_1 \times C_2 \times \ldots \times C_n \rightarrow C$ is continuous and $g_i : D_i \rightarrow C_i$ is continuous for each i, $1 \leq i \leq n$, then $f \circ (g_1, g_2, \ldots, g_n) : D_1 \times D_2 \times \ldots \times D_n \rightarrow C$, defined by $f \circ (g_1, g_2, \ldots, g_n) \langle x_1, x_2, \ldots, x_n \rangle = f \langle g_1(x_1), g_2(x_2), \ldots, g_n(x_n) \rangle$ is also continuous.

Proof: This is a straightforward application of the definition of continuity and is left as an exercise. ∎

The previous lemmas apply to functions on any domains. When considering the continuity of functionals, say

   $F : (D \rightarrow D) \rightarrow (D \rightarrow D)$ for some domain D

where F is defined by a rule of the form

   F f d = some expression in f and d,

a composition will probably involve the "independent" variable f—for example, in a functional such as

   $F : (N \rightarrow N) \rightarrow (N \rightarrow N)$ where

   F f n = n + (if n=0 then 0 else f(f(n-1))).

Lemma: If $F_1, F_2, \ldots, F_n$ are continuous functionals, say $F_i : (D^n \rightarrow D) \rightarrow (D^n \rightarrow D)$ for each i, $1 \leq i \leq n$, the functional $F : (D^n \rightarrow D) \rightarrow (D^n \rightarrow D)$ defined by $F(f) = f \langle F_1(f), F_2(f), \ldots, F_n(f) \rangle$ for all $f \in D^n \rightarrow D$ is also continuous.

Proof: Consider the case where n=1.
So $F_1 : (D \rightarrow D) \rightarrow (D \rightarrow D)$, $F : (D \rightarrow D) \rightarrow (D \rightarrow D)$, and $F(f) = f \langle F_1(f) \rangle$. Let $f_1 \subseteq f_2 \subseteq f_3 \subseteq \ldots$ be an ascending chain in $D \rightarrow D$. The proof shows that $lub\{F(f_i) \mid i \geq 1\} = F(lub\{f_i \mid i \geq 1\})$ in two parts.

Part 1: $lub\{F(f_i) \mid i \geq 1\} \subseteq F(lub\{f_i \mid i \geq 1\})$. For each $i \geq 1$, $f_i \subseteq lub\{f_i \mid i \geq 1\}$. Since F_1 is monotonic, $F_1(f_i) \subseteq F_1(lub\{f_i \mid i \geq 1\})$, which means that $F_1 f_i d \subseteq F_1 lub\{f_i \mid i \geq 1\} d$ for each $d \in D$.

Since f_i is monotonic, $f_i \langle F_1 f_i d \rangle \subseteq f_i \langle F_1 lub\{f_i \mid i \geq 1\} d \rangle$. But $F f_i d = f_i \langle F_1 f_i d \rangle$ and $f_i \langle F_1 lub\{f_i \mid i \geq 1\} d \rangle \subseteq lub\{f_i \mid i \geq 1\} \langle F_1 lub\{f_i \mid i \geq 1\} d \rangle$. Therefore, $F f_i d \subseteq lub\{f_i \mid i \geq 1\} \langle F_1 lub\{f_i \mid i \geq 1\} d \rangle$ for each $i \geq 1$ and $d \in D$. So by the Lub lemma, $lub\{F(f_i) \mid i \geq 1\} d = lub\{F f_i d \mid i \geq 1\} \subseteq lub\{f_i \mid i \geq 1\} \langle F_1 lub\{f_i \mid i \geq 1\} d \rangle = F lub\{f_i \mid i \geq 1\} d$ for each $d \in D$.

Part 2: $F(lub\{f_i \mid i \geq 1\}) \subseteq lub\{F(f_i) \mid i \geq 1\}$.

For any $d \in D$,

$F\ lub\{f_i \mid i \geq 1\}\ d = lub\{f_i \mid i \geq 1\} <F_1\ lub\{f_j\}\ d>$ by the definition of F

$= lub\{f_i \mid i \geq 1\} <lub\{F_1(f_j)\}\ d>$ since F_1 is continuous

$= lub\{lub\{f_i \mid i \geq 1\} <\{F_1(f_j)\}\ d>\}$ since $lub\{f_i \mid i \geq 1\}$ is continuous

$= lub\{lub\{f_i <\{F_1(f_j)\}\ d> \mid i \geq 1\}\}$ by the definition of $lub\{f_i \mid i \geq 1\}$. †

If $j \leq i$, then $f_j \subseteq f_i$, $F_1\ f_j \subseteq F_1\ f_i$ since F_1 is monotonic, $F_1\ f_j\ d \subseteq F_1\ f_i\ d$ for each $d \in D$, and $f_i <F_1\ f_j\ d> \subseteq f_i <F_1\ f_i\ d>$ since f_i is monotonic.

If $i < j$, then $f_i \subseteq f_j$ and $f_i <F_1\ f_j\ d> \subseteq f_j <F_1\ f_j\ d>$ for each $d \in D$ by the meaning of $\subseteq$.

Therefore $f_i <F_1\ f_j\ d> \subseteq lub\{f_n <F_1\ f_n\ d> \mid n \geq 1\}$ for each $i,j \geq 1$.
But $lub\{f_n <F_1\ f_n\ d> \mid i \geq 1\} = lub\{F\ f_n\ d \mid i \geq 1\} = lub\{F(f_n) \mid i \geq 1\}\ d$ by the definition of F. So $f_i <F_1\ f_j\ d> \subseteq lub\{F(f_n) \mid n \geq 1\}\ d$ for each $i,j \geq 1$,
and $lub\{f_i <F_1\ f_j\ d> \mid i \geq 1\} \subseteq lub\{F(f_n) \mid n \geq 1\}\ d$ for each $j \geq 1$.
Hence $lub\{lub\{f_i <F_1\ f_j\ d> \mid i \geq 1\} \mid j \geq 1\} \subseteq lub\{F(f_n) \mid n \geq 1\}\ d$.
Combining with † gives $F(lub\{f_i \mid i \geq 1\})\ d \subseteq lub\{F(f_n) \mid n \geq 1\}\ d$. ∎

Continuity Theorem: Any functional H defined by the composition of naturally extended functions on elementary domains, constant functions, the identity function, the if-then-else conditional expression, and a function parameter f, is continuous.

Proof: The proof follows by structural induction on the form of the definition of the functional. The basis is handled by the continuity of natural extensions, constant functions, and the identity function, and the induction step relies on the previous lemmas, which state that the composition of continuous functions, possibly involving f, is continuous. The details are left as an exercise. ∎

Example 14: Before proceeding, we work out the least fixed point of another functional by constructing approximating terms in the ascending chain.

$H : (N \rightarrow N) \rightarrow (N \rightarrow N)$ where

$H\ h\ n = n + (\text{if } n=0 \text{ then } 0 \text{ else } h(h(n-1)))$
$= \text{if } n=0 \text{ then } n \text{ else } n+h(h(n-1))$.

Consider the ascending chain $h_0 \subseteq h_1 \subseteq h_2 \subseteq h_3 \subseteq \ldots$ where $h_0\ n = H^0 \perp n = \perp(n)$ and $h_i\ n = H^i \perp n = H\ h_{i-1}\ n$ for $i \geq 1$. Calculate terms of this sequence until a pattern becomes apparent.

$h_0(n) = \perp(n) = \perp$

$h_1(n) = H\ h_0\ n = H \perp n$
$= \text{if } n=0 \text{ then } n \text{ else } n+h_0(h_0(n-1))$
$= \text{if } n=0 \text{ then } n \text{ else } n+\perp(\perp(n-1))$
$= \text{if } n=0 \text{ then } 0 \text{ else } \perp$

Note that the natural extension of + is strict in $\bot$.

$h_2(n) = H\ h_1\ n$
    $= \text{if } n=0 \text{ then } 0 \text{ else } n+h_1(h_1(n-1))$
    $= \text{if } n=0 \text{ then } 0 \text{ else } n+h_1(\text{if } n-1=0 \text{ then } 0 \text{ else } \bot)$
    $= \text{if } n=0 \text{ then } 0 \text{ else } n+h_1(\text{if } n=1 \text{ then } 0 \text{ else } \bot)$
    $= \text{if } n=0 \text{ then } 0 \text{ else } n+\text{if } n=1 \text{ then } h_1(0) \text{ else } h_1(\bot)$
    $= \text{if } n=0 \text{ then } 0 \text{ else if } n=1 \text{ then } n+0 \text{ else } n+\bot$
    $= \text{if } n=0 \text{ then } 0 \text{ else if } n=1 \text{ then } 1 \text{ else } \bot$

$h_3(n) = H\ h_2\ n$
    $= \text{if } n=0 \text{ then } 0 \text{ else } n+h_2(h_2(n-1))$
    $= \text{if } n=0 \text{ then } 0$
           $\text{else } n+h_2(\text{if } n-1=0 \text{ then } 0 \text{ else if } n-1=1 \text{ then } 1 \text{ else } \bot)$
    $= \text{if } n=0 \text{ then } 0$
           $\text{else } n+h_2(\text{if } n=1 \text{ then } 0 \text{ else if } n=2 \text{ then } 1 \text{ else } \bot)$
    $= \text{if } n=0 \text{ then } 0$
           $\text{else if } n=1 \text{ then } 1+h_2(0)$
                $\text{else if } n=2 \text{ then } 2+h_2(1) \text{ else } n+h_2(\bot)$
    $= \text{if } n=0 \text{ then } 0$
           $\text{else if } n=1 \text{ then } 1$
                $\text{else if } n=2 \text{ then } 3 \text{ else } \bot$

$h_4(n) = H\ h_3\ n$
    $= \text{if } n=0 \text{ then } 0 \text{ else } n+h_3(h_3(n-1))$
    $= \text{if } n=0 \text{ then } 0$
           $\text{else } n+h_3(\text{if } n-1=0 \text{ then } 0$
                    $\text{else if } n-1=1 \text{ then } 1$
                        $\text{else if } n-1=2 \text{ then } 3 \text{ else } \bot)$
    $= \text{if } n=0 \text{ then } 0$
           $\text{else } n+h_3(\text{if } n=1 \text{ then } 0$
                    $\text{else if } n=2 \text{ then } 1$
                        $\text{else if } n=3 \text{ then } 3 \text{ else } \bot)$
    $= \text{if } n=0 \text{ then } 0$
           $\text{else if } n=1 \text{ then } 1+h_3(0)$
                $\text{else if } n=2 \text{ then } 2+h_3(1)$
                    $\text{else if } n=3 \text{ then } 3+h_3(3) \text{ else } n+h_3(\bot)$
    $= \text{if } n=0 \text{ then } 0$
           $\text{else if } n=1 \text{ then } 1$
                $\text{else if } n=2 \text{ then } 3$
                    $\text{else if } n=3 \text{ then } \bot \text{ else } \bot$
    $= h_3(n)$

Therefore $h_k(n) = h_3(n)$ for each $k \geq 3$, and the least fixed point is $lub\{h_k \mid k \geq 0\} = h_3$. Note that the last derivation shows that $H\ h_3 = h_3$. ∎

Fixed points for Nonrecursive Functions

Consider the function $g(n) = n^2 - 6n$ defined on the natural numbers N. The function g allows two interpretations in the context of fixed-point theory.

First Interpretation: The natural extension $g^+: N^+ \to N^+$ of g is a continuous function on the elementary domain $N^+ = N \cup \{\bot\}$. Then the least fixed point of g^+, which will be an element of N^+, may be constructed as the least upper bound of the ascending sequence

$$\bot \subseteq g^+(\bot) \subseteq g^+(g^+(\bot)) \subseteq g^+(g^+(g^+(\bot))) \subseteq \dots.$$

But $g^+(\bot) = \bot$, and if $(g^+)^{k-1}(\bot) = \bot$, then $(g^+)^k(\bot) = g^+((g^+)^{k-1}(\bot)) = g^+(\bot) = \bot$. So by induction $(g^+)^k(\bot) = \bot$ for any $k \geq 1$.

Therefore $lub\{(g^+)^k(\bot) \mid k \geq 0\} = lub\{\bot \mid k \geq 0\} = \bot$ is the least fixed point.

In fact, g^+ has three fixed points in $N \cup \{\bot\}$: $g^+(0) = 0$, $g^+(7) = 7$, and $g^+(\bot) = \bot$.

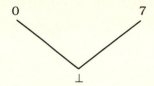

Second Interpretation: Think of $g(n) = n^2 - 6n$ as a rule defining a "recursive" function that just has no actual recursive call of g.

The corresponding functional $G : (N \to N) \to (N \to N)$ is defined by the rule
$$G\ g\ n = n^2 - 6n.$$

A function g satisfies the definition $g(n) = n^2 - 6n$ if and only if it is a fixed point of G—that is, $G\ g = g$.

The fixed point construction proceeds as follows:
$$G^0 \bot n = \bot(n) = \bot$$
$$G^1 \bot n = n^2 - 6n$$
$$G^2 \bot n = n^2 - 6n$$
$$\vdots$$
$$G^k \bot n = n^2 - 6n$$
$$\vdots$$

Therefore the least fixed point is $lub\{G^k(\bot) \mid k \geq 0\} = \lambda n . n^2 - 6n$, which follows the same definition rule as the original function g.

In the first interpretation we computed the least fixed point of the original function g, while in the second we obtained the least fixed point of a functional related to g. These two examples show that the least fixed point construction can be applied to any continuous function, although its importance comes from giving a consistent semantics to functions specified by actual recursive definitions.

Revisiting Denotational Semantics

In Chapter 9 we were tempted to define the meaning of a **while** command in Wren recursively with the semantic equation

> *execute* [[**while** E **do** C]] sto =
>> if *evaluate* [[E]] sto = *bool*(true)
>>> then *execute* [[**while** E **do** C]](*execute* [[C]] sto) else sto.

But this approach violates the principle of compositionality that states that the meaning of any syntactic phrase may be defined only in terms of the meanings of its proper subparts. This circular definition disobeys the principle, since the meaning of *execute* [[**while** E **do** C]] is defined in terms of itself.

Now we can solve this problem by using a fixed-point operator in the definition of the **while** command. The function *execute* [[**while** E **do** C]] satisfies the recursive definition above if and only if it is a fixed point of the functional

> W = λf . λs . if *evaluate* [[E]] s = *bool*(true) then f(*execute* [[C]] s) else s
>> = λf . λs . if *evaluate* [[E]] s = *bool*(true) then (f∘*execute* [[C]]) s else s.

Therefore we obtain a nonrecursive and compositional definition of the meaning of a **while** command by means of

> *execute* [[**while** E **do** C]] = *fix* W.

We gain insight into both the **while** command and fixed-point semantics by constructing a few terms in the ascending chain whose least upper bound is *fix* W,

> $W^0 \subseteq W^1 \subseteq W^2 \subseteq W^3 \subseteq \ldots$ where *fix* W = *lub*{$W^i(\bot)$ | i≥0}.

The fixed-point construction for W proceeds as follows:

$W^0(\bot)$ = λs . $\bot$

$W^1(\bot)$ = $W(W^0 \bot)$
> = λs . if *evaluate* [[E]] s = *bool*(true) then $\bot$(*execute* [[C]] s) else s
> = λs . if *evaluate* [[E]] s = *bool*(true) then $\bot$ else s

Let exC stand for the function *execute* [[C]] and continue the construction.

$W^2(\bot)$ = $W(W^1 \bot)$
> = λs . if *evaluate* [[E]] s = *bool*(true) then $W^1 \bot$ (exC s) else s
> = λs . if *evaluate* [[E]] s = *bool*(true)
>> then (if *evaluate* [[E]] (exC s) = *bool*(true)
>>> then $\bot$ else exC s)
>
> else s

$W^3(\bot) = W(W^2\ \bot)$

   $= \lambda s$. if $evaluate\ [\![E]\!]\ s = bool(\text{true})$ then $W^2\ \bot\ (\text{exC } s)$ else s

   $= \lambda s$. if $evaluate\ [\![E]\!]\ s = bool(\text{true})$

       then (if $evaluate\ [\![E]\!]\ (\text{exC } s) = bool(\text{true})$

          then (if $evaluate\ [\![E]\!]\ (\text{exC } (\text{exC } s)) = bool(\text{true})$

             then $\bot$ else exC (exC s))

       else (exC s))

     else s

   $= \lambda s$. if $evaluate\ [\![E]\!]\ s = bool(\text{true})$

       then (if $evaluate\ [\![E]\!]\ (\text{exC } s) = bool(\text{true})$

          then (if $evaluate\ [\![E]\!]\ (\text{exC}^2\ s) = bool(\text{true})$

             then $\bot$ else (exC^2 s))

       else (exC s))

     else s

$W^4(\bot) = \lambda s$. if $evaluate\ [\![E]\!]\ s = bool(\text{true})$

       then (if $evaluate\ [\![E]\!]\ (\text{exC } s) = bool(\text{true})$

          then (if $evaluate\ [\![E]\!]\ (\text{exC}^2\ s) = bool(\text{true})$

             then (if $evaluate\ [\![E]\!]\ (\text{exC}^3\ s) = bool(\text{true})$

                then $\bot$ else (exC^3 s))

            else (exC^2 s))

       else (exC s))

     else s

In general,

$W^{k+1}(\bot) = W(W^k\ \bot)$

   $= \lambda s$. if $evaluate\ [\![E]\!]\ s = bool(\text{true})$

       then (if $evaluate\ [\![E]\!]\ (\text{exC } s) = bool(\text{true})$

          then (if $evaluate\ [\![E]\!]\ (\text{exC}^2\ s) = bool(\text{true})$

            then (if $evaluate\ [\![E]\!]\ (\text{exC}^3\ s) = bool(\text{true})$

                $\vdots$

             then (if $evaluate\ [\![E]\!]\ (\text{exC}^k\ s) = bool(\text{true})$

              then $\bot$ else (exC^k s))

            else (exC^{k-1} s))

             $\vdots$

          else (exC^2 s))

       else (exC s))

     else s

The function $W^{k+1}(\bot)$ allows the body C of the **while** to be executed up to k times, which means that this approximation to the meaning of the **while** command can handle any instance of a **while** with at most k iterations of the body. Any application of a **while** command will have some finite number of iterations, say n. Therefore its meaning is subsumed in the approximation $W^{n+1}(\bot)$. The least upper bound of this ascending sequence provides semantics for the **while** command: $execute \, [\![\textbf{while } E \textbf{ do } C]\!] = fix \, W = lub\{W^i(\bot) \mid i{\geq}0\}$. Unlike previous examples of fixed-point constructions, we cannot derive a closed form representation of the least fixed point because of the complexity of the definition.

Another way to view the definition of $execute \, [\![\textbf{while } E \textbf{ do } C]\!]$ is in terms of the fixed-point identity, $W(fix \, W) = fix \, W$, where

$$W = \lambda f \, . \, \lambda s \, . \, \text{if } evaluate \, [\![E]\!] \, s = bool(\text{true}) \text{ then } f(execute \, [\![C]\!] \, s) \text{ else } s.$$

In this context, $execute \, [\![\textbf{while } E \textbf{ do } C]\!] = fix \, W$. Now define loop = $fix \, W$.

Then
$execute \, [\![\textbf{while } E \textbf{ do } C]\!] = \text{loop}$
$\qquad\qquad\qquad$ where loop s = (W loop) s
$\qquad\qquad = \text{loop}$
$\qquad\qquad\qquad$ where loop s = if $evaluate \, [\![E]\!] \, s = bool(\text{true})$
$\qquad\qquad\qquad\qquad\qquad$ then loop($execute \, [\![C]\!] \, s$) else s.

The local function "loop" is the least fixed point of W. Following this approach produces the compositional definition of $execute \, [\![\textbf{while } E \textbf{ do } C]\!]$ that we used in our specification of Wren in Figure 9.11.

Fixed-Point Induction

Since recursively defined functions get their meaning from the least fixed-point construction, properties of these functions can be established by means of induction on the construction of the least fixed point $lub\{F^i(\bot) \mid i{\geq}0\}$. For instance, alternate definitions and properties of "closed form" definitions can frequently be proved using fixed-point induction.

Let $\Phi(f)$ be a predicate that describes a property for an arbitrary function f defined recursively. To show Φ holds for the least fixed point F_{fp} of the functional F corresponding to a recursive definition of f, two conditions are needed.

Part 1: Show by induction that Φ holds for each element in the ascending chain
$$\bot \subseteq F(\bot) \subseteq F^2(\bot) \subseteq F^3(\bot) \subseteq \dots.$$

Part 2: Show that Φ remains true when the least upper bound is taken.

Part 2 is handled by defining a class of predicates with the necessary property, the so-called admissible predicates.

Definition: A predicate is called **admissible** if it has the property that whenever the predicate holds for each term in an ascending chain of functions, it also must hold for the least upper bound of that chain. ∎

Theorem: Any finite conjunction of inequalities of the form $\alpha(F) \subseteq \beta(F)$, where α and β are continuous functionals, is an admissible predicate. This includes terms of the form $\alpha(F) = \beta(F)$.

Proof: The proof of this theorem is beyond the scope of this text. See the further readings at the end of the chapter. ∎

Mathematical induction is used to verify the condition in Part 1.

Given a functional $F : (D{\rightarrow}D){\rightarrow}(D{\rightarrow}D)$ for some domain D and an admissible predicate $\Phi(f)$, show the following properties:

(a) $\Phi(\bot)$ holds where $\bot : D{\rightarrow}D$.

(b) For any $i \geq 0$, if $\Phi(F^i(\bot))$, then $\Phi(F^{i+1}(\bot))$.

An alternate version of condition (b) is

(b') For any $f : D{\rightarrow}D$, if $\Phi(f)$, then $\Phi(F(f))$.

Either formulation is sufficient to infer that the predicate Φ holds for every function in the ascending chain $\{F^i(\bot) \mid i \geq 0\}$.

We illustrate fixed-point induction with a simple example.

Example 15: Let $f : N{\rightarrow}N$ be defined by $f(n) =$ if $n=0$ then 1 else $3n^2{-}n{+}f(n{-}1)$. Prove that $f \subseteq \lambda n . n^3{+}n^2$. The recursively defined function f corresponds to the functional $F : (N{\rightarrow}N){\rightarrow}(N{\rightarrow}N)$ given by

F f n = if $n=0$ then 0 else $3n^2{-}n{+}f(n{-}1)$.

Let $\Phi(f)$ be the predicate $f \subseteq \lambda n . n^3{+}n^2$.

(a) Since $\bot \subseteq \lambda n . n^3{+}n^2$, $\Phi(\bot)$ holds.

(b') Suppose $\Phi(f)$—that is, $f \subseteq \lambda n . n^3{+}n^2$.

$$\begin{aligned}
\text{Then F f n} =\ & \text{if } n{=}0 \text{ then } 0 \text{ else } 3n^2{-}n{+}f(n{-}1) \\
\subseteq\ & \text{if } n{=}0 \text{ then } 0 \text{ else } 3n^2{-}n{+}(n{-}1)^3{+}(n{-}1)^2 \\
=\ & \text{if } n{=}0 \text{ then } 0 \text{ else } 3n^2{-}n{+}n^3{-}3n^2{+}3n{-}1{+}n^2{-}2n{+}1 \\
=\ & \text{if } n{=}0 \text{ then } 0 \text{ else } n^3{+}n^2 = n^3{+}n^2 \text{ for } n{\geq}0. \quad \blacksquare
\end{aligned}$$

A property proved by fixed-point induction may involve two functions, say $\Phi(f,g)$. Then satisfying the hypothesis (Part 1) for induction involves the following two steps:

(a) $\Phi(\bot,\bot)$.

(b') For any f and g given by functionals F and G, $\Phi(f,g)$ implies $\Phi(F(f),G(g))$.

Example 16: A recursive definition of a function is called **tail recursive** if each recursive call of the function is the last computation performed by the function. For example, the factorial function can be defined recursively by

   fac n = if n=0 then 1 else n•fac(n-1)

or it can be given a tail recursive definition using

   tailfac (n,p) = if n=0 then p else tailfac(n-1,n•p)

where the factorial of n results from the call, tailfac(n,1).

The correctness of the tail-recursive approach can be verified by fixed-point induction. The functionals that correspond to these two recursive definitions have the form

   $F : (N{\to}N){\to}(N{\to}N)$, where F f n = if n=0 then 1 else n•f(n-1)

and

   $G : (NxN{\to}N){\to}(NxN{\to}N)$, where G g (n,p) = if n=0 then p else g(n-1,n•p).

We want to prove that F_{fp} n = G_{fp} (n,1) for all n$\in$N. The result follows from a stronger assertion—namely, that p•F_{fp}(n) = G_{fp} (n,p) for all n,p$\in$N.

Let $\Phi(f,g)$ be the predicate "p•f(n) = g(n,p) for all n,p$\in$N".

(a) Since f_0 n= $\perp$ = g_0(n,p) for all n,p$\in$N, $\Phi(f_0,g_0)$ holds.

(b) Suppose $\Phi(f_i,g_i)$—that is, p•f_i(n) = g_i(n,p) for all n,p$\in$N. Note that for some values of n, both sides of this equation are $\perp$.

Then g_{i+1}(n,p) = G g_i (n,p)

$\qquad\qquad\qquad$ = if n=0 then p else g_i(n-1,n•p)

$\qquad\qquad\qquad$ = if n=0 then p else n•p•f_i(n-1)   (induction hypothesis)

$\qquad\qquad\qquad$ = p•(if n=0 then 1 else n•f_i(n-1))

$\qquad\qquad\qquad$ = p•f_{i+1}(n).

Therefore by fixed-point induction $\Phi(F_{fp},G_{fp})$ holds—that is,

   p•F_{fp}(n) = G_{fp} (n,p) for all n$\in$N.

The verification of fac n = tailfac(n,1) follows taking p=1, since fac is F_{fp} and tailfac is G_{fp}. ∎

The property p•fac n = tailfac(n,p) can be verified using normal mathematical induction on n as well.

Exercises

1. Show that the converse of the theorem about natural extensions is not true—namely,

False Theorem: Let g be an extension of a function between two sets D and C so that g is a total function from D^+ to C^+. If g is monotonic and continuous, then g is the natural extension of f.

2. Use the construction of the functions h_i as in the example in this section to find the least fixed point for these functionals. State the recursive definitions that give rise to these functionals.

   a) H f n = if n=0 then 3 else f(n+1)

   b) H f n = if n=0 then 0 else (2n–1)+f(n–1)

3. Prove by induction that the approximating functions for the recursive definition

$$\text{fac n = if n=0 then 1 else n•fac(n-1)}$$

   have the form

$$\text{fac}_0 \text{ n} = \perp$$
$$\text{fac}_i \text{ n = if n<i then n! else} \perp \text{ for } i \geq 1.$$

4. Prove that the "unnatural" extension of a constant function is continuous.

5. Complete the proof that if : TxNxN→N is continuous and also show that if : T→N→N→N is continuous.

6. Prove that a generalized composition of continuous functions is continuous.

7. Find a simple (nonrecursive) definition for each of these functions in N→N using a fixed-point construction.

   a) g(n) = if n>0 then 2+g(n–1) else 0

   b) h(n) = if n=0 then 0 else if n=1 then h(n+1)–1 else h(n–1)+1

   c) f(n) = if n=0 then 0 else if n=1 then f(n-1)+1 else n^2

   d) g(n) = if n=0 then 1 else 2n+g(n–1)

   e) h(n) = if n=0 then 1 else if n=1 then 2 else 4n–4+h(n–2)

   f) f(n) = if n=0 then f(n+1)+1 else 1

   g) f(n) = if n>100 then n–10 else f(f(n+11)) (McCarthy's 91 function)

8. Consider the following functional defined on functions over the natural numbers:

$$G : (N→N)→(N→N)$$
$$G = \lambda g . \lambda n . \text{ if n=0 then 2 else g(n)}$$

a) Give and justify a recursive definition that corresponds to this functional—that is, an operational definition of a function that will be a fixed point of G.

b) Define four different functions, g_0, g_1, g_2, and g_3, that are fixed points of the functional G, including the least fixed point, g_0. Carefully prove that g_0 and g_1 are fixed points of G.

c) Draw a diagram showing the relationship "is less defined than or equal" between these four functions.

d) Informally describe the operational behavior of the recursive definition in part a). Which of the four fixed-point functions has the closest behavior to the operational view?

9. Let $T = \{\perp, true, false\}$ be the elementary domain of Boolean values with the bottom element $\perp$. The function $and : T \times T \to T$ must agree with the following truth table:

and	true	false	$\perp$
true	true	false	?
false	false	false	?
$\perp$	?	?	?

Complete this truth-table in *two* ways to produce two different monotonic versions of the function *and* defined on T. Explain how these two *and* functions correspond to the possible interpretations of the predefined Boolean **and** function in a programming language such as Pascal.

10. Prove the Continuity Theorem:

Any functional H defined by the composition of naturally extended functions on elementary domains, constant functions, the identity function, the if-then-else conditional expression, and a function variable f, is continuous.

11. Use fixed-point induction to prove the equality of the following functions in $N \to N$:

$f(n) =$ if $n>5$ then $n-5$ else $f(f(n+13))$

$g(n) =$ if $n>5$ then $n-5$ else $g(n+8)$

12. Use fixed point-induction to prove the equality of the following functions in $N \times N \to N$:

$f(m,n) =$ if $m=0$ then n else $f(2 \bullet m,n)+3$

$g(m,n) =$ if $m=0$ then n else $g(2 \bullet m,n+3)$

Hint: Let $\Phi(f,g)$ be $\forall m>0 \forall n[f(m,n)=g(m,n)$ and $g(m,n+3)=g(m,n)+3]$.

13. Let $f : N \rightarrow N$ be a function defined by a recursive rule of the form

    $$f(n) = \text{if } p(n) \text{ then } n \text{ else } f(f(h(n))),$$

    where $p:N \rightarrow T$ and $h:N \rightarrow N$ are two arbitrary functions.

    Use fixed-point induction to show that $f \circ f = f$ (f is idempotent). *Hint*: Let $\Phi(g)$ be "$f(g(n)) = g(n)$ for all $n \in N$".

14. Let D be the set of natural numbers. Prove that the fixed-point operator

    $$fix : (D \rightarrow D) \rightarrow D \text{ where}$$
    $$fix = \lambda F \, . \, lub\{F^i(\bot) \mid i \geq 0\}$$

    is monotonic and continuous.

15. Let N be the domain of natural numbers. The set of finite lists of natural numbers can be specified by the recursive definition $L = \{nil\} \cup (\mathbf{N} \times L)$, where *nil* is a special constant symbol. One way to give meaning to such a recursive definition is to take L to be the least fixed point of the function $F(X) = \{nil\} \cup (\mathbf{N} \times X)$—namely, $L = F(L)$.

    a) Define and prove those properties that F must satisfy to guarantee the existence of a least fixed point.

    b) Carefully describe the first four terms in the ascending chain that is used in constructing the least fixed point for F.

16. (Thanks to Art Fleck at the University of Iowa for this problem.) Context-free grammars can be viewed as systems of equations where the nonterminals are regarded as variables (or unknowns) over sets of strings; the solution for the start symbol yields the language to be defined. In general, such an equation system has solutions that are tuples of sets, one for each nonterminal. Such solutions can be regarded as fixed points in that when they are substituted in the right-hand side, the result is precisely the solution again. For example (using ε for the null string), the grammar

    A ::= aAc | B
    B ::= bB | C
    C ::= ε | C

    corresponds to the transformation on triples <X,Y,Z> of sets defined by

    $$f(<X,Y,Z>) = <\{a\} \bullet X \bullet \{c\} \cup Y, \{b\} \bullet Y \cup Z, \{\varepsilon\} \cup Z>,$$

    whose fixed point <A, B, C> then satisfies the set equations

    A = {a}•A•{c} ∪ B
    B = {b}•B ∪ C
    C = {ε} ∪ C

    for appropriate $A,B,C \subseteq \{a,b,c\}^*$. For instance, the equations above are satisfied by the sets $A = \{a^n b^* c^n \mid n \geq 0\}$, $B = b^*$, $C = \{\varepsilon\}$.

Show that the equation system corresponding to the grammar above has more than one possible solution so that simply seeking an arbitrary solution is insufficient for formal language purposes. However, the *least* fixed point solution provides exactly the language normally defined by the grammar. Illustrate how the first few steps of the ascending chain in the fixed-point construction lead to the desired language elements for the grammar above, and discuss the connection with derivations in the grammar.

Note: We have the natural partial order for tuples of sets where
$$<S_1, ..., S_k> \subseteq <T_1, ... , T_k> \text{ if } S_i \subseteq T_i \text{ for all } i,\ 1 \leq i \leq k.$$

17. Prove Park's Induction Principle: If $f : D \rightarrow D$ is a continuous function on a domain D and $d \in D$ such that $f\, d \subseteq d$, it follows that *fix* $f \subseteq d$.

18. Let A and B be two domains with functions $f : A \rightarrow B$ and $g : B \rightarrow A$. Prove that *fix* $(f \circ g) = f(fix\ (g \circ f))$.

10.4 LABORATORY: RECURSION IN THE LAMBDA CALCULUS

Before we implement a fixed-point finder to provide recursively defined functions in the lambda calculus evaluator presented in Chapter 5, we describe how a definition mechanism, like a macro system, can be added to the evaluator. An example showing the definition and use of symbols follows.

```
>>> Evaluating the Lambda Calculus <<<
Enter name of source file: cube
    define Thrice = (L f x (f (f (f x))))
    define Sqr = (L x (mul x x))
    define Cube = (L x (mul x (Sqr x)))
    (Thrice Cube 2)
Successful Scan
Successful Parse
Result =  134217728
yes
```

Without the capability of forming definitions, the lambda expressions that we want to evaluate get extremely large. Now the file submitted to the evaluator will contain zero or more definitions followed by one lambda expression to be evaluated. Symbols defined in earlier lines may be used in later definitions.

The system maintains definitions of new symbols in a definition table Tab using predicates extendTab and applyTab in the same with way that environments are handled with the SECD machine in Chapter 8 and Pelican in Chapter 9. Processing the definitions decomposes into two parts: (1) elaboration and (2) expansion. As the list of definitions is processed, the right side of each definition must be expanded and a new binding added to the table.

```
elaborate(Tab,[def(X,E)|Defns],NewTab) :- expand(E,Tab,[ ],NewE),
                                          extendTab(Tab,X,NewE,TempTab),
                                          elaborate(TempTab,Defns,NewTab).
elaborate(Tab,[ ],Tab).
```

The expansion mechanism keeps track of the variable occurrences that have been bound since only free occurrences of symbols are replaced. Moving inside of an abstraction appends the lambda variable to the set of bound variables BV.

```
expand(var(X),Tab,BV,var(X)) :- member(X,BV).          % X is bound
expand(var(X),Tab,BV,E) :- applyTab(Tab,X,E).          % X is free and defined
expand(var(X),Tab,BV,var(X)).                          % X is a free variable
expand(con(C),Tab,BV,con(C)).                          % C is a constant
expand(comb(Rator,Rand),Tab,BV,comb(NewRator,NewRand)) :-
     expand(Rator,Tab,BV,NewRator), expand(Rand,Tab,BV,NewRand).
expand(lamb(X,E),Tab,BV,lamb(X,NewE)) :-
     concat(BV,[X],NewBV), expand(E,Tab,NewBV,NewE).
```

The definition table is manipulated by two predicates. We add a binding Ide ↦ Exp to the definition table Tab using extendTab.

```
extendTab(Tab,Ide,Exp,tab(Ide,Exp,Tab)).
```

We look up an identifier Ide in the definition table Tab using applyTab, which fails if the identifier is not found.

```
applyTab(tab(Ide,Exp,Tab),Ide,Exp).
applyTab(tab(Ide1,Exp1,Tab),Ide,Exp) :- applyTab(Tab,Ide,Exp).
```

The scanner must be altered to recognize the reserved word define and the equal symbol. The parser then produces a list of definitions of the form def(X,E) together with the lambda expression to be evaluated. The definitions are elaborated starting with an empty table nil, the lambda expression is expanded, and then the new expression can be evaluated.

```
go :- nl,write('>>> Evaluating the Lambda Calculus <<<'), nl, nl,
      write('Enter name of source file: '), nl, readfile(File), nl,
      see(File), scan(Tokens), nl, write('Successful Scan'), nl, !,
      seen, program(prog(D,E),Tokens,[eop]), write('Successful Parse'), nl, !,
      elaborate(nil,D,Tab), expand(E,Tab,[ ],Expr), !,
      evaluate(Expr,Result), nl, write('Result = '), pp(Result),nl.
```

Conditional Expressions

Recursive definitions require some way of choosing between the basis case and the recursive case. An expression-oriented language such as the lambda calculus (or a functional programming language) uses a conditional expression

(if e_1 e_2 e_3) = if e_1 then e_2 else e_3.

Recall that function application is left associative so that the abstract syntax tree for this expression takes the form

comb(comb(comb(con(if),e1),e2),e3)

where if has been added as another constant to the applied lambda calculus. To see how to evaluate comb(con(if),e1), consider the behavior that we expect when the value of e1 is true or false.

Case 1: e1 evaluates to true. We want the value of comb(con(if),e1) to be a selector function that takes the next value e2 and ignores the value e3 after it. Therefore take the value of comb(con(if),e1) to be the parsed lambda expression lamb(x,lamb(y, var(x))). Then

comb(comb(comb(con(if),true),e2),e3)
$\Rightarrow$ comb(comb(lamb(x,lamb(y,var(x))),e2),e3)
$\Rightarrow$ comb(lamb(y,e2),e3)
$\Rightarrow$ e2

Case 2: e1 evaluates to false. Now we want the value of comb(con(if),e1) to select the second value, and so we take its value to be lamb(x,lamb(y,var(y))). The expression comb(comb(comb(con(if),false),e2),e3) is left for the reader to reduce.

The Prolog code to carry out the evaluation of "if" is shown below.

```
compute(if, true, lamb(x,(lamb(y,var(x))))).
compute(if, false, lamb(x,(lamb(y,var(y))))).
```

Now we can express a functional corresponding to a recursive definition in the applied lambda calculus.

define Fac = (L f n (if (zerop n) 1 (mul n (f (sub n 1))))).

Notice here the use of a predicate "zerop" that tests whether its argument is equal to zero or not.

Paradoxical Combinator

Given a mechanism (conditional expressions) for describing the functionals corresponding to recursive definitions of functions, the next step is to provide an implementation of the fixed-point operator *fix*. The (untyped) lambda calculus contains expressions that can replicate parts of themselves and thereby act as fixed-point finders satisfying the fixed-point identity. The best know such expression, called the **paradoxical combinator**, is given by

   define **Y** = λf . (λx . f (x x)) (λx . f (x x))

or for the lambda calculus evaluator

   define Y = (L f ((L x (f (x x))) (L x (f (x x))))).

A reduction proves that **Y** satisfies the fixed-point identity.

   Y E =   (λf . (λx . f (x x)) (λx . f (x x))) E
   ⇒   (λx . E (x x)) (λx . E (x x))
   ⇒   E ((λx . E (x x)) (λx . E (x x)))
   ⇒   E (λh . (λx . h (x x)) (λx . h (x x)) E)
   ⇒   E (**Y** E).

The careful reader will have noticed that this calculation follows normal order reduction, a necessary prerequisite for having the **Y** combinator satisfy the fixed-point identity. Following an applicative order strategy leads to a nonterminating reduction.

   Y E =   (λf . (λx . f (x x)) (λx . f (x x))) E
   ⇒   (λf . (λx . f (x x)) (λx . f (x x))) E
   ⇒   (λf . (λx . f (x x)) (λx . f (x x))) E
   ⇒   ....

As motivation for the definition of **Y**, consider a lambda expression W with a free variable f

   define W = λx . f (x x),

and notice what happens when it is applied to itself.

   W W =   (λx . f (x x)) (λx . f (x x)) ⇒ f((λx . f (x x)) (λx . f (x x)))
   =   f(W W) ⇒ f(f((λx . f (x x)) (λx . f (x x))))
   =   f(f(W W)) ⇒ f(f(f((λx . f (x x)) (λx . f (x x)))))
   =   f(f(f(W W))) ⇒ f(f(f(f(W W)))) ⇒ ....

By continuing this reduction, as many copies of f can be created as are needed. The fixed-point operator (W W) for f replicates the function f any number of times. The fixed-point operator **Y** can then be defined for an arbitrary function f by

   Y f = W W

or abstracting the f

   Y = λf . W W.

Actually, the lambda calculus has an infinite number of expressions that can act as fixed-point operators. Three of these are given in the exercises.

Using the paradoxical combinator, we can execute a function defined recursively as shown by the following transcript of a computation with the factorial function.

```
>>> Evaluating the Lambda Calculus <<<
Enter name of source file: fact8
   define Y = (L f ((L x (f (x x))) (L x (f (x x)))))
   define Fac = (L f n (if (zerop n) 1 (mul n (f (sub n 1)))))
   define Factorial = (Y Fac)
   (Factorial 8)
Successful Scan
Successful Parse
Result =   40320
yes
```

Without the mechanism for defining symbols, the expression must be written in its expanded form,

```
((L f ((L x (f (x x))) (L x (f (x x)))))
    (L f n (if (zerop n) 1 (mul n (f (sub n 1)))))
        8),
```

but the results obtained from the lambda calculus evaluator are the same.

Fixed-Point Identity

A second approach to providing a fixed-point operator in the evaluator is to code *fix* in the evaluator as a constant satisfying the fixed-point identity

$$F(fix\ F) = fix\ F.$$

All we have to do is add a reduction rule that carries out the effect of the fixed-point identity from right to left so as to replicate the functional F— namely, $fix\ F \Rightarrow F(fix\ F)$. In the Prolog code for the evaluator, insert the following clause just ahead of the clause for reducing other constants.

```
reduce(comb(con(fix),E),comb(E,comb(con(fix),E))).     % Fixed Point Operator
```

Also the constant "fix" must be added to the scanner and parser. A sample execution follows.

```
Enter name of source file: fixfact8
   define Fac = (L f n (if (zerop n) 1 (mul n (f (sub n 1)))))
   (fix Fac 8)
Successful Scan
Successful Parse
Result =   40320
yes
```

To provide a better understanding of the effect of following the fixed-point identity, consider the definition of factorial with its functional again.

fac n = if n=0 then 1 else n•fac(n-1) and

Fac = λf . λn . if n=0 then 1 else n•f(n-1).

The least fixed point of Fac, (*fix* Fac), serves as the definition of the factorial function. The function (*fix* Fac) is not recursive and can be "reduced" using the fixed-point identity

fix Fac $\Rightarrow$ Fac(*fix* Fac).

The replication of the function encoded in the *fix* operator enables a reduction to create as many copies of the original function as it needs.

(*fix* Fac) 4 $\Rightarrow$ (Fac (*fix* Fac)) 4
$\Rightarrow$ (λf . λn . if n=0 then 1 else n•f(n-1)) (*fix* Fac) 4
$\Rightarrow$ (λn . if n=0 then 1 else n•(*fix* Fac)(n-1)) 4
$\Rightarrow$ if 4=0 then 1 else 4•(*fix* Fac)(4-1)
$\Rightarrow$ 4•((*fix* Fac) 3) $\Rightarrow$ 4•((Fac (*fix* Fac)) 3)
$\Rightarrow$ 4•((λf . λn . if n=0 then 1 else n•f(n-1)) (*fix* Fac) 3)
$\Rightarrow$ 4•((λn . if n=0 then 1 else n•(*fix* Fac)(n-1)) 3)
$\Rightarrow$ 4•(if 3=0 then 1 else 3•(*fix* Fac)(3-1))
$\Rightarrow$ 4•3•((*fix* Fac) 2) $\Rightarrow$ 4•3•(Fac (*fix* Fac))(2)
$\Rightarrow$ 4•3•((λf . λn . if n=0 then 1 else n•f(n-1)) (*fix* Fac) 2)
$\Rightarrow$ 4•3•((λn . if n=0 then 1 else n•(*fix* Fac)(n-1)) 2)
$\Rightarrow$ 4•3•(if 2=0 then 1 else 2•(*fix* Fac)(2-1))
$\Rightarrow$ 4•3•2•((*fix* Fac) 1) $\Rightarrow$ 4•3•2•((Fac (*fix* Fac)) 1)
$\Rightarrow$ 4•3•2•((λf . λn . if n=0 then 1 else n•f(n-1)) (*fix* Fac) 1)
$\Rightarrow$ 4•3•2•((λn . if n=0 then 1 else n•(*fix* Fac)(n-1)) 1)
$\Rightarrow$ 4•3•2•(if 1=0 then 1 else 1•(*fix* Fac)(1-1))
$\Rightarrow$ 4•3•2•1•((*fix* Fac) 0) $\Rightarrow$ 4•3•2•1•((Fac (*fix* Fac)) 0)
$\Rightarrow$ 4•3•2•1•((λf . λn . if n=0 then 1 else n•f(n-1)) (*fix* Fac) 0)
$\Rightarrow$ 4•3•2•1•((λn . if n=0 then 1 else n•(*fix* Fac)(n-1)) 0)
$\Rightarrow$ 4•3•2•1•(if 0=0 then 1 else 0•(*fix* Fac)(0-1))
$\Rightarrow$ 4•3•2•1•1 = 24

Exercises

1. Add the definition mechanism to the lambda calculus evaluator.

2. Extend the lambda calculus evaluator to recognize and interpret the conditional expression (if). Remember to add if to the list of reserved words in the scanner.

3. Show that each of the following expressions is a fixed-point operator in the lambda calculus:

   $\mathbf{Y_r} = \lambda h \ . \ (\lambda g \ . \ \lambda x \ . \ h \ (g \ g) \ x) \ (\lambda g \ . \ \lambda x \ . \ h \ (g \ g) \ x)$

   $\mathbf{Y_f} = \lambda h \ . \ (\lambda x \ . \ h \ (\lambda y \ . \ x \ x \ y)) \ (\lambda x \ . \ h \ (\lambda y \ . \ x \ x \ y))$

   $\mathbf{Y_g} = (\lambda x \ . \ \lambda y \ . \ y \ (x \ x \ y)) \ (\lambda x \ . \ \lambda y \ . \ y \ (x \ x \ y))$

4. Using the following definitions, calculate fib 4 by applying the Fixed-Point Identity.

   $G = \lambda g \ . \ \lambda n \ . \ \text{if } n=0 \text{ then } 0 \text{ else if } n=1 \text{ then } 1 \text{ else } g(n-1) + g(n-2)$

   fib = *fix* G = *fix* $(\lambda g \ . \ \lambda n \ . \ \text{if } n<2 \text{ then } n \text{ else } g(n-1) + g(n-2))$.

5. Add several relational operators, such as = and <, to the lambda calculus evaluator and use them to test other recursive definitions.

10.5 FURTHER READING

Many of the books that contain material on denotational semantics also treat domain theory. In particular, see [Allison86], [Schmidt88], [Stoy77], and [Watt91]. David Schmidt's book has a chapter on recursively defined domains, including the inverse limit construction that justifies their existence. [Paulson87] also contains material on domain theory. For a more advanced treatment of domain theory, see [Mosses90] and [Gunter90]. Dana Scott's description of domains and models for the lambda calculus may be found in [Scott76], [Scott80], and [Scott82].

The early papers on fixed-point semantics [Manna72] and [Manna73] are a good source of examples, although the notation shows its age. Much of this material is summarized in [Manna74]. This book contains a proof of the theorem about admissible predicates for fixed-point induction. [Bird76] also contains considerable material on fixed-point semantics.

Most books on functional programming or the lambda calculus contain discussions of the paradoxical combinator and the fixed-point identity. Good examples include [Field88], [Peyton Jones87], and [Reade89]. For an advanced presentation of recursion in the lambda calculus, see [Barendregt84].

Chapter 11
AXIOMATIC SEMANTICS

The techniques for operational semantics, introduced in Chapters 5 through 8, and denotational semantics, discussed in Chapters 9 and 10, are based on the notion of the "state of a machine". For example, in the denotational semantics of Wren, the semantic equation for the execution of a statement is a mapping from the current machine state, represented by the store, input stream and output stream, to a new machine state.

Based on methods of logical deduction from predicate logic, axiomatic semantics is more abstract than denotational semantics in that there is no concept corresponding to the state of the machine. Rather, the semantic meaning of a program is based on assertions about relationships that remain the same each time the program executes. The relation between an initial assertion and a final assertion following a piece of code captures the essence of the semantics of the code. Another piece of code that defines the algorithm slightly differently yet produces the same final assertion will be semantically equivalent provided any initial assertions are also the same. The proofs that the assertions are true do not rely on any particular architecture for the underlying machine; rather they depend on the relationships between the values of the variables. Although individual values of variables change as a program executes, certain relationships among them remain the same. These invariant relationships form the assertions that express the semantics of the program.

11.1 CONCEPTS AND EXAMPLES

Axiomatic semantics has two starting points: a paper by Robert Floyd and a somewhat different approach introduced by C. A. R. Hoare. We use the notation presented by Hoare. Axiomatic semantics is commonly associated with proving a program to be correct using a purely static analysis of the text of the program. This static approach is in clear contrast to the dynamic approach, which tests a program by focusing on how the values of variables change as a program executes. Another application of axiomatic semantics is to consider assertions as program specifications from which the program code itself can be derived. We look at this technique briefly in section 11.5.

Axiomatic semantics does have some limitations: Side effects are disallowed in expressions; the **goto** command is difficult to specify; aliasing is not allowed; and scope rules are difficult to describe unless we require all identifier names to be unique. Despite these limitations, axiomatic semantics is an attractive technique because of its potential effect on software development:

- The development of "bug free" algorithms that have been proved correct.

- The automatic generation of program code based on specifications.

Axiomatic Semantics of Programming Languages

In proving the correctness of a program, we use an applied predicate (first-order) logic with equality whose individual variables correspond to program variables and whose function symbols include all the operations that occur in program expressions. Therefore we view expressions such as "2*n+1" and "x+y>0" as terms in the predicate logic (mathematical terms) whose values are determined by the current assignment to the individual variables in the logic language. Furthermore, we assume the standard mathematical and logical properties of operations modeled in the logic—for example, $2*3+1 = 7$ and $4+1>0 =$ true.

An **assertion** is a logical formula constructed using the individual variables, individual constants, and function symbols in the applied predicate calculus. When each variable in an assertion is assigned a value (determined by the value of the corresponding program variable), the assertion becomes valid (true) or invalid (false) under a standard interpretation of the constants and functions in the logical language.

Typically, assertions consist of a conjunction of elementary statements describing the logical properties of program variables, such as stating that a variable takes values from a particular set, say m < 5, or defining a relation among variables, such as $k = n^2$. In many cases, assertions correspond directly to Boolean expressions in Wren, and the two notions are frequently confused in axiomatic semantics. We maintain a distinction between assertions and Boolean expressions by always presenting assertions in an italic font *like this*. In some instances, assertions use features of predicate logic that go beyond what is expressible in Boolean expressions—namely, when universal quantifiers, existential quantifiers, and implications occur in formulas.

For the purposes of axiomatic semantics, a program reduces to the meaning of a command, which in the abstract syntax includes a sequence of commands. We describe the semantics of a program by annotating it with assertions that are always valid when the control of the program reaches the points of the assertions. In particular, the meaning or correctness of a command (a program) is described by placing an assertion, called a **precondition**, before a command and another assertion, called a **postcondition**, after the command:

{ PRE } C *{ POST }*.

Therefore the meaning of command C can be viewed as the ordered pair *<PRE, POST>*, called a specification of C. We say that the command C is **correct with respect to the specification** given by the precondition and postcondition provided that if the command is executed with values that make the precondition true, the command halts and the resulting values make the postcondition true. Extending this notion to an entire program supplies a meaning of program correctness and a semantics to programs in a language.

Definition: A program is **partially correct** with respect to a precondition and a postcondition provided that if the program is started with values that make the precondition true, the resulting values make the postcondition true when the program halts (if ever). If it can also be shown that the program terminates when started with values satisfying the precondition, the program is called (**totally**) **correct.**

Partial Correctness = (Precondition and Termination ⊃ Postcondition)

Total Correctness = (Partial Correctness and Termination). ∎

We focus on proofs of partial correctness for programs in Wren and Pelican in the next two sections and briefly look at proofs of termination in section 11.4. The goal of axiomatic semantics is to provide axioms and proof rules that capture the intended meaning of each command in a programming language. These rules are constructed so that a specification for a given command can be deduced, thereby proving the partial correctness of the command relative to the specification. Such a deduction consists of a finite sequence of assertions (formulas of the predicate logic) each of which is either the precondition, an axiom associated with a program command, or a rule of inference whose premises have already been established.

Before considering the axioms and proof rules for Wren, we need to discuss the problem of specifications briefly. Extensive literature has dealt with the difficult problem of accurate specifications of algorithms. Programmers frequently miss the subtlety inherent in precise specifications. As an example, consider the following specification of the problem of finding the smaller of two nonnegative integers:

PRE = *{ m≥0 and n≥0 }*

POST = *{ minimum≤m and minimum≤n and minimum≥0 }*.

Unhappily, this specification is satisfied by the command "minimum := 0", which does not satisfy the informal description. We do not have space in this text to consider the problems of accurate specifications, but correctness proofs of programs only serve the programmer when the proof is carried out relative to correct specifications.

11.2 AXIOMATIC SEMANTICS FOR WREN

Again Wren serves as the initial programming language for semantic specification. In the next section we expand the presentation to Pelican with constants, procedures, blocks, and recursion. For each of these languages, axiomatic semantics focuses on assertions that describe the logical relationships between the values of program variables at points in a program.

An axiomatic analysis of Wren program behavior concentrates on the commands of the programming language. In the absence of side effects, expressions in Wren can be treated as mathematical expressions and be evaluated using mathematical rules. We assume that any program submitted for semantic analysis has already been verified as syntactically correct, including adherence to all context conditions. Therefore the declarations (of variables only) in Wren can be ignored in describing its axiomatic semantics. In the next section we investigate the impact of constant and procedure declarations on this approach to semantics.

Assignment Command

The first command we examine is assignment, beginning with three examples of preconditions and postconditions for assignment commands:

Example 1: $\{\,k = 5\,\}$ k := k + 1 $\{\,k = 6\,\}$

Example 2: $\{\,j = 3 \text{ and } k = 4\}$ j := j + k $\{\,j = 7 \text{ and } k = 4\,\}$

Example 3: $\{\,a > 0\,\}$ a := a − 1 $\{\,a \geq 0\,\}$.

For these simple examples, correctness is easy to prove either proceeding from the precondition to the postcondition or from the postcondition to the precondition. However, many times starting with the postcondition and working backward to derive the precondition proves easier (at least initially). We assume expressions with no side effects in the assignment commands, so only the the target variable is changed. "Working backward" means substituting the expression on the right-hand side of the assignment for every occurrence of the target variable in the postcondition and deriving the precondition, following the principle that whatever is true about the target variable after the assignment must be true about the expression before the assignment. Consider the following examples:

Example 1

> { k = 6 }   postcondition
> { k + 1 = 6 }   substituting k + 1 for k in postcondition
> { k = 5 }   precondition, after simplification.

Example 2

> { j = 7 and k = 4 }   postcondition
> { j + k = 7 and k = 4 }   substituting j + k for j in postcondition
> { j = 3 and k = 4}   precondition, after simplification.

Example 3

> { a ≥ 0 }   postcondition
> { a − 1 ≥ 0 }   substituting a − 1 for a in postcondition
> { a ≥ 1 }   simplification
> { a > 0 }   precondition, since a≥1 ≡ a>0 assuming a is an integer.

Given an assignment of the form V := E and a postcondition P, we use the notation P[V→E] (as in Chapter 5) to indicate the consistent substitution of E in place of each free occurrence of V in P. This notation enables us to give an axiomatic definition for the assignment command as

$$\{ P[V{\rightarrow}E] \}\ V := E\ \{ P \} \qquad\qquad \text{(Assign)}$$

The substitution operation P[V→E] needs to be defined carefully since formulas in the predicate calculus allow both free and bound occurrences of variables. This task will be given as an exercise at the end of this section.

If we view assertions as predicates—namely, Boolean valued expressions with a parameter—the axiom can be stated

$$\{ P(E) \}\ V := E\ \{ P(V) \}.$$

A proof of correctness following the assignment axiom can be summarized by writing

> { a > 0 } ⊃
>
> { a ≥ 1 } ⊃
>
> { a − 1 ≥ 0 } = { P(a−1) }
>
>   a := a−1
>
> { a ≥ 0 } = { P(a) }

where ⊃ denotes logical implication. The axiom that specifies "V := E" essentially states that if we can prove a property about E before the assignment, the same property about V holds after the assignment.

At first glance the assignment axiom may seem more complicated than it needs to be with its use of substitution in the precondition. To appreciate the subtlety of assignment, consider the following unsound axiom:

$$\{ \textit{true} \} \ V := E \ \{ V = E \}.$$

This apparently reasonable axiom for assignment is unsound because it allows us to prove false assertions—for example,

$$\{ \textit{true} \} \ m := m+1 \ \{ m = m+1 \}.$$

Input and Output

The commands **read** and **write** assume the existence of input and output files. We use "IN = " and "OUT = " to indicate the contents of these files in assertions and brackets to represent a list of items in a file; so [1,2,3] represents a file with the three integers 1, 2 and 3. We consider the left side of the list to be the start of the file and the right side to be the end. For example, affixing the value 4 onto the end of the file [1,2,3] is represented by writing [1,2,3][4]. In a similar way, 4 is prefixed to the file [1,2,3] by writing [4][1,2,3]. Juxtaposition means concatenation.

Capital letters are used to indicate some unspecified item or sequence of items; [κ]L thus represents a file starting with the value κ and followed by any sequence L, which may or may not be empty. For contrast, small caps denote numerals, and large caps denote lists of numerals. Exploiting this notation, we specify the semantics of the **read** command as removing the first value from the input file and "assigning" it to the variable that appears in the command.

$$\{ IN = [\kappa]L \ and \ P[V{\rightarrow}\kappa] \} \ \textbf{read} \ V \ \{ IN = L \ and \ P \} \tag{Read}$$

The **write** command appends the current value denoted by the expression to the end of the output file. Our axiomatic rule also specifies that the value of the expression is not changed and that no other assertions are changed.

$$\{ OUT=L \ and \ E=\kappa \ and \ P \} \ \textbf{write} \ E \ \{ OUT=L[\kappa] \ and \ E=\kappa \ and \ P \} \tag{Write}$$

where P is any arbitrary set of additional assertions.

The symbols acting as variables in the Read axiom serve two different purposes. Those symbols that describe the input list, a numeral and a list of numerals, stay constant throughout any deduction containing them. We refer to symbols of this type as logical variables, meaning that their bindings are frozen during the deduction (see Appendix A for a discussion of logical variables in Prolog). In contrast, the variable V and any variables in the expression E correspond to program variables and may represent different values during a verification. The values of these variables depend on the current assignment of values to program variables at the point where the assertion containing them occurs. When applying the axioms and proof rules of axiomatic semantics, we will use uppercase letters for logical variables and lowercase letters for individual variables corresponding to program variables.

The axioms and rules of inference in an axiomatic definition of a programming language are really axiom and rule schemes. The symbols "V", "E", and "P" need to be replaced by actual variables, expressions, and formulas, respectively, to form instances of the axioms and rules for use in a deduction.

Rules of Inference

For other axiomatic specifications, we introduce rules of inference that have the form

$$\frac{H_1, \ H_2, \ ..., \ H_n}{H}$$

This notation can be interpreted as

If H_1, H_2, ..., H_n have all been verified, we may conclude that H is valid.

Note the similarity with the notation used by structural operational semantics in Chapter 8. The sequencing of two commands serves as the first example of a rule of inference:

$$\frac{\{P\} \ C_1 \ \{Q\}, \ \{Q\} \ C_2 \ \{R\}}{\{P\} \ C_1; C_2 \ \{R\}} \qquad \text{(Sequence)}$$

This rule says that if starting with the precondition P we can prove Q after executing C_1 and starting with Q we can prove R after C_2, we can conclude that starting with the precondition P, R is true after executing C_1; C_2. Observe that the middle assertion Q is "forgotten" in the conclusion.

The **if** command involves a choice between alternatives. Two paths lead through an **if** command; therefore, if we can prove each path is correct given the appropriate value of the Boolean expression, the entire command is correct.

$$\frac{\{P \text{ and } B\} \ C_1 \ \{Q\}, \ \{P \text{ and } (\text{not } B)\} \ C_2 \ \{Q\}}{\{P\} \ \textbf{if} \ B \ \textbf{then} \ C_1 \ \textbf{else} \ C_2 \ \textbf{end if} \ \{Q\}} \qquad \text{(If-Else)}$$

Note that the Boolean expression B is used as part of the assertions in the premises of the rule. The axiomatic definition for the single alternative **if** is similar, except that for the false branch we need to show that the final assertion can be derived directly from the initial assertion P when the condition B is false.

$$\frac{\{P \text{ and } B\} \ C \ \{Q\}, \ (P \text{ and } (\text{not } B)) \supset Q}{\{P\} \ \textbf{if } B \textbf{ then } C \textbf{ end if } \{Q\}} \qquad \text{(If-Then)}$$

Before presenting the axiomatic definition for **while**, we examine some general rules applicable to all commands and verify a short program. Sometimes the result that is proved is stronger than required. In this case it is possible to weaken the postcondition.

$$\frac{\{P\} \ C \ \{Q\}, \ Q \supset R}{\{P\} \ C \ \{R\}} \qquad \text{(Weaken)}$$

Other times the given precondition is stronger than necessary to complete the proof.

$$\frac{P \supset Q, \ \{Q\} \ C \ \{R\}}{\{P\} \ C \ \{R\}} \qquad \text{(Strengthen)}$$

Finally, it is possible to relate assertions by the logical relationships *and* and *or*.

$$\frac{\{P_1\} \ C \ \{Q_1\}, \ \{P_2\} \ C \ \{Q_2\}}{\{P_1 \text{ and } P_2\} \ C \ \{Q_1 \text{ and } Q_2\}} \qquad \text{(And)}$$

$$\frac{\{P_1\} \ C \ \{Q_1\}, \ \{P_2\} \ C \ \{Q_2\}}{\{P_1 \text{ or } P_2\} \ C \ \{Q_1 \text{ or } Q_2\}} \qquad \text{(Or)}$$

Example: For a first example of a proof of correctness, consider the following program fragment.

```
read x; read y;
if x < y   then write x
           else write y
end if
```

To avoid the runtime error of reading from an empty file, the initial assertion requires two or more items in the input file, which we indicate by writing two items in brackets before the rest of the file. The output file may or may not be empty initially.

Precondition: $P = \{ IN = [M,N]L_1 \text{ and } OUT = L_2 \}$

The program writes to the output file the minimum of the two values read. To specify this as an assertion, we consider two alternatives:

Postcondition: $Q = \{ (OUT = L_2[M] \text{ and } M < N) \text{ or } (OUT = L_2[N] \text{ and } M \geq N) \}$

The correct assertion after the first **read** command is

$R = \{ IN = [N]L_1 \text{ and } OUT = L_2 \text{ and } x = M \},$

and after the second **read** command the correct assertion is

$$S = \{ IN = L_1 \text{ and } OUT = L_2 \text{ and } x = M \text{ and } y = N \}.$$

We obtain these assertions by working the axiom for the **read** command backward through the first two commands. The verification of these assertions can then be presented in a top-down manner as follows:

$\{ IN = [M,N]L_1 \text{ and } OUT = L_2 \} \supset$
$\{ IN = [M,N]L_1 \text{ and } OUT = L_2 \text{ and } M = M \} = P'$
    read x;
$\{ IN = [N]L_1 \text{ and } OUT = L_2 \text{ and } x = M \} \supset$
$\{ IN = [N]L_1 \text{ and } OUT = L_2 \text{ and } x = M \text{ and } N = N \} = R'$
    read y;
$\{ IN = L_1 \text{ and } OUT = L_2 \text{ and } x = M \text{ and } y = N \} = S.$

Since $\{ x < y \text{ or } x \geq y \}$ is always true, we can add it to our assertion without changing its truth value. After manipulating this assertion using the logical equivalence (using the symbol $\equiv$ for equivalence),

$$(P_1 \text{ and } (P_2 \text{ or } P_3)) \equiv ((P_1 \text{ and } P_2) \text{ or } (P_1 \text{ and } P_3)),$$

we have the assertion:

$S' = \{ (IN = L_1 \text{ and } OUT = L_2 \text{ and } x = M \text{ and } y = N \text{ **and** } (x < y \text{ **or** } x \geq y) \} \equiv$

$\{ (IN = L_1 \text{ and } OUT = L_2 \text{ and } x = M \text{ and } y = N \text{ **and** } x < y) \text{ **or** }$
    $(IN = L_1 \text{ and } OUT = L_2 \text{ and } x = M \text{ and } y = N \text{ **and** } x \geq y) \}.$

Representing this assertion as $\{ P_1 \text{ or } P_2 \}$, we now must prove the validity of

$\{ P_1 \text{ or } P_2 \}$
    if x < y **then write** x
              else write y
    end if
$\{ Q \}$

where Q is $\{ (OUT = L_2[M] \text{ and } M < N) \text{ or } (OUT = L_2[N] \text{ and } M \geq N) \}$. Therefore we must prove valid

$$\{ (P_1 \text{ or } P_2) \text{ and } B \} \text{ **write** } x \{ Q \}$$

and $\{ (P_1 \text{ or } P_2) \text{ and } (\text{not } B) \} \text{ **write** } y \{ Q \}$

where B is $\{ x < y \}$.

$\{ (P_1 \text{ or } P_2) \text{ and } B \}$ simplifies to

$$T_1 = \{ IN = L_1 \text{ and } OUT = L_2 \text{ and } x = M \text{ and } y = N \text{ and } x < y \}.$$

After executing "**write** x", we have

$$\{ IN = L_1 \text{ and } OUT = L_2[M] \text{ and } x = M \text{ and } y = N \text{ and } M < N \}.$$

Call this Q_1. Similarly $\{$ $(P_1$ or $P_2)$ and (not $B)$ $\}$ simplifies to

  $T_2 = \{$ $IN = L_1$ and $OUT = L_2$ and $x = M$ and $y = N$ and $x \geq y$ $\}$.

After the "**write** y" we have

  $\{IN = L_1$ and $OUT = L_2[N]$ and $x = M$ and $y = N$ and $M \geq N\}$.

Call this Q_2. Since $Q_1 \supset (Q_1$ or $Q_2.)$ and $Q_2 \supset (Q_1$ or $Q_2)$ we replace each individual assertion with

  Q_1 or $Q_2 \equiv$
    $((IN = L_1$ and $OUT = L_2[M]$ and $x = M$ and $y = N$ and $M < N)$ or
    $(IN = L_1$ and $OUT = L_2[N]$ and $x = M$ and $y = N$ and $M \geq N))$.

Finally we weaken the conclusion by removing the parts of the assertion about the input file and the values of x and y to arrive at our final assertion, the postcondition. Figure 11.1 displays the deduction as proof trees using the abbreviations given above. Note that we omit "**end if**" to save space. ∎

$$\frac{P \supset P', \quad \{P\} \text{ read } x \{R\}}{\{P\} \text{ read } x \{R\}} \qquad \frac{R \supset R', \quad \{R\} \text{ read } y \{S\}, \quad S \supset S', \quad S' \supset (P_1 \text{ or } P_2)}{\{R\} \text{ read } y \{P_1 \text{ or } P_2\}}$$
$$\frac{}{\{P\} \text{ read } x \; ; \text{ read } y \{P_1 \text{ or } P_2\}}$$

$$\frac{(((P_1 \text{ or } P_2) \text{ and } B) \supset T_1), \quad \{T_1\} \text{ write } x \{Q_1\}}{\{(P_1 \text{ or } P_2) \text{ and } B\} \text{ write } x \{Q_1\}, \qquad Q_1 \supset (Q_1 \text{ or } Q_2)}$$
$$\frac{}{\{(P_1 \text{ or } P_2) \text{ and } B\} \text{ write } x \{Q_1 \text{ or } Q_2\}}$$

$$\frac{(((P_1 \text{ or } P_2) \text{ and (not } B)) \supset T_2), \quad \{T_2\} \text{ write } y \{Q_2\}}{\{(P_1 \text{ or } P_2) \text{ and (not } B)\} \text{ write } y \{Q_2\}, \qquad Q_2 \supset (Q_1 \text{ or } Q_2)}$$
$$\frac{}{\{(P_1 \text{ or } P_2) \text{ and (not } B)\} \text{ write } y \{Q_1 \text{ or } Q_2\}}$$

$$\frac{\{(P_1 \text{ or } P_2) \text{ and } B\} \text{ write } x \{Q_1 \text{ or } Q_2\}, \quad \{(P_1 \text{ or } P_2) \text{ and (not } B)\} \text{ write } y \{Q_1 \text{ or } Q_2\}}{\{P_1 \text{ or } P_2\} \text{ if } x < y \text{ then write } x \text{ else write } y \quad \{Q1 \text{ or } Q_2\}, \qquad (Q_1 \text{ or } Q_2) \supset Q}$$
$$\frac{}{\{P_1 \text{ or } P_2\} \text{ if } x < y \text{ then write } x \text{ else write } y \{Q\}}$$

$$\frac{\{P\} \text{ read } x \; ; \text{ read } y \{P_1 \text{ or } P_2\}, \quad \{P_1 \text{ or } P_2\} \text{ if } x < y \text{ then write } x \text{ else write } y \{Q\}}{\{P\} \text{ read } x \; ; \text{ read } y \; ; \text{ if } x < y \text{ then write } x \text{ else write } y \{Q\}}$$

Figure 11.1: Derivation Tree for the Correctness Proof

While Command and Loop Invariants

Continuing the axiomatic definition of Wren, we specify the **while** command:

$$\frac{\{\,P \text{ and } B\,\}\ C\ \{\,P\,\}}{\{\,P\,\}\ \textbf{while } B \textbf{ do } C \textbf{ end while }\ \{\,P \text{ and } (\text{not } B)\,\}} \qquad \text{(While)}$$

In this definition P is called the **loop invariant**. This assertion captures the essence of the **while** loop: It must be true initially, it must be preserved after the loop body executes, and, combined with the exit condition, it implies the assertion that follows the loop. Figure 11.2 illustrates the situation.

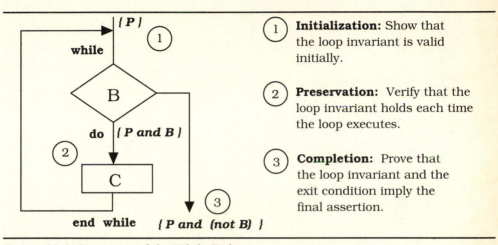

① **Initialization:** Show that the loop invariant is valid initially.

② **Preservation:** Verify that the loop invariant holds each time the loop executes.

③ **Completion:** Prove that the loop invariant and the exit condition imply the final assertion.

Figure 11.2: Structure of the While Rule

The purpose of the Preservation step is to verify the premise for the While rule shown above. The Initialization and Completion steps are used to tie the **while** loop into its surrounding code and assertions.

Example: Discovering the loop invariant requires insight. Consider the following program fragment that calculates factorial, as indicated by the final assertion. Remember, we use lowercase letters for variables and uppercase (small caps) to represent numerals that remain constant.

```
{ N ≥ 0 }
    k := N;  f := 1;
    while k > 0 do          { loop invariant }
            f := f * k;   k := k – 1;
    end while
{ f = N! }
```

The loop invariant involves a relationship between variables that remains the same no matter how many times the loop executes. The loop invariant also involves the **while** loop condition, $k > 0$ in the example above, modified to include the exit case, which is $k = 0$ in this case. Combining these conditions, we have $k \geq 0$ as part of the loop invariant. Other components of the loop invariant involve the variables that change values as a result of loop execution, f and k in the program above. We also look at the final assertion after the loop and notice that N! needs to be involved. For this program, we can discover the loop invariant by examining how N! is calculated for a simple case, say $N = 5$. We examine the calculation in progress at the end of the loop where k has just been decremented to 3.

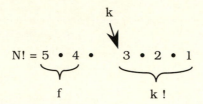

The variable f has stored the part of the computation completed so far, $5 \cdot 4$, and k has the starting value for the remaining computation. So k! represents the rest of the value to be computed. The complete value is $f \cdot k!$, which, at all times, must equal N!. We can show this in a table:

k	k!	f	f•k!
5	120	1	120
4	24	5	120
3	6	20	120
2	2	60	120
1	1	120	120
0	1	120	120

Now we have our loop invariant: $\{ f \bullet k! = N! \text{ and } k \geq 0 \}$.

We show the loop invariant is initially true by deriving it from the initialization commands and the precondition.

$\{ N \geq 0 \} \supset$
$\{ N! = N! \text{ and } N \geq 0 \}$
   k := N;
$\{ k! = N! \text{ and } k \geq 0 \} \supset$
$\{ 1 \bullet k! = N! \text{ and } k \geq 0 \}$
   f := 1;
$\{ f \bullet k! = N! \text{ and } k \geq 0 \}$

Note that N! = N! is a tautology when N ≥ 0, so we can replace it with true. We also know for any clause P that (P and true) is equivalent to P. Thus we can begin with the initial assertion N ≥ 0. Some of these implications are actually logical equivalences, but we write implications because that is all we need for the proofs.

To show that the loop invariant is preserved, we start with the invariant at the bottom of the loop and push it back through the body of the loop to prove { P and B }, the loop invariant combined with the entry condition at the top of the loop. Summarizing the proof gives us the following:

$$\{\, f{\bullet}k! = \text{N}! \text{ and } k > 0 \,\} \supset$$
$$\{\, f{\bullet}k{\bullet}(k{-}1)! = \text{N}! \text{ and } k > 0 \,\}$$
$$\qquad f := f * k;$$
$$\{\, f{\bullet}(k{-}1)! = \text{N}! \text{ and } k > 0 \,\} \supset$$
$$\{\, f{\bullet}(k{-}1)! = \text{N}! \text{ and } k{-}1 \geq 0 \,\}$$
$$\qquad k := k - 1;$$
$$\{\, f{\bullet}k! = \text{N}! \text{ and } k \geq 0 \,\}$$

We rely on the fact that k is an integer to transform the condition k > 0 into the equivalent condition k−1 ≥ 0.

Finally, we must prove the assertion after the **while** loop can be derived from (P and not B).

$$\{\, f \bullet k! = \text{N}! \text{ and } k \geq 0 \text{ and } (\text{not } k > 0) \,\} \supset$$
$$\{\, f \bullet k! = \text{N}! \text{ and } k \geq 0 \text{ and } k \leq 0 \,\} \supset$$
$$\{\, f \bullet k! = \text{N}! \text{ and } k = 0 \,\} \supset$$
$$\{\, f = \text{N}! \text{ and } k = 0 \,\} \supset \{\, f = \text{N}! \,\}$$

The last simplification is a weakening of the assertion { f = N! and k = 0 }. ∎

While proving this algorithm to be correct, we avoid some problems that occur when the algorithm is executed on a real computer. For example, the factorial function grows very rapidly, and it does not take a large value of N for N! to exceed the storage capacity for integers on a particular machine. However, we want to develop a machine-independent definition of the semantics of a programming language, so we ignore these restrictions. We summarize our axiomatic definitions for Wren in Figure 11.3, including the Skip axiom, which makes no change in the assertion.

Assign	$\{ P[V{\rightarrow}E] \} \ V := E \ \{ P \}$
Read	$\{ IN = [\kappa]L \ and \ P[V{\rightarrow}K] \} \ \textbf{read} \ V \ \{ IN = L \ and \ P \}$
Write	$\{ OUT=[L] \ and \ E=\kappa \ and \ P \} \ \textbf{write} \ E \ \{ OUT= L[\kappa] \ and \ E=\kappa \ and \ P \}$
Skip	$\{ P \} \ \textbf{skip} \ \{ P \}$
Sequence	$\dfrac{\{P\} \ C_1 \ \{Q\}, \ \ \{Q\} \ C_2 \ \{R\}}{\{P\} \ C_1; C_2 \ \{R\}}$
If-Then	$\dfrac{\{P \ and \ B\} \ C \ \{Q\}, \ \ (P \ and \ not \ B) \supset Q}{\{P\} \ \textbf{if} \ B \ \textbf{then} \ C \ \textbf{end if} \ \{Q\}}$
If-Else	$\dfrac{\{P \ and \ B\} \ C_1 \ \{Q\}, \ \ \{P \ and \ not \ B\} \ C_2 \ \{Q\}}{\{P\} \ \textbf{if} \ B \ \textbf{then} \ C_1 \ \textbf{else} \ C_2 \ \textbf{end if} \ \{Q\}}$
While	$\dfrac{\{P \ and \ B\} \ C \ \{P\}}{\{P\} \ \textbf{while} \ B \ \textbf{do} \ C \ \textbf{end while} \ \{P \ and \ not \ B\}}$
Weaken Postcondition	$\dfrac{\{P\} \ C \ \{Q\}, \ \ Q \supset R}{\{P\} \ C \ \{R\}}$
Strengthen Precondition	$\dfrac{P \supset Q, \ \ \{Q\} \ C \ \{R\}}{\{P\} \ C \ \{R\}}$
And	$\dfrac{\{P\} \ C \ \{Q\}, \ \ \{P'\} \ C \ \{Q'\}}{\{P \ and \ P'\} \ C \ \{Q \ and \ Q'\}}$
Or	$\dfrac{\{P\} \ C \ \{Q\}, \ \ \{P'\} \ C \ \{Q'\}}{\{P \ or \ P'\} \ C \ \{Q \ or \ Q'\}}$

Figure 11.3 Axiomatic Semantics for Wren

More on Loop Invariants

Constructing loop invariants for **while** commands in a program provides the main challenge when proving correctness with an imperative language. Although no simple formula solves this problem, several general principles can help in analyzing the logic of the loop when finding an invariant.

- A loop invariant describes a relationship among the variables that does not change as the loop is executed. The variables may change their values, but the relationship stays constant.
- Constructing a table of values for the variables that change often reveals a property among variables that does not change.
- Combining what has already been computed at some stage in the loop with what has yet to be computed may yield a constant of some sort.

- An expression related to the test B for the loop can usually be combined with the assertion { *not B* } to produce part of the postcondition.
- A possible loop invariant can be assembled to attempt to carry out the proof. We need enough to produce the final postcondition but not so much that we cannot establish the initialization step or prove the preservation of the loop invariant.

Example: Consider a short program that computes the exponential function for two nonnegative integers, M and N. The code specified by means of a precondition and postcondition follows:

```
{ M>0 and N≥0 }
    a := M;  b := N;  k := 1;
    while b>0 do
        if b=2*(b/2)
            then a := a*a;  b := b/2
            else b := b-1;  k := k*a
        end if
    end while
{ k = Mᴺ }
```

Recall that division in Wren is integer division. We begin by tracing the algorithm with two small numbers, M=2 and N=7, and thereby build a table of values to search for a suitable loop invariant. The value M^N = 128 remains constant throughout the execution of the loop. Since the goal of the code is to compute the exponential function, we add a column to the table for the value of a^b, since a is the variable that gets multiplied.

a	b	k	a^b
2	7	1	128
2	6	2	64
4	3	2	64
4	2	8	16
16	1	8	16
16	0	128	1

Observe that a^b changes exactly when k changes. In fact, their product is constant, namely 128. This relationship suggests that $k \bullet a^b = M^N$ will be part of the invariant. Furthermore, the loop variable b decreases to 0 but always stays nonnegative. The relation b≥0 seems to be invariant, and when combined with "not B", which is b≤0, establishes b=0 at the end of the loop. When b=0 is joined with $k \bullet a^b = M^N$, we get the postcondition $k = M^N$. Thus we have as a loop invariant:

$$\{ b \geq 0 \text{ and } k \bullet a^b = M^N \}.$$

Finally, we verify the program by checking that the loop invariant is consistent with an application of the rule for the **while** command in the given setting.

Initialization

$\{$ *M>0 and N$\geq$0* $\}$ $\supset$
$\{$ *M=M>0 and N=N$\geq$0 and 1=1* $\}$
$\qquad$ a := M; b := N; k := 1;
$\{$ *a=M>0 and b=N$\geq$0 and k=1* $\}$ $\supset$
$\{$ *b$\geq$0 and k$\bullet$a^b=M^N* $\}$

Preservation

Case 1: b is even, that is, b = 2i $\geq$ 0 for some i $\geq$ 0.
$\qquad$ Then b=2$\bullet$(b/2) $\geq$ 0 and b/2 = i $\geq$ 0.
$\qquad\qquad$ $\{$ *b$\geq$0 and k$\bullet$a^b=M^N and b>0* $\}$ $\supset$
$\qquad\qquad$ $\{$ *b>0 and k$\bullet$a^b=M^N* $\}$ $\supset$
$\qquad\qquad$ $\{$ *b/2>0 and k$\bullet$(a$\bullet$a)$^{b/2}$=M^N* $\}$
$\qquad\qquad\qquad$ a := a*a; b := b/2
$\qquad\qquad$ $\{$ *b>0 and k$\bullet$a^b=M^N* $\}$ $\supset$ $\{$ *b$\geq$0 and k$\bullet$a^b=M^N* $\}$

Case 2: b is odd, that is, b = 2i+1 > 0 for some i $\geq$ 0.
$\qquad$ Then b<>2$\bullet$(b/2).
$\qquad\qquad$ $\{$ *b$\geq$0 and k$\bullet$a^b=M^N and b 0* $\}$ $\supset$
$\qquad\qquad$ $\{$ *b>0 and k$\bullet$a^b=M^N* $\}$ $\supset$
$\qquad\qquad$ $\{$ *b–1$\geq$0 and k$\bullet$a$\bullet$a^{b-1}=M^N* $\}$
$\qquad\qquad\qquad$ b := b–1; k := k*a
$\qquad\qquad$ $\{$ *b$\geq$0 and k$\bullet$a^b=M^N* $\}$

These two cases correspond to the premises in the rule for the **if** command. The conclusion of the axiom establishes:

$\{$ *b$\geq$0 and k$\bullet$a^b=M^N and b>0* $\}$
$\qquad$ **if** b=2*(b/2) **then** a := a*a; b := b/2
$\qquad\qquad\qquad$ **else** b := b–1; k := k*a **end if**
$\{$ *b$\geq$0 and k$\bullet$a^b=M^N* $\}$

Completion

$\{$ *b$\geq$0 and k$\bullet$a^b=M^N and b$\leq$0* $\}$ $\supset$
$\{$ *b=0 and k$\bullet$a^b=M^N* $\}$ $\supset$ $\{$ *k=M^N* $\}$ ∎

Nested While Loops

Example: We now consider a more complex algorithm with nested **while** loops. In addition to a precondition and postcondition specifying the goal of the code, each **while** loop is annotated by a loop invariant to be supplied in the proof.

> *{ IN = [A] and OUT = [ ] and A ≥ 0 }*
>> **read** x;
>> m := 0; n := 0; s := 0;
>> **while** x>0 **do**   *{ outer loop invariant: C }*
>>> x := x–1; n := m+2; m := m+1;
>>> **while** m>0 **do** *{ inner loop invariant: D }*
>>>> m := m–1; s := s+1
>>> **end while**;
>>> m := n
>> **end while**;
>> **write** s
> *{ OUT = [A²] }*

Imagine for now that an oracle has provided the invariants for this program. Later we discuss how the invariants might be discovered. Given the complexity of the problem, it is convenient to introduce predicate notation to refer to the invariants. The outer invariant C is

$$C(x,m,n,s) = (x{\geq}0 \text{ and } m{=}2(A{-}x) \text{ and } m{=}n{\geq}0 \text{ and } s{=}(A{-}x)^2 \text{ and } OUT{=}[\;]).$$

Initialization (outer loop): First we prove that this invariant is true initially by working through the initialization code. Check the deduction from bottom to top.

> *{ IN = [A] and OUT = [ ] and A≥0 }* ⊃
> *{ A≥0 and 0=2(A–A) and 0=(A–A)² and IN = [A][ ] and OUT=[ ] }*
>> **read** x;
> *{ x≥0 and 0=2(A–x) and 0=(A–x)² and IN = [ ] and OUT=[ ] }* ⊃
> *{ x≥0 and 0=2(A–x) and 0=0 and 0=(A–x)² and IN = [ ] and OUT=[ ] }*
>> m := 0;
> *{ x≥0 and m=2(A–x) and m=0 and 0=(A–x)² and OUT=[ ] }* ⊃
> *{ x≥0 and m=2(A–x) and m=0 and 0≥0 and 0=(A–x)² and OUT=[ ] }*
>> n := 0;
> *{ x≥0 and m=2(A–x) and m=n and n≥0 and 0=(A–x)² and OUT=[ ] }*
>> s := 0;
> *{ x≥0 and m=2(A–x) and m=n≥0 and s=(A–x)² and OUT=[ ] }.*

Completion (outer loop): Next we show that the outer loop invariant and the exit condition, followed by the **write** command, produce the desired final assertion.

{ C(x,m,n,s) and x≤0 }
> ⊃ *{ x≥0 and m=2(A–x) and m=n≥0 and s=(A–x)² and OUT=[ ] and x≤0 }*
> ⊃ *{ x=0 and m=2(A–x) and m=n≥0 and s=(A–x)² and OUT=[ ] }*
> ⊃ *{ s=A² and OUT=[ ] }*

and
> *{ s=A² and OUT=[ ] }* **write** s *{ s=A² and OUT=[A²] }* ⊃ *{ OUT=[A²] }.*

Preservation (outer loop): Showing preservation of the outer loop invariant involves executing the inner loop; we thus introduce the inner loop invariant D, again obtained from the oracle:

D(x,m,n,s) =
$$(x \geq 0 \text{ and } n=2(A-x) \text{ and } m \geq 0 \text{ and } n \geq 0 \text{ and } m+s=(A-x)^2 \text{ and } OUT=[\ ]).$$

Initialization (inner loop): We show that the inner loop invariant is initially true by starting with the outer loop invariant, combined with the loop entry condition, and pushing the result through the assignment commands before the inner loop.

{ C(x,m,n,s) and x>0 }
$$\equiv \{\ x \geq 0 \text{ and } m=2(A-x) \text{ and } m=n \geq 0 \text{ and } s=(A-x)^2 \text{ and } OUT=[\ ] \text{ and } x>0\ \}$$
$$\supset \{\ x-1 \geq 0 \text{ and } m+2=2(A-x+1) \text{ and } m+1 \geq 0 \text{ and } m+2 \geq 0$$
$$\text{and } m+1+s=(A-x+1)^2 \text{ and } OUT=[\ ]\ \}$$
$$\equiv \{\ D(x-1,m+1,m+2,s)\ \}$$
since $(s=(A-x)^2 \text{ and } m+2=2(A-x+1)) \supset m+1+s=(A-x+1)^2.$

Therefore, using the assignment rule, we have

{ C(x,m,n,s) and x>0 } $\supset$ { D(x-1,m+1,m+2,s) }
        x := x-1; n := m+2; m := m+1
{ D(x,m,n,s) }.

Preservation (inner loop): Next we need to show that the inner loop invariant is preserved, that is,

{ D(x,m,n,s) and m>0 } m := m-1; s := s+1 { D(x,m,n,s) }.

It suffices to show

(D(x,m,n,s) and m>0)
$$\supset (x \geq 0 \text{ and } n=2(A-x) \text{ and } m \geq 0 \text{ and } n \geq 0$$
$$\text{and } m+s=(A-x)^2 \text{ and } OUT=[\ ] \text{ and } m>0)$$
$$\supset (x \geq 0 \text{ and } n=2(A-x) \text{ and } m-1 \geq 0 \text{ and } n \geq 0$$
$$\text{and } m-1+s+1=(A-x)^2 \text{ and } OUT=[\ ])$$
$$\equiv D(x,m-1,n,s+1).$$

The preservation step is complete because after the assignments, m replaces m-1 and s replaces s+1 to produce the loop invariant D(x,m,n,s).

Completion (inner loop): To complete our proof, we need to show that the inner loop invariant, combined with the inner loop exit condition and pushed through the assignment m := n, results in the outer loop invariant:

{ D(x,m,n,s) and m≤0 } m := n { C(x,m,n,s) }.

It suffices to show (D(x,m,n,s) and m≤0) $\supset$ C(x,n,n,s):

(D(x,m,n,s) and m≤0)
    ⊃ (x≥0 and n=2(A–x) and m≥0 and n≥0
                      and m+s=(A–x)^2 and OUT=[ ] and m≤0)
    ⊃ (x≥0 and n=2(A–x) and n=n≥0 and s=(A–x)^2 and OUT=[ ])
    ≡ C(x,n,n,s).

Thus the outer loop invariant is preserved. ∎

The previous verification suggests a derived rule for assignment commands:

$$\frac{P \supset Q[V \rightarrow E]}{\{P\}\ V := E\ \{Q\}}$$

We used an application of this derived rule when we proved

$$(C(x,m,n,s) \text{ and } x>0) \supset D(x{-}1,m{+}1,m{+}2,s)$$

from which we deduced

   { C(x,m,n,s) and x>0 }
     x := x–1; n := m+2; m := m+1
   { D(x,m,n,s) }.

Proving a program correct is a fairly mechanical process once the loop invariants are known. We have already suggested that one way to discover a loop invariant is to make a table of values for a simple case and to trace values for the relevant variables. To see how tracing can be used, let A = 3 in the previous example and hand execute the loops. The table of values is shown in Figure 11.4.

The positions where the invariant C(x,m,n,s) for the outer loop should hold are marked by arrows. Note how the variable s takes the values of the perfect squares—namely, 0, 1, 4, and 9—at these locations. The difficulty is to determine what s is the square of as its value increases.

Observe that x decreases as the program executes. Since A is constant, this means the value A–x increases: 0, 1, 2, and 3. This gives us the relationship s = (A–x)^2. We also note that m is always even and increases: 0, 2, 4, 6. This produces the relation m = 2(A–x) in the outer invariant.

For the inner loop invariant, s is not always a perfect square, but m+s is. Also, in the inner loop, n preserves the final value for m as the loop executes. So n also obeys the relationship n = 2(A–x).

Finally, the loop entry conditions are combined with the exit condition. For the outer loop, x>0 is combined with x=0 to produce the condition x≥0 for the outer loop invariant. In a similar way, m>0 is combined with m=0 to give m≥0 in the inner loop invariant.

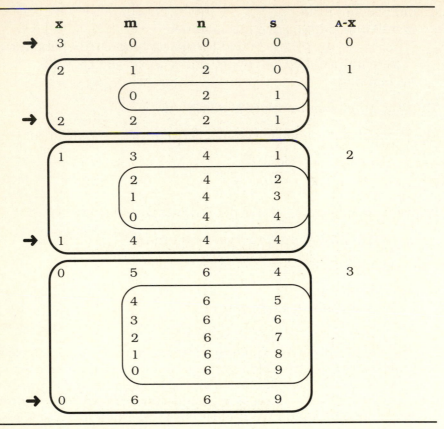

	x	m	n	s	A-X
→	3	0	0	0	0
	2	1	2	0	1
		0	2	1	
→	2	2	2	1	
	1	3	4	1	2
		2	4	2	
		1	4	3	
		0	4	4	
→	1	4	4	4	
	0	5	6	4	3
		4	6	5	
		3	6	6	
		2	6	7	
		1	6	8	
		0	6	9	
→	0	6	6	9	

Figure 11.4: Tracing Variable Values

Since finding the loop invariant is the most difficult part of proving a program correct, we present one more example. Consider the following program:

> { *IN* = [*A*] *and* *A*≥2 }
>   **read** n; b := true; d := 2;
>   **while** d<n **and** b **do** { *loop invariant* }
>   **if** n = d*(n/d) **then** b := false **end if**;
>   d := d+1
>   **end while**
> { b ≡ ∀k[2≤k<*A* ⊃ *not* ∃j[k•j = *A*]] }

The Boolean variable b is a flag, remaining true if no divisor of n, other than 1, is found—in other words, if n is prime. If a divisor is found, b is set to false and remains false. Here the invariant needs to record the partial results computed so far as the loop is executed.

At each stage in the loop, the potential divisors have been checked success-fully up to but not including the current value of d. We use the final assertion as a guide for constructing the invariant that expresses the portion of the computation completed so far.

Invariant = ([b ≡ ∀k[2≤k<d ⊃ not ∃j[k•j = A]]] and n=A≥2 and 2≤d≤n).

The remainder of the proof is left as an exercise.

Exercises

1. Give a deduction that verifies the specification of the following program fragment:

    { x=A and y=B } z:=x; x:=y; y:=z *{ x=B and y=A }*.

2. Define a proof rule for the repeat command.

    { P } **repeat** C **until** B *{ Q and B }*

    Use this proof rule to verify the partial correctness of the program segment shown below:

    { m = A > 0 and n = B ≥ 0 }
        p := 1;
        repeat
            p := p*n; m := m−1
        until m = 0
    { p = B^A }

3. Prove the partial correctness of the following program for integer multiplication by repeated addition.

    { B ≥ 0 }
        x := A; y := B; product := 0;
        while y > 0 **do**
            product := product+x; y := y−1
        end while
    { product = A•B }

4. Prove the partial correctness of this more efficient integer multiplication program.

    { m = A and n = B ≥ 0 }
        x := m; y := n; product := 0;
        while y > 0 **do**
            if 2*(y/2) <> y **then** product := product+x **end if**;
            x := 2*x; y := y/2
        end while;
    { product = A•B }

    Hint: Consider the two cases where y is even (y = 2k) and y is odd (y = 2k+1). Remember that / denotes integer division.

5. Finish the proof of the prime number detection program.

6. The **least common multiple** of two nonnegative integers m and n, LCM(m,n), is the smallest integer k such that k=i*m and k=j*n for some integers i and j. Write a Wren program segment that for integer variables m and n will set another variable, say k, to the value LCM(m,n). Give a formal proof of the partial correctness of the program fragment.

7. Provide postconditions for these code fragments and show their partial correctness.

    a) $\{\, m = A \geq 0\,\}$
    ```
        r := 0;
        while (r+1)*(r+1)<=m do r:=r+1 end while
    ```
    { *Postcondition* }

    b) $\{\, m = A \geq 0\,\}$
    ```
        x:=0; odd:=1; sum:=1;
        while sum<=m do
            x:=x+1; odd:=odd+2; sum:=sum+odd
        end while
    ```
    { *Postcondition* }

    c) $\{\, A \geq 0 \text{ and } B \geq 0\,\}$
    ```
        sum:=0; m:=A;
        while m≥0 do
            count := 0;
            while count≤B do
                sum := sum+1; count := count+1
            end while;
            m := m−1
        end while
    ```
    { *Postcondition* }

8. Write a fragment of Wren code C satisfying the following specification:
    $$\{\, M \geq 0\,\}$$
    $$C$$
    { *result*=b_K and $M=b_0+b_1 \bullet 2+ \ldots +b_j \bullet 2^j+ \supset$ *where* $b_j=0$ *or* 1 }.
    Prove that the code is partially correct with respect to the specification.

9. Carefully define the substitution operation P[V→E] for the predicate calculus. Be careful to avoid the problem of free variable capture. See substitution for the lambda calculus in Chapter 5.

10. Supply proofs of partial correctness for the following examples:

a) *{ N ≥ 0 }*
    ```
    sum:=0;  exp:=0; term:=1;
    while exp<N do
        sum := sum+term; exp := exp+1; term := term*2
    end while
    ```
    { sum = 2^N–1 }

b) *{ N ≥ 0 and D > 0 }*
    ```
    q:=0; r:=N;
    while r>=D do
        r := r–D; q := q+1
    end while
    ```
    { N = q•D+r and 0≤r<D }

c) *{ true }*
    ```
    k:=1; c:=0; sum:=0;
    while s<=1000 do
        sum := sum+k*k; c := c+1; k := k+1
    end while
    ```
    *{ "c is the smallest number of consecutive squares
       starting at 1 whose sum is greater than 1000" }*

d) *{ N >0 and N is odd }*
    ```
    sum:=1;  term:=1;
    while term<>N do
        term := term+2; sum := sum+2*term–1;
    end while
    ```
    { sum = N•(N+1)/2 }

e) *{ true }*
    ```
    sum:=0;  term:=1;
    while term<10000 do
        sum := sum+term; term := 10*term;
    end while
    ```
    { sum = 1111 }

f) *{ N ≥ 0 }*
    ```
    k:=N;  fact:=1; p:=1;
    while k<>1 do
        k := k–1; temp := fact;
        fact := k*(p+fact); p := p+temp
    end while
    ```
    { fact = N! }

g) $\{ A \geq 0 \ and \ B \geq 0 \}$

```
    m := A; n := B; product := 0;
    while m<>0 do
        while 2*(m/2)=m do
            n := 2*n; m := m/2
        end while;
        product := product+n; m := m–1
    end while
```

$\{ product = A{\bullet}B \}$

11. Suppose Wren has been extended to include an exponentiation operation $\uparrow$. Prove the partial correctness of the following code segment.

$\{ m = A \geq 1 \}$

```
    s := 1; k := 0;
    while s < m do
        s := s + 2↑k; k := k+1
    end while
```

$\{ log_2 A \ \leq \ k \ < \ 1+log_2 A \}$

11.3 AXIOMATIC SEMANTICS FOR PELICAN

Pelican, first introduced in Chapter 9, is an extension of Wren that includes the following features:

- Declarations of constants, procedures with no parameters, and procedures with a single parameter.
- Anonymous blocks with a declaration section and a command section.
- Procedure calls as commands.

Figure 11.5 restates the abstract syntax of Pelican.

Now we need to include the declarations in the axiomatic semantics. We assume that all programs have been checked independently to satisfy all syntactic rules and that only syntactically valid programs, including those that adhere to the context sensitive-conditions, are analyzed semantically. Some restrictions on the choice of identifier names will be introduced so that our presentation of the axiomatic semantics of Pelican does not become bogged down with syntactic details.

Since we do not have an underlying model for environments that can differentiate between different uses of the same identifier in different scopes, we require that all identifiers be named uniquely throughout the program. No generality is lost by such a restriction since any program with duplicate identifier names can be transformed into a program with unique names by systematic substitutions of identifier names within the scope of the identifier. For example, consider the following Pelican program with duplicate identifier names:

```
program squaring is
    var x, y: integer;
    procedure square(x : integer) is
        var y: integer;
        begin
            y := x * x; write y
        end
begin
    read x; read y; square(x); square(y)
end
```

Abstract Syntactic Domains

P : Program	C : Command	N : Numeral
B : Block	E : Expression	I : Identifier
D : Declaration	O : Operator	L : Identifier[+]
T : Type		

Abstract Production Rules

Program ::= **program** Identifier **is** Block

Block ::= Declaration **begin** Command **end**

Declaration ::= ε | Declaration Declaration
       | **const** Identifier = Expression
       | **var** Identifier : Type | **var** Identifier Identifier[+] : Type
       | **procedure** Identifier **is** Block
       | **procedure** Identifier (Identifier : Type) **is** Block

Type ::= **integer** | **boolean**

Command ::= Command **;** Command | Identifier **:=** Expression
       | **read** Identifier | **write** Expression | **skip** | **declare** Block
       | **if** Expression **then** Command **else** Command
       | **while** Expression **do** Command | Identifier
       | **if** Expression **then** Command | Identifier(Expression)

Expression ::= Numeral | Identifier | **true** | **false** | – Expression
       | Expression Operator Expression | **not**(Expression)

Operator ::= **+** | **–** | ***** | **/** | **or** | **and** | **<=** | **<** | **=** | **>** | **>=** | **<>**

Figure 11.5: Abstract Syntax for Pelican

The renaming works as follows: The first occurrence of the identifier name remains unchanged while each other occurrence in a different scope is systematically substituted with the same name followed by a numeric suffix (1, 2, 3, ..., as needed) that makes the name unique. To make sure this substitution does not result in duplication of other declarations, we mark it with a unique character, such as the sharp sign # shown below, that is not allowed in the original syntax. Using this scheme, the program given above becomes:

```
program squaring is
   var x, y: integer;
   procedure square(x#1 : integer) is
      var y#1: integer;
      begin
            y#1 := x#1 * x#1; write y#1
      end
   begin
      read x; read y; square(x); square(y)
   end
```

We inherit all of the axioms from Wren: Assign, Read, Write, Skip, Sequence, If-Then, If-Else, While, Weaken Postcondition, Strengthen Precondition, And, and Or. We also need to introduce an alternative form for rules of inference:

$$\frac{H_1, H_2, ..., H_n \vdash H_{n+1}}{H}$$

This rule can be interpreted as follows:

If H_{n+1} can be derived from $H_1, H_2, ..., H_n$, we may conclude H.

Blocks

Although we do not need to retain declaration information for context checking, which we assume has already been performed, we do need a mechanism for retaining pertinent declaration information, such as constant values, the bodies of procedure declarations, and their formal parameters, if applicable. This task is accomplished by two assertions, Procs and Const, which will depend on the declarations in the program being analyzed. We define Procs to be a set of assertions constructed as follows:

- If p is a declared parameterless procedure with body B, add body(p) = B to Procs.

- If p is a declared procedure with formal parameter F and body B, add parameter(p)=F and body(p)=B to Procs.

Constant declarations are handled by adding an assertion Const such that, for each declared constant c with value N, Const contains an assertion c = N.

For a constant declaration with an arbitrary expression, c = E, the assertion takes the form c = κ where κ is the current value of E. In the event that there are no declared constants, Const ≡ true. With these mechanisms, we can give an axiomatic definition for a block:

$$\frac{Procs \vdash \{\,P\ and\ Const\,\}\ \ C\ \{\,Q\,\}}{\{\,P\,\}\ \ D\ \textbf{begin}\ C\ \textbf{end}\ \{\,Q\,\}} \qquad\qquad \text{(Block)}$$

Example: Before continuing with the development of other new axiomatic definitions, we demonstrate how the block rule works for the following anonymous block, **declare** B, with a constant declaration:

```
declare
    constant x = 10;
    var y : integer;
begin
    read y; y := x + y; write y
end
```

Suppose we want to prove that

{ *IN* = *[7]L and OUT* = *[ ]* } B { *OUT* = *[17]* }.

Since no procedures are declared, Procs contains no assertions, but Const contains the assertion x = 10. We must show

{ *IN* = *[7]L and OUT* = *[ ] and x* = *10* }
    read y; y := x + y; **write** y
{ *OUT* = *[17]* }.

The proof proceeds as follows:

{ *IN* = *[7]L and OUT* = *[ ] and x* = *10* } ⊃
{ *IN* = *[7]L and OUT* = *[ ] and x* = *10 and 7* = *7* }
    read y
{ *IN* = *L and OUT* = *[ ] and x* = *10 and y* = *7* } ⊃
{ *IN* = *L and OUT* = *[ ] and x* = *10 and x+y* = *10+7* }
    y := x + y
{ *IN* = *L and OUT* = *[ ] and x* = *10 and y* = *17* }
    write y
{ *IN* = *L and OUT* = *[17] and x* = *10 and y* = *17* } ⊃
{ *OUT* = *[17]* }. ∎

Nonrecursive Procedures

Pelican requires four separate axiomatic definitions for procedure calls: nonrecursive calls without and with a parameter and recursive calls without and with a parameter. Calling a nonrecursive procedure without a parameter involves proving the logical relation of assertions around the execution of the body of the procedure. The subscript on the name of the rule indicates no parameter for the procedure.

$$\frac{\{P\}\ B\ \{Q\},\quad body(proc) = B}{\{P\}\ \text{proc}\ \{Q\}} \qquad\qquad (\text{Call}_0)$$

Example: Consider this anonymous block **declare** B that squares the existing value of x:

```
declare
    procedure square is
        begin
            x := x * x
        end
begin
    square
end
```

For this block, Procs is the assertion

$$body(square) = (x := \ x * x)$$

and Const is the true assertion. So, using the Block rule, we need to show

$$body(square) = (x:= x*x)\ \vdash\ \{\ x = N\ and\ true\}\ square\ \{x = N*N\ \}.$$

The first assertion in the hypothesis of Call_0 requires that we prove $\{\ x = N\ and\ true\ \}\ B\ \{\ x = N{\bullet}N\ \}$.

Since $\{\ P\ and\ true\ \}$ is equivalent to P, using the rule for a procedure invocation without a parameter, we need to prove

$$\{\ x = N\ \}\ x := x*x\ \{\ x = N*N\ \}.$$

Substituting $x*x$ for x in the postcondition, we have $\{\ x*x = N*N\ \}$. Because we know $\{x = N\} \supset \{\ x*x = N*N\ \}$, we strengthen the precondition to obtain the initial assertion. ∎

If a procedure P has a formal parameter F and the procedure invocation has an expression E as the actual parameter, we add the binding of F to E in both the precondition and postcondition to prove the procedure call is correct.

$$\frac{\{P\} \ B \ \{Q\}, \quad body(proc) = B, \quad parameter(proc) = F}{\{ \ P[F{\rightarrow}E] \ \} \ proc(E) \ \{ \ Q[F{\rightarrow}E] \ \}} \qquad (Call_1)$$

If we can show the relation $\{P\}$ B $\{Q\}$ is true about F where B = body(proc), we may conclude that the relation $\{ \ P[F{\rightarrow}E] \ \}$ proc(E) $\{ \ Q[F{\rightarrow}E] \ \}$ is true about E.

Example: Consider an anonymous block **declare** B that increments the existing value of a nonlocal variable x by an amount specified as a parameter:

> **declare**
> > **procedure** increment(step : **integer**) **is**
> > > **begin**
> > > > x := x + step
> > > **end**
> > **begin**
> > > increment(y)
> > **end**

We want to prove $\{ \ x = M \ and \ y = N\}$ B $\{ \ x = M + N \ and \ y = N\}$.

For this block, Procs contains the conjunction of the assertions

> body(increment) = (x := x+step)
>
> parameter(increment) = step,

and Const is the true assertion. We thus need to show

> body(increment) = (x:=x+step), parameter(increment) = step
> > $\vdash \{ \ x{=}M \ and \ y{=}N \ and \ true \ \}$ increment(y) $\{ \ x{=}M{+}N \ and \ y{=}N \ \}$.

We can eliminate the "*and true*"; then using our rule for a procedure invocation with parameter, we have to show

> $\{ \ x = M \ and \ step = N \ \}$
> > x := x + step
> $\{ \ x = M + N \ and \ step = N \ \}$

Substituting "x+step" for x in the postcondition, we have

> $\{ \ x + step = M + N \ and \ step = N \ \} \ \supset$
> $\{ \ x + N = M + N \ and \ step = N \ \} \ \supset$
> $\{ \ x = M \ and \ step = N \ \}$

the desired precondition. Therefore, by the rule Call$_1$, we may conclude
> $\{ \ x{=}M \ and \ y{=}N \ and \ true \ \}$ increment(y) $\{ \ x{=}M{+}N \ and \ y{=}N \ \}$.   ∎

Although not illustrated by the previous example, we must introduce some restrictions on parameter usage so as to avoid aliasing and thereby proving false assertions. Neither of these restrictions results in any loss of generality. Since we want to have parameters passed by value, any changes in the formal parameter inside the procedure should not be visible outside the procedure. This situation becomes a problem if the actual parameter is a variable.

We avoid the problem by not allowing the formal parameter to change value inside the procedure command sequence. Any program violating this restriction can be transformed into an equivalent program that obeys the restriction by declaring a new local variable, assigning this variable the value of the parameter, and then using the local variable in the place of the parameter throughout the procedure. For example, the code on the left allows the formal parameter f to change value but the corresponding code on the right permits only a local variable to change value.

```
procedure p (f : integer) is          procedure p (f : integer) is
begin                                     var local#f : integer;
    f := f * f;                        begin
    write f                                local#f := f;
end                                        local#f := local#f * local#f;
                                           write local#f
                                       end
```

The second restriction requires that if the actual parameter is a variable that is manipulated globally inside the procedure body, no change is made to the value of the formal parameter for which it is substituted. The procedure given below changes two nonlocal variables. We are concerned only with changes made to the variable x, which happens to be the actual parameter. The constraint adds a new variable at the level of invocation, assigning the value of the "manipulated" variable to the new variable, and passing the new variable as a parameter. This transformation is illustrated below by altering the variable "x" by appending "new#"in the calling environment and passing "new#x" as the actual parameter.

```
procedure q (f : integer ) is         procedure q (f : integer ) is
begin                                  begin
    read x;                                read x;
    y := y + f                             y := y + f
end                                    end
    :                                      :
p(x);                                  new#x := x;
                                       p(new#x);
```

Exercises at the end of this section provide Pelican programs for which erroneous semantics can be proved using the Call$_1$ rule when these transformations are ignored.

Recursive Procedures

Next we discuss recursive procedures without a parameter. Consider the following procedure that reads and discards all zeros until the first nonzero value is encountered.

> **procedure** nonzero **is**
>   **begin**
>   **read** x;
>   **if** x = 0 **then** nonzero **end if**
>   **end**

We cannot use the rule for a nonrecursive procedure without a parameter because we will have an endless sequence of applications of the same rule. To see how to avoid this problem, we use a technique similar to mathematical induction. Recall that with induction we have to show a base case and to prove that the proposition is true for n assuming that it is true for n–1. With recursion, we use a similar approach: We prove that the current call is correct if we assume that the result from any previous call is correct. The basis case corresponds to the situation in which the procedure is called, but it does not call itself again.

$$\frac{\{P\} \ \text{proc} \ \{Q\} \ \vdash \{P\} \ C \ \{Q\}, \ \ \text{body(proc)} = C}{\{P\} \ \text{proc} \ \{Q\}} \qquad \text{(Recursion}_0)$$

Example: For the procedure nonzero given above, suppose that the input file contains a sequence Z of zero or more 0's followed by a nonzero value, call it N, followed by any sequence of values L. We want to prove

> { $IN = Z[N]L$ and Z contains only zeros and $N \neq 0$} = P
>   nonzero
> { $IN = L$ and $x = N \neq 0$ } = Q.

To prove the correctness of the procedure call relative to the given specification, we need to show the following correctness specification for the body of the procedure

> { $IN = Z[N]L$ and Z contains only zeros and $N \neq 0$ } = P
>   **read** x;
>   **if** x = 0 **then** nonzero **end if**
> { $IN = L$ and $x = N \neq 0$ } = Q

where we are allowed to use the recursive assumption when nonzero is called from within itself. We make an assertion between the **read** command and the **if** command that takes into account two cases: Either x is zero or x is nonzero.

In the case that the sequence of zeros is not empty, we can write

$Z = [0]Z'$, where Z' contains zero or more 0's,

and in the other case, Z is empty. Therefore the precondition P is equivalent to

$((IN = [0]Z'[N]L$ and Z' contains only zeros and $N \neq 0)$ or $(IN = [N]L$ and $N \neq 0))$

Case 1: Z is not empty.

$\{ IN = [0]Z'[N]L$ and Z' contains only zeros and $N \neq 0 \}$
    read x
$\{ IN = Z'[N]L$ and Z' contains only zeros and $N \neq 0$ and $x = 0 \}$.

Case 2: Z is empty.

$\{ IN = [N]L$ and $N \neq 0 \}$ **read** x $\{ IN = L$ and $x = N \neq 0 \}$.

Applying the Or rule allows us to conclude the following assertion, called R, after the **read** command:

$R = ((IN = Z'[N]L$ and Z' contains only zeros and $N \neq 0$ and $x = 0)$
      or $(IN = L$ and $x = N \neq 0))$.

Using the If-Then rule, we must show:

$\{ R$ and $x = 0 \}$ nonzero $\{ IN = L$ and $x = N \neq 0 \}$ and
$(R$ and $x \neq 0) \supset (IN = L$ and $x = N \neq 0)$.

The second assertion holds directly since $(R$ and $x \neq 0)$ implies the final assertion. The first assertion involving the recursive call simplifies to

$\{ IN = Z'[N]L$ and $N \neq 0$ and $x = 0 \}$ nonzero $\{IN = L$ and $x = N \neq 0 \}$.

This is a stronger precondition than we require, so it suffices to prove:

$\{ IN = Z'[N]L$ and $N \neq 0 \}$ nonzero $\{ IN = L$ and $x = N \neq 0 \}$.

But this is exactly the recursive assertion, $\{P\}$ nonzero $\{Q\}$, which we may assume to be true (the induction hypothesis), so the proof is complete.   ∎

Finally, we consider an inference rule for a recursively defined procedure with a parameter. The axiomatic definition follows directly from recursion without a parameter, modified by the changes inherent in calling a procedure with a parameter.

$$\frac{\forall f \, (\{P[F \rightarrow f]\} \ \ \text{proc}(f) \ \{Q[F \rightarrow f]\}) \vdash \{P\} \ \ C \ \{Q\}, \ \text{body(proc)}=C, \ \text{parameter(proc)}=F}{\{ P[F \rightarrow E] \} \ \ \text{proc}(E) \ \{ Q[F \rightarrow E] \}} \qquad \text{(Recursion}_1)$$

The induction hypothesis allows us to assume the correctness of a recursive call of the procedure with any expression that satisfies the precondition as the actual parameter.

Example: To see how this rule works, we prove the correctness of a recursively defined factorial program. Since we do not have procedures that return values, we depend on a global variable "fact" to hold the current value as we return from the recursive calls.

> **procedure** factorial(n : **integer**) **is**
> > **begin**
> > > **if** n = 0 **then** fact := 1
> > > > **else** factorial(n–1); fact := n*fact;
> > > **end if**;
> > **end**;

We want to prove

> $\{\, num = \kappa \geq 0 \,\}$ $= P[F{\rightarrow}E]$
> > factorial(num)
> $\{\, fact = num!\ and\ num = \kappa \,\} = Q[F{\rightarrow}E]$, which implies fact = $\kappa!$.

In the proof below, "num" refers to the original actual parameter (called E in the rule) and "n" refers to the formal parameter (called F) in the recursive definition. Substituting the body of the procedure, we must show

> $\{\, n = \kappa \geq 0 \,\}$ $= P$
> > **if** n = 0 **then** fact := 1
> > > **else** factorial(n–1); fact := n*fact;
> > **end if**;
> $\{\, fact = n!\ and\ n = \kappa \,\}$ $= Q$

assuming as an induction hypothesis

> $\forall f(\{\, f = \kappa \geq 0 \,\}$ $= P[F{\rightarrow}f]$
> > factorial(f)
> > $\{\, fact = f!\ and\ f = \kappa \,\}$ $= Q[F{\rightarrow}f]).$

Case 1: n = 0.
Use the If-Else rule for the case when the condition is true:

> $\{\, n = \kappa \geq 0\ and\ n = 0 \,\} \supset$
> $\{\, n = \kappa = 0\ and\ 1 = 0! = \kappa! \,\}$
> > fact := 1
> $\{\, n = \kappa = 0\ and\ fact = 0! = n! \,\} \supset \{\, fact = n!\ and\ n = \kappa \,\}.$

Case 2: $n > 0$.

The recursive assumption gives

$\{ n = \kappa \geq 0 \ \ and \ n > 0 \} \supset$
$\{ n = \kappa > 0 \ and \ f = \kappa - 1 \geq 0 \}$
 factorial(f)
$\{ n = \kappa > 0 \ and \ fact = f! \ and \ f = \kappa - 1 \} \supset$
$\{ n = \kappa \ and \ fact = (\kappa - 1)! = (n-1)! \}$

The Assign rule gives

$\{ n = \kappa \ and \ fact = (\kappa - 1)! = (n-1)! \} \supset$
$\{ n = \kappa \ and \ n \bullet fact = n \bullet (n-1)! \}$
 fact := n * fact
$\{ n = \kappa \ and \ fact = n \bullet (n-1)! = n! \}$, which is the desired postcondition.   ∎

The complete axiomatic definition for Pelican is presented in Figure 11.6.

Assign	$\{ P[V \rightarrow E] \} \ V := E \ \{ P \}$
Read	$\{ IN = [\kappa]L \ and \ P[V \rightarrow K] \} \ \ \textbf{read} \ V \ \{ IN = L \ and \ P \}$
Write	$\{ OUT = [L] \ and \ E = \kappa \ and \ P \} \ \ \textbf{write} \ E \ \{ OUT = L[\kappa] \ and \ E = \kappa \ and \ P \}$
Skip	$\{ P \} \ \ \textbf{skip} \ \{ P \}$
Sequence	$\dfrac{\{P\} \ C_1 \ \{Q\}, \ \ \{Q\} \ C_2 \ \{R\}}{\{P\} \ C_1 ; C_2 \ \{R\}}$
If-Then	$\dfrac{\{P \ and \ B\} \ C \ \{Q\}, \ \ (P \ and \ not \ B) \supset Q}{\{P\} \ \textbf{if} \ B \ \textbf{then} \ C \ \textbf{end if} \ \{Q\}}$
If-Else	$\dfrac{\{P \ and \ B\} \ C_1 \ \{Q\}, \ \ \{P \ and \ not \ B\} \ C_2 \ \{Q\}}{\{P\} \ \textbf{if} \ B \ \textbf{then} \ C_1 \ \textbf{else} \ C_2 \ \textbf{end if} \ \{Q\}}$
While	$\dfrac{\{P \ and \ B\} \ C \ \{P\}}{\{P\} \ \textbf{while} \ B \ \textbf{do} \ C \ \textbf{end while} \ \{P \ and \ not \ B\}}$
Block	$\dfrac{Procs \vdash \{ P \ and \ Const \} \ C \ \{ Q \}}{\{ P \} \ D \ \textbf{begin} \ C \ \textbf{end} \ \{ Q \}}$

  where for all declarations "**procedure** I **is** B" in D,
      "body(I) = B" is contained in Procs;

    for all declarations "**procedure** I(F) **is** B" in D,
      "body(I) = B and parameter(I) = F" is contained in Procs; and

    Const consists of a conjunction of true and $c_i = E_i$
      for each constant declaration of the form "**const** $c_i = E_i$" in D.

Figure 11.6: Axiomatic Semantics for Pelican (Part 1)

Call without Parameter (Call$_0$)

$$\frac{\{P\}\ \ B\ \{Q\},\ \ body(proc) = B}{\{P\}\ \ proc\ \{Q\}}$$

Call with Parameter (Call$_1$)

$$\frac{\{P\}\ \ B\ \{Q\},\ \ body(proc) = B,\ parameter(proc) = F}{\{\ P[F{\rightarrow}E]\ \}\ \ proc(E)\ \{\ Q[F{\rightarrow}E]\ \}}$$

Recursion without Parameter (Recursion$_0$)

$$\frac{\{P\}\ \ proc\ \{Q\}\ \vdash\ \{P\}\ \ B\ \{Q\},\ \ body(proc) = B}{\{P\}\ \ proc\ \{Q\}}$$

Recursion with Parameter (Recursion$_1$)

$$\frac{\forall f(\{P[F{\rightarrow}f]\}\ \ proc(f)\{Q[F{\rightarrow}f]\})\vdash\{P\}\ \ B\{Q\},\ body(proc){=}B,\ parameter(proc){=}F}{\{\ P[F{\rightarrow}E]\ \}\ \ proc(E)\ \{\ Q[F{\rightarrow}E]\ \}}$$

Weaken Postcondition	$\dfrac{\{P\}\ \ C\ \{Q\},\ \ Q \supset R}{\{P\}\ \ C\ \{R\}}$
Strengthen Precondition	$\dfrac{P \supset Q,\ \ \{Q\}\ \ C\ \{R\}}{\{P\}\ \ C\ \{R\}}$
And	$\dfrac{\{P\}\ \ C\ \{Q\},\ \ \{P'\}\ \ C\ \{Q'\}}{\{P\ and\ P'\}\ \ C\ \{Q\ and\ Q'\}}$
Or	$\dfrac{\{P\}\ \ C\ \{Q\},\ \ \{P'\}\ \ C\ \{Q'\}}{\{P\ or\ P'\}\ \ C\ \{Q\ or\ Q'\}}$

Figure 11.6: Axiomatic Semantics for Pelican (Part 2)

Exercises

1. Prove that the following two program fragments are semantically equivalent, assuming the declaration of the procedure increment given in this section.

   read x;   **read** x;
   write x;   increment(-4);
                                    increment(1);
                                    increment(3);
                                    write x

2. Give an example where an invalid assertion can be proved if we allow duplicate identifiers to occur at different levels of scope.

3. Prove that the following procedure copies all nonzero values from the input file to the output file up to, but not including, the first zero value.

    procedure copy **is**
        var n : **integer**;
        begin
            read n; **if** n ≠ 0 **then write** n; **copy end if**
        end

4. Prove that the procedure "power" raises a to the power specified by the parameter value and leaves the result in the global variable product.

    procedure power(b: **integer**) **is**
        begin
            if b = 0 **then** product := 1
                            else power(b – 1); product := product * a
            end if
        end

5. Prove the partial correctness of this program relative to its specification.
    { B ≥ 0 }
        program sum is
            var m,n : **integer**;
            procedure incrementm(x : **integer**) **is**
                begin m := m+x **end**;
        begin
            m := 0; n := B;
            while n>0 **do**
                incrementm(A); n := n – 1
            end while
        end
    { m = A+B }

6. Consider the following procedure:

    procedure outputsequence(n: integer) **is**
        begin
            if n > 0 **then write** n; outputsequence(n–1) **end if**
        end
    Prove that
        {val = A ≥ 0 and OUT = [ ]}
                outputsequence(val)
        {OUT = [A, A-1, A-2, ... , 2, 1]}

7. Modify outputsequence in problem 6 so that it outputs values from 1 up to A. Prove the procedure correct.

8. Prove the partial correctness of the following Pelican program:

$\{$ κ≥0 and IN = [κ] and OUT = [ ] $\}$

```
program recurrence is
      var num,ans : integer;
      procedure fun(m : integer) is
            var temp : integer;
      begin
            if m = 0
                  then ans := 1
                  else temp := 2*m+1; fun(m−1); ans := ans + temp
            end if
      end;
      begin
            read num; fun(num); write ans
      end
```

$\{$ OUT = $[(κ+1)^2]$ $\}$

9. Illustrate the need for the transformation of procedures with a parameter that is changed in the body of the procedure by proving the spurious "correctness" of the following code using the Call$_1$ rule:

$\{$ OUT = [ ] $\}$

```
program problem1 is
      var a : integer;
      procedure p (b : integer) is
            begin  b := 5  end;
      begin
            a := 21;  p(a);  write a
      end
```

$\{$ OUT = [5] $\}$

10. Justify the need for the transformation of a one parameter procedure that makes a nonlocal change in the actual parameter by proving the spurious "correctness" of the following code using the Call$_1$ rule:

$\{$ OUT = [ ] $\}$

```
program problem2 is
      var m : integer;
      procedure q (f : integer) is
            begin  m := 8  end;
      begin
            m := 55;  q(m);  write m
      end
```

$\{$ OUT = [55] $\}$

11. Show what modifications will have to be made to the axiomatic definitions of Pelican to allow for procedures with several value parameters.

11.4 PROVING TERMINATION

In the proofs studied so far, we have considered only partial correctness, which means that the program must satisfy the specified assertions *only if* it ever halts, reaching the final assertion. The question of termination is frequently handled as a separate problem.

Termination is not an issue with many commands, such as assignment, selection, input/output, and nonrecursive procedure invocation. That these commands must terminate is contained in their semantics. Two language constructs require proofs of termination:

• Indefinite iteration (**while**)

• Invocation of a recursively defined procedure

The first case can be handled as a consequence of (well-founded) induction on an expression that is computed each pass through the loop, and the second can be managed by induction on some property possessed by each recursive call of the procedure.

Definition: A partial order $>$ or $\geq$ on a set W is **well-founded** if there exists no infinite decreasing sequence of distinct elements from W.   ∎

This means that given a sequence of elements $\{x_i \mid i \geq 1\}$ from W such that $x_1 \geq x_2 \geq x_3 \geq x_4 \geq \ldots$, there must exist an integer k such that $\forall i,j \geq k$, $x_i = x_j$.

If the partial order is **strict**, meaning that it is irreflexive, any decreasing sequence must have only distinct elements and so must be finite.

Examples of Well-founded Orderings

1. The natural numbers N ordered by $>$.

2. The Cartesian product NxN ordered by a lexicographic ordering defined as: $<m_1,m_2> \, > \, <n_1,n_2>$ if $([m_1 > n_1]$ or $[m_1 = n_1$ and $m_2 > n_2])$.

3. The positive integers, P, ordered by the relation "properly divides": $m > n$ if $(\exists k[m = n \bullet k]$ and $m \neq n)$.

Steps in Showing Termination

With indefinite iteration, termination is established by showing two steps:

1. Find a set W with a strict well-founded ordering >.

2. Find a **termination expression** E with the following properties:

    a) Whenever control passes through the beginning of the iterative loop, the value of E is in W.

    b) E takes a smaller value with respect to > each time the top of the iterative loop is passed.

In the context of a **while** command—for example, "**while** B **do** C **end while**" with invariant P—the two conditions take the following form:

a) (P and B) $\supset$ E$\in$W

b) { *P and B and E=A* } C { *A* > *E* }.

Example: Consider the following program that calculates the factorial of a natural number:

read n;
k := 0; f := 1;
while k < n **do**
    k := k + 1; f := k * f
end while;
write f

Take W = N, the set of natural numbers, as the well-founded set and E = n – k as the termination expression. Therefore, m$\in$W if and only if m $\geq$ 0. The loop invariant P is

$$(n \geq 0 \text{ and } k \leq n \text{ and } f = k! \text{ and } OUT = [\,]).$$

The conditions on the termination expression must hold at the top of the **while** loop where the invariant holds.

The two conditions follow immediately:

a) *(n $\geq$ 0 and k $\leq$ n and f = k! and OUT = [ ] and k < n) $\supset$ (n – k $\geq$ 0)*

b) *{ n $\geq$ 0 and k $\leq$ n and f = k! and OUT = [ ] and k < n and n – k = A } $\supset$*
    { n – (k + 1) = A – 1 }
        *k := k + 1; f := k * f*
    { n – k = A – 1 < A } ∎

Example: As another example, consider the program with nested loops from section 11.1.

```
read x;
m := 0; n := 0; s := 0;
while x > 0 do
    x := x-1; n := m+2; m := m+1;
    while m > 0 do
            m := m-1;  s := s+1
    end while;
    m := n
end while;
write s
```

With nested loops, each loop needs its own termination expression. In this example, they share the natural numbers as the well-founded set. The termination expressions can be defined as follows:

- For the outer loop: $E_o = x$

- For the inner loop: $E_i = m$

The code below shows the loop invariants used to verify that the termination expressions are adequate.

```
read x;
m := 0;  n := 0;  s := 0;
while x>0 do                  { x≥0 and m=2(A–x) and m=n≥0 and s=(A–x)² }
    x := x-1;  n := m+2;  m := m+1;
    while m>0 do              { x≥0 and n=2(A–x) and m≥0
        m := m-1;  s := s+1              and n≥0 and m+s=(A–x)2 }
    end while;
    m := n
end while;
write s
```

We leave the verification that the expressions E_o and E_i defined above satisfy the two conditions needed to prove termination as an exercise at the end of this section. ∎

Note that the termination expression method described above depends on identifying some loop control "counter" that cannot change forever.

Termination of Recursive Procedures

A procedure defined recursively contains the seeds of an induction proof for termination, if only a suitable property about the problem can be identified on which to base the induction.

Example: Consider a Pelican procedure to read and write input values until the value zero is encountered.

> **procedure** copy **is**
>   **var** n: **integer**;
>   **begin**
>   **read** n;
>   **if** n ≠ 0 **then write** n; copy **end if**
>   **end**

This procedure terminates (normally) only if the input stream contains the value zero. For a particular invocation of the procedure "copy", the depth of recursion depends on the number of nonzero integers preceding the first zero. We describe the input stream as IN $= L_1[0]L_2$ where L_1 contains no zero values.

Lemma: Given input of the form IN $= L_1[0]L_2$ where L_1 contains no zero values, the command "copy" halts.

Proof: By induction on the length of L_1, leng(L_1).

Basis: leng(L_1)=0.
    Then the input list has the form IN $= [0]L_2$, and after "**read** n", n=0.
    Calling copy causes execution of only the code
>   **read** n;
    which terminates.

Induction Step: leng(L_1)=k>0.
    As an induction hypothesis, assume that copy halts when
    leng(L_1)=k–1≥0. Then copy causes the execution of the code
>   **read** n;
>   **write** n;
>   copy
    which terminates because for this inner copy, leng(L_1)=k–1.   ∎

The complete proof of correctness of the procedure copy is left as an exercise.

Exercises

1. Formally prove that the factorial program in section 11.1 terminates. What happens to the termination proof if we remove the precondition $N{\geq}0$?

2. Prove that the following program terminates. Also show partial correctness.

   $\{ A \geq 0 \text{ and } B > 0 \}$
       m := A; n := B; k := 1;
       while n > 0 **do**
           if 2*(n/2) = n
                   then m := n*n; n := n/2
                   else n := n–1; k := k*m
           end if
       end while
   $\{ k = A^B \}$

3. For the nested loop problem in this section, verify that the expressions E_0 and E_i satisfy the two conditions needed to prove termination.

4. Prove that the following program terminates. Also show partial correctness.

   $\{ A{\geq}0 \text{ and } B{\geq}0 \text{ and } (A{\neq}0 \text{ or } B{\neq}0) \}$
       m := A; n := B;
       while m > 0 **do**
           if m ≤ n **then** n := n–m
                       else x := m; m := n; n := x
           end if
       end while
   $\{ n \text{ is the greatest common divisor of } A \text{ and } B \}$

   Verify each of the following termination expressions:

   - E_1 = <m,n> with the lexicographic ordering on NxN.

   - E_2 = 2m+n with the "greater than" ordering on N.

5. Prove the termination of the prime number program at the end of section 11.2.

6. Prove the termination of the program fragments in exercise 10 of section 11.2.

11.5 INTRODUCTION TO PROGRAM DERIVATION

In the first three sections of this chapter we started with programs or procedures that were already written, added assertions to the programs, and proved the assertions to be correct. In this section we apply axiomatic semantics in a different way, starting with assertions that represent program specifications and then deriving a program to match the assertions.

Suppose that we want to build a table of squares where T[k] contains k^2. A straightforward approach is to compute $k*k$ for each k and store the values in the table. However, multiplicative operations are inherently inefficient compared with additive operations, so we ask if this table can be generated using addition only. Actually this problem is not difficult; an early Greek investigation of "square" numbers provides a solution. As indicated by the table below, each square is the sum of consecutive odd numbers.

Square	Summation
1	1
4	1 + 3
9	1 + 3 + 5
16	1 + 3 + 5 + 7
25	1 + 3 + 5 + 7 + 9

The algorithm follows directly.

Table of Cubes

We now propose a slight variation of this problem: Construct a table of cubes using only additive methods. Given the ease of the solution for the table of squares, it may seem that we can find the answer quickly with just a little thought by playing with the numbers, but this problem turns out to be nontrivial. During a SIGCSE tutorial, David Gries reported that he assigned this problem to an advanced class in computer science and, even given several weeks, no one was able to come up with a correct solution. However, a solution can be produced directly if the techniques of program derivation are used.

We start with the final assertion that expresses the result of our program:

$\{ T[k] = k^3 \text{ for all } 0 \leq k \leq N \}$.

We build the table from the zeroth entry through the Nth entry, so for any particular value $m \leq N+1$, we know that all preceding table entries have been generated. This property becomes part of the loop invariant:

$\{\ T[k] = k^3 \text{ for all } 0 \le k < m\ \}$.

The value of m will increase until it reaches N+1, at which time the loop terminates. This condition gives us the other part of the loop invariant:

$\{\ 0 \le m \le N+1\ \}$.

We now have enough information to begin writing the program, starting with a skeleton describing the structure of the program.

```
m := 0;
while m < N + 1 do        { T[k] = k³ for all 0 ≤ k < m and  0 ≤ m ≤ N+1 }
    T[m] := ???
        :  :
    m := m + 1
end while
{ T[k] = k³ for all 0 ≤ k ≤ N }.
```

We introduce a new variable x whose value is assigned to T[m] each time the loop executes, adding to our loop invariant the requirement that $x = m^3$. Since x can only be changed by addition, we introduce another variable y and the assignment command x := x + y. The new value of x in the next iteration has to be $(m+1)^3$, so we have

$$x + y = (m+1)^3 = m^3 + 3m^2 + 3m + 1.$$

But we already have in our loop invariant the requirement that $x = m^3$, so this means that $y = 3m^2 + 3m + 1$ must be added to the loop invariant. Since m is initially zero, this means the initial values for x and y are 0 and 1, respectively. Here is the derived program so far.

```
m := 0;
x := 0;
y := 1;
while m < N + 1 do        { T[k] = k³ for all 0 ≤ k < m and  0 ≤ m ≤ N+1
                            and x = m³ and y = 3m² + 3m + 1 }

    T[m] := x;
    x := x + y;
     :  :
    m := m + 1
end while
{ T[k] = k³ for all 0 ≤ k ≤ N }.
```

The variable y can change only by addition, so we introduce a new variable z and the assignment y := y + z. The next time through the loop, m is incremented by one so that value of y must become

$$3(m + 1)^2 + 3(m + 1) + 1 = 3m^2 + 9m + 7.$$

But this new value equals y + z, so

$$y + z = 3m^2 + 9m + 7.$$

If we subtract the invariant $y = 3m^2 + 3m + 1$ from this equation, we end up with the requirement

$$z = 6m + 6,$$

which is added to the invariant. This relationship also means that z must be initialized to 6. So the code now becomes

```
m := 0;
x := 0;
y := 1;
z := 6;
while m <> N + 1 do        { T[k] = k³ for all 0 ≤ k < m and  0 ≤ m ≤ N+1
                              and x = m³
    T[m] := x;                and y = 3m² + 3m + 1
    x := x + y;               and z = 6m + 6 }
    y := y + z;
      :   :
    m := m + 1
end while
{ T[k] = k³ for all 0 ≤ k ≤ N }.
```

The next time through the loop, the new value of z must equal

$$6(m + 1) + 6 = 6m + 6 + 6 = \text{(old value of z)} + 6.$$

This equality tells us that z must be incremented by 6 each time through the loop, and therefore the computation meets the requirement of consisting of additive operations. So now we have the complete program.

```
m := 0;
x := 0;
y := 1;
z := 6;
while m < N + 1 do         { T[k] = k³ for all 0 ≤ k < m and  0 ≤ m ≤ N+1
                              and x = m³
    T[m] := x;                and y = 3m² + 3m + 1
    x := x + y;               and z = 6m + 6 }
    y := y + z;
    z := z + 6;
    m := m + 1
end while
{ T[k] = k³ for all 0 ≤ k ≤ N }
```

In the event that this formal derivation does not offer convincing enough proof that the above program works as expected, we present a small table of values following the algorithm.

m	x	y	z
0	0	1	6
1	1	7	12
2	8	19	18
3	27	37	24
4	64	61	30

Binary Search

The example above illustrates the technique of program derivation to produce a simple program, but it is tempting to ask if program derivation techniques can generate "really useful" programs. We conclude this section with the derivation of a binary search algorithm, an algorithm commonly presented in the study of data structures. We assume the following precondition for the sorted array A:

> { A[0..N] is a sequence of integers such that
>   A[i] ≤ A[i+1] for all $0 \le i < N$ and x is an integer and A[0] $\le x <$ A[N] }.

We want to determine if there exists at least one i such that $0 \le i < N$ and x = A[i]. However, x may not be present so we cannot require x = A[i] as part of the postcondition. Specifying the postcondition takes some insight. Notice that the precondition specifies that x be contained in the interval [A[0], A[N]), where [m,n) indicates an interval defined by the set { k | m≤k<n }. The basic idea will be to narrow that interval continually until it contains only a single element. We specify this by using indices i and j for the interval limits and requiring that ultimately j = i + 1. So the postcondition is

> { A[i] $\le x <$ A[j] and j = i + 1 }.

The test determining whether A[i] = x is made independently of this algorithm, but we will be able to guarantee that if A[i] ≠ x then x is not present anywhere in [A[0], A[N]).

The basic idea of the algorithm is that the subinterval [A[i],A[j]) becomes smaller and smaller, yet always contains x, until the postcondition is satisfied. We can now start construction of our program based on the following observations:

- The loop invariant is A[i] $\le x <$ A[j].
- The loop will repeat until j = i+1, so the loop entry condition is j ≠ i+1.

- The loop invariant is implied by the precondition if we set i to 0 and j to N.

Here is the initial program framework:

{ A[0..N] is a sequence of integers such that
A[i] ≤ A[i+1] for all 0 ≤ i < N and x is an integer and A[0] ≤ x < A[N] }
   i := 0;
   j := N;
   while j ≠ i + 1 **do** *{ A[i] ≤ x < A[j] }*
        : : :
   end while
{ A[i] ≤ x < A[j] and j = i + 1 }

We make the interval [A[i],A[j]) shrink by either increasing i or decreasing j. Suppose that we divide the interval "in half" by introducing the variable k = (i + j)/2, using integer division. Now x either lies in the interval [A[i],A[k]) or the interval [A[k],A[j]). It should be pointed out that x might lie in both intervals if A contains duplicate copies of x. However, in this case it does not matter which subinterval is chosen since both satisfy the loop invariant, and our algorithm requires only that we find one index, even though several may exist. If x < A[k], then setting j to k maintains the loop invariant. Otherwise A[k] ≤ x and setting i to k maintains the loop invariant. Here is the completed algorithm.

{ A[0..N] is a sequence of integers such that
A[i] ≤ A[i+1] for all 0 ≤ i < N and x is an integer and A[0] ≤ x < A[N] }
   i := 0;
   j := N;
   while j ≠ i + 1 **do**   *{ A[i] ≤ x < A[j] }*
      k := (i + j) / 2;
      if x < A[k] **then** j := k
                 else i := k
      end if
   end while
{ A[i] ≤ x < A[j] and j = i + 1 }

Exercises

1. Derive a program that constructs a table with $T[k] = k^4$, using only additive methods. This is similar to the table of cubes example except that four new variables have to be introduced with four assignment commands changing the values of these variables by addition.

2. Suppose that N is a fixed integer greater than or equal to zero (so the precondition is $\{N \geq 0\}$). Derive a program to find the integer square root of N. The integer square root is the largest integer that is less than or equal to the square root of N. This can be expressed as the postcondition:

$$\{ a \geq 0 \text{ and } 0 \leq a^2 \text{ and } a^2 \leq N \text{ and } N < (a + 1)^2 \}$$

Hint: Use two variables, a and b, initialized to 0 and N+1, respectively. As in the binary search problem, find the midpoint of a and b and change one of the values until the desired subinterval is found.

11.6 FURTHER READING

The original idea of verifying the correctness of a program using the techniques of logic first appears in papers by Robert Floyd [Floyd67] and C. A. R. Hoare [Hoare69]. These papers still serve as excellent introductions to axiomatic semantics. An early application of this method to programming language specification can be found in the definition of Pascal in [Hoare73].

The books dealing with the analysis of programs and languages in the framework of the predicate logic can be divided into two groups:

*   Books that develop axiomatic methods primarily to prove the correctness of programs as a tool of software engineering [Alagic78], [Backhouse86], [Francez92], [Gries81], and [Gumb89]. These authors concentrate on describing techniques of program construction and verification based on the predicate logic. The discussion of program derivation in section 11.5 falls into this classification. A book on program derivation by Geoff Dromey [Dromey89] gives numerous examples of this approach to program construction. The related method of "weakest precondition" is discussed in [Dijkstra76].

*   Books that view axiomatic methods as a means of programming language definition [Meyer90], [Nielson92], [Pagan81], [Tennent91], and [Winskel93]. Although correctness is discussed in these books, the emphasis is on using logic to specify the semantics of programming languages in a manner similar to the presentation of Wren and Pelican in this chapter.

For a review of predicate logic see [Enderton72], [Mendelson79], or [Reeves90].

Chapter 12
ALGEBRAIC SEMANTICS

The formal semantic techniques we have studied so far include denotational semantics, whose mathematical foundations lie in recursive function theory, and axiomatic semantics, whose foundations depend on predicate logic. In this chapter we study algebraic semantics, another formalism for semantic specification whose foundations are based on abstract algebras. Algebraic semantics involves the algebraic specification of data and language constructs. The basic idea of the algebraic approach to semantics is to name the different sorts of objects and the operations on the objects and to use algebraic axioms to describe their characteristic properties.

The methodology of algebraic semantics is customarily used to specify abstract data types (ADTs). The basic principle in specifying an ADT involves describing the logical properties of data objects in terms of properties of operations (some of which may be constants) that manipulate the data. The actual representation of the data objects and the implementations of the operations on the data are not part of the specification. For instance, we specify the abstract type whose values are stacks by defining the properties of the operations that push or pop items from the stacks, avoiding a description of a physical representation of the objects that serve as stacks.

In this chapter we introduce the basic ideas of algebraic specifications (syntax) and the corresponding algebras (semantics) that serve as models of specifications. As we will see, algebraic specifications extend from low-level objects, such as truth values with Boolean operations, through high-level objects, such as programs with operations to perform type checking and to interpret source code. Algebraic semantics is a broad field of study, and in this brief overview we can only suggest the underlying mathematical foundations. Some of the fundamental notions developed here will be used in the next chapter when we investigate our final approach to semantics, action semantics.

12.1 CONCEPTS AND EXAMPLES

Before exploring examples, we introduce some of the vocabulary of algebraic specification. The types in a programming language serve to classify the data processed by programs. Here we refer to types as **sorts**. An algebraic specification defining one or more sorts contains two parts: the **signature** and the **equations** (or axioms).

Definition: A **signature** Σ of an algebraic specification is a pair <Sorts, Operations> where Sorts is a set containing names of sorts and Operations is a family of function symbols indexed by the functionalities of the operations represented by the function symbols.   ∎

We use the terms "functions" and "operations" interchangeably, but when considering specifications, these terms refer to formal function symbols. The set of operations in a specification provides the syntax of the functions that are defined on the sorts of data. Suppose we want to specify an abstract type whose values are lists of integers. We provide three sorts in the specification:

Sorts = { Integer, Boolean, List }.

The elements of Sorts are only names; we can assume nothing about the properties of these sorts. The set of operations may include the function symbols given below with their signatures:

zero	: Integer
one	: Integer
plus (_ , _)	: Integer, Integer $\rightarrow$ Integer
minus (_ , _)	: Integer, Integer $\rightarrow$ Integer
true	: Boolean
false	: Boolean
emptyList	: List
cons (_ , _)	: Integer, List $\rightarrow$ List
head (_)	: List $\rightarrow$ Integer
tail (_)	: List $\rightarrow$ List
empty? (_)	: List $\rightarrow$ Boolean
length (_)	: List $\rightarrow$ Integer

The family of operations can be decomposed into eight sets of function symbols indexed by the domain-codomain constraints on the functions. We list several of the sets of operations in the family:

$Opr_{Boolean}$ = { true, false }

$Opr_{Integer,Integer \rightarrow Integer}$ = { plus, minus }

$Opr_{List \rightarrow Integer}$ = { head, length }

Other sets of operations are indexed by Integer, List, (Integer,List→List), (List→List), and (List→Boolean). Observe that operations with no domain represent constants of a particular sort—for example, zero, one, true, false, and emptyList. The signature of a specification can be compared with the declarations in a program—a specification defines the kinds of objects to which names will refer. The signature shown above tells us how we may use identifiers such as List, cons, and length but does not describe the behavior of the corresponding functions.

The equations in a specification act to constrain the operations in such a way as to indicate the appropriate behavior for the operations. They serve as axioms specifying an algebra, similar to the properties of associativity and commutativity of operations that we associate with abstract algebras in mathematics. Equations may involve variables representing arbitrary values from the various sorts in the specification. The variables in an equation are universally quantified implicitly. Listed below are several equations (axioms) that may appear in a specification of lists.

head (cons (m, s))   = m

empty? (emptyList)   = true

empty? (cons (m, s)) = false

The first equation stands for the closed assertion:

$\forall$m:Integer, $\forall$s:List [head (cons (m, s)) = m].

Since indexed sets can challenge our tolerance of notation, algebraic specifications are commonly represented using a module-like syntactic structure that encapsulates the pertinent information concerning the signature and the equations of the specification. We have already seen how the family of operations will be specified when we used the "function header" notation above:

cons (_ , _) : Integer,List → List.

The syntax of the function symbol is spelled out as a pattern, with underscores representing the parameter positions and the Cartesian product indicated by a comma forming the domain. These notational conventions have become common practice in algebraic specifications.

Another advantage of the module representation of algebraic specifications is that it lends itself to decomposing definitions into relatively small components. We break the specification of lists of integers into three smaller modules for integers, Boolean values, and then lists, using a mechanism to import the signature and equations of one module into another. We view an algebraic specification as a sequence of modules, so that when one module imports another module, the sorts and functions in the signature can be used in the importing module. Relative to this importing mechanism, we define sorts and functions to be either exported or hidden. Hidden symbols are visible only in the module where they are first defined. Later we see that modules can be parameterized to define generic abstract data types. With parameterized specifications, certain portions of the module are left unspecified until the module is instantiated by specifying values for the formal parameters.

A Module for Truth Values

We now turn our attention to a module that gives an algebraic specification of truth values.

module Booleans
    exports
        sorts Boolean
        operations

true	: Boolean
false	: Boolean
errorBoolean	: Boolean
not (_)	: Boolean $\rightarrow$ Boolean
and (_ , _)	: Boolean, Boolean $\rightarrow$ Boolean
or (_ , _)	: Boolean, Boolean $\rightarrow$ Boolean
implies (_ , _)	: Boolean, Boolean $\rightarrow$ Boolean
eq? (_ , _)	: Boolean, Boolean $\rightarrow$ Boolean

    end exports

    operations
        xor (_ , _) : Boolean, Boolean $\rightarrow$ Boolean

    variables
        b, b_1, b_2 : Boolean

    equations

[B1]	and (true, b)	=	b
[B2]	and (false, true)	=	false
[B3]	and (false, false)	=	false
[B4]	not (true)	=	false
[B5]	not (false)	=	true
[B6]	or (b_1, b_2)	=	not (and (not (b_1), not (b_2)))
[B7]	implies (b_1, b_2)	=	or (not (b_1), b_2)
[B8]	xor (b_1, b_2)	=	and (or (b_1, b_2), not (and (b_1, b_2)))
[B9]	eq? (b_1, b_2)	=	not (xor (b_1, b_2))

end Booleans

The sort Boolean has two "normal" constant values, true and false, and an error value errorBoolean. We discuss the handling of errors in conjunction with the next module that specifies natural numbers. The functions not, and, or, and eq? are exported, whereas the function xor (exclusive or) is hidden. The module has no hidden sorts. Remember that the variables in equations are universally quantified implicitly, so that equation [B1] represents the axiom:

$\forall$b:Boolean [and (true, b) = b].

The equations in a specification may allow several variations that result ultimately in the same definition. For example, the semantics of or can be specified directly by

or (true, true) = true

or (true, false)= true

or (false, b)   = b.

Although these different definitions of or suggest different evaluation strategies, the equations in a specification are purely declarative and do not imply any particular evaluation order. The xor is defined in terms of and, or, and not. In order to illustrate hidden functions, we have elected not to make xor public. The eq? function is defined as the logical negation of xor. A direct definition of eq? is also possible.

Module Syntax

Before turning our attention to more sample modules, we examine the structure of a typical module. Each of the components specified below may be omitted in defining a particular module.

module <module-name>

    imports

        <list of modules>

    parameters

        sorts <sort names>

        operations <function symbols with their signatures>

        variables <list of variables and their sorts>

        equations <unconditional and conditional equations>

    end

    exports

        sorts <list of public sorts>

        operations <list containing signatures of public function symbols>

    end exports

sorts <hidden sort names>

operations
    <hidden function symbols with their signatures>

variables
    <list of variables and their sorts>

equations
    <unconditional and conditional equations>
end <module-name>

The second section contains parameters that are defined in terms of formal parameter symbols. The actual values (arguments) are supplied when the module is instantiated by naming the parameterized module and supplying already defined sorts and operations for each of the formal sort names and function symbols in the parameter. The functionality (syntax) of the actual operations must agree with the formal parameters, and the argument functions must satisfy the equations in the parameters section that specify properties of the formal parameters. We have shown the format for a single parameter, but multiple parameters are also possible. When modules are imported, items in them may be renamed. We show the syntax for renaming later in the section.

The syntax of function application may be represented using several forms, but in this chapter we rely on ordinary prefix notation with parentheses delimiting the arguments. This notation eliminates the need for precedence rules to disambiguate the order of execution of the corresponding operations. In the next chapter we consider some variations on this notation for function application. Functions can also return multiple values as tuples—for example:

$$h : S_1 \rightarrow S_2, S_3.$$

Tupled outputs are a notational convenience and can be replaced by a single sort. These details are left as an exercise.

Equations specifying the properties of operations can be unconditional, as in the Booleans module, or conditional. A **conditional equation** has the form

$$lhs = rhs \; when \; lhs_1 = rhs_1, lhs_2 = rhs_2, ..., lhs_n = rhs_n.$$

Finally, we mention that modules cannot be nested.

A Module for Natural Numbers

In the rest of this section, we give more sample modules to illustrate the ideas introduced above, concentrating on specifications that will be needed to define the semantics of Wren. The next module specifies the natural numbers, containing constant function symbols 0, 1, 10 and errorNatural, a function succ used to construct terms for the specification, the numeric operations add, sub, mul, div, and the predicate operations eq?, less?, and greater?. An exercise asks the reader to add an exponentiation operation exp to Naturals. This function is used when Naturals is imported by a module called Strings.

module Naturals
    imports Booleans
    exports
        sorts Natural
        operations

0	: Natural
1	: Natural
10	: Natural
errorNatural	: Natural
succ (_)	: Natural $\rightarrow$ Natural
add (_ , _)	: Natural, Natural $\rightarrow$ Natural
sub (_ , _)	: Natural, Natural $\rightarrow$ Natural
mul (_ , _)	: Natural, Natural $\rightarrow$ Natural
div (_ , _)	: Natural, Natural $\rightarrow$ Natural
eq? (_ , _)	: Natural, Natural $\rightarrow$ Boolean
less? (_ , _)	: Natural, Natural $\rightarrow$ Boolean
greater? (_ , _)	: Natural, Natural $\rightarrow$ Boolean

    end exports

    variables
        m, n : Natural

    equations

[N1]	1	= succ (0)
[N2]	10	= succ (succ (succ (succ (succ (succ (succ (succ (succ (succ (0))))))))))
[N3]	add (m, 0)	= m
[N4]	add (m, succ (n))	= succ (add (m, n))
[N5]	sub (0, succ(n))	= errorNatural
[N6]	sub (m, 0)	= m
[N7]	sub (succ (m), succ (n))	= sub (m, n)
[N8]	mul (m, 0)	= 0 *when* m≠errorNatural
[N9]	mul (m, 1)	= m
[N10]	mul (m, succ(n))	= add (m, mul (m, n))
[N11]	div (m, 0)	= errorNatural
[N12]	div (0, succ (n))	= 0 *when* n≠errorNatural

[N13] div (m, succ (n)) $= if\,(\text{less? (m, succ (n))},$
$\qquad\qquad\qquad\qquad\qquad\qquad 0,$
$\qquad\qquad\qquad\qquad\qquad\qquad \text{succ(div(sub(m,succ(n)),succ(n))))}$

[N14]	eq? (0, 0)	= true	
[N15]	eq? (0, succ (n))	= false	*when n≠errorNatural*
[N16]	eq? (succ (m), 0)	= false	*when m≠errorNatural*
[N17]	eq? (succ (m), succ (n))	= eq? (m, n)	
[N18]	less? (0, succ (m))	= true	*when m≠errorNatural*
[N19]	less? (m, 0)	= false	*when m≠errorNatural*
[N20]	less? (succ (m), succ (n))	= less? (m, n)	
[N21]	greater? (m, n)	= less? (n, m)	

end Naturals

Each sort will contain an error value to represent the result of operations on values outside of their normal domains. We assume that all operations propagate errors, so that, for example, the following properties hold:

succ (errorNatural)	= errorNatural
mul (succ (errorNatural), 0)	= errorNatural
or (true, errorBoolean)	= errorBoolean
eq? (succ(0), errorNatural)	= errorBoolean.

Propagating errors in this manner requires that some equations have conditions that restrict the operations to nonerror values. Without these conditions, the entire sort reduces to the error value, as witnessed by a deduction using [N8] and ignoring the condition:

$\qquad$ 0 = mul(succ(errorNatural),0) = mul(errorNatural,0) = errorNatural.

Without the condition on [N8], all the objects in Natural can be shown to equal errorNatural:

$\qquad$ succ(0) = succ(errorNatural) = errorNatural,

$\qquad$ succ(succ(0)) = succ(errorNatural) = errorNatural,

$\qquad$ and so on.

The equations that require conditions to avoid this sort of inconsistency—namely, [N8], [N12], [N15], [N16], [N18], and [N19] in the Naturals module—are those in which the variable(s) on the left disappear on the right. As a notational convention to enhance readability, we use n≠errorNatural for eq? (n,errorNatural) = false and similar abbreviations for the other sorts.

The module Naturals has no equation defining properties for the succ function. This operation is called a **constructor**, since together with the constant 0, succ can be used to construct representations of the values that form the natural numbers. In a model of this specification, we assume that values are equal only when their identity can be derived from the equations. Since there are no equations for succ, 0 does not equal succ(0), which does not equal succ(succ(0)), and so forth. So the terms 0, succ(0), succ(succ(0)), ... can be viewed as characterizing the natural numbers, the objects defined by the module.

The element errorNatural can be derived from the equations in two cases: subtracting a number from another number smaller than itself and dividing any number by zero. Thus we say that the terms that can be generated in the natural numbers specification consist of the values 0, succ(0), succ(succ(0), succ(succ(succ(0))), ... and errorNatural. This set serves as the universe of values or the **carrier set** for one of the algebras that acts as a model of the specification. We will define this so-called term algebra model carefully when we discuss the mathematical foundations of algebraic specifications in the next section.

This method of interpreting the meaning of the equations is known as **initial algebraic semantics**. In an initial model, the equality of items can be proved only as a direct result of equations in the module; otherwise they are never considered to be the same. This characteristic is called the **no confusion** property. The **no junk** property of the initial model says that all terms in the carrier set of a model of the specification correspond to terms generated from the signature of the module. We will examine the no confusion and no junk properties again in the next section when we discuss the construction of an initial algebra and describe its properties.

The constant functions 1 and 10 are convenient renamings of particular natural numbers for easy reference outside of the module. Addition is defined recursively with the second operand being decremented until it eventually reaches 0, the base case. The other operations, sub, mul, and div are defined recursively in similar ways. The rule [N9] is redundant since its values are included in [N10]. The div equations introduce the built-in polymorphic function *if*, which is used to determine when div has reached the base case (the dividend is less than the divisor).

$$\text{div (m, succ (n))} = \textit{if}\,(\text{ less? (m, succ (n)),}$$
$$0,$$
$$\text{succ (div (sub (m, succ (n)), succ (n))))}$$

A generic *if* operation cannot be specified by an algebraic specification itself since its arguments range over all possible sorts. However, it is always possible to eliminate the *if* by writing multiple conditional equations. For example,

div (m, succ (n)) = 0   *when* less? (m, succ (n)) = true
div (m, succ (n)) = succ (div (sub (m, succ (n)), succ (n))))
                                               when less? (m, succ (n)) = false
div (m, succ (n)) = errorNatural   *when* less? (m, succ (n)) = errorBoolean.

Given this equivalence, we will continue to use *if* as a notational convenience
without sacrificing the underlying foundations of algebraic semantics. Observe that using *if* requires that the module Booleans be imported to provide
truth values.

A Module for Characters

The Characters module presented below defines an underlying character set
adequate for Wren identifiers. Although this character set is limited to digits
and lowercase characters, the module can be easily extended to a larger
character set.

module Characters
    imports Booleans, Naturals
    exports
        sorts Char
        operations
            eq? (_ , _) : Char, Char $\rightarrow$ Boolean
            letter? (_) : Char $\rightarrow$ Boolean
            digit? (_)   : Char $\rightarrow$ Boolean
            ord (_)   : Char $\rightarrow$ Natural
            char-0   : Char
            char-1   : Char
              :   :
            char-9   : Char
            char-a   : Char
            char-b   : Char
            char-c   : Char
              :   :
            char-y   : Char
            char-z   : Char
            errorChar   : Char
    end exports
    variables
        c, c_1, c_2 : Char
    equations
    [C1]   ord (char-0) = 0

[C2]   ord (char-1) = succ (ord (char-0))
[C3]   ord (char-2) = succ (ord (char-1))
  :   :   :
[C10]   ord (char-9) = succ (ord (char-8))
[C11]   ord (char-a) = succ (ord (char-9))
[C12]   ord (char-b) = succ (ord (char-a))
[C13]   ord (char-c) = succ (ord (char-b))
  :   :   :
[C35]   ord (char-y) = succ (ord (char-x))
[C36]   ord (char-z) = succ (ord (char-y))
[C37]   eq? (c_1, c_2) = eq? (ord (c_1), ord (c_2))
[C38]   letter? (c)   = and (not (greater? (ord (char-a), ord (c))),
                              not (greater? (ord (c), ord (char-z))))
[C39]   digit? (c)   = and (not (greater? (ord (char-0), ord (c))),
                              not (greater? (ord (c) ord (char-9))))

end Characters

Observe that the equation "ord (char-9) = 9" cannot be derived from the equations in the module, since 9 is not a constant defined in Naturals. Rather than add the constants 2 through 9 and 11 through 35 to Naturals (for this character set), we rely on the repeated application of the successor function to define the ordinal values. The ord function here does not produce ascii codes as in Pascal but simply gives integer values starting at 0. Note that eq? refers to two different operations in [C37]. The first represents the equality operation on the characters currently being defined, and the second symbolizes equality on the natural numbers imported from Naturals. The sorts of the arguments determine which of the overloaded eq? operations the function symbol represents.

A Parameterized Module and Some Instantiations

The next example shows a parameterized module for homogeneous lists where the type of the items in the lists is specified when the module is instantiated.

module Lists
    imports Booleans, Naturals

    parameters Items
        sorts Item
        operations
            errorItem : Item
            eq?   : Item, Item → Boolean

variables
    a, b, c : Item
equations
    eq? (a,a) = true   *when* a≠errorItem
    eq? (a,b) = eq? (b,a)
    implies (and (eq? (a,b), eq? (b,c)), eq? (a,c)) = true
                                   when a≠errorItem, b≠errorItem, c≠errorItem
end Items

exports
    sorts List
    operations
        null   : List
        errorList   : List
        cons (_ , _)   : Item, List → List
        concat (_ , _) : List, List   → List
        equal? (_ , _) : List, List   → Boolean
        length (_)   : List → Natural
        mkList (_)   : Item → List
    end exports

variables
    i, i$_1$, i$_2$: Item
    s, s$_1$, s$_2$: List

equations
[S1]   concat (null, s)   = s
[S2]   concat (cons (i, s$_1$), s$_2$) = cons (i, concat (s$_1$, s$_2$))
[S3]   equal? (null, null)   = true
[S4]   equal? (null, cons (i, s)) = false   *when* s≠errorList, i≠errorItem
[S5]   equal? (cons (i, s), null) = false   *when* s≠errorList, i≠errorItem
[S6]   equal? (cons (i$_1$, s$_1$), cons (i$_2$, s$_2$)) = and (eq? (i$_1$, i$_2$), equal? (s$_1$, s$_2$))
[S7]   length (null)   = 0
[S8]   length (cons (i, s))   = succ (length (s))   *when* i≠errorItem
[S9]   mkList (i)   = cons (i, null)
end Lists

The three parameters for Lists define the type of items that are being joined, an error value, and an equality test required for comparing the items. The equations in the parameter section ensure that the operation associated with the formal symbol eq? is an equivalence relation. The symbols that act as parameters are unspecified until the module is instantiated when imported into another module. The operation null is a constant that acts as a constructor representing the empty list, and cons is a constructor function, having no defining equations, that builds nonempty lists. The structures formed by applications of the constructor functions represent the values of the sort List.

The length function is defined recursively with the base case treating the null list and the other case handling all other lists. The operation mkList is a convenience function to convert a single item into a list containing only that item. Since cons and null are exported, the user can do this task directly, but having a named function improves readability.

The process of renaming is illustrated in the following example of a list of integers, called Files, that will be used for input and output in the specification of Wren. Sometimes sorts and operations are renamed purely for purposes of documentation. Items that are not renamed on import retain their original names. For example, the constructor for Files will still be cons. See the further readings at the end of this chapter for more on these issues.

module Files
    imports Booleans, Naturals,
        instantiation of Lists
            bind Items **using** Natural **for** Item
                      using errorNatural **for** errorItem
                      using eq? **for** eq?
            rename **using** File **for** List
                    using emptyFile **for** null
                    using mkFile **for** mkList
                    using errorFile **for** errorList
    exports
        sorts File
        operations
            empty? (_) : File → Boolean
    end exports
    variables
        f : File
    equations
    [F1]   empty? (f) = equal? (f, emptyFile)
end Files

The identifiers created by renaming are exported by the module as well as the identifiers in the exports section. Note that we extend the instantiated imported module Lists with a new operation empty?. The Strings module, which is used to specify identifiers in Wren, also contains an instantiation of Lists.

module Strings
    imports Booleans,Naturals, Characters,
            instantiation of Lists
                bind Items **using** Char **for** Item
                      using errorChar **for** errorItem
                      using eq? **for** eq?
              rename using String **for** List
                    using nullString **for** null
                    using mkString **for** mkList
                    using strEqual **for** equal?
                    using errorString **for** errorList
    exports
        sorts String
        operations
            string-to-natural (_) : String $\rightarrow$ Boolean, Natural
    end exports
    variables
        c : Char
        b : Boolean
        n : Natural
        s : String
    equations
    [Str1]   string-to-natural (nullString) = <true,0>
    [Str2]   string-to-natural (cons (c, s))=
            if (and (digit? (c), b),
                <true, add (mul (sub (ord (c), ord (char-0)),
                                exp (10, length (s)))), n)>,
                <false, 0>)
                    when <b,n> = string-to-natural (s)
end Strings

The string-to-natural function returns a pair: The first value is a truth value that indicates whether the conversion was successful, and the second value is the numeric result. We introduced the constant 10 in Naturals to make this specification more readable. The operation exp is added to Naturals in an exercise.

A Module for Finite Mappings

The final modules of this section are Mappings and an instantiation of Mappings. A mapping associates a domain value of some sort with an item taken from some range (codomain) sort. Both the domain and range sorts are specified by parameters and determined at the time of instantiation. We use two mappings later in an algebraic specification of Wren. The type checking module associates Wren types with variable names modeling a symbol table, and the evaluation (or execution) module associates numeric values with variable names, modeling a store. Both of these sorts result from instantiations of Mappings.

module Mappings
    imports Booleans
    parameters Entries
        sorts Domain, Range
        operations
            equals (_ , _) : Domain, Domain $\rightarrow$ Boolean
            errorDomain : Domain
            errorRange   : Range

        variables
            a, b, c : Domain

        equations
            equals (a, a) = true   *when* a≠errorDomain
            equals (a, b) = equals (b, a)
            implies (and (equals (a, b), equals (b, c)), equals (a, c)) = true
                    when a≠errorDomain, b≠errorDomain, c≠errorDomain
      end Entries
    exports
        sorts Mapping
        operations
            emptyMap   : Mapping
            errorMapping   : Mapping
            update (_ , _ , _) : Mapping, Domain, Range $\rightarrow$ Mapping
            apply (_ , _)   : Mapping, Domain $\rightarrow$ Range
    end exports
    variables
        m   : Mapping
        d, d_1, d_2 : Domain
        r   : Range
    equations
  [M1]   apply (emptyMap, d)   = errorRange
  [M2]   apply (update (m, d_1, r), d_2) = r
                    when equals (d_1, d_2) = true, m≠errorMapping
  [M3]   apply (update (m, d_1, r), d_2) = apply (m, d_2)
                    when equals (d_1, d_2) = false, r≠errorRange
    end Mappings

The operation emptyMap is a constant, and the update operation adds or changes a pair consisting of a domain value and a range value in a mapping. The operation apply returns the range value associated with a domain value or returns errorRange if the mapping has no value for that domain element. Observe the similarity between terms for this specification and the Prolog terms we used in implementing environments and stores earlier in the text. The finite mapping [a|→8,b|→13] corresponds to the term

>   update (update (emptyMap, a, 8), b, 13),

which represents an object of sort Mapping.

A store structure that associates identifiers represented as strings with natural numbers can be defined in terms of Mappings. The following module instantiates Mappings using the types String and Natural for the domain and range sorts of the mappings, respectively. The operations are renamed to fit the store model of memory.

> **module** Stores
>   **imports** Strings, Naturals,
>   **instantiation of** Mappings
>   **bind** Entries **using** String **for** Domain
>   **using** Natural **for** Range
>   **using** strEqual **for** equals
>   **using** errorString **for** errorDomain
>   **using** errorNatural **for** errorRange
>   **rename using** Store **for** Mapping
>   **using** emptySto **for** emptyMap
>   **using** updateSto **for** update
>   **using** applySto **for** apply
> **end** Stores

We have introduced enough basic modules to develop an algebraic specification of Wren in section 12.4. However, the notation is sometimes less convenient than desired—for example,

>   succ (succ (succ (0))) stands for the natural number written as 3 (base-ten)

and

>   cons (char-a, cons (char-b, nullString)) represents the string literal "ab".

Additional specification modules can be developed to provide a more conventional notation (see Chapter 6 of [Bergstra89]), but these notational issues are beyond the scope of this book. We also ignore the problem of conflict resolution when several imported modules extend some previously defined module by defining operations with the same name in different ways. Since this topic is dealt with in the references, our presentation will concentrate on semantic rather than syntactic issues. We take a brief look at the mathematical foundations of algebraic semantics in the next section.

Exercises

1. Give the equation(s) for a direct definition of eq? in the module Booleans.

2. Show how the output of tuples can be eliminated by introducing new sorts. Develop a specific example to illustrate the technique.

3. Add function symbols lesseq? and greatereq? to the module Naturals and provide equations to specify their behavior.

4. Add a function symbol exp representing the exponentiation operation to Naturals and provide appropriate equations to specify its behavior.

5. Extend the module for Naturals to a module for Integers by introducing a predecessor operator.

6. Consider the module Mappings. No equations are provided to specify the sort Mapping, so two mappings are equal if they are represented by the same term. Does this notion of equality agree with the normal meaning of equal mappings? What equation(s) can be added to the module to remedy this problem?

7. Define a module that specifies binary trees with natural numbers at its leaf nodes only. Include operations for constructing trees, selecting parts from a tree, and several operations that compute values associated with binary trees, such as "sum of the values at the leaf nodes" and "height of a tree".

8. Redo exercise 7 for binary trees with natural numbers at interior nodes in addition to the leaf nodes.

9. Consider the signature defined by the module Mixtures. List five terms of sort Mixture. Suggest some equations that we may want this specification to satisfy. *Hint*: Consider algebraic properties of the binary operation.

   module Mixtures
      exports
        sorts Mixture
        operations
           flour   : Mixture
           sugar   : Mixture
           salt   : Mixture
           mix (_ , _): Mixture, Mixture $\rightarrow$ Mixture
      end exports
   end Mixtures

12.2 MATHEMATICAL FOUNDATIONS

Some very simple modules serve to illustrate the mathematical foundations
of algebraic semantics. We simplify the module Booleans to include only the
constants false and true and the function not. In a similar way, we limit Naturals
to the constant 0, the constructor succ, and the function symbol add. By
limiting the operations in this way, we avoid the need for error values in the
sorts. See the references, particularly [Ehrig85], for a description of error
handling in algebraic specifications.

module Bools
    exports
        sorts Boolean
        operations
            true   : Boolean
            false   : Boolean
            not (_) : Boolean $\rightarrow$ Boolean
    end exports

    equations
    [B1]   not (true) = false
    [B2]   not (false) = true
end Bools

module Nats
    imports Bools
    exports
        sorts Natural
        operations
            0   : Natural
            succ (_) : Natural $\rightarrow$ Natural
            add (_ , _): Natural, Natural $\rightarrow$ Natural
    end exports

    variables
        m, n : Natural

    equations
    [N1]   add (m, 0)   = m
    [N2]   add (m, succ (n)) = succ (add (m, n))
end Nats

Ground Terms

In the previous section we pointed out function symbols that act as constructors provide a way of building terms that represent the objects being defined by a specification. Actually, all function symbols can be used to construct terms that stand for the objects of the various sorts in the signature, although one sort is usually distinguished as the type of interest. We are particularly interested in those terms that have no variables.

Definition: For a given signature Σ = <Sorts,Operations>, the set of **ground terms** T_Σ for a sort S is defined inductively as follows:

1. All constants (nullary function symbols) of sort S in Operations are ground terms of sort S.

2. For every function symbol $f : S_1,...,S_n \to S$ in Operations, if $t_1,...,t_n$ are ground terms of sorts $S_1,...,S_n$, respectively, then $f(t_1,...,t_n)$ is a ground term of sort S where $S_1,...,S_n,S \in$ Sorts. ∎

Example: The ground terms of sort Boolean for the Bools module consist of all those expressions that can be built using the constants true and false and the operation symbol not. This set of ground terms is infinite.

true, not(true), not(not(true)), not(not(not(true))), ...
false, not(false), not(not(false)), not(not(not(false))), ... ∎

Example: The ground terms of sort Natural in the Nats module are more complex, since two constructors build new terms from old; the patterns are suggested below:

0,	add(0,0),	
succ(0),	add(0,succ(0)),	add(succ(0),0),
succ(succ(0)),	add(0,succ(succ(0))),	add(succ(succ(0)),0),
	add(succ(0),succ(0)),	
succ(succ(succ(0))),	add(0,succ(succ(succ(0)))),	add(succ(succ(succ(0))),0),
	add(succ(0),succ(succ(0))),	add(succ(succ(0)),succ(0)),
:	:	: ∎

If we ignore the equations in these two modules for now, the ground terms must be mutually distinct. On the basis of the signature only (no equations), we have no reason to conclude that not(true) is the same as false and that add(succ(0),succ(0)) is the same as succ(succ(0)).

Σ-Algebras

Algebraic specifications deal only with the syntax of data objects and their operations. Semantics is provided by defining algebras that serve as models of the specifications. **Homogeneous algebras** can be thought of as a single set, called the **carrier**, on which several operations may be defined—for example, the integers with addition and multiplication form a ring. Computer science applications and some mathematical systems, such as vector spaces, need structures with several types. **Heterogeneous** or **many-sorted algebras** have a number of operations that act on a collection of sets. Specifications are modeled by Σ-algebras, which are many-sorted.

Definition: For a given signature Σ, an algebra A is a Σ-**algebra** under the following circumstances:

- There is a one-to-one correspondence between the carrier sets of A and the sorts of Σ.

- There is a one-to-one correspondence between the constants and functions of A and the operation symbols of Σ so that those constants and functions are of the appropriate sorts and functionalities.　▌

A Σ-algebra contains a set for each sort in S and an actual function for each of the function symbols in Σ. For example, let Σ = <Sorts, Operations> be a signature where Sorts is a set of sort names and Operations is a set of function symbols of the form $f : S_1,...,S_n \rightarrow S$ where S and each S_i are sort names from Sorts. Then a Σ-algebra A consists of the following:

1. A collection of sets $\{ S_A \mid S \in \text{Sorts} \}$, called the **carrier sets**.

2. A collection of functions $\{ f_A \mid f \in \text{Operations} \}$ with the functionality

$$f_A : (S_1)_A,...,(S_n)_A \rightarrow S_A$$

   for each $f : S_1,...,S_n \rightarrow S$ in Operations.

Σ-algebras are called heterogeneous or many-sorted algebras because they may contain objects of more than one sort.

Definition: The **term algebra** T_Σ for a signature Σ = <Sorts, Operations> is constructed as follows. The carrier sets $\{ S_{T_\Sigma} \mid S \in \text{Sorts} \}$ are defined inductively.

1. For each constant c of sort S in Σ we have a corresponding constant "c" in S_{T_Σ}.

2. For each function symbol $f : S_1,...,S_n \rightarrow S$ in Σ and any n elements $t_1 \in (S_1)_{T_\Sigma}, ...,t_n \in (S_n)_{T_\Sigma}$, the term "$f(t_1,...,t_n)$" belongs to the carrier set $(S)_{T_\Sigma}$.

The functions in the term algebra, corresponding to the function symbols in Operations, are defined by simply forming the literal term that results from applying the function symbol to terms. For each function symbol $f : S_1,...,S_n \rightarrow S$ in Σ and any n elements $t_1 \in (S_1)_{T_\Sigma}, ...,t_n \in (S_n)_{T_\Sigma}$, we define the function f_{T_Σ} by $f_{T_\Sigma}(t_1, ..., t_n)$ = "$f(t_1, ..., t_n)$".　▌

The elements of the carrier sets of T_Σ consist of strings of symbols chosen from a set containing the constants and function symbols of Σ together with the special symbols "(", ")", and ",". For example, the carrier set for the term algebra T_Σ constructed from the module Bools contains all the ground terms from the signature, including

> "true", "not(true)", "not(not(true))", ...
> "false", "not(false)", "not(not(false))", ...

Furthermore, the function not_{T_Σ} maps "true" to "not(true)", which is mapped to "not(not(true))", and so forth.

This term algebra clearly does not specify the intended meaning of Bools since the carrier set is infinite. Also, "false" $\neq$ "not(true)", which is different from our understanding of the *not* function in Boolean logic. So far we have not accounted for the equations in a specification and what properties they enforce in an algebra.

Definition: For a signature Σ and a Σ-algebra A, the **evaluation function** $eval_A : T_\Sigma \rightarrow A$ from ground terms to values in A is defined as:

$eval_A$ ("c") = c_A for constants c and

$eval_A$("f(t_1,...,t_n)") = $f_A(eval_A(t_1),...,eval_A(t_n))$
    where each term t_i is of sort S_i for f : $S_1,...,S_m \rightarrow S$ in Operations.   ∎

For any Σ-algebra A, the evaluation function from T_Σ must always exist and have the property that it maps function symbols to actual functions in A in a conformal way to be defined later. The term algebra T_Σ is a symbolic algebra—concrete but symbolic.

A Congruence from the Equations

As the function symbols and constants create a set of ground terms, the equations of a specification generate a congruence $\equiv$ on the ground terms. A congruence is an equivalence relation with an additional "substitution" property.

Definition: Let Spec = $<\Sigma,E>$ be a specification with signature Σ and equations E. The **congruence $\equiv_E$ determined by E on T_Σ** is the smallest relation satisfying the following properties:

1. Variable Assignment: Given an equation lhs = rhs in E that contains variables $v_1,...,v_n$ and given any ground terms $t_1,...,t_n$ from T_Σ of the same sorts as the respective variables,

$$lhs[v_1 \mapsto t_1, ..., v_n \mapsto t_n] \equiv_E rhs[v_1 \mapsto t_1, ..., v_n \mapsto t_n]$$

where $v_i \mapsto t_i$ indicates substituting the ground term t_i for the variable v_i. If the equation is conditional, the condition must be valid after the variable assignment is carried out on the condition.

2. Reflexive: For every ground term $t \in T_\Sigma$, $t \equiv_E t$.

3. Symmetric: For any ground terms $t_1, t_2 \in T_\Sigma$, $t_1 \equiv_E t_2$ implies $t_2 \equiv_E t_1$.

4. Transitive: For any terms $t_1, t_2, t_3 \in T_\Sigma$,
$$(t_1 \equiv_E t_2 \text{ and } t_2 \equiv_E t_3) \text{ implies } t_1 \equiv_E t_3.$$

5. Substitution Property: If $t_1 \equiv_E t_1',\dots,t_n \equiv_E t_n'$ and $f : S_1,\dots,S_n \to S$ is any function symbol in Σ, then $f(t_1,\dots,t_n) \equiv_E f(t_1',\dots,t_n')$. ∎

Normally, we omit the subscript E and rely on the context to determine which equations apply. To generate an equivalence relation from a set of equations, we take every ground instance of all the equations as a basis, and allow any derivation using the reflexive, symmetric, and transitive properties and the rule that each function symbol preserves equivalence when building ground terms.

For the Bools module, all ground terms are congruent to true or to false.

true ≡ not(false) ≡ not(not(true)) ≡ not(not(not(false))) ≡ ....
false ≡ not(true) ≡ not(not(false)) ≡ not(not(not(true))) ≡ ....

These congruences are easy to prove since no variables are involved. For the Nats module, all ground terms are congruent to one of 0, succ(0), succ(succ(0)), succ(succ(succ(0))), and so forth. For example, the following four terms are congruent:

succ(succ(0)) ≡ add(0,succ(succ(0))) ≡
add(succ(succ(0)),0) ≡ add(succ(0),succ(0)).

We show the proof for add(succ(0),succ(0)) ≡ succ(succ(0)).

add(succ(0),succ(0))
  ≡ succ(add(succ(0),0)) using [N2] from Nats and a variable
                  assignment with [m ↦ succ(0), n ↦ 0]
  ≡ succ(succ(0)) using [N1] from Nats and a variable
                  assignment with [m ↦ succ(0)].

Definition: If Spec is a specification with signature Σ and equations E, a Σ-algebra A is a **model** of Spec if for all ground terms t_1 and t_2, $t_1 \equiv_E t_2$ implies $\text{eval}_A(t_1) = \text{eval}_A(t_2)$. ∎

Example: Consider the algebra A = <{off, on}, {off, on, switch}>, where off and on are constants and switch is defined by

switch(off) = on and switch(on) = off.

Then if Σ is the signature of Bools, A is a Σ-algebra that models the specification defined by Bools.

Boolean$_A$ = {off, on} is the carrier set corresponding to sort Boolean.

Operation symbols of Σ	**Constants/functions of A**
true : Boolean	true$_A$ = on : Boolean$_A$
false : Boolean	false$_A$ = off : Boolean$_A$
not : Boolean $\to$ Boolean	not$_A$ = switch : Boolean$_A$ $\to$ Boolean$_A$

For example, not(true) $\equiv$ false and in the algebra A,

eval$_A$(not(true)) = not$_A$(eval$_A$(true)) = not$_A$(true$_A$) = switch(on) = off, and
eval$_A$(false) = off.   ▮

There may be many models for Spec. We now construct a particular Σ-algebra, called the **initial algebra**, that is guaranteed to exist. We take this initial algebra *to be the meaning* of the specification Spec.

The Quotient Algebra

The term algebra T_Σ serves as the starting point in constructing an initial algebra. We build the quotient algebra Q from the term algebra T_Σ of a specification <Σ,E> by factoring out congruences.

Definition: Let <Σ,E> be a specification with Σ = <Sorts, Operations>. If t is a term in T_Σ, we represent its congruence class as [t] = { t' | t $\equiv_E$ t' }. So [t] = [t'] if and only if t $\equiv_E$ t'. These congruence classes form the members of the carrier sets { S_{T_Σ} | S$\in$ Sorts } of the **quotient algebra**, one set for each sort S in the signature. We translate a constant c into the congruence class [c]. The functions in the term algebra define functions in the quotient algebra in the following way:

Given a function symbol f : S_1,...,S_n $\to$ S in Σ, f_Q([t_1],...,[t_n]) = [f(t_1,...,t_n)] for any terms t_i : S_i, with 1$\leq$i$\leq$n, from the appropriate carrier sets.

The function f_Q is well-defined, since $t_1 \equiv_E t_1'$, ..., $t_n \equiv_E t_n'$ implies $f_Q(t_1,...,t_n) \equiv_E$ $f_Q(t_1',...,t_n')$ by the Substitution Property for congruences.   ▮

Consider the term algebra for Bools. There are two congruence classes, which we may as well call [true] and [false]. From our previous observation of the congruence of ground terms, we know that the congruence class [true] contains

"true", "not(false)", "not(not(true))", "not(not(not(false)))", ...

and the congruence class [false] contains
"false", "not(true)", "not(not(false))", "not(not(not(true)))", ...

The function not_Q is defined in the following way:

$not_Q([false]) = [not(false)] = [true]$, and
$not_Q([true]) = [not(true)] = [false]$.

So the quotient algebra has the carrier set { [true], [false] } and the function not_Q. This quotient algebra is, in fact, an initial algebra for Bools. Initial algebras are not necessarily unique. For example, the algebra

A = <{off, on}, {off, on, switch}>

is also an initial algebra for Bools.

An initial algebra is "finest-grained" in the sense that it equates only those terms required to be equated, and, therefore, its carrier sets contain as many elements as possible. Using the procedure outlined above for developing the term algebra and then the quotient algebra, we can always guarantee that at least one initial algebra exists for any specification.

Homomorphisms

Functions between Σ-algebras that preserve the operations are called Σ-homomorphisms. See Chapter 9 for another description of homomorphisms. These functions are used to compare and contrast algebras that act as models of specifications.

Definition: Suppose that A and B are Σ-algebras for a given signature Σ = <Sorts, Operations>. Then h is a Σ-**homomorphism** if it maps the carrier sets of A to the carrier sets of B and the constants and functions of A to the constants and functions of B, so that the behavior of the constants and functions is preserved. In other words, h consists of a collection { h_S | S∈ Sorts } of functions $h_S : S_A \rightarrow S_B$ for S∈ Sorts such that

$h_S(c_A) = c_B$ for each constant symbol c : S, and

$h_S(f_A(a_1,...,a_n)) = f_B(h_{S_1}(a_1),...,h_{S_n}(a_n))$ for each function symbol

   $f : S_1,...,S_n \rightarrow S$ in S and any n elements $a_1 \in (S_1)_A,...,a_n \in (S_n)_A$.   ∎

If there is a Σ-homomorphism h from A to B and the inverse of h is a Σ-homomorphism from B to A, then h is an **isomorphism** and—apart from renaming carrier sets, constants, and functions—the two algebras are exactly the same.

The notion of Σ-homomorphism is used to define the concept of initial algebra formally.

Definition: A Σ-algebra I in the class of all Σ-algebras that serve as models of a specification with signature Σ is called **initial** if for any Σ-algebra A in the class, there is a unique homomorphism h : I $\rightarrow$ A. ∎

The quotient algebra Q for a specification is an initial algebra. Therefore for any Σ-algebra A that acts as a model of the specification, there is a unique Σ-homomorphism from Q to A. The function $eval_A : T_\Sigma \rightarrow A$ induces the Σ-homomorphism h from Q to A using the definition:

$$h([t]) = eval_A(t) \text{ for each } t \in T_S.$$

The homomorphism h is well defined because if $t_1 \equiv t_2$, $h([t_1]) = eval_A(t_1) = eval_A(t_2) = h([t_2])$.

Any algebra isomorphic to Q is also an initial algebra. So since the quotient algebra Q and the algebra A = <{off, on}, {off, on, switch}> are isomorphic, A is also an initial algebra for Bools. We can now formally define the terms junk and confusion, introduced earlier in this chapter.

Definition: Let <Σ,E> be a specification, let Q be the quotient algebra for <Σ,E>, and let B be an arbitrary Σ-algebra.

1. If the homomorphism from Q to a Σ-algebra B is not onto (not surjective), then B contains **junk** since B contains values that do not correspond to any terms constructed from the signature.

2. If the homomorphism from Q to B is not one-to-one (not injective), then B exhibits **confusion** since two different values in the quotient algebra correspond to the same value in B. ∎

Consider the quotient algebra for Nats with the infinite carrier set [0], [succ(0)], [succ(succ(0))], and so on. Suppose that we have a 16-bit computer for which the integers consist of the following set of values:

{ -32768, -32767, ..., -1, 0, 1, 2, 3, ..., 32766, 32767 }.

The negative integers are junk with respect to Nats since they cannot be images of any of the natural numbers. On the other hand, all positive integers above 32767 must be confusion. When mapping an infinite carrier set onto a finite machine, confusion must occur.

Consistency and Completeness

Consistency and completeness are two issues related to junk and confusion. The following examples illustrate these notions. Suppose we want to add a predecessor operation to naturals by importing Naturals (the original version) and defining a predecessor function pred.

module Predecessor$_1$

    imports Booleans, Naturals

    exports

        operations

            pred (_) : Natural → Natural

    end exports

    variables

        n : Natural

    equations

    [P1]   pred (succ (n)) = n

end Predecessor$_1$

We say that Naturals is a subspecification of Predecessor$_1$ since the signature and equations of Predecessor$_1$ include the signature and equations of Naturals. We have added a new congruence class [pred(0)], which is not congruent to 0 or any of the successors of 0. We say that [pred(0)] is junk and that Predecessor$_1$ is not a **complete extension** of Naturals. We can resolve this problem by adding the equation [P2] pred(0) = 0 (or [P2] pred(0) = errorNatural).

Suppose that we define another predecessor module in the following way:

module Predecessor$_2$

    imports Booleans, Naturals

    exports

        operations

            pred (_) : Natural → Natural

    end exports

    variables

        n : Natural

    equations

    [P1]   pred (n) = sub (n, succ (0))

    [P2]   pred (0) = 0

end Predecessor$_2$

The first equation specifies the predecessor by subtracting one, and the second equation is carried over from the "fix" for Predecessor$_1$. In the module Naturals, we have the congruence classes:

    [errorNatural], [0], [succ(0)], [succ(succ(0))], ...

With the new module Predecessor$_2$, we have pred(0) = sub(0,succ(0)) = errorNatural by [P1] and [N5], and pred(0) = 0 by [P2]. So we have reduced the number of congruence classes, since [0] = [errorNatural]. Because this has introduced confusion, we say that Predecessor$_2$ is not a **consistent extension** of Naturals.

Definition: Let Spec be a specification with signature Σ = <Sorts, Operations> and equations E. Suppose SubSpec is a subspecification of Spec with sorts SubSorts (a subset of Sorts) and equations SubE (a subset of E). Let T and SubT represent the terms of Sorts and SubSorts, respectively.

- Spec is a **complete extension** of SubSpec if for every sort S in SubSorts and every term t_1 in T, there exists a term t_2 in SubT such that t_1 and t_2 are congruent with respect to E.

- Spec is a **consistent extension** of SubSpec if for every sort S in SubSorts and all terms t_1 and t_2 in T, t_1 and t_2 are congruent with respect to E if and only if t_1 and t_2 are congruent with respect to SubE. ∎

Exercises

1. Describe an initial algebra for the simplified Nats module given in this section.

2. Use the specification of Booleans in section 12.1 to prove the following congruences:

    a) and(not(false),not(true)) $\equiv$ false

    b) or(not(false),not(true)) $\equiv$ true

3. Use the specification of Naturals in section 12.1 to prove the following congruences:

    a) sub (10, succ (succ (succ (succ (succ (succ(0)))))))
    $$\equiv \text{succ (succ (succ (succ (0))))}$$

    b) mul (succ (succ (0)), succ (succ (0))) $\equiv$ succ (succ (succ (succ (0))))

    c) less? (succ (0), succ (succ (succ (0)))) $\equiv$ true

4. Each of the following algebras are Σ-algebras for the signature of Nats. Identify those that are initial and define the homomorphisms from the initial algebras to the other algebras. Do any of these algebras contain confusion or junk?

    a) A = <{ 0, 1, 2, 3, ... }, {0_A, succ$_A$, add$_A$}> where 0_A = 0, succ$_A$ = λn . n+1, and add$_A$ = λm . λn . m+n.

    b) B = <{ 0, 1, 2 }, {0_B, succ$_B$, add$_B$}> where 0_B = 0, succ$_B$(0)= 1, succ$_B$(1)= 2, succ$_B$(2)= 0, and add$_B$ = λm . λn . m+n (modulo 3).

c) $C = <\{ ..., -2, -1, 0, 1, 2, 3, ... \}, \{0_C, succ_C, add_C\}>$ where $0_C = 0$, $succ_C = \lambda n . n+1$, and $add_C = \lambda m . \lambda n . m+n$.

d) $D = <\{ zero, succ(zero), succ(succ(zero)), ... \}, \{0_D, succ_D, add_D\}>$ where $0_D = zero$, $succ_D = \lambda n . succ(n)$, $add_D(m,zero) = m$, and $add_D(m,succ(n)) = succ(add_D(m,n))$.

5. List five different terms in the term algebra T_Σ for the specification of stores in the module at the end of section 12.1. Describe the quotient algebra for Mappings, including two additional equations:

[M4]   update (update (m, d_1, r_1), d_2, r_2) = update (update (m, d_2, r_2), d_1, r_1)
                                                                          when $d_1 \neq d_2$

[M5]   update (update (m, d_1, r_1), d_1, r_2) = update (m, d_1, r_2).

5. Consider the following module that defines a specification $<\Sigma,E>$ with signature Σ and equations E. Ignore the possibility of an errorBoolean value in the sort.

> **module** Booleans
> > **exports**
> > > **sorts** Boolean
> > > **operations**
> > > > true : Boolean
> > > > false : Boolean
> > > > not (_) : Boolean $\rightarrow$ Boolean
> > > > nand (_ , _) : Boolean, Boolean $\rightarrow$ Boolean
> > **end exports**
> > **variables**
> > > b : Boolean
> > **equations**
> > > [B1]   nand (false, false) = true
> > > [B2]   nand (false, true) = false
> > > [B3]   nand (true, false) = false
> > > [B4]   nand (true, true) = false
> > > [B5]   not (b) = nand (b, b)
>
> **end** Booleans

a) Give an induction definition of the carrier set of the term algebra T_Σ for this Σ.

b) Carefully describe the quotient algebra Q for this specification.

c) Describe another algebra A whose carrier set has only *one* element and that models this specification. Define a homomorphism from Q to A.

d) Describe another algebra B whose carrier set has *three* elements and that models this specification. Define a homomorphism from Q to B.

12.3 USING ALGEBRAIC SPECIfiCATIONS

Before considering the algebraic semantics for Wren, we take a detour to discuss several other uses of algebraic specifications. Defining abstract data types has proved to be the most productive application of these specification methods so far. In the first part of this section we develop and discuss the specification of abstract data types using algebraic methods. Then in the second part of this section we return to the concept of abstract syntax and see that it can be put on a more formal foundation by exploiting algebraic specifications and their corresponding algebras.

Data Abstraction

The main problem in creating large software systems is that their complexity can exceed the programmers' powers of comprehension. Using abstraction provides a fundamental technique for dealing with this complexity. Abstraction means that a programmer concentrates on the essential features of the problem while ignoring details and characteristics of concrete realizations in order to moderate the magnitude of the complexity.

Abstraction aids in the constructing, understanding, and maintaining of systems by reducing the number of details a programmer needs to understand while working on one part of the problem. The reliability of a system is enhanced by designing it in modules that maintain a consistent level of abstraction, and by permitting only certain operations at each level of abstraction. Any operation that violates the logical view of the current level of abstraction is prohibited. A programmer uses procedural and data abstractions without knowing how they are implemented (called **information hiding**). Unnecessary details of data representation or of an operation's implementation are hidden from those who have no need to see them.

Data abstraction refers to facilities that allow the definition of new sorts of data and operations on that data. Once the data and operations have been defined, the programmer forgets about the implementation and simply deals with their logical properties. The goal of data abstraction is to separate the logical properties of the data and operations from the implementation. Programmers work with abstract data types when they use the predefined types in a programming language. The objects and operations of integer type are used in a program based solely on their logical characteristics; programmers need know nothing of the representation of integers or of the implementation of the arithmetic operations. This information hiding allows them to consider problems at a higher level of abstraction by ignoring implementation details. High-level strategies should not be based on low-level details.

The full power of abstraction becomes evident only when programmers can create abstract data types for themselves. Many modern programming languages provide support for the specification of ADTs. Three facilities are desirable in a programming language for the creation of ADTs:

1. **Information Hiding**: The compiler should ensure that the user of an ADT does not have access to the representation (of the values) and implementation (of the operations) of an ADT.

2. **Encapsulation**: All aspects of the specification and implementation of an ADT should be contained in one or two syntactic unit(s) with a well-defined interface to the users of the ADT. The Ada package, the Modula-2 module, and the class feature in object-oriented programming languages are examples of encapsulation mechanisms.

3. **Generic types** (parameterized modules): There should be a way of defining an ADT as a template without specifying the nature of all its components. Such a generic type will be instantiated when the properties of its missing component values are instantiated.

Instead of delving into the definition of ADTs in programming languages, we return now to a more formal discussion of data abstraction in the context of algebraic specification as already examined in the first two sections of this chapter.

A Module for Unbounded Queues

We start by giving the signature of a specification of queues of natural numbers.

module Queues
    imports Booleans, Naturals
    exports
        sorts Queue
        operations
            newQ   : Queue
            errorQueue   : Queue
            addQ (_ , _) : Queue, Natural $\rightarrow$ Queue
            deleteQ (_) : Queue $\rightarrow$ Queue
            frontQ (_)   : Queue $\rightarrow$ Natural
            isEmptyQ (_): Queue $\rightarrow$ Boolean
    end exports
end Queues

Given only the signature of Queues, we have no justification for assuming any properties of the operations other than their basic syntax. Except for the names of the operations, which are only meaningless symbols at this point, this module could be specifying stacks instead of queues. One answer to this ambiguity is to define the characteristic properties of the queue ADT by describing informally what each operation does—for example:

- The function isEmptyQ(q) returns true if and only if the queue q is empty.
- The function frontQ(q) returns the natural number in the queue that was added earliest without being deleted yet.
- If q is an empty queue, frontQ(q) is an error value.

Several problems arise with this sort of informal approach. The descriptions are ambiguous, depending on terms that have not been defined—for example, "empty" and "earliest". The properties depend heavily on the names used for the operations and what they suggest. The names will be of no use with a completely new data type. On the other hand, a programmer may be tempted to define the meaning of the operations in terms of an implementation of them, say as an array with two index values identifying the front and rear of the queue, but this defeats the whole intent of data abstraction, which is to separate logical properties of data objects from their concrete realization.

A more formal approach to specifying the properties of an ADT is through a set of axioms in the form of module equations that relate the operations to each other. We insert the following sections into the module Queues:

variables
    q : Queue
    m : Natural

equations

[Q1]   isEmptyQ (newQ)   = true

[Q2]   isEmptyQ (addQ (q,m)) = false   *when* q≠errorQueue, m≠errorNatural

[Q3]   delete (newQ)   = newQ

[Q4]   deleteQ (addQ (q,m))   = *if* (isEmptyQ(q), newQ, addQ(deleteQ(q),m))
                                      when m≠errorNatural

[Q5]   frontQ (newQ)   = errorNatural

[Q6]   frontQ (addQ (q,m))   = *if* (isEmptyQ(q), m, frontQ(q))
                                      when m≠errorNatural

The decision to have delete(newQ) return newQ is arbitrary. Some other time we might want delete(newQ) to be errorQueue when describing the behavior of a queue.

Implementing Queues as Unbounded Arrays

Assuming that the axioms correctly specify the concept of a queue, they can be used to verify that an implementation is correct. A realization of an abstract data type will consist of a representation of the objects of the type, implementations of the operations, and a **representation function** Φ that maps terms in the model onto the abstract objects in such a way that the axioms are satisfied. For example, say we want to represent queues as arrays with two pointers, one to the front of the queue and one to the rear. Note that the implementation is simplified by defining unbounded arrays, since the queues that have been described are unbounded.

To enhance the readability of this presentation, we use abbreviations such as "m=n" for eq?(m,n) and "m≤n" for not(greater?(m,n)) from now on. The notion of an unbounded array is presented as an abstract data type in the following module:

module Arrays
  imports Booleans, Naturals
  exports
      sorts Array
      operations
          newArray : Array
          errorArray : Array
          assign (_ , _ , _) : Array, Natural, Natural → Array
          access (_ , _)   : Array, Natural → Natural
  end exports

  variables
      arr   : Array
      i, j, m : Natural

  equations
  [A1]   access (newArray, i) = errorNatural
  [A2]   access (assign (arr, i, m), j) = *if* (i = j, m, access(arr,j))
$$\text{\textit{when} m≠errorNatural}$$

end Arrays

The implementation of the ADT Queue using the ADT Array has the following set of triples as its objects:

  ArrayQ = { <arr,f,e> | arr : Array and f,e : Natural and f≤e }.

The operations over ArrayQ are defined as follows:

  [AQ1]   newAQ = <newArray,0,0>

  [AQ2]   addAQ (<arr,f,e>, m)   = <assign(arr,e,m),f,e+1>

[AQ3]   deleteAQ (<arr,f,e>)   = if (f = e, <newArray,0,0>, <arr,f+1,e>)

[AQ4]   frontAQ (<arr,f,e>)   = if (f = e, errorNatural, access(arr,f))

[AQ5]   isEmptyAQ (<arr,f,e>) = (f = e) $when$ arr≠errorArray

The array queues are related to the abstract queues by a homomorphism, called a representation function,

Φ : { ArrayQ,Natural,Boolean } → { Queue,Natural,Boolean },

defined on the objects and operations of the sort. We use the symbolic terms "Φ(arr,f,e)" to represent the abstract queue objects in Queue.

For arr : Array, m : Natural, and b : Boolean,

Φ (<arr,f,e>) = Φ(arr,f,e) $when$ f≤e

Φ (<arr,f,e>) = errorQueue $when$ f>e

Φ (m) = m

Φ (b) = b

Φ (newAQ) = newQ

Φ (addAQ) = addQ

Φ (deleteAQ) = deleteQ

Φ (frontAQ) = frontQ

Φ (isEmptyAQ) = isEmptyQ

Under the homomorphism, the five equations that define operations for the array queues map into five equations describing properties of the abstract queues.

[D1]   newQ   = Φ(newArray,0,0)
[D2]   addQ (Φ(arr,f,e), m) = Φ(assign(arr,e,m),f,e+1)
[D3]   deleteQ (Φ(arr,f,e)) = if (f = e, Φ(newArray,0,0), Φ(arr,f+1,e))
[D4]   frontQ (Φ(arr,f,e))   = if (f = e, errorNatural, access(arr,f))
[D5]   isEmptyQ (Φ(arr,f,e)) = (f = e)

As an example, consider the image of [AQ2] under Φ.

Assume [AQ2] addAQ (<arr,f,e>,m) = <assign (arr,e,m),f,e+1>.

Then addQ (Φ(arr,f,e),m) = Φ(addAQ) (Φ(<arr,f,e>),Φ(m)>)

                = Φ(addAQ (<arr,f,e>,m))

                = Φ(assign(arr,e,m),f,e+1),

which is [D2].

The implementation is correct if its objects can be shown to satisfy the queue axioms [Q1] to [Q6] for arbitrary queues of the form $q = \Phi(\text{arr},f,e)$ with $f \le e$ and arbitrary elements m of Natural, given the definitions [D1] to [D5] and the equations for arrays. First we need a short lemma.

Lemma: For any queue $\Phi(a,f,e)$ constructed using the operations of the implementation, $f \le e$.

Proof: The only operations that produce queues are newQ, addQ, and deleteQ, the constructors in the signature. The proof is by induction on the number of applications of these operations.

Basis: Since $\text{newQ} = \Phi(\text{newArray},0,0)$, $f \le e$.

Induction Step: Suppose that $\Phi(a,f,e)$ has been constructed with n applications of the operations and that $f \le e$.

Consider a queue constructed with one more application of these functions, for a total of $n+1$.

Case 1: The $n+1^{st}$ operation is addQ.
    But $\text{addQ }(\Phi(a,f,e),m) = \Phi(\text{assign }(a,f,m), f, e+1)$ has $f \le e+1$.

Case 2: The $n+1^{st}$ operation is deleteQ.
    But $\text{deleteQ }(\Phi(a,f,e)) = if\ (f = e,\ \Phi(\text{arr},f,e),\ \Phi(\text{arr},f+1,e)\ )$.
    If $f=e$, then $f \le e$, and if $f<e$, then $f+1 \le e$.   ∎

The proof of the lemma is an example of a general principle, called **structural induction** because the induction covers all of the ways in which the objects of the data type may be constructed (see the discussion of structural induction in Chapter 8). The goal is to prove a property that holds for all the values of a particular sort, and the induction applies to those operations (the constructors) that produce elements of the sort. For the lemma, the constructors for Queue consist of newQ, addQ, and deleteQ. The general principle can be described as follows:

> **Structural Induction**: Suppose f_1, f_2, ..., f_n are the operations that act as constructors for an abstract data type S, and P is a property of values of sort S. If the truth of P for all arguments of sort S for each f_i implies the truth of P for the results of all applications of f_i that satisfy the syntactic specification of S, it follows that P is true of all values of the data type. The basis case results from those constructors with no arguments—namely, the constants of sort S.

To enable the verification of [Q4] as part of proving the validity of this queue implementation, it is necessary to extend Φ for the following values:
    For any f : Natural and arr : Array, $\Phi(\text{arr},f,f) = \text{newQ}$.

This extension is consistent with definition [D1].

Verification of Queue Axioms

Let $q = \Phi(a,f,e)$ be an arbitrary queue and let m be an arbitrary element of Natural.

[Q1] isEmptyQ (newQ) = isEmptyQ (Φ(newArray,0,0)) by [D1]
$\qquad\qquad\qquad\qquad$ = (0 = 0) = true by [D5].

[Q2] isEmptyQ (addQ (Φ(arr,f,e),m))
$\qquad\qquad\qquad$ = isEmptyQ (Φ(assign(arr,e,m),f,e+1) by [D2]
$\qquad\qquad\qquad$ = (f = e+1) = false, since f$\le$e by [D5] and the lemma.

[Q3] deleteQ (newQ) = deleteQ (Φ(newArray,0,0)) by [D1]
$\qquad\qquad\qquad$ = Φ(newArray,0,0) = newQ by [D3] and [D1].

[Q4] deleteQ (addQ (Φ(arr,f,e), m))
$\qquad\qquad\qquad\qquad$ = deleteQ (Φ(assign(arr,e,m),f,e+1)) by [D2]
$\qquad\qquad\qquad\qquad$ = Φ(assign(arr,e,m),f+1,e+1) by [D3].

Case 1: f = e, that is, isEmptyQ (Φ(arr,f,e)) = true.
Then Φ(assign(arr,e,m),f+1,e+1) = newQ by [D1].

Case 2: f < e, that is, isEmptyQ (Φ(arr,f,e)) = false.
Then Φ(assign(arr,e,m),f+1,e+1) = addQ (Φ(arr,f+1,e), m) by [D2]
$\qquad\qquad\qquad\qquad\qquad$ = addQ (deleteQ (Φ(arr,f,e)), m) by [D3].

[Q5] frontQ (newQ) = frontQ (Φ(newArray,0,0)) by [D1]
$\qquad\qquad\qquad$ = errorNatural since 0 = 0 by [D4].

[Q6] frontQ (addQ (Φ(arr,f,e), m)) = frontQ (Φ(assign(arr,e,m),f,e+1)) by [D2]
$\qquad\qquad\qquad\qquad\qquad$ = access (assign(arr,e,m), f) by [D4].

Case 1: f = e, that is, isEmptyQ (Φ(arr,f,e)) = true.
So access (assign(arr,e,m), f) = access (assign (arr,e,m), e) = m by [A2].

Case 2: f < e, that is, isEmptyQ (Φ(arr,f,e)) = false.
Then access (assign (arr,e,m), f) = access (arr,f)
$\qquad\qquad\qquad\qquad\qquad$ = frontQ (Φ(arr,f,e)) by [A2] and [D4].

Since the six axioms for the unbounded queue ADT have been verified, we know that the implementation via the unbounded arrays is correct. ∎

ADTs As Algebras

In the previous section we defined Σ-algebras, the many-sorted algebras that correspond to specifications with signature Σ. Now we apply some of the results to the queue ADT. Recall that any signature Σ defines a Σ-algebra T_Σ of all the terms over the signature, and that by taking the quotient algebra Q defined by the congruence based on the equations E of a specification, we get an initial algebra that serves as the finest-grained model of a specification $\langle \Sigma, E \rangle$.

Example: An instance of the queue ADT has operations involving three sorts of objects—namely, Natural, Boolean, and the type being defined, Queue. Some authors designate the type being defined as the **type of interest**. In this context, a graphical notation has been suggested (see Figure 12.1) to define the **signature** of the operations of the algebra.

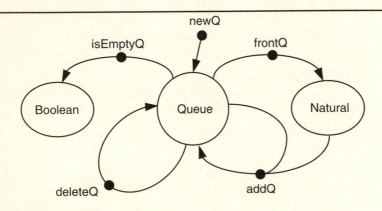

Figure 12.1: Signature of Queues

The signature of the queue ADT defines a term algebra T_Σ, sometimes called a **free word algebra**, formed by taking all legal combinations of operations that produce queue objects. The values in the sort Queue are those produced by the constructor operations. For example, the following terms are elements of T_Σ (we use common abbreviations for natural numbers now, such as 5 for succ(succ(succ(succ(succ(0)))))):

>   newQ.

>   addQ (newQ,5), and

>   deleteQ (addQ (addQ (deleteQ (newQ),9),15)).

The term **free** for such an algebra means that the operations are combined in any way satisfying the syntactic constraints, and that all such terms are distinct objects in the algebra. The properties of an ADT are given by a set E of equations or axioms that define identities among the terms of T_Σ.

So the queue ADT is not a free algebra, since the axioms recognize certain terms as being equal. For example:

>   deleteQ (newQ) = newQ and

>   deleteQ (addQ (addQ (deleteQ (newQ), 9), 15)) = addQ (newQ, 15).

The equations define a congruence $\equiv_E$ on the free algebra of terms as described in section 12.2. That equivalence relation defines a set of equivalence classes that partition T_Σ.

$$[\,t\,]_E = \{\,u \in T_\Sigma \mid u \equiv_E t\,\}$$

For example, $[\,\text{newQ}\,]_E = \{\,\text{newQ, deleteQ(newQ), deleteQ(deleteQ(newQ))}, \ldots \}$.

The operations of the ADT can be defined on these equivalence classes as in the previous section:

> For an n-ary operation $f \in S$ and $t_1, t_2, \ldots, t_n \in T_\Sigma$,
> let $f_Q([t_1],[t_2],\ldots,[t_n]) = [f(t_1, t_2, \ldots, t_n)]$.

The resulting (quotient) algebra, also called $T_{\Sigma,E}$, *is* the abstract data type being defined. When manipulating the objects of the (quotient) algebra $T_{\Sigma,E}$ the normal practice is to use representatives from the equivalence classes.

Definition: A **canonical** or **normal form** for the terms in a quotient algebra is a set of distinct representatives, one from each equivalence class. ∎

Lemma: For the queue ADT $T_{\Sigma,E}$ each term is equivalent to the value newQ or to a term of the form $\text{addQ(addQ(}\ldots\text{addQ(addQ(newQ,}m_1\text{),}m_2\text{),}\ldots\text{),}m_{n-1}\text{),}m_n\text{)}$ for some $n \geq 1$ where $m_1, m_2, \ldots, m_n$: Natural.

Proof: The proof is by structural induction.

Basis: The only constant in T_Σ is newQ, which is in normal form.

Induction Step: Consider a queue term t with more than one application of the constructors (newQ, addQ, deleteQ), and assume that any term with fewer applications of the constructors can be put into normal form.

Case 1: $t = \text{addQ(q,m)}$ will be in normal form when q, which has fewer constructors than t, is in normal form.

Case 2: Consider $t = \text{deleteQ(q)}$ where q is in normal form.

> **Subcase a**: $q = \text{newQ}$. Then $\text{deleteQ(q)} = \text{newQ}$ is in normal form.
>
> **Subcase b**: $q = \text{addQ(p,m)}$ where p is in normal form.
>
> Then $\text{deleteQ(addQ(p,m))} = if\ (\text{isEmptyQ(p), newQ,addQ(deleteQ(p),m))}$.
>
> If p is empty, $\text{deleteQ(q)} = \text{newQ}$ is in normal form.
>
> If p is not empty, $\text{deleteQ(q)} = \text{addQ(deleteQ(p),m)}$. Since deleteQ(p) has fewer constructors than t, it can be put into normal form, so that deleteQ(q) is in normal form. ∎

A canonical form for an ADT can be thought of as an "abstract implementation" of the type. John Guttag [Guttag78b] calls this a **direct implementation** and represents it graphically as shown in Figure 12.2.

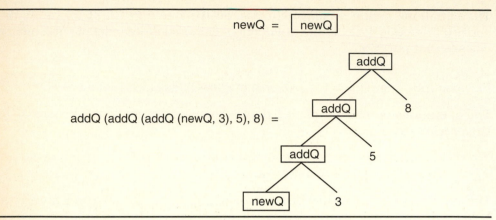

Figure 12.2: Direct Implementation of Queues

The canonical form for an ADT provides an effective tool for proving proper-ties about the type.

Lemma: The representation function Φ that implements queues as arrays is an onto function.

Proof: Since any queue can be written as newQ or as addQ(q,m), we need to handle only these two forms. By [D1], Φ(newArray,0,0) = newQ.

Assume as an induction hypothesis that q = Φ(arr,f,e) for some array. Then by [D2], Φ(assign(arr,e,m),f,e+1) = addQ (Φ(arr,f,e),m).

Therefore any queue is the image of some triple under the representation function Φ.   ∎

Given an ADT with signature Σ, operations in Σ that produce an element of the type of interest have already been called **constructors**. Those operations in Σ whose range is an already defined type of "basic" values are called **selectors**. The operations of Σ are partitioned into two disjoint sets, Con the set of constructors and Sel the set of selectors. The selectors for Queues are frontQ and isEmptyQ.

Definition: A set of equations for an ADT is **sufficiently complete** if for each ground term $f(t_1,t_2,....,t_n)$ where f∈ Sel, the set of selectors, there is an element u of a predefined type such that $f(t_1,t_2,....,t_n) \equiv_E u$. This condition means there are sufficient axioms to make the derivation to u.

Theorem: The equations in the module Queues are sufficiently complete.

Proof:
1. Every queue can be written in normal form as newQ or as addQ(q,m).

2. isEmptyQ(newQ) = true, isEmptyQ(addQ(q,m)) = false, frontQ(newQ) = errorNatural, and frontQ(addQ(q,m)) = m or frontQ(q) (use induction).   ∎

Abstract Syntax and Algebraic Specifications

Throughout the text we have emphasized the importance of abstract syntax in the definition of programming language semantics. In particular, we have stressed several points about abstract syntax:

- In a language definition we need to specify only the meaning of the syntactic forms given by the abstract syntax, since this formalism furnishes all the essential syntactic constructs in the language. Details in the concrete syntax (BNF) may be ignored. No harm arises from an ambiguous abstract syntax since its purpose is not syntactic analysis (parsing). Abstract syntax need only delineate the structure of possible language constructs that can occur in the programs to be analyzed semantically.

- The abstract syntax of a programming language may take many different forms, depending on the semantic techniques that are applied to it. For instance, the abstract syntax for structural operational semantics has little resemblance to that for denotational semantics in its format.

The variety of abstract syntax and its tolerance of ambiguity raises questions concerning the nature of abstract syntax and its relation to the language defined by the concrete syntax. Answers to these questions can be found by analyzing the syntax of programming languages in the context of algebraic specifications.

To illustrate how a grammar can be viewed algebraically, we begin with a small language of integer expressions whose concrete syntax is shown in Figure 12.3.

<expr> ::= <term>

<expr> ::= <expr> + <term>

<expr> ::= <expr> – <term>

<term> ::= <element>

<term> ::= <term> * <element>

<element> ::= <identifier>

<element> ::= (<expr>)

Figure 12.3: Concrete Syntax for Expressions

To put this syntactic specification into an algebraic setting, we define a signature Σ that corresponds exactly to the BNF definition. Each nonterminal becomes a sort in Σ, and each production becomes a function symbol whose syntax captures the essence of the production. The signature of the concrete syntax is given in the module Expressions.

module Expressions
   exports
      sorts Expression, Term, Element, Identifier
      operations

expr (_)	: Term	→ Expression
add (_ , _)	: Expression, Term	→ Expression
sub (_ , _)	: Expression, Term	→ Expression
term (_)	: Element	→ Term
mul (_ , _)	: Term, Element	→ Term
elem (_)	: Identifier	→ Element
paren (_)	: Expression	→ Element

   end exports
end Expressions

Observe that the terminal symbols in the grammar are "forgotten" in the signature since they are embodied in the unique names of the function symbols. Now consider the collection of Σ-algebras following this signature. Since the specification has no equations, the term algebra T_Σ is initial in the collection of all Σ-algebras, meaning that for any Σ-algebra A, there is a unique homomorphism h : $T_\Sigma \to$ A. The elements of T_Σ are terms constructed using the function symbols in Σ. Since this signature has no constants, we assume a set of constants of sort Identifier and represent them as structures of the form ide(x) containing atoms as the identifiers. Think of these structures as the tokens produced by a scanner. The expression "x * (y + z)" corresponds to the following term in T_Σ:

t = expr (mul (term (elem (ide(x))),
                    paren (add (expr (term (elem (ide(y)))),
                        term (elem (ide(z)))))))).

Constructing such a term corresponds to parsing the expression. In fact, the three algebras, the term algebra T_Σ, the collection of expressions satisfying the BNF definition, and the collection of parse (derivation) trees of expressions are isomorphic. Consider the two trees in Figure 12.4. The one on the left is the derivation tree for "x * (y + z)", and the other one represents its associated term in T_Σ.

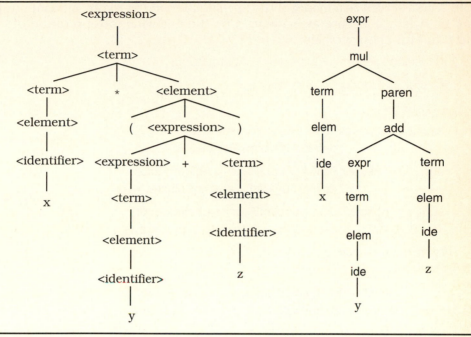

Figure 12.4: Derivation Tree and Algebraic Term

If the concrete syntax of a programming language coincides with the initial term algebra of a specification with signature Σ, what does its abstract syntax correspond to? Consider the following algebraic specification of abstract syntax for the expression language.

module AbstractExpressions
    exports
        sorts AbstractExpr, Symbol
        operations
            plus (_ , _) : AbstractExpr, AbstractExpr $\rightarrow$ AbstractExpr
            minus (_ , _) : AbstractExpr, AbstractExpr $\rightarrow$ AbstractExpr
            times (_ , _) : AbstractExpr, AbstractExpr $\rightarrow$ AbstractExpr
            ide (_)   : Symbol $\rightarrow$ AbstractExpr
    end exports
end AbstractExpressions

Employing the set Symbol of symbolic atoms used as identifiers in the expression language, we can construct terms with the four constructor function symbols in the AbstractExpressions module to represent the abstract syntax trees for the language. These freely constructed terms form a term algebra, call it A, according to the signature of AbstractExpressions. In addition, A also serves as a model of the specification in the Expressions module; that is, A is a Σ-algebra as evidenced by the following interpretation of the sorts and function symbols:

$\text{Expression}_A = \text{Term}_A = \text{Element}_A = \text{AbstractExpr}$

$\text{Identifier}_A = \{ \text{ide}(x) \mid x : \text{Symbol} \}.$

Operations:

expr_A : $\text{AbstractExpr} \to \text{AbstractExpr}$
defined by $\text{expr}_A (e) = e$

add_A : $\text{AbstractExpr}, \text{AbstractExpr} \to \text{AbstractExpr}$
defined by $\text{add}_A (e_1,e_2) = \text{plus}(e_1,e_2)$

sub_A : $\text{AbstractExpr}, \text{AbstractExpr} \to \text{AbstractExpr}$
defined by $\text{sub}_A (e_1,e_2) = \text{minus}(e_1,e_2)$

term_A : $\text{AbstractExpr} \to \text{AbstractExpr}$
defined by $\text{term}_A (e) = e$

mul_A : $\text{AbstractExpr}, \text{AbstractExpr} \to \text{AbstractExpr}$
defined by $\text{mul}_A (e_1,e_2) = \text{times}(e_1,e_2)$

elem_A : $\text{Identifier} \to \text{AbstractExpr}$
defined by $\text{elem}_A (e) = e$

paren_A: $\text{AbstractExpr} \to \text{AbstractExpr}$
defined by $\text{paren}_A (e) = e$

Under this interpretation of the symbols in Σ, the term t, shown in Figure 12.4, becomes a value in the Σ-algebra A:

t_A = (expr (mul (term (elem (ide(x))),
$\qquad$ paren (add (expr (term(elem (ide(y)))), term (elem (ide(z))))))))$_A$

= expr_A (mul_A (term_A (elem_A (ide(x))),
$\qquad$ paren_A (add_A (expr_A (term_A (elem_A (ide(y)))), term_A(elem_A (ide(z))))))

= expr_A (mul_A (term_A (ide(x)),
$\qquad$ paren_A (add_A (expr_A (term_A (ide(y))), term_A (ide(z))))))

= expr_A (mul_A (ide(x), paren_A (add_A (expr_A (ide(y)), ide(z)))))

= mul_A (ide(x), add_A (ide(y), ide(z)))

= times (ide(x), plus (ide(y), ide(z)))

The last term in this evaluation represents the abstract syntax tree in A that corresponds to the original expression "x * (y + z)".

Each version of abstract syntax is a Σ-algebra for the signature associated with the grammar that forms the concrete syntax of the language. Furthermore, any Σ-algebra serving as an abstract syntax is a homomorphic image of T_Σ, the initial algebra for the specification with signature Σ. Generally, Σ-algebras acting as abstract syntax will contain confusion; the homomorphism from T_Σ will not be one-to-one. This confusion reflects the abstracting process: By confusing elements in the algebra, we are suppressing details in the syntax. The expressions "x+y" and "(x+y)", although distinct in the concrete syntax and in T_Σ, are indistinguishable when mapped to plus(ide(x),ide(y)) in A.

Any Σ-algebra for the signature resulting from the concrete syntax can serve as the abstract syntax for some semantic specification of the language, but many such algebras will be so confused that the associated semantics will be trivial or absurd. The task of the semanticist is to choose an appropriate Σ-algebra that captures the organization of the language in such a way that appropriate semantics can be attributed to it.

Exercises

1. Define suitable canonical forms for the following ADTs, and prove their correctness:

   a) Unbounded Array

   b) Stack of natural numbers

2. Define a parameterized module for queues in which the items in the queues are unspecified until the module is instantiated. Give an instantiation of the module.

3. Define a module that specifies the integers including operations for successor, predecessor, addition, equality, and less than. Determine the form of canonical terms for the (initial) quotient algebra for the specification, proving that the forms chosen are adequate.

4. Determine the form of canonical terms for the (initial) quotient algebra generated by the following module that specifies lists of natural numbers. Prove that the canonical forms are sufficient and argue that the choice is minimal.

   module NatLists
       imports Booleans, Naturals
       exports
       sorts List
       functions
           emptyList   : List
           mkList (_)   : Natural $\rightarrow$ List
           concat (_ , _) : List, List $\rightarrow$ List

```
        consL ( _ , _ )  :  Natural, List → List
        consR ( _ , _ )  :  List, Natural → List
        empty? ( _ )     :  List → Boolean
        length ( _ )     :  List → Natural
```
end exports

variables
```
        s, s₁, s₂, s₃  :  List
        m             :  Natural
```

equations

[NL1]	concat (s, emptyList)	= s
[NL2]	concat (emptyList, s)	= s
[NL3]	concat (concat (s_1, s_2), s_3)	= concat (s_1, concat (s_2, s_3))
[NL4]	consL (m, s)	= concat (mkList (m), s)
[NL5]	consR (s, m)	= concat (s, mkList (m))
[NL6]	empty? (emptyList)	= true
[NL7]	empty? (mkList (m))	= false *when* m ≠ errorNatural
[NL8]	empty? (concat (s_1, s_2))	= and (empty? (s_1), empty? (s_2))
[NL9]	length (emptyList)	= 0
[NL10]	length (mkList (m))	= 1 *when* m ≠ errorNatural
[NL11]	length (concat (s_1, s_2))	= add (length (s_1), length (s_2))

end NatLists

5. Define alternate abstract syntax for the expression language by specifying a signature with a module and an Σ-algebra for the signature Σ of Expressions that does the following:

   a) Describes only the structure of an expression, so that the abstract syntax tree for "x * (y + z)" is opr (ide(x), opr (ide(y), ide(z))).

   b) Identifies only the first identifier in an expression, so that the abstract syntax tree for "x * (y + z)" is ide(x).

6. Specify modules for the concrete syntax and the abstract syntax of Wren as described in Chapter 1 and show how its term algebra of the abstract syntax module can be interpreted as a Σ-algebra for the signature of the module for the concrete syntax.

12.4 ALGEBRAIC SEMANTICS FOR WREN

We have seen that there are many aspects in specifying the syntax and semantics of a programming language. In Chapter 1 we studied BNF and its variants; in Chapter 2 we built a lexical analyzer and parser for Wren. Context checking was demonstrated using three approaches: attribute grammars (Chapter 3), two-level grammars (Chapter 4), and denotational semantics (Chapter 9). Programming language semantics has been handled in a variety of ways: self-definition (Chapter 6), translational semantics (Chapter 7), structural operational semantics (Chapter 8), denotational semantics (Chapter 9), and axiomatic semantics (Chapter 11). Each technique has its strengths and weaknesses. For example, denotational semantics can perform type checking and program interpretation, but it does not stress lexical analysis and parsing beyond the abstract production rules. Axiomatic semantics does not deal with lexical analysis, parsing, or type checking. Most techniques rely on knowledge of well-known domains, such as truth values with logical operations or numbers with arithmetic operations.

Of the techniques studied so far, algebraic semantics is perhaps the most versatile in its ability to perform all of the functions mentioned above. Modules can be developed to perform lexical analysis, parsing, type checking and language evaluation. Basic domains, such as truth values, natural numbers, and characters, are carefully specified using fundamental concepts, such as zero and the successor function for natural numbers. The initial algebras constructed as quotient algebras represent the meaning of these domains, apart from the renaming of constants and functions. Because of the length of a complete presentation, we elect not to develop the lexical analyzer and parser for Wren using algebraic specifications. See [Bergstra89] for the missing specification techniques. Rather, we concentrate on showing how the methodology can be used to perform type checking and program interpretation. In particular, we develop the following modules:

- WrenTypes specifies the allowed types for Wren programs.
- WrenValues specifies the permissible value domains.
- WrenASTs specifies the output of the parser, the abstract syntax trees.
- WrenTypeChecker returns a Boolean value resulting from context checking.
- WrenEvaluator interprets a Wren program given an input file.
- WrenSystem calls the evaluator if type checking is successful.

For simplicity, we have limited the domain of arithmetic values to natural numbers. To reduce the complexity of the example, declarations allow only a single identifier. Boolean variables can be declared, but we leave their manipulation as an exercise at the end of this section. We also leave the handling of runtime errors, such as division by zero and reading from an empty file, as an exercise. Since nonterminating programs cause technical difficulties in an algebraic specification, we plan to describe only computations (programs and input) that terminate. We want our equations for the Wren evaluator to be sufficiently complete; that is, every program and input list can be reduced to an equivalent term in the sort of lists of natural numbers (output lists). We lose the property of sufficient completeness when we include configurations that produce nonterminating computations.

Types and Values in Wren

The first module, WrenTypes, specifies four constant functions, naturalType, booleanType, programType, and errorType, along with a single Boolean operation to test the equality of two types.

module WrenTypes
    imports Booleans
    exports
        sorts WrenType
        operations
            naturalType   : WrenType
            booleanType : WrenType
            programType : WrenType
            errorType   : WrenType
            eq? (_ , _)   : WrenType, WrenType → Boolean
    end exports

    variables
        t, t_1, t_2 : WrenType

    equations
    [Wt1]   eq? (t, t) = true   *when* $t \neq$ errorType
    [Wt2]   eq? (t_1, t_2) = eq? (t_2, t_1)
    [Wt3]   eq? (naturalType, booleanType)   = false
    [Wt4]   eq? (naturalType, programType)   = false
    [Wt5]   eq? (naturalType, errorType)   = false
    [Wt6]   eq? (booleanType, programType) = false
    [Wt7]   eq? (booleanType, errorType)   = false
    [Wt8]   eq? (programType, errorType)   = false
end WrenTypes

The next module, WrenValues, specifies three functions for identifying natural numbers, Boolean values, and an error value. These function symbols perform the same role as the tags in a disjoint union. Two values are equal only if they come from the same domain and if they are equal in that domain.

module WrenValues
    imports Booleans, Naturals
    exports
        sorts WrenValue
        operations
            wrenValue (_) : Natural $\rightarrow$ WrenValue
            wrenValue (_) : Boolean $\rightarrow$ WrenValue
            errorValue   : WrenValue
            eq? (_ , _)   : WrenValue, WrenValue $\rightarrow$ Boolean
    end exports

    variables
       x, y   : WrenValue
       n, n_1, n_2 : Natural
       b, b_1, b_2 : Boolean

    equations
    [Wv1] eq? (x, y) = eq? (y,x)
    [Wv2] eq? (wrenValue(n_1), wrenValue(n_2)) = eq? (n_1,n_2)
    [Wv3] eq? (wrenValue(b_1), wrenValue(b_2)) = eq? (b_1,b_2)
    [Wv4] eq? (wrenValue(n), wrenValue(b))   = false
                                         when m $\neq$ errorNatural, b $\neq$ errorBoolean
    [Wv5] eq? (wrenValue(n), errorValue)   = false   *when* n $\neq$ errorNatural
    [Wv6] eq? (wrenValue(b), errorValue)   = false   *when* b $\neq$ errorBoolean
end WrenValues

Abstract Syntax for Wren

The abstract syntax tree module specifies the form of a Wren program that has been parsed successfully. As noted previously, we show only the structure of the abstract syntax trees, not how they are constructed.

module WrenASTs
    imports Naturals, Strings, WrenTypes
    exports
        sorts WrenProgram, Block, DecSeq, Declaration,
               CmdSeq, Command, Expr, Ident
        operations
            astWrenProgram (_ , _) : Ident, Block $\rightarrow$ WrenProgram
            astBlock (_ , _)   : DecSeq, CmdSeq $\rightarrow$ Block
            astDecs (_ , _)   : Declaration, DecSeq $\rightarrow$ DecSeq
            astEmptyDecs   : DecSeq
            astDec (_ , _)   : Ident, WrenType $\rightarrow$ Declaration

astCmds (_ , _)	: Command, CmdSeq	→ CmdSeq
astOneCmd (_)	: Command	→ CmdSeq
astRead (_)	: Ident	→ Command
astWrite (_)	: Expr	→ Command
astAssign (_ , _)	: Ident, Expr	→ Command
astSkip	: Command	
astWhile (_ , _)	: Expr, CmdSeq	→ Command
astIfThen (_ , _)	: Expr, CmdSeq	→ Command
astIfElse (_ , _ , _)	: Expr, CmdSeq, CmdSeq	→ Command
astAddition (_ , _)	: Expr, Expr	→ Expr
astSubtraction (_ , _)	: Expr, Expr	→ Expr
astMultiplication (_ , _)	: Expr, Expr	→ Expr
astDivision (_ , _)	: Expr, Expr	→ Expr
astEqual (_ , _)	: Expr, Expr	→ Expr
astNotEqual (_ , _)	: Expr, Expr	→ Expr
astLessThan (_ , _)	: Expr, Expr	→ Expr
astLessThanEqual (_ , _)	: Expr, Expr	→ Expr
astGreaterThan (_ , _)	: Expr, Expr	→ Expr
astGreaterThanEqual (_ , _)	: Expr, Expr	→ Expr
astVariable (_)	: Ident	→ Expr
astNaturalConstant (_)	: Natural	→ Expr
astIdent (_)	: String	→ Ident

    end exports

end WrenASTs

If we define a module for the concrete syntax of Wren based on its BNF specification, an algebra modeling WrenASTs will be a homomorphic image of the term algebra over that concrete syntax.

A Type Checker for Wren

The WrenTypeChecker module exports an overloaded function check that returns a Boolean result indicating if the context conditions are satisfied. Calling check with a declaration sequence performs an additional vital function: It builds the symbol table that associates names with types.

module WrenTypeChecker
    imports Booleans, WrenTypes, WrenASTs,
            instantiation of Mappings
                bind Entries **using** String **for** Domain
                          using WrenType **for** Range
                          using eq? **for** equals

> **using** errorString **for** errorDomain
>
> **using** errorType **for** errorRange
>
> **rename using** SymbolTable **for** Mapping
>
> **using** nullSymTab **for** emptyMap

exports

   operations

check (_)	: WrenProgram	$\rightarrow$ Boolean
check (_ , _)	: Block, SymbolTable	$\rightarrow$ Boolean
check (_ , _)	: DecSeq, SymbolTable	$\rightarrow$ Boolean, SymbolTable
check (_ , _)	: Declaration, SymbolTable	$\rightarrow$ Boolean, SymbolTable
check (_ , _)	: CmdSeq, SymbolTable	$\rightarrow$ Boolean
check (_ , _)	: Command, SymbolTable	$\rightarrow$ Boolean

end exports

operations

   typeExpr : Expr, SymbolTable $\rightarrow$ WrenType

variables

block	: Block
decs	: DecSeq
dec	: Declaration
cmds, $cmds_1$, $cmds_2$	: CmdSeq
cmd	: Command
expr, $expr_1$, $expr_2$	: Expr
type	: WrenType
symtab, $symtab_1$	: SymbolTable
m	: Natural
name	: String
b, b_1, b_2	: Boolean

equations

[Tc1]   check (astWrenProgram (astIdent (name), block))
        = check (block, update(nullSymTab, name, programType))

[Tc2]   check (astBlock (decs, cmds), symtab)
        = and (b_1,b_2)
            when   <b_1,$symtab_1$> = check (decs, symtab),
                    b_2 = check (cmds, $symtab_1$),

[Tc3]   check (astDecs (dec, decs), symtab)
        = <and (b_1,b_2), $symtab_2$>
            when   <b_1,$symtab_1$> = check (dec, symtab),
                    <b_2,$symtab_2$> = check (decs, $symtab_1$)

[Tc4]   check (astEmptyDecs, symtab)
          = <true, symtab>

[Tc5]   check (astDec (astIdent (name), type), symtab)
          = *if* (apply (symtab, name) = errorType,
                  <true, update(symtab, name, type)>,
                  <false, symtab>)

[Tc6]   check (astCmds (cmd, cmds), symtab)
          = and (check (cmd, symtab), check (cmds, symtab))

[Tc7]   check (astOneCmd (cmd), symtab)
          = check (cmd, symtab)

[Tc8]   check (astRead (astIdent (name)), symtab)
          = eq?(apply (symtab, name), naturalType)

[Tc9]   check (astWrite (expr, symtab)
          = eq? (typeExpr (expr, symtab), naturalType)

[Tc10] check (astAssign (astIdent (name), expr), symtab)
          = eq? (apply(symtab, name), typeExpr (expr, symtab))

[Tc11] check (astSkip, symtab)
          = true

[Tc12] check (astWhile (expr, cmds), symtab)
          = *if* (eq? (typeExpr (expr, symtab), booleanType),
                  check (cmds, symtab),
                  false)

[Tc13] check (astIfThen (expr, cmds), symtab)
          = *if* (eq? (typeExpr (expr, symtab), booleanType),
                  check (cmds, symtab),
                  false)

[Tc14] check (astIfElse (expr, cmds$_1$, cmds$_2$), symtab)
          = *if* (eq? (typeExpr (expr, symtab), booleanType),
                  and (check (cmds$_1$, symtab), check (cmds$_2$, symtab)),
                  false)

[Tc15] typeExpr (astAddition (expr$_1$, expr$_2$), symtab)
          = *if* (and (eq? (typeExpr (expr$_1$, symtab), naturalType),
                              eq? (typeExpr (expr$_2$, symtab), naturalType)),
                  naturalType,
                  errorType)

[Tc16] typeExpr (astSubtraction (expr$_1$, expr$_2$), symtab)
  = *if* (and (eq? (typeExpr (expr$_1$, symtab), naturalType),
                eq? (typeExpr (expr$_2$, symtab), naturalType)),
        naturalType,
        errorType)

[Tc17] typeExpr (astMultiplication (expr$_1$, expr$_2$), symtab)
  = *if* (and (eq? (typeExpr (expr$_1$, symtab), naturalType),
                eq? (typeExpr (expr$_2$, symtab), naturalType)),
        naturalType,
        errorType)

[Tc18] typeExpr (astDivision (expr$_1$, expr$_2$), symtab)
  = *if* (and(eq? (typeExpr (expr$_1$, symtab), naturalType),
                eq? (typeExpr (expr$_2$, symtab), naturalType)),
        naturalType,
        errorType)

[Tc19] typeExpr (astEqual (expr$_1$, expr$_2$), symtab)
  = *if* (and (eq? (typeExpr (expr$_1$, symtab), naturalType),
                eq? (typeExpr (expr$_2$, symtab), naturalType)),
        booleanType,
        errorType)

[Tc20] typeExpr (astNotEqual (expr$_1$,expr$_2$), symtab)
  = *if* (and (eq? (typeExpr (expr$_1$, symtab), naturalType),
                eq? (typeExpr (expr$_2$, symtab), naturalType)),
        booleanType,
        errorType)

[Tc21] typeExpr (astLessThan (expr$_1$, expr$_2$), symtab)
  = *if* (and (eq? (typeExpr (expr$_1$, symtab), naturalType),
                eq? (typeExpr (expr$_2$, symtab), naturalType)),
        booleanType,
        errorType)

[Tc22] typeExpr (astLessThanEqual (expr$_1$, expr$_2$), symtab)
  = *if* (and (eq? (typeExpr (expr$_1$, symtab), naturalType),
                eq? (typeExpr (expr$_2$, symtab), naturalType)),
        booleanType,
        errorType)

[Tc23] typeExpr (astGreaterThan (expr$_1$,expr$_2$),symtab)
  = *if* (and (eq? (typeExpr (expr$_1$, symtab), naturalType),
                eq? (typeExpr (expr$_2$, symtab), naturalType)),
        booleanType,
        errorType)

[Tc24] typeExpr (astGreaterThanEqual (expr$_1$, expr$_2$), symtab)
 = *if* (and (eq? (typeExpr (expr$_1$, symtab), naturalType),
  eq? (typeExpr (expr$_2$, symtab), naturalType)),
  booleanType,
  errorType)

[Tc25] typeExpr (astNaturalConstant (m), symtab)
 = naturalType

[Tc26] typeExpr (astVariable (astIdent(name)), symtab)
 = apply (symtab, name)

end WrenTypeChecker

Most of the type-checking equations are self-evident; we point out only general features here. Equations [Tc1], [Tc3], and [Tc5] build the symbol table from the declarations while ensuring that no identifier is declared twice. [Tc1] adds the program name with programType to the table. Most of the equations for commands pass the symbol table information along for checking at lower levels. The following equations perform the actual type checking:

[Tc5]   No identifier is declared more than once.

[Tc8]   The variable in a **read** command has naturalType.

[Tc9]   The expression in a **write** command has naturalType.

[Tc10]   The assignment target variable and expression have the same type.

[Tc12-14] The expressions in **while** and **if** commands have booleanType.

[Tc15-18] Arithmetic operations involve expressions of naturalType.

[Tc19-24] Comparisons involve expressions of naturalType.

An Interpreter for Wren

The WrenEvaluator module is used to specify semantic functions that give meaning to the constructs of Wren. The top-level function meaning takes a Wren program and an input file and returns the output file resulting from executing the program. We assume that the output file is initially empty. The declaration sequence builds a store that associates each declared variable with an initial value, zero for naturalType and false for booleanType. Commands use the current store, input file, and output file to compute a new store, a new input file, and a new output file. Evaluating an expression produces a WrenValue.

module WrenEvaluator

imports Booleans, Naturals, Strings, Files, WrenValues, WrenASTs,

instantiation of Mappings

bind Entries **using** String **for** Domain

using WrenValue **for** Range

using eq? **for** equals

using errorString **for** errorDomain

using errorValue **for** errorRange

rename using Store **for** Mapping

using emptySto **for** emptyMap

using updateSto **for** update

using applySto **for** apply

exports

operations

meaning (_ , _)	: WrenProgram, File	$\rightarrow$ File
perform (_ , _)	: Block, File	$\rightarrow$ File
elaborate (_ , _)	: DecSeq, Store	$\rightarrow$ Store
elaborate (_ , _)	: Declaration, Store	$\rightarrow$ Store
execute (_ , _ , _ , _)	: CmdSeq, Store, File, File	$\rightarrow$ Store, File, File
execute (_ , _ , _ , _)	: Command, Store, File, File	$\rightarrow$ Store, File, File
evaluate (_ , _)	: Expr, Store	$\rightarrow$ WrenValue

end exports

variables

input, $input_1$, $input_2$	: File
output, $output_1$, $output_2$	: File
block	: Block
decs	: DecSeq
cmds, $cmds_1$, $cmds_2$	: CmdSeq
cmd	: Command
expr, $expr_1$, $expr_2$	: Expr
sto, sto_1, sto_2	: Store
value	: WrenValue
m,n	: Natural
name	: String
b	: Boolean

equations

[Ev1]   meaning (astWrenProgram (astIdent (name), block), input)
= perform (block, input)

[Ev2]   perform (astBlock (decs,cmds), input)
= execute (cmds, elaborate (decs, emptySto), input, emptyFile)

[Ev3]   elaborate (astDecs (dec, decs), sto)
           = elaborate (decs,elaborate(dec, sto))

[Ev4]   elaborate (astEmptyDecs, sto)
           = sto

[Ev5]   elaborate (astDec (astIdent (name), naturalType), sto)
           = updateSto(sto, name, wrenValue(0))

[Ev6]   elaborate (astDec (astIdent (name), booleanType), sto)
           = updateSto(sto, name, wrenValue(false))

[Ev7]   execute (astCmds (cmd, cmds), sto_1, $input_1$, $output_1$)
           = execute (cmds, sto_2, $input_2$, $output_2$)
           when <sto_2, $input_2$, $output_2$> = execute (cmd, sto_1, $input_1$, $output_1$)

[Ev8]   execute (astOneCmd (cmd), sto, input, output)
           = execute (cmd, sto, input, output)

[Ev9]   execute (astSkip, sto, input, output)
           = <sto, input, output>

[Ev10]   execute (astRead(astIdent (name)), sto, input, output)
           = *if* (empty? (input),
                error case left as an exercise
                <updateSto(sto, name, first), rest, output>)
                              when input = cons(first,rest)

[Ev11]   execute (astWrite (expr), sto, input, output)
           = <sto, input, concat (output, mkFile (evaluate (expr, sto)))>

[Ev12]   execute (astAssign (astIdent (name), expr), sto, input, output)
           = <updateSto(sto, name, evaluate (expr, sto)), input, output>

[Ev13]   execute (astWhile (expr, cmds), sto_1, $input_1$, $output_1$)
           = *if* (eq? (evaluate (expr, sto_1), wrenValue(true))
                execute (astWhile(expr, cmds), sto_2, $input_2$, $output_2$)
                     when <sto_2, $input_2$, $output_2$> =
                                   execute (cmds, sto_1, $input_1$, $output_1$),
           <sto_1, $input_1$, $output_1$>)

[Ev14]   execute (astIfThen (expr, cmds), sto, input, output)
           = *if* (eq? (evaluate (expr, sto), wrenValue(true))
                execute (cmds, sto, input, output),
                <sto, input, output>)

[Ev15]   execute (astIfElse (expr, $cmds_1$, $cmds_2$), sto, input, output)
           = *if* (eq? (evaluate (expr, sto), wrenValue(true))
                execute ($cmds_1$, sto, input, output)
                execute ($cmds_2$, sto, input, output))

[Ev16] evaluate (astAddition (expr$_1$, expr$_2$), sto)
          = wrenValue(add (m,n))
          when wrenValue(m) = evaluate (expr$_1$, sto),
              wrenValue(n) = evaluate (expr$_2$, sto)

[Ev17] evaluate (astSubtraction (expr$_1$, expr$_2$), sto)
          = wrenValue(sub (m,n))
          when wrenValue(m) = evaluate (expr$_1$, sto),
              wrenValue(n) = evaluate (expr$_2$, sto)

[Ev18] evaluate (astMultiplication (expr$_1$, expr$_2$), sto)
          = wrenValue(mul (m,n))
          when wrenValue(m) = evaluate (expr$_1$, sto),
              wrenValue(n) = evaluate (expr$_2$, sto)

[Ev19] evaluate (astDivision (expr$_1$, expr$_2$), sto)
          = wrenValue(div (m,n))
          when wrenValue(m) = evaluate (expr$_1$, sto),
              wrenValue(n) = evaluate (expr$_2$, sto)

[Ev20] evaluate (astEqual (expr$_1$, expr$_2$), sto)
          = wrenValue(eq? (m,n))
          when wrenValue(m) = evaluate (expr$_1$, sto),
              wrenValue(n) = evaluate (expr$_2$, sto)

[Ev21] evaluate (astNotEqual (expr$_1$, expr$_2$), sto)
          = wrenValue(not (eq? (m,n)))
          when wrenValue(m) = evaluate (expr$_1$, sto),
              wrenValue(n) = evaluate (expr$_2$, sto)

[Ev22] evaluate (astLessThan (expr$_1$, expr$_2$), sto)
          = wrenValue(less? (m,n))
          when wrenValue(m) = evaluate (expr$_1$, sto),
              wrenValue(n) = evaluate (expr$_2$, sto)

[Ev23] evaluate (astLessThanEqual (expr$_1$, expr$_2$), sto)
          = wrenValue(not(greater? (m,n)))
          when wrenValue(m) = evaluate (expr$_1$, sto),
              wrenValue(n) = evaluate (expr$_2$, sto)

[Ev24] evaluate (astGreaterThan (expr$_1$, expr$_2$), sto)
          = wrenValue(greater? (m,n))
          when wrenValue(m) = evaluate (expr$_1$, sto),
              wrenValue(n) = evaluate (expr$_2$, sto)

[Ev25]   evaluate (astGreaterThanEqual (expr$_1$, expr$_2$), sto)
         = wrenValue(not(less? (m,n)))
         when wrenValue(m) = evaluate (expr$_1$, sto),
              wrenValue(n) = evaluate (expr$_2$, st)

[Ev26]   evaluate (astNaturalConstant (m), sto)
         = wrenValue(m)

[Ev27]   evaluate (astVariable (astIdent (name)), sto)
         = applySto (sto, name)

end WrenEvaluator

Each equation should be self-explanatory. Observe that [Ev10] is incomplete, as we have only indicated that error handling is needed for reading from an empty file. Also [Ev17] might cause an error when a larger number is subtracted from a smaller number, or [Ev19] when any number is divided by zero. We have elected not to show this error handling since it requires modifications to almost all equations to propagate the error to the top level, and this introduces unwanted complexity. Two exercises deal with alternative error-handling techniques.

A Wren System

Our final module, WrenSystem, invokes the type checker and, if it succeeds, calls the evaluator. If type checking fails, the empty file is returned. Remember that we have assumed the program interpretation completes successfully to avoid technical issues relating to sufficient completeness.

module WrenSystem
    imports WrenTypeChecker, WrenEvaluator
    exports
        operations
            runWren : WrenProgram, File → File
    end exports

    variables
        input   : File
        program : WrenProgram

    equations
    [Ws1]   runWren (program, input) = *if* (check (program),
                                         meaning (program, input),
                                         emptyFile)
         -- return an empty file if context violation, otherwise run program
end WrenSystem

This completes the development of an algebraic specification for Wren. In the next section, we implement part of this specification in Prolog.

Exercises

1. What changes, if any, would be needed in the modules presented in this section if an Integers module were used in place of a Naturals module?

2. Complete the syntactic and semantic functions and equations for Boolean expressions. The comparisons given in this section will be only one possible alternative for a Boolean expression.

3. One technique of error handling is to assign default values such as zero when an item is read from an empty file. For division by zero, consider introducing a constant representing a maximum allowed natural number. Assuming WordSize is imported from a module called ComputerSystem, how can such a value be defined? Indicate by revising the equations how all arithmetic operations have to guard against exceeding such a value.

4. Halting evaluation due to a fatal runtime error, such as reading from an empty file or division by zero, is difficult to specify. Briefly indicate how this problem can be handled by returning a Boolean value (in addition to other values) to indicate whether each operation is successful.

12.5 LABORATORY: IMPLEMENTING ALGEBRAIC SEMANTICS

As with other semantic definitions, algebraic specifications can be translated directly into Prolog. In the development presented in this section, we assume that the lexical analyzer and parser given in Chapter 2 provide input to the interpreter. The user is asked to specify a file containing a Wren program and an input file (a list of natural numbers). Interpreting the program produces the output file. Numerals in the input file are translated into natural number notation for processing, and when a **write** statement is encountered, values in natural number notation are translated to base-ten numerals.

We show the implementation of three modules: Booleans, Naturals, and WrenEvaluator. We have not translated identifier names into the Strings notation based on a Characters module; these modules are left as an exercise at the end of this section. Implementation of the modules for Files and Mappings is also left as an exercise. Observe that we have no mechanism for implementing generic modules, such as Lists, in Prolog, so we simply implement the instantiated modules directly. Finally, we have not implemented the WrenTypeChecker; that project has also been left as an exercise.

Before examining the implementations of the modules, we inspect the expected behavior of the system, including the output of the parser to remind us of the format produced by the language-processing system. This program converts a list of binary digits into the corresponding decimal number using any integer greater than 1 to terminate the list.

```
>>> Interpreting Wren via Algebraic Semantics <<<
Enter name of source file: frombinary.wren
    program frombinary is
      var sum,n : integer;
    begin
      sum := 0; read n;
      while n<2 do
        sum := 2*sum+n; read n
       end while;
      write sum
    end
Scan successful
Parse successful
prog([dec(integer,[sum,n])],
    [assign(sum,num(0)),read(n),
      while(exp(less,ide(n),num(2)),
       [assign(sum,exp(plus,exp(times,num(2),ide(sum)),ide(n))),
          read(n)]),
      write(ide(sum))])
Enter an input list followed by a period: [1,0,1,0,1,1,2].
Output = [43]
yes
```

Module Booleans

The implementation of the module Booleans includes the constants true and false and the functions not, and, or, xor, and beq (note the name change to avoid confusion with equality in the Naturals module).

```
boolean(true).
boolean(false).

bnot(true, false).
bnot(false, true).
```

```
and(true, P, P).
and(false, true, false).
and(false, false, false).

or(false,P,P).
or(true,P,true) :- boolean(P).

xor(P, Q, R) :- or(P,Q,PorQ), and(P,Q,PandQ),
                        bnot(PandQ,NotPandQ), and(PorQ,NotPandQ, R).

beq(P, Q, R) :- xor(P,Q,PxorQ), bnot(PxorQ,R).
```

We have followed the specifications given in the module Booleans closely except for the direct definition of or. We misspell not as bnot to avoid conflict with the predefined predicate for logical negation that may exist in some Prolog implementations.

Module Naturals

The implementation of Naturals follows directly from the algebraic specification. The predicate natural succeeds with arguments of the form

zero, succ(zero), succ(succ(zero)), succ(succ(succ(zero))), and so on.

Calling this predicate with a variable, such as natural(M), generates the natural numbers in this form if repeated solutions are requested by entering a semicolon after each successful answer to the query.

```
natural(zero).
natural(succ(M)) :- natural(M).
```

The arithmetic functions follow the algebraic specification. Rather than return an error value for subtraction of a larger number from a smaller number or for division by zero, we print an appropriate error message and abort the program execution. The comparison operations follow directly from their definitions. Observe how the conditions in the specifications are handled in the Prolog clauses. We give a definition of the exponentiation operation now for completeness.

```
add(M, zero, M) :- natural(M).
add(M, succ(N), succ(R)) :- add(M,N,R).

sub(zero, succ(N), R) :- write('Error: Result of subtraction is negative'), nl, abort.
sub(M, zero, M) :- natural(M).
sub(succ(M), succ(N), R) :- sub(M,N,R).
```

```
mul(M, zero, zero) :- natural(M).
mul(M, succ(zero), M) :- natural(M).
mul(M, succ(succ(N)), R)  :- mul(M,succ(N),R1), add(M,R1,R).

div(M, zero, R) :- write('Error: Division by zero'), nl, abort.
div(M, succ(N), zero) :- less(M,succ(N),true).
div(M,succ(N),succ(Quotient)) :- less(M,succ(N),false),
                                 sub(M,succ(N),Dividend),
                                 div(Dividend,succ(N),Quotient).

exp(succ(M), zero, succ(zero)) :- natural(M).
exp(M, succ(zero), M) :- natural(M).
exp(M, succ(N), R) :- exp(M,N,MexpN), mul(M, MexpN, R).

eq(zero,zero,true).
eq(zero,succ(N),false) :- natural(N).
eq(succ(M),zero,false) :- natural(M).
eq(succ(M),succ(N),BoolValue) :- eq(M,N,BoolValue).

less(zero,succ(N),true) :- natural(N).
less(M,zero,false) :- natural(M).
less(succ(M),succ(N),BoolValue) :- less(M,N,BoolValue).

greater(M,N,BoolValue) :- less(N,M,BoolValue).

lesseq(M,N,BoolValue) :- less(M,N,B1), eq(M,N,B2), or(B1,B2,BoolValue).

greatereq(M,N,BoolValue) :- greater(M,N,B1), eq(M,N,B2), or(B1,B2,BoolValue).
```

We add two operations not specified in the Naturals module that convert base-ten numerals to natural numbers as defined in the module Naturals using successor notation and vice versa. Specifically, toNat converts a numeral to natural notation and toNum converts a natural number to a base-ten numeral. For example, toNat(4,Num) returns Num = succ (succ (succ (succ (zero)))).

```
toNat(0,zero).
toNat(Num, succ(M)) :- Num>0, NumMinus1 is Num-1, toNat(NumMinus1, M).

toNum(zero,0).
toNum(succ(M),Num) :- toNum(M,Num1), Num is Num1+1.
```

Declarations

The clauses for elaborate are used to build a store with numeric variables initialized to zero and Boolean variables initialized to false.

```
elaborate([Dec|Decs],StoIn,StoOut) :-                          % Ev3
                        elaborate(Dec,StoIn,Sto),
                        elaborate(Decs,Sto,StoOut).

elaborate([ ],Sto,Sto).                                        % Ev4

elaborate(dec(integer,[Var]),StoIn,StoOut) :-                  % Ev5
                        updateSto(StoIn,Var,zero,StoOut).

elaborate(dec(boolean,[Var]),StoIn,StoOut) :-                  % Ev6
                        updateSto(StoIn,Var,false,StoOut).
```

Commands

For a sequence of commands, the commands following the first command are evaluated with the store produced by the first command. The Prolog code is simpler if we allow an empty command sequence as the base case.

```
execute([Cmd|Cmds],StoIn,InputIn,OutputIn,              %Ev7
                        StoOut,InputOut,OutputOut) :-
              execute(Cmd,StoIn,InputIn,OutputIn,Sto,Input,Output),
              execute(Cmds,Sto,Input,Output,StoOut,InputOut,OutputOut).

execute([ ],Sto,Input,Output,Sto,Input,Output).                % Ev8
```

The **read** command removes the first item from the input file, converts it to natural number notation, and places the result in the store. The **write** command evaluates the expression, converts the resulting value from natural number notation to a numeric value, and appends the result to the end of the output file.

```
execute(read(Var),StoIn,emptyFile,Output,StoOut,_,Output) :-    % Ev10
              write('Fatal Error: Reading an empty file'), nl, abort.

execute(read(Var),StoIn,[FirstIn|RestIn],Output,StoOut,RestIn,Output) :-   % Ev10
              toNat(FirstIn,Value),
              updateSto(StoIn,Var,Value,StoOut).

execute(write(Expr),Sto,Input,OutputIn,Sto,Input,OutputOut) :-    % Ev11
              evaluate(Expr,StoIn,ExprValue),
              toNum(ExprValue,Value),
              mkFile(Value,ValueOut),
              concat(OutputIn,ValueOut,OutputOut).
```

Assignment evaluates the expression using the current store and then updates that store to reflect the new binding. The **skip** command makes no changes to the store or to the files.

```
execute(assign(Var,Expr),StoIn,Input,Output,StoOut,Input,Output) :-    % Ev12
        evaluate(Expr,StoIn,Value).
        updateSto(StoIn,Var,Value,StoOut).

execute(skip,Sto,Input,Output,Sto,Input,Output).                       % Ev9
```

The two forms of **if** commands test the Boolean expressions and then let a predicate select carry out the appropriate actions. Observe how the one-alternative **if** command passes an empty command sequence to select. If the comparison in the **while** command is false, the store and files are returned unchanged. If the comparison is true, the **while** command is reevaluated with the store and files resulting from the execution of the **while** loop body. These commands are implemented with auxiliary predicates, select and iterate, to minimize the amount of backtracking the system must do.

```
execute(if(Expr,Cmds),StoIn,InputIn,OutputIn,StoOut,InputOut,OutputOut) :-
    evaluate(Expr,StoIn,BoolVal),                                      % Ev14
    select(BoolVal,Cmds,[ ],StoIn,InputIn,OutputIn,StoOut,InputOut,OutputOut).

execute(if(Expr,Cmds1,Cmds2),StoIn,InputIn,OutputIn,StoOut,InputOut,OutputOut) :-
    evaluate(Expr,StoIn,BoolVal),                                      % Ev15
    select(BoolVal,Cmds1,Cmds2,StoIn,InputIn,OutputIn,StoOut,InputOut,OutputOut).

select(true,Cmds1,Cmds2,StoIn,InputIn,OutputIn,StoOut,InputOut,OutputOut) :-
    execute(Cmds1,StoIn,InputIn,OutputIn,StoOut,InputOut,OutputOut).

select(false,Cmds1,Cmds2,StoIn,InputIn,OutputIn,StoOut,InputOut,OutputOut) :-
    execute(Cmds2,StoIn,InputIn,OutputIn,StoOut,InputOut,OutputOut).

execute(while(Expr,Cmds),StoIn,InputIn,OutputIn, StoOut,InputOut,OutputOut) :-
    evaluate(Expr,StoIn,BoolVal),                                      % Ev13
    iterate(BoolVal,Expr,Cmds,StoIn,InputIn,OutputIn,StoOut,InputOut,OutputOut).

iterate(true,Expr,Cmds,StoIn,InputIn,OutputIn,StoOut,InputOut,OutputOut) :-
    execute(Cmds,StoIn,InputIn,OutputIn,Sto,Input,Output),
    execute(while(Expr,Cmds),Sto,Input,Output,StoOut,InputOut,OutputOut).

iterate(false,Expr,Cmds,Sto,Input,Output,Sto,Input,Output).
```

Expressions

The evaluation of arithmetic expressions is straightforward. Addition is shown below; the other three operations are left as exercises. Evaluating a variable involves looking up the value in the store. A numeric constant is converted to natural number notation and returned.

```
evaluate(exp(plus,Expr1,Expr2),Sto,Result) :-          % Ev16
            evaluate(Expr1,Sto,Val1),
            evaluate(Expr2,Sto,Val2),
            add(Val1,Val2,Result).
```

```
evaluate(num(Constant),Sto,Value) :- toNat(Constant,Value).     %Ev26
```

```
evaluate(ide(Var),Sto,Value) :- applySto(Sto,Var,Value).        % Ev27
```

Evaluation of comparisons is similar to arithmetic expressions; the equal comparison is given below, and the five others are left as an exercise.

```
evaluate(exp(equal,Expr1,Expr2),Sto,Bool) :-          % Ev20
            evaluate(Expr1,Sto,Val1),
            evaluate(Expr2,Sto,Val2),
            eq(Val1,Val2,Bool).
```

The Prolog implementation of the algebraic specification of Wren is similar to the denotational interpreter with respect to command and expression evaluation. Perhaps the biggest difference is in not relying on Prolog native arithmetic to perform comparisons and numeric operations. Instead, the Naturals module performs these operations based solely on a number system derived from applying a successor operation to an initial value zero.

More elaborate approaches are possible in which the original specification module is read and interpreted. These tasks are beyond the scope of this book; interested readers can consult the further readings at the end of this chapter.

Exercises

1. Complete the interpreter as presented by adding the modules Files and Mappings and by completing the remaining arithmetic operations and comparison operations.

2. As an extension of exercise 2 in section 12.4, implement the syntactic and semantic functions and equations for Boolean expressions in Prolog.

3. Add modules for Characters and Strings. Translate identifiers from the parser, such as ide(name), into Strings, such as cons(char-n, cons(char-a, cons(char-m, cons(char-e, nullString)))).

4. Implement the modules WrenTypeChecker and WrenSystem. If a context violation is encountered, print an appropriate error message, indicating where the error occurred. Process the remainder of the program for other context violations, but do not evaluate the program.

5. Change the Naturals module to be an Integers module. Be sure to change other parts of the program, such as removing the error on subtraction, accordingly.

12.6 FURTHER READING

Ehrig and Mahr [Ehrig85] present the best overall discussion of algebraic specifications and the algebras that model them with a clear presentation of the theory. This subject matter developed from the work done on abstract data types by the ADJ group in the 1970s [Goguen78]. Watt's book on formal semantics [Watt91] also serves as a good introduction to algebraic specifications supported by many examples. The short paper by Burstall and Goguen [Burstall82] provides a concise but well-motivated discussion of specifications. For a more advanced treatment of the subject, see [Wirsing90].

The algebraic specification of data types has been developed primarily by John Guttag and the ADJ group. The best presentations of abstract data types can be found in [Guttag78a], [Guttag78b], [Guttag78c], and [Guttag80]. [Goguen77] and [Broy87] both discuss the use of algebraic specifications to model abstract syntax. For more on abstract syntax, see [Noonan85] and [Pagan83].

Using algebraic methods to specify the semantics of a programming language is covered in considerable detail in [Bergstra89]. Our specification of Wren is largely based on the ideas in his book. Another presentation of algebraic semantics can be found in [Broy87].

Chapter 13
ACTION SEMANTICS

The formal methods discussed in earlier chapters, particularly denotational semantics and structural operational semantics, have been used extensively to provide accurate and unambiguous definitions of programming languages. Unlike informal definitions written in English or some other natural language, formal definitional techniques can serve as a basis for proving properties of programming languages and the correctness of programs. Although most programmers rely on informal specifications of languages, these definitions are often vague, incomplete, and even erroneous. English does not lend itself to precise and unambiguous definitions.

In spite of the arguments for relying on formal specifications of programming languages, programmers generally avoid them when learning, trying to understand, or even implementing a programming language. They find formal definitions notationally dense, cryptic, and unlike the way they view the behavior of programming languages. Furthermore, formal specifications are difficult to create accurately, to modify, and to extend. Formal definitions of large programming languages are overwhelming to both the language designer and the language user, and therefore remain mostly unread.

Programmers understand programming languages in terms of basic concepts such as control flow, bindings, modifications of storage, and parameter passing. Formal specifications often obscure these notions to the point that the reader must invest considerable time to determine whether a language follows static or dynamic scoping and how parameters are actually passed. Sometimes the most fundamental concepts of the programming language are the hardest to understand in a formal definition.

Action semantics, which attempts to answer these criticisms of formal methods for language specification, has been developed over the past few years by Peter Mosses with the collaboration of David Watt. The goal of their efforts has been to produce formal semantic specifications that directly reflect the ordinary computational concepts of programming languages and that are easy to read and understand. In this chapter we present an introduction to the methods of action semantics by specifying three languages: the calculator language from Chapter 9, Wren, and Pelican.

13.1 CONCEPTS AND EXAMPLES

Action semantics has evolved out of the tradition of denotational semantics, where syntactic entities (abstract syntax trees) are mapped compositionally by semantic functions into semantic entities that act as the denotations of the syntactic objects. The chief difference between the two methods of formal specification lies in the nature of the semantic entities. The semantic functions of denotational semantics map syntactic phrases into primitive mathematical values, structured objects, and such higher-order functions as are found in the lambda calculus where functions can be applied to other functions. In contrast, action semantics uses three kinds of first-order entities as denotations: **actions**, **data**, and **yielders**. "First-order" means that actions cannot be applied to other actions.

- The semantic entities known as **actions** incorporate the performance of computational behavior, using values passed to them to generate new values that reflect changes in the state of the computation. Actions are the engines that process data and yielders.

- The **data** entities consist of mathematical values, such as integers, Boolean values, and abstract cells representing memory locations, that embody particles of information. Data are classified into sorts so that the kinds of information processed by actions are well specified in a language definition. Sorts of data are defined by algebraic specifications in the manner discussed in Chapter 12.

- **Yielders** encompass unevaluated pieces of data whose values depend on the current information incorporating the state of the computation. Yielders are entities that, depending on the current storage and environment, can be evaluated to yield data.

We begin our discussion of action semantics by considering the meaning of several simple language constructs from Pelican (see section 9.5), first viewing denotational definitions and then introducing enough action notation to describe the constructs in action semantics. Figure 13.1 displays the semantic equations for a denotational specification of constant and variable declarations and identifier evaluation.

Denotational semantics expresses the details of a semantic equation functionally, so we see many parameters being passed to, and values returned from, the semantic functions explicitly. In contrast, each action in action semantics entails particular modes of control and data flow implicitly. Much of the information processed by an action is manipulated automatically when the action is performed.

---

elaborate ⟦**const** I = E⟧ env sto = (*extendEnv*(env,I,*evaluate* E env sto), sto)

elaborate ⟦**var** I : T⟧ env sto = (*extendEnv*(env,I,*var*(loc)), sto_1)
         where (sto_1, loc) = *allocate* sto

evaluate ⟦I⟧ env sto =
        if dval = *int*(n) or dval = *bool*(p)
            then dval
            else if dval = *var*(loc)
                    then if *applySto*(sto,loc) = *undefined*
                        then *error*
                        else *applySto*(sto,loc)
        where dval = *applyEnv*(env,I)

Figure 13.1: Denotational Semantics for Part of Pelican

In action semantics, the meaning of a programming language is defined by mapping program phrases to actions. The performance of these actions models the execution of the program phrases. To define these few constructs from Pelican, we need to describe several primitive actions, two operations that yield data, and two composite actions. Primitive actions can store data in storage cells, bind identifiers to data, compute values, test Boolean values, and so on. The following primitive actions include the ones needed to define the fragment of Pelican plus a few others as examples:

complete	Terminate normally the action being performed.
fail	Abort the action being performed.
give _	Give the value obtained by evaluating a yielder.
allocate a cell	Allocate a memory location.
store _ in _	Store a value in a memory location.
bind _ to _	Bind an identifier to data produced by a yielder.

These examples illustrate a syntactic convention wherein parameters to operations are indicated by underscores. Operations in action semantics can be prefix, infix, or outfix. Outfix operators have only internal place holders such as in "sum(_,_)". The last two examples above are considered prefix since they end with a place holder. Infix operators begin and end with argument places—for example, "_ or _". The operations are evaluated with prefix having the highest precedence and outfix the lowest. Prefix operators are executed from right to left, and infix from left to right.

Other operations—the yielders in action semantics—give values that depend on the current information, such as the current storage and the current bindings:

the _ stored in _	Yield the value of a given type stored in a memory location.

the _ bound to _   Yield the object of a certain type bound to an identifier.

the given _   Yield the value of the specified type given to the action.

Action combinators are binary operations that combine existing actions, using infix notation, to control the order in which subactions are performed as
well as the data flow to and from the subactions. Action combinators are
used to define sequential, selective, iterative, and block structuring control
flow as well as to manage the flow of information between actions. The following two combinators model sequential control and nondeterministic choice,
respectively:

_ then _

Perform the first action; when it completes, perform the second action
taking the data given by the first action.

_ or _

Perform either one of the two actions, choosing one arbitrarily; if it fails,
perform the other action using the original state.

With these operations, we specify the two declarations and identifier evaluation from Pelican in Figure 13.2.

---

elaborate [[**var** I : T]] =
                    allocate a cell
          then
                    bind I to the given Cell

elaborate [[**const** I = E]] =
                    evaluate E
          then
                    bind I to the given Value

evaluate [[I]] =
                    give the Value stored in the Cell bound to I
          or
                    give the Value bound to I

Figure 13.2: Action Semantics for Part of Pelican

These examples convey the basic idea of action specifications. Since prefix
operations are evaluated from right to left, we may omit the parentheses in
"bind I to (the given Cell)" and "give (the Value stored in (the Cell bound to I))".
Observe that one of the actions in the last semantic equation must fail, thereby
producing either the constant binding or the variable binding to the identifier. In the sequel we describe these primitive actions, yielders, and action
combinators in more detail.

A specification of a programming language using action semantics naturally breaks into the two parts shown in the diagram below.

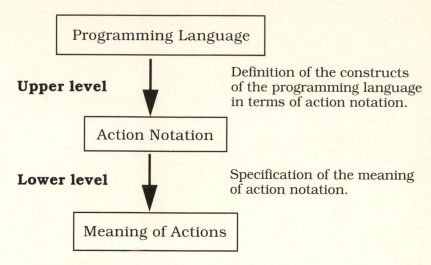

The description of action semantics in the book by Peter Mosses [Mosses92] specifies the meaning of action notation (the lower level, which is also known as microsemantics) formally using algebraic axioms to present the notation and structural operational semantics to give the semantics of action performance. Here we describe action notation using examples, short English definitions, and diagrams, concentrating our efforts in the upper level, also known as macrosemantics, where semantics is bestowed on a programming language in terms of action notation.

Data and Sorts

The data manipulated by a programming language need to be specified in a semantic definition of the language. These data are static, mathematical objects that include entities such as cells, tuples, and maps—as well as the expected sets of integers and Boolean values. These entities are required to describe the behavior of programs in the language.

In action semantics, data are classified into sorts, which are sets of mathematical objects equipped with assorted operations on those objects. These sorts are defined by algebraic specifications. The languages presented in this chapter require the sorts TruthValue and Integer, which can be specified in a way similar to the modules in Chapter 12. In the spirit of action semantics, we define the sorts TruthValue and Integer following the syntax for algebraic specifications found in [Mosses92]. We omit the equations in the specifications and refer the reader to Chapter 12 for examples.

module TruthValues
    exports
        sorts TruthValue
        operations
            true   : TruthValue
            false : TruthValue
            not _ : TruthValue $\rightarrow$ TruthValue
            both (_ , _) : TruthValue, TruthValue $\rightarrow$ TruthValue
            either (_ , _): TruthValue, TruthValue $\rightarrow$ TruthValue
            _ is _ : TruthValue, TruthValue $\rightarrow$ TruthValue   -- the equality relation
    end exports
    equations
      :
end TruthValues

module Integers
    imports TruthValues
    exports
        sorts Integer
        operations
            0 : Integer
            1 : Integer
            10 : Integer
            successor _   : Integer $\rightarrow$ Integer
            predecessor _   : Integer $\rightarrow$ Integer
            sum (_ , _)   : Integer, Integer $\rightarrow$ Integer
            difference (_ , _) : Integer, Integer $\rightarrow$ Integer
            product (_ , _)   : Integer, Integer $\rightarrow$ Integer
            integer-quotient (_ , _) : Integer, Integer $\rightarrow$ Integer
            _ is _ : Integer, Integer $\rightarrow$ TruthValue   -- the equality relation
            _ is less than _   : Integer, Integer $\rightarrow$ TruthValue
            _ is greater than _ : Integer, Integer $\rightarrow$ TruthValue
    end exports
    equations
      :
end Integers

Sort operations allow sorts to be compared and combined to form new sorts. These operations correspond to normal set operations.

Definition: Let S_1 and S_2 be two sorts.

a) The **join** or union of S_1 and S_2 is denoted by $S_1 \mid S_2$.

b) The **meet** or intersection of S_1 and S_2 is denoted by $S_1 \,\&\, S_2$.

c) The notation $S_1 \leq S_2$ means that S_1 is a **subsort** of S_2. ∎

The sorts used in an action semantics specification form a lattice according to the partial order $\leq$. Every sort automatically includes a special element, called nothing, representing the absence of information in much the same way as $\perp$ was used in domain theory. We use the sort Datum to include all the values manipulated by actions and refer to tuples each of whose components is a Datum as Data. Every Datum can be viewed as a member of Data (Datum $\leq$ Data), since a singleton tuple is identified with the individual in the tuple. Using this notation, we can make a few assertions about sorts of data:

• The expressible values in Wren constitute the sort (Integer | TruthValue).

• (Integer | TruthValue) $\leq$ Datum.

• (Integer & TruthValue) = nothing.

The special value nothing plays a particularly important role in action specifications, representing the result of any operation or action that terminates abnormally. Every sort automatically contains the value nothing, which represents the empty sort. Most actions and operations specify the sort of values that will be used and produced by their performance. Whenever the wrong kind of value appears, the result will be nothing. As with any semantic methodology, programs are expected to be syntactically correct—adhering to both the context-free syntax (BNF) and the context-sensitive syntax (context constraints dealing with type checking)—before they are submitted to semantic analysis. In spite of this, action semantics follows a strict type discipline in specifying the meaning of language constructs. This careful delineation of the types of objects manipulated by actions adds to the information conveyed by the semantic descriptions. Performing an action corresponding to a language construct that violates type constraints results in failure. An operation (yielder) that fails for any reason produces the value nothing, and an action that contains such an operation simply fails.

Although we can describe the sort of actions, actions themselves do not form a subsort of Datum, since actions, which work on data, cannot manipulate actions. Later we will see that actions can, however, be encapsulated into data, called abstractions, that can be "enacted", thereby causing the performance of the actions. This mechanism enables action semantics to model subprogram declaration and invocation.

Action semantics classifies data according to how far they tend to be propagated during action performance.

- **Transient** Data or tuples of data given as the immediate results of action performance are called transients. These values model the data given by expressions. They must be used immediately or be lost.

- **Scoped** These data consist of bindings of tokens (identifiers) to data as in environments. They are accessible (visible) throughout the performance of an action and its subactions, although they may be hidden temporarily by the creation of inner scopes.

- **Stable** Stable data model memory as values stored in cells (or locations) defined in a language's specification. Changes in storage made during action performance are enduring, so that stable data may be altered only by explicit actions.

When we describe actions themselves later, we will see that actions are also classified by the fundamental kind of data that they modify. This classification gives rise to the so-called **facets** of action semantics that are determined by the kind of information principally involved in an action's performance.

Yielders

During the performance of an action, certain **current information** is maintained implicitly, including:

- The transients given to and given by actions
- The bindings received by and produced by actions
- The current state of the storage

Terms that evaluate to produce data, depending on the current information, are called **yielders**. The yielders in an action semantics specification select information for processing by actions from transients, bindings, and storage, verifying its type consistency. Below we describe four yielders that play an important role in language specification.

the given _ : Data → Yielder

Yield the transient data given to an action, provided it agrees with the sort specified as Data.

the given _ # _ : Datum, PositiveInteger → Yielder

Yield the nth item in the tuple of transient data given to an action, provided it agrees with the sort specified as Datum, where n is the second argument.

the _ bound to _ : Data, Token → Yielder

> Yield the object bound to an identifier denoted by the Token in the current bindings, after verifying that its type is the sort specified as Data.

the _ stored in _ : Data, Yielder → Yielder

> Yield the value of sort Data stored in the memory location denoted by the cell yielded by the second argument.

Token denotes a subsort of Yielder that gives identifiers. PositiveInteger is a subsort of Integer. These yielders are evaluated during action performance to produce values (Data) to be used by and given by actions.

Actions

Actions are dynamic, computational entities that model the operational behavior of programming languages. When performed, actions accept the data passed to them in the form of the current information—namely, the given transients, the received bindings, and the current state of storage—to give new transients, produce new bindings, and/or update the state of the storage. If no intermediate result is to be passed on to the next action, the transient is simply the empty tuple. Similarly, the empty binding, with every identifier unbound, is passed to the next action if the action produces no bindings.

Depending on the principal type of information processed, actions are classified into several different facets, including:

- **Functional Facet**: actions that process transient information
- **Imperative Facet**: actions that process stable information
- **Declarative Facet**: actions that process scoped information
- **Basic Facet**: actions that principally specify flow of control
- **Reflective Facet**: actions that handle abstractions (subprograms)
- **Hybrid Action Notation**: actions that deal with recursive bindings

An action performance may **complete** (terminate normally), **fail** (terminate abnormally), or **diverge** (not terminate at all).

The Functional Facet

Actions and yielders classified in the functional facet primarily manipulate the transients given to and given by actions. First we consider composite actions in the functional and basic facets, a few of the so-called action combinators. These combinators may also process scoped information, but we defer the discussion of bindings until a later section in this chapter.

Action combinators have the signature

$$\text{combinator : Action, Action} \rightarrow \text{Action}$$

and are normally written using infix notation. At this point we are concerned only with control flow and the processing of transients.

The basic combinator "A_1 and then A_2" performs the first action and then performs the second. We illustrate the control flow between the two actions by a dashed line in a diagram that indicates that the first action must terminate normally (complete) before the second action can be performed.

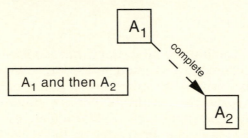

Both actions can use the transients passed to the combined action. The transients given by each action are concatenated and given by the combined action. We depict the concatenation of transients (tuples) by joining the data flow lines. The transient from the first action precedes that from the second in the concatenation, which is ordered from left to right. Adding the processing of the transients to "A_1 and then A_2" gives the following diagram:

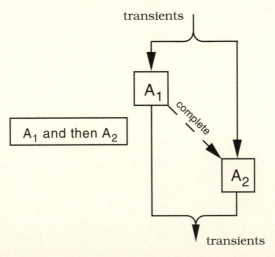

The basic action combinator "A_1 and A_2" allows interleaving of the performance of the two actions. The diagram below shows no control dependency between the two actions, suggesting that they can be performed collaterally. Both actions use the transients passed to the combined action. The transients given by each action are concatenated and given by the combined action.

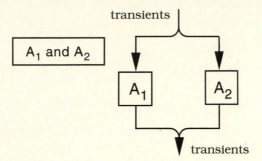

The functional action combinator "A_1 then A_2" performs the first action using the transients given to the combined action and then performs the second action using the transients given by the first action. The transients given by the combined action are those given by the second action. The dashed line shows the control dependency.

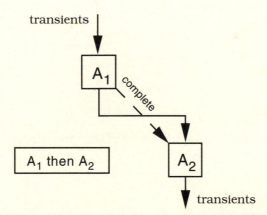

For each of these action combinators, if one of the actions gives the value nothing, the result of the composite action is nothing. We say these combinators are **strict** in the value nothing.

The sample language in the next section—namely, the calculator language from section 9.2—uses a primitive functional action give : Yielder $\rightarrow$ Action, which was mentioned earlier; "give Y" where Y is a yielder (a term that evaluates to a data value) gives the value computed from Y as its transient.

The yielder "the given S" where S is a sort of data, retrieves and type checks the datum in the given transient. The yielder takes a parameter that is a sort to document the type of the datum in the transient.

The yielder "the given S#n" retrieves and type checks the nth datum in the given transient tuple.

For example, the composite action

   give sum (the given Integer#1, the given Integer#2)
and
   give (the given Integer#1 is the given Integer#2)

provided with the tuple (3,5) as a transient, gives the tuple (8,false) as its result. The operation is serves as equality for integers.

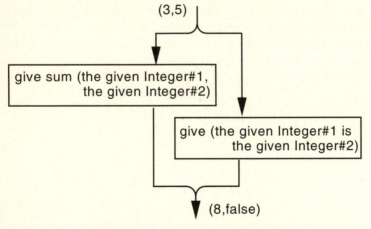

The tuple (3,3) given as a transient will result in the tuple (6,true) as the transient given by this composite action.

The Imperative Facet

Actions and yielders in the imperative facet deal with storage, allocating memory locations, updating the contents of locations, and fetching values from memory. All actions work on a common store consisting of an unlimited number of **cells**, which are data of the sort Cell. Initially all cells are considered unused. When an object of sort Cell is allocated, it changes from being unused to containing a special value called undefined. The values that may be stored in memory belong to a sort called Storable, corresponding to the storable values in denotational semantics. Thus when specifying an imperative programming language, we need to specify the sort Storable. Any action may alter the state of a cell, and such a modification remains in effect until some other action modifies the cell again by storing a different value in it or by deallocating the cell. Therefore we think of the data stored in cells as **stable** information.

Cells form a sort of data that can be left unspecified. This abstract data type requires only that cells are distinguishable and that we have an unlimited number of them, although only a finite number will be in use at any one time. We can view the current storage as a finite mapping from cells to the sort (Storable | undefined).

Two primitive imperative actions allocate and update storage cells.

allocate a cell

> Find an unused cell, storing the value undefined in it, and give the (object of sort) Cell as the transient of the action.

The actual allocation algorithm is not important, as long as it always yields an unused cell when performed. In [Mosses92] the allocate operation is a hybrid action defined in terms of primitive actions from the imperative and functional facets. We treat it as a primitive action to simplify the discussion. The precedence rules for action semantics allow us to use multiword operation names without any confusion. The expression "allocate a cell" represents a nullary operation. A primitive action defines the modification of a memory cell.

store Y_1 in Y_2

> Update the cell yielded by Y_2 to contain the Storable yielded by Y_1.

The imperative facet has no special action combinators, but any action has the potential of altering storage. In the combination "A_1 and then A_2", any changes to storage by A_1 precede those made by A_2. In contrast, if both A_1 and A_2 in "A_1 and A_2" modify memory, the results are unpredictable because of the possible interleaving.

The yielder "the S stored in Y" gives the datum currently stored in the cell yielded by evaluating Y provided that the value given is a datum of sort S. Otherwise, the yielder gives nothing.

Suppose that two locations, denoted by $cell_1$ and $cell_2$, have been allocated and currently contain the value undefined. Also assume that the next cell to be allocated is $cell_3$. Figure 13.3 shows snapshots of the current storage as a composite action is performed.

The first subaction to the combinator then gives $cell_3$ as a transient to the second subaction that stores a value there. Observe how indenting determines the grouping of the actions.

Initial storage:

cell$_1$	undefined
cell$_2$	undefined

store 3 in cell$_1$

cell$_1$	3
cell$_2$	undefined

and then

cell$_1$	3
cell$_2$	5

store 5 in cell$_2$

and then

allocate a cell

then

store sum (the Integer stored in cell$_1$,

the Integer stored in cell$_2$)

in the given Cell

cell$_1$	3
cell$_2$	5
cell$_3$	8

Figure 13.3: Current Storage While Performing an Action

Exercises

1. Assuming the value 5 as the given transient, diagram the following composite actions:

   a)   give -7

       and

            give the given integer

      then

      give product (the given Integer#1, the given Integer#2)

   b)   give difference (0,the given Integer)

      then

            give successor(the given Integer)

       and

            give predecessor(the given Integer)

      then

      give sum (the given Integer#1, the given Integer#2)

2. Actions from the functional facet can be viewed as describing a simple language of expressions that define functions that take a value (the tran-

sient) and give a result (the new transient). Describe the functions defined by the following actions:

a)   give successor (the given Integer)
      then
         give product (the given Integer, the given Integer)

b)   give product (2, the given Integer)
      then
         give successor (the given Integer)

c)   give successor (the given Integer)
      and then
         give product (the given Integer, the given Integer)

d)   give predecessor (the given Integer)
      and
             give successor (the given Integer)
      then
         give product (the given Integer#1, the given Integer#2)

3. Suppose that the following action is given a cell containing the integer 5 as a transient. What (possible) numbers can be stored in the cell after performing this action?

       store 0 in the given Cell
    and
             store successor (the Integer stored in the given Cell) in the given Cell
         and then
             store sum (the Integer stored in the given Cell, 10) in the given Cell

4. Suppose that the current storage contains only two defined cells: { $cell_1 \mapsto 6$, $cell_2 \mapsto -2$ }. Describe the current storage after performing the following action:

             give Integer stored in $cell_1$
         and
             give 10
         then
             store product (the given Integer#1, the given Integer#2) in the given $cell_1$
         then
             give successor (the Integer stored in $cell_2$)
         then
             store difference (the given Integer, the Integer stored in $cell_1$) in $cell_2$

Assuming that $cell_1$ corresponds to the variable x and $cell_2$ to y, what assignment command(s) are modeled by the performance of this action?

13.2 ACTION SEMANTICS OF A CALCULATOR

We use the calculator from section 9.2 as the first example of a complete specification by means of action semantics. Here the definition of the calculator semantics is somewhat simplified by using the imperative facet to provide a storage location for the calculator memory. A module describes the necessary imperative features needed for the specification.

module Imperative
    imports Integers, Mappings
    exports
        sorts   Storable = Integer,
                Storage = Mapping [Cell to (Storable | undefined)],
                Cell ≤ Datum
        operations
                $cell_1$: Cell
                allocate a cell : Action
                store _ in _ : Yielder, Yielder → Action
                the _ stored in _ : Storable, Yielder → Yielder
                    :
    end exports
    equations
      :
end Imperative

The module Imperative imports the module Mappings that specifies objects to model finite functions, instantiating an object of sort Mapping using the notation "Mapping [domain to codomain]". We use slightly different (from Chapter 12) but equivalent notation–namely, Storage = Mapping [Cell to (Storable | undefined)]— to instantiate the parameters to the Mappings module and to rename (really give synonyms for) identifiers from the imported module. Using Mappings, Imperative can specify an empty map, a mechanism for adding a new ordered pair to the map, a way to change the image of a domain element, and notation for applying the map to a domain item. Here we only name the operations, actions, data, and yielders, used to manipulate storage in action notation.

For reference we repeat the abstract syntax of the calculator language in Figure 13.4, slightly modified for the action semantic specification. It is a common practice to fit the definition of the abstract syntax to the method used for the semantic specification. For example, we used different definitions of abstract syntax in Chapter 8 and Chapter 9. However, since the concrete syntax of the calculator language is unchanged from Chapter 9, we are specifying the semantics of the same language.

Abstract Syntactic Domains

P : Program   E : Expression   D : Digit

S : ExprSequence   N : Numeral

Abstract Production Rules

Program ::= ExprSequence

ExprSequence ::= Expression | Expression ExprSequence

Expression ::= Numeral | $\mathbf{M^R}$ | **Clear** | Expression **+** Expression

        | Expression **–** Expression | Expression **x** Expression

        | Expression $\mathbf{M^+}$ | Expression **=** | Expression $\mathbf{^+/\text{-}}$

Numeral ::= Digit | Numeral Digit

Digit ::= **0** | **1** | **2** | **3** | **4** | **5** | **6** | **7** | **8** | **9**

Figure 13.4: Abstract Syntax for the Calculator Language

Semantic Functions

As with denotational semantics, meaning is ascribed to the calculator language via semantic functions, mostly mapping syntactic domains to actions. Because of the expressiveness of action semantics using the imperative facet, we need fewer semantic functions.

meaning _   : Program → Action

perform _   : ExprSequence → Action

evaluate _   : Expression → Action

the value of _   : Numeral → Integer   -- uses only nonnegative integers

digit value _   : Digit → Integer

The action that serves as the meaning of a program gives a value that can be taken as the semantics of the program in the calculator language. This value, corresponding to an expressible value in denotational semantics, is the integer shown in the display as a result of executing the program. We describe its sort, a subsort of Datum, by the definition

Value = Integer   -- expressible values.

The sort Action includes many operational behaviors but conveys no specifics about the nature of individual actions. To make specifications more precise, entities of sort Action can be qualified by describing the **outcome**, the sort of information produced by an action, and the **income**, the sort of information used by an action. A subsort of Action can be defined by writing

Action [outcome] [income].

We omit the details that describe possible income and outcome entities formally, but the terminology itself suggests the intent of the qualifications. The semantic functions for the calculator are more accurately specified by the following signatures:

meaning _ : Program → Action [completing | giving a Value | storing]
                                        [using current storage]

perform _   : ExprSequence → Action [completing | giving a Value | storing]
                                        [using current storage]

evaluate _ : Expression → Action [completing | giving a Value | storing]
                                        [using current storage]

Note that the symbol |, which denotes the join or union of sorts, is an associative operation.

Semantic Equations

The semantic function evaluate does the bulk of the work in specifying the calculator language. The value given by performing the action resulting from evaluate, and from the functions meaning and perform, is the value shown in the display of the calculator. Although the display value can be considered as the semantics of a phrase in the calculator language, meaning is more fully specified by describing the activities performed to obtain this value. The actions of action semantics are designed to model these activities.

The evaluate function takes the nine different forms of expressions as its actual parameter. For each we describe the intended operational behavior, and then give the semantic equation that describes this behavior as an action. Observe how closely the definition in action notation parallels the informal description.

- **Numeral**

   To evaluate a numeral, simply display its integer value on the display.

   evaluate N = give the value of N

   The value given as a transient by the action give is the displayed integer.

- **Memory Recall**

   Display the value stored in the single memory location that we assume has been allocated initially and named $cell_1$. The module Imperative asserts the existence of a constant cell, $cell_1$, to serve this purpose.

   evaluate $\mathbf{M^R}$ = give Integer stored in $cell_1$

   Again the transient given by the action is the displayed value.

- **Clear**

  The clear operation resets the memory location to zero and displays zero.

  > evaluate **Clear** =
  >> store 0 in cell$_1$
  >
  > and
  >> give 0

  Since we have no reason to perform one of these subactions before the other, the composite action uses the and combinator. If interference were possible between the two activities, we could use and then to establish order. In the case of **Clear**, choosing an order of performance over-specifies the behavior.

- **Addition of Two Expressions**

  This binary operation gives the sum of the integers that result from the two expressions. The left expression must be evaluated first since it may involve a side effect by storing a value in the calculator memory.

  > evaluate $[\![E_1 + E_2]\!]$ =
  >> evaluate E_1
  >
  > and then
  >> evaluate E_2
  >
  > then
  >> give sum (the given Integer#1, the given Integer#2)

  The first combinator forms a tuple (a pair) consisting of the values of the two expressions, which are evaluated from left to right. That tuple is given to the sum operation, which adds the two components. Action semantics uses indenting to describe the evaluation order of action operations. Parentheses are also allowed for this purpose, but generally the indenting convention is easier to follow. For comparison, consider the semantic equation for addition written using parentheses.

  > evaluate $[\![E_1 + E_2]\!]$ = (evaluate E_1 and then evaluate E_2) then
  >> (give sum (the given Integer#1, the given Integer#2))

  Since evaluate is a prefix operation, it takes precedence over the and then combinator. Actually none of these parentheses are necessary, but composite actions are easier to read if they employ some grouping mechanism.

- **Difference of Two Expressions**
- **Product of Two Expressions**

  Subtraction and multiplication are handled in the same way as addition, but difference and product are used to implement the operations.

- **Add to Memory**

  Display the value of the current expression and add it to the calculator memory.

  > evaluate $[\![E\ \mathbf{M^+}]\!]$ =
  >> evaluate E
  >
  > then
  >>> store sum (the Integer stored in $cell_1$, the given Integer) in $cell_1$
  >> and
  >>> give the given Integer

  The second subaction to then must propagate the transient from the first subaction so that it can be given by the composite action. The primitive action "store _ in _" yields no transient, which is represented by an empty tuple. The action "give the given Integer" propagates the integer from the evaluation of E. Action semantics views a single datum as identical to a singleton tuple containing the same value. Concatenating the empty tuple and the singleton tuple produces the value of E as the transient of the and combinator. Without the subaction "give the given Integer", the value from E will be lost. It must be propagated as the resulting transient from the entire action.

  Action semantics has a primitive action regive that abbreviates "give the given Data". We use this abbreviation in some of the remaining examples, although using regive reduces the information since the sort of the Data is not specified.

- **Equal**

  The equal key terminates an evaluation, displaying the value from the current expression.

  > evaluate $[\![E\ \mathbf{=}]\!]$ = evaluate E

- **Change Sign**

  The $\mathbf{^+/\text{-}}$ key flips the sign of the integer produced by the latest expression evaluation.

  > evaluate $[\![E\ \mathbf{^+/\text{-}}]\!]$ =
  >> evaluate E
  >
  > then
  >> give difference (0, the given Integer)

The meaning function initializes the calculator by storing zero in the memory location and then evaluates the expression sequence. The storing operation gives an empty transient. The semantic function perform evaluates the expressions in the sequence one at a time, ignoring the given transients. The semantic functions value of and digit value have essentially the same behavior as the corresponding functions in denotational semantics. All of the semantic equations for the action semantics of the calculator language are collected in Figure 13.5.

---

meaning P =
           store 0 in $cell_1$
   and then
           perform P

perform $[\![E\ S]\!]$ =
           evaluate E
   and then
           perform S

perform E = evaluate E

evaluate N = give the value of N

evaluate $\mathbf{M^R}$ = give Integer stored in $cell_1$

evaluate **Clear** =
           store 0 in $cell_1$
   and
           give 0

evaluate $[\![E_1 + E_2]\!]$ =
              evaluate E_1
       and then
              evaluate E_2
   then
           give sum (the given Integer#1, the given Integer#2)

evaluate $[\![E_1 - E_2]\!]$ =
              evaluate E_1
       and then
              evaluate E_2
   then
           give difference (the given Integer#1, the given Integer#2)

evaluate $[\![E_1 \times E_2]\!]$ =
              evaluate E_1
       and then
              evaluate E_2
   then
           give product (the given Integer#1, the given Integer#2)

Figure 13.5: Semantic Equations for the Calculator Language (Part 1)

---

evaluate $[\![E\ \mathbf{M^+}]\!]$ =
        evaluate E
    then
          store sum (the Integer stored in $cell_1$, the given Integer) in $cell_1$
      and
        regive   -- give the given Data

evaluate $[\![E\ =]\!]$ = evaluate E

evaluate $[\![E\ \mathbf{^+/\text{-}}]\!]$ =
        evaluate E
    then
        give difference (0, the given Integer)

the value of $[\![N\ D]\!]$ = sum (product (10,the value of N), the value of D)

the value of D = digit value D

digit value $\mathbf{0}$ = 0
$\vdots$
digit value $\mathbf{9}$ = 9

Figure 13.5: Semantic Equations for the Calculator Language (Part 2)

The use of the combinator "and then" in the definition of meaning and perform is only used to sequence the control flow since the transients are ignored between the subactions.

Action semantics uses the emphatic brackets "$[\![$" and "$]\!]$" slightly differently than denotational semantics. Semantic functions are applied to abstract syntax trees. In action semantics the notation "$[\![E_1 + E_2]\!]$" denotes the abstract syntax tree composed of a root and three subtrees, E_1, $+$, and E_2. Since E_1 is already an abstract syntax tree, we have no need for another set of brackets in the expression "evaluate E_1". We omit the brackets in each semantic equation that gives meaning to an abstract syntax tree that consists of a single subtree (a single object) as in "evaluate **Clear**".

A Sample Calculation

As an example, consider the calculator program elaborated in Figure 9.7:

$\mathbf{12 + 5\ ^+/\text{-} = x\ 2\ M^+\ 123\ M^+\ M^R\ ^+/\text{-} - 25 = + M^R =}$

This sequence of calculator keystrokes parses into three expressions, so that the overall structure of the action semantics evaluation has the form

meaning $[\![\mathbf{12 + 5\ ^+/\text{-} = x\ 2\ M^+\ 123\ M^+\ M^R\ ^+/\text{-} - 25 = + M^R =}]\!]$

= store 0 in $cell_1$
   and then
       perform $[\![12 + 5\ {}^+/\text{-} = x\ 2\ M^+\ 123\ M^+\ M^R\ {}^+/\text{-} - 25 = +\ M^R =]\!]$

= store 0 in $cell_1$
   and then
       evaluate $[\![12 + 5\ {}^+/\text{-} = x\ 2\ M^+]\!]$
   and then
       evaluate $[\![123\ M^+]\!]$
   and then
       evaluate $[\![M^R\ {}^+/\text{-} - 25 = +\ M^R =]\!]$

The first expression begins with an empty transient and with $cell_1$ containing the value 0. We show the transient (as a tuple) given by each of the subactions as well as the value stored in $cell_1$.

	Transient	$cell_1$
evaluate $[\![12 + 5\ {}^+/\text{-} = x\ 2\ M^+]\!]$ =	( )	0
give the value of 12	(12)	0
and then		
give the value of 5	(5)	0
then		
give difference (0, the given Integer)	(-5)	0
then	(12,-5)	0
give sum (the given Integer#1, the given Integer#2)	(7)	0
and then		
give the value of 2	(2)	0
then	(7,2)	0
give product (the given Integer#1, the given Integer#2)	(14)	0
then		
store sum (the Integer stored in $cell_1$, the given Integer) in $cell_1$	( )	14
and		
regive	(14)	14

This action gives the value 14, which is also the value in $cell_1$. The second expression starts with 14 in memory, ignoring the given transient, and results in the following action:

evaluate $[\![123\ M^+]\!]$ =		
give the value of 123	(123)	14
then		
store sum(the Integer stored in $cell_1$,the given Integer) in $cell_1$	( )	137
and		
regive	(123)	137

This action gives the value 123 and leaves the value 137 in cell$_1$. The third expression completes the evaluation, starting with 137 in memory, as follows:

evaluate $[\![\mathbf{M^R} \ ^+/- - 25 = + \mathbf{M^R} =]\!]$ =

give Integer stored in cell$_1$	(137)	137
then		
give difference (0, the given Integer)	(-137)	137
and then		
give the value of 25	(25)	137
then	(-137,25)	137
give difference (the given Integer#1, the given Integer#2)	(-162)	137
and then		
give Integer stored in cell$_1$	(137)	137
then	(-162,137)	137
give sum (the given Integer#1, the given Integer#2)	(-25)	137

This final action gives the value -25, leaving the value 137 in the calculator's memory.

Exercises

1. Evaluate the semantics of these combinations of keystrokes using the action semantics definition in this section:

    a) $8 \ ^+/- + 5 \ \text{x} \ 3$ =

    b) $7 \ \text{x} \ 2 \ \mathbf{M^+} \ \mathbf{M^+} \ \mathbf{M^+} - 15 + \mathbf{M^R}$ =

    c) $10 - 5 \ ^+/\text{-} \ \mathbf{M^+} \ 6 \ \text{x} \ \mathbf{M^R} \ \mathbf{M^+}$ =

    Consult the concrete syntax of the calculator language in section 9.2 when parsing these programs. For instance, the program in part a is grouped in the manner as shown by the parentheses below:

    $$((((8 \ ^+/\text{-}) + 5) \ \text{x} \ 3) =)$$

2. Add to the calculator a key **sqr** that computes the square of the value in the display. Alter the semantics to model the action of this key. Its syntax should be similar to that of the $^+/\text{-}$ key.

3. Prove that for any expression E, meaning $[\![E = \mathbf{M^+}]\!]$ = meaning $[\![E \ \mathbf{M^+} =]\!]$.

4. Some calculators treat "=" differently than the calculator in this section, repeating the most recent operation, so that "**2 + 5 = =**" leaves 12 on the display and "**2 + 5 = = =**" leaves 17. Consider the changes that must be made in the action semantics to model this alternative interpretation.

13.3 THE DECLARATIVE FACET AND WREN

Actions and yielders in the declarative facet deal primarily with scoped information in the form of bindings between identifiers, represented as tokens,
and various semantic entities such as constants, variables, and procedures.
In this section we illustrate several fundamental concepts from the declarative facet, along with a couple of actions dealing with control flow from the
basic facet, in specifying the programming language Wren. Since Wren has
such a simple structure with respect to declarations—namely, a single global
scope—only a few features of the declarative facet are introduced. More complicated actions from the declarative facet are discussed in section 13.4, where
we provide an action specification of Pelican.

One aspect of defining a programming language involves specifying what
kinds of values can be bound to identifiers, the so-called denotable values in
denotational semantics. In action semantics the subsort of Datum that consists of entities that can be bound to identifiers is known as the sort Bindable.
Wren allows binding identifiers only to simple variables, which are modeled
as cells in action semantics. The algebraic specification in a module called
Declarative suggests the salient aspects of the entities in the declarative facet.

module Declarative
     imports Imperative, Mappings
     exports
         sorts   Token
                 Variable = Cell,
                 Bindable = Variable,
                 Bindings = Mapping [Token to (Bindable | unbound)]
         operations
                 empty bindings : Bindings
                 bind _ to _ : Token, Yielder $\rightarrow$ Action
                 the _ bound to _ : Data, Token $\rightarrow$ Yielder
                 produce _ : Yielder $\rightarrow$ Action
                       :
     end exports
     equations
       :
end Declarative

The term "empty bindings" denotes bindings with every identifier unbound.
Action semantics establishes a binding using the primitive declarative action
"bind T to Y", which produces a singleton binding mapping that we represent
informally by [T$\mapsto$B] where B is the datum of sort Bindable yielded by Y.

A declarative yielder finds the value associated with an identifier in the current bindings. The term "the S bound to T" evaluates to the entity bound to the Token T provided it agrees with the sort S; otherwise the yielder gives nothing. The action "produce Y" creates the bindings consisting of the map yielded by Y. It corresponds to the action "give Y" in the functional facet.

Before considering composite actions from the declarative facet, we observe that the action combinators defined earlier process bindings as well as transients. Although the action combinators introduced as part of the functional and basic facets do not concentrate on processing bindings, they receive bindings as part of the current information and produce possibly new bindings as a result of their subactions. The bindings of two actions can combine in two fundamental ways:

merge(bindings$_1$,bindings$_2$):

> Merging the sets of bindings means to form their (disjoint) union with the understanding that if any identifier has bindings in both sets, the operation fails, producing nothing.

overlay(bindings$_1$,bindings$_2$):

> The bindings are combined in such a way that the associations in bindings$_1$ take precedence over those in bindings$_2$.

In the following diagrams, scoped information flows from left to right whereas transients still flow from top to bottom. We depict the merging of bindings by having the lines for scoped information connected by a small circle suggesting a disjoint union. Later when action combinators use the overlay operation, the lines show a break indicating which set of bindings takes precedence.

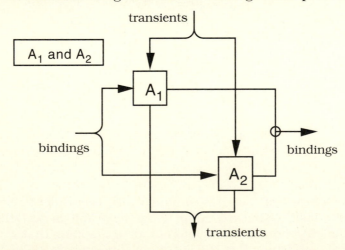

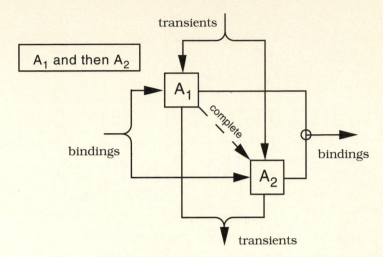

For both of the combinators and and and then, each action receives the bindings for the composite action, and the bindings produced by the subactions are merged. The only difference between these two action combinators is that and then enforces an ordering in the performance of the two subactions.

The action combinator then has the same declarative behavior as the combinator and then.

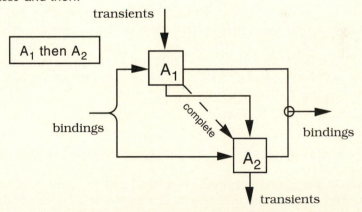

The only primarily declarative action combinator required in the Wren specification is the composite action hence. This combinator sequences the bindings with the first subaction receiving the original bindings, the second subaction receiving the bindings produced by the first, and the bindings produced by the combined action being those produced by the second subaction. The combinator hence processes transients in the same way as the combinator and then.

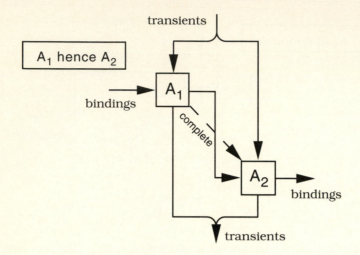

The Programming Language Wren

We now turn to describing an action specification of Wren (see section 1.3 or 9.3 for the syntax of Wren). We omit that part of action semantics used to describe input and output, so the **read** and **write** commands from Wren are ignored in this chapter. Input and output require the communicative facet, a topic beyond the scope of our presentation. In the action semantics description of Wren, we specify the declarative information of the language despite the simplicity of its scope rules. The kinds of information processed by Wren can be specified as the three sorts:

sorts Value = Integer | TruthValue,   -- expressible values
           Storable = Integer | TruthValue,   -- storable values
           Bindable = Variable   -- denotable values (Variable = Cell)

Four new semantic functions provide meaning to the phrases of Wren. The signatures below include the outcome and income to help describe the behavior of the resulting actions.

    run _ : Program → Action [completing | diverging | storing]
                    [using current storage]
    elaborate _ : Declaration → Action [completing | binding | storing]
                      [using current bindings | current storage]
    execute _ : Command → Action [completing | diverging | storing]
                    [using current bindings | current storage]

evaluate _ : Expression → Action [completing | giving a Value]
            [using current bindings | current storage]

For each syntactic construct, we give a brief informal description of its semantics and then provide its definition in action semantics.

- **Program**

  First elaborate the declarations, which involve only variables, and then execute the body of the program using the resulting bindings. The program identifier is ignored, serving as documentation only.

  run $[\![$**program** I **is** D **begin** C **end**$]\!]$ = elaborate D hence execute C

- **Variable Declaration**

  Allocate a cell from storage and then bind the identifier to that cell. The definition handles declarations of a single variable only. Multiple variable declarations can be treated as a sequence of declarations.

  elaborate $[\![$**var** I : T$]\!]$ =
            allocate a cell
     then
            bind I to the given Cell

- **Empty Declaration**

  Produce no bindings. "$[\![\ ]\!]$" denotes an empty tree.

  elaborate $[\![\ ]\!]$ = produce empty bindings

- **Sequence of Declarations**

  Elaborate the first declaration and then elaborate the second using the bindings from the first and producing the combined bindings.

  elaborate $[\![D_1\ D_2]\!]$ = elaborate D_1 and then elaborate D_2

  The bindings in D_1 should be visible to the second declaration, although in Wren D_2 has no way to refer to an identifier in D_1. For this reason, the "and then" combinator suffices to specify declaration sequencing in Wren. With and then each subaction constructs bindings independently, and the two sets of bindings are merged. In a program that satisfies the context constraints for Wren, no conflict can arise between the declarations in D_1 and D_2 when they merge. The combinator then could be used as well since the transients play no role in these declarations.

- **Sequence of Commands**

  Execute the first command and then execute the second.

  execute $[\![C_1\ ;\ C_2]\!]$ = execute C_1 and then execute C_2

- **Skip**

    Do nothing.

    execute **skip** = complete

- **Assignment**

    Find the cell bound to the identifier and evaluate the expression. Then store the value of the expression in that cell.

    execute $[\![$I := E$]\!]$ =
    >   give the Cell bound to I and evaluate E
    >   then
    >   store the given Value#2 in the given Cell#1

    The parameters to the and combinator are presented without indentation. The "bound to" yielder and the give action take precedence because prefix operations are always performed before infix ones. Parentheses can be used to alter precedence or to enhance clarity.

To describe the decision process in **if** and **while** commands, we need an action combinator that belongs to the basic facet and a primitive action from the functional facet. The action combinator or models nondeterministic choice. "A_1 or A_2" arbitrarily chooses one of the subactions and performs it with the given transients and the received bindings. If the chosen action fails, the other subaction is performed with the original transients and bindings. The effect of or is shown in the diagram below with $k = 1$ or $k = 2$, but which one is not specified by action semantics.

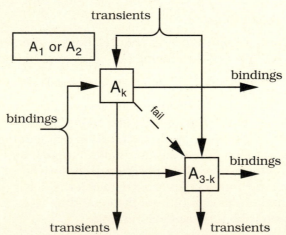

Although most action combinators are strict relative to failure (if one of the subactions fails, the composite action also fails), "A_1 or A_2" can complete (succeed) even though one of its subactions fails. However, if the chosen action fails after making a change to storage, the change is irrevocable, the other action is ignored, and the whole action fails.

The primitive functional action "check Y", where Y is a yielder that gives a TruthValue, completes if Y yields true and fails if it yields false. The action gives empty transients and produces empty bindings. The action check acts as a guard, which when combined with the composite action or enables a specification to carry out decision making.

- **If Commands**

    The **if** commands evaluate the Boolean expression that serves as the test, and then they perform the **then** command or the **else** command depending on the test. If the **else** part is missing, the command does nothing when the condition is false.

    execute $[\![$**if** E **then** C_1 **else** $C_2$$]\!]$ =
    >   evaluate E
    > then
    >>   check (the given TruthValue is true) and then execute C_1
    >   or
    >>   check (the given TruthValue is false) and then execute C_2

    execute $[\![$**if** E **then** C$]\!]$ =
    >   evaluate E
    > then
    >>   check (the given TruthValue is true) and then execute C
    >   or
    >>   check (the given TruthValue is false) and then complete

The operation is acts as equality for the sort TruthValue. Observe that for each of the **if** commands only one of the conditions supplied to the action check can be true. The phrase "and then complete" may be omitted from the second definition. It simply provides symmetry to the or combinator. Also, the first check test can read

>   check (the given TruthValue) and then execute C.

To complete the specification of commands in Wren, we need two more actions, unfolding _ and unfold, from the basic facet to define the **while** command. These actions serve only to determine the flow of control during the performance of subactions.

unfolding _

    The composite action unfolding : Action → Action performs its argument action, but whenever the dummy action unfold is encountered, the argument action is performed again in place of unfold.

unfold

The primitive action unfold is a dummy action, standing for the argument action of the innermost enclosing unfolding.

The diagram below suggests the behavior of the action unfolding A. Whenever the action A performs unfold, it is restarted with the transients and bindings that are given to unfold. Eventually we expect A to complete producing the final transients and bindings.

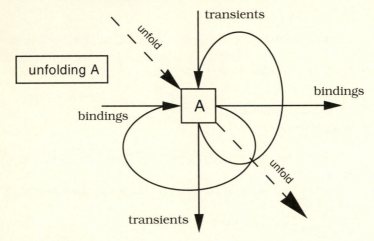

The actions unfolding and unfold are used to describe indefinite iteration—in this case, the **while** command in Wren. Inside a performance of unfolding, an invocation of unfold has the effect of restarting the original action.

- **While Command**

    The Boolean expression is evaluated first. If its value is true, the body of the loop is executed and then the **while** command is started again when the execution of loop body completes; otherwise, the command terminates.

    execute [[**while** E **do** C]] =
            unfolding
                    evaluate E
            then
                        check (the given TruthValue is true)
                            and then execute C
                                and then unfold
                    or
                        check (the given TruthValue is false) and then complete

We conclude the specification of Wren by giving the semantic equations for evaluate, the function that defines the meaning of expressions.

- **Variable Name**

  Give the value stored in the memory location bound to the variable.

  evaluate I = give Value stored in the Cell bound to I

  The precedence rules of action semantics assume that this action is interpreted as "give (the Value stored in (the Cell bound to I))".

- **Literal**

  Give the value of the literal.

  evaluate N = give the value of N

  evaluate **true** = give true

  evaluate **false** = give false

- **Arithmetic on Two Expressions**

  Evaluate the two expressions and give the sum of their values.

  evaluate $[\![E_1 + E_2]\!]$ =

                 evaluate E_1

       and

                 evaluate E_2

     then

            give sum (the given Integer#1, the given Integer#2)

  Since Wren allows no side effects in expressions, we have no need to specify an order of evaluation of the components in a binary expression. Subtraction, multiplication, and division are handled in a similar manner. If the integer-quotient operation is given zero as a divisor, the operation gives nothing, and that causes the action to fail.

  evaluate $[\![E_1 \,/\, E_2]\!]$ =

                 evaluate E_1

       and

                 evaluate E_2

     then

            give integer-quotient (the given Integer#1, the given Integer#2)

- **Unary Minus**

  Evaluate the expression and give the negation of the resulting value.

  evaluate $[\![- E]\!]$ =

            evaluate E

     then

            give difference (0, the given Integer)

- **Relational Expressions**

  Evaluate the two expressions and give the result of applying the appropriate relation operation to the two values.

  evaluate $[\![E_1 < E_2]\!] =$

                  evaluate E_1

          and

                  evaluate E_2

      then

               give (the given Integer#1 is less than the given Integer#2)

- **Binary Boolean Operations**

  Evaluate the two expressions and give the result of applying the appropriate Boolean operation to the two values.

  evaluate $[\![E_1 \textbf{ and } E_2]\!] =$

                  evaluate E_1

          and

                  evaluate E_2

      then

               give both (the given TruthValue#1, the given TruthValue#2)

- **Boolean Not**

  Evaluate the expression and give the logical negation of the given value.

  evaluate $[\![\textbf{not}(E)]\!] =$

                evaluate E

      then

             give not (the given TruthValue)

Exercises

1. Add these language constructs to Wren and define them using action semantics.

   a) repeat-until commands

         Command ::= ... | **repeat** Command **until** Expression

   b) conditional expressions

         Expression ::= ... | **if** Expression **then** Expression **else** Expression

   c) expressions with side effects

         Expression ::= ... | **begin** Command **return** Expression **end**

2. Provide a definition of conditional (short-circuit) **and** and **or** in action semantics. Use the syntactic forms "E_1 **and then** E_2" and "E_1 **or else** E_2" for these expressions.

3. Extend Wren to allow constant declarations and explain how the action specification needs to be modified.

4. Give an action specification of the vending machine in exercise 8 of section 9.3.

13.4 THE REFLECTIVE FACET AND PELICAN

The major changes when we move from Wren to Pelican (see section 9.5) have to do with declarations: Identifiers can now also be bound to constant values and to procedures. Therefore the sort Bindable includes two more possibilities.

sorts Bindable = Variable | Value | Procedure   -- denotable values

In action semantics procedure objects are modeled as abstractions, which are yielders that encapsulate actions. We defer specifying procedures until later in this section. Now we consider the scope rules of Pelican, which are more complicated than those in Wren, requiring several additional declarative actions.

rebind

> This primitive declarative action reproduces all of the received bindings. The action rebind propagates bindings in a manner analogous to the way regive propagates transients. The effect of rebind is to extend the scope of the current bindings.

_ moreover _

> As with the combinator and, moreover allows the performance of the two actions to be interleaved. Both actions use the transients and bindings passed to the combined action. The bindings produced by the combined action are the bindings produced by the first action overlaid by those produced by the second. Transients are handled as with the and combinator.

The diagram below shows the blending of the bindings using the overlay operation by means of a broken line. The bindings that follow the solid line take precedence.

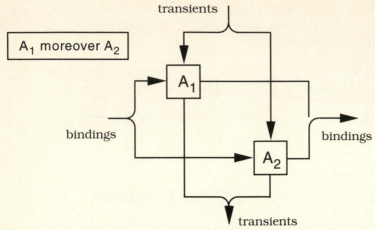

_ before _

The declarative action combinator **before** performs the first action using the transients and the bindings passed to the combined action, and then performs the second action using the transients given to the combined action and the bindings received by the combined action overlaid by those produced by the first action. The combined action produces the bindings produced by the first action overlaid with those produced by the second. The transients given by the combined action are those given by the first action concatenated with those given by the second.

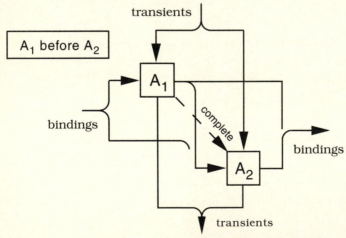

Pelican allows several more kinds of bindings than Wren. We give the three sorts that specify the kinds of information processed by Pelican, noting that only **Bindable** is different from the specification for Wren.

sorts Value = Integer | TruthValue,   -- expressible values

Storable = Integer | TruthValue,   -- storable values

Bindable = Variable | Value | Procedure   -- denotable values

The semantic functions for Pelican have the same signatures as in the specification of Wren, but we need to add several semantics equations for the additional language constructs in Pelican. We postpone describing procedures for now and concentrate on constant declarations and the **declare** command.

- **Constant Declaration**

  Evaluate the expression and then bind its value to the identifier.

  elaborate [[**const** I = E]] =

  　　　　evaluate E

  　then

  　　　　bind I to the given Value

- **Sequence of Declarations**

  Elaborate the declarations sequentially. Since the scope rules for Pelican are more complicated, allowing nested scopes, we use the composite action before to combine the bindings from the two declarations so that D_1 overlays the enclosing environment and D_2 overlays D_1.

  　　elaborate [[D_1 D_2]] = elaborate D_1 before elaborate D_2

  The "and then" combinator no longer suffices for declaration sequencing. Pelican requires that each declaration has access to the identifiers that are defined earlier in the same block as well as those in any enclosing block, as illustrated by the declaration sequence below:

  　　const max = 50;

  　　　　max1 = max+1;

  Pelican allows "dynamic expressions" in constant definitions. Using before ensures that identifiers elaborated in D_1 are visible when D_2 is elaborated. Pelican does not require that D_2 overlay D_1, since declarations in a sequence must have distinct identifiers. They may just as well be merged, but no problems arise when before performs an overlay at two points in the processing of bindings. Now that we have the combinator before, it can also be used in place of and then in defining declaration sequencing in Wren.

- **Variable Name or Constant Identifier**

  An identifier can be bound to a constant value or to a variable. Evaluating an identifier gives the constant or the value assigned to the variable.

evaluate ⟦I⟧ =
>> give the Value stored in the Cell bound to I
> or
>> give the Value bound to I

Only one of the subactions to the or combinator succeeds, so that the action gives the appropriate value denoted by the identifier I.

- **Anonymous Block (declare)**

  Elaborate the declarations in the block, producing bindings that overlay the bindings received from the enclosing block, and execute the body of the block with the resulting bindings. The bindings created by the local declaration are lost after the block is executed.

  execute ⟦**declare** D **begin** C **end**⟧ =
  >> rebind moreover elaborate D
  > hence
  >> execute C

  The action rebind propagates the bindings given to it. Therefore the action "rebind moreover elaborate D" overlays the received bindings (from the enclosing block) with the local bindings from D to provide the environment in which C will execute.

As an illustration of this mechanism for handling the declarations in Pelican, consider the following program.

```
program scope is
    const c = 5;
    var n : integer;
begin
    declare
            const m = c+8;        -- D₁
            const n = 2*m;        -- D₂
        begin
            :                     -- C
        end;
    :
end
```

Assuming that the first cell allocated is cell$_1$, the action that elaborates the first two declarations produces the bindings [c ↦ 5, n ↦ cell$_1$], which are received by the body of the program and therefore by the **declare** command. The following action models the execution of the declare command.

execute $[\![$**declare** D_1; D_2; **begin** C **end**$]\!]$ =
              rebind moreover elaborate $[\![D_1\ D_2]\!]$
       hence
              execute C

Working from the inside, we first elaborate the declarations

elaborate $[\![D_1\ D_2]\!]$ = elaborate D_1 before elaborate D_2.

The diagram below, with the empty transients omitted, illustrates the activities carried out by the before combinator.

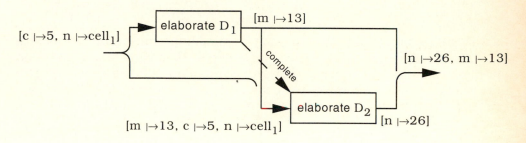

This action, elaborate $[\![D_1\ D_2]\!]$, serves as the second subaction in

rebind moreover elaborate $[\![D_1\ D_2]\!]$,

which is depicted in the next diagram.

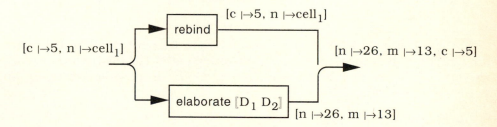

Therefore the body of the anonymous block will execute in an environment containing three bindings, $[n \mapsto 26, m \mapsto 13, c \mapsto 5]$.

The Reflective Facet and Procedures

The reflective facet addresses those actions and yielders that allow the description of subprogram declaration and invocation. The activity of a procedure in Pelican can be modeled by the performance of an action. Recall that actions themselves are not data but can be incorporated in data called ab-

stractions. Objects that can be bound to identifiers in Pelican include procedures, which are modeled as abstractions.

sorts Procedure = Abstraction
Bindable = Variable | Value | Procedure

View an abstraction datum as an entity with three components, the action
itself and the transients and bindings, if any, that will be given to the action
when it is performed.

$$\text{Abstraction} = \begin{array}{|c|c|} \hline & \text{Transients} \\ \text{Action} & \\ \cline{2-2} & \text{Bindings} \\ \hline \end{array}$$

As with subprograms in a programming language, we concern ourselves with
two aspects: the creation of a procedural object by means of a declaration
and the invocation of the object that sets it intoction. When a Pelican procedure declaration is elaborated, the code of the procedure modeled as an action is incorporated into an abstraction using an operation that acts as a
yielder.

abstraction of _ : Action → Yielder

The yielder "abstraction of A" encapsulates the action A into an abstraction
together with no transients and no bindings.

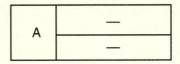

If we want the action inside an abstraction to be performed with certain
transients and bindings, they must be supplied after the abstraction is constructed. The current bindings are inserted into an abstraction using an
operation on yielders.

closure of _ : Yielder → Yielder

The yielder "closure of Y" incorporates the bindings received by the enclosing action into the abstraction given by Y. Attaching the declaration-
time bindings, those bindings in effect when the subprogram is declared,
ensures that the resulting action performs the defined procedure in its
static environment, thereby producing static scoping for resolving references to nonlocal identifiers. Assuming that StaticBindings denotes the
current bindings in effect when the declaration is elaborated, the term
"closure of abstraction of A" yields the object shown below. In this example,
bindings are inserted into an abstraction at abstraction-time.

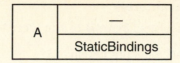

Once bindings are incorporated into an abstraction, no further changes can be made to the bindings. A later performance of "closure of _" will have no effect. Dynamic scoping ensues if bindings are attached at enaction-time— that is, when a procedure is called and the action in its abstraction is to be performed. We define the execution of a procedure using a reflective action enact that takes as its parameter a yielder that gives an abstraction.

enact _ : Yielder → Action

> The action "enact Y" activates the action encapsulated in the abstraction yielded by Y, using the transients and bindings that are included in the abstraction. If no transients or bindings have been incorporated into the abstraction, the enclosed action is given empty transients or empty bindings at enaction-time.

Procedures Without Parameters

We now have enough action notation to specify parameterless procedures in Pelican, handling both their declaration and call, but first we repeat that procedures are represented by the subsort of Datum known as Abstraction in the action specification.

> **sorts** Procedure = Abstraction

- **Procedure Declaration (no parameter)**

  Bind the identifier of the declaration to a procedure object that incorporates the body of the procedure, so that it will be executed in the declaration-time environment.

  > elaborate [[**procedure** I **is** D **begin** C **end**]] =
  >   bind I to
  >   closure of
  >   abstraction of
  >   rebind moreover elaborate D
  >   hence
  >   execute C

The abstraction bound to I incorporates the current (static) bindings and empty transients. Executing the body of the procedure resembles the execution of a **declare** command (see the semantic equation for **declare**).

- **Procedure Call (no parameter)**

  Execute the procedure object bound to the identifier.

  execute $[\![I]\!]$ = enact the Procedure bound to I

  Recall that the procedure object, an abstraction, brings along its static environment. The action corresponding to a parameterless procedure expects no transients, and the abstraction bound to I has empty transients.

Procedures With A Parameter

We need a mechanism that allows an actual parameter to be passed to the procedure. Another operation on yielders constructs an unevaluated term— a yielder—that provides a way for the current transient to be incorporated into the abstraction.

application of _ to _ : Yielder, Yielder → Yielder

  The yielder "application of Y_1 to Y_2" attaches the argument value yielded by Y_2 as the transient that will be given to the action encapsulated in the abstraction yielded by Y_1 when that action is enacted. As with bindings, a further supply of transients to an abstraction is ignored. The argument, a value, is inserted into the abstraction when the procedure is called.

- **Procedure Call (one parameter)**

  Evaluate the actual parameter, an expression, and then execute the procedure bound to the identifier with the value of the expression.

  execute $[\![I\ (E)]\!]$ =
          evaluate E
      then
          enact application of (the Procedure bound to I) to the given Value

  Assuming that Abs, the abstraction bound to I, incorporates the action A and the bindings StaticBindings, and that Val is the value of the expression E, "application of Abs to the given Value" creates the abstraction that will be enacted. The actual parameter(s) to a procedure provide the only transient information that is relevant at enaction-time.

A	(Val)
	StaticBindings

To specify the declaration of procedures with one parameter, we need another action combinator thence that combines the behavior of then for transients and hence for bindings. Therefore both transients and bindings flow sequentially through the two actions.

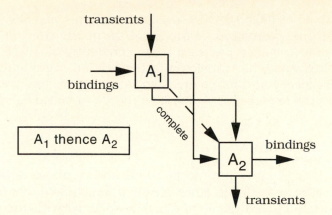

The action encapsulated in an abstraction formed by a declaration of a procedure with a parameter expects a value, the actual parameter, to be given to it as a transient. This value is stored in a new memory location allocated by the action. The command that constitutes the body of the procedure is executed in an environment that consists of the original static environment, inserted into the abstraction using "closure of", overlaid by the binding of the formal parameter to the allocated variable, and then overlaid by the local declarations.

- **Procedure Declaration (one parameter)**

  Bind the procedure identifier in the declaration to a procedure object that incorporates the body of the procedure, so that when it is called, it will be executed in the declaration-time environment and will allocate a local variable for the actual parameter passed to the procedure.

  elaborate $[\![$ **procedure** I_1 (I_2) **is** D **begin** C **end**$]\!]$ =
        bind I_1 to
            closure of
                abstraction of
                    allocate a cell and give the given Value and rebind
                thence
                        rebind
                moreover
                        bind I_2 to the given Cell#1
                    and
                        store the given Value#2 in the given Cell#1
                hence
                    rebind moreover elaborate D
                hence
                    execute C

The three uses of rebind ensure that the bindings at each stage of the specification are extensions of the bindings at the previous stage. The first argument to thence passes a tuple consisting of a Cell and a Value (Integer or TruthValue) as transients to the second argument. The action combinators thence and hence are associative, so we have no need of indentation in the expression "A_1 thence A_2 hence A_3 hence A_4".

Recursive Definitions

The specifications of procedure declarations shown above do not allow recursive calls of the procedures, since the identifiers (procedure names) being declared are not included in the bindings associated with the abstractions created by the declarations. The details of the hybrid actions that implement recursive bindings are beyond the scope of our discussion of action semantics. We can, however, describe a hybrid action for establishing recursive bindings that is defined in terms of more primitive actions.

recursively bind _ to _ : Token, Bindable → Action

> The action "recursively bind T to abstraction of A" produces the binding of T, an identifier, to an abstraction Abs so that the bindings attached to the action A incorporated in Abs include the binding being produced.

$$
Abs = \quad
\begin{array}{|c|c|}
\hline
\multirow{2}{*}{A} & - \\
\cline{2-2}
 & [T \mapsto Abs] \\
\hline
\end{array}
$$

Therefore the action "recursively bind _ to _" permits the construction of a circular binding.

> elaborate [[**procedure** I **is** D **begin** C **end**]] =
>   recursively bind I to
>   closure of
>   abstraction of
>   rebind moreover elaborate D
>   hence
>   execute C

To illustrate the effects of a recursive declaration, consider the bindings created by a Pelican program.

> **program** example **is**
>   **const** c = 5;
>   **var** b : **boolean**;
>   **procedure** p **is** ... **begin** ... **end**;
> **begin** ... **end**

Let A denote the action corresponding to the body of the procedure. The action "closure of abstraction of A" creates the abstraction Abs shown below, which does not allow a recursive call of the procedure.

$$\text{Abs} = \boxed{\begin{array}{c|c} A & \overline{} \\ & [c \mapsto 5,\ b \mapsto \text{cell}_1] \end{array}}$$

The action "bind p to closure of abstraction of A" produces the binding [p $\mapsto$ Abs]. Any reference to the procedure identifier p inside the procedure is an illegal reference, yielding nothing. In contrast, the action "recursively bind p to closure of abstraction of A" changes the abstraction Abs into a new abstraction Abs' whose attached bindings include the association of the procedure abstraction with p. Now a recursive call is permitted.

$$\text{Abs'} = \boxed{\begin{array}{c|c} A & \overline{} \\ & [p \mapsto \text{Abs'},\ c \mapsto 5,\ b \mapsto \text{cell}_1] \end{array}}$$

The recursive action produces the binding [p $\mapsto$ Abs'], which when overlaid on the previous (enclosing) bindings, produces the bindings [p $\mapsto$ Abs', c $\mapsto$ 5, b $\mapsto$ cell$_1$] to be received by the procedure p and the body of the program.

Figure 13.6 collects the definitions for an action semantic specification of Pelican. Observe how many of the definitions are identical to those of Wren.

Translating to Action Notation

Action notation can be viewed as a metalanguage for the semantic specification of programming languages. The semantic equations in Figure 13.6 define a translator from Pelican programs into action notation, which can act as an intermediate language in an interpreter or a compiler. By providing an interpreter of action notation, we can obtain a prototype implementation of any programming language with a specification in action semantics. A translator of action notation into a machine language produces a compiler of the language.

The metalanguage of action semantics can also be used to verify semantic equivalence between language phrases. Although an action specification can be read at an informal level, it is a formal definition. Furthermore, action notation can be manipulated algebraically using properties such as associativity, commutativity, and identity laws to prove the equivalence of certain action expressions. Two language phrases are semantically equivalent if their translations into action notation are equivalent. Discovering the algebraic properties of action notation is an area of ongoing research. See the further readings for more on this topic.

run _ : Program → Action [completing | diverging | storing]
[using current storage]

run [[**program** I **is** D **begin** C **end**]] = elaborate D hence execute C

elaborate _ : Declaration → Action [completing | binding | storing]
[using current bindings | current storage]

elaborate [[ ]] = produce empty bindings

elaborate [[D$_1$ D$_2$]] = elaborate D$_1$ before elaborate D$_2$

elaborate [[**var** I : T]] =
        allocate a cell
    then
        bind I to the given Cell

elaborate [[**const** I = E]] =
        evaluate E
    then
        bind I to the given Value

elaborate [[**procedure** I **is** D **begin** C **end**]] =
    recursively bind I to
        closure of
            abstraction of
                rebind moreover elaborate D
            hence
                execute C

elaborate [[**procedure** I$_1$ (I$_2$) **is** D **begin** C **end**]] =
    recursively bind I$_1$ to
        closure of
            abstraction of
                allocate a cell and give the given Value and rebind
            thence
                    rebind
                moreover
                    bind I$_2$ to the given Cell#1
                and
                    store the given Value#2 in the given Cell#1
            hence
                rebind moreover elaborate D
            hence
                execute C

Figure 13.6: Semantic Equations for Pelican (Part 1)

---

execute _ : Command → Action [completing | diverging | storing]
                             [using current bindings | current storage]

execute ⟦C₁ ; C₂⟧ = execute C₁ and then execute C₂

execute ⟦**declare** D **begin** C **end**⟧ =
                 rebind moreover elaborate D
         hence
                 execute C

execute **skip** = complete

execute ⟦I := E⟧ =
                 give the Cell bound to I and evaluate E
         then
                 store the given Value#2 in the given Cell#1

execute ⟦**if** E **then** C⟧ =
                 evaluate E
         then
                     check (the given TruthValue is true) and then execute C
             or
                     check (the given TruthValue is false) and then complete

execute ⟦**if** E **then** C₁ **else** C₂⟧ =
                 evaluate E
         then
                     check (the given TruthValue is true) and then execute C₁
             or
                     check (the given TruthValue is false) and then execute C₂

execute ⟦**while** E **do** C⟧ =
         unfolding
                     evaluate E
             then
                         check (the given TruthValue is true) and then
                             execute C and then unfold
                 or
                         check (the given TruthValue is false) and then complete

execute I = enact the Procedure bound to I

execute ⟦I (E)⟧ =
                 evaluate E
         then
                 enact application of (the Procedure bound to I) to the given Value

---

Figure 13.6: Semantic Equations for Pelican (Part 2)

---

evaluate _ : Expression → Action [completing | giving a Value]
                                [using current bindings | current storage]

    evaluate I =
           give the Value stored in the Cell bound to I
       or
           give the Value bound to I

    evaluate N = give the value of N

    evaluate **true** = give true

    evaluate **false** = give false

    evaluate $[\![E_1 + E_2]\!]$ =
           evaluate E_1 and evaluate E_2
      then
           give sum (the given Integer#1, the given Integer#2)
    ⋮   ⋮

    evaluate $[\![- E]\!]$ =
           evaluate E
      then
           give difference (0, the given Integer)

    evaluate $[\![E_1 >= E_2]\!]$ =
           evaluate E_1 and evaluate E_2
      then
           give not (the given Integer#1 is less than the given Integer#2)
    ⋮   ⋮

    evaluate $[\![E_1 \text{ **or** } E_2]\!]$ =
           evaluate E_1 and evaluate E_2
      then
           give either (the given TruthValue#1, the given TruthValue#2)
    ⋮   ⋮

    evaluate $[\![\textbf{not}(E)]\!]$ =
           evaluate E
      then
           give not (the given TruthValue)

Figure 13.6: Semantic Equations for Pelican (Part 3)

We conclude this section by translating a Pelican program into its equivalent action notation. This task is aided by the property of compositionality: Each phrase is defined solely in terms of the meaning of its immediate subphrases. Furthermore, any phrase may be substituted for a semantically equivalent phrase without changing the meaning of the program.

We illustrate a translation of the following Pelican program annotated as shown below:

```
program action is
      const max = 50;           -- D₁
      var sum : integer;         -- D₂
      var switch : boolean;      -- D₃
      procedure change is        -- D₄
          begin
              n := n+3;
              switch := not(switch)
          end;
begin
      sum := 0;                  -- C₁
      n := 1;                    -- C₂
      switch := true;            -- C₃
      while n<=max do            -- C₄
          if switch then sum := sum+n end if;
          change
      end while
end
```

The overall structure of the translation takes the form

run $[\![$**program** I **is** $D_1 D_2 D_3 D_4$ **begin** $C_1; C_2; C_3; C_4$ **end**$]\!]$

= elaborate $[\![D_1 D_2 D_3 D_4]\!]$ hence execute $[\![C_1; C_2; C_3; C_4]\!]$

= elaborate D_1 before elaborate D_2 before elaborate D_3 before elaborate D_4 hence

execute C_1 and then execute C_2 and then execute C_3 and then execute C_4

The elaboration uses the property that the combinators and then and before are both associate. We proceed by elaborating the four declarations in the program.

elaborate D_1 = give the value of 50 then bind max to the given Value

elaborate D_2 = allocate a cell then bind sum to the given Cell

elaborate D_3 = allocate a cell then bind switch to the given Cell

elaborate D_4 =
    recursively bind change to closure of(abstraction of(
              rebind
          moreover
            produce empty bindings
       hence
               give the Cell bound to n
            and
                  give the Value stored in Cell bound to n
              or
                  give the Value bound to n
            and
              give the value of 3
          then
            give sum(the given Integer#1,the given Integer#2)
       then
         store the given Value#2 in the given Cell#1
     and then
          give the Cell bound to switch
        and
            give the Value stored in Cell bound to switch
        or
            give the Value bound to switch
      then
        give not(the given Truthvalue)
    then
      store the given Value#2 in the given Cell#1))

The translation of the Pelican program is completed by expanding the four commands.

execute C_1 =   give the Cell bound to sum and give the value of 0
      then
        store the given Value#2 in the given Cell#1

execute C_2 =   give the Cell bound to n and give the value of 1
      then
        store the given Value#2 in the given Cell#1

execute C_3=   give the Cell bound to switch and give true
      then
        store the given Value#2 in the given Cell#1

execute C_4 =
   unfolding
               give the Value stored in Cell bound to n
       or
            give the Value bound to n
     and
            give the Value stored in Cell bound to max
       or
            give the Value bound to max
    then
      give not(the given Integer#1 is greater than the given Integer#2)
  then
       check (the given Truthvalue is true)
      and then
           give the Value stored in Cell bound to switch
        or
         give the Value bound to switch
       then
         check the given Truthvalue is true
        and then
             give the Cell bound to sum
           and
              give the Value stored in Cell bound to sum
           or
             give the Value bound to sum
          and
             give the Value stored in Cell bound to n
          or
            give the Value bound to n
        then
         give sum(the given Integer#1,the given Integer#2)
       then
        store the given Value#2 in the given Cell#1
      or
        check the given Truthvalue is false
       and then
        complete
     and then
      enact the Procedure bound to change
     and then unfold
   or
      check the given Truthvalue is false and then complete

Exercises

1. Suppose that the current bindings contain two pairs: $[\,x \mapsto cell_1, y \mapsto 2\,]$. Consider two actions:

$$A_1 = \text{bind y to 15}$$
$$A_2 = \text{bind x to successor(the Integer bound to y)}$$

What are the (possible) current bindings after performing the following composite actions?

a) A_1 and then A_2

b) A_1 hence A_2

c) A_1 and A_2

d) A_1 moreover A_2

e) A_1 before A_2

2. Extend Pelican to include a definite iteration command using the syntax

$$\textbf{for } I := E_1 \textbf{ to } E_2 \textbf{ do } C \textbf{ end for}$$

and assuming iteration over integer values only. Following the semantics of the **for** command in Pascal and Ada, provide an action specification of this command. Observe the difference in how Pascal and Ada treat the loop variable I:

a) Pascal: Assume I has been declared in the block containing the **for** command.

b) Ada: The **for** command implicitly declares I to have the subrange $E_1..E_2$ and to have scope extending through the body of the command only.

3. Modify Pelican so that parameters are passed by

a) reference

b) value-result

4. Modify Pelican so that it uses dynamic scoping to resolve nonlocal variable references.

5. Suppose that Pelican is extended to include functions of one parameter, passed by value. The abstract syntax now has productions of the form

Declaration ::= ... | **function** Identifier$_1$ (Identifier$_2$) **is** Declaration
begin Command **return** Expression **end**

and

Expressions ::= ... | Identifier (Expression).

Make all the necessary changes in the action definition of Pelican to incorporate this new language construct.

6. A unit for a binary operation @ : A,A → A is an element u of A such that for all a∈A, a@u = u@a = a. Using the primitive actions complete, fail, regive, and rebind, identify units for the following action combinators:

   and then, and, then, or, hence, moreover, before, and thence.

7. Which of the binary combinators in exercise 6 are associative, commutative, and/or idempotent?

8. Translate the following Pelican programs into action notation:

   a) **program** facwhile **is**
         var n : **integer**;
         var f : **integer**;
     begin
           n := 8; f := 1;
           while n>1 **do**
               f := f*n; n := n−1
           end while
     end

   b) **program** facproc **is**
         const num = 8;
         var n : **integer**;
         var f : **integer**;
         procedure fac(n : **integer**) **is**
             procedure mul(m : **integer**) **is**
                 begin f := f*m **end**;
             begin
                 if n=0 **then** f := 1 **else** fac(n−1); mul(n) **end if**
             end;
       begin n := num; fac(n) **end**

13.5 LABORATORY: TRANSLATING INTO ACTION NOTATION

Prolog serves well as an implementation language for a translator from Pelican to action notation. The compositional definitions of the meaning of Pelican given in Figure 13.6 convert to Prolog clauses directly. The resulting actions can be represented as Prolog structures by writing actions, yielders, and auxilliary operations with prefix syntax. First we show a sample execution of the translator. The output has been edited (indented) to make the scope of the actions easier to determine.

```
>>> Translating Pelican into Action Semantics   <<<
Enter name of source file: small.pelican
    program small is
       const c = 34;
       var n : integer;
      begin
        n := c+21
      end
Translated Action:
hence(
  before(
    then(give(valueof(34)),bind(c,given(Value))),
      before(then(allocateacell,bind(n,given(Cell))),
             produce(emptybindings))),
  andthen(
    then(
      and(give(boundto(Cell,n)),
          then(and(or(give(storedin(Value,boundto(Cell,c))),
                      give(boundto(Value,c))),
                  give(valueof(21))),
                give(sum(given(Integer,1),given(Integer,2)))))),
      storein(given(Value,2),given(Cell,1))),
    complete))
yes
```

Since this translation is purely a static operation, we need not be concerned with stores and environments—these are handled when action notation is interpreted or compiled. At the top level a predicate run translates a program. Observe that we have dispensed with the syntactic category of blocks to match the specification in Figure 13.6, thereby giving another example of tailoring the abstract syntax to the specification method. Several small changes will be needed in the parser to reflect this alteration in the abstract syntax.

```
run(prog(Decs,Cmds),hence(ElaborateD,ExecuteC)) :-
                              elaborate(Decs,ElaborateD),
                              execute(Cmds,ExecuteC).
```

The Prolog predicate that implements the translation of programs builds Prolog structures that represent the equivalent action using calls to the predicates elaborate and execute to construct pieces of the structure. Two clauses deal with sequences of the declarations.

```
elaborate([ ],produce(emptybindings)).
```

```
elaborate([Dec|Decs],before(ElaborateDec,ElaborateDecs)) :-
                              elaborate(Dec,ElaborateDec),
                              elaborate(Decs,ElaborateDecs).
```

Individual declarations are translated by Prolog clauses that match the action definitions in Figure 13.6 in their logical structure.

```
elaborate(var(T,var(Ide)),then(allocateacell,bind(Ide,given('Cell')))).
```

```
elaborate(con(Ide,E),then(EvaluateE,bind(Ide,given('Value')))) :-
                              evaluate(E,EvaluateE).
```

```
elaborate(proc(Ide,param(Formal),Decs,Cmds),
recursivelybind(Ide,
   closureof(abstractionof(
      hence(hence(
               thence(and(allocateacell,and(give(given('Value')),rebind)),
                     moreover( rebind,
                              and( bindto(Formal,given('Cell',1)),
                                   storein(given('Value',2),given('Cell',1))))),
               moreover(rebind,ElaborateD)),
            ExecuteC))))) :- elaborate(Decs,ElaborateD),
                     execute(Cmds,ExecuteC).
```

We leave the clause for procedures with no parameters as an exercise. Commands are translated by the predicate execute. We provide several examples and leave the remaining clauses as exercises.

```
execute([Cmd|Cmds],andthen(ExecuteCmd,ExecuteCmds)) :-
                              execute(Cmd,ExecuteCmd),
                              execute(Cmds,ExecuteCmds).
```

```
execute([ ],complete).
```

```
execute(declare(Decs,Cmds),hence(moreover(rebind,ElaborateD),ExecuteC)) :-
                              elaborate(Decs,ElaborateD),
                              execute(Cmds,ExecuteC).
```

```
execute(skip,complete).
```

```
execute(assign(Ide,Exp),then(and(give(boundto('Cell',Ide)),EvaluateE),
                     storein(given('Value',2),given('Cell',1)))) :-
                              evaluate(Exp,EvaluateE).
```

```
execute(if(Test,Then),
    then(EvaluateE,or( andthen(check(is(given('Truthvalue'),true)),ExecuteC),
                    andthen(check(is(given('Truthvalue'),false)),complete))))  :-
                                        evaluate(Test,EvaluateE),
                                        execute(Then,ExecuteC).

execute(while(Test,Body),unfolding(
    then(EvaluateE,or( andthen(check(is(given('Truthvalue'),true)),
                                andthen(ExecuteC,unfold)),
                    andthen(check(is(given('Truthvalue'),false)),complete)))))  :-
                                        evaluate(Test,EvaluateE),
                                        execute(Body,ExecuteC).

execute(call(Ide,E),
    then(EvaluateE,enact(application(boundto('Procedure',Ide),given('Value')))))  :-
                                        evaluate(E,EvaluateE).
```

Expressions are translated by the Prolog predicate evaluate. Again we show several of the clauses, leaving the rest as exercises. Observe how closely the Prolog clauses agree with the action specifications.

```
evaluate(ide(Ide),or( give(storedin('Value',boundto('Cell',Ide))),
                    give(boundto('Value',Ide)))).

evaluate(num(N),give(valueof(N))).

evaluate(minus(E),then(EvaluateE,give(difference(0,given('Integer')))))  :-
                                        evaluate(E,EvaluateE).

evaluate(plus(E1,E2), then(and(EvaluateE1,EvaluateE2),
                    give(sum(given('Integer',1),given('Integer',2)))))  :-
                                        evaluate(E1,EvaluateE1),
                                        evaluate(E2,EvaluateE2).

evaluate(neq(E1,E2), then(and(EvaluateE1,EvaluateE2),
                    give(not(is(given('Integer',1),given('Integer',2))))))  :-
                                        evaluate(E1,EvaluateE1),
                                        evaluate(E2,EvaluateE2).

evaluate(and(E1,E2), then(and(EvaluateE1,EvaluateE2),
                give(both(given('Truthvalue',1),given('Truthvalue',2)))))  :-
                                        evaluate(E1,EvaluateE1),
                                        evaluate(E2,EvaluateE2).
```

This action notation translator is just the first step in building a prototype implementation of Pelican. To complete the task, we need to construct an interpreter for actions. Although this code can be written in Prolog, the number of parameters may make the clauses cumbersome. For example, a predicate for interpreting an action combinator (a binary operation) will require six parameters for incoming transients, bindings, and store and three parameters for the resulting information. A language that allows us to maintain the store imperatively may produce more readable code. See the further readings at the end of this chapter for an alternative approach.

Exercises

1. Complete the implementation in Prolog of the action notation translator by writing the missing clauses.

2. Add these language constructs to Pelican and extend the translator by defining clauses that construct the appropriate action notation.

   a) repeat-until commands
   > Command ::= ... | **repeat** Command **until** Expression

   b) conditional expressions
   > Expression ::= ... | **if** Expression **then** Expression **else** Expression

   c) expressions with side effects
   > Expression ::= ... | **begin** Command **return** Expression **end**

   d) definite iteration commands
   > Command ::= ...
   > | **for** Identifier := Expression **to** Expression **do**
   > Command **end for**

3. Write a Prolog predicate that prints the resulting action following the indenting conventions of action semantics. Use the example at the end of section 13.4 as a model.

4. Write an interpreter for action notation in Prolog or some other programming language to produce a prototype system for this subset of Pelican (no input and output).

13.6 FURTHER READING

The standard reference for action semantics is the book by Peter Mosses [Mosses92]. He uses a subset of Ada to illustrate the full power of action semantics, including the communicative facet, which is beyond the scope of our presentation. Mosses also gives a formal specification of action notation (the lower level) using structural operational semantics. This book contains an extensive description of the literature that covers the development of action semantics over the past ten years. Note that action notation has evolved over this time frame from a more symbolic notation to a more English-like presentation. Mosses uses a slightly different framework for the algebraic specification of data, the so-called unified algebras [Mosses89].

A shorter introduction to action semantics can be found in a technical report [Mosses91]. These works contain extensive bibliographies that point to the earlier literature on action semantics. When consulting the earlier papers, note that the notation of action semantics has evolved considerably during its development.

David Watt [Watt91] has a lengthy description of action semantics with many examples, culminating in a complete action specification of Triangle, his example imperative programming language. Watt is also involved in a project, called ACTRESS, using action semantics to construct compilers [Brown92].

We mentioned in section 9.5 that Prolog may not be the best language in which to write an action interpreter. Functional programming provides a better paradigm for manipulating actions. Watt suggests implementing action semantics in ML [Watt91]. A full description of using ML to develop semantic prototypes of programming languages can be found in [Ruei93]. In this report a programming language is translated into ML functions that represent the actions and yielders. These ML functions are executed directly to provide a prototype interpreter for the language Triangle.

Appendix A
LOGIC PROGRAMMING WITH PROLOG

I mperative programming languages reflect the architecture of the underlying von Neumann stored program computer: Programs consist of instructions stored in memory with a program counter determining which instruction to execute next. Programs perform their computations by updating memory locations that correspond to variables. Programs are prescriptive—they dictate precisely how a result is to be computed by means of a sequence of commands to be performed by the computer. Assignment acts as the primary operation, updating memory locations to produce a result obtained by incremental changes to storage using iteration and selection commands.

An alternative approach, logic programming, allows a programmer to describe the logical structure of a problem rather than prescribe how a computer is to go about solving it. Based on their essential properties, languages for logic programming are sometimes called:

1. **Descriptive or Declarative Languages**: Programs are expressed as known facts and logical relationships about a problem that hypothesize the existence of the desired result; a logic interpreter then constructs the desired result by making inferences to prove its existence.

2. **Nonprocedural Languages**: The programmer states only *what* is to be accomplished and leaves it to the interpreter to determine *how* it is to be proved.

3. **Relational Languages**: Desired results are expressed as relations or predicates instead of as functions; rather than define a function for calculating the square of a number, the programmer defines a relation, say sqr(x,y), that is true exactly when $y = x^2$.

Imperative programming languages have a descriptive component, namely expressions: "3*p + 2*q" is a description of a value, not a sequence of computer operations; the compiler and the run-time system handle the details. High-level imperative languages, like Pascal, are easier to use than assembly languages because they are more descriptive and less prescriptive.

The goal of logic programming is for languages to be purely descriptive, specifying only what a program computes and not how. Correct programs will be easier to develop because the program statements will be logical descriptions of the problem itself and not of the execution process—the assumptions made about the problem will be directly apparent from the program text.

Prolog

Prolog, a name derived from "Programming in Logic", is the most popular language of this kind; it is essentially a declarative language that allows a few control features in the interest of acceptable execution performance. Prolog implements a subset of predicate logic using the Resolution Principle, an efficient proof procedure for predicate logic developed by Alan Robinson (see [Robinson65]). The first interpreter was written by Alain Colmerauer and Philippe Roussel at Marseilles, France, in 1972.

The basic features of Prolog include a powerful pattern-matching facility, a backtracking strategy that searches for proofs, uniform data structures from which programs are built, and the general interchangeability of input and output.

Prolog Syntax

Prolog programs are constructed from **terms** that are either constants, variables, or structures.

Constants can be either atoms or numbers:

- **Atoms** are strings of characters starting with a lowercase letter or enclosed in apostrophes.
- **Numbers** are strings of digits with or without a decimal point and a minus sign.

Variables are strings of characters beginning with an uppercase letter or an underscore.

Structures consist of a **functor** or **function symbol**, which looks like an atom, followed by a list of terms inside parentheses, separated by commas. Structures can be interpreted as **predicates** (relations):

>   likes(john,mary).
>   male(john).
>   sitsBetween(X,mary,helen).

Structures can also be interpreted as **structured objects** similar to records in Pascal:

> person(name('Kilgore','Trout'),date(november,11,1922))
>
> tree(5, tree(3,nil,nil), tree(9,tree(7,nil,nil),nil))

Figure A.1 depicts these structured objects as trees.

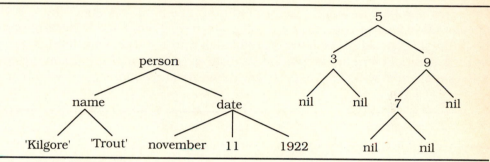

Figure A.1: Structured objects

A Prolog program is a sequence of statements, called **clauses**, of the form

> P_0 :- P_1, P_2, ..., P_n.

where each of P_0, P_1, P_2, ..., P_n is an atom or a structure. A **period** terminates every Prolog clause. A clause can be read declaratively as

> P_0 is true if P_1 and P_2 and ... and P_n are true

or procedurally as

> To satisfy goal P_0, satisfy goal P_1 and then P_2 and then ... and then P_n.

In a clause, P_0 is called the **head** goal, and the conjunction of goals P_1, P_2, ..., P_n forms the **body** of the clause. A clause without a body is a **unit clause** or a **fact**:

> "P." means "P is true" or "goal P is satisfied".

A clause without a head, written

> ":- P_1,P_2, ..., P_n." or "?- P_1,P_2, ..., P_n."

is a **goal clause** or a **query** and is interpreted as

> "Are P_1 and P_2 and ... and P_n true?" or
>
> "Satisfy goal P_1 and then P_2 and then ... and then P_n".

To program in Prolog, one defines a database of facts about the given information and conditional clauses or **rules** about how additional information can be deduced from the facts. A query sets the Prolog interpreter into action to try to infer a solution using the database of clauses.

BNF Syntax for Prolog

Prolog is a relatively small programming language as evidenced by a BNF specification of the core part of Prolog given in Figure A.2. The language contains a large set of predefined predicates and notational variations such as infix symbols that are not defined in this specification. In addition, Prolog allows a special syntax for lists that will be introduced later.

<program> ::= <clause list> <query> | <query>

<clause list> ::= <clause> | <clause list> <clause>

<clause> ::= <predicate> . | <predicate> :- <predicate list> .

<predicate list> ::= <predicate> | <predicate list> , <predicate>

<predicate> ::= <atom> | <atom> (<term list>)

<term list> ::= <term> | <term list> , <term>

<term> ::= <numeral> | <atom> | <variable> | <structure>

<structure> ::= <atom> (<term list>)

<query> ::= ?- <predicate list> .

<atom> ::= <small atom> | ' <string> '

<small atom> ::= <lowercase letter> | <small atom> <character>

<variable> ::= <uppercase letter> | <variable> <character>

<lowercase letter> ::= **a** | **b** | **c** | **d** | ... | **x** | **y** | **z**

<uppercase letter> ::= **A** | **B** | **C** | **D** | ... | **X** | **Y** | **Z** | **_**

<numeral> ::= <digit> | <numeral> <digit>

<digit> ::= **0** | **1** | **2** | **3** | **4** | **5** | **6** | **7** | **8** | **9**

<character> ::= <lowercase letter> | <uppercase letter>
            | <digit> | <special>

<special> ::= **+** | **-** | ***** | **/** | **** | **^** | **~** | **:** | **.** | **?** | **@** | **#** | **$** | **&**

<string> ::= <character> | <string> <character>

Figure A.2: BNF for Prolog

A Prolog Example

The simple example in this section serves as an introduction to Prolog programming for the beginner. Remember that a Prolog program consists of a collection of facts and rules defined to constrain the logic interpreter in such a way that when we submit a query, the resulting answers solve the problems at hand. Facts, rules, and queries can all be entered interactively, but usually a Prolog programmer creates a file containing the facts and rules, and then after "consulting" this file, enters only the queries interactively. See the documentation for instructions on consulting a file with a particular implementation of Prolog.

We develop the example incrementally, adding facts and rules to the database in several stages. User queries will be shown in boldface followed by the response from the Prolog interpreter. Comments start with the symbol % and continue to the end of the line.

Some facts:
```
parent(chester,irvin).
parent(chester,clarence).
parent(chester,mildred).
parent(irvin,ron).
parent(irvin,ken).
parent(clarence,shirley).
parent(clarence,sharon).
parent(clarence,charlie).
parent(mildred,mary).
```

Some queries:

?- parent(chester,mildred).
yes

?- parent(X,ron).
X = irvin
yes

?- parent(irvin,X).
X = ron;
X = ken;   % The user-typed semicolon asks the system for
no   %   more solutions.

?- parent(X,Y).
X =chester
Y = irvin   % System will list all of the parent pairs, one at a time,
yes   %   if semicolons are entered.

Additional facts:
```
male(chester).      female(mildred).
male(irvin).        female(shirley).
```

```
male(clarence).      female(sharon).
male(ron).           female(mary).
male(ken).
male(charlie).
```

Additional queries:

?- parent(clarence,X), male(X).
X = charlie
yes

?- male(X), parent(X,ken).
X = irvin
yes

?- parent(X,ken), female(X).
no

Prolog obeys the "closed world assumption" that presumes that any predicate that cannot be proved must be false.

?- parent(X,Y), parent(Y,sharon).
X = chester
Y = clarence
yes

These queries suggest definitions of several family relationships.

Some rules: father(X,Y) :- parent(X,Y), male(X).

grandparent(X,Y) :- parent(X,Z), parent(Z,Y).

paternalgrandfather(X,Y) :- father(X,Z), father(Z,Y).

sibling(X,Y) :- parent(Z,X), parent(Z,Y).

The scope of a variable in Prolog is solely the clause in which it occurs.

Additional queries:

?- paternalgrandfather(X,ken).
X = chester
yes

?- paternalgrandfather(chester,X).
X = ron;
X = ken;
X = shirley;   % Note the reversal of the roles of input and output.
X = sharon;
X = charlie;
X = mary;
no

?- **sibling(ken,X).**
X = ron;
X = ken;
no

The inference engine concludes that ken is a sibling of ken since parent(irvin,ken) and parent(irvin,ken) both hold. To avoid this consequence, the description of sibling needs to be more carefully constructed.

Predefined Predicates

1. The equality predicate = permits infix notation as well as prefix.

    ?- **ken = ken.**
    yes

    ?- **=(ken,ron).**
    no

    ?- **ken = X.**   % Can a value be found for X to make it the same as ken?
    X = ken
    yes   % The equal operator represents the notion of unification.

2. "not" is a unary predicate:
        not(P) is true if P cannot be proved and false if it can.

    ?- **not(ken=ron).**
    yes

    ?- **not(mary=mary).**
    no

The closed world assumption governs the way the predicate "not" works since any goal that cannot be proved using the current set of facts and rules is assumed to be false and its negation is assumed to be true. The closed world assumption presumes that any property not recorded in the database is not true. Some Prolog implementations omit the predefined predicate not because its behavoir diverges from the logical not of predicate calculus in the presence of variables (see [Sterling86]). We have avoided using not in the laboratory exercises in this text.

The following is a new sibling rule (the previous rule must be removed):

    sibling(X,Y) :- parent(Z,X), parent(Z,Y), not(X=Y).

Queries:

    ?- **sibling(ken,X)**.
    X = ron;
    no

```
?- sibling(X,Y).
X = irvin
Y = clarence;            % Predicate sibling defines a symmetric relation.
X = irvin                % Three sets of siblings produce six answers.
Y = mildred;
X = clarence             % The current database allows 14 answers.
Y = irvin;
X = clarence
Y = mildred;
X = mildred
Y = irvin;
Y = mildred
X = clarence             % No semicolon here.
yes
```

A relation may be defined with several clauses:

```
closeRelative(X,Y) :- parent(X,Y).
closeRelative(X,Y) :- parent(Y,X).
closeRelative(X,Y) :- sibling(X,Y).
```

There is an implicit **or** between the three definitions of the relation closeRelative. This disjunction may be abbreviated using semicolons as

```
closeRelative(X,Y) :- parent(X,Y) ; parent(Y,X) ; sibling(X,Y).
```

We say that the three clauses (or single abbreviated clause) define(s) a "procedure" named closeRelative with arity two (closeRelative takes two parameters). The identifier closeRelative may be used as a different predicate with other arities.

Recursion in Prolog

We want to define a predicate for "X is an ancestor of Y". This is true if

```
parent(X,Y) or
parent(X,Z) and parent(Z,Y) or
parent(X,Z), parent(Z,Z1), and parent(Z1,Y) or
    :                      :
```

Since the length of the chain of parents cannot be predicted, a recursive definition is required to allow an arbitrary depth for the definition. The first possibility above serves as the basis for the recursive definition, and the rest of the cases are handled by an inductive step.

```
ancestor(X,Y) :- parent(X,Y).
ancestor(X,Y) :- parent(X,Z), ancestor(Z,Y).
```

Add some more facts:

        parent(ken,nora).   female(nora).
        parent(ken,elizabeth).   female(elizabeth).

Since the family tree defined by the Prolog clauses is becoming fairly large,
Figure A.3 shows the parent relation between the twelve people defined in
the database of facts.

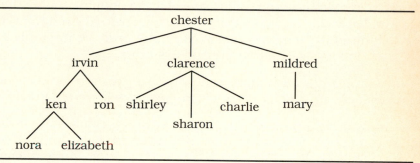

Figure A.3: A Family Tree

Some queries:

?- **ancestor(mildred,mary).**
yes   % because parent(mildred,mary).

?- **ancestor(irvin,nora).**
yes   % because
         %   parent(irvin,ken)
         %   and ancestor(ken,nora) because parent(ken,nora).

?- **ancestor(chester,elizabeth).**

yes   % because
         %   parent(chester,irvin)
         %   and ancestor(irvin,elizabeth)
         %   because parent(irvin,ken)
         %   and ancestor(ken,elizabeth) because parent(ken,elizabeth).

?- **ancestor(irvin,clarence).**
no   % because parent(irvin,clarence) is not provable and
     %   whoever is substituted for Z it is impossible to
     %   prove parent(irvin,Z) and ancestor(Z,clarence).

All possibilities for Z are tried that make parent(irvin,Z) true, namely Z=ron
and Z=ken, and both ancestor(ron,clarence) and ancestor(ken,clarence) fail.

The reader is encouraged to write Prolog definitions for other predicates dealing with family relationships—for example, mother, child, uncle, niece, maternal grandfather, first cousin, and descendant.

Control Aspects of Prolog

In pure logic programming, the predicates in a goal question may be considered in any order or in parallel since logical conjunction (and) is commutative and associative. Furthermore, alternate rules defining a particular predicate (procedure) may be considered in any order or in parallel since logical disjunction (or) is commutative and associative.

Since Prolog has been implemented with a concern for efficiency, its interpreters act with a deterministic strategy for discovering proofs.

1. In defining a predicate, the order in which clauses are presented to the system (the **rule order** or **clause order**) is the order in which the interpreter tests them—namely, from top to bottom. Here the term "rule" includes any clause, including facts (clauses without bodies).

   Rule order determines the order in which answers are found. Observe the difference when the two clauses in ancestor are reversed.

   ```
   ancestor2(X,Y) :- parent(X,Z), ancestor2(Z,Y).
   ancestor2(X,Y) :- parent(X,Y).
   ```

   ?- ancestor(irvin,Y).
   Y = ron, ken, nora, elizabeth   % Four answers returned separately.

   ?- ancestor2(irvin,Y).
   Y = nora, elizabeth, ron, ken   % Four answers returned separately.

   Depending on the nature of the query, different rule orders may have different execution speeds when only a yes or no, or only one solution is desired.

2. In defining a rule with a clause, the order in which terms (subgoals) are listed on the right-hand side (the **goal order**) is the order in which the interpreter will try to satisfy them—namely, from left to right.

   Goal order determines the shape of the search tree that the interpreter explores in its reasoning. In particular, a poor choice of goal order may permit a search tree with an infinite branch in which the inference engine will become lost. The version below is ancestor2 with the subgoals in the body of the first clause interchanged.

   ```
   ancestor3(X,Y) :- ancestor3(Z,Y), parent(X,Z).
   ancestor3(X,Y) :- parent(X,Y).
   ```

?- **ancestor(irvin,elizabeth).**

yes

?- **ancestor3(irvin,elizabeth).**

This query invokes a new query

ancestor3(Z,elizabeth), parent(irvin,Z).

which invokes

ancestor3(Z1,elizabeth), parent(Z,Z1), parent(irvin,Z).

which invokes

ancestor3(Z2,elizabeth), parent(Z1,Z2), parent(Z,Z1), parent(irvin,Z).

which invokes ...

The eventual result is a message such as

"Out of local stack during execution; execution aborted."

The problem with this last definition of the ancestor relation is the left recursion with uninstantiated variables in the first clause. If possible, the leftmost goal in the body of a clause should be nonrecursive so that a pattern match occurs and some variables are instantiated before a recursive call is made.

Lists in Prolog

As a special notational convention, a list of terms in Prolog can be represented between brackets: [a, b, c, d]. As in Lisp, the head of this list is a, and its tail is [b, c, d]. The tail of [a] is [ ], the empty list. Lists may contain lists: [5, 2, [a, 8, 2], [x], 9] is a list of five items.

Prolog list notation allows a special form to direct pattern matching. The term [H | T] matches any list with at least one element:

H matches the head of the list, and

T matches the tail.

A list of terms is permitted to the left of the vertical bar. For example, the term [X,a,Y | T] matches any list with at least three elements whose second element is the atom a:

X matches the first element,

Y matches the third element, and

T matches the rest of the list, possibly empty, after the third item.

Using these pattern matching facilities, values can be specified as the intersection of constraints on terms instead of by direct assignment.

Although it may appear that lists form a new data type in Prolog, in fact they are ordinary structures with a bit of "syntactic sugar" added to make them easier to use. The list notation is simply an abbreviation for terms constructed with the predefined "." function symbol and with [ ] considered as a special atom representing the empty list. For example,

[a, b, c] is an abbreviation for .(a, .(b, .(c, [ ])))

[H | T] is an abbreviation for .(H, T)

[a, b | X] is an abbreviation for .(a, .(b, X))

Note the analogy with the relationship between lists and S-expressions in Lisp. In particular, the "list" object [a | b] really represents an object corresponding to a dotted pair in Lisp—namely, .(a,b).

List Processing

Many problems can be solved in Prolog by expressing the data as lists and defining constraints on those lists using patterns with Prolog's list representation. We provide a number of examples to illustrate the process of programming in Prolog.

1. Define last(L,X) to mean "X is the last element of the list L".

    The last element of a singleton list is its only element.
        last([X], X).

    The last element of a list with two or more elements is the last item in its tail.
        last([H|T], X) :- last(T, X).

    ?- **last([a,b,c], X).**
    X = c
    yes

    ?- **last([ ], X).**
    no

Observe that the "illegal" operation of requesting the last element of an empty list simply fails. With imperative languages a programmer must test for exceptional conditions to avoid the run-time failure of a program. With logic programming, an exception causes the query to fail, so that a calling program can respond by trying alternate subgoals. The predicate last acts as a generator when run "backward".

?- **last(L, a).**
L = [a];
L = [_5, a];   % The underline indicates system-generated variables.
L = [_5, _9, a];
L = [_5, _9, _13, a] ...

The variable H in the definition of last plays no role in the condition part (the body) of the rule; it really needs no name. Prolog allows **anonymous variables**, denoted by an underscore:

last([_ |T], X) :- last(T, X).

Another example of an anonymous variable can be seen in the definition of a father relation:

father(F) :- parent(F, _), male(F).

The scope of an anonymous variable is its single occurrence. Generally, we prefer using named variables for documentation rather than anonymous variables, although anonymous variables can be slightly more efficient since they do not require that bindings be made.

2.   Define member(X,L) to mean "X is a member of the list L".

For this predicate we need two clauses, one as a basis case and the second to define the recursion that corresponds to an inductive specification.

The predicate succeeds if X is the first element of L.

member(X, [X|T]).

If the first clause fails, check if X is a member of the tail of L.

member(X, [H|T]) :- member(X,T).

If the item is not in the list, the recursion eventually tries a query of the form member(X,[ ]), which fails since the head of no clause for member has an empty list as its second parameter.

3.   Define delete(X,List,NewList) to mean
"The variable NewList is to be bound to a copy of List with all instances of X removed".

When X is removed from an empty list, we get the same empty list.

delete(X,[ ],[ ]).

When an item is removed from a list with that item as its head, we get the list that results from removing the item from the tail of the list (ignoring the head).

delete(H,[H|T],R) :- delete(H,T,R).

If the previous clause fails, X is not the head of the list, so we retain the head of L and take the tail that results from removing X from the tail of the original list.

delete(X,[H|T],[H|R]) :- delete(X,T,R).

4. Define union(L1,L2,U) to mean

"The variable U is to be bound to the list that contains the union of the elements of L1 and L2".

If the first list is empty, the result is the second list.

union([ ],L2,L2).   % clause 1

If the head of L1 is a member of L2, it may be ignored since a union does not retain duplicate elements.

union([H|T],L2,U) :- member(H,L2), union(T,L2,U).   % clause 2

If the head of L1 is a not member of L2 (clause 2 fails), it must be included in the result.

union([H|T],L2,[H|U]) :- union(T,L2,U).   % clause 3

In the last two clauses, recursion is used to find the union of the tail of L1 and the list L2.

5. Define concat(X,Y,Z) to mean "the concatenation of lists X and Y is Z". In the Prolog literature, this predicate is frequently called append.

concat([ ], L, L).   % clause α

concat([H|T], L, [H|M]) :- concat(T, L, M).   % clause β

?- **concat([a,b,c], [d,e], R).**
R = [a,b,c,d,e]
yes

The inference that produced this answer is illustrated by the search tree in Figure A.4. When the last query succeeds, the answer is constructed by unwinding the bindings:

R = [a | M] = [a | [b | M1]] = [a,b | M1] = [a,b | [c | M2]]
   = [a,b,c | M2] = [a,b,c | [d,e]] = [a,b,c,d,e].

Figure A.5 shows the search tree for another application of concat using semicolons to generate all the solutions.

To concatenate more than two lists, use a predicate that joins the lists in parts.

concat(L,M,N,R) :- concat(M,N,Temp), concat(L,Temp,R).

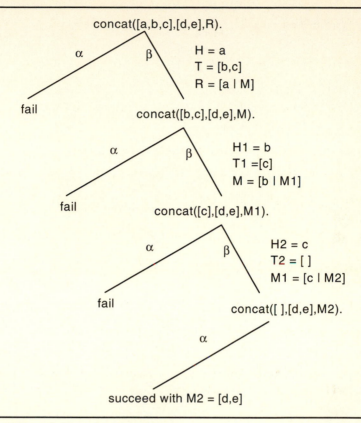

Figure A.4: A Search Tree for concat

No confusion results from using the same name for this predicate, since the two versions are distinguished by the number of parameters they take (the arities of the predicates).

6. Define reverse(L,R) to mean "the reverse of list L is R".

> reverse([ ], [ ]).
> reverse([H|T], L) :- reverse(T, M), concat(M, [H], L).

In executing concat, the depth of recursion corresponds to the number of times that items from the first list are attached (cons) to the front of the second list. Taken as a measure of complexity, it suggests that the work done by concat is proportional to the length of the first list. When reverse is applied to a list of length n, the executions of concat have first argument of lengths, n-1, n-2, ..., 2, 1, which means that the complexity of reverse is proportional to n^2.

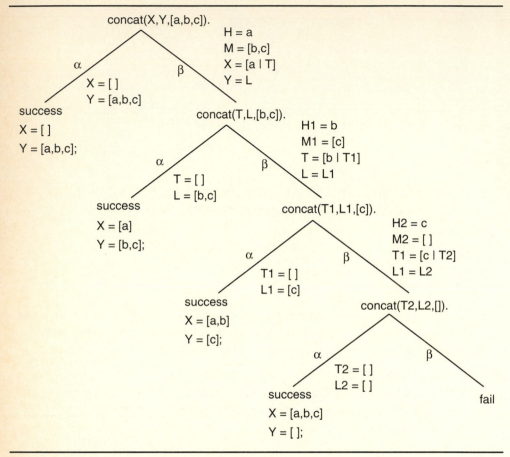

Figure A.5: Another Search Tree for concat

7. An improved reverse using an accumulator:

    rev(L, R) :- help(L, [ ], R).

    help([ ], R, R).
    help([H|T], A, R) :- help(T, [H|A], R).

The predicate help is called n times if the original list is of length n, so the complexity of rev is proportional to n. Observe that the predicat help is tail recursive.

Sorting in Prolog

A few relations are needed for comparing numbers when sorting a list of numbers (equal and not equal are described later):

M < N, M =< N, M > N, M >= N.

These relations demand that both operands be numeric atoms or arithmetic expressions whose variables are bound to numbers.

Insertion Sort

If a list consists of head H and tail T, the idea with the insertion sort is to sort the tail T (recursively) and then insert the item H into its proper place in the tail.

    insertSort([ ], [ ]).
    insertSort([X|T], M) :- insertSort(T, L), insert(X, L, M).

    insert(X, [H|L], [H|M]) :- H<X, insert(X, L, M).
    insert(X, L, [X|L]).

Observe that the clauses for insert are order dependent. The second clause is executed when the first goal of the first clause fails—namely, when H>=X. If these clauses are switched, the definition of insert is no longer correct.

Although this dependence on the rule order of Prolog is common in Prolog programming and may be slightly more efficient, a more logical program is constructed by making the clauses that define insert independent of each other:

    insert(X, [ ], [X]).
    insert(X, [H|L], [X,H|L]) :- X=<H.
    insert(X, [H|L], [H|M]) :- X>H, insert(X,L,M).

Now only one clause applies to a given list. The original clause insert(X, L, [X|L]). must be split into two cases depending on whether L is empty or not.

Quick Sort

The quick sort works by splitting the list into those items less than or equal to a particular element, called the **pivot**, and the list of those items greater than the pivot. The first number in the list can be chosen as the pivot. After the two sublists are sorted (recursively), they are concatenated with the pivot in the middle to form a sorted list.

The splitting operation is performed by the predicate partition(P, List, Left, Right), which means P is a pivot value for the list List, Left = { X∈ List | X≤P }, and Right = { X∈ List | X>P }.

```
partition(P, [ ], [ ], [ ]).
partition(P, [A|X], [A|Y], Z) :- A=<P, partition(P, X, Y, Z).
partition(P, [A|X], Y, [A|Z]) :- A>P, partition(P, X, Y, Z).

quickSort([ ], [ ]).
quickSort([H|T], S) :-  partition(H, T, Left, Right),
                        quickSort(Left, NewLeft),
                        quickSort(Right, NewRight),
                        concat(NewLeft, [H|NewRight], S).
```

The clauses for both partition and quickSort can be entered in any order since they are made mutually exclusive either by the patterns in their head terms or by the "guard" goals at the beginning of their bodies. The goals in the definition of partition may be turned around without affecting correctness but with a severe penalty of diminished efficiency since the recursive call will be made whether it is needed or not. An empirical test showed the sorting of 18 integers took 100 times longer with the goals switched than with the original order.

The Logical Variable

A variable in an imperative language is not the same concept as a variable in mathematics:

1. A program variable refers to a memory location that may have changes in its contents; consider an assignment N := N+1.

2. A variable in mathematics simply stands for a value that once determined will not change. The equations $x + 3y = 11$ and $2x - 3y = 4$ specify values for x and y—namely, $x=5$ and $y=2$—which will not be changed in this context. A variable in Prolog is called a **logical variable** and acts in the manner of a mathematical variable.

3. Once a logical variable is bound to a particular value, called an **instantiation** of the variable, that binding cannot be altered unless the pattern matching that caused the binding is undone because of backtracking.

4. The destructive assignment of imperative languages, where a variable with a value binding is changed, cannot be performed in logic programming.

5. Terms in a query change only by having variables filled in for the first time, never by having a new value replace an existing value.

6. An iterative accumulation of a value is obtained by having each instance of a recursive rule take the values passed to it and perform computations of values for new variables that are then passed to another call.

7. Since a logical variable is "write-once", it is more like a constant identifier with a dynamic defining expression as in Ada (or Pelican) than a variable in an imperative language.

The power of logic programming and Prolog comes from using the logical variable in structures to direct the pattern matching. Results are constructed by binding values to variables according to the constraints imposed by the structures of the arguments in the goal term and the head of the clause being matched. The order that variables are constrained is generally not critical, and the construction of complex values can be postponed as long as logical variables hold their places in the structure being constructed.

Equality and Comparison in Prolog

Prolog provides a number of different ways to compare terms and construct structures. Since beginning Prolog programmers often confuse the various notions of equality and related predicates, we provide a brief overview of these predicates.

Unification

"T1 = T2"   Succeed if term T1 can be unified with term T2.

```
| ?- f(X,b) = f(g(a),Y).
X = g(a)
Y = b
yes
```

Numerical Comparisons

"=:=", "=\=", "<", ">", "=<", ">="

Evaluate both expressions and compare the results.

```
| ?- 5<8.
yes

| ?- 5 =< 2.
no

| ?- N =:= 5.
! Error in arithmetic expression: not a number (N not instantiated to a number)
no

| ?- N = 5, N+1 =< 12.
N = 5                    % The unification N = 5 causes a binding of N to 5.
yes
```

Forcing Arithmetic Evaluation (is)

"N is Exp"   Evaluate the arithmetic expression Exp and try to unify the resulting number with N, a variable or a number.

| ?- **M is 5+8.**
M = 13
yes

| ?- **13 is 5+8.**
yes

| ?- **M is 9, N is M+1.**
M = 9
N = 10
yes

| ?- **N is 9, N is N+1.**
no   % N is N+1 can never succeed.

| ?- **6 is 2*K.**
! Error in arithmetic expression: not a number (K not instantiated to a number)
no

The infix predicate is provides the computational mechanism to carry out arithmetic in Prolog. Consider the following predicate that computes the factorial function:

The factorial of 0 is 1.

    fac(0,1).

The factorial of N>0 is N times the factorial of N-1.

    fac(N,F) :- N>0, N1 is N-1, fac(N1,R), F is N*R.

| ?- **fac(5,F).**
F = 120
yes

Identity

"X == Y"   Succeed if the terms currently instantiated to X and Y are literally identical, including variable names.

| ?- **X=g(X,U), X==g(X,U).**
yes

| ?- **X=g(a,U), X==g(V,b).**
no

| ?- **X\==X.**   % "X \== X" is the negation of "X == X"

no

Term Comparison (Lexicographic)

"T1 @< T2", "T1 @> T2", "T1 @=< T2", "T1 @>= T2"

| ?- ant @< bat.
yes

| ?- @<(f(ant),f(bat)).   % infix predicates may also be entered
yes   %   as prefix

Term Construction

"T =.. L"   L is a list whose head is the atom corresponding to the
                   principal functor of term T and whose tail is the argument
                   list of that functor in T.

| ?- T =.. [@<,ant,bat], call(T).
T = ant@<bat
yes

| ?- T =.. [@<,bat,bat],call(T).
no

| ?- T =.. [is,N,5], call(T).
N = 5,
T = (5 is 5)
yes

| ?- member(X,[1,2,3,4]) =.. L.
L = [member,X,[1,2,3,4]]
yes

Input and Output Predicates

Several input and output predicates are used in the laboratory exercises. We describe them below together with a couple of special predicates.

get0(N)   N is bound to the ascii code of the next character from the current input stream (normally the terminal keyboard). When the current input stream reaches its end of file, a special value is bound to N and the stream is closed. The special value depends on the Prolog system, but two possibilities are:

        26, the code for control-Z or

        -1, a special end of file value.

put(N)   The character whose ascii code is the value of N is printed on the current output stream (normally the terminal screen).

see(F)   The file whose name is the value of F becomes the current input stream.

seen   Close the current input stream.

tell(F)   The file whose name is the value of F becomes the current output stream.

told   Close the current output stream.

read(T)   The next Prolog term in the current input stream is bound to T. The term in the input stream must be followed by a period.

write(T)   The Prolog term bound to T is displayed on the current output stream.

tab(N)   N spaces are printed on the output stream.

nl   Newline prints a linefeed character on the current output stream.

abort   Immediately terminate the attempt to satisfy the original query and return control to the top level.

name(A,L)   A is a literal atom or a number, and L is a list of the ascii codes of the characters comprising the name of A.

> | ?- **name(A,[116,104,101]).**
> A = the
>
> | ?- **name(1994,L).**
> L = [49, 57, 57, 52]

call(T)   Assuming T is instantiated to a term that can be interpreted as a goal, call(T) succeeds if and only if T succeeds as a query.

This Appendix has not covered all of Prolog, but we have introduced enough Prolog to support the laboratory exercises in the text. See the further readings at the end of Chapter 2 for references to more material on Prolog.

Appendix B
FUNCTIONAL PROGRAMMING WITH SCHEME

The languages usually studied in computer science—namely, Pascal, C, Modula-2, and Ada—are considered imperative languages because the basic construct is a command. These languages are heavily influenced by the "von Neumann architecture" of computers, which includes a store (memory) and an instruction counter used to identify the next instruction to be fetched from the store. The computation model has control structures that determine the sequencing of instructions, which use assignments to make incremental modifications to the store.

Imperative languages are characterized by the following properties:

- The principal operation is the assignment of values to variables.
- Programs are command oriented, and they carry out algorithms with statement level sequence control, usually by selection and repetition.
- Programs are organized as blocks, and data control is dominated by scope rules.
- Computing is done by effect, namely by changes to the store.

The computing by effect intrinsic to imperative programming plays havoc with some of the mathematical properties that are essential to proving the correctness of programs. For example, is addition commutative in an imperative program? Does "write(a+b)" always produce the same value as "write(b+a)"? Consider the following Pascal program:

```
program P (output);
    var b : integer;
    function a : integer;
            begin b := b+2; a := 5 end;
    begin
            b := 10
            write(a+b)  or  write(b+a)
    end.
```

In fact, implementations of Pascal will most likely give different results for the two versions of this program, depending on the order of evaluation of expressions. This anomaly is caused by the side effect in the expression being evaluated, but programming by effect lies at the heart of imperative programming. If we depend on imperative programs, we must discard many of the basic properties of mathematics, such as associative and commuative laws of addition and multiplication and the distributive law for multiplication over addition.

The functional programming paradigm provides an alternative notion of programming that avoids the problems of side effects. Functional languages are concerned with data objects and values instead of variables. Values are bound to identifiers, but once made, these bindings cannot change. The principal operation is function application. Functions are treated as first-class objects that may be stored in data structures, passed as parameters, and returned as function results. A functional language supplies primitive functions, and the programmer uses function constructors to define new functions. Program execution consists of the evaluation of an expression, and sequence control depends primarily on selection and recursion. A pure functional language has no assignment command; values are communicated by the use of parameters to functions. These restrictions enforce a discipline on the programmer that avoids side effects. We say that functional languages are referentially transparent.

Principle of Referential Transparency: The value of a function is determined by the values of its arguments and the context in which the function application appears, and it is independent of the history of the execution. ∎

Since the evaluation of a function with the same argument produces the same value every time that it is invoked, an expression will produce the same value each time it is evaluated in a given context. Referential transparency guarantees the validity of the property of substituting equals for equals.

Lisp

Work on Lisp (**Lis**t **p**rocessing) started in 1956 with an artificial intelligence group at MIT under John McCarthy. The language was implemented by McCarthy and his students in 1960 on an IBM 704, which also had the first Fortran implementation. Lisp was an early example of interactive computing, which played a substantial role in its popularity. The original development of Lisp used S-expressions (S standing for symbolic language) with the intention of developing an Algol-like version (Lisp 2) with M-expressions (M for metalanguage). When a Lisp interpreter was written in Lisp with S-expressions, Lisp 2 was dropped. The principal versions, which are based on Lisp 1.5, include Interlisp, Franz Lisp, MacLisp, Common Lisp, and Scheme.

Lisp has a high-level notation for lists. Functions are defined as expressions, and repetitive tasks are performed mostly by recursion. Parameters are passed to functions by value. A Lisp program consists of a set of function definitions followed by a list of expressions that may include function evaluations.

Scheme Syntax

The Scheme version of Lisp has been chosen here because of its small size and its uniform treatment of functions. In this appendix we introduce the fundamentals of functional programming in Scheme. When we say Scheme, we are referring to Lisp. The basic objects in Scheme, called S-expressions, consist of atoms and "dotted pairs":

> <S-expr> ::= <atom> | (<S-expr> . <S-expr>)

The only terminal symbols in these productions are the parentheses and the dot (period). The important characteristic of an S-expression is that it is an atom or a pair of S-expressions. The syntactic representation of a pair is not crucial to the basic notion of constructing pairs.

Atoms serve as the elementary objects in Scheme. They are considered indivisible with no internal structure.

> <atom> ::= <literal atom> | <numeric atom>
>
> <literal atom> ::= <letter> | <literal atom> <letter> | <literal atom> <digit>
>
> <numeric atom> ::= <numeral> | – <numeral>
>
> <numeral> ::= <digit> | <numeral> <digit>

Literal atoms consist of a string of alphanumeric characters usually starting with a letter. Most Lisp systems allow any special characters in literal atoms as long as they cannot be confused with numbers. The numeric atoms defined here represent only integers, but most Lisp systems allow floating-point numeric atoms.

Since S-expressions can have arbitrary nesting when pairs are constructed, Scheme programmers rely on a graphical representation of S-expressions to display their structure. Consider the following diagrams illustrating the S-expression (a . (b. c)):

Lisp tree (or L-tree):

Cell diagram (or box notation):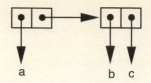

We prefer using the box notation for S-expressions. Atoms are represented as themselves, and if the same atom is used twice in an S-expression, a single value can be shared since atoms have unique occurrences in S-expressions.

Functions on S-expressions

The simplicity of Scheme (and Lisp) derives from its dependence on several basic functions for constructing pairs and selecting components of a pair. Two selector functions are used to investigate a pair:

car   Applied to a nonatomic S-expression, car returns the left part.

cdr   Applied to a nonatomic S-expression, cdr returns the right part.

On the IBM 704, car stood for "**c**ontents of **a**ddress **r**egister" and cdr for "**c**ontents of **d**ecrement **r**egister". Some authors have suggested that "head" and "tail" or "first" and "rest" are more suggestive names for these functions, but most Lisp programmers still use the traditional names.

The following examples that use brackets [ ] to delimit arguments do not follow correct Scheme syntax, which will be introduced shortly:

car [((a . b) . c)] = (a . b)

cdr [((a . b) . c)] = c

An error results if either function is applied to an atom.

An abstract implementation of the selector functions can be explained in terms of a box diagram:

car returns the left pointer.

cdr returns the right pointer.

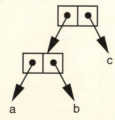

A single constructor function cons builds a pair given two S-expressions:

cons   Applied to two S-expressions, cons returns a dotted pair contain-
          ing them.

For example:

cons[p , q] = (p . q)

cons[(a . b) , (a . c)] = ((a . b) . (a . c))

As an abstract implementation, we allocate a new cell and set its left and
right components to point to the two arguments. Observe that the atom a is
shared by the two pairs.

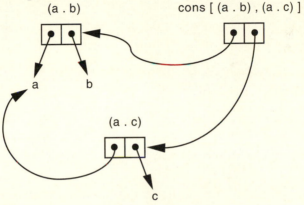

Lists in Scheme

The notion of an S-expression is too general for most computing tasks, so
Scheme primarily deals with a subset of the S-expressions. A list in Scheme
is an S-expression with one of two forms:

1. The special atom ( ) is a list representing the empty list. Note that ( ) is the
    only S-expression that is both an atom and a list.

2. A dotted pair is a list if its right (cdr) element is a list.

S-expressions that are lists use special notation:

(a . ( ))	is represented by	(a)
(b . (a . ( )))	is represented by	(b a)
(c . (b . (a . ( ))))	is represented by	(c b a)

Cell diagrams for lists are usually drawn with a horizontal "spine" that
stretches from left to right. The spine contains as many boxes as the list has
elements at its top level.

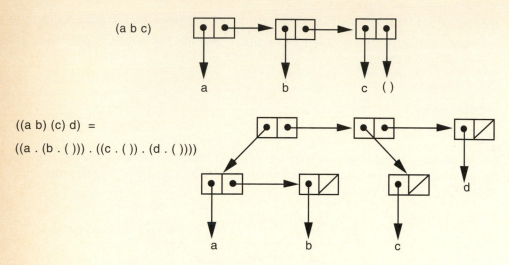

Observe the abbreviation of a slash through the cell at the end of a list to represent a pointer to an empty list ( ).

The elementary constructor and selectors for S-expressions have special properties when applied to lists.

car   When applied to a nonempty list, car returns the first element of the list.

cdr   When applied to a nonempty list, cdr returns a copy of the list with the first element removed.

cons   When applied to an arbitrary S-expression and a list, cons returns the list obtained by appending the first argument onto the beginning of the list (the second argument).

For example:

car [(a b c)] = a   cdr [(a b c)] = (b c)

car [((a))] = (a)   cdr [((a))] = ( )

cons [(a) , (b c)] = ((a) b c)   cons [a , ( )] = (a)

Syntax for Functions

In Scheme, the application of a function to a set of arguments is expressed as a list:

     (function-name   sequence-of-arguments)

This prefix notation is known as **Cambridge Polish Form** since it was developed at MIT in Cambridge. We illustrate the notation by introducing many of the predefined Scheme numeric functions.

Unary functions:

(add1 5)	returns 6
(sub1 0)	returns -1
(abs (add1 -5))	returns 4

Binary functions:

(- 6 9)	returns -3
(quotient 17 5)	returns 3
(/ 17 5)	returns 3.4
(* 10 12)	returns 120
(- (* 10 2) (+ 13 3))	returns 4
(modulo 53 5)	returns 3

N-ary functions:

(+ 1 2 3 4 5)	returns 15
(* 1 2 3 4 5)	returns 120
(max 2 12 3 10)	returns 12
(min (* 4 6) (+ 4 6) (- 4 6))	returns -2

Miscellaneous functions:

(expt 2 5)	returns 32
(expt 5 -2)	returns 0.04
(sqrt 25)	returns 5
(sqrt 2)	returns 1.4142135623730951

Functions that return Boolean values are called predicates. In Scheme predicates return either the atom #t, which stands for true, or #f, the value for false. Scheme programmers usually follow the convention of naming a predicate with identifiers that end in a question mark.

(negative? -6)	returns #t		(= 6 2)	returns #f
(zero? 44)	returns #f		(< 0.5 0.1)	returns #f
(positive? -33)	returns #f		(>= 3 30)	returns #f
(number? 5)	returns #t		(<= -5 -3)	returns #t
(integer? 3.7)	returns #f		(odd? 5)	returns #t
(real? 82)	returns #f		(even? 37)	returns #f
(> 6 2)	returns #t			

Scheme Evaluation

When the Scheme interpreter encounters an atom, it evaluates the atom:

• Numeric atoms evaluate to themselves.

- The literal atoms #t and #f evaluate to themselves.
- Each other literal atom evaluates to the value, if any, that has been bound to it.

The define operation may be used to bind a value to an atom. The operation makes the binding and returns a value:

```
(define a 5)    returns  a
(define b 3)    returns  b
a               returns  5
(+ a b)         returns  8
(+ a c)         returns an error since c has no value bound to it.
```

Although the value returned by define is unspecified in the Scheme standard, most Schemes return the name of the identifier that has just been bound.

When the Scheme interpreter evaluates a list, it expects the first item in the list to be an expression that represents a function. The rest of the items in the list are evaluated and given to the function as argument values.

```
(* a (add1 b))   returns  20
```

Suppose now that we want to apply car to the list (a b c). Evaluating the expression (car (a b c)) means that a must represent a function, which will be applied to the values of b and c, and the resulting value is passed to car. Since we want to apply car to the list (a b c) without evaluating the list, we need a way to suppress that evaluation. Scheme evaluation is inhibited by the quote operation.

```
(quote a)                    returns the symbol a
(quote (a b c))              returns (a b c) unevaluated
(car (quote (a b c)))        returns a
(cdr (quote (a b c)))        returns (b c)
(cons (quote x) (quote (y z)))   returns the list (x y z)
```

The quote operation may be abbreviated by using an apostrophe.

```
(cdr '((a) (b) (c)))   returns  ((b) (c))
(cons 'p '(q))         returns  (p q)
(number? 'a)           returns  #f
'a                     returns  a
'(1 2 3)               returns  (1 2 3)
```

The car and cdr functions may be abbreviated to simplify expressions. (car (cdr '(a b c))) may be abbreviated as (cadr '(a b c)). Any combination of a's and d's between c and r (up to four operations) defines a Scheme selector function.

Now that we have a mechanism for suppressing evaluation of a literal atom or a list, several more fundamental functions can be described.

pair?   When applied to any S-expression, pair? returns #t if it is a dotted pair, #f otherwise.

> (pair? 'x)   returns #f
> (pair? '(x)) returns #t

atom?   When applied to any S-expression, atom? is the logical negation of pair?. (atom? is not standard in Scheme.)

null?   When applied to any S-expression, null? returns #t if it is the empty list, #f otherwise.

> (null? '( ))   returns #t
> (null? '(( ))) returns #f

eq?   When applied to two *literal atoms*, eq? returns #t if they are the same, #f otherwise.

> (eq? 'xy 'x)   returns #f
> (eq? (pair? 'gonzo) #f) returns #t
> (eq? '(foo) '(foo))   returns #f

The reader may find the equality function eq? somewhat confusing since it may appear that the expression (foo) should be equal to itself. To explain this unusual version of equality, we develop a short example. We use the define operation to create two bindings.

(define x '(a b))
(define y '(a b))

To explain why (eq? x y) returns #f, consider the cell diagram below. Each time the Scheme interpreter processes an S-expression, such as (define x '(a b)), it creates a new copy of the structure being processed.

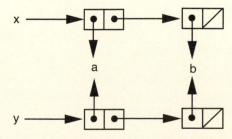

Although the values appear to be the same, they are two different copies of the same S-expression. The test (eq? x y) returns #f because x and y point to two different objects. We can view eq? as testing pointer equality. On atoms eq? acts as an equality test since atoms are treated as unique objects. The equality of numeric atoms can be tested using the = function. The equality of general S-expressions will be considered later.

Special Forms

All the operations considered so far do not act in the same way. Scheme functions, such as +, car, null?, =, and user-defined functions, always evaluate their arguments. In fact, when (+ (car '(2 4 6)) 5) is submitted to the interpreter, each of the expressions +, (car '(2 4 6)), and 5 are evaluated:

+   evaluates to the predefined addition operation,

(car '(2 4 6))   evaluates to the number 2, and

5   evaluates to the number 5.

On the other hand, several of the operations described so far do not and cannot evaluate all of their operands. (quote a) simply returns its operand unevaluated. (define x (+ 5 6)) evaluates its second argument, but leaves its first argument unevaluated.

These operations are called **special forms** to distinguish them from normal Scheme functions. A complete list of the special forms in Scheme follows:

and	delay	let	quasiquote
begin	do	let*	quote
case	if	letrec	set!
cond	lambda	or	while
define			

For some of these special forms, the determination of which arguments are evaluated is made on a dynamic basis using the results of evaluations performed so far. We will not take the time to describe all of the special forms in Scheme. The description of those not used in this appendix can be found in the references for Scheme.

Defining Functions in Scheme

The special form define returns the name of the function (or other object) being defined; more importantly, it has the side effect of binding an object that may be a function to the name.

> (define name (lambda (list-of-parameters) expression))

The use of lambda here will be explained later. The basic idea is that executing the function defined by the expression (lambda (list-of-parameters) expression) involves evaluating the expression in an environment that contains binding of the parameters in the list to actual arguments. We give examples to illustrate user-defined Scheme functions below.

- Calculate the hypotenuse given the legs of a right triangle.

    (define hypotenuse (lambda (a b) (sqrt (+ (* a a) (* b b)))))

    (hypotenuse 3 4)   returns 5.0
    (hypotenuse 10 20)   returns 22.360679774997898

- Find the first item in a list (a synonym for car).

    (define first (lambda (L) (car L)))

    (first '((a b c))) returns (a b c)

- Find the second item in a list.

    (define second (lambda (L) (cadr L)))

    (second '((a) (b) (c))) returns (b)

What if the value bound to L does not have a first or second element? We use revisions to these two functions to illustrate conditional expressions in Scheme. We plan to change the definition so that

> If L is empty, both functions return #f.

> If L has only one element, second returns #f.

A mechanism for making decisions is needed to carry out these revisions. Decisions in Scheme are represented as conditional expressions using the special form cond:

    (cond (c_1 e_1) (c_2 e_2) ... (c_n e_n) (else e_{n+1})),

which is equivalent to   **if** c_1 **then** return e_1

$\qquad\qquad$ **else if** c_2 **then** return e_2

$\qquad\qquad\qquad$:

$\qquad\qquad$ **else if** c_n **then** return e_n

$\qquad\qquad$ **else** return e_{n+1}

If all of c_1, c_2, ..., c_n are false and the else clause is omitted, the cond result is unspecified, although many implementations return an empty list. The function cond is a special form since it does not evaluate all its arguments. For the purposes of testing, any non-#f value represents true.

Now we use cond to revise the definitions of the functions first and second.

    (define first (lambda (L)
        (cond ((null? L) #f)
            (else (cdr L)))))

```
(define  second  (lambda (L)
    (cond  ((null? L)  #f)
           ((null? (cdr L))  #f)
           (else  (cadr L))  )))
```

Both cond and the body of function definitions allow more generality, allowing a sequence of expressions. Each expression is evaluated and the value of the last one is the result returned. The other expressions are evaluated for their side effects (a non-functional aspect of Scheme).

```
(define  categorize  (lambda (n)
    (cond  ((= n 0)  (display 'zero) 0)
           ((positive? n)  (display 'positive) 1)
           (else  (display 'negative) -1))  ))
```

Another special form for decision making is the if operation:

```
(if test then-expression else-expression)
```

For example,   (define safe-divide (lambda (m n)
                    (if (zero? n)
                        0
                        (/ m n))))

Recursive Definitions

The main control structure in Scheme is recursion. Functions that require performing some sequence of operations an arbitrary number of times can be defined inductively. These definitions translate directly into recursive definitons in Scheme. In the next two examples, we define a function using mathematical induction and then translate that definition using recursion.

* Exponentiation (assume $m \neq 0$)

$$m^0 = 1$$
$$m^n = m \bullet m^{n-1} \text{ for } n > 0$$

```
(define  power  (lambda (m n)
                (if (zero? n)
                    1
                    (* m (power m (sub1 n)))  )))
```

A sample execution of the power function demonstrates how the recursion unfolds. In reality, the induction hypothesis inherent in a recursion definition ensures that the result computes what we want.

```
(power  2  3)
        = 2 • (power  2  2)
            = 2 • [2 • (power  2  1)]
```

$$= 2 \cdot [2 \cdot [2 \cdot (\text{power } 2 \ 0)]]$$
$$= 2 \cdot [2 \cdot [2 \cdot 1]]$$
$$= 2 \cdot [2 \cdot 2] \ = \ 2 \cdot 4 \ = \ 8$$

- Fibonacci

    fib(0) = 1

    fib(1) = 1

    fib(n) = fib(n-1) + fib(n-2) for n>1

```
(define fib (lambda (n)
         (cond  ((zero? n) 1)
                ((zero? (sub1 n)) 1)
                (else (+ (fib (sub1 n)) (fib (- n 2)) )) ))))
```

Lambda Notation

Scheme contains a mechanism for defining anonymous functions, as was the case in the lambda calculus (see Chapter 5). The lambda expression $\lambda x,y \ . \ y^2+x$ becomes the S-expression (lambda (x y) (+ (* y y) x)) in Scheme. An anonymous function can appear anywhere that a function identifier is allowed. For example, we can apply the previous function as follows:

    ((lambda (x y) (+ (* y y) x)) 3 4) returns 19.

In fact, the expression that we use to define a function is simply making a binding of an identifier to a lambda expression representing an anonymous function. For example, the expression (define fun (lambda (x y) (+ (* y y) x))) binds the name fun to the anonymous function (lambda (x y) (+ (* y y) x))). Scheme permits an abbreviation of such a definition using notation that shows the pattern of a call of the function as in

    (define (fun x y) (+ (* y y) x)).

Recursive Functions on Lists

Many functions in Scheme manipulate lists. Therefore we develop three examples that show the basic techniques of processing a list recursively.

1. Count the number of occurrences of atoms in a list of atoms. For example, (count1 '(a b c b a)) returns 5.

    Case 1: List is empty $\Rightarrow$ return 0

    Case 2: List is not empty

    $\Rightarrow$ it has a first element that is an atom

    $\Rightarrow$ return (1 + number of atoms in the cdr of the list).

In Scheme, cond can be used to select one of the two cases.

```
(define  count1  (lambda (L)
                  (cond ((null? L)  0)
                        (else  (add1 (count1 (cdr L)))) )))
```

2. Count the number of occurrences of atoms at the "top level" in an arbitrary list. For example, (count2 '(a (b c) d a)) returns 3.

    Case 1: List is empty ⇒ return 0

    Case 2: List is not empty.
    > **Subcase a**: First element is an atom (it not is a pair)
    > > ⇒ return (1 + number of atoms in the cdr of the list).
    > **Subcase b**: First element is not an atom
    > > ⇒ return the number of atoms in the cdr of the list.

    We write this algorithm in Scheme as the function

    ```
    (define  count2  (lambda (L)
                      (cond ((null? L)  0)
                            ((atom? (car L))  (add1 (count2 (cdr L))))
                            (else  (count2 (cdr L))) )))
    ```

3. Count the number of occurrences of atoms at all levels in an arbitrary list. For example, (count2 '(a (b c) d (a))) returns 5.

    Case 1: List is empty ⇒ return 0

    Case 2: List is not empty.
    > **Subcase a**: First element is an atom
    > > ⇒ return (1 + number of atoms in the cdr of the list).
    > **Subcase b**: First element is not an atom
    > > ⇒ return (the number of atoms in the car of the list
    > > + the number of atoms in the cdr of the list).

    The corresponding Scheme function is defined below.

    ```
    (define  count3  (lambda (L)
                      (cond ((null? L)  0)
                            ((atom? (car L))  (add1 (count3 (cdr L))))
                            (else  (+ (count3 (car L)) (count3 (cdr L)) )) )))
    ```

Now that we have seen the basic patterns for defining functions that process lists, we describe a number of useful list manipulation functions, most of which are predefined in Scheme. We give them as user-defined functions as a means of explaining their semantics and to provide additional examples of Scheme code. In many Scheme systems the identifiers associated with pre-defined functions may not be redefined since they are reserved words. There-fore the names of the following user-defined functions may have to be altered to avoid confusion.

- **Length of a list**

```
(define length (lambda (L)
                (if (null? L)
                    0
                    (add1 (length (cdr L))) )))
```

The function length will work identically to the predefined length function in Scheme except that the execution may be slower or a stack may overflow for long lists since the predefined functions may be more efficiently imple-mented.

- **The nth element of a list**

```
(define nth (lambda (n L)
             (if (zero? n)
                 (car L)
                 (nth (sub1 n) (cdr L)) )))
```

This function finds the nth element of a list using zero as the position of the first item. So the first element is called the 0th.

- **Equality of arbitrary S-expressions**

The strategy for the equality function is to use = for numeric atoms, eq? for literal atoms, and recursion to compare the left parts and right parts of dotted pairs. The corresponding predefined function is called equal?.

```
(define equal? (lambda (s1 s2)
                (cond ((number? s1) (= s1 s2))
                      ((atom? s1) (eq? s1 s2))
                      ((atom? s2) #f)
                      ((equal?(car s1) (car s2)) (equal? (cdr s1) (cdr s2)))
                      (else #f) )))
```

- **Concatenate two lists**

```
(define concat (lambda (L1 L2)
                (cond ((null? L1) L2)
                      (else (cons (car L1) (concat (cdr L1) L2))) )))
```

For example, (concat '(a b c) '(d e)) becomes

 (cons 'a (concat '(b c) '(d e)))

    = (cons 'a (cons 'b (concat '(c) '(d e))))

      = (cons 'a (cons 'b (cons 'c (concat '( ) '(d e)))))

       = (cons 'a (cons 'b (cons 'c '(d e))))

        = (cons 'a (cons 'b '(c d e)))

         = (cons 'a '(b c d e))

          = (a b c d e)

Although its name may suggest otherwise, this is a pure function, so neither argument is altered. If length(L1) = n, concat requires n applications of cons; this is a measure of how much work is done. The predefined function for concatenating lists is called append and allows an arbitrary number of lists as its arguments. User functions with an arbitrary number of arguments can be defined several ways, but that topic is beyond the scope of this presentation.

- **Reverse a list**

  (define reverse (lambda (L)
     (if (null? L)
      '( )
      (concat (reverse (cdr L)) (list (car L))))))

The diagram below shows the way reverse handles a list with four elements. Observe that we assume that the function works correctly on lists of length three (the induction hypothesis).

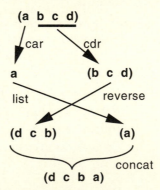

- **Membership (at the top level) in a list**

  (define member (lambda (e L)
     (cond ((null? L) #f)
      ((equal? e (car L)) L)
      (else (member e (cdr L))))))

We might expect this Boolean function to return #t (true) or #f (false), but it returns the rest of the list starting with the matched element for true. This behavior is consistent with the interpretation that any non-#f object represents true. If the item is not in the list (the first case in the cond expression), member returns #f.

- **Logical operations**

        (define and (lambda (s1 s2) (if s1 s2 #f)))

        (define or (lambda (s1 s2) (if s1 s2 #t)))

The predefined "and" and "or" operations (actually special forms) allow an arbitrary number of S-expressions as arguments. In these functions and in our user-defined functions, the arguments are tested from left to right until a decision can be made. For and, the first false argument makes the result #f. For or, the first true argument makes the result non-#f.

Since we defined and and or as regular functions, all of the arguments in a call must be evaluated even if they are not all needed. The special forms and and or evaluate only as many operands as are needed to make a decision.

Scope Rules in Scheme

In Lisp 1.5 and many of its successors, access to nonlocal identifiers is resolved by dynamic scoping: the calling chain (along dynamic links) is followed until the identifier is found local to a program unit (a function in Lisp). McCarthy claims that he intended for Lisp to have static scoping but that a mistake was made in implementing the early versions of Lisp(see [Wexelblat81]). In fact, dynamic scoping is easier to implement for Lisp.

Scheme and Common Lisp use static scoping; nonlocal references in a function are resolved at the point of function definition. Static scoping is implemented by associating a closure (instruction pointer and environment pointer) with each function as it is defined. The calling stack maintains static links for nonlocal references.

Top-level define's create a global environment composed of the identifiers being defined that is visible everywhere. A new scope is created in Scheme when the formal parameters, which are local identifiers, are bound to actual values when a function is invoked. The following transcript shows the creation of a global identifier a and a local (to f) identifier a.

    >>> (define a 22)
    a
    >>> a
    22

```
>>> (define f (lambda (a) (* a a)))
f
>>> (f 7)
49
>>> a
22
```

Local scope can also be created by various versions of the let expression in Scheme. The basic let expression, actually a special form, elaborates the bindings simultaneously and then evaluates the expression expr in the current environment augmented by these bindings.

(let ((id_1 val_1) ... (id_n val_n)) expr)

The expression (let ((a 5) (b 8)) (+ a b)) is an abbreviation of the function application ((lambda (a b) (+ a b)) 5 8); both expressions return the value 13. The let expression used to illustrate static scoping in section 8.2 takes the following form in Scheme:

```
>>> (let ((x 5))
        (let ((f (lambda (y) (+ x y))))
            (let ((x 3))
                (f x))))
   8
```

The translation into function applications is not as easy to read.

```
>>> ((lambda (x)
        ((lambda (f)
            ((lambda (x) (f x))
                3))
            (lambda (y) (+ x y))))
      5)
   8
```

Scheme also has a sequential let, called let*, that evaluates the bindings from left to right.

(let* ((a 5) (b (+ a 3))) (* a b)) is equivalent to

```
>>> (let ((a 5))  (let ((b (+ a 3)))  (* a b)))
40.
```

Finally, letrec must be used to bind an identifier to a function that calls the identifier—namely, a recursive definition. The following expression defines fact as an identifier local to the expression.

```
>>> (letrec ((fact (lambda (n)
                 (cond  ((zero? n) 1)
                        (else (* n (fact (sub1 n)))))))))
      (fact 5))
120
```

See Chapter 10 for an explanation of the meaning of letrec in terms of fixed points.

Proving Correctness in Scheme

Reasoning about the correctness of programs in imperative languages can be a formidable challenge (see Chapter 11).

- Execution depends on the contents of each memory cell (each variable).
- Loops must be executed statically by constructing a loop invariant.
- The progress of the computation is measured by "snapshots" of the state of the computation after every instruction.
- Side effects in programs can make correctness proofs very difficult.

Functional languages are much easier to reason about because of referential transparency: Only those values immediately involved in a function application need to be considered. Programs defined as recursive functions usually can be proved correct by an induction proof. Consider a Scheme function that computes the sum of the squares of a list of integers.

```
(define sumsqrs (lambda (L)
                 (cond ((null?  L)  0)
                       (else  (+  (*  (car L) (car L))  (sumsqrs (cdr L)))))))
```

Notation: If L is a list, let L_k denote the kth element of L.

Precondition: L is a list of zero or more integers.

Postcondition: (sumsqrs L) $= \Sigma_{1 \le k \le length(L)} L_k^2$

Proof of correctness: By induction on the length n of L.

Basis: n = length(L) = 0

Then $\Sigma_{1 \le k \le length(L)} L_k^2 = 0$ and (sumsqrs L) returns 0.

Induction step: Suppose that for any list M of length n,

(sumsqrs M) $= \Sigma_{1 \le k \le length(M)} M_k^2$.

Let L be a list of length n+1. Note that (cdr L) is a list of length n.

Therefore (sumsqrs L) $= L_1^2 +$ (sumsqrs (cdr L))

$$= L_1^2 + \Sigma_{2 \le k \le length(L)} L_k^2 = \Sigma_{1 \le k \le length(L)} L_k^2.$$

Higher-Order Functions

Much of the expressiveness of functional programming comes from treating functions as first-class objects with the same rights as other objects—namely, to be stored in data structures, to be passed as parameters to subprograms, and to be returned as function results.

In Scheme, functions can be bound to identifiers using define and may also be stored in structures:

```
(define fn-list (list  add1  −  (lambda (n) (* n n))))
```

or alternatively

```
(define fn-list  (cons add1
                  (cons −
                  (cons (lambda (n) (* n n)) '( )))))
```

defines a list of three unary functions.

```
fn-list returns (#<PROCEDURE add1> #<PROCEDURE −> #<PROCEDURE>).
```

A Scheme procedure can be defined to apply each of these functions to a number:

```
(define construction
        (lambda (fl x)
              (cond ((null? fl) '( ))
          ,            (else (cons ((car fl) x) (construction (cdr fl) x))))))
```

so that

```
(construction fn-list 5)  returns  (6 −5 25).
```

The function construction is based on an operation found in FP, a functional language developed by John Backus (see [Backus78]). It illustrates the possibility of passing functions as arguments.

Since functions are first-class objects in Scheme, they may be stored in any sort of structure. It is possible to imagine an application for a stack of functions or even a tree of functions.

Definition: A function is called **higher-order** if it has one or more functions as parameters or returns a function as its result. ∎

Higher-order functions are sometimes called functional forms since they allow the construction of new functions from already defined functions. The expressiveness of functional programming comes from the use of functional forms that allow the development of complex functions from simple functions using abstract patterns—for example, construction defined above. We continue, describing several of the most useful higher-order functions.

- **Composition**

      (define compose (lambda (f g) (lambda (x) (f (g x)))))

      (define inc-sqr (compose add1 (lambda (n) (* n n))))

      (define sqr-inc (compose (lambda (n) (* n n)) add1))

  Note that the two functions inc-sqr and sqr-inc are defined without the use of parameters.

  (inc-sqr 5) returns 26

  (sqr-inc 5) returns 36

- **Apply to all**

  In Scheme, map is a predefined function that applies a functional argument to all the items in a list. It takes a unary function and a list as arguments and applies the function to each element of the list returning the list of results.

  (map add1 '(1 2 3)) returns (2 3 4)

  (map (lambda (n) (* n n)) '(1 2 3)) returns (1 4 9)

  (map (lambda (ls) (cons 'a ls)) '((b c) (a) ( ))) returns ((a b c) (a a) (a))

  The function map can be defined as follows:

      (define map (lambda (proc lst)
                    (if (null? lst)
                    '( )
                    (cons (proc (car lst)) (map proc (cdr lst))))))

- **Reduce**

  Higher-order functions are developed by abstracting common patterns from programs. For example, consider the functions that find the sum or the product of a list of numbers:

      (define sum (lambda (ls)
                    (cond ((null? ls) 0)
                          (else (+ (car ls) (sum (cdr ls)))))))

      (define product (lambda (ls)
                        (cond ((null? ls) 1)
                              (else (* (car ls) (product (cdr ls)))))))

  The common pattern can be abstracted as a higher-order function reduce (also called foldright):

      (define reduce (lambda (proc init ls)
                        (cond ((null? ls) init)
                              (else (proc (car ls) (reduce proc init (cdr ls)))))))

Reduce can be used to compute both the sum and product of a list of numbers.

```
>>> (reduce + 0 '(1 2 3 4 5))
15

>>> (reduce * 1 '(1 2 3 4 5))
120

>>> (reduce concat '( ) '((1 2 3) (4 5) (6 7 8)))
(1 2 3 4 5 6 7 8)
```

Now sum and product can be defined in terms of reduce:

```
(define sum  (lambda (ls) (reduce + 0 ls)))

(define product  (lambda (ls) (reduce * 1 ls)))
```

- **Filter**

  By passing a Boolean function, it is possible to "filter" in only those elements from a list that satisfy the predicate.

  ```
  (define filter (lambda (proc ls)
              (cond ((null? ls)  '( ))
                    ((proc (car ls)) (cons (car ls) (filter proc (cdr ls))))
                    (else (filter proc (cdr ls))) )))
  ```

  (filter even? '(1 2 3 4 5 6)) returns (2 4 6).

  (filter (lambda (n) (> n 3)) '(1 2 3 4 5)) returns (4 5).

Currying

A binary function—for example, + or cons—takes both of its arguments at the same time. For example, (+ a b) will evaluate both a and b so that their values can be passed to the addition operation.

Having a binary function take its arguments one at a time can be an advantage. Such a function is called **curried** after Haskell Curry. (See the discussion of currying in Chapter 5.)

```
(define curried+ (lambda (m) (lambda (n)  (+ m n)) ))
```

Note that if only one argument is supplied to curried+, the result is a function of one argument.

```
(curried+ 5) returns #<procedure>

((curried+ 5) 8) returns 13
```

Unary functions can be defined using curried+, as shown below:

```
(define add2  (curried+ 2))
(define add5  (curried+ 5))
```

In some functional languages—for example, Standard ML and Miranda—all functions are automatically defined in a curried form. In Scheme, curried functions must be defined explicitly by nested lambda expressions.

- **Curried Map**

```
(define cmap (lambda (proc)
                (lambda  (lst)
                    (if  (null? lst)
                        '( )
                        (cons (proc (car lst)) ((cmap proc) (cdr lst)))))))
```

(cmap add1) returns #<procedure>

((cmap add1) '(1 2 3)) returns (2 3 4)

((cmap (cmap add1)) '((1) (2 3) (4 5 6))) returns ((2) (3 4) (5 6 7))

(((compose cmap cmap) add1) '((1) (2 3) (4 5 6))) returns ((2) (3 4) (5 6 7))

The notion of currying can be applied to functions with more than two arguments.

Tail Recursion

One criticism of functional programming centers on the heavy use of recursion that is seen by some critics as overly inefficient. Scheme and some other functional languages have a mechanism whereby implementations optimize certain recursive functions by reducing the storage on the run-time execution stack.

Example: Factorial

```
(define factorial (lambda (n)
                    (if  (zero? n)
                        1
                        (* n (factorial (sub1 n))) )))
```

When (factorial 6) is invoked, activation records are needed for six invocations of the function—namely, (factorial 6) through (factorial 0). Without each of these stack frames, the local values of n—namely, n=6 through n=0—will be lost so that the multiplication at the end cannot be carried out correctly.

At its deepest level of recursion all the information in the expression

(* 6 (* 5 (* 4 (* 3 (* 2 (* 1 (factorial 0))))))))

is stored in the run-time execution stack.   ∎

Definition: A function is **tail recursive** if its only recursive call is the last action that occurs during any particular invocation of the function. ∎

Example: Factorial with Tail Recursion

```
(define fact (lambda (n)
             (letrec ((fact-help
                       (lambda (prod count)
                         (if  (> count n)
                             prod
                             (fact-help  (* count prod)
                                         (add1 count)) ))))
       (fact-help 1 1))))
```

Note that although fact-help is recursive, there is no need to save its local environment when it calls itself since no computation remains after that call. The result of the recursive call is simply passed on as the result of the current activation.

The execution of (fact 6) proceeds as follows:

```
(fact 6)
     (fact-help 1 1)
     (fact-help 1 2)
     (fact-help 2 3)
     (fact-help 6 4)
     (fact-help 24 5)
     (fact-help 120 6)
     (fact-help 720 7)
```

The final call is the base case, which returns 720 directly. Note that the static scope rules make the value of n visible in the function fact-help. ∎

Scheme is a small, elegant but amazingly powerful programming language. We have been able to present only a few of its features in this overview and have not shown the full range of data types, mutation of data structures (imperative programming in Scheme), object-oriented programming techniques, stream processing, declaring and using macros, or continuations (as briefly discussed in section 9.7). However, we have presented enough concepts so that the reader can write simple Scheme functions and understand the use of Scheme in this text.

Bibliography

[Abelson85]
Harold Abelson, Gerald Jay Sussman, and Julie Sussman, *Structure and Interpretation of Computer Programs*, MIT Press, Cambridge, MA, 1985.

[Aho86]
Alfred Aho, Ravi Sethi, and Jeffrey Ullman, *Compilers: Principles, Techniques, and Tools*, Addison-Wesley, Reading, MA, 1986.

[Alagic78]
Suad Alagic and Michael Arbib, *The Design of Well-Structured and Correct Programs*, Springer-Verlag, New York, 1978.

[Allison86]
Lloyd Allison, *A Practical Introduction to Denotational Semantics*, Cambridge University Press, Cambridge, UK, 1986.

[Anderson76]
E. R. Anderson, F. C. Belz, and E. K. Blum, "SEMANOL (73) A Metalanguage for Programming the Semantics of Programming Languages", *Acta Informatica*, 6, 1976, pp. 109–131.

[Astesiano91]
Egidio Astesiano, "Inductive and Operational Semantics", In *Formal Description of Programming Concepts*, edited by Erich Neuhold, et al, Springer-Verlag, Berlin, 1991.

[Backhouse79]
Roland Backhouse, *Syntax of Programming Languages: Theory and Practice*, Prentice Hall International, Hemel Hempstead, UK, 1979.

[Backhouse86]
Roland Backhouse, *Program Construction and Verification*, Prentice Hall International, Englewood Cliffs, NJ, 1986.

[Backus78]
John Backus, "Can Programming Be Liberated from the von Neumann Style? A functional Style and Its Algebra of Programs", *Communications of the ACM*, 21.8, August 1978, pp. 613–641.

[Barendregt84]
H. P. Barendregt, *The Lambda Calculus, Its Syntax and Semantics*, North-Holland, Amsterdam, 1984.

[Bennett90]
Jeremy Bennett, *Introduction to Compiling Techniques*, McGraw-Hill, New York, 1990.

[Bergstra89]
J. Bergstra, J. Heering, and Paul Klint, *Algebraic Specification*, Addison-Wesley, Reading, MA, 1989.

[Bird76]
Richard Bird, *Programs and Machines*, Wiley, New York, 1976.

[Bochman76]
Gregor Bochman, "Semantic Evaluation from Left to Right", *Communications of the ACM*, 19.2, February 1976, pp. 55–62.

[Bochman78]
Gregor Bochman and P. Ward, "Compiler Writing System for Attribute Grammars", *The Computer Journal*, 21.2, May 1978, pp. 144–148.

[Bratko90]
Ivan Bratko, *Prolog: Programming for Artificial Intelligence*, Second Edition, Addison-Wesley, Reading, MA, 1990.

[Brown92]
Deryck Brown, Hermano Moura, and David Watt, "ACTRESS: an Action Semantics Directed Compiler Generator", *Proceeding of the 1992 Workshop on Compiler Construction*, Paderborn, Germany, Lecture Notes in Computer Science, 641, Springer-Verlag, Berlin, 1992, pp. 95–109.

[Broy87]
Manfred Broy, Martin Wirsing, and Peter Pepper, "On the Algebraic Definition of Programming Languages", *ACM Transactions on Programming Languages and Systems*, 9.1, 1987, pp. 54–99.

[Bryant86a]
Barrett Bryant, Balanjaninath Edupuganty, San-Jon Chao, and Danny Deng, "Two-Level Grammar as a Programming Language for Data Flow and Pipelined Algorithms", *Proceedings of the IEEE Computer Society 1986 International Conference on Computer Languages*, 1986, pp. 136–143.

[Bryant86b]
Barrett Bryant, Balanjaninath Edupuganty, and Lee Hull, "Two-Level Grammar as an Implementable Metalanguage for Axiomatic Semantics", *Computer Languages*, 11.3/4, 1986, pp. 173–191.

[Bryant88]
Barrett Bryant, et al, "Two-Level Grammar: Data Flow English for Functional and Logic Programming", *Proceedings of the 1988 ACM Computer Science Conference*, pp. 469–474.

[Burstall82]
R. M. Burstall and J. A. Goguen, "Algebras, theories and freeness: an introduction for computer scientists", In *Theoretical Foundations of Programming Methodology*, edited by M. Broy and G. Schmidt, Reidel, Dordreckt, Holland, 1982, pp. 329–348.

[Campbell84]
J. A. Campbell, editor, *Implementations of Prolog*, Ellis Horwood, Chichester, UK, 1984.

[Chomsky56]
Noam Chomsky, "Three Models for the Description of Language", IRE *Transactions on Information Theory*, IT-2, 1956, pp. 113–124.

[Chomsky59]
Noam Chomsky, "On Certain Formal Properties of Grammars", *Information and Control*, 2, 1959, pp. 137–167.

[Cleaveland77]
J. C. Cleaveland and R. C. Uzgalis, *Grammars for Programming Languages*, Elsevier North-Holland, New York, 1977.

[Clocksin87]
W. F. Clocksin and C. S. Mellish, *Programming in Prolog*, Third Edition, Springer-Verlag, Berlin, 1987.

[Cohen79]
Rina Cohen and Eli Harry, "Automatic Generation of Near-Optimal Translators for Noncircular Attribute Grammars", *Sixth Annual ACM Symposium on Principles of Programming Languages*, 1979, pp. 121–134.

[Colmerauer78]
Alain Colmerauer, "Metamorphosis Grammars", In *Natural Language Communication with Computers*, edited by Leonard Bolc, Springer-Verlag, Berlin, 1978, pp. 133–189.

[Covington88]
Michael Covington, Donald Nute, and Andre Vellino, *Prolog Programming in Depth*, Scott, Foresman, Glenview, IL, 1988.

[Demers85]
A. Demers, A. Rogers, and F. K. Zadeck, "Attribute propagation by message passing", *ACM SIGPLAN Notices*, 20.7, July 1985, pp. 43–59.

[Deransart90]
P. Deransart and M. Jourdan, editors, *Attribute Grammars and their Applications*, LNCS 461, Springer-Verlag, Berlin, 1990.

[Deussen75]
P. Deussen, "A Decidability Criterion for van Wijngaarden Grammars", *Acta Informatica*, 5, 1975, pp. 353–375.

[Diller88]
Antoni Diller, *Compiling Functional Languages*, Wiley, Chichester, UK, 1988.

[Dijkstra76]
Edsger Dijkstra, *A Discipline of Programming*, Prentice Hall, Englewood Cliffs, NJ, 1976.

[Dromey89]
  Geoff Dromey, *Program Derivation: The Development of Programs from Speci-fications*, Addison-Wesley, Reading, MA, 1989.

[Dybvig87]
  Kent Dybvig, *The Scheme Programming Language*, Prentice Hall, Englewood Cliffs, NJ, 1987, pp. 33–42.

[Edupuganty85]
  Balanjaninath Edupuganty and Barrett Bryant, "Two-Level Grammars for Automatic Interpretation", *Proceedings of the 1985 ACM Annual Conference*, Denver, pp. 417–423.

[Edupuganty88]
  Balanjaninath Edupuganty and Barrett Bryant, "Two-Level Grammar: An Implementable Metalanguage for Denotational Semantics", Technical Report CIS-TR-88-05, University of Alabama at Birmingham, 1988.

[Edupuganty89]
  Balanjaninath Edupuganty and B. R. Bryant, "Two-Level Grammar as a Functional Programming Language", *The Computer Journal*, 32.1, 1989, pp. 36–44.

[Ehrig85]
  Hartmut Ehrig and Bernd Mahr, *Fundamentals of Algebraic Specification 1: Equations and Initial Semantics*, Springer-Verlag, Berlin, 1985.

[Enderton72]
  Herbert Enderton, *A Mathematical Introduction to Logic*, Academic Press, New York, 1972.

[Farrow84]
  Rodney Farrow, "Generating a Production Compiler from an Attribute Grammar", *IEEE Software*, 1.4, October 1984, pp. 77–93.

[Farrow89]
  Rodney Farrow and Alec Stanculescu, "A VHDL Compiler Based on Attribute Grammar Methodology", *SIGPLAN Notices*, 24.7, 1989, pp. 120–130.

[Field88]
  Anthony Field and Peter Harrison, *Functional Programming*, Addison-Wesley, Wokingham, UK, 1988.

[Fischer91]
  Charles Fischer and Richard LeBlanc, Jr., *Crafting a Compiler with C*, Benjamin/Cummings, Redwood City, CA, 1991.

[Floyd67]
  Robert Floyd, "Assigning Meaning to Programs", *AMS Symposia in Applied Mathematics*, 19, 1967, pp. 19–67.

[Francez92]
  Nissim Francez, *Program Verification*, Addison-Wesley, Reading, MA, 1992.

[Friedman92]
Daniel Friedman, Mitchell Wand, and Christopher Haynes, *Essentials of Programming Languages*, McGraw-Hill, New York, 1992.

[Glaser84]
Hugh Glaser, Chris Hankin, and David Till, *Principles of Functional Programming*, Prentice Hall International, Hemel Hempstead, UK, 1984.

[Goguen77]
J. A. Goguen, J. W. Thatcher, E. G. Wagner, and J. B. Wright, "Initial Algebra Semantics and Continuous Algebras", *Journal of the ACM*, 24.1, January 1977, pp. 68–95.

[Goguen78]
J. A. Goguen, J. W. Thatcher, and E. G. Wagner, "An Initial Algebra Approach to the Specification, Correctness, and Implementation of Abstract Data Types", In *Current Trends in Programming Methodology IV: Data Structuring*, edited by Raymond Yeh, Prentice Hall, Englewood Cliffs, NJ, 1978, pp. 80–149.

[Gordon79]
Michael Gordon, *The Denotational Description of Programming Languages*, Springer-Verlag, New York, 1979.

[Gordon88]
Michael Gordon, *Programming Language Theory and its Implementation*, Prentice Hall International, Hemel Hempstead, UK, 1988.

[Gries81]
David Gries, *The Science of Programming*, Springer-Verlag, New York, 1981.

[Gumb89]
Raymond Gumb, *Programming Logics: An Introduction to Verification and Semantics*, Wiley, New York, 1989.

[Gunter90]
Carl Gunter and Dana Scott, "Semantic Domains", In *Handbook of Theoretical Computer Science: Volume B, Formal Models and Semantics*, edited by Jan van Leeuwen, MIT Press, Cambridge, MA, 1990.

[Gunter92]
Carl Gunter, *Semantics of Programming Languages: Structures and Techniques*, MIT Press, Cambridge, MA, 1992.

[Guttag78a]
John Guttag and J. J. Horning, "The Algebraic Specification of Abstract Data Types", *Acta Informatica*, 10, 1978, pp. 27–52.

[Guttag78b]
John Guttag, Ellis Horowitz, and David Musser, "Abstract Data Types and Software Validation", *Communications of the ACM*, 21.12, December 1978, pp. 1048–1064.

[Guttag78c]
John Guttag, Ellis Horowitz, and David Musser, "The Design of Data Type Specification", In *Current Trends in Programming Methodology IV: Data Structuring*, edited by Raymond Yeh, Prentice Hall, Englewood Cliffs, NJ, 1978, pp. 60–79.

[Guttag80]
John Guttag, "Notes on Type Abstraction (Version 2)", *IEEE Transactions on Software Engineering*, SE-6.1, January 1980, pp. 13–23.

[Hennessy90]
Matthew Hennessy, *The Semantics of Programming Languages: An Elementary Introduction Using Structural Operational Semantics*, Wiley, New York, 1990.

[Henson87]
Martin Henson, *Elements of Functional Languages*, Blackwell Scientific, Oxford, UK, 1987.

[Hoare69]
C. A. R. Hoare, "An Axiomatic Basis for Computer Programming", *Communications of the ACM*, 12.10, October 1969, pp. 576–580.

[Hoare73]
C. A. R. Hoare and Niklaus Wirth, "An Axiomatic Definition of the Programming Language Pascal", *Acta Informatica*, 2, 1973, pp. 335–355.

[Hopcroft79]
John Hopcroft and Jeffrey Ullman, *Introduction to Automata Theory, Languages, and Computation*, Addison-Wesley, Reading, MA, 1979.

[Janssen86]
T. M. V. Janssen, *Foundations and Applications of Montague Grammar, Part I*, Volume 19 of *CWI Tracts*, Center for Mathematics and Computer Science, Amsterdam, 1986.

[Johnson78]
S. C. Johnson, "YACC - Yet Another Compiler-Compiler", Bell Laboratories, Murray Hill, NJ, July 1978.

[Johnson85]
G. F. Johnson, and C. N. Fischer, "A Meta-language and System for Nonlocal Incremental Evaluation in Language-based Editors", *Twelfth ACM Symposium on Principles of Programming Languages*, New Orleans, 1985, ACM, New York, pp. 141–151.

[Kahn87]
Giles Kahn, "Natural Semantics", In *Fourth Annual Symposium on Theoretical Aspects of Computer Science*, edited by F. Bandenburg, G. Vidal-Naquet, and M. Wirsing, Lecture Notes in Computer Science, 247, Springer-Verlang, Berlin, 1987, pp. 22–39.

[Kamin90]
Samuel Kamin, *Programming Languages: An Interpreter-Based Approach*, Addison-Wesley, Reading, MA, 1990.

[Kastens80]
U. Kastens, "Ordered Attribute Grammars", *Acta Informatica*, 13.3, 1980, pp. 229–256.

[Kennedy76]
K. Kennedy and S. K. Warren, "Automatic Generation of Efficient Evaluators for Attribute Grammars", *Third ACM Symposium of Principles of Programming Languages*, Atlanta, GA, 1976, ACM, New York.

[Kennedy79]
K. Kennedy and J. Ramanathan, "A Deterministic Attribute Grammar Evaluator Based on Dynamic Sequencing", *ACM Transactions on Programming Languages and Systems*, 1.1, 1979, pp. 142–160.

[Kluzniak85]
Feliks Kluzniak and Stanislaw Szpakowicz, *Prolog for Programmers*, Academic Press, London, 1985.

[Knuth68]
Donald Knuth, "Semantics of Context-Free Languages", *Mathematical Systems Theory*, 2, 1968, pp. 127–145. Correction in 5, 1971, p. 95.

[Kowalski79]
Robert Kowalski, "Algorithm = Logic + Control", *Communications of the ACM*, 22.7, July 1979, pp. 424–436.

[Kupka80]
I. Kupka, "van Wijngaarden Grammars as a Special Information Processing Model", In *Mathematical Foundations of Computer Science*, Lecture Notes in Computer Science, 88, edited by P. Dembinski, Springer-Verlag, Berlin, 1980, pp. 387–401.

[Kurtz91]
Barry Kurtz, "Laboratory Activities for Studying the Formal Semantics of Programming Languages", *SIGCSE Bulletin*, 23.1, March 1991, pp. 162–168.

[Landin64]
Peter Landin, "The Mechanical Evaluation of Expressions", *The Computer Journal*, 6.4, January 1964, pp. 308–320.

[Landin66]
Peter Landin, "A λ-Calculus Approach", In *Advances in Programming and Non-numerical Computation*, edited by Leslie Fox, Pergamon Press, Oxford, UK, 1966, pp. 97–141.

[Lesk75]
M. E. Lesk, "Lex - A Lexical Analyzer Generator", Computer Science Technical Report 39, Bell Laboratories, Murray Hill, NJ, October 7, 1975.

[Lewis74]
P. M. Lewis, D. J. Rosenkrantz, and R. E. Stearns, "Attributed Translations", *Journal of Computer and Systems Sciences*, 9, 1974, pp. 279–307.

[MacLennan90]
Bruce MacLennan, *Functional Programming Methodology: Practice and Theory*, Addison-Wesley, Reading, MA, 1990.

[Malpas87]
John Malpas, *Prolog: A Relational Language and its Applications*, Prentice Hall, Englewood Cliffs, NJ, 1987.

[McCarthy60]
John McCarthy, "Recursive Functions of Symbolic Expressions and Their Computation by Machine", *Communications of the ACM*, 3.4, April 1960, pp. 184–195.

[McCarthy65a]
John McCarthy, "A Basis for a Mathematical Theory of Computation", In *Computer Programming and Formal Systems*, edited by P. Braffort and D. Hirschberg, North-Holland, Amsterdam, 1965, pp. 33–70.

[McCarthy65b]
John McCarthy, et al, *LISP 1.5 Programmer's Manual*, Second Edition, MIT Press, Cambridge, MA, 1965.

[Maluszynski84]
Jan Maluszynski, "Towards a Programming Language Based on the Notion of Two-Level Grammar", *Theoretical Computer Science*, 28, 1984, pp. 13–43.

[Manna72]
Zohar Manna and Jean Vuillemin, "Fixpoint Approach to the Theory of Computation", *Communications of the ACM*, 15.7, July 1972, pp. 528–536.

[Manna73]
Zohar Manna, Stephen Ness, and Jean Vuillemin, "Inductive Methods for Proving Properties of Programs", *Communications of the ACM*, 16.8, August 1973, pp. 491–502.

[Manna74]
Zohar Manna, *Mathematical Theory of Computation*, McGraw-Hill, New York, 1974.

[Manna93]
Zohar Manna and Richard Waldinger, *The Deductive Foundations of Computer Programming*, Addison-Wesley, Reading, MA, 1993.

[Marcotty76]
Michael Marcotty, Henry Ledgard, and Gregor Bochmann, "A Sampler of Formal Definitions", *Computing Surveys*, 8.2, 1976, pp. 191–276.

[Martin91]
John C. Martin, *Introduction to Languages and the Theory of Computation*, McGraw-Hill, New York, 1991.

[Mayoh81]
B. H. Mayoh, "Attribute Grammars and Mathematical Semantics", *SIAM Journal on Computing*, 10.3, August 1981, pp. 503–518.

[Meek90]
Brian Meek, "The Static Semantic File", *SIGPLAN Notices*, 25.4, 1990, pp. 33–42.

[Mendelson79]
Elliott Mendelson, *Introduction to Mathematical Logic*, Second Edition, D. Van Nostrand Company, New York, 1979.

[Meyer90]
Bertrand Meyer, *Introduction to the Theory of Programming Languages*, Prentice Hall, Hemel Hempstead, UK, 1990.

[Michaelson89]
Greg Michaelson, *An Introduction to Functional Programming through Lambda Calculus*, Addison-Wesley, Wokingham, UK, 1989.

[Mosses89]
Peter Mosses, "Unified Algebras and Action Semantics", In *STACS'89, Proceedings Symposium on Theoretical Aspects of Computer Science*, Paderborn, Germany, Lecture Notes in Computer Science, 349, Spring-Verlag, Berlin, 1989.

[Mosses90]
Peter Mosses, "Denotational Semantics", In *Handbook of Theoretical Computer Science: Volume B, Formal Models and Semantics*, edited by Jan van Leeuwen, MIT Press, Cambridge, MA, 1990.

[Mosses91]
Peter Mosses, "An Introduction to Action Semantics", Technical Report, DAIMI PB-370, Computer Science Department, Aarhus University, Aarhus, Denmark, November 1991.

[Mosses92]
Peter Mosses, *Action Semantics*, Cambridge University Press, Cambridge, UK, 1992.

[Naur63]
Peter Naur, editor, "Revised Report on the Algorithmic Language Algol 60", *Communications of the ACM*, 6.1, January 1963, pp. 1–20.

[Nielson92]
Hanne Riis Nielson and Flemming Nielson, *Semantics with Applications: A Formal Introduction*, Wiley, Chichester, UK, 1992.

[Nilsson84]
M. Nilsson, "The World's Shortest Prolog Interpreter?", In *Implementations of Prolog*, edited by J.A. Campbell, Ellis Horwood, Chichester, UK, 1984, pp. 87–92.

[Noonan85]
Robert Noonan, "An Algorithm for Generating Abstract Syntax Trees", *Computer Language*, 10.3/4, 1985, pp. 225–236.

[Pagan76]
Frank Pagan, "On Interpreter-oriented Definitions of Programming Languages", *Computer Journal*, 2, 1976, pp. 151–155.

[Pagan81]
Frank Pagan, *Formal Specification of Programming Languages: A Panoramic Primer*, Prentice Hall, Englewood Cliffs, NJ, 1981.

[Pagan83]
Frank Pagan, "A Diagrammatic Notation for Abstract Syntax and Abstract Structured Objects", *IEEE Transactions on Software Engineering*, SE-9.3, May 1983, pp. 280–289.

[Parsons92]
Thomas W. Parsons, *Introduction to Compiler Construction*, Computer Science Press, New York, 1992.

[Paulson87]
Lawrence Paulson, *Logic and Computation*, Cambridge University Press, Cambridge, UK, 1987.

[Peyton Jones87]
Simon Peyton Jones, *Implementation of Functional Programming Languages*, Prentice Hall International, Hemel Hempstead, UK, 1987.

[Pittman92]
Thomas Pittman and James Peters, *The Art of Compiler Design: Theory and Practice*, Prentice Hall, Englewood Cliffs, NJ, 1992.

[Plotkin81]
Gordon Plotkin, "A Structural Approach to Operational Semantics", Technical Report, DAIMI FN-19, Computer Science Department, Aarhus University, Aarhus, Denmark, 1981.

[Prawitz65]
Dag Prawitz, *Natural Deduction: A Proof-Theoretical Study*, Almqvist & Wiksell, Stockholm, 1965.

[Reade89]
Chris Reade, *Elements of Functional Programming*, Addison-Wesley, Wokingham, UK, 1989.

[Reeves90]
Steve Reeves and Michael Clarke, *Logic for Computer Science*, Addison-Wesley, Reading, MA, 1990.

[Reps89]
T. Reps and T. Teitelbaum, *The Synthesizer Generator: A System for Constructing Language-based Editors*, Springer-Verlag, New York, 1989.

[Revesz88]
Gyorgy Revesz, *Lambda-Calculus, Combinators, and Functional Programming*, Cambridge University Press, Cambridge, UK, 1988.

[Robinson65]
J. A. Robinson, "A Machine-Oriented Logic Based On the Resolution Principle", *Journal of the ACM*, 12, pp. 23–41, January 1965.

[Ross89]
Peter Ross, *Advanced Prolog: Techniques and Examples*, Addison-Wesley, Reading, MA, 1989.

[Rosser84]
J. Barkley Rosser, "Highlights of the History of the Lambda-Calculus", *IEEE Annals of the History of Computing*, 1984, pp. 337–349.

[Ruei93]
Ruth Ruei and Ken Slonneger, "Semantic Prototyping: Implementing Action Semantics in Standard ML", Technical Report 93-08, The University of Iowa, Department of Computer Science, Iowa City, IA, 1993.

[Saint-Dizier90]
Patrick Saint-Dizier and Stan Szpakowicz, *Logic and Logic Grammars for Language Processing*, Ellis Horwood, Chichester, UK, 1990.

[Schmidt88]
David Schmidt, *Denotational Semantics: A Methodology for Language Development*, Wm. C. Brown Publishers, Dubuque, IA, 1988.

[Scott76]
Dana Scott, "Data Types as Lattices", *SIAM Journal on Computing*, 5.3, September 1976, pp. 522–587.

[Scott80]
Dana Scott, "Lambda Calculus: Some Models, Some Philosophy", In *The Kleene Symposium*, North-Holland, Amsterdam, 1980, pp. 223–265.

[Scott82]
Dana Scott, "Domains for Denotational Semantics", In *Automata, Languages and Programming IX*, Springer-Verlag, Berlin, pp. 577–613.

[Sebesta93]
Robert Sebesta, *Concepts of Programming Languages*, Benjamin/Cummings, Redwood City, CA , 1993.

[Sethi89]
Ravi Sethi, *Programming Languages: Concepts and Constructs*, Addison-Wesley, Reading, MA, 1989.

[Sintzoff67]
M. Sintzoff, "Existence of a van Wijngaarden Syntax for Every Recursively Enumerable Set", *Ann. Soc. Sci. Bruxelles 81*, 1967, 2, pp. 115–118.

[Slonneger91]
  Ken Slonneger, "An Exercise in Denotational Semantics", *SIGCSE Bulletin*, 23, 1, March 1991, pp. 178–183.

[Slonneger93]
  Ken Slonneger, "Executing Continuation Semantics: A Comparison", *Software — Practice and Experience*, 23.12, December 1993.

[Springer89]
  George Springer and Daniel Friedman, *Scheme and the Art of Programming*, MIT Press, Cambridge, MA, 1989.

[Stepney93]
  Susan Stepney, *High Integrity Compilation: A Case Study*, Prentice Hall International, Hemel Hempstead, UK, 1993.

[Sterling94]
  Leon Sterling and Ehud Shapiro, *The Art of Prolog*, Second Edition, MIT Press, Cambridge, MA, 1994.

[Stoy77]
  Joseph Stoy, *Denotational Semantics: The Scott-Strachey Approach to Programming Language Theory*, MIT Press, Cambridge, MA, 1977.

[Strachey66]
  Christopher Strachey, "Towards a Formal Semantics", In *Formal Language Description Languages*, edited by T. B. Steele, North-Holland, Amsterdam, 1966, pp. 198–220.

[Strachey72]
  Christopher Strachey, "The Varieties of Programming Language", In *Proceedings of the International Computing Symposium*, Cini Foundation, Venice, 1972, pp. 222–233.

[Sundararaghavan87]
  K. R. Sundararaghavan, Balanjaninath Edupuganty, and Barrett Bryant, "Towards a Two-Level Grammar Interpreter", *Proceedings of the ACM 25th Annual Southeast Regional Conference*, 1987, Birmingham, AL, pp. 81–88.

[Tarski55]
  Alfred Tarski, "A Lattice-Theoretical Fixpoint Theorem and its Applications", *Pacific Journal of Mathematics*, 5, 1955, pp. 285–309.

[Tennent76]
  R. D. Tennent, "The Denotational Semantics of Programming Languages", *Communications of the ACM*, 19.8, August 1976, pp. 437–453.

[Tennent81]
  R. D. Tennent, *Principles of Programming Languages*, Prentice Hall International, Englewood Cliffs, NJ, 1981.

[Tennent91]
  R. D. Tennent, *Semantics of Programming Languages*, Prentice Hall International, Hemel Hempstead, UK, 1991.

[Turner84]
S. J. Turner, "W-Grammars for Logic Programming", In *Implementations of Prolog*, edited by J. A. Campbell, Ellis Horwood, Chichester, UK, 1984, pp. 352–368.

[van Wijngaarden66]
Aad van Wijngaarden, "Recursive Definition of Syntax and Semantics", In *Formal Language Description Languages for Computer Programming*, edited by T. B. Steel, North-Holland, Amsterdam, 1966, pp. 13–24.

[van Wijngaarden76]
Aad van Wijngaarden, et al, *Revised Report on the Algorithmic Language ALGOL 68*, Springer-Verlag, Berlin, 1976.

[van Wijngaarden82]
Aad van Wijngaarden, "Languageless Programming", In *The Relationship Between Numerical Computation and Programming Languages*, edited by J. K. Reid, North-Holland, Amsterdam, 1982, pp. 361–371.

[Wagner78]
E. G. Wagner, T. W. Thatcher, and J. B. Wright, "Programming Languages as Mathematical Objects", *Mathematical Foundations of Computer Science*, Lecture Notes in Computer Science, 45, 1978, Springer-Verlag, Berlin, 1978.

[Waite84]
William Waite and Gerhard Goos, *Compiler Construction*, Springer-Verlag, New York, 1984.

[Warren80]
David H. D. Warren, "Logic Programming and Compiler Writing", *Software—Practice and Experience*, 10, 1980, pp. 97–125.

[Watt79]
David Watt, "An Extended Attribute Grammar for PASCAL", *SIGPLAN Notices*, 14.2, 1979, pp. 60–74.

[Watt90]
David Watt, *Programming Language Concepts and Paradigms*, Prentice Hall International, Hemel Hempstead, UK, 1990.

[Watt91]
David Watt, *Programming Language Syntax and Semantics*, Prentice Hall International, Hemel Hempstead, UK, 1991.

[Watt93]
David Watt, *Programming Language Processors*, Prentice Hall International, Hemel Hempstead, UK, 1993.

[Wegner72]
Peter Wegner, "The Vienna Definition Language", *Computing Surveys*, 4.1, March 1972, pp. 5–63.

[Wexelblat81]

Richard Wexelblat, *The History of Programming Languages*, Academic Press, New York, 1981.

[Winskel93]

Glynn Winskel, *The Formal Semantics of Programming Languages*, MIT Press, Cambridge, MA, 1993.

[Wirsing90]

Martin Wirsing, "Algebraic Specification", In *Handbook of Theoretical Computer Science: Volume B, Formal Models and Semantics*, edited by Jan van Leeuwen, MIT Press, Cambridge, MA, 1990.

[Woodcock88]

Jim Woodcock and Martin Loomes, *Software Engineering Mathematics: Formal Methods Demystified*, Pitman, London, 1988.

Index

625

Y